Handbook of Budgeting

Sixth Edition

WILLIAM R. LALLI

Editor

John Wiley & Sons, Inc.

Library of Congress Cataloging-in-Publication Data:

Handbook of budgeting / [edited by] William R. Lalli. — 6th ed.
   p. cm.
  Includes index.
  ISBN 978-0-470-92045-9 (cloth); ISBN 978-1-118-17059-5 (ebk);
  ISBN 978-1-118-17060-1 (ebk); ISBN 978-1-118-17061-8 (ebk)
 1. Budget in business.   I. Lalli, William Rea.
  HG4028.B8H36 2012
  658.15′4—dc23
                                    2011029142

10 9 8 7 6 5 4 3 2 1

Founded in 1807, John Wiley & Sons is the oldest independent publishing company in the United States. With offices in North America, Europe, Asia, and Australia, Wiley is globally committed to developing and marketing print and electronic products and services for our customers' professional and personal knowledge and understanding.

The Wiley Corporate F&A series provides information, tools, and insights to corporate professionals responsible for issues affecting the profitability of their company, from accounting and finance to internal controls and performance management.

Contents

PART THREE: PREPARATION OF SPECIFIC BUDGETS

Foreword

The idea of budgeting often brings fear, even loathing, to the minds of most persons. Perhaps that is because many of us were first introduced to the term by trying to figure out how to spend our seemingly unfairly small "allowances" as children. It was not easy to figure out how much candy we could buy and still go to the movies on the weekend. These days our children buy more movies (and video games) than they attend, but the principles (and the sweets) are the same.

In its simplest sense, budgeting is any plan, usually expressed in financial or mathematical terms. As an expression of expectations, a budget generally aligns resources with needs to accomplish a specific goal. As mileposts and measuring sticks, budgets provide invaluable benchmarks that can be used every day in reacting to management challenges.

Some see budgets as a necessary evil, but in reality they are underrated tools that can greatly enhance any business process.

The greatest value of budgets—arming management with key decision-making tools—is often overlooked. To the uninitiated, a budget succeeds or fails based on how close actual results compare to expectations. While it is great fun to predict the future accurately, to win a bet as they say, life's best lessons are often learned in analyzing why you were wrong.

In reality, analyzing the reasons actual results differ from expected results is a far more useful tool than the often disappointing attempt to accurately predict the future. This cannot be done effectively without a budget to compare things to. Like the weather, financial futures are difficult to predict and sometimes correlate only with predictions as result of an accident, good luck or otherwise. Were these assumptions wrong? Were needs incorrectly calculated? Did the business environment change? Did the world change? Was a better method or process discovered? Were there unanticipated challenges? By studying what is different and the reasons for differences, we can continually improve both performance and our ability to predict the future. We have certainly come a long way in improving our ability to predict the weather, but expectations for accuracy have also increased. Similarly, the art and science of budgeting has advanced dramatically over the years since the handbook was first published. Revisions in this edition reflect alterations and improvements comparing these budgets to older ones.

Budgets are clearly not just for children to manage their allowances and meager earnings. They are not just for big businesses either, as some would incorrectly perceive. Budgets are for everyone.

In modern times, budgets are often (unfortunately) utilized only by midsize businesses when they are in trouble. They would likely be in trouble less frequently if they used budgets more often. Certainly there is less superficial need to manage resources when revenues seem to flow effortlessly well beyond the costs needed to sustain a business. The lack of need in these cases is invariably only superficial; easy money is a fleeting concept. Darwinian pressures on business provide survival only to the fittest and most prepared.

As can be learned by studying the various budgets in this book, time, money, and processes can be budgeted. Planning for the future enhances our understanding of the present. Budgets reduce the chances of repetition of past errors, and while nothing can prevent the commission of new errors or the introduction of new challenges, effective budgeting can lead to the preparedness necessary to deal with adversity and opportunity when either is on your doorstep.

This handbook is a resource that will help you identify the right type of budget to use and which tools to implement in actually completing the budget and provide insight into analyzing your budget against actual expectations.

David A. Lifson, CPA
Crowe Horwath LLP

 David Lifson, CPA, is a partner with Crowe Horwath LLP and leads the New York City tax and business consultancy practice, where he develops business strategies and personal financial plans utilizing both his and the firm's broad range of accounting, audit, tax, and business consulting backgrounds, both domestically and internationally. He specializes in advising clients on managing various types of business change within tax, economic, and other related constraints and dealing with the tax compliance challenges that accompany change. This includes starting or closing a business; buying, merging, or selling one; or trying to change or value an existing operation.

Mr. Lifson is the recipient of the American Institute of CPAs 2009 Arthur J. Dixon Memorial Award, the accounting profession's highest award in the area of taxation. He has chaired the Tax Executive Committee, served as a member of the AICPA Board of Directors and on its council, and has chaired or served on various committees, task forces, and technical resource panels over the years. He is also a former president of the New York State Society of CPAs and has served in various capacities on its behalf. Mr Lifson has chaired the Small Business and Self Employed subgroup of the Internal Revenue Service's Advisory Council (IRSAC) while serving on the council. IRSAC meets regularly to advise the Commissioner of the IRS and key IRS group leaders on how to administer the tax system effectively.

Preface

 ## THE NEED TO IMPROVE YOUR BUDGETING PROCESSES

Despite advances in technology and finance, we have not reached the limit of knowledge or made the most advanced achievements in reaching our financial goals. That is a definition of a frontier that we face in these times.

There are many types of budgeting, and most of them are covered in this book. The need for sound, dependable information as the basis for quality decision making based on reliable budgets, I contend, has never been stronger. That is the reason I proposed revising this book to present this sixth edition of the *Handbook of Budgeting*.

I could report on the state of the economy and economic trends, citing a variety of sources and experts; however, my only point is that in bad times more than in good times, budgeting can be key to an entity's survival or prosperity.

This book is intended as a business tool. I shall leave it to the academicians to analyze what might work better. Instead, our authors present 35 chapters of tried-and-true experiences taken from frontline business exposure that will enlighten you as to how you may incorporate real changes in your environment.

I became the second editor of this book after its founding editor died. One reason I was selected to replace him was due to the extensive work I was doing at the time in the budgeting area for delivering continuing professional education to senior financial executives. One day at a conference, an attendee approached me, realized I was the book editor, and paid me the highest compliment I ever received. She told me that she worked with a copy of the book open on her desk.

There is no outer limit in any field of endeavor, especially one in which the opportunities for research and development have not been exploited. This is the new frontier that must be met with technology and information management in finance in modern times which companies must master in order to survive and prosper. Use every tool at your disposal.

 ## THE FORECAST ON BUDGETING

The *Handbook of Budgeting* has been revised in this sixth edition to retain some "evergreen" knowledge from previous contributors, augmented by new experts on new topics.

More contributions from corporate perspectives translate into more opportunities for you to take this information to your team and to implement the lessons this book contains company-wide.

Chief financial officers, chief information officers, chief operating officers; vice presidents of fnance; controllers and assistant controllers; directors and managers of budgeting, forecasting, financial planning, analysis, business planning, strategic planning, performance measurement, and finance; financial consultants; budget analysts; and financial analysts will all find that this book has been designed with their specific needs in mind.

Our contributors and I believe that budgeting is the most important component of an overall dynamic business planning process. When it is combined with available technology, you may quickly analyze its impact on your business, which will lead you to more effective decisions that improve the profitability of your company.

Please note that the term "budgeting" is used in its broadest context and includes the major process components of strategic planning, target setting, operational planning, financial planning, reporting, and forecasting.

According to research referred to in the pages of this book, forward-looking companies spend significantly more time (44 percent of the total time spent in planning) on forecasting and action-planning activities that can actually improve business performance. They also focus on what is important by implementing best practices throughout the planning process.

You will also find information in the *Handbook of Budgeting* on the latest business-planning software that allows you to develop budgets quickly by employing Web-based technology to process information over the Internet. Companies that use the latest technology can also quickly assess the impact to their bottom line based on competition, economic slowdowns, and consumer behavior. Always remember that the consequences of inadequate action planning and forecasting can be severe when a company's performance fails to meet Wall Street expectations.

It is the intention of John Wiley & Sons, Inc., that the *Handbook of Budgeting* will help you to meet the challenges of this new frontier.

William Rea Lalli, Editor
January 2012

PART ONE

Introduction to the Budgeting Process

CHAPTER ONE

Integrating the Balanced Scorecard for Improved Planning and Performance Management

Antosh G. Nirmul
Balanced Scorecard Collaborative, Inc.

 **OVERVIEW**

The balanced scorecard is a management tool developed by Drs. Robert Kaplan and David Norton in the early 1990s. Since that time, the scorecard has become a standard management practice adopted by large and small organizations throughout the world. The balanced scorecard is based on the simple premise that people and organizations respond and perform based on what is measured. Often this is described as "People respond to what is inspected, not expected." Measurement becomes a language that communicates clear priorities to the organization.

Because the primary goal of any organization (commercial, governmental, or non-profit) is to create value for its stakeholders and because the strategy is the way the organization intends to create value, the measurement system should be closely linked to the strategy. The balanced scorecard provides a measurement system that translates the strategy into operational terms through a series of causal relationships defined around four key perspectives (see Exhibit 1.1):

1. *Financial perspective.* For commercial organizations, the financial perspective defines the value created for the shareholders. For noncommercial organizations, the expectations of the financial stakeholders are defined.

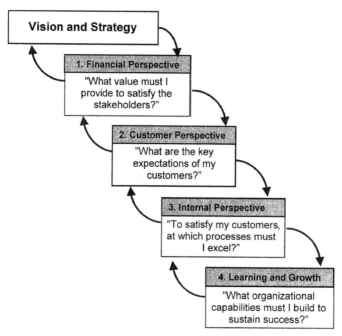

EXHIBIT 1.1 Four Perspectives of the Balanced Scorecard

2. *Customer perspective.* The targeted customers and the value they receive from the organization are defined in the customer perspective. The value expectations of the customers typically are developed around the standard attributes of cost, quality, service, and time.
3. *Internal perspective.* The key processes at which the organization must excel are defined in the internal perspective. Often these processes are grouped into a few key themes, such as operation excellence, customer intimacy, and innovation.
4. *Learning and growth perspective.* The key capabilities of the organization in terms of people, skills, technology, and culture are defined in the learning and growth perspective. These organizational attributes are the foundation for future strategic success.

By specifying and measuring the organization's key priorities within these four perspectives, a balanced view can be obtained. One element of this balance is the traditional mix of financial and nonfinancial factors, but the other, more innovative balance, is in the timing of strategic impact. In terms of fostering long-term sustainable success, each of the four perspectives has a time-specific impact that contributes to the concept of balanced management. Even though the overall goal may be financial or shareholder value, each of the other perspectives contributes differently to the outlook for that goal.

The financial perspective measures financial performance for a past period (last quarter, last year, etc.). The customer perspective measures the value delivered to and the overall satisfaction of customers which will have a short-term future impact on the financial performance. The internal perspective measures the ability of the organization to execute its processes that will have a short-term future impact on customer value and a medium-term impact on financial performance. The learning and growth perspective measures the development of organizational capabilities that will have a short-term impact on operational execution, a medium-term impact on customer satisfaction, and a long-term impact on financial performance.

By analyzing and measuring the strategy across all four perspectives, organizations achieve balance between the leading and lagging indicators of performance as well as between financial and nonfinancial factors. The combination of these multiple dimensions of balance allows a more holistic understanding of the organization's strategic execution and ultimate strategic success. Management should be able to use the scorecard results to obtain a snapshot of the current performance and a forecast of future strategic performance for the organization. This snapshot should highlight any key issues and be a valuable tool in steering the business through the allocation of resources and prioritization of strategic initiatives.

ELEMENTS OF A BALANCED SCORECARD

The primary elements of a balanced scorecard are the strategic objectives, performance measures, execution targets, and strategic initiatives (see Exhibit 1.2). These elements must be clearly defined and properly aligned among the four perspectives to create a useful management tool. Once these elements are aligned, their combination should be able to tell the story of the strategy in a clear and common framework. A well-defined framework will become a standard strategic language that can be used throughout the organization to better understand and manage strategy.

Strategic Objectives

The strategic objectives are short statements of the strategy that are used to highlight the key priorities of the organization. Specifying the objectives is the first and most strategically important step in designing a balanced scorecard. The objectives should be designed to reflect a midterm version of the strategy, typically the priorities over the next five years. The strategic objectives should highlight the most important priorities for the organization to

Element	Strategic Objective	Performance Measure	Execution Target	Strategic Initiative
Description	A short statement of the strategic priority	The way the organization will measure success	The expected performance for successful execution	The necessary actions to achieve success
Example	Cross-sell the Product lines	Percentage of customers buying more than one product line	45% Year 1 50% Year 2 60% Year 3	Cross-training program for sales force

EXHIBIT 1.2 Primary Elements of the Balanced Scorecard

focus on during this time period. These objectives typically are formatted in a verb-adjective-noun format similar to activities (see Exhibit 1.3 for examples). To show the emphasis on the customer's expectations, objectives for the customer perspective generally are specified in the words of the customer. The formatting of customer objectives is represented as the key attributes of the organization's products and services that represent value to the customer.

The definition of the strategic objectives is an area that clearly makes the balanced scorecard a strategic management tool rather than a simple key performance measure framework. The identification of the priorities of the organization across each perspective requires a well-developed strategy that is understood by the organization. Senior management involvement is especially critical during the definition of the objectives. To define strategic objectives, an organization must understand these questions:

- *Financial.* What is the primary financial outcome for the organization? What are the key financial levers necessary to achieve that outcome?
- *Customer.* Who are my primary customers or customer groups? What attributes differentiate my products or services to these customers? What is most important to the customer?
- *Internal.* What areas of my internal processes must excel to satisfy the customers? How do these processes link together to meet specific customer needs? What is the internal focus of my organization: operational excellence, innovation, customer knowledge, and other key goals?
- *Learning and growth.* What skills and capabilities are necessary to execute the strategy in the future? What type of people and culture will enable the organization's success? How should we manage technology and information to leverage these assets for tangible results?

Only after the organization has clearly articulated its strategy through the strategic objectives can the subject of performance measures be properly addressed. A large organization can typically expect to define between 20 and 25 strategic objectives for a

Perspective	Sample Objectives
Financial	Increase shareholder value Grow core revenue Reduce overhead costs
Customer	Lowest-cost provider Highest-quality service Long-term relationships
Internal	Understand customer needs Improve operational efficiency Develop innovative products Improve risk management processes
Learning and Growth	Retain top-performing employees Build stronger relationship skills Increase knowledge sharing Improve information infrastructure

EXHIBIT 1.3   Sample Strategic Objectives

clearly articulated strategy. More than 25 objectives would indicate a lack of clear priorities for the organization. Fewer objectives can be sufficient if they are defined specifically enough to communicate the strategy effectively.

The definition of the strategic objectives should highlight areas of inconsistency in the strategy. An organization cannot seek to be all things to all customers. The strategic objective process is designed to highlight the most important outcomes that define value for the shareholders and customers as well as the few key processes and organizational attributes that contribute most to that value. The objectives will not cover every activity performed by the organization but should highlight those that will be most critical over the strategic horizon.

Performance Measures

As a measurement framework, the balanced scorecard often is judged by the quality of the performance measures. Performance measures serve to further clarify the priorities of an organization by directly identifying the most important priorities for strategic execution. The performance measures identify how the organization will judge success. Most organizations already have some type of indicators defined throughout the various levels of the business. The issue in defining the scorecard is to identify the most important measures that will reflect the execution of the strategy.

The performance measures on a balanced scorecard often are compared to the dashboard on an automobile. While the driver of the car looks at only a few key metrics (speed, fuel level, etc.), the car itself monitors hundreds of other pieces of information. In our case, the executives of the organization use the scorecard as the key performance information they need to monitor and steer the business while other more operational metrics are looked at within the business. The other operational metrics can be brought forward to the executives only when there is an unusual problem. Major changes (intended or not) in performance and execution should be visible through the scorecard measures.

A number of different types of performance measures can be used on a balanced scorecard (see Exhibit 1.4). The choice of specific performance measures is a very

Type of Measure	Sample Measures
Numbers	Revenue per employee Total operating cost Mean time between failure (MTBF)
Rankings	Performance against benchmark Relative market share Customer satisfaction ranking
Percentages	Revenue growth Customer retention Calls answered without hold
Indices	Core process efficiency Combined system reliability
Survey	Employee satisfaction Customer satisfaction Climate of change

EXHIBIT 1.4 Types of Performance Measures

individual decision for the organization. There is no template set of scorecard measures that will be appropriate for any strategy. There are, however, a few guidelines that can assist an organization in choosing appropriate measures:

▪ Choose at least one measure for each strategic objective. Total measures should be around 25 for a large organization.
▪ Choose quantitative rather than subjective measures where possible.

The goal of these guidelines is to create the most useful set of measures possible. The existence of any strategic objective that cannot be described by a measure should call into question the validity of that strategy. Experience with senior management has shown that using more than 25 indicators makes it very difficult for executives to understand and focus on the results. The clearest measures are those that result in a specific and understandable number (e.g., dollars, number of employees, etc.). Generally, more subjective measures, such as indices and survey results, are more difficult to measure, communicate, and understand. While it is impossible to create a scorecard with only objective measures, the balance should be toward more numerical and less subjective indicators.

Another key factor to consider when choosing measures is the frequency of data reporting. The organization cannot expect to have executive discussions on scorecard results each quarter if its data are available only on an annual basis. The choice of measures should correspond to the frequency of desired reporting. Most organizations review their scorecard performance and strategic focus on a quarterly basis. In this case, at least 75 percent of an organization's scorecard measures should be available at that frequency.

Execution Targets

The setting and communication of targets are key steps necessary to operationalize a scorecard. While the measures communicate where management focus will be, the targets communicate the expected level of performance. For example, a measure such as customer retention shows a strategic focus: The difference between a 90 percent target and a 60 percent target represents a major shift in strategy. The setting of appropriate targets can be a difficult and painful process.

An important distinction in setting targets is the difference between standard performance targets and "stretch" targets. Stretch targets typically are used in areas of new or enhanced strategic focus and are meant to move the organization in new directions. Typically these targets are multiyear in nature, and their implementation approach is not fully defined when they are initially set. For an established organization, a target such as doubling revenue in three years would require significant changes. Often the precise steps needed to reach that target are not yet defined. The use of a stretch target forces innovation and change in an organization.

Obviously, an organization cannot set 25 stretch targets and hope to achieve all of them. Most execution targets will be more traditional incremental advances that reflect successful execution of the strategy. The choice of where to use stretch versus incremental targets strongly defines the emphasis in the strategy. Stretch targets create inspirational goals for the organization; incremental targets supplement those goals with core areas that need continual focus for sustained success.

The key point in choosing appropriate execution targets, whether stretch or incremental, is evaluating the capabilities of an organization and its resources. Incremental targets should be clearly reachable given the available resources and capabilities. The setting of unreasonable targets undermines employee faith and accountability in the performance management process. While the achievement of stretch targets may not be easily envisioned initially, the targets should come into clearer focus as the time period for the stretch goals is crossed. Every stretch target should have a measurable time period attached and should be updated throughout that time frame. Typically, stretch targets would be set at a maximum of 20 percent of the total measures and with 80 percent of targets remaining as incremental improvements.

Strategic Initiatives

Strategic initiatives are actions or projects that represent the primary path through which organizations create new skills, capabilities, or infrastructure to achieve strategic goals. In this definition, strategic initiatives are different from projects or actions that simply create incremental improvement over or maintain the existing skills, capabilities, or infrastructure of an organization. For example, in a financial organization, a project to build a new online ability to process self-service customer transactions could be a strategic initiative while a project to improve the interface of existing online tools or extend the online services would be considered an incremental upgrade of existing capabilities.

The criteria that an organization uses to define which actions are considered strategic versus basic projects are unique to its strategy and circumstances. Typically, a strategic initiative has a certain strategic importance, size, and breadth of influence that makes it more than an operational project (see Exhibit 1.5). The goal in identifying actions that are strategic initiatives versus operational projects or activities is to be able to allocate resources in a more strategic manner using the scorecard and strategy. This distinction is explored further in the separation of operational versus strategic budgets when the scorecard is integrated into the planning process.

Criteria	Sample Threshold
Size	At least $1 million budget Requires 10 or more FTEs Must be approved by executive board
Reach	Crosses multiple business units Requires more than a year to implement
Importance	Is necessary to meet stretch targets Must succeed to achieve the strategy Meets multiple strategic objectives

EXHIBIT 1.5 Key Criteria that Separate Strategic Initiatives

When creating a balanced scorecard, an organization should be able to identify its existing strategic initiatives and map them across the strategic objectives and measures on the scorecard. The mapping process is particularly important in that it can identify areas of strategic alignment (see Exhibit 1.6). Any identified initiative that cannot be mapped directly to a scorecard objective may not truly be a priority effort for executing the current strategy. Conversely, a key strategy with stretch targets that does not have an initiative associated with the strategy will be difficult to achieve (the target). Initiatives are particularly important for instances where stretch targets are defined, which by definition requires the development of new organization abilities.

In Exhibit 1.6 you can see certain gaps where there are no identified initiatives for the specified objectives. These gaps need to be carefully analyzed based on their context before any decisions are made. Financial objectives typically do not have many initiatives attached to them because as ultimate outcomes all initiatives eventually support the financial goals. Most initiatives will directly support the internal and learning and growth perspectives that represent the strategic processes being implemented to achieve the customer and financial outcomes. The lack of an initiative for a specific objective may mean that the organization can achieve that goal with incremental effort or that there is a strategic gap. In performing this analysis, the relation of the overall execution

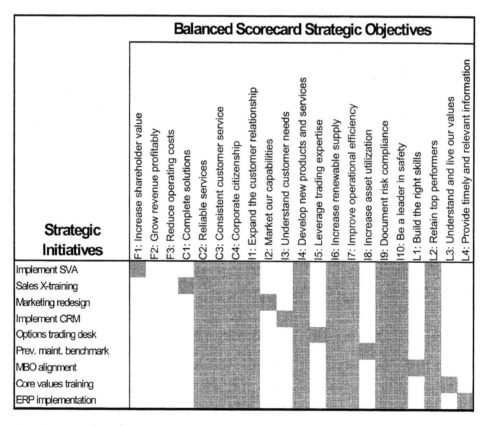

EXHIBIT 1.6   Sample Initiative Mapping

targets to the organization's current capabilities is particularly important. While initiative mapping often helps an organization to eliminate unaligned activities, it should not become an exercise in creating initiatives simply to fill gaps in a mapping diagram.

USE OF STRATEGY MAPS

As the use of balanced scorecards has increased, organizations have found value in a number of processes that expand on the original concepts. The strategy map is one of these additional value-added concepts that helps to organize the strategic objectives into a logical cause-and-effect chain. At its simplest, a strategy map is a diagram that organizes the strategic objectives visually into the four perspectives and attempts to show linkages between them with a series of arrows. Exhibit 1.7 offers one example; there is an almost infinite number of ways to display these objectives and linkages graphically.

Regardless of the graphical choices, the strategy map is designed for one key function: to tell the story of the strategy. The cause-and-effect linkages should explain how your organization will attempt to take intangible assets, such as knowledge and information (found in the learning and growth perspective), and turn them into tangible outcomes, such as customer satisfaction and shareholder value (found in the customer and financial perspectives). The key translators in this case are the core organizational processes found in the internal perspective.

If you examine the left side of the strategy map in Exhibit 1.7, you can read one part of the strategic story for this organization. By building the right skills, particularly customer-focused skills, the organization will be better able to understand the needs of

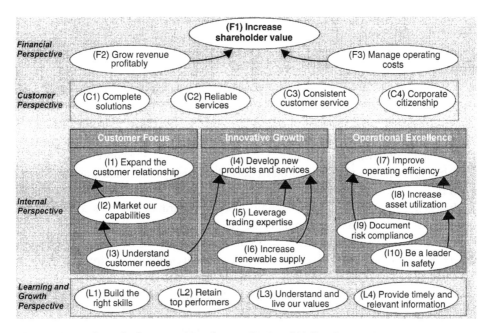

EXHIBIT 1.7 Sample Strategy Map from a Fictional Utility Company

its customers. This understanding will help it more effectively market its products and services to the target audiences, which should result in stronger and deeper customer relationships. The combination of better marketing and broader relationships will help it to be viewed by its target customers as a complete provider of solutions. By broadening relationships with existing customers and reaching target customers more effectively, revenue growth and ultimately shareholder value can be achieved.

The fact that strategy maps can be used to explain the effect of intangible assets on overall results makes them useful communications tools. Organizations use such maps to help individuals understand their role in executing the strategy. It is much easier for human resource managers to understand that their efforts to build an organization's skills and climate result in better relationships with the customer than to try to understand how those efforts directly influence revenue growth or shareholder value. The key to mobilizing an organization around a strategy is having individuals understand how they can impact strategic success. The strategy map is an important tool that, when combined with the scorecard, allows employees to understand and focus on the key priorities to achieve the vision.

SCORECARD CASCADING

Just as the strategy is clearly articulated through the four perspectives for the overall organization, it should be done in a similar manner for each of the operating and support groups. The cascade process creates aligned scorecards at multiple levels of the organization to focus resources and attention on the key strategic priorities. There are typically a number of key themes where focus is needed throughout the organization for sustained success. In a utility organization, this might be reliability; for a manufacturing organization, it could be quality; a service organization may have customer relationships; and so on. For any of these core themes, each subsidiary organization must contribute, whether it is marketing, production, or information technology. The scorecard helps to create better strategic alignment among the units toward achieving the organization's goals.

Ideally, the overall corporate scorecard will be developed first to articulate the core themes. Given the strategic priorities for the overall organization, each subsidiary group can analyze its own strategic destination and approach. The actual maps and scorecards may look different based on the organization's strategy at each group's own level. Most market-facing operating units will be focused toward a specific subset of the overall organization's customer base and product portfolio. These groups should develop a customer perspective aligned to their specific market focus.

Independent elements of the value chain (assembly, distribution, etc.) or shared service units (information technology, human resources, etc.) will designate internal customers for their key outcomes. The customer perspective in this case must identify the key needs of the internal customers and the relationships the internal customers desire. The financial perspectives for the internal-facing units typically are focused on process efficiency and effectiveness. They must deliver a specific type of value to the market-facing organizations to drive overall shareholder value. An example of this is shown for a supply chain organization in Exhibit 1.8. Here you can see how a map for an internal-facing organization has a very different internal and customer focus from one for the overall organization.

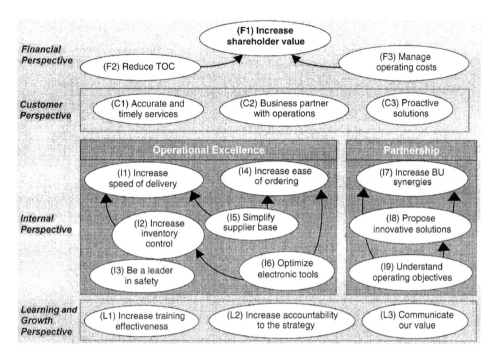

EXHIBIT 1.8   Sample Strategy Map for a Supply Chain Organization

Typically, an organization will designate a few key strategic objectives and measures that every part of the organization must use. These shared objectives often include the overall shareholder value measurement, a focus on employee satisfaction or development, a consistent risk management process, and so on. These shared objectives are the initial building blocks for the cascaded scorecards. The remainder of the scorecard will be based on the units' unique and aligned strategy. In Exhibit 1.8, a few key objectives, such as F1, have been mandated throughout the organization. Other objectives, such as L1, have been taken and interpreted for the specific organization.

Much has been written on the right number of scorecards for an organization. There is no magic number. As you develop past two or three levels, the scorecards begin to become smaller and more focused. Some organizations have cascaded down to personal scorecards for individuals that combine the key shared metrics of the organization with specific goals for the person, his or her team, and business unit. While organizations have derived great value from the cascading of scorecards to individuals, it is recommended that an initial implementation of the balanced scorecard focus on the first two to three levels of an organization. Further cascading should take place in subsequent management cycles and leverage the learning from the initial implementation.

BRINGING IT ALL TOGETHER

As discussed, the balanced scorecard is designed to create management focus on the strategy by translating that strategy into operational terms through the use of strategic objectives, measures, targets, and initiatives. The implementation of a good balanced scorecard requires a number of elements:

- *Leadership involvement.* The scorecard is designed around the strategy, and senior leadership must commit to articulating and communicating the strategy through the framework. They must unfreeze the organization to implement effective change in the management process.
- *Cause-and-effect relationships.* Each element of the scorecard must be linked to the key outcomes through a clear cause-and-effect chain. The lack of these relationships typically identifies gaps in the strategy.
- *Performance measures.* There must be a complete and balanced set of outcome and driver measures that can report data necessary to steer the organization. A lack of key measures or the data to support them will invalidate the value of the scorecard.
- *Stakeholder value.* The value to the stakeholders (shareholders, customers, employees, etc.) must be clearly articulated. The cause-and-effect chains should lead directly to the creation of value for these groups.
- *Initiatives that create change.* The portfolio of strategic initiatives must be defined to move the organization toward the strategic destination. A lack of initiatives may impede strategic success while too many can reduce focus and overstretch resources.

An effective scorecard must have all of these elements and be clearly linked to the other management processes within the organization. The rest of this discussion focuses on the linkages of the scorecard with the strategic planning and budgeting process as well as the use of the scorecard as a continuous management tool. Without continued focus and attention on the strategy, an organization cannot reach its goals.

INTEGRATING THE SCORECARD WITH PLANNING AND PERFORMANCE

A successful balanced scorecard process is one that does not exist on its own but is seamlessly integrated with the overall planning and performance management processes of the organization. The scorecard brings value to the integrated processes by providing a focus on strategy with a common language and organizing framework. Many organizations have used the balanced scorecard as a way to streamline and standardize their management processes. The ability of the scorecard to leverage its common elements and lexicon at the corporate, business group, division, or even individual level provides an ability to synchronize and align previously disparate processes.

The integration of the balanced scorecard with planning and performance processes must happen in two key ways:

1. *Annual planning process.* The balanced scorecard represents a significant improvement in the ability to link the periodic strategic planning process with the budgeting process.

2. *Ongoing strategic management.* The balanced scorecard allows the organization to review its performance based on the successful execution of the strategy as well as traditional financial and budgetary concerns. Better information allows the organization to make strategic decisions faster and with better results.

The value the scorecard brings in putting strategy at the forefront of measurement and performance is achieved only through continuous focus. Successful organizations have used the balanced scorecard as a key tool in communicating the strategic priorities of the organization during the annual planning process as well as a measurement tool for assessing ongoing execution success.

BALANCED SCORECARD AND ANNUAL PLANNING

For most organizations, integrating the balanced scorecard with their annual planning process represents a way to streamline and align existing processes rather than develop and implement a totally new process. The scorecard can add value to almost any type of planning cycle. For purposes of this discussion, we focus on a traditional annual budgeting process.

Exhibit 1.9 shows where the scorecard process fits in the planning cycle (primarily as the link between strategic planning and the budgeting process). We also see that the scorecard can have a profound influence on the budgeting process and should influence the priorities of the strategic planning process.

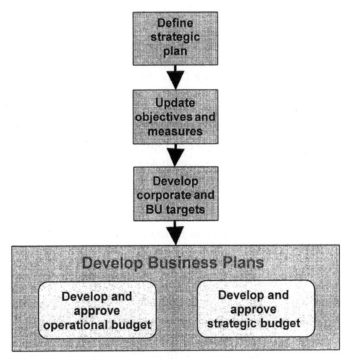

EXHIBIT 1.9   Key Steps in an Integrated Scorecard Planning Process

Integration with Strategic Planning

The widespread use of scenario planning techniques has helped to standardize and improve the effectiveness of strategic planning processes. The scenario plan should identify the key factors in the marketplace and regulatory environment that will impact the organization's strategy. In terms of integration with the scorecard, the scenario plans should include a major focus on the targeted customer groups. To properly define the strategy and strategic objectives, the shifting needs and expectations of the target customers must be forecasted accurately. Additionally, the competitive landscape for these target customers must be examined closely to determine if the differentiating factors for the organization will still be relevant in future periods.

Understanding future customer and market conditions through the scenario plans will also have a major impact on the internal process priorities. In situations in which the competitive advantage of an organization is forecast to decline, a new focus on customer acquisition or product development activities is likely to be necessary. Obviously any change to the operational focus will also require corresponding changes in the organization and its skills and culture.

The outcome of the scenario planning process should be a primary scenario that details the key market and environmental conditions for the planning horizon of the strategic plan. Alternative scenarios should also be retained to allow contingency plans to be integrated with the overall strategic plan. The executives should be able to understand and discuss these scenarios to develop the final overall strategic plan.

The resulting strategic plan should focus on two key points:

1. *Strategic destination.* The destination identifies the primary goals for the organization over the plan horizon. This destination may be expressed in financial terms, market position, and/or desired customer relationships.
2. *Strategic approach.* The approach should focus on identifying the key priorities and milestones along the path to the destination.

The destination must be stated in a way that communicates the guiding principles behind strategic decisions and may have multiple components. For example, a company may wish to achieve the largest market share while leading its industry in employee satisfaction ratings. While the destination always should be a large and ideally inspiring goal for the organization, it should not be contradictory or seem impossible. For example, an organization is unlikely to be the lowest-cost provider while achieving the highest customer satisfaction. The clarity of the strategic destination is the key to enabling effective strategic management.

The approach should specify the available resources that will be deployed to reach the destination. The available resources must be aligned with the destination to communicate a reachable but inspiring goal for the organization. The approach should be specific in terms of organizational changes that need to occur and include reorganizations, skill transitions, or acquisition/divestiture intent. The approach must be precise enough to allow for proper resource alignment and strategic focus.

The combination of a clearly articulated strategic destination and approach will allow the organization to effectively measure progress and steer the organization toward the destination through the strategic management process driven by the scorecard.

Update Objectives and Measures

Once a clear strategic plan has been identified, the scorecard elements must be updated to reflect any changes. The financial and customer perspectives must be aligned to the strategic destination. The financial perspective will state the overall financial destination and the key financial levers that will enable value creation. For example, an organization that is moving toward a cost-leadership strategy may need to put more emphasis on the cost and asset utilization objectives rather than revenue growth. The customer perspective should identify the target customer groups and the key value that those groups will expect. For this example, the organization should have customer objectives focused on cost, consistency, and efficient service.

The internal and learning and growth perspectives will typically be focused on articulating the strategic approach. The primary internal process focus areas should be identified in strategic themes that collect related objectives. Continuing the example, an *operational excellence* theme might contain objectives focused on machine reliability (to drive asset utilization), supply chain efficiency (to drive cost leadership and cycle time), and safety. The learning and growth perspective should articulate the changes in skills (through development or acquisition), culture (through training or accountability processes), and information (through systems or process changes). In this example, the organization may need to increase its skills in process management, move accountability closer to the operational decision makers, and improve its ability to analyze operational performance for continuous improvement.

As the objectives in each perspective are adjusted, the measures must change as well. In general, any change in the objective will require a change in the measure. Measures should also be evaluated for objectives that have not changed. The key factor in the evaluation of existing measures should be the quality of information that was provided by the measure and the resulting ability to make decisions based on that information. In many cases, the organization may change the frequency of collection or the underlying calculation of the measure to improve information quality.

Traditionally, organizations tried not to change their performance measures in order to gain long-term trending and comparability information. The balanced scorecard does not dispute that goal but seeks only to ensure proper alignment between the strategy and measures by updating them together. Because the scorecard objectives and measures are designed to highlight the most important priorities, successful organizations will find that they have reached their goals and no longer need to retain certain measures over time. For our example, once supply chain efficiency has been moved to a sustainable goal, the focus may shift to product development cycle time.

The adjustment of the strategic objectives and measures must be first carried out for the overall corporate scorecard and then cascaded down to the operating and support units. As discussed in the cascading section, common objectives and measures should be used where strategic themes cross organizational boundaries. These common strategies should be a key focus for the final alignment of the cascaded objectives and measures.

Develop Corporate and Business Unit Targets

The use of the balanced scorecard to communicate key targets before the primary budgeting phase delivers significant value to organizations with integrated processes. In a traditional planning process, the operational units begin a bottom-up budgeting process based on their prior year's performance. Because this process typically begins before the communication of new strategies and resource commitments, it results in misalignment with top management priorities and multiple corrective iterations that add time and frustration to the process. The use of scorecard targets to provide direct input into the budgeting process of operating units can help eliminate this frustration and reduce time spent in iterations by aligning the expectations of senior management with those of the operating units.

At the conclusion of the strategic planning process, the organization should be able to clearly articulate the targeted customers and the mix of products and services that will be provided to them. The strategic destination and approach should be formalized by setting the primary scorecard targets in the financial and customer perspectives for the overall corporation. The financial targets should communicate expectations for overall shareholder value broken down into revenue, expense, and capital allocation components. The customer targets will articulate the market share, customer segmentation, and product portfolio expectations.

There should not be an expectation that all scorecard targets will be known before the more detailed operational plans and budgets are created. The strategic planning process should easily be able to set the financial and customer targets based on the overall strategic destination. The strategic approach should also be able to specify at least some of the key internal and learning and growth targets at the corporate level. The primary goal should be to cascade the financial and customer targets to the level of the key operating and business units. The scorecards for the operating units will then be updated with the overall strategic destination and performance expectations for the corporation.

While the core strategy for the organization is set at the corporate level, the actual execution of that strategy happens within the operational units. Even though the overall strategic approach will have set out some key focus areas, the business units will develop their detailed approach to implementing the strategy during their operational and strategic planning, processes that will allow them to set their final targets in the internal and learning areas of the scorecard.

The value in setting the corporate and business unit targets for the financial and customer dimensions is achieved by communicating them early enough and at a sufficient level of detail to align the detailed business unit planning before that process is under way. In many organizations, the time spent by in reconciling the detailed budgets of the operating units with the financial expectations of the corporations at the end of the planning process is essentially wasted effort. By better aligning the expectations at the beginning of the process and aligning the planning schedules of the operational units to wait for the strategic targets, the overall planning effort is reduced and the overall satisfaction with this effort is increased at both management and executive levels.

Develop Business Plans

Once the strategic planning process has concluded with the strategic destination and approach specified and translated into key financial and customer targets, the operational and support units should create their detailed business plans that will articulate their specific approach to deploying their assets and resources to meet the strategic goals. Much has been written on the level of detail that these plans need to encompass. The clearest guidance is that the business plans for each unit should be as short and as streamlined as possible while providing sufficient management information for the organization.

The basic business planning methodology includes an articulation of the strategy and the budget for each of the participating units. In integrating the scorecard, the strategy components of the business plan should be easily cascaded from the corporate strategic plan using the predefined strategic targets. The important strategy components for the operating units are no different from those at the corporate level, mainly the key financial goals, targeted customers, product portfolios, and organizational approach to meet those goals. The focus of this discussion is on the budgeting elements of the business plans.

In implementing strategic management processes and aligning them to budgeting, the key learning is that the budgeting process must be split into an operational budget, which is directly influenced by the strategic targets, and a strategic budget, which becomes an integral part of the strategic management process. The split between these key elements is illustrated in Exhibit 1.10. This split is very different from a traditional

EXHIBIT 1.10   Split between Operational and Strategic Budgets

alignment based on capital versus operational expenses and is discussed further in the sections on operational and strategic budgeting.

Aligning the Operational Budget

The operational budget is made up of a number of line items that can be representative of both capitalized and expensed items. In working with utility companies, they refer to this budget as what is necessary to keep the lights on. Basically, the operational budget refers to those activities that are ongoing and necessary to maintain the current capabilities of the organization to produce, sell, and service its core products and services provided to the customer base. The operational activities may include marketing, customer service, operations, overhead, support, maintenance, and so forth. The primary difference between this and the strategic budget is that strategic line items are discretionary in nature and designed to build new capabilities that are beyond the core customers, products, and operations of the existing organization.

The operational budget by far makes up the major component of the expenditures of most organizations. Most operational budgets comprise up to 90% of the total expenditures for the organization. The approach to developing this budget is no different from that discussed in other best-practice budgeting approaches. Ideally, the budget should be defined in a top-down manner using activity-based budgeting techniques that result in the minimum number of line items for effective management.

The only key difference in this process for scorecard organizations is the use of the targets. The problem most organizations have in implementing activity-based budgeting is the need to know precisely what products and services will be provided to what customers at what levels of service. The previously discussed target setting based on the strategic plan should focus on providing exactly this information. Once an organization's core activity performance is understood, the creation of the specific line items should be more of a systematic journey from the targets rather than an incremental update from prior-year performance (i.e., last year plus 10 percent, etc.).

The delivery of clear outcome targets from the strategy should allow the operating units to better understand the resources they will require to implement the strategy. The inclusion of the resource constraints of the organization with the outcome targets allows the budgeting process to be done with the confidence that these resources needs will be approved and implemented. The confidence given by early targets greatly improves both the accuracy of the process and the organizational commitment to using it as a key business tool.

Aligning the Strategic Budget

While the strategic budget often represents only 10 percent of an organization's total expenditures, it is the key means to implementing new strategies and transforming the organization for future success. The management of a separate strategic budget differently from the operational budget components is new to most organizations. The linkage to a scorecard-based strategic management system is clear because the strategic budget is composed of the key strategic initiatives for the organization.

As discussed, strategic initiatives are those actions or programs that help to implement new organizational capabilities that close a strategic gap in the current abilities of an organization versus its ability to achieve the strategic destination. Criteria that define a strategic initiative were discussed in the initiatives section of the balanced scorecard overview. A further key delineation is that strategic budget items are discretionary in nature; they represent a choice to allocate resources to a new area versus a mandatory expenditure to maintain the current capabilities. For example, constructing an additional product assembly line would be a strategic initiative while maintaining or replacing existing machinery would be an operational initiative.

Each operating unit should try to find the key initiatives that will enable it to reach the long-term strategic goals of the organization. These initiatives may involve the development of new products, an expansion of current production capabilities, expansion of the customer base, and so on. The goals of the initiatives should directly impact or be sufficient to meet the stretch targets for the operating unit or the corporation as a whole.

The identification and analysis of proposed initiatives should result in the preparation of a short business case describing the implementation time frame, resource usage, risks, and benefits. Each operating unit should use a standard template for the business case that will allow comparison across other units. The key to this process is a cross-business unit evaluation of proposed initiatives. The corporation should designate a diverse central team that can analyze multiple initiatives and prioritize them based on the available resources.

The initiative evaluation team should implement a scoring model for the proposed initiatives that takes into account both the financial and overall strategic benefits and risks from implementation. A sample scoring framework is shown in Exhibit 1.11. Each of the dimensions in the framework will break down into specific evaluation criteria.

Strategic Alignment (30 pts.)	• Overall importance of initiative to successful execution of the strategy
	   • Breadth of support to strategy
	   • Impact on strategic measures and targets

Financial Benefits (20 pts.)	• Financial benefits calculated through net revenue (NPV)
	   • Cost
	   • Revenue

Cost (20 pts.)	• The total cost of the initiative • The internal resource requirements

Other Benefits (30 pts.)	• The additional benefits from implementation
	   • Social benefits (employees, community)
	   • Environmental benefits
	   • Legal/regulatory exposure

Risk Factors (−30 pts.)	• A collection of factors designed to measure the overall risk and complexity of implementation • Technology, external opposition, time to implement, risk planning and analysis, legislative involvement, etc.

EXHIBIT 1.11   Sample Scoring Priorities for Strategic Initiatives

The organization should predetermine the individual elements that will result in a normalized initiative prioritization score before the planning process begins. The scoring criteria should be built into the business case template that each operating unit uses to define its proposed initiatives.

The use of a centralized evaluation team and a standard prioritization template greatly increases the communication across the organization during the strategic budgeting process. This process is designed to maximize the value from the total organization strategic budget by evaluating initiatives in a holistic way. The communication of the organization's priorities through the standard business case and template helps to streamline the operating unit's identification process and provides a common set of expectations regarding the availability of resources.

Once the cross-business evaluation team has prioritized the complete set of initiatives, it will create a short list that can be sent to senior management. This process will assure senior management that all areas of the business have cooperated to find the best use of strategic resources. An executive committee then should approve the final set of initiatives based on the prioritized list. One of the key goals of using a standardized and numerical evaluation process is to help remove elements of politics and perceived favoritism from the initiative approval process.

Once the approved initiatives are designated, each operating unit should include those business cases as well as any smaller locally approved initiatives in its strategic budget as part of its overall business plan. Each operating unit will likely have a series of other initiatives that due to their size or scope will be part of the unit's internal local budget rather than needing a special distribution of strategic resources.

Finalizing the Business Plans

Once each operating unit has completed its operational and strategic budgeting processes, these budgets along with their completed strategies, scorecards, and targets should be combined into a consolidated business plan for approval by senior management. Because targets were established at the beginning of the process and the distribution of strategic resources was agreed to during the initiative evaluation, there should be a minimum of iteration or rework at this time. Senior management should already know what the key strategic outcomes and approaches will be for each operating unit. The focus of the process should be to communicate early and often to reduce the overall planning workload and increase the accuracy and effectiveness of the process.

CONTINUOUS STRATEGIC MANAGEMENT WITH THE SCORECARD

While the balanced scorecard clearly can be used as an organizing framework to streamline the planning and budgeting process, the core value from the scorecard is derived from using it as a continuous management tool that puts strategy at the center of performance analysis and decision making. The scorecard must be used throughout the organization, both to communicate the strategy and to help the organization understand its success or failure at executing the strategy. For performance management, a consistent and defined process must be implemented that reports scorecard information to the right level of management to take strategic actions.

Most large organizations choose to review their scorecard performance on at least a quarterly basis. Organizations in fast-evolving markets or industries may choose to review their performance on a monthly basis as well. The actual performance of the organization against the defined measures and targets should be reported using an easily understood format. The concept of traffic lighting, or using red, yellow, and green indicators for each measure to signify below target, slightly below target, or on target, is the generally accepted means for reporting this information.

Even more important than the simple traffic light information is the strategic narrative that accompanies the performance. For each measure, the organization should report the critical information that shows why the performance is at the specified level. This information is especially crucial for areas that are below target or in danger of falling below target. For these yellow or red measures, a specific exception template should also be prepared that clearly articulates the understanding, options, and recommendations for strategic actions that should occur to improve performance.

The concept of using exception-based reporting helps to transform the executive meeting process. Where in a traditional organization serial reporting is used to report results and activities in each business area, a scorecard and exception-focused reporting process immediately draws attention to only those areas that need strategic action. Three steps are necessary to implement this type of reporting process:

1. *Early communication.* The scorecard results and analysis should be prepared and distributed with enough time for executives to review the results before the meeting. In this case, strategies that are performing at expected levels should not need to be discussed further during the actual meeting.
2. *Standardized reporting.* A set of standard templates for measures that are both on or off target must be developed that will allow reporting at a consistent level of detail. The standardization allows for easy consumption of the information and forces the prior consideration of strategic implications and actions for the owners of each measure.
3. *Consistent use of the scorecard.* Each of the cascaded scorecards should be reported using standard templates to its management before the organization's senior management discusses the strategy. These premeetings allow for a deeper understanding of the progress of the overall strategy and help clients to be able to report subsidiary performance results using the scorecards in a concise manner that highlights only those areas of strategic issue.

The most important resource for any executive is time. By transforming the meeting process using the scorecard as an organizing framework, the time spent in executive meetings can be reduced by as much as half. These meetings should be a dynamic setting where strategic issues are clearly presented with options and recommendations being prepared and communicated in advance. Time that normally would be spent presenting an issue and its background is now shifted to the meeting preparation and information distribution that takes place between meetings. The actual meeting discussion should be focused on strategic implications and on making key decisions.

Once the level of performance has been communicated and strategic decisions have been made, the organization then can understand the expectations for future performance. Organizations that use rolling forecast processes should update their forecasts based on the strategic environment and execution expectations. As discussed, a well-designed scorecard will have predictive value for future performance based on the results reported against the different perspectives. An organization would be unwise to expect continued strong financial performance if customer and internal indicators suggest a lack of execution ability.

Most executives spend very little time discussing strategy outside of the strategic planning process. The strategy should be the living focus of any management discussion. The combination of a strategic framework for discussion, a standardized method for reporting information against that framework, and a clear focus on decision making will increase the effectiveness of the management process. These benefits are easily achieved with a well-designed and properly implemented scorecard process.

SUMMARY

The success of the balanced scorecard as a strategic management framework is based on the concept that you cannot manage what you cannot measure. This concept is further illuminated by the concept that you cannot measure what you cannot understand. The scorecard allows an organization to articulate and communicate its key strategic priorities by identifying them in the four perspectives of financial, customer, internal, and learning and growth. The scorecard framework forces the organization to better understand and communicate the strategy. The scorecard then allows the organization to effectively measure the execution of the strategy by defining specific performance indicators and targets that communicate the expected level of performance.

The value of a well-implemented scorecard can be seen in both a better understanding of the strategy by the organization and a better set of tools to help manage that strategy. The integration of the scorecard with the planning process allows that framework to put strategy at the center of resource allocation and prioritization decisions. While value is achieved by the exploration of the strategy in scorecard design, lasting value is achieved by effective implementation and use.

2

Strategic Balanced Scorecard–Based Budgeting and Performance Management

Robert E. Paladino, CPA, MBA

Senior Vice President of Global Performance
Crown Castle International (CCI)

INTRODUCTION: WHY MOST COMPANIES FAIL TO IMPLEMENT THEIR STRATEGIES

Corporate America is littered with examples of failed strategies, mergers and acquisitions, and bankruptcies that have left large groups of investors dismayed and perplexed. As a result, public outcry has increased for increased regulatory action and controls and reporting transparency to protect investors. Publicly traded companies now face increased disclosure and mandatory compliance with the Sarbanes-Oxley Act, one of the most far-reaching acts of its kind in recent memory. How could so many bright and energetic executives and their teams fail to understand the key drivers of value in their businesses and poorly execute their company strategies? Unfortunately, some companies resorted to the unsavory practice of fabricating results rather than executing on sound business strategies supported by solid budget and performance management practices. But just what are the barriers to success? How do balanced scorecard-based budgets support achievement of company strategy objectives?

Exhibit 2.1 provides some empirical evidence to help us understand the reasons why nine of ten companies fail to implement their strategies.

The *vision barrier* postulates that only 5 percent of company employees fully understand the company strategy. Why is it so hard for employees to understand the company's direction? The strategy has not been explained in terms that relate to their everyday objectives, roles, and responsibilities. Is it any wonder that companies are challenged to harness the creativity and energy of their arguably most valuable resource?

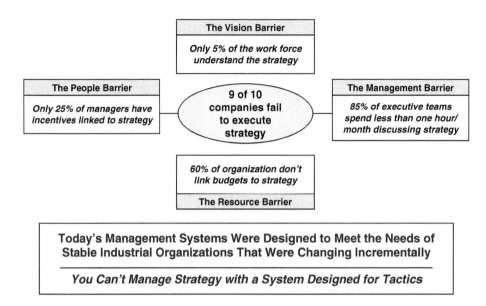

EXHIBIT 2.1   Why Do Nine of Ten Companies Fail to Implement Their Strategy?

Source: Balanced Scorecard Collaborative, *Strategy Focused Organization*, January 15, 2001.

The *management barrier* indicates that 85 percent of executive teams spend far less time discussing strategies and strategic issues. Is it any wonder that implementation rates are so low? Why do businesspeople spend so much time in company meetings but fail to grasp the message conveyed by their reports and analyses? This barrier may help explain why there are disconnects among financial, customer, and operational objectives, measures, and targets.

The *resource barrier* shows us that most companies do not link budgets to strategies. In short, companies may be pursuing financial strategies that differ from or, worse, may be in conflict with their company business and customer strategies. For instance, an operating unit is making its financial targets at the expense of not investing in preventive maintenance, only deferring inevitable poor performance until next year.

The *people barrier* shows us that management incentives link to the company strategy only 25 percent of the time. By default, it is pursuing objectives that in most cases may not support the company direction.

How do these four barriers relate to budgeting, and what can be done to overcome these barriers? Why do some companies understand and overcome these barriers and deliver exceptional performance? What do they understand that many other companies do not? In this chapter, we further explore these issues to understand solutions that involve strategic balanced scorecard-based budgeting and performance management.

WHY A FEW COMPANIES PRODUCE EXCEPTIONAL RESULTS

Kaplan and Norton are credited with developing one of the most exciting and innovative management tools of the past century—the strategy map and balanced scorecard (BSC).

Bain & Company's research suggests that 50 percent of the Fortune 1,000 and 40 to 45 percent of larger companies in Europe use the BSC.[1] No doubt many have scorecards in place, but do they all follow the rigors set forth in their methodology? I can say from direct experience that companies encounter problems with a cafeteria-plan approach to strategic management; they run the risk of leaving out a vital part of an integrated management framework. How would your car accelerate with only seven out of eight cylinders working? How about four out of eight?

The strategy map and BSC focus on objectives and measures vital to executing company strategy. Central to the strategy map and BSC is a focus on selected key objectives and measures. At this juncture we shall explore Pareto's law, often referred to as the 80/20 law, named after the Italian economist Vilfredo Pareto, as it relates to the BSC. Born in 1848, the son of a Genoese father and a French mother, Pareto studied engineering at the University of Turin, Italy. The five-year course in civil engineering, the first two years of which were devoted to mathematics, deeply influenced Pareto's future intellectual outlook. His first work, *Cours d'Economie Politique* (1896–1897), included his famous law of income distribution, a complicated mathematical formulation in which he attempted to prove that the distribution of incomes and wealth in society is not random and that a consistent pattern appears throughout history, in all parts of the world and in all societies, where 80 percent of the income is controlled by 20 percent of the population. This principle has found application across many business situations. You may have noticed in your company that 80 percent of the revenue is derived from 20 percent of the customers, or that 80 percent of operating results come from 20 percent of the plants, and so on. One does not slavishly follow this principle, but business leaders and managers recognize the power of understanding the concentration of drivers and values. The BSC leverages Pareto's law by focusing on the vital few objectives that drive value.

I had the distinct honor of working directly with Kaplan and Norton while leading the telecommunications and utility consulting practice at their firm, the Balanced Scorecard Collaborative. It was truly gratifying to apply this leading-edge strategic management framework at dozens of companies and as an executive at Crown Castle International (CCI). I can say from experience with companies in the field that piecemeal application of the BSC methodology increases risk of failure to implement company strategy fully. Conversely, disciplined implementation of their methodology tailored to your company's needs will yield mind-numbing results. CCI is one of the few companies to win the coveted Balanced Scorecard Collaborative Hall of Fame Award for its BSC implementation and results. Other winners are listed in Exhibit 2.2.

Strategy Map and Objectives

We begin with an in-depth review of the strategy map and strategic and operational objectives to set the foundation. In the next section, we build on this foundation by linking key measures to these objectives. Once we have developed well-aligned objectives and measures, we review how balanced scorecard-based budgets play a key role

---

[1] Peter Brewer, "Putting Strategy Into the Balanced Scorecard," *Strategic Finance*, January 1, 2002.

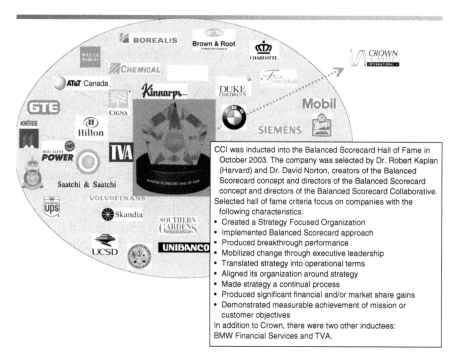

CCI was inducted into the Balanced Scorecard Hall of Fame in October 2003. The company was selected by Dr. Robert Kaplan (Harvard) and Dr. David Norton, creators of the Balanced Scorecard concept and directors of the Balanced Scorecard concept and directors of the Balanced Scorecard Collaborative. Selected hall of fame criteria focus on companies with the following characteristics:

- Created a Strategy Focused Organization
- Implemented Balanced Scorecard approach
- Produced breakthrough performance
- Mobilized change through executive leadership
- Translated strategy into operational terms
- Aligned its organization around strategy
- Made strategy a continual process
- Produced significant financial and/or market share gains
- Demonstrated measurable achievement of mission or customer objectives

In addition to Crown, there were two other inductees: BMW Financial Services and TVA.

EXHIBIT 2.2 Balanced Scorecard Hall of Fame: Crown Castle International Winner

in driving strategy through the organization through effective meeting management. Finally, we review how the links between key objectives and measures and employee incentive compensation reinforce desired behaviors.

The *strategy map* is a one-page graphical representation of your company's strategy. To put this in context, if you wanted an investor to review your financial results, you would provide her with your financial reports consisting of an income statement and a balance sheet. Similarly, if you want the investor to see how well your company is achieving its vision and implementing its strategy, you would share your corporate strategy map and BSC. Now we focus on the strategy map for Pareto Inc. (honorary name for our model company). (See Exhibit 2.3.) The next sections provide a more in-depth discussion of its design and the company as a case study throughout this chapter.

Case Study Summary: Pareto Inc. High-Technology Company Strategy Map

The strategy map shows Pareto Inc.'s vision and business strategy on one page. It shows how the executive team believes the organization will achieve the company's strategic objectives. The strategy map also functions as a communications tool so you will be able to explain your company strategy map to your people inside of 30 minutes. Keep in mind that no single employee will be responsible for achieving all of these objectives; rather, each employee would be responsible for a select subset of two to four objectives

Vision: We will delight our enterprise customers as the preferred provider of integrated network solutions and services

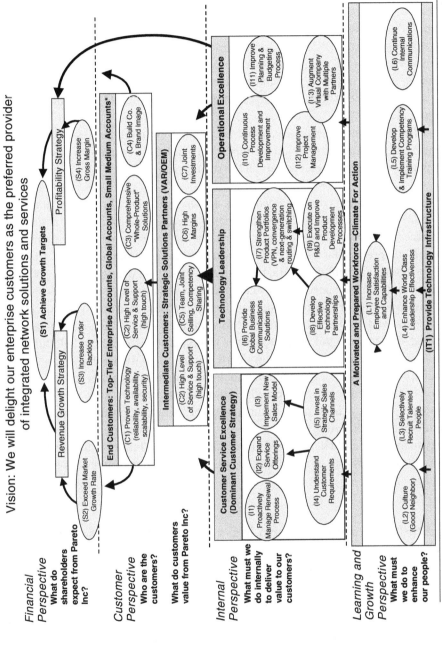

EXHIBIT 2.3 Pareto Inc. Strategy Map

Financial Perspective
What do shareholders expect from Pareto Inc?

Customer Perspective
Who are the customers?

What do customers value from Pareto Inc?

Internal Perspective
What must we do internally to deliver value to our customers?

Learning and Growth Perspective
What must we do to enhance our people?

(S1) Achieve Growth Targets

Profitability Strategy

Revenue Growth Strategy

(S4) Increase Gross Margin

(S3) Increase Order Backlog

(S2) Exceed Market Growth Rate

End Customers: Top-Tier Enterprise Accounts, Global Accounts, Small Medium Accounts*

(C1) Proven Technology (reliability, availability, scalability, security)

(C2) High Level of Service & Support (high touch)

(C3) Comprehensive "Whole-Product" Solutions

(C4) Build Co. & Brand Image

Intermediate Customers: Strategic Solutions Partners (VAR/OEM)

(C2) High Level of Service & Support (high touch)

(C5) Team, Joint Selling, Competency Sharing

(C6) High Margins

(C7) Joint Investments

Customer Service Excellence (Dominant Customer Strategy)

(I1) Proactively Manage Renewal Process

(I2) Expand Service Offerings

(I3) Implement New Sales Model

(I4) Understand Customer Requirements

(I5) Invest in Strategic Sales Channels

Technology Leadership

(I6) Provide Global Business Communications Solutions

(I7) Strengthen Product Portfolios (VPN, convergence & next-generation routing & switching)

(I8) Develop Effective Technology Partnerships

(I9) Execute on R&D and Improve Product Development Processes

Operational Excellence

(I10) Continuous Process Development and Improvement

(I11) Improve Planning & Budgeting Process

(I12) Improve Project Management

(I·3) Augment Virtual Company with Multiple Partners

A Motivated and Prepared Workforce –Climate For Action

(L1) Increase Employee Satisfaction and Capabilities

(L2) Culture (Good Neighbor)

(L3) Selectively Recruit Talented People

(L4) Enhance World Class Leadership Effectiveness

(L5) Develop & Implement Competency Training Programs

(L6) Continue Internal Communications

(IT1) Provide Technology Infrastructure

* (C2) High Touch Relationship would not apply to Small – Medium customers

29

that later will be linked to compensation. The executive team followed the Kaplan and Norton methodology and developed a strategy map with four perspectives (listed down the left side of the map):

1. *Financial perspective.* What do shareholders value from Pareto Inc.? What do they expect the company to deliver to them?
2. *Customer perspective.* What are our intermediary and end customer segments and what have they told us they expect from us? What is our value proposition?
3. *Internal processes perspective.* What are the key business processes we must excel at to be able to deliver the value to customers, which translates into value for the shareholders?
4. *Learning and growth perspective.* What are the foundational factors—the people, skills, culture, and information technology (IT) infrastructure—we have to have in place to enable the achievement of the strategy?

This strategy map is also referred to as a cause-and-effect or linkage diagram. When read from the bottom to the top, the map is intended to capture key drivers that affect successive perspectives moving upward. For instance, if we excel at becoming a motivated and prepared workforce in the learning and growth perspective, then we can excel at our performance in the internal processes that drive customer satisfaction in the customer perspective. If the company has satisfied customers realizing the benefits from its network solutions and services, then the company will be successful at its revenue and profitability strategies. In summary, Pareto Inc. has a balanced, integrated strategy across four perspectives that can be measured to help fulfill its vision. The next section provides an in-depth discussion of the strategy map to help advance understanding of this valuable tool and the linkages between and among objectives. It should also provide you with a litmus test I refer to as the new employee test. Imagine you have been hired as the new sales trainer at Pareto Inc. and the vice president (VP) of sales (also your new boss) is walking you through the company's strategy map. You should have a solid understanding of your new company's strategy in about 30 minutes and be able to see where your position contributes to driving Pareto Inc.'s strategy.

Case Study Continued: Pareto Inc.'s Four Perspectives—An In-Depth Look

Financial Perspective—What Do Shareholders Expect from Pareto Inc.?

From the shareholders' perspective, they will expect us to Achieve Growth Targets (S1) as depicted in the first ellipse on the map in Exhibit 2.3. The investment climate today has shown that Wall Street rewards growth companies that also demonstrate free cash flow. Consequently, to deliver on its growth targets, Pareto Inc.'s financial strategy will be driven primarily by a Revenue Growth strategy (on the left side of the map) balanced with a Profitability strategy (on the right side of the map). That is, the Revenue strategy is defined by two strategic objectives:

1. Exceed Market Growth Rate (S2)
2. Increase Order Backlog (S3)

The Profitability strategy, Increase Gross Margin (S4), recognizes that we must meet a gross margin threshold to attract and retain investors. We now turn to the customer perspective.

Customer Perspective — What Do Our End Customers and Channel Partners Value from Pareto Inc.?

Pareto Inc. has identified and targeted three end customer segments as depicted in the top box consisting of top-tier enterprise accounts, global accounts, and small to medium accounts. These customers primarily value four things:

1. Proven Technology (C1)
2. High Level of Service and Support (C2)
3. Comprehensive Whole Product Solutions (C3)
4. Build Company and Brand Image (C4)

To achieve its aggressive financial growth objectives, Pareto Inc. will pursue what is called a "high-touch" channel strategy to leverage the sales forces of various partners (intermediate customers) as shown in the Strategic Solutions box consisting of value-added resellers (VARs) and original equipment manufacturers (OEMs). Using this model, Pareto Inc. will not only derive the benefit from its hundreds of salespeople but also the selling power of several thousand intermediate direct partner salespeople to touch end customers. These Strategic Solutions partners' value propositions differ from the end customers described above. They value four things:

1. High Level of Service and Support (C2)
2. Team, Joint Selling, Competency Sharing (C5)
3. High Margins (C6)
4. Joint Investments (C7)

Pareto Inc.'s goal is to shift and increase sales through the Strategic Solutions partners shown. Pareto Inc. will embark on a program to train the indirect sales force and their supporting staff on our products to help achieve this goal. This is the clearest linkage to your new sales training position.

Internal Process Perspective—A Closer Look at Three Operations Strategies

Business research has identified and defined three types of customer strategies, and studies have shown that high-performing organizations major in *one strategy* and minor in the remaining two. Many companies have failed by losing focus and have attempted to pursue all three strategies. This singular focus also later ties into balanced scorecard-based budgeting.

The three strategies include (1) Customer Service Excellence/Customer Intimacy, which has a relationship focus; (2) Technology Leadership, which has a product focus; and (3) Operational Excellence, which has a low-cost provider focus. Pareto Inc. is pursuing strategy 2, Customer Intimacy, as its dominant customer strategy; this is shown in the middle box. This should help clarify the sales organization's focus and help you develop your sales training materials. Let us review our dominant or major strategy first.

Customer Service Excellence Theme
The future of our company is centered on leveraging the talents of solutions partners to enhance sales volume, maintain high-quality relationships with end customers, and accelerate growth. The Customer Service Excellence strategic theme consists of three substrategies:

1. Proactively Manage Renewal Process (I1) to improve our customer relationship and encourage greater renewal rates.
2. Expand Service Offerings (I2), which will be driven by Understand Customer Requirements (I4).
3. Implement New "High Touch" Sales Model (I3), which will require Invest in Strategic Sales Channels (I5).

We also recognize our strengths in two other strategic themes: Technology Leadership to develop and/or acquire new solutions, and Operational Excellence to deliver solutions on time.

Technology Leadership Theme
Pareto Inc. will focus on providing solutions consisting of products developed in-house, through partners, and from acquisitions. This strategy consists of achieving one key objective: Provide Global Business Communications Solutions (I6); this in turn is supported directly by Strengthen Product Portfolios (I7) to include virtual private networks (VPNs), convergence and next-generation routing and switching. Strengthen Product Portfolios (I7) is driven by two other objectives: Develop Effective Technology Partnerships (I8) and Execute on R&D and Improve the Product Development Processes (I9).

Operational Excellence Theme
Pareto Inc. will achieve better operational efficiencies in its processes to support better margins.

Continuous Process Development and Improvement (I10) focuses on four "customer-facing" processes to make it easier for customers to do business with the company. These include:

1. Integrated Planning, essentially matching demand and supply of products
2. Integrated Order Management, linked with all solutions partners
3. Problem Resolution, to solve customer problems in a timely manner
4. Invoicing, to increase the speed and accuracy of invoices to drive cash flow

Improve Planning and Budgeting (I11) is internally focused on allocation of scarce capital to key strategic projects to achieve the strategic objectives.

Improve Project Management (I12) is focused on the discipline of managing projects to completion, on time and on budget.

Augment Virtual Company with Partners (I13) is focused on linking suppliers and customers to internal systems and processes to speed up cycle times, improve information flows, and reduce errors.

Learning and Growth Perspective Motivated and Prepared Workforce Theme
Pareto Inc.'s success is dependent on realizing the full potential of its human capital. This is manifested in Increase Employee Satisfaction and Capabilities (L1). Five strategies contribute to achieving this objective:

1. *Culture (L2).* Given the influx of many new people, the company will maintain a culture of contribution to the United Way and executive positions on local nonprofit boards, for example.
2. *Selectively Recruit Talented People (L3).* This area is focused on assessing skills needs as an enterprise and deploying a focused approach to recruiting resources to close gaps.
3. *Enhance World Class Leadership Effectiveness (L4).* The executive team recognizes its responsibility to excel at skills such as communications and motivation.
4. *Develop and Implement Competency Programs (L5).* This area focuses on leaders receiving 360-degree feedback, employees implementing career development plans, and Pareto Inc. providing top-notch training to all its employees to enhance its human capital.
5. *Continue Internal Communications (L6).* We recognize that a lot has been done to improve communications, but rapid growth and increasingly complex business creates challenges. We will continue to aggressively communicate to ensure employees are all focused on achieving our vision through our strategic objectives. We will continue to aggressively communicate to ensure employees are all focused on achieving our vision through our strategic objectives.

Provide Technology Infrastructure (IT1) recognizes increased reliance on technology, whether voice or data for communications or enterprise resource planning ERP to manage a global multifaceted supply chain.

How have we done with the new employee test? Do you have a better understanding of Pareto Inc.'s strategy? Could you train the next new employee? What could be more important to Pareto Inc.'s employees understanding and executing its strategy? This clarity will help overcome the four barriers (vision, management, resource, and people) to companies successfully implementing their strategies. The executive team challenged itself to regularly communicate Pareto Inc.'s strategy map and objectives to its employees—think of the power of several thousand people understanding the company direction, including the creativity and motivation that would unleash. With the strategy map and objectives clearly defined, we now direct our attention to Pareto

Inc.'s BSC measures, targets, and initiatives. These will be discussed in more depth in the next section.

MEASURE YOUR STRATEGY WITH BALANCED SCORECARD

The BSC mirrors and supports the strategy map described earlier. Each strategy map strategic objective is linked to a measure on the BSC to enable management to track implementation of the company strategy. In Exhibit 2.4, we displayed the dominant operations strategy described earlier: Customer Excellence, including its key objectives, measures, measure target, executive sponsor, and related initiatives . This construct provides clarity or line-of-sight accountability for strategy execution and supports management meetings focused on accountability and performance.

For instance, in your area of expertise, Implement New Sales Model (I3) will be measured by Percent Revenue from Channel Partners, which has a target of 15 percent for the year. The objective, measure, and target are owned by the VP of Sales, who has also kicked off the sales training project that you support to manage this transition with the team. Back to the new employee test: Here is where the VP of Sales would provide more granular details on sales-related objectives, measures, and targets.

Categories and Types of Measures

The BSC is composed of many different *categories* of measures or ways to express measures as shown above. Some examples include:

	Objective	Measure	Target	Sponsor	Initiative
(I1) Proactively Manage Renewal Process (I3) Implement New Sales Model (I2) Expand Service Offerings (I4) Understand Customer Requirements (I5) Invest in Strategic Sales Channels	I1. Proactively Manage Renewal Process	Renewal %	80%+	VP Sales	Contract Renewal IT Project
	I2. Expand Service Offerings	$ Revenue from New Offerings	$50 million	VP Sales	
	I3. Implement New Sales Model	**% Revenue from Channel Partners**	**15%**	**VP Sales**	**Sales Training Project**
	I4. Understand Customer Requirements	# User Group Members	20 Sessions	VP Sales	
	I5. Invest in Strategic Sales Channels	# New Partners	Grow by 20%	VP Sales	

EXHIBIT 2.4　Pareto Inc. Internal Perspective: Customer Service Excellence

- *Percentages.* Free cash flow percent growth rate, repairs and maintenance percent reduction rates, customer percent retention rate, or process sales percent closure rate
- *Absolute dollars.* New product revenue, payroll expenses, or ground lease expense
- *Ordinal numbers.* Sulfur dioxide or nitrogen dioxide emissions in thousands of tons
- *Survey ratings.* Customer satisfaction on a seven-point scale
- *Time.* Cycle time expressed in seconds, minutes, hours, days, weeks, and so on
- *Ratios.* Safety loss worker days per 1,000 hours worked
- *Indices.* System average interruption duration index or customer average interruption duration index
- *Rankings.* Top ten in size, assets, market capitalization, or customer satisfaction

While there are many categories of measures, one can also sort and group them into complementary *types*. We examine four types of measures consisting of two pairs that complement each other: lead and lag and efficiency and output.

Lead and Lag Measures

Leading measures are often referred to as early-warning measures. These indicators are generally more prevalent in the operations and learning and growth perspectives of your BSC to provide a month or quarter heads-up to activities or events that will manifest themselves later in the financial results measures. On occasion, however, you will see a lead measure in the financial perspective. In Pareto Inc.'s BSC, you see *Front-Log* expressed as the number and dollar value of proposals submitted to its customers for consideration. Another leading measure includes *Backlog*, a measure of customer contract commitments that have not yet been recognized as revenue.

Lagging measures, or rearview-mirror-based measures, such as Free Cash Flow, record history of what took place last month, last quarter, or last year. While these measures provide a historical perspective, they are not always reliable predictors of future performance. Would you drive that eight-cylinder car in reverse? You need the visibility provided by leading indicators about the road ahead.

Efficiency (Process) and Effectiveness (Output) Measures

Efficiency (process) measures provide visibility into how well a given process or set of processes is functioning. Process measures are closely linked to quality efforts whether we are focusing on ISO 9000, Baldrige Award criteria, or Six Sigma. In quality terms, these are called your drivers, or Xs. While a complete discussion of any of these quality disciplines has embodied many entire books, the context here is understanding and appreciating how the BSC and process quality measures are reinforcing. Fundamentally, your BSC should be tracking key attributes of processes or an index of several processes. Examples of process measures include productivity measures such as process cost per unit of output (economic), turnaround time (cycle time), and process reliability and repeatability.

Effectiveness (output) measures complement efficiency measures and provide instruction on the quality of process outputs. In quality terms, these are your customer-facing deliverables, or so-called Ys. Examples include percent defective items, number of errors, and invoicing accuracy.

A call center example at this stage would highlight the Efficiency and Effectiveness measure relationship. The (X) Efficiency/Process measure of "Answer Speed" by company operators would help drive the (Y) Effectiveness/Output measure of "Call Abandon Rate." Quality programs will look at improving the Xs that drive the Y results.

Bringing things together, Pareto Inc. has a new sales objective, Implement New Sales Model (I3), that will be measured by a Percent Revenue from Channel Partners. This measure fits into the *Percent Category* and is a *Lagging, Output* Y measure. Your training program, however, is a leading X indicator where you may adopt submeasures, such as number of classes taught or number of salespeople trained. Each measure has approximately 20 attributes to ensure it is properly developed, budgeted, and managed; attributes include, for instance, measure owner, measure reporter, data source system, measure definition and calculation, and many other attributes. It is critical to stabilize the attributes and provide transparency so everyone is clear about the rules of the road. Your BSC program will lose creditability without healthy debate and consensus on what is being measured and how.

Measure Targets

Once a company has defined its objectives and measures, it must establish targets (we use the terms "targets" and "budgets" synonymously) against which it can track performance. For our purposes, we discuss targets in the context of annual planning, generally consisting of annual figures. The next section breaks this down into a more detailed budget discussion. Targets set and communicate the expected performance level for the organization and focus the organization on improvement. Each target should match a measure, one for one, and be quantifiable.

Exhibit 2.5 explains the four primary methods for setting targets.

Pareto Inc. has a new sales objective, Implement New Sales Model (I3), that will be measured by a Percent Revenue with a *15 Percent Target* for Revenue from Channel Partners. This should provide a clear, quantifiable target for your sales training program to help the sales team achieve.

Four Target-Setting Methods	Measure	Target	
		2005	Stretch
Derived from overall goal	Revenue	$39,774	$111,482
Benchmark industry leaders	Cycle time	100 Days	60 Days
Incremental improvement based on historical performance	Employee retention	85%	90%
Establish baseline and define targets over time	Mystery caller program in place Benchmark established? (y/n)	Yes	90% compliance rating

EXHIBIT 2.5 Four Primary Methods for Setting Targets

Some key points to consider when setting targets as a company are listed next.

- Targets should be defined as a comprehensive set.
- Be sure the order of magnitude is appropriate to close any performance gaps.
- When in doubt, look back to the strategy map and the performance gap.
- Large performance gaps require a definitive action plan supported by appropriate resources if the stretch target is to be achieved.

BALANCED SCORECARD–BASED BUDGETS

The sections on strategy maps, objectives, measures, and targets have laid the foundation for balanced scorecard-based budgeting and later performance management, both critical parts of your BSC program. When budgeting for BSC measures, you are setting more granular monthly or quarterly targets for each so you can effectively monitor and manage performance.

Best practice companies will run parallel financial budget and BSC budget processes. The rationale is establishing synchronization and clear links between the financial budgets and related financial BSC measures. In this case, Pareto Inc. will establish an annual revenue target based on business plan assumptions on the overall market, customer analyses, sales plans, and so on. Once the financial plan is approved (by the board), the BSC will focus on a subset of the scores or hundreds of line items in keeping with the Pareto principle (80/20 rule). In this case, Pareto Inc. will focus on three financial measures: one for (S1) Achieve Growth Targets and two for (S4) Profitability Growth Strategy, which includes Margin percent and Operating Expenses $.

After locking in the financial perspective between the budget and the BSC, measure owners will focus on disaggregating the annual targets to monthly, quarterly, and weekly figures. Setting targets involves negotiation among core operations groups and functional support groups to arrive at the right integration of values among objectives and across time. Experience has shown cross-functional collaboration is needed to set meaningful balanced scorecard-based budgets.

For example, in your new position as sales trainer, you are expected to help drive Implement New Sales Model (I3) with a target of increasing revenue 15 percent. How will you spread the accomplishment of this goal across months? Will you assume a straight-line approach evenly distributed month to month? Will you front-end load or back-end load the accomplishment? But wait; you noticed that you will need to work with the owner of a predecessor or supporting objective, Invest in Strategic Sales Channels (I5). You and this owner of (I5) will have to work out the relationship between your objectives, including the timing of how and when they will be accomplished. You also see value in establishing your own leading indicators, *Number of Training Classes Delivered* and *Number of Salespeople Trained.*

Once you have agreed and submitted your balanced scorecard-based budget for approval, you are now ready to proactively manage performance.

PERFORMANCE MANAGEMENT

One of the first things you will need to focus on is linking job descriptions and bonus compensation to balanced scorecard-based objectives, measures, and targets. This is a powerful link that cannot be underestimated and will also support productive meeting management.

Linking Compensation to Strategy

There are several different approaches to total compensation, and this chapter does not attempt to cover this vast subject matter area. Rather, I provide a basic example for the sales manager position in Pareto Inc. Your new position with a base salary of $100,000 has provided for 30 percent or $30,000 salary bonus potential. But what would you base success on? Pareto Inc. believes that your bonus should be split 80 percent (or $24,000) based on BSC results for your measure and 20 percent (or $6,000) based on demonstrating leadership values and behaviors. Did this example capture your attention? How important is it for you to now set leading indicators to help ensure your own success? Again, would you front-load your training in Q1 this year (probably yes)? As a new sales manager, you now have clear line-of-sight accountability and rewards linked to performance that can be actively monitored and tracked.

Meeting Management Preparation

Focused preparation for operational review meetings is probably the most overlooked aspect of proactive management. I am not saying people do not work hard to prepare for budget review meetings; I am saying they are narrowly focused on just finances rather than the vital financial, customer, and operations objectives, and measures that drive value (recall Vilfredo Pareto). How often have you sat in meetings where every income statement and balance sheet line-item variance was dissected for discussion? Probably too often. Invariably, the explanations include changes in the weather influencing more or less selling days, one-time events, and changes in methods of accounting. Leading companies are reviewing the few exceptions to their strategy map depicted in stoplight terms: Green is exceeding target, yellow is within say 10 percent of achieving target, and red is more than 10 percent below target.

At Pareto Inc., you are preparing for an operations review meeting and you consult your BSC dashboard to find that both Achieve Growth Targets (S1) and Exceed Market Growth Rate (S2) are green, or exceeding target. But you are alerted to some cautionary yellow lights on leading indicators that could derail (S1) and (S2) lagging indicators *next quarter*. One of these includes Implement New Sales Model (I3)—*your objective*. What do you do? Do not panic—prepare your presentation on why this objective is yellow, and present corrective actions to move the dial to green.

Meeting Management

Today is the operations review meeting, and the VP of Sales has asked you to explain your yellow variance as shown in the strategy map and balanced scorecard-based budget report. You sigh with relief since you were alerted the week prior to the meeting. You are fully in control and have a good solid presentation to support this rating. You should acknowledge the caution light but then proceed to show that your first leading indicator of *Number of Training Classes Delivered* is green. (You have conducted one per week for the past month.) But here is where you shine—you brilliantly show that your second leading indicator, *Number of Sales People Trained,* is glowing red (because you're more than 10 percent below target) since attendance has been low, plagued by cancellations.

You open up the discussion and find that while salespeople have signed up for your classes, they have not been released by their directors to attend classes. You have determined the root cause and during the meeting the VP of Sales reaffirms his commitment to having all salespeople attend your class. This meeting therefore very effectively dealt with a performance exception on the strategy map and balanced scorecard-based budget that became visible through your adoption of two department-level leading indicators. This new training represents an investment in future quarters' sales results. Had this been a financial (only) budget review, would your company have identified this shortcoming this month, or would you have found out a few months later in the financial numbers when it was too late for corrective action? Successful companies recognize the value of leading indicators and reviewing financial, customer, and operational measures results.

SUMMARY

In this chapter we have focused on understanding why companies fail to implement their strategies (the four barriers) and the vital role of the strategy map and balanced scorecard-based budgeting. The tools are based on the Pareto principle (80/20 rule) focused on the vital (few) objectives, measures, and targets that support strategy implementation, management, and control. Further, as Pareto Inc.'s new sales trainer, you passed the new employee test by reviewing the strategy map and establishing leading indicators to help you secure position success and to attain incentive compensation.

3

Budgeting and the Strategic Planning Process

Albert A. Fried

DEFINITION OF STRATEGIC PLANNING

Strategic planning is actually a simple, familiar concept. *Webster's New Collegiate Dictionary* defines planning as the "devising of a method for making or doing something to attain an end." Planning is thus a daily, almost unconscious activity for everyone. The unique aspect of strategic planning as currently applied in sophisticated business management stems from the connotations of the word "strategic"—that is, important, clever, and skillful.

As applied to business management, "strategic planning" is characterized by these attributes:

- It is directed at accomplishment of a specific, defined set of objectives.
- It examines alternate ways of doing the job and provides an estimate of resources required.
- It provides a benchmark to measure how much has been done.

Even in this sense, strategic planning per se is not new. Caesar, Hannibal, Napoleon, and all other great leaders were superb strategists. Andrew Carnegie and Henry Ford devised very effective strategic plans for their businesses based largely on brilliant intuition. The use of *formal* strategic planning systems in business management is a relatively recent phenomenon that has developed because an increasingly complex and rapidly changing environment has made decision making too difficult to rely solely on intuitive judgment. (Even intuitive geniuses such as Ford blundered when they failed to assess and react to environmental and competitive change.)

It is important to note that the terms "long-range forecasting" and "strategic planning" are not synonymous. Forecasting, regardless of whether it is of long or short range, is an attempt to predict future events and conditions. Strategic planning devises a set of actions and programs that should be implemented *now* (or at least within the next year). Environmental analysis and forecasting are very important inputs into the planning process. A good plan provides actions that are responsive to the opportunities and threats identified as a consequence of the environmental analysis and forecast.

PLANNING CYCLE

Exhibit 3.1 illustrates the typical progression of planning and budgeting through a corporation. (For clarity, only one business unit is shown below the dotted line. Most corporations consist of multiple business units. For purposes of this illustration, unit A should be considered representative of a number of units.)

At the top of the exhibit representing the corporate level—that is, the chief executive officer (CEO) and his or her staff—is the corporate strategic plan. This is the CEO's plan for the company. It sets corporate policy; defines the business units and their individual missions and goals; establishes guidelines for corporate development activities, particularly with regard to major acquisitions and divestitures; and determines the financial policies, including dividend policy and debt structure.

Details of corporate strategic planning processes are beyond the scope of this chapter. There are, however, several points regarding this process that should be mentioned.

1. Many companies, especially loosely tied conglomerates, do not have a formal corporate strategic plan. All companies have policies and goals, whether they have been reduced to writing or not. It is important that these policies and goals be understood by the unit manager. If the corporate strategy is unclear and but leaves no doubt as to what they mean, the planning cycle will be considerably less efficient because the plans are likely to be inconsistent with the corporate objectives.
2. The corporate strategic plan does not have to be formulated each year; nor does it need to be tied to an annual planning and budgeting cycle. It must be updated, however, when inputs from environment analysis, forecasts, and/or budgets indicate that significant changes are occurring.

The next elements of the planning cycle are the business unit's strategic plan and operation plan. These two closely linked processes are the first steps in an effective budgeting process and are the principal subjects of this chapter. It is important to prepare and review these plans *before* starting to develop a detailed budget because they will determine the directions the business will follow and the tasks it intends to undertake. If the annual budgeting cycle is designed to allow for such development, review, and management approval before preparation of the budget, much unnecessary effort will be eliminated. If the budget is not prepared *after* agreement on the strategic plan, these problems can occur:

- The budget must be redone—often under tight time constraints and stress, with considerable wasted effort—as a result of a revision in the direction of the plans.

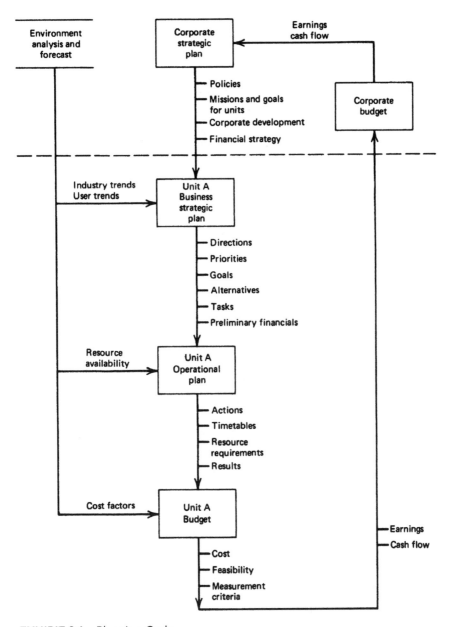

EXHIBIT 3.1 Planning Cycle

- An unrealistic set of goals and measurements is established for the business because of insufficient time or resources to redo the budget.

The strategic planning process uses inputs of the environmental analysis, the forecasts (particularly of industry and user trends), and the corporate objectives for the business. The strategic plan provides direction, priorities, a set of goals, alternatives (including the preferred alternative), an outline of the tasks to be undertaken, and a first approximation of the financial implications. The operational plan uses the output of the strategic plan to develop the detailed actions and timetable for the budget period. This plan serves as the guideline for the various segments of the business and provides a means of integrating the activities to reach a common goal. The next step is the preparation of the budget in which the financial implications of the operational plan are determined.

As a business proceeds through this cycle, the level of detail becomes progressively greater. The strategic plan must contain some description of the tasks and a preliminary indication of the financial implications in order to permit a meaningful assessment of the plan. A preliminary operating plan often is prepared together with the strategic plan to better allow assessment of the proposed strategies. It is important, however, to retain flexibility during the strategic planning process; therefore, operational plans and budgets should not be prepared in great detail at this stage of the cycle.

The planning cycle shown in Exhibit 3.1 also contains two important feedback loops. The first loop feeds the results of the budget back to strategic planning. This permits reassessment of the strategy selected, based on more detailed and up-to-date information. (The strategic plan, as we shall see later in this chapter, is a dynamic concept rather than a fixed, permanent program. It should be adjusted and revised as new information becomes available.)

The second loop takes the sum of the unit budgets up to a total corporate budget, which then determines the corporate earnings, cash flow, and related financial parameters. This must be fed back to the corporate strategic plan to permit a reassessment of its feasibility.

In many companies with a formal planning cycle, the strategic plan and a preliminary operation plan are prepared and reviewed with management during the second quarter of the year to ensure that there is substantial agreement and understanding on the business direction before work starts on the detailed operational plan and annual budget. The detailed operational plan is then prepared during the third quarter of the year and the annual budget is prepared during the fourth quarter.

STRATEGIC PLANNING PROCESS: A DYNAMIC CYCLE

The strategic planning process has been shown to be part of the total corporate planning cycle. It is also a cycle within itself, as indicated in Exhibit 3.2.

For convenience in describing the process, each part of the cycle is described as a discrete "step." Actually, a good planning process has continual interaction and reiteration among the parts so that there is less distinction among the parts of the process than this illustration might imply.

The first step in the process is the *situation analysis*. In this step, the business is broken down into appropriate segments for planning; the environmental analysis, including competitor and industry assessments, is integrated; and the critical issues facing the business are defined.

The second step is the *business direction/concept*, in which the leverage points (i.e., the situations or elements that have the highest payoff potential) are identified and a concept for the business is developed that will enable it to exploit its unique advantages.

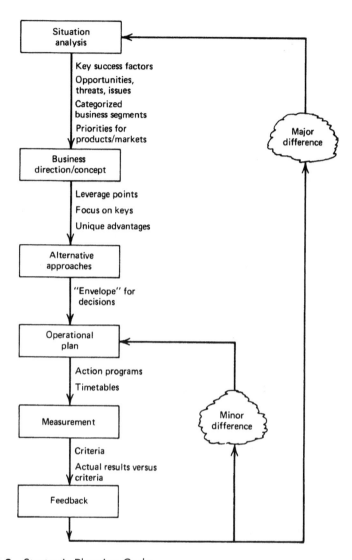

EXHIBIT 3.2 Strategic Planning Cycle

The third step is the development of *alternate approaches* for moving the business in the proposed direction. This step provides an envelope of realistic possibilities from which a decision can be made.

The fourth step is the *operational plan*, which sets out the action programs and the timetable required to achieve the desired goals. This plan is included as an integral part of the strategic plan in this review. In practice, however, where the strategic planning is done well in advance of the budget preparation, the operational plan is usually done in two stages—(1) a preliminary plan, which is integral to the strategic plan, and (2) a detailed plan, which is prepared just prior to preparing the annual budget. The difference between the two is in the level of detail. The preliminary plan lists major actions and their timing and provides an estimate of the resource requirements. The detailed plan lists actions, timing, and resources for each function of the business. It serves as an integrating tool for the business as well as a planning tool.

The fifth step in the cycle is *measurement*. This involves the establishment of criteria against which the effectiveness of the actions can be measured and a monitoring system to permit timely assessments. The monitoring system should be designed so as to be a part of the regular financial reporting system for the business. The data obtained provide the basis for the last step in the cycle, the *feedback*.

This step is critical to making the entire strategic planning process a useful management tool. Most businesses operate in a rapidly changing environment, and the only way to keep the plan up to date and usable is to adjust it continually according to the feedback of the results. The type of modifications made depend on the extent of the difference between the results and the plan. Minor differences may require some adjustment in the timetable or in the sequence of actions. A major difference should precipitate a reexamination of the assumptions used in the situation analysis and a change in business direction.

SITUATION ANALYSIS

This step in the planning process (also called the environmental assessment) consists of three interrelated parts: (1) describing the environment; (2) positioning the business(es); and (3) defining the opportunities, threats, and critical issues. For clarity, each is discussed separately.

Describing the Environment

Use of Forecasts

The environmental forecast and analysis are important inputs. In many larger companies, forecasts of the economy and of specific industries are prepared by a corporate staff. Smaller companies use a variety of external forecasts that range from subscription services offered by consulting organizations, financial institutions, and universities, to special studies to published documents issued by governmental agencies, industry associations, and trade publications. The collection and analysis of such data are an important activity. For an example of how one large company uses this concept, see Exhibit 3.3.

Identifying Key Success Factors

An effective way of identifying success factors in a particular business is to compare the winners and the losers in that industry. The attributes that the successful and unsuccessful businesses have in common are the key success factors.

Development of an explicit understanding of these factors has ramifications far beyond the efficiency of the strategic planning process. As discussed in a subsequent section of this chapter, use of key success factors is a vital element in the business

EXHIBIT 3.3 Examples of the Use of Environmental Analysis by a Large Company

Product Line: _____

Country: ____ U.S.A. ____

Description of Expected Event/Change	Timing	Significance to Business		Management Reaction
Increasing price inflation will lead to user demand for high-yield product. Competitors A and B believed to have product in test	Competitor A market introduction 4Q 2010	$X million of sales threatened by lower price/unit usage	1.	Get complete tests on competitive products; develop quality campaign by December 2010.
			2.	Develop offset product by 1Q 2010.
Growth of generic products	Continuing over next 3 years	Could affect up to 20% of segment sales	1.	Start research and development program for differentiated product—target introduction by 4Q 2010.

Product Line: ____ Overall Country ____

Country: ____ Brazil ____

Description of Expected Event/Change	Timing	Significance to Business		Management Reaction
Brazil agrees to Tokyo Round of General Agreement on Tariffs and Trade reduced import tariffs and removes all export subsidies.	July 1, 2010	1. Aggressive import competition in _____ and _____ products	1.	Increase efforts on cost reduction project.
		2. $X millions of export sales threatened	2.	Determine which export products are competitive without subsidy and focus efforts in 2010–2014 on reinforcing their position.
		3. Items 1 and 2 combine to produce excess capacity in Brazil	3.	Delay expansion to 2012?
		4. Availability of lower-cost packaging materials	4.	Start development and testing of new packages for _____ and _____ products.

47

positioning process and, in turn, in the development of strategies. Even more important is the application of these factors in the ongoing management and control of a business. Executives who understand the key success factors and develop their priorities are likely to be more effective than those who do not have this focus.

Segmenting the Business

Selection of the proper business segments is also critical in the planning process and deserves careful attention. The segment or business unit used for planning does *not* have to correspond to the existing organization unit. That particular organization may be efficient for management and control, but it is not necessarily the most relevant division of the business for planning. In a business that produces a family of products such as thermometers, it may be efficient to have a broad range of products within one management organization, but there are sufficient differences among product application, customer type, specifications, and marketing channels to warrant different plans.

Some guidelines for selecting appropriate segments for planning are listed next.

- *Use the smallest practical segment.* For example, "imported beer" is more meaningful than "beer," which in turn is more precise than "alcoholic beverages." However, the segment should be large enough to have some available industry data.
- *Use segments only if there is a meaningful difference between them.* (A meaningful difference is one that allows for different actions, especially where they have an effect on the key success factors.) Typical differences are product characteristics, users, competitors, and geography.
- *A segment should contain all of the direct competitors.* For example, imported automobiles were once considered in a different segment from domestic automobiles. Yet the competition between a Mercedes and a Cadillac, or between a Honda and a Chevrolet, is more meaningful than the competition between a Honda and a Mercedes. In this case, the meaningful difference is price rather than country of origin.

A product/application matrix such as that illustrated in Exhibit 3.4 is sometimes used as a guide for developing appropriate segments. By entering dollar or unit volume numbers, the relative importance of specific products—both current and potential—can be identified easily. The example also is keyed to allow the identification of the strongest competitor in each product/application box. This display also can be useful as an initial guide to market opportunities that might be exploited and to potential competitive threats.

Positioning the Business(es)

Business Gridding

The concept of business gridding was designed as an aid to developing different strategies and actions for responding to different business environments. The premises behind this approach are listed next.

- It is easier to generate profits from a business operating in a favorable environment. (Oil companies usually have better returns than tanneries.)

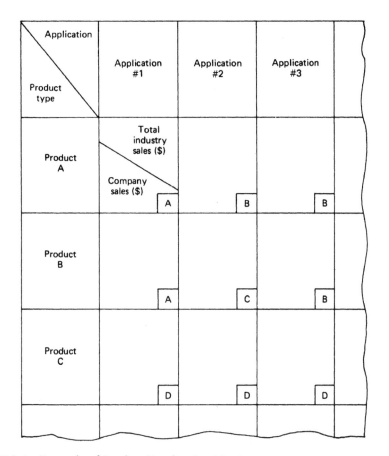

EXHIBIT 3.4 Example of Product/Application Matrix

- The strongest competitors in an industry are usually more profitable.
- It is usually easier and less costly to maintain and build on existing strength than to attempt to overtake a competitor.

The strategic position of a business (or, more appropriately, a business segment) is a primary input to development of an effective strategy. The business grid provides a means of identifying this position based on an assessment of the industry's attractiveness and of the competitive strength of the company.

There are several different versions of this grid in use. Two of the most popular are the 2 × 2 matrix, developed by the Boston Consulting Group, and the 3 × 3 matrix, developed by McKinsey and the General Electric Company.

In the Boston Consulting Group's matrix, industry growth rate is used as a proxy for industry attractiveness and market share is used as a proxy for competitive strength. Using this grid, businesses are positioned as shown in Exhibit 3.5, with different strategies for each position.

- *Star (high share, high growth).* Maintain or increase market strength.

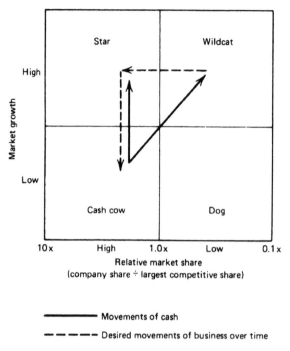

EXHIBIT 3.5   Boston Consulting Group's 2 × 2 Matrix

- *Cash cow (high share, low growth).* Slow growth minimizes investment needs; use business to generate cash for investment in "wildcat" below.
- *Wildcat (low share, high growth).* Investment and effective strategies to fulfill their potential; move into "star" category.
- *Dog (low share, low growth).* No future; exit from the business.

The 3 × 3 matrix system developed by McKinsey and General Electric, shown in Exhibit 3.6, provides for a more inclusive assessment of the strategic position of the business by using a combination of factors (which can be tailored to individual businesses) rather than the single measurements of industry growth and market share. Industry attractiveness is rated high, medium, or low and is assigned to the appropriate column. Company strength is also rated high, medium, or low.

Rating Industry Attractiveness

There is no valid cookbook approach for evaluating industry attractiveness for a specific business segment. There are, however, some common characteristics, such as market size and industry growth, that usually are important for all business segments. In addition, there may be some unique characteristics that are especially significant for a particular business and not for others. For example, government regulations are much more significant for the medical equipment business than for the plastic film business.

Some guidelines are listed next.

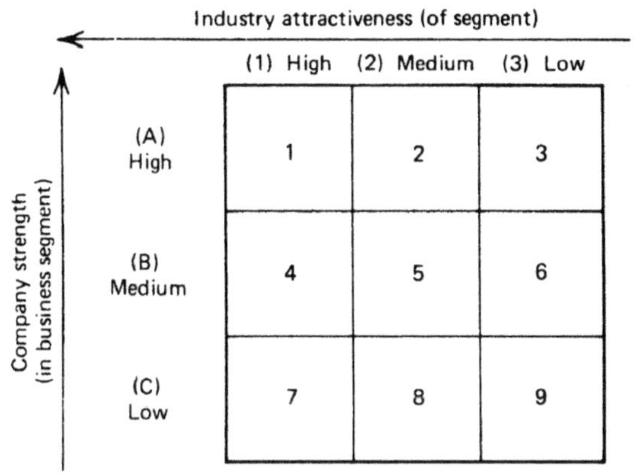

Industry attractiveness (of segment)

EXHIBIT 3.6 McKinsey/General Electric Company 3 × 3 Matrix

▪ *The evaluation of attractiveness should not be based on just one or two characteristics.* A large, growing market does not automatically result in an attractive industry for all participants—witness the sad experience of General Electric and RCA in computers, for example.

▪ *The number of characteristics should be limited to the five or six most important ones.* Use of more tends to complicate and confuse the analysis, without adding much insight. Use of the key success factors described previously will aid in selection.

▪ *Hard factual information should be used, and an effort to collect such information should be made before undertaking this analysis.* However, some useful analysis can be done even if the information base is incomplete by using informal guesswork.

▪ *The process should be considered a repetitive one.* As the analysis proceeds, data gaps will be identified; some of these can be filled, and the analysis can be modified.

The next characteristics are usually among the most important:

▪ Market size and growth potential
▪ Industry profitability (average margins)
▪ Competitive structure
▪ User attitude shifts/opportunities for differentiation
▪ Legislative impacts

Exhibit 3.7 is an example of a format used in one company to assess industry attractiveness. In this example, the company actually used a numerical rating system by assigning an importance weighting to each of the factors. Each factor in the business was given a rating of 1, 2, or 3, based on benchmarks related to company objectives, as indicated in an industry attractiveness worksheet, shown in Exhibit 3.8. Returning to Exhibit 3.7, note that the format for assessing industry attractiveness includes entries for trends in each factor and implications for action of the ratings in each factor.

EXHIBIT 3.7 Example of Format for Rating Industry Attractiveness

Product Line/Category _____

Division _____

Factor	Importance		Trends					Implications for Opportunities, Threats, and Issues	Rating	
	2010	2011				Compound Growth Rate			2010	2011
			2009	2010	2011	2009–2011	2007–2008			
Market Size and Growth										
Market definition:										
Total $										
Total units										
Industry Profitability										
Ability to pass on cost Increases										
Gross margin levels										
Competitive Structure										
Ease of entry/technological barriers										
Ease of share acquisition										
Competitive stability										
Dominant competitors										
Extent of industry overcapacity										
Customer/User Outlook										
Key user segment growth trend										
Changing consumer attitudes and/or legislation/regulation										
Opportunity										
Chance to gain franchise or preemptive position with unique product, positioning, or appeal										
Other										
Other										

EXHIBIT 3.8   Industry Attractiveness Worksheet

BPU_____

Year_____

Factor	Importance	Ratings and Benchmarks			Final Rating (Weighted)
		3	2	1	
Market Size and Growth					
Size: $ value of the market in 2010–2011 or 2014 as measured by manufacturer's shipments		Less than $50MM	$50–$150MM	More than $150MM	
Growth: Compound annual growth projected on *real* $ for 2009–2011		Less than 2%	2%–5%	More than 5%	
Industry Profitability					
Ability to pass on cost increases in higher prices		Difficult	Sometimes possible	Relatively easy	
Industry gross margin levels		Less than 20%	20%–40%	More than 40%	
Competitive Structure					
Ease of entry (existence of technological or other barriers)		Easy (low barriers to entry)	Moderately difficult (some barriers)	Difficult (high barriers to entry)	
Ease of share acquisition		New competitor can easily pick up share	Moderately difficult	Very difficult to acquire share	
Competitive stability		Several new competitors in market	Some new entrants	Few or no new market entrants of consequence	
Dominant competitor		Major competitor holds 50% of higher share of market	Major competitor holds 30%–50% share	Major competitor holds less than 30% share	
Extent of industry overcapacity		High	Medium	Low	

EXHIBIT 3.8 *(Continued)*

| | | BPU_____ | | | |
| | | Year_____ | | | |

Factor	Importance	Ratings and Benchmarks			Final Rating (Weighted)
		3	2	1	
Customer/User Outlook					
Key user segment growth trend (see date package)		Little growth or decline in key user/ customer segment	Some growth in key user segment	Major growth in key user/ customer segment forecast	
Changing consumer attitudes or legislation/ regulation		Negative impact	Little or no impact	Positive impact	
Opportunity					
Chance to gain franchise or preemptive position with unique product, positioning, or appeal		None identified	Some potential	Clearly exists	
Others					

Rating Company Strengths

Again, there is no valid cookbook approach. In rating company strengths, two aspects should be considered:

1. *Company performance in key success factors.* How well the company does in *each* of the factors makes the difference between success and failure.
2. *Defendable competitive strengths.* What strengths the company has compared to its competitors and whether those strengths can be defended and maintained. For example, a patent is a strength, provided that it (a) will not expire shortly and (b) cannot be circumvented.

The general guidelines mentioned in the comments on rating industry attractiveness are also applicable. The important factors are:

- Share
- Product quality
- Unique/proprietary product features
- Relative manufacturing costs
- Distribution
- Patent position

Exhibit 3.9 gives an example of a format used by one company to rate company strengths. As in the illustration in Exhibit 3.7, the company used a numerical rating by assigning an importance weighting to each factor. It then ranked itself on a scale of 1 to 3 against its two most important competitors for each factor. The format in Exhibit 3.9 also requires entry of

EXHIBIT 3.9 Company/Competitor Strength Evaluation Format: Product Line Review

Product Line Category_____

Country_____

Factor	Importance	Relative Rating * A B	Relevant Data/Support	Comments on Company's Advantages/ Disadvantages	Action
Share (enter below)			%		
			Segment Total Co. A B		
Company share					
_____					
Competitor A					
_____					
Company + Competitor A					
_____					
Product quality/ perception of quality					
Unique or proprietary product features			Product features	Ability to defend against competitors	
			Leader or follower		
Pricing			Company		
			_____		
			_____		
Relative manufacturing cost					
			% National Distribution		
Distribution/ coverage			Company 2009 2010 2011		
			_____		
			_____		
Sales force effectiveness (direct; indirect)					
			Total $ Exp. 2009 2010 2011		
Advertising and consumer promotion			_____		
Trade promotion			_____		

supporting data, comments on the company's advantages and disadvantages related to each factor, and the implications of the ratings for each factor for future action.

Defining Opportunities, Threats, and Critical Issues

Opportunities and Threats

An *opportunity* is a combination of time, place, and circumstances that offers potentially favorable results for the business. It usually results from an ongoing or potential change in government, market, or competitive environment. It is a potential short- and/or long-term competitive edge for the business that can be exploited by undertaking an appropriate action. If no action is required to attain the benefit, then the change should be considered part of the forecast rather than an opportunity. If the action required to take advantage of the potential benefits is unfeasible, there is no opportunity.

A *threat* is a combination of time, place, and circumstances that could have a negative impact on the future performance of the business. A threat usually results from an ongoing or potential change in the government, market, or competitive environment and provides some advantage to a competitor, which can result in a decline in share, earnings, and so on, unless an appropriate action is undertaken.

An opportunity can become a threat if a competitor seizes it first. A threat can become an opportunity if it forces a response that has side benefits. A business is likely to be faced with a multitude of opportunities and threats. For planning purposes, it is important to set priorities and to focus on the most important ones. There are three factors to consider in establishing priorities:

1. *Probability.* Likelihood that the event or condition will occur
2. *Impact.* The probable change in the business result if action is taken
3. *Timing.* How urgently an action is required

Use of an array, such as that shown in Exhibit 3.10, can help in sorting priorities. It may be useful to use several such displays (e.g., separate ones for opportunities and threats and for the long range and the short range).

Critical Issues

The opportunities and threats that have the highest priority are *critical issues* for the strategic plan. Additional critical issues may emerge from examination of internal situations. For example: Should we add additional capacity? How much? Should we move the operation to a lower labor cost area?

The purpose of defining issues is to indicate the principal decisions that need to be made and, where feasible, to identify the alternate choices that should be considered. Where the specific decision and options are not yet clear, the issue should carefully frame the question that, when resolved, will lead to action. Therefore, issues typically are of three types:

1. *Position issues.* Issues related to the current and future grid position, which will determine the basic strategic direction. Examples: How large is the potential market? How will new technology affect our competitive position—can we use it to

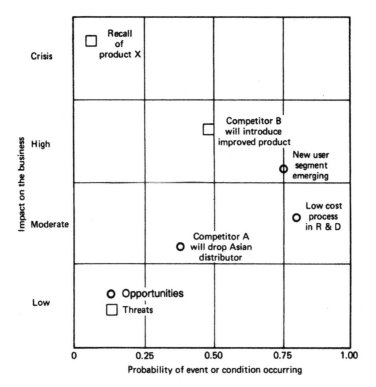

EXHIBIT 3.10   Priority Assessment Array for Opportunities and Threats

develop a proprietary position? How will entry of a competitor affect our share and/ or profitability, considering potential effect on prices, advertising, and promotion?

2. *Decision issues.* Issues related to specific near-term decisions that have a significant impact on the conduct of the business during the next several years. Examples: Should we exit the business? Should we expand our production capacity in a foreign country?

3. *Tactical issues.* Issues related to the programs to implement a particular strategy. Examples: Pricing strategy and tactics and evaluating the desirability of using the company name on a new premium product versus a new brand-name umbrella that conveys premium quality.

A list of critical issues for the business should be agreed to by all levels of management involved in the planning and budgeting process before the strategic plan is completed. A consensus as to which items will be addressed and regarding the degree of detail with which they will be treated facilitates a more efficient and more useful planning effort.

 BUSINESS DIRECTION/CONCEPT

Setting Differentiated Objectives

Different matrix positions will have different characteristics and different problems. Using the McKinsey/General Electric matrix shown in Exhibit 3.6, for example, four broad business classifications can be defined. Each classification has different characteristics and problems and should have different objectives. This is illustrated in Exhibit 3.11.

Use of the matrix approach to differentiating business segments facilitates the establishment of priorities among businesses. It allows a rational approach to making basic decisions regarding the setting of objectives for each business and the determination of which priority decisions to resolve first. This, in turn, will provide a basis for allocating resources among the different businesses and for resolving conflicts between the short and the long term.

Identifying Leverage Points and Unique Advantages

The business direction or concept is developed by first identifying the important economic leverage points of the business and then devising a means for building and/or preserving a unique advantage against the competitors. This is not an easy task, because it requires a combination of rigorous analysis (of the company's strengths and weaknesses) and creative insights. Some useful guidelines may facilitate the process.

- The key success factors described previously are good indicators of the critical economic leverage points and may be identical.
- Leverage points must be measurable and related to the economic outcome in the business. It is useful to undertake a sensitivity analysis for each proposed leverage point to verify that it is significant to the business.
- The unique advantage must be economically measurable. Although many intangibles can reinforce a business, the basic concepts of the strategy must be developed around advantages that can be translated into economic benefits; otherwise, the plan will be unclear and contain generalities that do not provide useful direction. For example, a plastics producer's concept directed at "enhancing the company's reputation as a high-quality supplier" is not as explicit as a concept directed at "maintaining

EXHIBIT 3.11 Matrix Approach to Differentiating Business Segments

Box Numbers	1, 2, 3	4, 5, 6	7, 8	9
Business Class	Invest/Grow	Selectivity/Earnings	Harvest	Divest
Characteristics	Long-term growth Worldwide Changes coming rapidly Uses cash	Plateaued or weakening Limited long-term opportunities Short-term profits Self-financing	Declining profits High-risk opportunities with questionable future Special situations	"Dogs"
Typical problems	Digestion Containing risk	Protecting position without excessive resource commitment	Keeping positions from eroding too fast Avoiding unrealistic rebuilds	Stemming operating losses
Principal objective	Build market position for long-term profit	Self-financing with high short-term earnings	Maximize cash flow	Exit with minimum loss

product leadership through the introduction of a family of products that provide greater strength and lower density." The more explicit concept permits evaluation to determine: (1) Is it feasible, considering the relative strengths of the company? (2) What is the advantage worth in terms of price and/or market share? (3) Are there off-setting advantages (e.g., product service, ease of use) that might be more important?

■ The unique advantage must be preservable. In the preceding example, if competitors respond quickly with comparable or better products, the concept will not result in a winning strategy. The company must have some unique capability to maintain the proposed product leadership (e.g., patents, special know-how, long-term production, and cost advantage) for this to be the foundation of a viable strategy.

Use of the Matrix Position as a Guide

The position of the business or business segments often suggests appropriate directions for development of concepts, as indicated in Exhibit 3.12. It should be recognized that the elements used to determine the matrix position are dynamic, and that a position will change. In developing the concept, both the current matrix position and the anticipated future direction (especially with regard to the industry attractiveness) should be considered.

Industry attractiveness →

		High	Medium	Low
Business strengths	High	Maximum investment Diversify worldwide Consolidate position Accept moderate near-term profits	Investment in selected segments Earnings where share ceiling Seek attractive new segments to apply strength	Defend strengths Focus on attractive subsegments Evaluate opportunities for market revitalization Monitor for H/D timing
	Medium	Build selectively on strengths Define implications of leadership challenge Avoid vulnerability—fill out weaknesses	Segment business further to develop differentiated product strategies	No essential commitment Position to divest or to shift to more attractive segments
	Low	Ride market Seek niches, specialization Increase strength opportunistically (e.g., acquisition)	Action to preserve/increase cash flow Opportunistic sale or Opportunistic rationalization to increase strength	Exit/prune Timing to maximize return

EXHIBIT 3.12 Matrix Position as a Guide to Concept Development

ALTERNATIVE APPROACHES

This stage of planning addresses, over a broad spectrum, the basic choices available for running the business. It produces an envelope of possibilities for decision making. Each strategy alternative must be a realistic possibility (not merely set up to prove that the preferred alternative is the best).

The selection of alternatives poses a problem for the planning team in that a complete range of alternatives must be included to ensure that a significantly better choice is not overlooked, yet there must be a limited number (usually no more than five; otherwise the planning effort will get bogged down).

Some organizations find it helpful to have the planning team review the proposed alternatives with the next higher level of management before starting to undertake a detailed evaluation. This is a good point in the planning process at which to conduct a preliminary review because it allows top managers to participate at the conceptual stage, when they can provide input to make the process more effective. Such a review will eliminate alternatives that are inconsistent with other corporate objectives before much evaluation effort is expended. Also, additional alternatives may surface, which can be addressed more efficiently at this stage than after the completion of the total planning cycle.

Evaluation of Alternatives

The first step in the evaluation of a proposed alternative is to test it for completeness and usefulness to the development of the plan.

- *Critical issues.* The proposed concept must provide an answer to the major issues and/or choices identified in the situation analysis.
- *Benefits and risks.* The benefits and the risks must be identified and cross-checked against the conclusions reached in the situation analysis. Specifically, do they exploit the identified opportunities and/or meet the threats? What is the probable impact on competitors and their likely reaction? How much do the uncertainties in the forecast increase the potential benefit or risk?
- *Competitive advantage.* A successful strategy develops or maintains a significant advantage over competitors. An alternative should describe how this will be accomplished.
- *Program oriented.* The alternative must be explicit enough to permit a set of operating plans to be readily derived from it.
- *Differentiated.* There must be a meaningful difference in the strategic approach between alternatives; otherwise, too much effort will be expended on analysis of minor variations. For a meaningful difference to exist, there must be a significant difference in some of the key actions in each alternative.

The next step in the evaluation of alternatives is to itemize the principal actions, the timing, and the resources required to implement the proposed alternative. This is, in essence, a "preliminary" operating plan, different from the "final" operating plan only in its level of detail. In the preliminary plan, activities are defined in sufficient detail to permit an economic assessment of each alternative; in the final plan, programs and related tasks should be defined in sufficient detail to permit development of budgets and measurements for each function in each business unit.

If the alternatives are truly differentiated, the financial forecasts, based on the cost/ benefits implications, usually will be sufficiently different to permit approximations based on estimates rather than on a detailed account-by-account buildup. For example, if one of the key programs in an alternative were product development to achieve improved product properties, it would probably be sufficient to estimate the number of person-years required in each year and to multiply it by a representative average cost/person-year. In development of the final plan, more specific programs, manpower, description, and associated cost would be developed.

OPERATIONAL PLAN

In describing the overall strategic planning cycle shown in Exhibit 3.2, the point was made that the operational plan is usually done in two stages, especially when the strategic plan is prepared well in advance of the budget. The preliminary plan, which is integral to the strategic plan, serves to define and refine the strategy alternatives and to provide a basis for selecting between them, as described earlier in this chapter. The final operational plan is much more detailed and serves as the basis for establishing annual budgets, business measurements, and individual performance measurement. It is also an effective device for integrating and communicating between the functions in a business.

Contents of Operational Plan

The operation plan is essentially a summary of the principal action programs. The plan should contain this information for each of these programs:

- Description of the program and how it relates to the strategy objective
- Resource requirements, including manpower and costs
- Expected results
- Time schedule to reach key decision points
- Assignment of responsibilities
- Support or input required from other organizations within the company

The amount of detail included will differ considerably between new developmental activities and those that are part of an ongoing program.

The presentation of the operational plan to management requires careful abstracting and highlighting in order to keep the volume of material down to manageable proportions. Most companies use simplified formats for summarizing and presenting the operational plan. An example of one such format is shown in Exhibit 3.13. (This is a highly condensed version of a two-page format.)

EXHIBIT 3.13　Illustration of Format for Summarizing and Presenting the Operational Plan

Strategy and Programs Summary	
Product Group _____	**Division** _____
Recommended strategy	Opportunities/threats/issues addressed by strategy
Second-best alternative strategy	Reasons for not recommending alternative
Key programs	
Description	How does it implement strategy?

Level of effort $	Manpower	Investment	Milestones Description	Date	Responsibility	Benefits $ Income before taxes	$ Cash
2008						2009	
2009						2010	
2010						2011	

Consistency of Actions with Strategic Approach

The actions outlined in the operational plan should be a logical extension of the selected strategic alternative. Previously in this chapter, it was demonstrated how the business position in a 3 × 3 matrix can be used as a guide for concept development. This technique can also be carried a step further, using the four basic business classes to develop appropriate differentiated actions for elements of the operational plan. Exhibit 3.14 provides an array for testing the consistency of the operational plans and actions with the business position as determined in the situation analysis.

Successive Commitments

An operational plan must balance the need to commit to a strategy with the need to maintain sufficient flexibility—to allow for changes or shifts as new information becomes available in order to resolve uncertainties that were present at the time the plan was prepared. This can be accomplished by adopting a progressive approach in which only those commitments that are necessary are made at the onset. The next elements are essential for developing a plan with successive commitments:

- Identification of the key decision points
- Timetable to trigger key decisions
- Level of resource investment (money, people, etc.) at each decision point
- Criteria and measurements by which key decisions are to be made

It is possible to step up the level of commitment to a program as results are obtained and as the degree of risk is reduced.

EXHIBIT 3.14 Specific Actions Based on Matrix Position

	Objective			
Plan elements	Build market position for long-term profit	High short-term earnings; medium cash flow	Maximize cash generation	Exit
Financial commitment	Maximum digestible	Selective/high-return segments	Minimum	Dispose
Risk	Accept/contain	Limit	Avoid	No new risk
Markets	Expand into new segments	Concentrate on core	Withdraw from marginal segments	Maintain if possible
Products	Lead, diversify new categories	Differentiate specialization line extension value/cost	Prune	Maintain where needed for sale of business
Share	Build, create preservable competitive advantage	Target growth/protect position	Forgo share for profit	Forgo share
Pricing/promotion	Aggressively heavy merchandising	Stabilize for maximum contribution	Up, even at expense of volume	Pricing up, no promotion
Advertising	Heavy creativity	Limit creativity	Cut	Minimize
Distribution	Build coverage, performance	Protect coverage	Pull out of marginal regions businesses	Isolate if practical from other
Purchasing	Ensure adequate forward coverage	Protect cost competitiveness	Limit extended commitments	No long-term commitment
Cost/capacity	Utilize scale, not thrift, capacity ahead of demand	Aggressive reduction of variable; economize on fixed balance capacity	"Variabilize" by cutting consolidation	Major effort to reduce overhead
Management	Entrepreneurs—high variable compensation	Skeptical—balanced	Disciplined—strong cost control, high base salary	Entrepreneurs—high variable, commitment after exit

The next example illustrates this approach: Consider a business in which unit sales volume has grown at a compound annual rate of 12 percent per year for the past five years. The environmental analysis and forecast indicate that the market will continue to grow at approximately 12 percent per year. An aggressive new marketing plan is being activated, and, as a result, unit sales volume is forecast to increase at a compound annual rate of 14 percent per year for the next five years. If this were achieved, the production facility would be beyond capacity, with no room to expand in the present site in three years. If the marketing plan were more successful than forecast, growth could be as high as 20 percent per year, which would result in an out-of-capacity condition in two years. However, the sales growth rate might be as low as 5 percent per year if foreign competitors successfully entered the market. If this occurred, present facilities would be adequate for at least five years. The three forecasts and their relation to the current capacity are summarized in Exhibit 3.15.

A new plant involves a major investment, with the amount heavily dependent on the size of the facility. Exhibit 3.16 is representative of the timing and the level of commitment at various stages. Because the entire process would take at least 24 months, the program would have to be started immediately in order to avoid an out-of-capacity condition if the high-case forecast were achieved. (This is a serious risk for the business, because it provides an opportunity for foreign competitors to establish a position in the market.) If growth were slowed to the 5 percent per year rate, the company might have a substantial investment tied up in a facility that would not be used for four or five more years. It is possible in this case to avoid delay and not to take an imprudent risk by using successive commitments.

Exhibit 3.16 illustrates that a considerable amount of the preliminary program work (which is time consuming) can be done without making a major commitment. The first step—selection of a new site—can be started immediately with a very small investment commitment and low risk. The next decision point and step up in level of commitment would come in the ninth month with a decision on whether to proceed with detailed engineering design. At this time, the results of the first year of the new marketing plan, the imminence of the foreign competitive threat, and the likelihood of achieving the high forecast would all be much better defined. A decision on the major commitment does not have to be made until the fifteenth month.

Use of successive, progressive commitments enables rapid action to exploit opportunities that might develop faster and be larger than planned, yet it contains the risk at a level consistent with the level of certainty. It is not buying time or a way of avoiding decisions that should be made. In fact, as the previously described example illustrates, it can facilitate a more aggressive action plan.

	Year	Plan (14%/year)	High (20%/year)	Low (5%/year)
	Current	7000/month	7000/month	7000/month
	1	8,000	8,499	7,350
Current capacity 10,000/ month	2	9,100	10,080	7,720
	3	10,400	12,100	8,100
	4	11,800	14,500	8,500
	5	13,500	17,400	8,930

EXHIBIT 3.15 Sales Volume at Three Forecast Levels for Illustrative Case

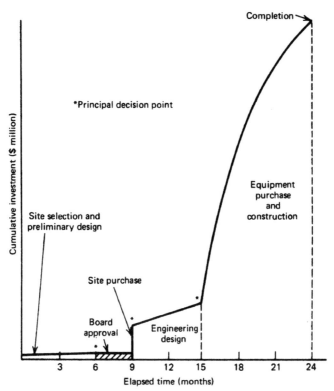

EXHIBIT 3.16   Example of Program Timing and Commitment Level for New Facility

MEASUREMENT

The concept of a dynamic strategic plan, in which actual results are compared to expectations and revisions are made to accommodate the plan, is essential to use of such a plan as a management tool in running the business. Each program in the operational plan must have a finite, quantifiable result as an objective. The result must also be time dependent. The plan should specify interim results, not just a final objective (especially if the program is of relatively long duration). Examples of some usable program objectives are illustrated in the table on the following page.

These examples were selected to illustrate the type of results that are not normally reported in the monthly or other periodic financial reports. It is just as important to track these results as it is to measure the usual financial parameters in the business. In many instances, the nonroutinely reported results will provide early warning signals that the financial objectives will not be met or will be greatly exceeded and that the plans should be modified.

FEEDBACK

There is nothing worse in planning than an irrevocable commitment to an unworkable strategy. A feedback system will help avoid such a situation.

Program	Objective	Time
Develop high-strength product	Demonstrate feasibility of Polymer X with laboratory samples	Month 2
(Polymer X)	Achieve consistent test results on five laboratory batches—impact strength—density	Month 4
	Complete detailed economic evaluation with price below 85¢/pound	Month 6
Improve distribution to hospitals	Identify 10 qualified distributors	Month 1
	Sign three distributors	Month 3
	Obtain $100,000/month sales in hospital through new distributors	Month 9

All planning processes, whether they are formal or informal, are built on a series of assumptions regarding the internal and external environment and the principal changes that are likely to occur. A major benefit of a formal planning process is that it compels an explicit statement of the underlying assumptions. It also provides a direct link between these assumptions and the business positioning, the business direction, and, eventually, the action plans.

The strategic plan can be used effectively as a day-to-day management guide only if objective measurements are established for the action plans and the results are compared to these objectives periodically. Doing this enables revisions in the plan based on the latest information. Maintaining an ability to shift and modify keeps the plan realistic and, provided that the changes are consistent with the strategy, still allows an orderly approach to managing a complex business in the face of uncertainty.

In some companies with sophisticated planning systems, detailed monthly financial reports are prepared that are tied to the annual financial budget, but there are no regular reports on those program objectives that are not directly measured in the financial results. Without regular reports on those results, the plan cannot be kept current. If the plan is outdated before it is printed, it loses credibility. The business management will tend to regard the strategic planning effort as an exercise done primarily to satisfy higher management whims and consider it to be a diversion from the "real" job of running the business.

It is possible to develop regular reporting systems that compare actual results to the plan objectives. Minor differences may require only revision of the timetables in the operational plan. Major differences should evoke a reexamination of the situation analysis and the assumed business position, which, in turn, may lead to change in the business direction and strategic concept for the business. If the plan is prepared with a feedback system as an integral element, necessary changes are likely to be made in a more timely manner and with less resistance.

CONTINGENCY PLANNING

The preceding discussion on feedback focused on detecting changes in the environment or differences between results and plan expectations and on adjusting the plan to accommodate changes and/or differences. In some companies, an attempt is made to anticipate unexpected situations by preparing a responding course of action in advance. Doing this can help avoid surprise and enable an intelligent, rapid response to crises. If the response is ready when an emergency arises, presumably a more well-thought-out decision can be made without scrambling. Contingency planning can also help sharpen planning skills by forcing managers to stretch their look at the environment and to identify possibilities that might have been overlooked in preparing the strategic plan.

Contingency planning systems usually consist of a three-step process:

1. Identifying the possible event
2. Determining the trigger points
3. Developing responses to the event

Identifying the Possible Event

This step lists the possible events that might be important to the business and that have not been forecast in the base plan. The potential impact of each event on the business is determined, and the probability of its occurring is estimated. An array, similar to the one shown in Exhibit 3.10, is useful for assessing priorities and selecting the most important events for further work.

Determining the Trigger Points

In this step, the indicators that alert us to the impending occurrence are identified, and individuals are assigned to track these indicators and warn when the event appears imminent.

Developing Responses to the Event

To develop an appropriate response, it is assumed that the event will occur and that it will produce a result significantly different from what was assumed in the base plan. Thus, the approach is the same as previously described in the section on feedback. The difference from the base case assumption is evaluated to determine its impact on the assessment of the business situation and the business position. The necessary changes in business direction, and the consequent operational plan to exploit the new opportunities or to respond to the threats, are then determined, and a standby plan is developed.

Although the preceding description implies a formal, structured system comparable to the one employed for the base case, this is not the actual practice in most companies. Contingency planning is often done on an informal basis, with only verbalization or skeletal outlines. Emphasis is placed in many cases on the thought process which becomes part of the discussion in the review process rather than a documented plan.

There are several reasons for this. Many of the contingencies contemplated are radical. The development of a written plan and its inevitable dissemination may cause problems through exposure and discussion of unlikely events with highly negative connotations (e.g., plant shutdown or sale of business). In some cases, contingency actions have also created more damage than they tried to correct by causing managers to anticipate the contingency (especially a negative one) and to start cutting back even in advance of the triggers. Other problems with contingency planning are the added burden of managerial time and energy required to prepare additional plans and the possibility that contingency plans will be used as escape hatches for poor performance on the base plan.

Although contingency planning is a useful exercise, the need for formal contingency plans is considerably reduced if the initial plan is designed with flexibility, using a progressive commitment approach and employing measurement and feedback on a regular basis.

PROBLEMS IN IMPLEMENTING FORMAL STRATEGIC PLANNING SYSTEMS

G. A. Steiner surveyed 215 corporations in diverse industries[1] to identify the most common problems encountered in organizing and implementing formal long-range and strategic planning systems. His study, which has been supported by other investigations, found ten most important pitfalls to avoid:

1. Top management's assumption that it can delegate the planning function to the planner
2. Top management's becoming so engrossed in current problems that it spends insufficient time on long-range planning with the result that the process becomes discredited among other managers and staff
3. Failure to develop company goals suitable as a basis for formulating long-range plans
4. Failure to assure the necessary involvement in the planning process of major line personnel
5. Failing to use plans as standards for measuring managerial performance
6. Failure to create a climate in the company that is congenial and not resistant to planning

---

[1] G. A. Steiner, *Pitfalls in Comprehensive Long-Range Planning* (Oxford, OH: The Planning Executive Institute, 1972), pp. 52–54.

7. Assuming that corporate comprehensive planning is something separate from the entire management process
8. Injecting so much formality into the system that it lacks flexibility, looseness, and simplicity, thereby restraining creativity
9. Failure of top management to review with departmental and divisional heads the long-range plans that they have developed
10. Top management's consistently rejecting the formal planning mechanism by making intuitive decisions which conflict with the formal plans

Some of these problems have been addressed in the preceding section. It is important to recognize that these are dangers to successful implementation. Most of these problems can be overcome if the CEO is committed to a formal planning system. In the final analysis, the success of a formal planning system depends on three factors:

1. The involvement, dedication, and support of the CEO
2. The degree of practical business insight, experience, and credibility of the individuals responsible for designing and administering the system
3. The degree to which the planning system is tailored to the particular needs of the business (rather than fitting into a standardized planning package)

SUMMARY

Formal strategic planning systems are useful management tools that should serve as a day-to-day guide, not just as an annual exercise. The next characteristics distinguish a useful strategic plan:

- It is *oriented toward decision making*, not just a set of objectives or written plans.
- It is an *operational* tool, not just a long-term forecast. It is the foundation for the annual budget, all major programs, short-term actions, performance measurement, and so on.
- It is *competitor oriented*, aimed at developing economic, preservable advantages.
- It is *factual and analytical*: It avoids "motherhood" statements, using objectivity and detail where necessary to resolve issues.
- It is *selective*, focusing on the priorities of the business and on the most critical issues.
- It is *continuing and dynamic*, providing a framework for decisions rather than an excuse for indecision.

CHAPTER FOUR

Budgeting and Forecasting: Process Tweak or Process Overhaul?

Joseph M. Orlando

Partner, KPMG LLP, Risk Advisory Services

William E. Dailey

Managing Director, KPMG LLP, Risk Advisory Services

INTRODUCTION

The process of developing an annual budget or interim financial forecast should provide a company with the opportunity to integrate its strategic objectives with the budget proposals of its business units and functions. On the surface, this seems fairly straightforward. Yet the art and science of budgeting and forecasting have been at the center

Note: The information herein is of general nature and is not intended to address the specific circumstances of any individual or entity. The views and opinions expressed are those of the authors and do not necessarily represent the views and opinions of KPMG LLP. Although we endeavor to provide accurate and timely information, there can be no guarantee that such information is accurate as of the date it is received or that it will continue to be accurate in the future. No one should act upon such information without appropriate professional advice after a thorough examination of the particular situation.

KPMG LLP is the audit, tax, and advisory firm that has maintained a continuous commitment throughout its history to providing leadership, integrity, and quality. The Big Four firm with the strongest growth record over the past decade, KPMG turns knowledge into value for the benefit of its clients, people, communities, and the capital markets. Its professionals work together to provide clients access to global support, industry insights, and a multidisciplinary range of services. KPMG LLP (www.us.kpmg.com) is the U.S. member firm of KPMG International. KPMG International member firms have nearly 100,000 professionals, including 6,800 partners, in 148 countries.

of a highly charged discussion in recent years. Numerous magazine articles have pronounced budgeting and forecasting as evil, dead, or superfluous—often citing a lack of flexibility in a changing marketplace, excessive detail, and simply "taking too much time." In fact, Jack Welch[1] has called it "the bane of corporate America."

Whether the shortcomings of budgeting and forecasting processes are real or perceived, there has been no shortage of effort in this area during the last 20 years. Myriad approaches have been offered—zero-based budgeting, fixed and variable cost, balanced scorecard, and activity-based management—but none with staying power. Software applications ranging from "super spreadsheets" to enterprise resource planning (ERP) tools have promised but not delivered a silver bullet. Along the way, companies have tinkered with various components of the leading methodologies and tools, but in most cases ended up with unwieldy and inflexible processes that no longer meet their business needs.

Do companies now need to overhaul their budgeting and forecasting processes, or will continued tweaking fix their problems? Since the ultimate responsibility for resolving the budgeting and forecasting dilemma typically resides in the office of the chief financial officer, KPMG's CFO Advisory Services practice set out to find the answer. We conducted a survey of companies worldwide to gain insights into the current state of budgeting and forecasting. We then analyzed the results against our own notions of effective budgeting and forecasting practices.

SURVEY METHODOLOGY

The companies that participated in the survey had annual sales ranging from $250 million to well in excess of $5 billion and represented all major industry segments. Respondents included both finance and nonfinance professionals.

Exhibits 4.1, 4.2, and 4.3 show the demographics for the survey.

FINDINGS: BUDGETING PROCESS

The traditional budgeting process appears to be alive and well, since 95 percent of surveyed companies report that they do indeed prepare a budget. However, our data shows a wider range of results regarding approaches, uses, effectiveness, and other aspects of company budgets.

Replacing the Traditional Budget

Only 5 percent of the companies surveyed have replaced their traditional budgeting process—not surprising since this is a difficult task for a company of any size. Interestingly, companies that have made this transition had revenues of less than $1 billion.

Companies that have *considered* replacing their underlying approach to budgeting but have not yet done so (58 percent) favored a rolling-forecast process as their first choice of approaches (41 percent), followed by key performance indicators (KPIs) (32 percent), activity-based costing (19 percent), and others. The fact that well over half of

---

[1] Marshall Loeb, "Jack Welch Lets Fly on Budgets, Bonuses, and Buddy Boards," *Fortune*, May 29, 1995, p. 73.

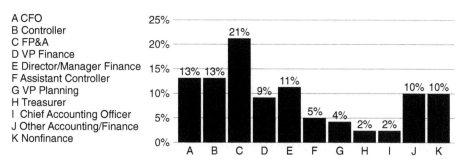

A CFO
B Controller
C FP&A
D VP Finance
E Director/Manager Finance
F Assistant Controller
G VP Planning
H Treasurer
I Chief Accounting Officer
J Other Accounting/Finance
K Nonfinance

EXHIBIT 4.1 Demographics Respondents by Job Title/Classification

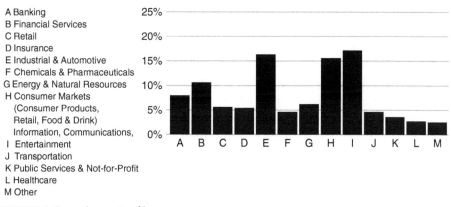

A Banking
B Financial Services
C Retail
D Insurance
E Industrial & Automotive
F Chemicals & Pharmaceuticals
G Energy & Natural Resources
H Consumer Markets
   (Consumer Products,
   Retail, Food & Drink)
   Information, Communications,
I Entertainment
J Transportation
K Public Services & Not-for-Profit
L Healthcare
M Other

EXHIBIT 4.2 Industry Profile

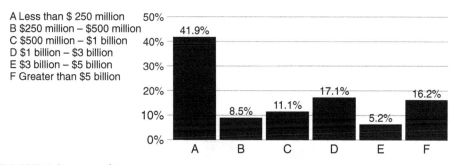

A Less than $ 250 million
B $250 million – $500 million
C $500 million – $1 billion
D $1 billion – $3 billion
E $3 billion – $5 billion
F Greater than $5 billion

EXHIBIT 4.3 Annual Revenue

the companies considered changing their approach indicates that companies recognize the need for fundamental change in their existing processes.

It is somewhat surprising that almost 42 percent of the companies that prepared an annual budget indicated that they have *not* considered changing their approach. While these companies may indeed be committed to a traditional approach, it is unlikely that they have been immune to the influences of other methodologies. These organizations may have added future periods to the traditional 12-month budget period or instituted a modified activity-based approach for specific departmental budgets while keeping their fundamental traditional budgeting process intact. Ultimately, such tweaks may or may not meet the needs of the company.

What explains the reluctance to change among the remaining 42 percent? We offer some observations:

- Since budgeting is a dynamic and relatively fluid process, it is sometimes easier to adjust budget methods continually—by starting earlier, adding or modifying requirements, or changing the review process for short-term results—rather than trying to revamp the entire process.
- Making fundamental changes in the budgeting process requires a monumental investment because budget creation tends to be vertically and horizontally integrated and involves all aspects and organizations within the company. The fact that a return on the investment is unlikely to be realized in the short term tends to discourage such investments.
- Budgets are not held to the same level of external scrutiny as actual financial results and, though budgets are important, companies can compensate for inadequacies with a rebudgeting or forecasting effort.
- Although the budget generally is viewed as a business process, the responsibility for driving the process typically resides with the finance department (more than 80 percent of the respondents indicated that finance drives the process), and finance may not have the authority to make the necessary radical changes.
- Some organizations may be complacent ("If it works, why change it?") or have a fear of the unknown.

Changing the Budgeting Process

Companies with revenue greater than $1 billion consider changing their budgeting processes more often than smaller companies do. These larger companies also expressed the greatest dissatisfaction with their budgeting processes.

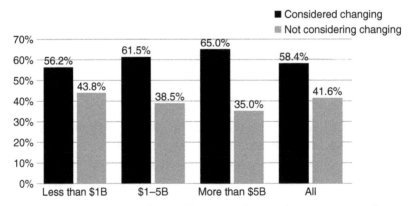

EXHIBIT 4.4 Companies Considering Changing Their Budgeting Process (by Annual Revenue)

A COMPARISON OF BUDGETING APPROACHES

TRADITIONAL BUDGETING PROCESS

- Focuses on achieving specified dollar objectives
- Establishes a finite planning horizon—typically one year
- Creates an environment of continual trade-offs between predetermined financial targets
- Is often disconnected from current and changing market conditions

ROLLING FORECAST PROCESS

- Establishes a rolling planning horizon of six to eight quarters, adding new periods as the current period ends
- Rapidly assimilates changes in the marketplace and facilitates reformulated plans
- Is supported by key operational metrics to keep strategic plans in focus
- Requires an ability to project key operational drivers, such as revenue and volume, for the entire planning horizon

KEY PERFORMANCE INDICATORS

- Identifies KPIs (internal and external) that are appropriate for the business
- Includes KPIs for operational and financial metrics
- Cascades the KPIs throughout the company
- Leaves specific details for achieving a KPI goal to local management
- Requires that KPIs be integrated and that they represent a balanced set of measurable goals

ACTIVITY-BASED COSTING

- Identifies key activities conducted by the company and isolates resources and costs associated with the activity
- Identifies key drivers of the activities, both revenue-producing and others
- Examines relationships between drivers and activities and develops forecasts for the drivers, which dictate required resources and costs

With more to lose, larger companies clearly have a greater sense of urgency over budgeting process issues than do smaller companies. Presumably, larger companies also have more resources for studying various budgeting approaches, which could enhance their willingness to change (see Exhibit 4.4).

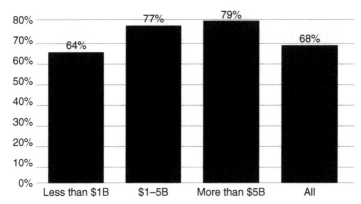

EXHIBIT 4.5 Companies Linking the Budgeting Process and Strategic Plan (by Annual Revenue)

What Is the Source of the Budget?

More than two-thirds of the companies in the survey indicated that the budgeting process is linked to their strategic or long-range plan. This linkage to a strategic planning process was more prevalent in larger companies than in smaller companies (see Exhibit 4.5).

The process of linking the budget to the strategic plan is an integral step in an effective financial planning effort and is generally considered an effective practice. Ideally, the strategic plan describes and quantifies the direction of the company and is endorsed by the stakeholders in terms of goals, objectives, and timing.

EFFECTIVE BUDGETING PRACTICES

- *Integrate the budget process with the strategic plan.* Establish top-down direction by using the first-year component of the strategic plan as the budget.
- *Include bottom-up planning.* In addition to setting expectations and providing direction from the top, ensure accountability by assimilating tactical plans from the bottom.
- *Manage the process.* Develop a comprehensive and integrated planning calendar that clearly identifies specific information required for the process, describe deliverables in detail, build in key checkpoints to ensure the process stays on schedule, and plan the review meeting to secure the participation of key individuals.
- *Define the scope.* Budget only meaningful items that can be measured and reported. Do not waste time attempting to plan or incorporate items that are not in the control of the budgeting organization.

Most Important				Least Important
Financial Planning	Performance Measurement	Financial Control	Executive Compensation	Cost/Pricing Strategy
#1	#2	#3	#4	#5

EXHIBIT 4.6   Most Important—Least Important Financial Management Processes

What Is the Budget Used For?

As shown in Exhibit 4.6, for more than half the companies, financial planning was the primary purpose for the budget. Performance measurement—a more appropriate use of budgeting—ranks second, followed by financial control.

In a well-formulated planning environment, financial planning focuses on long-term goals, budgeting focuses on current-year goals, and financial controls focus on day-to-day costs and resources. These three financial management processes differ in their level of detail or granularity—with financial planning being the least granular, financial controls the most granular, and budgeting somewhere in the middle.

Ideally, a budget should set current-year goals for business units and *exclude* both long-range planning goals and line items associated with operations. Such a budget can provide a baseline for measuring performance and thereby provide insight into the costs of executing strategy as well as progress in achieving long-range financial goals.

However, many companies are actually using budgeting for financial planning purposes. The budget is an effective mechanism for *executing* the first year of the financial plan but not for actual financial planning. Since the scope of the budget is typically short term—year 1 of the strategic plan—by definition it is ill-equipped to provide the broader context of long-range goals.

It may be appropriate for financial planning to become more tactical and less strategic in some industries. However, turning the budget into a planning mechanism—essentially a constant work in progress to reflect changing goals—is not the best use of the budgeting process. We can assume from this widespread practice that companies' bona fide financial planning processes are insufficiently robust to address future-year goals. In addition, companies simply may be failing to appreciate and exploit the potential efficiencies and value of the budget and other financial management processes (see Exhibit 4.7).

Budgeting Top Down, Bottom Up, or Hybrid

Does the strategic planning process drive development of the annual budget (top down) or does the budget emerge solely from operating units and budget preparers (bottom up)? As Exhibit 4.8 shows, the survey data are mixed, with more than half of respondents using a hybrid approach and the remainder evenly divided between top-down and bottom-up approaches (21 percent each).

EXHIBIT 4.7   Granularity in Planning, Budgeting, Operations, and Forecasting

Financial Management Processes	Granularity	Purpose	Horizon
Strategic Plan	Low	Long-range financial goals	3–5 years
Budget	Medium	Tactical execution of first year of financial plan: allows performance measurement against annual goals	1 year for traditional budget; 6–8 quarters for rolling budget
Operational Plans	High	Day-to-day financial controls	<1 year
Forecast	Low to medium	Adjusting short-term strategies and tactics	1–2 quarters

If a company's strategic plan has established overall direction (top down) and been ratified by the board and stakeholders, then execution of the plan is what the company expects—though not blind execution. Strategies need to be formulated, investments identified, trade-offs presented, emerging opportunities considered, tactics solidified, and a clear and measurable budget put in motion.

When a *purely* bottom-up approach prevails (21 percent of companies), the starting point for the budget cycle may be improperly staged and those responsible for preparing the budget may be more likely to start the process with a blank sheet of paper. As a result, they run the risk of incorporating elements that are inconsistent with long-range goals, such as investments, productivity improvements, or cost savings. Though these inconsistencies may emerge in the budget review process, over the long haul this type of do loop disenfranchises people from the budgeting process.

Conversely, communicating long-range financial goals at the beginning of the process (top down) can empower people to make rational contributions to the budget (bottom up). This hybrid approach enables the company to balance its budget purposes across the various constituencies while incorporating planning, measurement, and control, as shown in Exhibit 4.9.

In the hybrid approach, leadership focuses on long-range company goals and affordability, business units and segments focus on performance measurement based

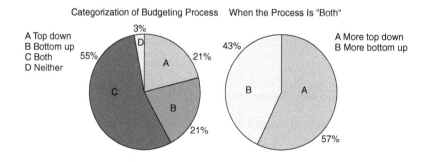

EXHIBIT 4.8   Categorization of Budgeting Process

EXHIBIT 4.9   The Hybrid Approach

on budget goals, and operational departments focus on applying resources and controlling costs.

A merging of top-down and bottom-up approaches can promote a healthy conflict between planners and operations. To foster a sense of ownership, the numbers need to roll up from the line and functional people who will execute the plan, manage the resources, spend the money, and deliver the results. However, the leadership team at the top is in a better position to understand what the company can afford. These opposing views define the battle lines for budget engagement.

The historical problem of top down/bottom up is that much time and effort is spent posturing, and the review and integration phase is not always approached in an open and honest manner by either side. Therefore, clear and direct communication is essential at the beginning of the budgeting process and throughout the budget cycle. From preparation through review, fundamental planning assumptions must be shared and applied consistently. These can range from salary planning assumptions to exchange rates and from outsourcing to growth in key skills. When all the participants have the same rulebook, the result is a better process and far greater accountability.

How Long Does It Take to Prepare a Budget?

As shown in Exhibit 4.10, the average cycle time for developing a budget according to the respondents was approximately 2.6 months, with 84 percent of companies requiring more than two months and almost one-third requiring more than three months.

The size and complexity of a company affects the duration of its budget cycle. However, any budgeting process that exceeds four to eight weeks from kickoff to board approval is probably too long. Under two months is generally considered the benchmark, after which the process typically begins to unravel. Exhibit 4.11 shows the impact of process delay on budget components.

However, factors that contribute to a protracted budget cycle are actually within the control of a company. The review process, the most important factor, may include a wildly excessive number of reviews, each with a redo cycle. Last-minute data gathering, typically resulting from inadequate reporting, can lead to inefficient use of resources, reporting inaccuracies, and reworking of numbers. Finally, filling out of forms, whether

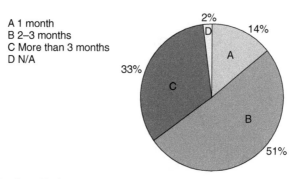

A 1 month
B 2–3 months
C More than 3 months
D N/A

2%
D
14%
A
33%
C
B
51%

EXHIBIT 4.10 Budget Cycle Preparation

manually or digitally, consumes resources, adds little value, and unnecessarily lengthens the budgeting process. Process breakdown can be avoided through rational planning, monitoring, and collaboration, as shown in Exhibit 4.12.

A well-formulated budget process has both top-down and bottom-up components.
However, any budget process that includes a bottom-up component tends to be length-
ened by the complexity of bottom-up communication channels. Companies with annual
revenue greater than $5 billion tend to use a hybrid budget process—bottom up *and* top
down—more than smaller companies do, and they also have the longest cycle times.

These companies may face larger-scale communication and coordination issues
than do smaller companies (see Exhibit 4.13).

We can assume that a hybrid approach, because of internal conflicts, would be sus-
ceptible to delays if strategy and tactics were not efficiently integrated. Budget development
without guidance from strategic planners could lead to revisions and delays, particularly

EXHIBIT 4.11 Impact of Process Delay on Budget Components

Budget Component	Companies using Component*	Purpose of Component
Volume/Revenue Planning Assumptions	92%	Provide guidance for year-over-year growth
Income Statement and Spending	92%	Baseline; targets for cost reduction, margin, and SG&A goals
Headcount Goals	69%	Measure productivity; complement spending targets
Capital Appropriation/ Expenditures	65.5%	Short- and long-term investment plan/cash/ equity requirements
Balance Sheet	59.3%	Goals, cash flows, asset account flows (inputs, outputs, etc.)

* Percentage of survey respondents indicating that this is a key part of their budget

EXHIBIT 4.12   Avoiding Budgeting Process Breakdown

How the Budgeting Process Can Break Down	Possible Solution	Comments
Failure to have a firm start and end date	A detailed event-based calendar with key dates and responsibilities that is broadly communicated and continually monitored	Key checkpoints for Go/No Go decisions
Lack of agreement of the volume planning assumptions resulting in individual budget entities developing their own assumptions	An integrated revenue planning process that incorporates collaboration across the vested parties but has one decision maker	Operational metrics for organizations not directly tied to the volume plan/units of measure in the plan (i.e., units, contract, revenue, etc.)
Failure to orchestrate structured review sessions with senior management and review plans using a standard approach (formats, comparative data, underlying assumptions)	Mandate executive participation	With agreement on the "total," the budget process becomes a zero-sum game
Too many reviews and lack of focus on results and decisions	Determine how deep into the organization the initial budgeting process needs to go	If the communicated goals are not met, arrange meetings and reviews during the budget cycle on the exceptions

if the roll-up comes from deep within the organization. However, as we have mentioned, despite the added complexity, bottom-up input is critical to achieving buy-in and execution of the plan, and a well-organized process can potentially make up for inherent difficulties.

What Do Companies Budget?

As shown in Exhibit 4.14, of the five major components typically found in a budget, all are included by more than half of the surveyed companies.

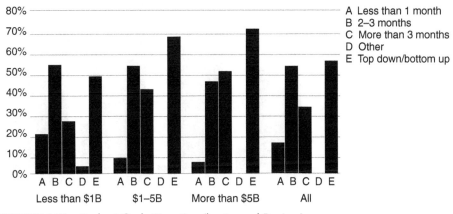

EXHIBIT 4.13   Budget Cycle Duration (by Annual Review)

EXHIBIT 4.14 What do Companies Budget?

Budget Component	Percentage of Respondents
Income Statement	92%
Balance Sheet	59
Cash Flow	60
Headcount	69
Capital Appropriations/Expenditures	66

If the primary purpose of the budget for 53 percent of the companies is financial planning, it is significant that 41 percent do *not* budget the balance sheet. This discrepancy raises questions about the quality and integration of the budgeting process, since the balance sheet is necessary for any financial planning effort.

Spending was budgeted by only 15 percent of the companies. Preferably, spending should be implicit in the income statement portion of the budget; as a line item, spending is more appropriate under operational controls. Clearly, only a few of the companies are using the budget for operational controls.

Exhibits 4.15 and 4.16 suggest that companies may develop budget items with a silo approach, which can lead to disconnects in the financial management of the business. In an effective budget process, the income statement and balance sheet are aligned and cash flow covers costs. It makes sense that a budget should include all three components—income statement, balance sheet, and cash flow. With less than two-thirds of the companies budgeting the balance sheet and cash flow, these companies need to examine how well they are integrating their budget components.

Disconnects among balance sheet, income statement, and cash flow can be further compounded when responsibility for goal setting and financial performance is poorly defined. While certain aspects of budgeting the balance sheet can be best served by leadership, unless the group with ultimate responsibility prepares, submits, and explains the entire financial picture, some level of ownership may be compromised. Furthermore, if a

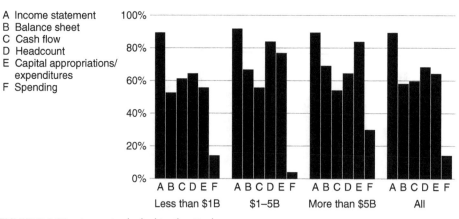

EXHIBIT 4.15 Items Included in the Budget

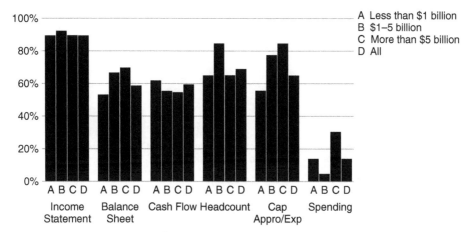

EXHIBIT 4.16 Comparison of Budget Items by Company Size (in Annual Revenue)

company has not integrated goals between the income statement and the balance sheet, it is possible that the achievement of one goal can end up adversely affecting another area. As an example, it could be possible for a manufacturing organization to meet the income statement budget by producing product that flows into inventory and avoids generating variances yet at the same time consumes cash, degrades the balance sheet, and creates more inventory than necessary.

Does the Budget Process Work?

Approximately 67 percent of the companies in the survey indicated that they "always" or "sometimes" change their budget during the year. For this majority of companies, the budget is malleable, in contrast to the traditional budget, which puts a stake in the ground to allow for performance measurement (see Exhibit 4.17).

As shown in Exhibit 4.18, companies had four overarching reasons for changing their budgets midstream. Two in particular suggest fundamental difficulties with the budget process: A full 27 percent changed their budgets because they deemed their plans unattainable, and 25 percent built budget changes right into the process with planned updates at regular intervals.

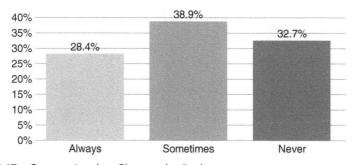

EXHIBIT 4.17 Companies that Change the Budget

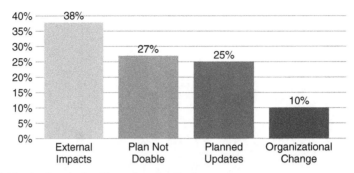

EXHIBIT 4.18   Rationale for Changing the Budget

The size of the company appears to be a factor in "working" the budgeting process for the surveyed companies, with the most "change" activity occurring among the largest and smallest companies (see Exhibit 4.19).

Smaller companies may be less able to absorb significant external pressures and may be forced to alter the budget in response. In large companies, budget goals may never permeate the organization, rendering the budget meaningless soon after the process is completed.

Are Companies Satisfied with the Budget Process?

Interestingly, companies under $1 billion in revenue expressed the highest level of overall satisfaction with the budget process while companies with revenue greater than $5 billion expressed the least satisfaction with the process (see Exhibit 4.20).

Overall dissatisfaction with the budgeting process is not as great as portrayed in the media. The fact that smaller companies are willing to change their budgets may alleviate some of the constraints and frustration with the process. In addition, as mentioned, the fact that most companies have regular forecasting processes in place—which can help communicate changes and update the plan—may contribute to lower dissatisfaction with the budget process.

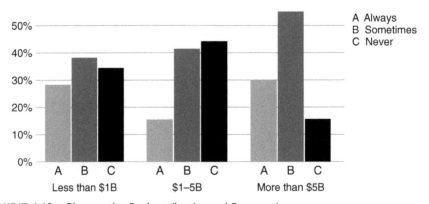

EXHIBIT 4.19   Change the Budget (by Annual Revenue)

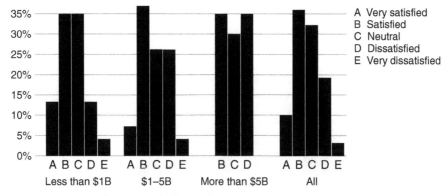

EXHIBIT 4.20   Satisfaction with the Budget Process

Among companies with revenue greater than $5 billion, the transition from planning to execution may simply take too long, with the result that the budgeting process does not meet the needs of the business. The ineffectiveness of the process naturally leads to budget changes during the year, which in turn undermines accountability.

Does Technology Hold the Answer?

Although software developers would have us believe that automation is the key to budget planning, technology cannot by itself improve the quality of the process. As with any technology implementation, "garbage in, garbage out" fully applies to budgeting. An exclusive focus on technology merely means "getting garbage faster."

However, technology can play a positive role—particularly in adding up and consolidating inputs and providing a host of reporting capabilities—if it is part of an overall redesign effort. As shown in Exhibit 4.21, indeed, survey participants were upbeat about the theoretical value of technology, with more than 65 percent indicating that technology could significantly improve their process.

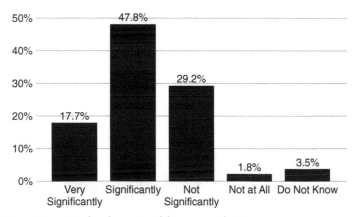

EXHIBIT 4.21   Extent Technology Would Improve the Process

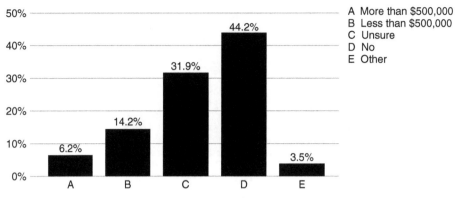

EXHIBIT 4.22 Investment Plans (Technology Next 12 Months)

Yet less than 21 percent of respondents were planning to make any investment in the next 12 months, perhaps because of questions and concerns about the maturity and stabilization of relevant software (see Exhibit 4.22).

As shown in Exhibit 4.23, spreadsheets are the technology mainstay for most companies (85 percent) and about half use more than one tool—which may impede integration of budget-oriented data.

FINDINGS: FORECASTING PROCESS

One purpose of financial forecasting is to allow companies to anticipate marketplace events and impacts on the business so they can make the tactical decisions necessary to deliver predictable financial results. Financial forecasting appears to be a well-established fixture: Almost every company in the survey did some level of financial forecasting, whether formal and scheduled (79 percent) or ad hoc (11 percent). With more than 41 percent of all the companies forecasting monthly and 37 percent forecasting quarterly, the forecasting process is clearly a key mechanism for keeping management informed.

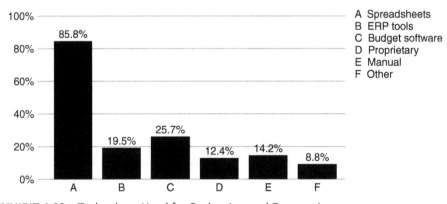

EXHIBIT 4.23 Technology Used for Budgeting and Forecasting

It is vital that a company keep track of the current financial outlook—particularly if it is in a volatile industry, at a crucial stage in its life cycle, or in turbulent times. However, if the process becomes highly institutionalized, detailed, and protracted, budgeting can be a waste of time since the information yielded by such a process will have lost its usefulness by the time submissions and reviews are completed.

What Do Companies Forecast?

In choosing what to forecast, almost all companies focused on the income statement (85 percent) while giving short shrift to other potential forecast components—cash flow, balance sheet, headcount, and capital appropriations and expenditures (see Exhibit 4.24). This approach is not surprising in our income statement–driven economy, where share price is the leading factor in business decision making. However, forecasting arguably requires the same degree of integration budgeting. Future estimates of income statement, balance sheet, cash flow, and other key components need to form a complete and accurate picture.

Who in the Organization Does the Forecasting?

As shown in Exhibit 4.25, forecasting appears to be the domain primarily of high-level groups within the organization, in contrast to the budgeting process, which requires multilevel involvement across the organization.

Are Companies Satisfied with the Forecasting Process?

Overall, the survey in Exhibit 4.26 indicates that the forecasting process meets company needs better than the budgeting process does. This makes sense, given that the forecasting process differs from the budgeting process in several key ways: It takes far less time, involves less detail, and is not complicated by top-down, bottom-up integration and negotiation.

What Is the Forecast Cycle Time?

For a forecast to be meaningful, its cycle time must be short enough that the results will be useful to management for developing contingency plans, taking corrective actions, warning investors, or carrying out similar time-sensitive responsibilities. If

EXHIBIT 4.24   Component—Companies Using Component

	Companies Using Component[1]	
Component	In Budgeting	In Forecasting
Income Statement	92%	85%
Balance Sheet	59	46
Cash Flow	60	55
Headcount	69	46
Capital Appropriations/ Expenditures	66	39

[1] Percentage of survey respondents who indicated this is a key part of their budget or forecast.

EFFECTIVE FORECASTING PRACTICES

- *Predictability.* By using an integrated forecasting process, companies can improve their short-term predictability and provide accurate and timely information to stakeholders. In addition, this messaging can bring about the necessary course corrections within the company to stay on track.
- *Accountability.* Since forecasts tend to be developed based on actual results, management can see the short-term implications of their decisions and make adjustments as required.
- *Flexibility.* As mentioned, since the forecasting process tends to be based on current market conditions, managers and executives can redeploy resources, change spending patterns, and align their plans with those of the company and marketplace.
- *Short cycle time.* The general nature of a forecasting process requires a short cycle time to have any effect on short-term results.
- *Rapid transition from planning to execution.* For the new tactics to be deployed, there must be a short forecast development cycle and a rapid communication of the new tactics.

a company develops forecasts on a monthly cycle and requires two weeks to develop each forecast, the results cannot be very useful. Exhibit 4.27 shows various forecast cycle durations.

What Would Improve the Forecasting Process?

When we asked the companies what could improve the forecasting process, no single factor stood out (see Exhibit 4.28). The processes companies have in place more or less meet their needs. However, among the companies as a whole, no single area is consis-

EXHIBIT 4.25 Who in the Organization Does the Budgeting and Forecasting?

Organizations	Budgeting	Forecasting
Department	55.8%	10.2%
Functional Areas	69.0	10.2
Plant/Site/Sales Office	31.9	1.9
Product Line	30.1	9.2
Business Unit	62.8	32.5
Division	43.4	9.2
Legal Entity	20.4	5.6
Geography	20.4	3.7
Territory	7.1	2.8
Corporate Only	11.5	4.6
Other	1.8	10.1

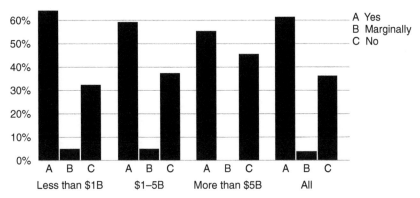

Forecasting Process Meeting the Needs of the Company

A Yes
B Marginally
C No

Less than $1B $1–5B   More than $5B   All

EXHIBIT 4.26 Forecasting Process Meeting the Needs of the Company

tently trouble free. One can speculate that companies have learned to adapt to their existing processes and may not be aware of potential areas for improvement.

REPORT SUMMARY

We set out to determine if companies need to overhaul their budgeting and forecasting processes or if continued tweaking could fix their problems. Here is what the respondents reported overall:

- The traditional budgeting and forecasting processes are still very much cornerstones of the corporate financial planning process and are likely to stay that way for the foreseeable future. In addition, the willingness of many companies to change their budget during the budget period ensures sufficient flexibility to accommodate changes in the marketplace.
- A significant percentage of companies rely exclusively on bottom-up input and consensus on the budget for the upcoming year without top-down direction. Others

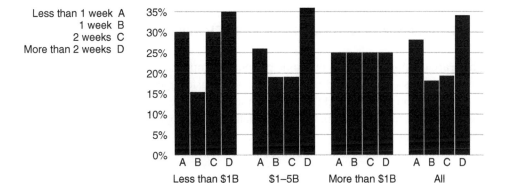

Less than 1 week A
1 week B
2 weeks C
More than 2 weeks D

Less than $1B $1–5B   More than $1B   All

EXHIBIT 4.27 Forecast Cycle Duration

EXHIBIT 4.28   What Would Make the Forecast Process More Effective?

Factor	Percentage of Respondents
Prior-period actuals	18.5
New unit sales plan	23.1
New revenue projection	22.2
Economic data	19.4
Other internal departments	20.4
Direct customer input	20.4
Other	24.1

become bogged down in the inherent, albeit healthy, conflict over budget direction between strategic planners and functional units.

▪ Budgeting and forecasting processes generally work for most companies, but only after being force-fitted to meet company needs. The budget is no longer widely seen as a stake in the ground. Instead, since almost all companies do some kind of financial forecasting during the year, they have the ability to continually modify their plans and apply the plans when needed.

Our conclusion is that while either overhauling or tweaking might be appropriate, companies need to (1) evaluate what is actually occurring in their budgeting and forecasting sphere as compared with leading budgeting and forecasting practices and (2) assess the alignment of these processes with their strategic objectives and goals.

Clearly, those companies that do not link the budgeting process with the strategic plan should set about doing so. And those companies that incur delays as a result of inefficient budget processes need to refine communication and planning mechanisms between operating units and strategic planners. However, until a company has a road map for change, it typically will hunker down and maintain the status quo even if its process is not working as it should.

 ## DEVELOPING A ROAD MAP FOR CHANGE

There are no quick solutions or magic potions for improving the budgeting and forecasting processes. The effort requires a back-to-basics approach to integrating the company vision with financial goals and measurement, rather than attempting to use budgeting and forecasting to mitigate deficiencies in operational controls or long-range planning.

Improving budget and forecasting processes typically occurs in four phases:

1. *Ensure that an effective strategic planning process is in place.* Obtain senior-level commitment to the planning process and sufficient granularity of output to provide guidance to businesses units.
2. *Develop a budget based on strategic goals.* Use KPIs (leading and lagging, internal and external), well-defined rules of engagement, and a clear path from planning to execution.
3. *Accommodate change.* Use forecasting to reflect changes in the marketplace (customer demand, market acceptance, currency volatility, etc.) and provide feedback on the strategic plan.
4. *Measure performance.* Implement tracking processes that measure progress toward attaining goals. The overall planning process should have a cascading effect within the company as the top-level direction flows down to the operating units—with the expectation of continuity and consistency through "one goal, one plan, one measurement."

CHAPTER FIVE

The Budget: An Integral Element of Internal Control

Jay H. Loevy, CPA, CFE
Edward Mendlowitz, CPA
WithumSmith+Brown

INTRODUCTION

No system can be effective without proper and adequate controls. It is abundantly evident from the body of technical literature (this book included) that the raison d'être of budgeting is its use as a control tool by management. The whole process—setting goals and objectives, establishing standards of performance, and analyzing and acting on results—is almost synonymous with the term "management control." It is the way management is assured that "people in the organization do what they are supposed to do."[1]

Yet the subject of this chapter deals with *internal control* rather than management control. The difference in terms lies with its use. "Internal control" appears to be used exclusively in the field of auditing. In its Statement on Auditing Standards 55, the American Institute of Certified Public Accountants (AICPA) states:

> *Although the internal control structure may include a wide variety of objectives and related policies and procedures, only some of these may be relevant to an audit of the entity's financial statements. Generally, the policies and procedures that are relevant*

---

[1] Robert N. Anthony, John Deardon, and Norton M. Bedford, *Management Control Systems* (Homewood, IL: Richard C. Irwin, 1984), p. 5.

to an audit pertain to the entity's ability to record, process, summarize, and report financial data consistent with the assertions embodied in the financial statements.[2]

Thus, staying with the more narrow definition of internal control, this chapter focuses on those controls relevant to financial records and reports but that exist within the total control framework of the company.

The "output" of an internal control system results from comparing actual results of operations with the results expected from the planning process. Through use of reports comparing planned with actual results, management could identify such problems as:

- Inaccurate information reported in the company's financial records
- Unauthorized operations, such as overextending credit or entering into higher-risk transactions
- Defalcations, such as conversion of company receipts, diversion of inventories, or unauthorized disbursements
- Reduction in planned profit for any number of reasons

The planning process as an integral element of internal control. Its relationship to the control environment is described in the next sections.

THE CONTROL ENVIRONMENT

Exhibit 5.1 illustrates the control environment and shows how this environment is divided between macrocontrols and microcontrols. The former are the framework for the control environment while the latter are systems and procedures that put them into action.

Macrocontrols

The four macrocontrol elements—corporate culture, organization, planning and reporting, and external controls—are interrelated, and management should ensure that all four exist within the company.

For example, companies that rely solely on the integrity and conscientiousness of their employees (organization) without planning systems and outside controls are imprudent. Likewise, planning and reporting systems that are not made a part of the corporate culture will likely be ineffective in guiding the way employees think and act.

Corporate Culture

This segment could be the most important of the four, yet it is the most difficult to define. Company culture is that unique combination of ideas, mission, policies, goals, and ways of personal interaction that are created by top management and echoed by other personnel. Control policies and procedures can become a code to live by in the company, or

---

[2] American Institute of Certified Public Accountants, Statement on Auditing Standards 55, *Consideration of the Internal Control Structure in a Financial Audit* (New York: Author, 1988), p. 4.

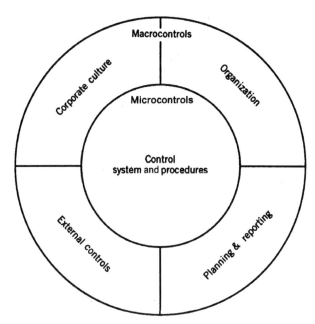

EXHIBIT 5.1 Control Environment

they can be given only lip service. Employees are very quick to discern the *real* control environment by the way management reacts to procedural and/or policy infractions or other operating problems. Thus, corporate culture sets the tone for the whole company, including its commitment to exercising control over its operations.

One of the ways management exercises this control and exhibits its commitment to a controlled environment is through the use of an internal audit section. Internal auditors are company employees, as differentiated from external auditors, who are independents, such as certified public accountants. While both internal and external auditors are concerned with controls, they approach the subject from a somewhat different perspective. The internal auditor's primary objective is to ascertain that the company's policies and procedures are being followed; the external auditor's primary objective is to express an opinion on the fairness of the company's financial statements.

Organization

In order for an internal control system to operate, there must be persons to whom management can assign authority and responsibility, a structure to define reporting relationships, and a means to communicate with others. This is accomplished by establishing an organization having a formal, well-defined structure in which the incumbents of all positions operate within the scope of their assigned authority and responsibility.

Planning and Reporting

This set of macrocontrols provides the means by which management can define the company's mission, set forth company goals and operating objectives, set performance standards, monitor performance of its operating units, and evaluate and control the managers who are responsible for such performance. As we will see in the next sections, planning and reporting are formal and structured methods, as differentiated from the corporate culture, which tends to be more anecdotal and unstructured.

External Controls

A company relies on certain controls exercised by organizations and persons external to the management of the company. They may include external auditors, the board of directors and committees thereof, regulatory agencies (especially in regulated industries), and the body of customers and suppliers who can be expected to complain of unfair or illegal treatment.

Microcontrols

In order to carry out the goals and objectives of management, a *system* must exist that governs the procedures for control over all relevant transactions. Such controls will encompass the processes known as management information systems, management control systems, operating policies and procedures, and other such descriptive titles.

Microcontrols differ from macrocontrols in that they are more *procedural* in nature. Consider, for example, how the subject of product pricing might be handled within the control environment.

During strategic planning sessions, it is determined that product pricing will be competitive with national companies. Product division heads are given the authority to adjust prices within certain limits without higher-level approval. In order to carry out these macrocontrol decisions, certain control microcontrol procedures are instituted. These require the division head to document the existence of national company pricing, determine that such pricing is not due only to short-term promotions, and document the actions taken to adjust and communicate revised pricing in the field.

The existence of microcontrol procedures in this example closes the loop, in that top management is able to review and analyze the actions taken by subordinates in carrying out policies that they had approved. This is further described later in this chapter in the section titled "Reporting Systems."

PLANNING SYSTEMS

Certified public accountants, in conducting financial audits, rely on the effectiveness of a company's planning and reporting system in forming an opinion on the company's financial statements. The AICPA's Statement 55 delineates these management methods, which should be present in a properly controlled environment:

> *Establishing planning and reporting systems that set forth management's plans and the results of actual performance. Such systems may include business planning; budgeting, forecasting, and profit planning; and responsibility accounting.*

Establishing methods that identify the status of actual performance and exceptions from planned performance, as well as communicating them to the appropriate levels of management.

Using such methods at appropriate management levels to investigate variances from expectations and to take appropriate and timely corrective action.[3]

Budgeting policy and procedures are termed the foundation of the discipline of budgeting. The term "discipline" is apt. Internal control depends on discipline, and thus the company's plans must be originate in a controlled, disciplined manner. The first step in this procedure is the setting of goals and objectives.

Goals and Objectives

In a well-controlled environment, all personnel are supposed to work toward common goals, using prescribed, authorized procedures. Management cannot expect employees to act effectively if they are unaware of, or do not fully subscribe to, the goals set forth by company policy.

In a military analogy, a battlefield commander can exercise control over troops only if subordinates understand the battlefield objectives and follow out orders accordingly. A platoon leader who is expected to render surveillance but instead attacks an enemy position could put the whole operation in jeopardy. Control within a company operates in a similar fashion, although it is not lives that are at stake; instead, it is money, jobs, and eventually the entity itself.

The importance of goal setting as a control element is directly proportional to the size and complexity of the organization. In a small, one-location organization, the company's goals are discussed frequently in one form or another. Even the morning coffee break can be a forum for reinforcing such goals. Conversely, if operating chiefs are thousands of miles away and do not communicate often with their superiors, company goals tend to become fuzzy and can eventually disappear.

Consider what happens in a football game. In the huddle, the players are close together and understand what the play will be and what will be expected of them. However, if the quarterback decides to call an "audible" at the line of scrimmage, his teammates behind him and at the far ends may not be able to hear over the crowd noise. Such lack of communication can result in a busted play.

Thus, the consequences of inadequate goal setting and the attendant communication of same is at best a dilution of companywide effectiveness; at worst it is a forerunner of the eventual collapse of the organization.

Assigning Responsibility for Performance

Plans will remain plans unless they are carried out. The assignment of responsibility for putting the goals and objectives into practice is an important link in the chain of controls. It should be done in a formal manner and should include:

---

[3] Ibid., p. 26.

- An organization chart showing at least the key operating personnel and the reporting relationship among and between them. In multidivision companies, there normally would be charts of the organization at different levels: operating unit, division, and total corporation, for example.
- Job descriptions for all positions, which should include title, reporting relationship, limits of authority, primary job responsibilities, and qualifications for the job.
- A written statement of the goals and objectives for the organizational unit, including a profit plan or budget and narrative description of the problems and opportunities faced by the unit.

Anthony, Deardon, and Bedford use the term "responsibility center" to denote any organization unit headed by a responsible manager. They further categorize such responsibility centers as revenue centers, expense centers, profit centers, and investment centers.[4] (Investment centers are also profit centers and for this chapter's purpose need not be separated.) The three latter categories could be illustrated as:

1. *Revenue centers.* Sales offices and marketing and sales promotion units
2. *Expense centers.* Administrative departments and units servicing other units, such as engineering or quality control
3. *Profit centers.* Manufacturing plants, retail operations, and operating companies

Budgets developed for responsibility centers should be both *relevant* to the type of center and *controllable* by it. There must be a clear and demonstrable relationship between the goals and objectives of the unit and the opportunity of the responsible manager to control results. For example, it would not be meaningful to a manufacturing department head to be responsible for profits if he or she had no opportunity to control sales or selling price. One would need to go higher in the organization, say to the vice president of manufacturing or the head of a product division, to properly assign profit responsibility.

The meaning of assigning responsibility within the internal control framework should be obvious: Only people can bear responsibility for budgetary results. (Thankfully, we have not yet assigned such responsibility to computers!) These people, the managerial group, form a required element in the internal control system. They are measured and controlled in comparison to the expectations developed in the goal-setting stage of planning.

The means by which top management exercises this control is the subject of the next section.

REPORTING SYSTEMS

In exercising their job responsibilities, company personnel make decisions that collectively influence the conduct of the company as a whole. Some individual decisions will

---

[4] Anthony, Deardon, and Bedford, *Management Control Systems*, pp. 194–210

have only a minor effect, such as selecting a forms vendor, while some will have more significance, such as the hiring of a key executive. According to Ackoff:

> *Control is the evaluation of decisions, including decisions to do nothing, once they have been implemented. The process of control involves four steps:*
>
> 1. *Predicting the outcomes of decisions in the form of performance measures.*
> 2. *Collecting information on actual performance.*
> 3. *Comparing actual with predicted performance.*
> 4. *When a decision is shown to have been deficient, correcting the procedure that produced it and correcting its consequences where possible.*[5]

The first item was previously discussed. In this section, we cover the collection, reporting, and analysis of information in order to close the control loop.

Decision making depends on reliable, accurate information. The more significant the decision, the more important it is to have confidence in the information on which the decision is based. Take the example of a manager who must decide on shutting down a division because it is unprofitable. He must be certain that profitability, as reported on division income statements, is accurate. A manager may be confident that the company's computer programs operate as intended, since no problems have arisen in this regard, but he or she may not be so sanguine about the control over input data.

Control over Input

All information begins with input of data to the management information system. Obviously, the output of the system is only as reliable as its input. Some of the considerations the manager might have regarding the accuracy of input to these reports are listed next.

Area of Concern	Possible Control Procedures by Management or Auditors
Have all sales been recorded?	Reconciliation of shipping and billing data
Are shipments to customers properly authorized?	Inventory verification and reconciliation with sales invoices
Has proper credit been given to intracompany sales?	Review and reconciliation of intracompany sales
Has unit pricing been applied correctly?	Periodic reporting and review of unit pricing tables billing program
Have unauthorized sales allowances been granted	Separation of duties involving approval and recording of sales allowances
Are sales allowances greater than an acceptable level?	Comparison of sales allowances to gross sales by customer
Have incorrect methods been used to calculate cost of goods sold?	Review and analysis of cost variances

(Continued)

---

[5] Russell L. Ackoff, *A Concept of Corporate Planning* (New York: John Wiley & Sons, 1970), p. 112.

(Continued)

Area of Concern	Possible Control Procedures by Management or Auditors
Have there been defalcations or errors affecting:	
−Cost of materials?	Independent matching of purchase, receiving, and payment data
−Receipt of inventory?	Rotation of duties and mandatory vacations of purchasing personnel
−Control of inventory?	Cycle counting of inventory
−Cost of labor?	Surprise inspections of payroll check issuance procedures
−Control of all costs and receipt of revenues	Rotation of duties and mandatory vacations of accounting personnel
Was the budget data entered correctly?	Review printout of budget after data entry

Reporting, Review, and Response

The last phases of the budgetary control process close the loop. This loop, which is illustrated in Exhibit 5.2, starts with the planning phase, then records actual transactions, and finally reports against the plan and generates management response.

Usually, one or more documents are produced in each phase of the control loop: the budget after the planning phase; reports comparing budget with actual after the execution phase; memos or reports analyzing results after evaluation; and action-type documents, containing management directives, in the response phase. The results of such actions are then included in the next period's planning.

Evaluation is based on reports of actual results for a responsibility center in comparison to budget and a calculation of the difference, or variance, therefrom. A very

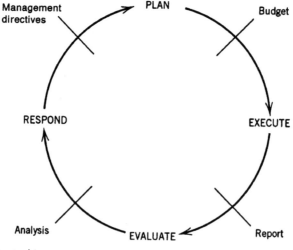

EXHIBIT 5.2   Control Loop

useful report format would include both current period and year to date, as in the next abbreviated example:

Current Period				Year to Date		
Budget	Actual	Variance		Budget	Actual	Variance
1,000	980	[20]	Sales	25,500	26,300	800
600	610	[10]	Cost of sales	16,600	16,400	[200]
250	210	20	Expenses	6,400	6,1	700
					00	
150	160	10	Net income	2,500	3,800	1,300

Note that unfavorable variances are bracketed, regardless of whether they are revenue or expense.

The most effective reports are those that deliver the message clearly and succinctly. What the message should be is determined by the circumstances, including the scope of responsibility of the recipient, the relevance and usefulness of detailed information, and the frequency of reporting. In any case, reports should be designed to highlight the most important parts of the message, so that the recipient does not have to waste time getting to the heart of the matter.

Interpretation and analysis of these reports is a vital control step, because budget variances, by themselves, will not necessarily provide guidance to the organization. For example, the fact that gross sales were lower than plan does not indicate what, if any, action should be taken. Was the difference caused by the number of units, the selling price per unit, the mix of products, or some combination thereof? The manager must go behind the top-level numbers to properly analyze cause and effect.

Often there are so many variables that it is extremely difficult to isolate the major cause or causes of variances. For example, in a multiproduct environment, sales of some products may be up, some down; some gross margins may be affected by special sales promotions and/or purchasing discounts; and all sales may have been affected by adverse weather conditions. Thus, without corroboration of these variables, the manager would be ill advised to take corrective action.

Instead, the manager should track one or more of the significant variables for a period of months to see if he or she can isolate the major causes for a degradation of gross profit. Doing this might necessitate creating specialized data input, processing, and reporting, such as separating all sales that resulted from special promotions or other such circumstances. When it appears that the cause or causes have been found, the manager should take steps to ameliorate the situation.

In a well-controlled environment, top management would be figuratively looking over the shoulder of the manager, since they would be receiving either the same reports or those at a higher level. In either case, any significant change in responsibility center gross profit should be noticeable. It is incumbent on management to see that the problem is being studied and that corrective action is taken or recommended.

SUMMARY

In order to express an opinion on the fairness of financial statements, the auditor must examine and evaluate the company's system of internal control. This system operates within the internal control structure, composed of macrocontrols and microcontrols. One of the four macrocontrol elements is planning and reporting.

Planning involves the establishment of goals and objectives for the company as a whole, as well as its components, which, for control purposes, are called responsibility centers. Reporting involves the comparison of actual results with plan. It is the manager's responsibility to analyze such results and develop action plans to try to correct any situations causing unfavorable variances from plan.

The proper conduct of such a system of internal controls provides assurance to the auditor that data have entered the accounting system in a controlled fashion and that any transactions that were materially inaccurate or unauthorized would be identified and corrected.

CHAPTER SIX

The Relationship between Strategic Planning and the Budgeting Process

Jeffrey L. Bass, MA, MPA
CEO, Executive Strategies Group LLC

INTRODUCTION

To fully understand and appreciate the functional relationship between strategic planning and budgeting, it is important to understand the purposes of strategic planning. For early-stage companies, business plans typically are seen as marketing tools in the capital formation process. As the company matures, strategic planning evolves into a process of assessing and responding to industry change. However, it may still be used to raise capital. As the company matures to Fortune 1000–100 status, the strategic planning process will become an institutionalized function designed to direct and control growth and direction, and it might be used to raise capital.

goal: strategic planning process.

This chapter examines the strategic planning process from the perspective of organizational, managerial, operational, marketing, and financial impacts. The role of budgeting in planning as well as in plan implementation and monitoring is explored.

HOW TO PLAN

Strategic planning *must not* be viewed merely as an expedient way to raising capital. First of all, sophisticated capital providers and their professional representatives will quickly understand and dismiss a business plan born of such reasoning. Perhaps the management team with such a limited view denies itself the opportunity to manage and control the company's growth and development objectively and methodically by requiring the definition of business objectives and identification of realistic market, operational, and financial targets, and the strategic planning process becomes an important weapon in management's arsenal. Actual performance can be measured against targets established through the planning process. Variations from these targets can be addressed and corrective actions taken—including modifying the strategic business plan—without resorting to crisis management. Impacts on revenues, cash flow, and profitability of product modification or new product development can be carefully assessed and adjusted. Changes in industry direction or consumer preference can be more easily monitored and addressed in a timely fashion so as to assure a sustained competitive, if not competitively advantaged, market position.

The strategic planning process also defines the need for and scheduled deployment of various resources and technologies. If undertaken objectively (i.e., in an egoless environment), the strategic planning process defines the talents and skills of management needed to assure successful company growth. Finally, the planning process facilitates the termination of financing requirements and financial performance.

In short, growing a company is like embarking on a trip to an unfamiliar destination. We could travel blindly, asking directions along the way and hoping that we are not being misdirected. If we arrive at our destination, it may be too late for it to be meaningful. Alternatively, we can research our destination to ensure that it is the place we want to be. We can plot our course, understand the directions and time and cost of travel alternatives, and arrive at our destination before the sun sets. This is how prudent business owners and managers plan: by developing a *road map* to set the course for their company's successful growth and development.

By the way, a business plan resulting from such an objective strategic planning process can more successfully be used as a capital-raising document (if for no other reason than it will convey to the capital provider the seriousness and maturity of the management team).

THE AUDIENCE FOR WHOM THE PLAN IS DESIGNED

The conventional belief is that because a strategic business plan is prepared to satisfy the assumed requirements of capital providers, these individuals or entities must be the most important readers of the document. However, the strategic business plan *should not* be formulated as a capital-raising document: It follows that capital providers should not be viewed as the primary audience of the plan document. As the strategic plan should be a product of a deliberate, methodical, and objective planning process, it stands to reason that the most important users are the business owner and managers. These individuals should use the plan as the operating tool it was designed to be.

A properly formulated strategic business plan assesses management and organization requirements and includes functional job descriptions and tables of organization.

[handwritten margin notes: Users of... ① owner/manager ② attorneys, accountants ③ suppliers / lg customers ④ capital providers]

Therefore, the plan could also be of value to attorneys drafting shareholder agreements, employment contracts, and private placement memoranda, among other documents. In addition, the company's accountants or compensation planners may find the business plan useful in helping management to formulate competitively advantaged compensation programs to attract and retain the highly qualified key employees needed by the company to achieve its stated business objectives.

Suppliers and large customers often like to review a company's business plan to find some assurance that they can expect to enjoy beneficial long-term relationships with the company. Finally, capital providers are, of course, important readers of the strategic business plan.

STRATEGIC BUSINESS PLANNING AND ITS ROLE IN BUDGETING

Budgets are documents that reflect management's best estimate of revenues and expenses at a future time. In a mature company (for the purposes of this discussion, a *mature company* is defined as one with at least one year of operating history), management has the luxury of experience and history. The older the company, the more confident management can be in using history as a component in the budget-making process. It can, at least in part, base its budget on the company's past financial performance. Understandably, a start-up company's management does not have the tool of history to work with. Formulating a budget for this group of managers is tantamount to sticking a wet thumb to the wind. Interestingly, what both sets of managers have in common is the unknown. How well future events are factored into the budget process will determine the efficacy of the resulting budget and its reliability as a financial and operating tool, and will also minimize the incidence of surprises, such as market or technological changes. Such modifications in the business dynamic could cause substantial deviations from budget and, importantly, could harm the company.

No one can, with 100 percent confidence, predict the future, regardless of the reliability of the data used; however, by engaging in a methodical and objective process of strategic planning, management of any size company can at least afford itself the ability to understand and factor into the analyses parameters of change. An institutionalized program of strategic business planning requires management to regularly assess the market within the context of the company's business objectives, product mix, marketing strategy, research and development program, management and organization structure, operations, *and budget.* Consequently, the effect(s) of market fluctuations on all functional areas of the organization can be analyzed easily. Budgets can be modified to reflect the new reality, and corrective management actions, if necessary, can be taken in a calm and deliberate manner.

What is important to understand is that budgeting is a component and actually a product of strategic planning. If we embrace the process of strategic planning and accept the premise that it should be institutionalized and repetitive, we can better understand its relationship to budget making, monitoring, and implementation.

PLANNING DIFFERENCES AMONG SMALL, MEDIUM, AND LARGE ORGANIZATIONS

If we lived in Utopia, all businesses, regardless of size, would have institutionalized strategic planning programs. In the real world in which we reside, this will never be the case except, perhaps, among Fortune 50 or 100 companies that have whole departments dedicated to strategic planning. AT&T and IBM are two examples. At the opposite end of the spectrum, we can hardly expect the neighborhood dry cleaner or grocer to do any kind of formalized planning. However, once again, all businesses are united by the common thread of market change and very often by internal threats or opportunities as well. Their ability to anticipate and respond to such changes will affect their competitive position, profitability, and cash flow and, in the case of the public company, stock price and market capitalization. Although the neighborhood dry cleaner likely will not engage in formal strategic planning, it must nevertheless be sensitive to the local competitive environment, consumer preferences and expectations, demographic changes, and technological changes within the industry. It is wise for such a small business to be alert to these elements to ensure, as best possible, business continuity and profitability. The only instance in which a business of this size would ever be asked for a business plan that includes detailed financial projections would be to satisfy the requirements for a loan application, particularly one that carries a guarantee of the United States Small Business Administration or other government agency or program.

Consider, though, the dry cleaner that has a good understanding of the market. This entity's owners might believe, perhaps, that the days of the single-store neighborhood dry cleaner are numbered. Due to the owners' entrepreneurial spirit, the company embarks on a program to consolidate neighborhood-based dry cleaners through strategic acquisition. The plan might also call for the creation of a central cleaning facility to service the acquired stores and achieve important economies of scale. The strategy is to acquire underperforming entities and improve them through various capital improvements and management changes. To realize the plan, this entity has to identify suitable acquisition targets, understand their respective markets, and develop an acquisition model. The cleaners will also need a definitive assessment of financial requirements and performance as well as an understanding of how the requisite financing will be obtained and used. In short, these entrepreneurs must engage in a strategic planning process to properly structure a growing acquisition-and-operating company that will require significant financing. Though the immediate motivation for such planning may be to secure capital, an objectively prepared strategic business plan will enable the entrepreneur to better manage invested proceeds and measure acquisition timing and actual store performance against targets.

Several years go by and the dry cleaning company now owns several thousand dry cleaning stores throughout the United States. Its stock is publicly traded on a major exchange. Earnings are increasing period for period, and the price/earnings ratio remains strong. The company is the clear leader in its industry. However, its ever-vigilant strategic planning department detects potential internal and external threats to the company's long-term success: On one hand, members of its labor force are agitated over what they believe to be noncompetitive wages and benefits. In addition, a new and apparently well-financed dry-cleaning Web site, providing 24-hour pickup and delivery at very competitive prices, is introduced with considerable fanfare and industry analyst excitement.

Having reviewed the analyses conducted by staff, the director of strategic planning confers with the company's vice president of human resources (HR) and information technology officer to formulate workable responses to these threats. The director then meets with the company's president, chief financial officer (CFO), and chief operating officer (COO) and recommends the timely implementation of a new compensation and benefits program, as well as changes in HR policies and procedures. Also recommended is a global expansion program, as well as modification of the company's Web site to offer 24-hour pickup and delivery utilizing the company's vast network of stores. When asked by the CFO to justify his recommendations, the director of strategic planning produces long-range analyses indicating steady and growing erosion of market share and dramatic escalation of labor costs if these actions are not implemented. In addition, the director provides analyses indicating that if these strategies are implemented, earnings per share and market capitalization will continue to rise. The director produces an implementation schedule linked to a detailed budget to show the effects of implementation. The chief executive officer, CFO, and COO confer further with the director of strategic planning. They make some modifications to the plan but approve it almost as recommended. The company's board of directors meets to review the plan. After considerable deliberation, the board approves implementation. Subsequently, industry analysts notified of the change react positively, believing that the company will maintain and expand its market share. Several upgrade the company's stock to a "strong buy." The strategic planning department will continually monitor the effects of implementation against plan and budget forecasts, even as staff maintains its vigilant watch over internal and external events that could affect the company's good health.

From the start-up to the stock market darling, all companies must strategically plan. The method and intensity of planning is a function only of stage of development.

COMPONENTS OF STRATEGIC PLANNING

Definition of Business Objectives

As the hackneyed Chinese proverb goes, "A journey of 1,000 miles begins with the first step." When applied to strategic planning, perhaps the proverb could be phrased "The road map to success begins with the definition of business objectives." The statement of business objectives establishes the direction the company will take to achieve the growth of which its owners and managers believe it is capable. The business objectives lay out clear expectations of what can be accomplished within a defined period. This statement is the reference point of the company's marketing strategy, organization and management development, operations growth, and financial performance. It begins the business planning process and sets the tone and direction of the business and its plan.

The typical time period covered by a business plan is three to five years. (Three years is much more realistic.) Therefore, strategic business planning should begin with the definition of an overall business objective, also known as a mission statement. The mission statement basically memorializes the purposes of the business's existence. It often discusses how the company, through its products and/or services, will succeed by filling a void in the market, improving on current products or technologies, or creating demand. The mission statement should continue with a discussion of the expected management philosophy and style of the company and how these are consistent with success.

Upon completion of the mission statement, the next task is to define short-term, interim, and long-term objectives. If planning for a three-year time period, these can often be linked to the first, second, and third years, respectively.

Critical Success Factors

Critical success factors can be viewed as milestones that must be reached if the company's stated business objectives are to be achieved. For example, a short-term objective of an early-stage company may be to obtain required financing. A critical success factor in accomplishing this objective would be to complete a strategic business plan. A later-stage company may have an objective to expand geographically. In this instance, critical success factors could include completion of detailed market analyses of targeted areas; acquisition of office, manufacturing, or warehouse space; completion of capital improvements; and hiring of required human resources. An understandable business objective of a public company would be (and should always be) to increase shareholder value. Critical success factors would include achieving cost reductions of some specified amount, revenue enhancement through introduction of new products by specified dates, and completion of strategic acquisitions within stated time frames.

Critical success factors are important because they constitute the mechanism through which a strategic business plan is implemented and monitored. They facilitate formulation of action plans, which, in turn, are linked to project budgets.

MANAGEMENT AND ORGANIZATION

Management

Many of us are familiar with the real estate professional's admonition that the three most important considerations in purchasing real property, of any type, are "location, location, location." Ask an astute investor to identify the most important criteria of an investment decision and he or she will tell you, "management, management, management."

A company can have a great product or family of products with a very accepting market. However, if the assembled management team is ill-suited to bring the products to market and/or to do so in a cost-efficient manner, it is highly unlikely that team members will attract the capital required by the company. This is as true of the mature company as it is of the start-up. In the case of the later-stage company, the founding management team may not have the skill or depth of experience needed to grow the entity to the next level; therefore, obtaining financing to fuel future growth may range from difficult to impossible.

As strategic business planning is an objective process, it stands to reason that the management team must be true to the process and to itself. Very simply put, founders or later-stage company managers must assess soberly whether they individually and collectively possess that combination of skills and experience needed to achieve the company's business objectives. Clearly, it is in management's interests to do this soul searching because both present-day income and future wealth accumulation depend on the outcome of this analysis.

The impact of this analysis on budget making may be obvious: If additions to the management team are necessary, cash flows will be affected by virtue of the impact on general and administrative expenses. Line items affected would include:

- Executive compensation
- Insurance
- Payroll taxes
- Rent
- Furniture and fixtures
- Leasehold improvements

Why would rent, furniture and fixtures, and leasehold improvements be affected? There is a simple answer: Each manager hired, depending on level of responsibility, will require work space. This can range from a cubicle to a 1,000-square-foot office with conference facilities. These offices may have to be built, and clearly they have to be furnished and equipped with computers and other office necessities. If additional space is required and is available in the same facility, rent will increase. If new space is needed, decisions will have to be made regarding buy/lease alternatives in terms of impact on earnings and cash flow.

Of course, higher-level executives likely will command superior compensation and benefits programs, which could include deferred compensation, bonuses, profit sharing, and use of company-leased automobiles. Obviously, these items have budget implications as well.

the on budget — salary & comp + Benefits!

Organization

Of no less importance to the company's success are its human resources below the executive management level. Sound strategic planning should not only include analyses of human resource requirements at every functional level but should also define organizational culture and management staff relations. A table of organization graphically depicts hierarchical reporting relationships. A functional table of organization also includes brief descriptions of responsibilities for each position included in the organization structure. These charts also identify the numbers of persons needed per position.

Although the tangible implications of human resource needs analysis on budget making are obvious, less clear is the impact on the budget and company success of the organizational culture. Unfortunately, some managers neglect consideration of this important element in human resource planning. Today's businesses not only empha-size and expect a high level of work ethics, solid performance, and productivity but also increasingly are providing workplace attributes that respond to workers' professional, physical, social, and emotional needs. Hierarchical reporting is necessary for supervision of less experienced workers by more experienced ones, but many organizations today also have some form of participative management system that allows workers at every level to provide input to management decision making.

In the early 1980s, the New York City Department of Sanitation embarked on a radical program to change its solid waste refuse collection system. It proposed to eliminate one worker from a then-conventional three-person truck crew. It also proposed to extend collection routes by approximately one-third, meaning that the two remaining workers would have to work 50 percent more. Understandably, the union representing the workers was vehemently opposed to such actions. However, through labor management committees, workers participated in a process of route design, productivity target formulation, and collection truck design. The result was deployment of a new collection system using two-member truck crews operating radically different trucks along longer routes. Notably, not one worker was laid off, New York City streets got demonstrably cleaner, and workers who met productivity targets received incremental shift differential pay. New York City's operating budget was reduced by more than $100 million. (The author was director of operations planning for the New York City Department of Sanitation at the time.)

Today, companies also provide day care, a variety of insurance and retirement benefits, flextime, and so forth. Though all these programs affect budget making, they nevertheless create a more cohesive and productive work environment with likely positive implications for the bottom line.

MARKET ANALYSIS

Total Available Market

The *total available market* refers to the overall industry in which a company participates. An understanding of this industry—from consumer preferences through the influence of technological change to competitive environment, profit, and pricing—is absolutely necessary to determine if a business should be started or continued in a particular industry. These analyses can and should be conducted regularly to afford companies at any stage of development the benefit of current market intelligence.

Segment Analysis

Segment analysis is simply a refinement of an analysis of the industry. For example, the wireless communications industry includes everything from cell phones to smartphones to notepad devices. But what if a company did nothing but distribute smartphones? Though management should certainly have intelligence about the total available market, it really has to focus on that segment of the industry focused on smartphones. The same demographic, competition, supplier, pricing, and profit analyses that will be conducted at the industry level will have to be more concentrated here. The distributor will have to know the segment very well to develop and sustain even a competitive—let alone a competitively advantaged—market position.

Total available market and segment analyses are not mutually exclusive. Indeed, there are compelling reasons to coordinate the two. First, every company, as part of its strategic planning process, must assess internal and external strengths, weaknesses, opportunities, and threats (SWOT analyses). Without getting into a very detailed discussion, suffice it to say that SWOT analysis defines the organization's strengths as well as its vulnerabilities. Armed with this information, management can more decisively and objectively formulate strategies and implementation actions to shore up the weak areas and capitalize on the strong ones. A thorough understanding of the market facilitates this process. In the example of the smartphone distributor, technological changes coupled with consumer preferences suggest a broader acceptance of cell phones as a preferred means of communicating. Indeed, most cell phones now feature texting capabilities. The distributor is one of the leaders in the industry and has a highly motivated and well-compensated sales force. Management makes the strategic decision to create a cell phone division. Not only will this action result in mitigating any falloff in smartphone sales, but it also would likely constitute a new growth area for the company.

Market research need not be a daunting task. For the start-up, most local area colleges have good libraries and business professors and students eager to assist with the research. The cost for such services is usually very nominal. Of course, entrepreneurs should immerse themselves in the process as much as possible, so that they can benefit from hands-on knowledge of the market.

Later-stage companies could purchase detailed and longer-range analyses from highly reputable market research firms. A number of these enable subscribers to access vast databases online.

Publicly held companies should have in-house market research capability. The rationale for this is simple: Financial institutions making a market in the company's stock have such a capability, in the persons of industry analysts. In addition to facilitating responsive management decision making in a dynamic environment, current data enable management to have the same body of knowledge as the analysts and to better fashion preemptive financial public relations that actually could influence the analysts' thinking.

FORMULATION OF MARKETING STRATEGIES

The formulation and implementation of marketing strategies have obvious implications for budget making. The more sophisticated the marketing strategies and supporting programs, the more costly they will be to implement. Simple preparation and distribution of product literature will incur one level of cost. A more complex strategy of establishing a competitively advantaged market position (e.g., through aggressive pricing, opening geographically dispersed sales offices, active trade show participation, and multimedia ad campaigns) will have a significantly different impact on projected revenues, general and administrative expenses, profit margins, cash flows, and, ultimately, net earnings.

The latter end of the spectrum is not reserved solely for later-stage companies. Start-up technology companies, for example, not only have to develop product literature in advance of going to market, they also often have to be present at trade shows and advertise in strategically selected journals.

The formulation of sound and realistic marketing strategies is critical because it constitutes the major vehicle for attaining the organization's strategic business objectives. Consequently, formulated strategies must respond to analyzed market conditions and opportunities. Whereas too aggressive a marketing program may be injurious to the company, very often a timid marketing program can have even more dire consequences, including erosion of lead time and dilution of competitive advantage. Therefore, market strategy formulation should not be constrained by budget making. It is wise to let the marketing strategies dictate budget requirements. It is always easier to shape marketing strategies after they have been formulated and analyzed for budget impact. Some careful pruning of too rich a program can be made. If too much scaling back has to be done, a wholesale reassessment of the market, business objectives, and marketing strategies must be initiated. In this respect, marketing strategy formulation constitutes the first "traffic signal." It either confirms or rejects the alignment of market data, strategic business objectives, and projected financial requirements and performance.

OPERATIONS ANALYSIS

Implementation and Monitoring

Careful monitoring of market strategy and operations plan implementation is important, not only from a budgetary perspective but also, significantly, from the perspective of attaining the organization's business objectives. If it is important for the company to actively participate in four trade shows in a given time frame, but the company participates only in three, there may be some cost savings—but the company's competitive position may be endangered. Alternatively, office or plant rental costs may be significantly higher than originally projected. This budgetary hit may be offset by the property's location or the perceived strategic compatibility of other tenants. An important component of implementation of a strategic business plan is monitoring timeliness as well as the actual versus projected costs of carrying out the plan. Discrete tasks and expected outcomes, assignment of task or project responsibility, task completion timelines, budgeted resources, and variance from budget reporting are all ingredients of sound plan implementation and monitoring. Exhibit 6.1 is a suggested task/output work plan. Exhibit 6.2 expands this plan to a monitoring and reporting tool.

Because human resources is responsible for the plan's success, it is important that all the appropriate people be involved in the strategic planning process. For the start-up, these would likely be the founders of the company. For the later-stage, more complex, and perhaps publicly held corporation, participants could include various officers of the entity (e.g., CEO, COO, CFO, chief information officer, executive vice president, marketing and sales vice president[s], etc.) and lower-level managerial or professional staff. The same individuals who formulate the strategic business plan should also have

EXHIBIT 6.1   Task/Output Work Plan

BUSINESS OBJECTIVE:

Tasks	Outputs

responsibility for its implementation, monitoring, and modification if this becomes necessary. Each responsible individual must have a thorough understanding of his or her responsibilities, deliverable due dates, and the implications of his or her assignment on the work of other team members and on the organization's attainment of its business objectives. Although Exhibits 6.1 and 6.2 facilitate this process, their usefulness will be diluted if the implementation team (which could also be thought of as a project team) does not have the discipline to meet regularly and take its responsibilities seriously. The entire strategic planning process will have been for naught if the same commitment to

EXHIBIT 6.2   Extended Task/Output Work Plan

BUSINESS OBJECTIVE:

Tasks	Outputs	Year 1 1 2 3 4 5 6 7 8 9 10 11 12	Year 2	Year 3	Resp. of	Budgeted Cost	Variance (Time or Cost)	Comments/Explanations

planning is not carried over to implementation and monitoring the success of implementation.

Selling the Plan

At the beginning of this chapter, we reviewed the potential audience or readership of the strategic business plan. The most important user of the plan is the management team itself; hence, the first selling effort must be of the strategic planning process. The onus is on executive management to communicate the benefits of strategic planning to these others who will be members of the planning team. Executive management of companies that have embraced contemporary management styles and techniques will have an easier time than its counterpart at companies that still support strictly top-down management decision making.

Other readers of the plan, including capital providers, suppliers, customers, and attorneys, must get a sense that the management is sincere and can propel the company to at least the performance levels defined in the strategic business plan document. Even with an established company, management will have to convince outsiders that it has the wherewithal to continue the entity's growth and development. For start-ups, the task is clearly more formidable. In either case, an objective strategic planning process resulting in a realistic, no-holds-barred business plan will go a long way to convince document readers of management's seriousness and its ability to sustain and grow the company in a profitable fashion.

SUMMARY

Strategic business planning is not easy. It requires commitment not only to the work of planning, implementation, and monitoring but also—more important—to the objectivity that is the essential ingredient of the process. Unless this commitment is there, regardless of the truths that may be born of objectivity (e.g., need for changes in management team composition or responsibilities), the plan will be useless. Not only will it not suffice as a capital-raising document, but it will also not serve as the "road map" to guide management for continued growth and development of the company. To the contrary, *subjective* planning will lead management astray and actually could result in underperformance at best and the company's demise at worst.

CHAPTER SEVEN

The Essentials of Business Valuation

Frank C. Evans, CBA, ASA, CPA/ABV
Principal, Evans and Associates

Edward Mendlowitz, CPA/ABV/CFF/PFS
Partner, WithumSmith+Brown

INTRODUCTION

What Makes Business Valuation a Unique Challenge

Most people's experience with valuation is limited to getting an appraisal on specific assets, such as real estate, a vehicle, or jewelry. These inanimate objects frequently are traded in a reasonably active market and there are often simple, reliable data available on recent sales of similar items. Although exceptions occur, appraising or valuing (the terms can be used interchangeably) these assets is not overly complicated, and the results are not subject to wide variation or difference of opinion.

Valuing a business is far more complex. Investors may purchase a minority or controlling interest in a business, either of which can convey a wide variety of rights and restrictions on those rights. The interest could be securities in a publicly traded company for which there is an active market and indications of value readily available, or interests in a closely held business—C corporation, S corporation, limited liability company, or partnership—for which little or no market may exist. Investors usually buy companies to acquire the anticipated future returns of the enterprise. They must estimate the risk involved in their investment and the future returns they expect to receive. The business may own a wide variety of assets that may or may not be essential to the future operations of the enterprise. Most businesses are operating entities that include people, products and/or services, technologies, customers, suppliers, competitors, and various other intangibles, many of which may change frequently. A properly prepared business valuation must take into account all of these factors to generate an accurate and credible result. This is clearly a detailed and complex process, but if it is done correctly, value can be determined accurately. This chapter reviews the theory and process of business valuation and emphasizes key points to consider to yield defendable estimates of value.

Reasons for Valuing a Business

Valuations of businesses or partial interests in them are prepared for a variety of reasons, with the most common being:

- Purchase, sale, dissolution, or merger
- Shareholder or buy-sell agreements
- Gift, estate, or inheritance taxes or related tax planning
- Equitable distribution related to a marital dissolution
- Allocation of value among categories of assets or classes of ownership interest for various tax or litigation purposes
- Employee stock ownership plans
- Transfers to successors
- Phantom stock, restricted stock and stock option plans, and employee compensation agreements
- Valuation in the owner's personal financial plan
- Credit purposes
- Financial statement uses

It is essential that the purpose of the appraisal be carefully considered because this influences numerous factors in the valuation process and the value that is ultimately determined.

Business Valuation Standards and Professional Organizations

To foster independence, integrity, and competence in the valuation profession, various appraisal organizations established the Appraisal Foundation in 1987. The Appraisal Standards Board of the Appraisal Foundation promulgates *Uniform Standards of Professional Appraisal Practice* (*USPAP*), which include standards, rules, statements, and advisory opinions on appraisal practice. The *USPAP* can be obtained from the Appraisal Foundation by calling 202-347-7722.

The American Institute of Certified Public Accountants issued its Statements on Standards for Valuation Services in 2007, which set forth the professional standards and rules to be followed by certified public accountants (CPAs) in the performance of valuations.

Another player with strict rules is the Internal Revenue Service, which has adopted rules for valuations that are used for tax purposes. These can be found in Revenue Ruling 59-60, Revenue Ruling 68-609, and subsequently issued rulings. The essence of Revenue Ruling 59-60 is an eight-factor key issue analysis that must be addressed. Readers should become familiar with these rulings prior to commencing a valuation that will be used for tax purposes.

Various organizations have developed professional designations in business valuation. Their requirements for certification and/or recertification vary substantially, and those retaining professional valuation services should consider these differences carefully. The primary organizations and their most common business valuation designations are listed next.

Organization	Certification
American Institute of Certified Public Accountants	Accredited in business valuation
888-777-7077	
American Society of Appraisers	Accredited Senior Appraiser
800-272-8258	
Institute of Business Appraisers	Certified Business Appraiser
954-584-1144	
National Association of Certified Valuation Analysts	Accredited Senior Appraiser
800-677-2009	

UNDERSTANDING THE VALUATION ASSIGNMENT

There is frequently a temptation to skip over the preliminary considerations of the purpose, the standard of value, and in some cases the date of the valuation to get to the computations. That decision usually results in errors or oversights. In a best-case scenario, making corrections just consumes more time. The greater danger is failure to recognize and understand mistakes and why the resulting value is inappropriate. A solid grasp of these fundamental points also enhances the appraiser's ability to clearly analyze details about the business as they arise. So, study the points discussed next carefully. It will be worth the effort.

Defining What Is to Be Valued

You can value a wide range of items, from assets to a specific security, such as preferred stock. Most commonly, however, business appraisals are prepared to determine the value of a whole or partial equity interest or the invested capital of the company. *Equity* interests most commonly are some or all of the common stock of the business. This can become more complex if there are varying classes of stock or when the shares of stock carry with them different rights or restrictions. Equity interests are frequently appraised for tax purposes, *employee share option plan* reporting requirements, shareholder agreements, or in litigation, including divorce.

EXHIBIT 7.1 Computation of Net Assets and Invested Capital

Balance Sheet	
Assets	**Liabilities**
	Trade and accrued payables
	Interest-bearing debt
	Total liabilities
	Equity
Total operating assets	Total liabilities and equity
Less trade and accrued payables	Less trade and accrued payables
Net operating assets	Invested capital

In the merger and acquisition setting, where interests in a business are actually purchased or sold, the appraisal is more often prepared on an *invested capital* basis. As Exhibit 7.1 illustrates, invested capital is the total of the interest-bearing debt and equity of the entity.

This is equivalent to the net operating assets, which is computed by subtracting the trade payables and accrued payables from total operating assets. Use of the invested capital model generates what is frequently referred to as *enterprise value* because it shows the value of the whole company as it is financed with debt and equity. This is contrasted with equity, which reflects only the value of a specific ownership interest in the business.

The distinction between equity and invested capital is critical for a comprehensive understanding of what is actually being valued. In actual transactions, buyers frequently focus on what they will have to pay to acquire a company while sellers concentrate on how much they will get from the sale. In the process, either party can inadvertently shift from one definition of the investment under consideration to the other without recognizing it. There are also many steps in the financial computations that must recognize the equity/invested capital distinction to avoid over- or underestimating value.

In addition to what is being valued, it is very important to determine the date of the valuation. This is particularly relevant when the valuation is done for a prior period or transaction or to back up a previous transaction. The appraiser should take into account only what was known at that date. If activities were in place at the time that would lead a reasonable person to assume a logical conclusion, then these can be considered, but be careful not to factor in things that occurred after that date, such as an unsolicited sale to an investment or strategic buyer that cropped up unexpectedly.

Definitions of Value

Failure to recognize or thoroughly understand the major definitions of value also frequently leads to errors and distortions. Many business executives have heard the term "fair market value" and may even be familiar with this commonly accepted definition:

> The cash or equivalent price at which property would change hands between a willing buyer and a willing seller, neither being under compulsion to buy or sell and both parties having reasonable knowledge of relevant facts.

However, they frequently fail to recognize that for valuation, the definition of fair market value includes four assumptions:

1. The hypothetical buyer is prudent but without synergistic benefit.
2. The business will continue as a going concern and not be liquidated.
3. The hypothetical sale will be for cash.
4. The parties are able as well as willing.

The *willing buyer* under fair market value is considered to be a *financial* and not a *strategic* buyer. That is, the buyer contributes only capital and management of equivalent competence to that of the current management. This assumption excludes the buyer who, because of other business activities, brings some value-added benefits to the company that will enhance the company being valued and/or the buyer's other business activities (e.g., being acquired by other companies in the same or a similar industry). This assumption also excludes consideration that the buyer may already be a shareholder, creditor, or related or controlled entity, which might be willing to acquire the interest at an artificially high or low price due to considerations not typical of the motivation of the arm's-length financial buyer.

The *willing seller* in the fair market value process is also hypothetical and is, therefore, imbued with knowledge of the relevant facts (i.e., the influences on value exerted by the market, the investment characteristics specific to the company's risk drivers, and the interest's degree of control and lack of marketability).

Particularly in the merger and acquisition setting, the appraiser must consider *investment value*, which is the value of the subject interest to a specific buyer given that party's unique circumstances. Parties who may bring value-creating characteristics to a company, such as buyers who operate in the same industry as the target, should compute both fair market value and investment value. The first is the target company's value to the present owners on a stand-alone basis. The second is the value to a specific buyer given the synergies, economies of scale, or other integration benefits that are created through the combined ownership. (See Exhibit 7.2.) The amount that investment value exceeds fair market value, up to the maximum of investment value, is the acquisition premium over fair market value that that buyer can afford to pay for the target. Paying above fair market value and below investment value creates value for the buyer; paying above investment value destroys value as the buyer pays more for the target than the present value of its anticipated future returns. Buyers should also recognize that as

EXHIBIT 7.2   Acquisition Premiums and Value Creation or Destruction

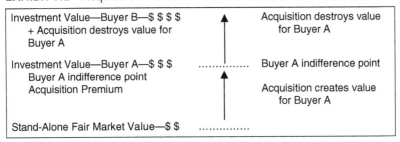

the price they are considering approaches investment value, the acquisition becomes increasingly less attractive because the value it creates is decreasing toward zero. A higher price also increases the pressure on the acquirer to achieve every possible synergy and other integration benefit at the earliest possible time to make the acquisition a success. When the price paid is too far above stand-alone fair market value, poor or negative returns often result because of lower synergies, delays in achievement of synergies, or failure for them to develop at all.

Both buyers and sellers should also recognize that a target's investment value is probably different for each potential acquirer because of variations in integration benefits. While sellers should attempt to identify the target where they fit best and create the highest value, buyers should attempt to estimate the target's value to them versus other bidders in assessing the offer they should make.

Fair value is a measure that applies in litigation scenarios such as a dissenting shareholder lawsuit. It is not the same as fair market value and is usually statutorily defined.

Going-Concern versus Liquidation Value

Businesses can be appraised on a *going-concern basis* or on a *liquidation basis*. Appraisals of operating companies that are generating profits are usually prepared on a going-concern basis, which assumes that the company's returns will continue to be generated, although they may change depending on future events. Under a going-concern premise, the value of assets is usually considered on an "in place, in use" basis rather than their value in liquidation.

The second premise is liquidation, which assumes that the value of the business will be realized through sale of the company's tangible and intangible assets. The liquidation procedure can further be delineated as either *orderly*, in which case adequate time exists to wind down the company's operations and sell the assets with reasonable care, or *forced*, which assumes the presence of pressure to liquidate, often under distressed conditions and typically at reduced prices. In either case, the value should take into consideration the costs incurred to execute the liquidation.

The going-concern versus liquidation premise is a fundamental one that should not be overlooked. Applying liquidation-based assumptions and resulting values to an operating entity is an example of application of flawed theory that commonly results in an inappropriate value.

RESEARCH AND INFORMATION GATHERING

Like business valuation theory, industry and competitive research is a topic that readers too often want to skip over to begin the mechanics of computing value. Inadequate research is a blueprint for computing an inappropriate value and, more dangerously, for not realizing why. So this topic requires careful attention.

Experienced appraisers, particularly those who value companies in many different industries, recognize that background industry research and competitive analysis is essential to understanding the company being appraised. For those who want to begin the appraisal by analyzing the target's financial statements, remember this: Financial statements and ratios show the results of historical performance and financial position, but they do not reveal the causes. The appraiser must identify and analyze these causes in assessing the company, its forecast of the future, and the probability of achieving that forecast.

Kinds of Information Needed

The information needed for every appraisal generally includes:

1. General economic information, detailed information about the industry in which the company operates, and a comparative analysis of the company versus its competitors
2. Information on the price at which other companies in the same industry have traded, the nature of these transactions, and how these companies compare in size and strength with the target. All shareholder, partnership, or member agreements in effect as of the valuation date and through date of this request.
4. Copy of the stock certificate or the legend, if any, appearing on stock certificates issued to the people transferring the interests being valued.
5. Listing of all the locations business is conducted from.
6. Organizational chart, if any.
7. All employment, consulting, management, or any other agreements in effect during last five years and through the date of this request.
8. Financial statements, if any, for the most recent five fiscal years with the accountants' report, and any financial statements issued after that date with an accountants' report.
9. Federal and all state tax returns for the most recent five years, including all schedules, statements, forms and attachments.
10. Copies of the W-2 and 1099 forms for the two immediately preceding two years.
11. Aged schedules of accounts receivable and accounts payable and accrued expenses as at the end of the last two fiscal years.
12. Listing of the five largest customers for each of last three years and sales to them each year.
13. Listing of the five largest suppliers for each of the last three years and purchases from them each year.
14. Copies of any contracts with customers or suppliers currently in effect.
15. Copies of any commitments to buy equipment.
16. Copy of all loan applications from the beginning of the second preceding fiscal year through the date of this request, including all statements and attachments.
17. Copy of all loan agreements, covenants, and notes from the beginning of the second preceding fiscal year through the date of this request including all statements and attachments. A schedule of the loan covenants and the company's compliance with them as of the end of the last fiscal year. Also copies of any bank correspondence after the loan was issued regarding the company's performance under the loan agreements.

18. Copy of any agreement, outline, term sheet, or proposed agreement for which this valuation is required, if any; or, if for estate planning or wealth transfer purposes, a listing of the individual gifts that are contemplated.
19. Independent appraisals of any real estate.
20. Independent appraisals of any equipment. In the event that equipment values are not significant, accept in lieu of the appraisal a representation letter by the company's management of what amount is acceptable as the value of the equipment in connection with our valuation.

This listing is not complete or definitive but an illustration of the types of information needed. In some instances, much of this information would be needed before a valuation is commenced to determine the standards of value, the premise of value, whether other appraisals would be needed such as for real estate and equipment, and overall scope of the project.

Critical Importance of Competitive Analysis

In appraising companies on a going-concern basis, the appraiser's focus is on the future—specifically, what returns can be expected from the company and what risks are associated with those returns. Accurate estimates require a thorough knowledge of the underlying market forces that are influencing the target and its competitors. These market forces can vary dramatically and usually include many of the drivers shown in Exhibit 7.3. Each of these and other relevant drivers must be identified, assessed, and weighted so that the appraiser has a clear sense of external and internal competitive forces and their effect on the company. Industry changes and trends, including growth, technology, market structure, and consolidation, must be considered for their impacts. The strengths and weaknesses of the company and its competition will help to reveal

EXHIBIT 7.3   Key Value Drivers and Risk Drivers

Technology	Regulatory changes
Market share	Market structure
Breadth of product or service line	Access to capital
Reputation and general goodwill	Brand names
Patents, copyrights, intellectual property	Reliance on key vendors or suppliers
Proprietary methods and processes	Pricing power
Management breadth and depth	Availability of skill workforce and associated morale
Distribution systems	Production and warehouse capacity
Barriers to entry	Environmental issues
Litigation	Quality of physical plant
Location of facilities, customers, and inventory	Relations with key customers or accounts
Customer loyalty or persistence	Quality of accounting information and Internal controls
Liquidity and financial leverage	Customer concentration

strategic advantages and disadvantages and the prospects for them to change. Research and surveys of existing, past, and prospective customers will reveal how the company is perceived in the market.

All of this research is essential to explain why and how a company achieved its present position and to assess its future prospects. Inadequate research leaves these issues uncertain and renders value conclusions unreliable.

Resources: Two resources for industry data are First Research (www.firstresearch. com) and Ibisworld (www.ibisworld.com) where you can purchase reports of updated industry situations. Another resource where you can compare financial data with a database of other companies in an industry is Profit Cents (www.profitcents.com).

 ## ADJUSTING AND ANALYZING THE FINANCIAL STATEMENTS

Normalization Adjustments to Reflect True Economic Performance

The financial statements of a business, even if prepared in accordance with generally accepted accounting principles (GAAP) and audited by an independent CPA firm, are frequently not appropriate for valuation purposes. Adjustments are usually necessary to allow the statements to depict the true economic performance of the business.

The most common *normalization adjustments* to an income statement are for nonrecurring income and expenses that are not expected to routinely occur and for nonoperating items that are not part of the ongoing operating activities of the company. With the nonoperating items removed, the operating value of the company can be computed, with the value of any nonoperating assets then added to determine the total value of the company. Interest income and expense are examples of nonoperating items, as is life insurance on the owner's life. However, life insurance on a key employee who is not an owner would be considered essential and would not be adjusted for.

If a controlling interest in the company is being appraised, normalization adjustments are also frequently made for compensation, fringe benefits, and other perquisites that are paid to shareholders/employees or related parties that are above a market-based compensation level. Once again, the objective is to determine the true economic performance of the business without distortion from payments to owners for tax planning or other purposes.

Where tax returns are provided without GAAP financial statements, adjustments would be needed to conform the statements to GAAP type of presentations. For instance, tax-based inventory includes adjustments for items that would not be appropriate for a GAAP report, does not usually include provisions for doubtful accounts receivable collections, and would have different depreciation expense deductions and lower entertainment expenses.

Analyzing the Financial Statements

Analyzing financial statements for valuation purposes includes the traditional horizontal and vertical analysis. Growth trends and rates of growth are especially important because they frequently reveal major value drivers. This discussion assumes that the reader is familiar with financial ratios and analysis techniques, so these are not reviewed. It is essential to emphasize, however, that even experienced analysts frequently commit an error of omission when analyzing statements for valuation purposes. The omission is failure to connect the conclusions of the analysis to their estimate of value. That is, in analyzing the various ratios that reflect financial position and operating performance, the resulting strengths, weaknesses, and trends must then be described in terms of their impact on the company's value. Failure to do this provides the reader with additional information without an understanding of how these factors affect value.

Another common mistake is to compare the target company's normalized financial statements, and ratios computed from them, against industry averages from a source such as Robert Morris Associates (RMA) Annual Statement Studies. The RMA data come from actual financial statements that reflect all of the tax planning and other owner motivations that commonly distort true economic performance. To compare normalized statements with this unadjusted industry average data is an apples-to-oranges analysis. Industry averages can and should be used when appropriate, but comparisons should be made using the company's unadjusted statements rather than the normalized data.

Selecting the Appropriate Ratios to Use

A financial analysis usually involves examination of the liquidity, activity, leverage, coverage, growth, and profitability ratios. These are all commonly included in an analysis for valuation purposes, although typically some categories of ratios will be considered more important than others in terms of their effect on value. For example, a buyer analyzing a target would commonly focus more on activity ratios that reflect management efficiency and margin ratios that reflect profitability than on liquidity or leverage ratios that may be eliminated by the buyer in the acquisition. Growth rates and growth trends also are frequently of greater interest in a valuation than in an analysis prepared for other purposes.

How to Review Forecasts

Business valuations frequently involve forecasts of future returns that determine the value of the company. In reviewing these forecasts, appraisers should be particularly sensitive to (i.e., suspicious of) certain numbers. Sales frequently yield the most important number in the forecast and the one that requires the most detailed verification. When possible, obtain detailed volume and pricing data by products or business segments to fully understand the sales data. Then carefully compare this with the competitive analysis of the industry and market to assess whether these volumes and prices are reasonable. Frequently, limits on market size, growth, and price pressures reveal sales forecasts to be unrealistic. A second area to closely review is gross profit and operating profit margins. Especially in those situations where the forecast shows significant improvements over historical performance or industry averages, talk to operating managers about how these improvements will be achieved. Without detailed, convincing explanations, these margins may have to be adjusted.

A third area of particular concern in a valuation-based analysis is activity ratios. Total asset turnover, computed as sales divided by assets, measures how efficiently the company uses assets to generate revenue. Subsets of this broad measure look at the most significant assets, which usually are receivables, inventory, and fixed assets. The receivable collection period, inventory turnover, and fixed asset turnover ratios should all be computed for each year of the forecast and then compared with historic performance and industry standards. Again, if major changes, particularly improvements, are suggested, operating managers should be able to explain how these efficiencies will be achieved.

THREE APPROACHES TO VALUING A BUSINESS

Companies can be appraised through the *income, market* or *asset* approaches. Compliance with *USPAP* requires the appraiser to consider all three approaches to ensure that all of the value characteristics of the company are considered in an appraisal. Frequently, however, one or more of the approaches is inappropriate, in that it fails to accurately portray the financial performance or position of the company. For a thorough analysis, the appraiser should attempt to use all three approaches. If one or two of the approaches, or specific methods within these approaches, are unacceptable, they should then be rejected. However, it is often a dangerous error to simply dismiss an approach without consideration and explanation of why it cannot be used.

INCOME APPROACH

Theory of the Income Approach

The value of a business can be determined by computing the future returns of the entity and discounting them to their present value at a rate of return that reflects the riskiness of the investment. This theory is both simple and convincing because it includes sound economic justification for the value determined. However, the devil is in the details. To apply the income approach effectively, you must accurately estimate the future returns of the company and accurately quantify the risk through a rate of return. Thus, this theoretically sound approach is dependent on estimates of returns and rates of return, both of which are subjective.

Advantages and Disadvantages of the Income Approach

The primary advantages of the income approach are that it is based on sound economic theory and it generally can be used with any operating business that generates positive returns. When applied correctly, it is also appropriate for appraisal of control or minority interests in a company.

Because the income approach is dependent on estimating returns and rates of return, it is less appropriate where this is not possible or when returns are not positive. It is also less appropriate for asset-intensive companies, such as holding companies, where value is more a function of the assets owned than the returns generated from them.

Methods within the Income Approach

The income approach can determine value either through a *multiperiod discounting* or a *single-period capitalization*. Each method closely follows the underlying theory but applies it under different assumptions.

The single-period capitalization, or *capitalized future returns method*, computes value by capitalizing the return of the company for a single year in this computation:

$$\text{Value} = \frac{\text{Return}}{\text{Capitalization Rate}}$$

This computation assumes that the company's performance can be accurately reflected in the return of a single period and that this return will grow to infinity at a constant rate. If either of these assumptions is inappropriate, then this method may not yield a realistic indication of value.

The multiperiod discounting or *discounted future returns* method requires a forecast of the company's future returns. The forecast can be of varying lengths with three, five, seven, or ten years commonly used. A major factor determining the length of the forecast is that it should extend until a stabilized or sustainable return has been achieved. As the next computation indicates, all returns beyond the forecast are then capitalized using the single-period capitalization computation:

$$V = \frac{R_1}{(1+d)} + \frac{R_2}{(1+d)^2} + \cdots \frac{R_n}{(1+d)^n} + \frac{\frac{R_n \times (1+g)}{(d-g)}}{(1+d)^n}$$

where

$$
\begin{aligned}
V &= \text{Value of equity} \\
R_1 &= \text{Return—year 1} \\
R_2 &= \text{Return—year 2} \\
R_n &= \text{Return—year } n \\
n &= \text{Number of years} \\
g &= \text{Long-term growth rate} \\
d &= \text{Discount rate}
\end{aligned}
$$

Through its forecast, the multiperiod discounting method reflects variations in the company's return for the forecast period. This is its advantage over the single-period capitalization, which uses only a single-period return and assumes that this return grows at a constant rate. Where significant variations in the return are expected to occur, the multiperiod discounting method should be used.

Since businesses are generally assumed to continue beyond the forecast period, a terminal value is computed, which is the present value of the capitalized future returns of the company from the end of the forecast period to infinity. This computation involves taking the return for the final year of the forecast, increasing it by the company's forecasted long-term growth rate, and capitalizing this amount to generate the capitalized value of the return beyond the forecast. Because this computation yields a capitalized value as of the end of the forecast, it is then discounted using the same discount factor that was applied to the last year of the forecast.

The terminal-period computation assumes that the returns of the company will grow at a constant rate to infinity. The choice of this long-term growth rate can have a huge effect on the value determined, particularly if the forecast period is relatively short—say three years. This long-term growth rate must be carefully analyzed and justified. For example, if an industry is projected to grow at 3 percent, the terminal computation based on a long-term growth rate of 6 percent implies that the company will grow at twice the rate of growth of its competitors to infinity. To achieve this, the company must continually take market share, which suggests very long-term strategic advantages.

Other options are to consider no returns (and, therefore, no value) beyond the forecast or to add the appraised value of the company's assets as of the end of the forecast as its terminal value.

Choosing the Return Stream

A company can generate many "returns," from top-line revenues to bottom-line net income after taxes, and cash flow is frequently considered superior to an income measure. Any return or benefit can be chosen as long as it is discounted or capitalized with an appropriate rate of return. Naturally, earnings reflect profitability and margins that revenue measures ignore and cash flows reflect non–income statement reinvestment requirements.

So which return is best? Sellers and investment bankers frequently prefer *earnings before interest and taxes* (EBIT) or *earnings before interest, taxes, depreciation and amortization* (EBITDA), because these are relatively high profit measures and they exclude financing charges. They are a return to invested capital but they fail to reflect the company's need for reinvestment in working capital and fixed assets.

Net cash flow, also called *free cash flow*, is the preferable return because it most closely parallels the returns available to investors in the public market. Net cash flow considers the company's need for reinvestment and represents dollars that are available to investors. Net cash flow to equity is computed as shown:

	Net Income After Taxes
+	Noncash charges
−	Capital expenditures
+ or −	Changes in working capital
+ or −	Changes in debt
=	Net cash flow to equity

Alternatively, net cash flow to invested capital is computed as shown:

Net Income Plus Tax-Adjusted Interest Expense	
+	Noncash charges
−	Capital expenditures
+ or −	Changes in working capital
=	Net cash flow for invested capital

Errors can be easily made in computing net cash flow to equity or invested capital. In the long term, which includes the single-period capitalization method and the terminal value computation in the multiperiod discounting method, in a growing company the capital expenditures should exceed noncash write-offs. So, carefully analyze net cash flow forecasts where capital expenditures are equal to or less than depreciation write-offs. Such forecasts suggest a company in decline and are probably inappropriate if management indicates the company will be growing.

A growing company should also experience growth in receivables, inventory, and payables—working capital—at a rate similar to the growth in sales. Typically the growth in receivables and inventory will exceed the growth in payables, causing working capital to reduce net cash flow.

In the computation of the net cash flow to equity over the long term, the change in long-term debt should increase positive cash flow. As the company grows, its profits increase equity, and long-term debt generally will grow proportionately as the company maintains a stable capital structure.

In computing the cash flow to invested capital, the tax-adjusted interest expense must be added back to income to achieve a predebt return. The principal proceeds or payments are omitted because the return is prior to consideration of flows to interest-bearing creditors.

The net cash flow return clearly portrays the dollars that are available to those who provide funds to the business. Net cash flow serves as an excellent proxy for the returns, either through dividends or stock appreciation that investors earn through ownership of public securities. Returns on the public securities provide excellent historical benchmarks of the rates of return that investors demand. And since these returns are net cash flow, they can be used to develop the discount rate for net cash flow. Other common returns, such as EBITDA, EBIT, or net income after taxes, do not have market rates of return available for reliable discounting.

To summarize, we can compute the value of either the invested capital or the equity of the company. Returns to invested capital—income before taxes and interest expense or cash flow before taxes, interest, and principal—yield invested capital value, whereas returns to equity—net income after taxes or net cash flow after interest and principal—yield equity value.

Rates of Return

Rates of return that reflect investor preferences can be derived from market evidence of returns that investors have received for the relative risks that they have assumed from different kinds of investments.

Discount rates can be viewed as required rates of return that investors demand on a given type of investment. They can also be thought of as opportunity costs, because in accepting one investment, others with varying rates of return and risk characteristics are forgone. They are applied to a future amount in computing its present value. Every discount rate contains three elements:

1. A risk-free or safe rate
2. A premium above this for accepting the added risk of investment in equity over the risk-free rate
3. An additional premium for risks unique to that specific investment

Capitalization rates, or *cap rates*, are discount rates from which the investment's long-term growth rate has been subtracted. Once the discount rate has been derived, the cap rate is determined by analyzing the company's long-term growth potential. The cap rate is then applied to a single-period return in a computation that assumes that the return will grow at the long-term growth rate to infinity.

Discount and cap rates are derived as costs of equity and are applied to a return to equity to determine a value of equity. Alternatively, the return can be to invested capital, in which case it must be discounted or capitalized by a cost of invested capital to determine the value of the interest-bearing debt and equity of the company—its invested capital. The cost of debt and equity is known as the *weighted average cost of capital* (WACC) and is derived in the format shown in Exhibit 7.4. The computation in the exhibit clearly demonstrates the advantages of financing with debt, which is tax deductible, versus equity, which is not.

Hurdle rates are usually developed internally or artificially chosen rates of return required by management for certain investments. For example, a company may have computed that it has a WACC of 14 percent and wishes to earn a return of least 2 percent

EXHIBIT 7.4   Weighted-Average Cost of Capital Discount Rate Applicable to Invested Capital

Applicable Rates:			
Cost of equity			20%
Nominal borrowing rate			10%
Tax bracket			40%
Capital Structure (market value):			
Equity			60%
Debt			40%

	Computation of WACC Discount Rate		
Component	**Net Rate**	**Ratio**	**Contribution to WACC**
Debt @ borrowing rate (1–.t)	6.0%	40%	2.4%
Equity	20.0%	60%	12.0%
WACC applicable to invested capital (based on market values)			**14.4%**

EXHIBIT 7.5   Returns, Rates of Return, and Resulting Value

Return	Rate of Return	Value of Investment
EBITDA	WACC	Invested capital
EBIT	WACC	Invested capital
Pretax net income	Cost of equity	Equity
After-tax net income	Cost of equity	Equity
N F to invested capital	WACC	Invested capital
N F to equity	Cost of equity	Equity

above this on all investments, which yields a hurdle rate of 16 percent. Exhibit 7.5 summarizes options regarding rates of return and the resulting value that is generated. Note that once invested capital value is computed, the company can subtract the market value of its debt from invested capital to compute the market value of equity. Regardless of which return is chosen, if it is properly matched with the appropriate rate of return, the same value should be computed for the company. That is, the company's value should not increase or decrease by switching from one return to another.

The best-known method for deriving discount rates is the *capital asset pricing model* (CAPM), which can be expressed in this way:

$$R_e = R_f + B \times (R_m - R_f)$$

In appraising closely held companies, the model is usually modified, as shown next, with additional premiums to reflect the small size and unique risk factors inherent in the typical closely held company versus a publicly traded one:

$$R_e = R_f + B \times (R_m - R_f) + R_s + R_u$$

where

$$
\begin{aligned}
R_e &= \text{Expected return on equity} \\
R_f &= \text{Risk-free rate of return as of the appraisal date} \\
B &= \text{Beta} \\
R_m - R_f &= \text{Long-term average market return on large public company common} \\
&\quad\;\; \text{stocks over long-term average risk-free rate} \\
R_s &= \text{Small company risk premium} \\
R_u &= \text{Unique risk premium}
\end{aligned}
$$

Enough has been written about the CAPM that we will not describe it here. As it applies to the appraisal of closely held companies, however, several points are appropriate. The beta in the computation is derived from betas of a peer group of publicly traded companies. These betas are computed and published by a variety of sources (note that each source does not compute betas in the same way), and reflect the riskiness of that peer group of companies and that industry versus the systematic risk of the market as a whole. The beta for the subject company is then derived by comparing it to the peer group of companies from which the beta was derived. Because closely held companies are usually much smaller and less diversified from the peer group of public companies, the additional factors in the modified CAPM are added.

Many appraisers find it difficult to apply the CAPM in the appraisal of closely held companies with sales of less than $25 to $50 million. This small size often renders these companies so much different from the peer group of public companies that even the modified CAPM is overly subjective. An alternative method developed by the business valuation profession and regularly used in the appraisal of medium- and smaller-size closely held companies is called the *buildup approach*. It recognizes the same three essential elements of a discount rate as CAPM but builds the rate with several elements that isolate size and specific company factors while assuming a beta of 1. The next computation illustrates the buildup method for deriving a discount rate for equity:

	R_f	Risk-free rate as of the appraisal date
+	$R_m - R_f$	Average market return of S&P 500–size common stocks
+	R_s	Benchmark premium for size
+	R_u	Adjustments for specific company risk factors
=		Discount rate for future net cash flow to equity

To the risk-free rate we add the long-term average return on Standard & Poor's 500–size stocks over the long-term average risk-free rate.

Because investors generally equate safety with size, they require higher returns for smaller companies to compensate for the greater risks they perceive in these investments. These returns have been quantified through studies of rates of return on public company securities categorized in deciles by market capitalization size. Over the long term, the smallest 10 percent to 20 percent of public companies generate a return of 3 percent (bottom 20 percent) to 6 percent (bottom 10 percent) higher than the largest public companies. This reflects investor requirements of higher returns on more risky investments. The betas also increase as size decreases, which shows the added volatility (i.e., risk) that varies inversely with size.

This risk premium for size is added if the target company is as small or smaller than the smallest publicly traded companies. The most common source of data on rates of equity returns, including details and an explanation of cost of capital and the equity risk premium, is *Stocks, Bonds, Bills and Inflation* by Ibbotson (1-800-758-3557), which is published annually.

The final element in the buildup method is the specific company's risk premium, which is subjectively determined through a review of risk drivers specific to the subject company. Factors commonly considered in determining the specific company risk premium include, but are not limited to:

- Profitability
- Liquidity
- Skill and depth of management
- Market size and structure
- Industry risks
- Customer concentration
- Growth

- Financial and operating leverage
- Breadth of product or service line
- Access to capital
- Size
- Vendor relations and reliance

The rate derived through CAPM or the buildup procedure is the discount rate for next year's net cash flow to equity. If the appraisal uses a different return, such as the latest historical year's net income, then the rate of return must be adjusted. Failure to make these adjustments is one of the most common ways that value is distorted in the income approach. Business appraisal experts agree that net cash flow most accurately measures the cash available to providers of capital and employs the rate of return for which the most detailed and reliable market data exist.

Multiples of EBITDA, EBIT, net income after taxes, or other returns can be derived, but often these are based on historical rather than future returns. The EBIT or EBITDA multiples are frequently quoted by sellers or their agents, such as investment bankers, who have a strong incentive to create high values. Carefully review the nature of the source of these data and the characteristics of the companies involved to ensure that they are appropriate for application to the target company. They may reflect isolated transactions or strategic considerations that do not apply to the target.

MARKET APPROACH

When the Market Approach Is Appropriate

Though used less often than the income approach, market procedures can often provide excellent indications of the value of a business. Based on the principal of substitution, which states that one will not pay more for an investment than the cost of an equally desirable substitute, the market approach determines value based on the price at which similar securities are traded in an active market. As with the income approach, the theory is straightforward and convincing, but the application is more difficult and provides ample opportunity for error.

This approach requires an adequate population of transactions to present a clear indication of market prices. The subject company must be similar enough in size, products, markets served, and other factors to create a convincing comparison. Where these conditions do not exist, the market approach cannot be employed.

Methods within the Market Approach

One factor that frequently contributes to confusion is misunderstanding of the distinctions between the two primary market approach methods. The first, called the *merger and acquisition* or *direct market comparison method*, looks at acquisitions of controlling interests in public or private companies. Buyers often are strategic because they already operate in that industry or a related one, and they often are expanding their product lines or geographic market or are integrating vertically. Because they can expect to

EXHIBIT 7.6   Primary Public and Private Company Transaction Sources

Mergerstat Review	(800) 455-8871
Merger & Acquisition Sourcebook	(800) 825-8763

achieve synergies or other economies and benefits through the acquisition, they usually pay a premium above the target's stand-alone fair market value. This is referred to as a control premium, which is misleading because it is usually the perceived synergies and economies that drive up the price rather than acquisition of control of the target. Because of the strategic nature of the underlying transactions, these data must be carefully analyzed when used to establish fair market value.

Common sources of data on sales of controlling interests in public and private company transactions in excess of $1 million are listed in Exhibit 7.6. Remember that these generally reflect the actions of strategic buyers acquiring a controlling interest and often reflect investment value rather than fair market value.

Several databases, including those in Exhibit 7.7, contain limited information on transactions in controlling interests in smaller privately held companies. For numerous lines of business, sufficient information exists from these sources to develop reliable indications of the value.

The public guideline company method is more widely used, which looks at the price at which minority interests in these companies are bought and sold in public markets by nonstrategic buyers. From these prices, fair market value on a minority, marketable basis is determined. When an adequate population of suitable guideline companies is available, the market approach determines value by establishing multiples of sale price to various operating performance or financial position measures from the companies that constitute the market (see Exhibit 7.8).

How to Select Guideline Companies

Selection of guideline companies can begin with companies that you know in that industry. Others can be identified through data searches, usually based on Standard Industry Classification (SIC) codes, which are available from numerous databases. The Securities and Exchange Commission (SEC) now requires public companies to file electronically and through their database, Electronic Data Gathering and Retrieval (EDGAR); extensive data on these companies can be gathered at nominal cost.

Once a population of potential guideline companies has been selected, each must be analyzed to determine whether it is appropriate to serve as an indication of market value for the target company. The key is to determine whether the public company is

EXHIBIT 7.7   Primary Closely Held Company Market Databases

BIZCOMPS	(800) 825-8763
Institute of Business Appraisers Market Data Base	(561) 732-3202
Pratt's Stats	(888) BUS-VALU

EXHIBIT 7.8 Common Market Approach Multiples

Multiple	Performance Measure	Investment Determined
Price to earnings	Common stock price/net income after taxes	Common stock value
Price to pretax earnings	Common stock price/net income before taxes	Common stock value
Price to gross cash flow	Common stock price/net income after taxes + noncash expenses	Common stock value
Price to equity	Common stock price/stockholders' equity	Common stock value
Market value of invested capital to EBIT	Invested capital/net income before interest and taxes	Invested capital value
Market value of invested capital to EBITDA	Invested capital/net income before interest, taxes, depreciation and amortization	Invested capital value
Market value of invested capital to sales	Invested capital/sales revenue	Invested capital value
Market value of invested capital to assets	Invested capital/total assets	Invested capital value

sufficiently similar in size, operations, products, and markets to serve as the market for the subject company. For example, a privately owned, local discount department store probably should not be compared with Wal-Mart or Penney's because they are simply too different to make a realistic comparison. Among the factors most commonly chosen as characteristics for comparison are those shown in Exhibit 7.9.

Deriving an Appropriate Multiple for the Target Company

The subject company must be compared with the guideline companies to determine where it would logically fall within the range of multiples presented. It is quite common for a privately held company, because of limited size and narrow product line, customer concentration, or weak management, to fall outside of the guideline company range entirely. Choosing the mean or median of the guideline companies implies that the subject company is, in general, equivalent to the guideline companies in terms of size, products, and other key characteristics, but this is seldom the case. The data in Exhibit 7.10 illustrate the development of a range and mean and median multiples of guideline companies for SIC Code 2511, *Furniture and Fixtures*.

EXHIBIT 7.9 Characteristics for Comparison

Size	Products
Geographic market	Customers

EXHIBIT 7.10   Equity Basis Price/Earnings Ratios of Guideline Companies for Most Recent Fiscal Year

Guideline Company	12/31/XX Stock Share Price		Latest Fiscal Year Earnings per Share		Stock Price/Earnings Multiple
Chromcraft	27.75	/	2.36	=	11.76
Pulaski	17.00	/	1.52	=	11.18
Rowe	8.00	/	.53	=	15.09
Stanley	10.88	/	1.76	=	6.18
Winsloew	9.75	/	.97	=	10.05
Median					10.85
Mean					11.18

Invested Capital Basis MVIC*/EBIT Ratios of Guideline Companies for Most Recent Fiscal Year

Guideline Company	12/31/XX MVIC Share Price		Latest Fiscal Year EBIT per Share		MVIC Price/EBIT Multiple
Chromcraft	31.18	/	3.98	=	7.84
Pulaski	33.15	/	3.20	=	10.36
Rowe	8.30	/	.88	=	9.43
Stanley	18.57	/	3.48	=	5.34
Winsloew	14.42	/	1.87	=	7.71
Median					7.84
Mean					8.14

*MVIC: Market value of invested capital

Invested Capital versus Equity Value

The distinction between invested capital and equity exists in the market approach as it does in the income approach. Where the operating measure represents a return to debt and equity—such as sales, EBIT, or assets—the computation yields invested capital value. Returns to equity—such as after-tax earnings—are compared with the price of common equity to yield equity value.

ASSET APPROACH

When the Asset Approach Is Appropriate

The value of a profitable operating company is usually determined by the income or market approach, which looks at what investors are willing to pay for the future returns that the business will generate. Companies that generate an inadequate return, nonoperating companies, holding companies, or asset-intensive companies are often valued through an asset approach that determines value based on a hypothetical sale of the underlying assets.

The asset approach is usually less appropriate for profitable companies because the present value of the future returns, reflected in the results of an income or market approach, exceeds the market value of the tangible and specific intangible assets. For operating companies, the asset approach may present the minimum value of the company. Its use suggests that the company's operations possess little or no value, or generate an inadequate return on investment.

Naturally, use of the asset approach is dependent on the ability to obtain reliable estimates of the fair market value of the underlying assets. Assets such as vehicles possess a ready market, whereas specialized equipment, inventory, or real estate may not. The value of these underlying assets usually must be determined through an appraisal.

Adjusted Book Value Method

The primary asset approach method is adjusted book value, which, as the name implies, adjusts the assets and liabilities on the company's books to their market value. Equity is then increased or decreased as required to balance the balance sheet and, in the process, equity or invested capital value is determined. This is not dissimilar to the description in the previous section.

Going-Concern versus Liquidation Value Premise

Although the asset approach determines value based on a hypothetical sale of the company's assets, it assumes that the company will continue as a going concern, so the assets are valued in place and in use.

If a liquidation of the company is anticipated, then liquidation value should be determined on either an orderly or forced liquidation basis. In either case, the costs to close down the company and liquidate the assets must be considered in the determination of value.

MAKING ADJUSTMENTS TO VALUE

Identify the Value Initially Determined

As with many topics in business valuation, adjustments to value, which most often are discounts and premiums, are frequently misunderstood. So, begin with a clear understanding of the nature of the value determined prior to consideration of premiums or discounts. More specifically, determine whether the initial value represents control or lack of control and is marketable or nonmarketable. Then compare this to the interest being appraised, and, when discrepancies exist, adjust value through the imposition of premiums or discounts. If this process is not followed, it is likely that premiums and discounts will be incorrectly applied.

Note, however, that in the income approach, minority versus control is generally determined through selection of a minority or control return rather than through imposition of premiums or discounts. That is, the income approach values a controlling interest through use of the return available to the controlling shareholder, not through imposition of a control premium to a value determined based on the return to a minority shareholder. Conversely, it determines the value of a minority interest with the return available to the minority shareholder rather than through application of a minority interest discount to a value determined on a control return. The premiums and discounts are based on market evidence, which justifies adjustments to value within a certain range. Because the return to a controlling shareholder may be many times greater than a minority return, this standard premium-and-discount adjustment range may not appropriately reflect these differences.

The concept of control or lack of marketability as herein used applies to the specific shares being valued, not the entire enterprise or its underlying assets. In the final analysis, the issue is what would a buyer pay for such shares in and the effect the lack of control or marketability would play in the determination of what they would pay for the shares.

How Investors Perceive Control and Liquidity

The concept of control and liquidity are conceptually depicted in Exhibit 7.11. Investors reward control because it creates the potential for an increased share of the total return, just as they recognize the vulnerability that lack of control creates. They also reward marketability or liquidity because it provides the ability to liquidate an investment and acquire cash rapidly, whereas illiquidity does not.

Most investments in public companies are minority interests in marketable securities. Investors recognize that they have little direct influence on the activities of the company but know that they can quickly abandon a company should they disagree with its policies or see events that threaten their stock value. Minority investors in closely held companies have a much weaker position because they often have much less accurate information on the company's performance and they lack the ability to quickly liquidate their shares. Thus, minority interests in closely held companies tend to sell at sharp discounts because they lack control and are illiquid.

Although control and liquidity are distinct, they are also related because the degree of control affects marketability. The minority shareholder in a closely held company has no direct access to the company's cash flow, lacks the ability to direct the company, and has no ready market through which to sell his or her stock. The controlling shareholder, within specific limits created by state laws, controls the company's cash flow, can sell their control shares and can liquidate the company if appropriate so the controlling interest enjoys far greater marketability.

In closely held companies, shareholder agreements and corporate bylaws frequently create significant restrictions on the transfer of shares. For example, shareholder

EXHIBIT 7.11   Value Elevator

Higher Value	Control	Marketable (liquid)
Lower Value	Lack of Control	Nonmarketable (illiquid)

agreements often include a right of first refusal that requires that shares for sale first be offered at a specified price to existing shareholders or the corporation or entity. Such restrictions can have a material effect on value. Also, recognize the vulnerability and interdependence that ownership arrangements create. For example, a 50 percent owner typically possesses the ability to block any initiatives proposed by other shareholders but lacks the ability to initiate any actions that are opposed by the remaining shareholders. This emphasizes how control or lack of control is gradual, and varies with the size of an ownership interest and the ownership distribution.

Acquisition Premiums: Control and Minority Interests

To quantify how investors value the benefits of control, studies of merger and acquisition data have been done over many years. These studies compare the price at which controlling interests in publicly held companies have been acquired versus their preacquisition price, which is assumed to be the company's fair market value on a minority non marketable basis. This price difference is commonly referred to as a *control premium*, although this term is misleading. As previously discussed under the market approach, acquisition by public companies of controlling interests in other public companies usually reflects the motives of a strategic buyer. Generally, this buyer is paying the higher price to achieve synergies, such as a larger market share, technologies, expanded product lines, or other benefits that extend far beyond ownership control. Thus, the premium would be described more accurately as an acquisition premium because of the breadth of benefits they are expected to carry. The primary control premium studies are published annually in *Mergerstat Review* (1-800-455-8871). Although the results vary, the typical control premiums fall into a range from approximately 27 percent to 35 percent.

Because there is no source of market data to quantify minority interest discounts, these are derived from the control premium studies. Where the control premium measures the premium over fair market value, the implied minority interest discount compares the same dollar premium to the control price, as shown next.

This implied minority interest discount, which is also computed in the studies referred to earlier, can be calculated through the next formula:

Control value $80	Control premium	
Acquisition premium $20	$\dfrac{\$20}{\$60}$	= 33⅓%
Fair market value $60		
	Implied minority interest discount	
	$\dfrac{\$20}{\$80}$	= 25%

$$\text{Minority interest discount} = 1 - (1/(1 + \text{control premium}))$$

$$25\% = 1 - (1/(1 + 33\ 1/3\%))$$

The Mergerstat studies indicate that, in general, the implied minority interest discount since 1983 has been approximately 22 percent to 26 percent.

These studies clearly indicate the magnitude of the market's desire for control and reflect the next attributes that typically accompany control.

- Appoint the board of directors.
- Change the corporate bylaws.
- Establish and pay dividends *and* control their timing.
- Set owner compensation and benefits.
- Incur indebtedness.
- Make capital expenditures.
- Liquidate the company.
- Purchase treasury stock.
- Implement business and operational changes
- Purchase, sell, convey, exchange, pledge, hypothecate, and encumber company's assets.
- Enter in and abrogate agreements on behalf of the entity.
- In general, cause the entity to do whatever it desires subject to constraints imposed by law, public policy, and shareholders' or owners' agreements.

Remember two final points:

1. Control comes in degrees based on ownership percentages.
2. Control versus lack of control is generally determined in the choice of the return stream in the income approach.

Simply put, a conclusion can be drawn that buyers of an interest in a business entity would pay less if they cannot control the destiny of their investment than they would if they were able to control it.

Discounts for Lack of Marketability

If the value initially determined is on a marketable basis and the interest being appraised is closely held (i.e. lacks marketability), then an adjustment must be made for this illiquidity. Similar to the treatment of control versus lack-of-control issues, studies have been done to quantify how investors discount securities that lack marketability.

Restricted stock studies have been conducted by the SEC and other organizations for many years. These studies compare the price of public securities that have been restricted from sale on the open market for a specified period with similar securities of the same company that are not subject to restrictions. These shares can be sold in private transactions, and because they are a security in a publicly traded company, their prices must be reported. The primary difference between the restricted shares and their freely traded counterparts is the restriction from sale on the open market, typically for a period of about one year.

The results of these studies, which vary from year to year, show a fairly consistent pattern of discounts in the range of 30 percent to 35 percent. That is, investors who own securities in publicly traded companies for which they know a ready market will become available within a period of roughly one to two years still must offer a discount of about one-third to liquidate their shares in private transactions. Thus, liquidity is highly valued.

A second source of research to quantify the discount for lack of marketability comes from pre–initial public offering (IPO) studies. These are studies of the price at which securities in privately held companies were sold during the period from approximately 5 to 36 months prior to the company going public versus their initial public offering price. These discounts also vary from year to year but generally tend to fall in the range of 40 percent to 50 percent. Many analysts regard the pre-IPO studies as a better indication of a discount for lack of marketability to apply to minority interest shares in a closely held company than the restricted stock studies, because the underlying securities in the pre-IPO studies are interests in closely held companies.

The conclusions of these studies should be emphasized. Typically when a company goes public, its IPO is preceded by significant speculation and anticipation by shareholders on the benefits of the public offering. Yet even in those circumstances where the closely held company was of the size and attractiveness that it was able to go public, its shareholders typically could sell their stock prior to the IPO at only slightly more than half of its IPO price. Thus, sellers had to offer deep discounts to dispose of their stock because of the uncertainty of the IPO and the illiquidity inherent in the security of the closely held company.

This naturally leads to the question of how large the discount should be for stock of a minority interest in a closely held company that does not anticipate going public. The data suggest that it should be at least 30 percent to 45 percent less than the freely traded value on a minority basis. The lack of liquidity, however, is a relative concept, and the factors that would tend to increase the size of the discount would include:

- The element and strength of control that is exercised by the controlling owners
- Restrictions on transfer of the stock
- Minimal or no dividends payments
- Little prospect for sale of company or a public offering
- Thin market for that size of block of stock
- Seller unwilling to sign a covenant not to compete

Among the factors that would tend to decrease the discount for lack of marketability are:

- Existence of a market for the interest being valued
- History of meaningful dividends payments
- High likelihood or potential for sale of the company or public offering
- Interest being valued is sufficient to cause liquidation, sale, or merger
- No restriction on the sale of the interest being valued
- Presence of a put option (with a reasonable prospect of being enforced and funded)

Buy/sell agreements and the ownership distribution of the remaining shares are factors that could increase or decrease the discount for lack of marketability.

It is essential to emphasize that these discounts apply to a minority interest. As discussed, the controlling interest in the closely held company typically possesses far greater liquidity through its ability to liquidate the company. Therefore, although the liquidation process may take a significant period of time and could involve significant transaction costs, the controlling interest possesses far greater liquidity along with the ability to somewhat control their destiny.

Minimal data exist to document the size of the lack of marketability discount, if any, for controlling interests in closely held companies. There seems to be a consensus in the valuation profession that it should not exceed 20 percent and may be 0 percent. Factors to consider begin with the fact that the controlling interest has access to the entity's cash flow—either from its operations or through its sale. The nature of the company and the time and cost that would have to be incurred to sell it are factors to consider. Also, there is an active market for some kinds of closely held companies, while others, particularly those in specialized or in narrow industries or poor locations, could be much more difficult to sell. Other factors include the time and costs to liquidate and convert the shares into cash and the in-place management and supervisory personnel.

 ## REACHING THE VALUATION CONCLUSION

Confirmation of the Valuation Assignment

For those with little or no experience in business valuation, it can be very frustrating to have employed the income, market, and asset approaches, derived at least one value from each, and then found that the results vary substantially. The resulting questions inevitably include:

- Which value is correct?
- Why are the others different?
- Has an error been made?
- How can one value be "better" than another?

The review and reconciliation process should begin with the valuation assignment: What specifically did you set out to appraise? This initial checklist should at least consider:

- What is being appraised—invested capital, equity, or something else?
- What is the standard of value—fair market value, investment value, or something else?
- What is the ownership interest—control, lack of control, or minority?
- Is the ownership interest marketable, or does it lack marketability?
- What is the date of the appraisal, and what were the conditions and known information at that time?

After these basics have been reviewed and confirmed, review the three approaches to value—income, market, and asset. Even if each is appropriate to this assignment, is one likely to be more appropriate than another or at least easier to research, document, and support? For example, if the income approach lacks an accurate forecast, the market approach lacks adequate guideline company information, or the asset approach lacks accurate asset appraisals, the reliability and appropriateness of each is reduced. Furthermore, if the income approach uses a return for which a rate of return is difficult to determine, if the market approach is based on companies that are not in exactly the same industry, or if the asset approach is used to appraise a minority interest, the answers are again less reliable and probably less appropriate.

A technique commonly employed when there is difficulty in identifying the most appropriate approach is to average the values that are determined. This method ignores the issues of reliability and appropriateness, as well as the appraiser's professional judgment, and frequently creates distortions. The averaging also disregards the higher value that has been determined by at least one of the approaches.

Keep in mind that each approach looks at the business from a different perspective. While the income approach looks at future returns and develops a rate of return to reflect risk, the market approach focuses on the price that similar investments have recently traded for, and the asset approach looks to valuing the underlying assets. Each of the approaches relies on the appraiser to generate information and statistics that lead to an opinion of value. Each of these building blocks of value—rates of return, value multiples, and asset appraisals—should be reviewed for their accuracy, reliability, and appropriateness to the subject company and the interest in it that is being appraised. As these building blocks are reviewed, the appraiser will most likely have a higher degree of confidence and comfort in certain information, assumptions, and computations than others. The report or analysis that accompanies the computation should reflect this. That is, the narrative should persuasively explain why some numbers or assumptions are more appropriate than others. The inability to explain these differences should suggest a lack of research or analysis and the need to do further work to raise the confidence level.

Go back and review the value drivers and risk drivers that the competitive analysis indicated had the largest influence on the company's value. Then analyze how well each valuation procedure considers and reflects these factors. Return streams, rates of return, and value multiples are the appraiser's primary tools to quantify these issues. Each procedure should be evaluated based on its ability to accurately portray these drivers as they affect the interest being valued.

Doing this really amounts to the process of preparing sanity checks, where the appraiser is asking what a well-informed, reasonable, hypothetical willing buyer or seller in a free and open market would do about this deal. If the answer to that question is in doubt, the issues that create that doubt and the value that appears too high or too low must once again be carefully analyzed. As this analysis takes place, the appraiser must continually be aware of control versus minority and marketable versus nonmarketable issues. For example, a value that may be appropriate on a control basis could be completely unrealistic for a minority interest.

Mathematical versus Subjective Weightings

When several different procedures have been employed, all of which appear to be appropriate, although perhaps at different levels, they may have to be weighted either subjectively or mathematically. Mathematical computations appear to be mechanical and may suggest an unrealistic level of precision. Subjective appraisals generally require the appraiser to describe and justify the final estimate of value, which tends to create an added degree of discipline and rigor to the process. In either case, it is constructive to include an explanation of why the approaches and methods that were not employed were rejected. This helps to clarify the process, identify the key value drivers and risk drivers involved, and builds confidence in the final estimate of value. Appraisers should also recognize that where significant uncertainties exist, or in dynamic markets where rapid changes occur, a range of value may be more appropriate than a single figure. Conversely, where substantial market data exist and reliable forecasts are available for relatively stable industries, consistent estimates of value should be achieved.

In business valuation, procedures and conclusions usually are not absolute and must be carefully weighed. The process is far less mechanical than most anticipate, and there is no substitute for extensive research, accurate computations, and seasoned judgment.

It is the author's experience that the typical beginner will take at least several years to master the body of knowledge contained in the following sources. Any serious student of business valuation should purchase these books and expect to spend many hours with them. After this is done, reread this chapter; it should make a lot more sense.

8

Moving Beyond Budgeting: Integrating Continuous Planning and Adaptive Control

Steve Player
Robin Fraser
Jeremy Hope
*Beyond Budgeting Round Table**

INTRODUCTION

The Beyond Budgeting Round Table (BBRT) was set up in response to growing dissatisfaction, indeed frustration, with traditional budgeting. Since its inception in January 1998, 60 organizations have participated in the BBRT. Though its origins are in the United Kingdom, it now has members from many countries, including Belgium, France, Germany, Holland, Norway, South Africa, Sweden, Switzerland, the United Kingdom, and the United States. There are also regional BBRT groups in North America and Australia.

All member companies joined because they recognized the budgeting process was too long, too expensive, added little value, and was increasingly out of kilter with their competitive environment. In fact, research suggests that between 80 to 90 percent of companies are dissatisfied with their planning and budgeting processes. This process takes, on average, between four and five months to complete.[1] It also involves many people and absorbs up to 20 to 30 percent of senior executives' and financial managers' time.[2] In a recent survey, financial directors ranked budgetary reform as their top priority.[3]

---

*The Beyond Budgeting Round Table (BBRT) is a not-for-profit research consortium group open to organizations seeking to advance planning and control processes. BBRT was founded in Europe in 1998 and expanded to North America in 2002. For more information on research and programs, please visit www.bbrt.org or call (214)744-6188.

[1] Hackett Benchmarking Solutions (www.thgi.com/pprfax.htm).

[2] Fran Littlewood, "Look Beyond the Budget," *The Times* (London), January 11, 2000.

[3] Economic Intelligence Unit Report, 2000, quoted in "Driving Value Through Strategic Planning and Budgeting—A Research Report from Cranfield School of Management and Accenture," 2001, p. 4.

Despite these concerns, however, few were convinced at the outset that there was a viable alternative. Our task was to provide this alternative. We did this by first identifying those companies that had abandoned the annual budgeting process, visiting them, and then (through case reports and presentations) reporting back to BBRT members. By extracting best practices, we gradually pieced together a coherent set of processes that can effectively replace the functions of budgeting without the undesirable side effects.

Our research also reminded us that budgets (or any planning and measurement frameworks for that matter) do not exist in a vacuum. They determine how people behave in any given situation. "If you can't measure it, you can't manage it" is one of the favorite aphorisms of management academics and practitioners alike. It is this link between measurement and behavior that has loomed much larger in our project than we anticipated. We can recall some particularly animated meetings when a number of people (all senior managers) admitted to engaging in dubious practices as they were put under pressure to meet year-end targets. It is these revelations, together with a torrent of media criticism about how many firms have been managing the numbers (especially following the Enron debacle), that have caused us to place much more emphasis on the link between the fixed-target element of the annual budgeting process and undesirable management practices.

Many organizations have recognized these problems and attempted to improve the budgeting process. But little difference has resulted. This chapter is about other organizations that have gone beyond tinkering with the existing budgeting process. They have abandoned it altogether. Some have seen the problems of budgeting in terms of an ineffective process that is too long, too costly, and fails to provide its users with sufficient value. They have seen the opportunity to build more responsive and value-adding processes, to make them less political, and to have fewer behavioral side effects. Others have seen the problem more in terms of how budgets reinforce bureaucracy and are barriers to cultural change (especially how they block decentralization initiatives). They have seen the opportunity to release the pent-up energy and imagination of thousands of front-line people and to open the way to (permanently) lower costs and more sustainable profitability. But the one common thread is that these organizations do not manage with an annual budget. And they have used the same principles to replace it.

ANNUAL BUDGETING TRAP

For most organizations, the annual budgeting process results in a fixed performance contract between superiors and subordinates. It typically sets fixed targets, attaches incentives to those targets, sets out a detailed plan and budget that must be followed, spells out the resources available to meet the budget, includes any cross-company commitments that must be met, and contains details of how performance will be evaluated and which reports must be produced. The litmus test of such a contract is the linking of fixed targets and financial incentives. According to a survey of 2000 global companies in 2002, this linkage was confirmed in 60 percent of cases. Another (1998) survey of U.S. companies indicated that 73 percent of the respondents had made major changes to their performance management plans over the preceding two years as they experimented with different ways to tie pay to individual performance.[4]

It is apparent that senior executives believe that such a contract represents the most effective way of maximizing the performance potential of the firm. The problem is that, as managers take whatever actions they feel are warranted to meet their contracted numbers, the negative effects may outweigh the positive effects. The result is, more often than not, that such contracts lead to an annual performance trap. Faced with missing the recognition and rewards that come from meeting agreed targets, managers invariably resort to a range of shady practices. At best it leads to managing their earnings (e.g., at Gillette,[5] Coca-Cola,[6] and Citicorp[7]) and at worse to outright fraud (e.g., at Enron and Wimpey[8]). Peter Senge put the problem in context when he said, "Once we become convinced that we must achieve a certain outcome, our universe collapses and we see everything through the narrow lens of the predetermined outcome. Our awareness diminishes. Our ability to invent totally new ways of responding to new challenges is lost. Fear of failure increases."[9]

The budgeting process assumes that managers can predict and control their way to the future. It provided a rational and coherent approach to managing performance when market conditions were relatively stable, capital was the primary constraint on growth and improvement, strategy and product life cycles were lengthy, and the management behavior required was one of compliance with plans and procedures. But in the competitive climate in which most organizations operate today, it is no longer effective.

WHY SOME ORGANIZATIONS ARE GOING BEYOND BUDGETING

Firms have been trying to come to terms with these problems for decades. In the 1970s and 1980s, for example, zero-based budgeting (ZBB) became a popular approach. ZBB starts with a blank sheet of paper in regard to discretionary expenditure. It proved to be a useful (though usually one-off) exercise to review discretionary overheads. In recent years, some firms have introduced more frequent and much-streamlined planning and budgeting processes. These include budgets done half-yearly or quarterly instead of annually, and rolling budgets that tend to have a 12-month horizon (updated every quarter). Though these approaches offer more current (and thus more relevant) numbers for managers to follow, they suffer from an increased workload (even if done with fewer line items) and thus, more often than not, even higher cost. Some firms, such as Ford, Electrolux, and Sprint, have made strenuous efforts to harness the power of their information databases to enable the budgeting process to be performed with more

---

[4] Jeffrey Pfeffer, "Six Dangerous Myths About Pay," *Harvard Business Review* (May-June 1998): 109–119.

[5] Carol J. Loomis, "The 15% Delusion," *Fortune*, February 5, 2001, p. 52.

[6] Ibid. p. 53.

[7] Ibid. p. 52.

[8] Charles Pretzlik, "Wimpey's Profits Hit by £4m Write Off," *Financial Times*, September 16, 1999.

[9] H. Thomas Johnson and Anders Bröms, *Profit Beyond Measure* (London: Nicholas Brealey Publishing, 2000) p. xv (foreword by Peter Senge).

relevant real-time data.[10] Others, like BP-Amoco and Asea Brown Boveri, have directed their efforts at integrating budgeting with strategy.[11]

Implementing strategic management models such as the balanced scorecard is another approach taken by an increasing number of firms that are trying to shift their emphasis from being *budget-focused* to being *strategy-focused* organizations. But the full power of the balanced scorecard is constrained by the short-term performance drivers of the annual budget. These, by and large, remain focused on *managing* the next year-end rather than supporting medium-term strategy.

Most of these improvements have been aimed at reducing the costs and increasing the relevance of budgeting. But few have attempted to break free from the fixed performance contract and the annual trap that it creates. Indeed the evidence from scorecard users is that the performance indicators used are predominantly financial (62 percent) and lagging (76 percent).[12] Our conclusion is that despite many attempts to change the budgeting process and the mind-set it encourages, it remains the predominant feature of performance management in most organizations today.

BEYOND BUDGETING: ENABLING A MORE ADAPTIVE PERFORMANCE MANAGEMENT PROCESS

Borealis A/S is at the leading edge of polymer research and development and is now the world's fourth largest producer with annual sales of $4 billion. The problem it faced was that the budgeting process provided the illusion of control when, in reality, its core assumptions were based on volatile oil prices and a highly unpredictable business cycle. So it replaced the target setting, planning, measurement, and control functions of the budgeting process by integrating them within a balanced scorecard that (freed from the constraining influence of short-term budgets) directed managerial attention toward a number of strategic themes that underpin medium-term goals (such as reducing fixed costs by 30 percent over five years).

Targets are now set by reference to industry benchmarks, and the annual review process takes only a few weeks compared with five months spent previously on the budget. Rolling forecasts support quarterly performance reviews, and costs are managed through key performance indicator (KPI) boundaries and trend analysis. Performance is now reviewed quarterly, and scorecard measures are a feature of Web pages and bulletin boards that inform everyone about strategic performance. Project leaders believe they have saved 95 percent of the time that was formerly spent on budgeting and forecasting.

Another (unexpected) benefit was the enhanced status of the finance people, who are no longer seen as bean counters but as people who really help front-line managers with operational decisions. Moreover, the finance people are pleased with the results, as project leader Bjarte Bogsnes, explains: "We now achieve what the planning and budgeting process did in a simpler, more direct way. In fact I would go further. The

---

[10] "Driving Value Through Strategic Planning and Budgeting—A Research Report from Cranfield School of Management and Accenture," pp. 4–5.

[11] Ibid.

[12] Press release by Answerthink, March 20, 2002.

new system is not just simpler—it gives us far more information and control than the traditional budget ever did."

The next sections briefly describe what organizations such as Borealis previously did with their budgeting processes and what they now do without them.

How Have Organizations *Set Targets* without Budgeting?

What They Used to Do

They set targets on the basis of financial and, more often than not, "negotiated" numbers between superiors and subordinates before the start of the year. The targets were fixed for the year ahead. They represented the key component of the annual fixed performance contract. All actions were then focused on meeting the numbers.

What They Do Now

They set targets using high-level KPIs. These are set by reference to internal and external benchmarks and based on medium-term (typically three- to five-year) "aspirational" goals. A rolling review process then reevaluates them every year. In some cases, they are set by the executive board and then cascaded down the business. In others, they are based on a few world-class KPIs that enable units to set targets on a trajectory that will take them to the top of the "premier league." They use targets to set a framework for strategy. But the most important change is that they are *not fixed for the year*. The benefits are that the process is fast, and, because the benchmarking bar is always being raised, it is more likely to maximize profit potential.

How Have Organizations *Rewarded* People without Budgeting?

What They Used to Do

Organizations assumed managers would be motivated and fairly rewarded if the right mix of targets and incentives was in place. Thus, rewards were linked to a fixed outcome agreed in advance. The benefits were that managers "knew where they stood and what they had to meet." It was then up to them to achieve the target and bonus. They knew (and thus accepted) that this element of the budget contract led to gaming. In one study of 402 U.S. firms, almost all respondents stated they engaged in one or more budget games. Managers either did not accept the budgetary targets and opted to beat the system, or they felt pressured to achieve budgetary targets at any cost.[13]

What They Do Now

Most evaluate and reward performance on the progress that both teams and the firm as a whole make toward achieving medium-term goals (using a range of KPIs). Performance evaluation is made "with hindsight" in light of how a unit performed against

---

[13] Robert Simons, *Levers of Control* (Boston: Harvard Business School Press, 1995), p. 83.

benchmarks and peers. One firm has dispensed with local rewards altogether and for the past 30 years has been using one group-wide profit-sharing plan based on a formula related to the competitive performance of the firm. One benefit is that all cases have seen a reduction in gaming behavior. (With no fixed contract, there is little point in gaming.)

How Have Organizations Managed *Action Planning* without Budgeting?

What They Used to Do

The planning process used to be either top down (prepared by leaders or central planning departments) or sometimes bottom up, with local teams preparing their plans and then negotiating and agreeing them with superiors. Moreover, many were based on departmental improvements that were not necessarily in accord with strategic objectives. After many months of discussion, the resulting plan provided clear guidelines that told people what they had to do in the year ahead. However, such a predetermined plan can be a liability when the business environment has become as unpredictable as it is today. But the evidence suggests that such problems are ignored. For example, only 20 percent of firms change their budgets within the fiscal cycle.[14]

What They Do Now

They review the medium-term outlook (usually a two- to five-year horizon) every year and the short-term outlook (typically, five to eight quarters ahead) every quarter. Both cycles are aimed at achieving rolling medium-term goals. Responsibility for these reviews is, by and large, devolved to business unit teams and, in some cases, front-line teams. The role of group executives is to set strategic objectives and medium-term goals and then challenge the plans and initiatives that managers propose to ensure their core assumptions and risks are reasonable and represent the best options available. Both cycles are "light touch" processes taking no more than a few weeks for the annual cycle and a few days for the quarterly cycle. Useful tools such as rolling forecasts, the balanced scorecard, and activity accounting support these performance reviews. Action plans are derived from them. The primary benefits of these various approaches are faster response and a sharper focus on achieving strategic goals and satisfying customers' needs.

How Have Organizations *Managed Resources* without Budgeting?

What They Used to Do

They allocated resources on the basis of budget contracts negotiated *in advance* together with a share of "central costs" that (in theory, if not in practice) were needed to support them. The benefit was that at one point in time all resources were allocated to one unit or another. No further management attention was needed until the following year's budget review. However, senior executives too often acted like central committees approving

---

[14] "Corporate Strategic Planning Suffers from Inefficiencies," *Hackett Benchmarking*, PR Newswire, October 25, 1999.

or disapproving investment proposals based on annual plans. It is little wonder that strategy expert Gary Hamel said this approach is "the last bastion of Soviet-style central planning and can be found in Fortune 500 companies."[15]

What They Do Now

They make resources available and accessible to front-line teams as and when required through fast-track approvals and easier access to operational resources. They also have a high-level team that manages the resource portfolio (with quarterly reviews). They manage operational resources by setting guidelines based on KPIs (such as a cost-to-income ratio) within which managers can operate. They are held accountable *after the event* for the deployment of these resources. Some have developed an internal market whereby resources can be acquired by operating units from central services providers at an agreed price. This approach overcomes much of the game playing associated with resource allocation. Devolving more resource decisions to front-line teams has the effect of making them more accountable for resource decisions. This, in turn, builds greater ownership and leads to less waste.

How Have Organizations *Coordinated Actions* without Budgeting?

What They Used to Do

They linked their plans through the central coordination of departmental and business unit budgets. For example, they ensured that production and sales were in tune, and marketing had the resources to support the sales plan. At that point in time, each unit plan linked with another, leading to a coherent plan for the whole firm. But while the plans of individual departments might have been coordinated with each other, it was doubtful whether this amounted to a coherent *strategy* for the firm as a whole. Departmental managers are often too keen to improve their own department without considering how this may fit with broader strategic goals. (One study concluded that 60 percent of firms fail to align their action plans with their strategy.)[16]

What They Do Now

They coordinate their plans and actions across the business, not through a central plan but through a process of managing customer demand. This can vary from dealing with customized requests to managing through agreed customer order cycles. Inside the firm, these arrangements take the form of service-level agreements that, in effect, are commitments from one process to another. These are fixed for a period appropriate to the demand cycle, but the key change is that operating units act as both suppliers and customers of products and services with needs that must be satisfied. With such an approach, the organization is more likely to act as an integrated system pursuing a common strategy rather than a number of disparate parts. It also encourages sharing and cooperation and focuses on providing the external (paying) customer with an excellent service.

---

[15] Gary Hamel, "Bringing Silicon Valley Inside," *Harvard Business Review* (September–October 1999): 76.
[16] Robert S. Kaplan and David P. Norton, *The Strategy Focused Organization* (Boston: Harvard Business School Press, 2001), p. 274.

How Have Organizations *Measured and Controlled Performance* without *Budgeting*?

What They Used to Do

They controlled performance against predetermined budgets and then took corrective action to ensure that performance remained on track. Thus local managers would need to explain any variances and provide updated budgets or forecasts as a basis of further action. They would rarely look beyond the next fiscal year-end. (In 77 percent of the 2000 global companies surveyed by the Hackett Group in 2002, the focus of the forecast process was solely on the current fiscal year.)

What They Do Now

Organizations find that with no budget to compare performance against, managers are not flying blind. On the contrary, they are more aware of where they are going than ever before as they have more relevant indicators to guide them. They use measures and controls to focus managerial attention on anticipating the future rather than explaining what went wrong in the past. Main features include comparisons with external benchmarks, performance league tables, leading indicators, and rolling forecasts. These are also combined with actual financial results, comparisons against prior years, and trend analysis to provide a rich (and constantly moving) performance picture.

CLIMBING THE TWIN PEAKS OF BEYOND BUDGETING

The overall effect of these changes is a performance management process based on a *relative performance contract* rather than fixed targets. Though freed from the fixed performance contract, managers must still perform to high levels of expectation. Otherwise they will fail to survive. The difference is that the performance emphasis has shifted from internally negotiated short-term contracts to externally benchmarked medium-term KPIs. This is, in essence, how organizations have gone *beyond* budgeting and broken free from the annual performance trap.

But there is an even greater prize on offer. It is only when most leaders have made a successful transition to adaptive processes that they have seen the opportunity of *radically decentralizing performance responsibility to front-line people.* Exhibit 8.1 shows how many companies have climbed the first peak (and achieved significant progress) only to see the greater opportunities of the second.

While adaptive processes offer the prospect of cost savings from not budgeting, less gaming, faster response, better strategic alignment, and more value from finance people, radical decentralization offers much more. For example, it promises permanent reductions in the cost structure, more capable people, more innovation, more loyal customers, more ethical reporting, and the release of the full potential of management systems and tools. Abandoning the burdensome bureaucracy and the budgeting process that supports it is the key.

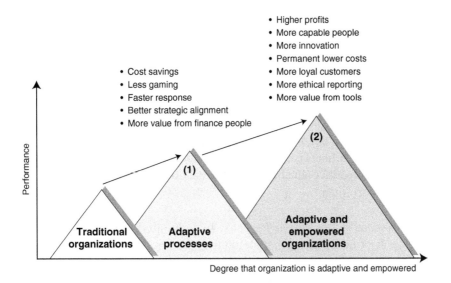

EXHIBIT 8.1   The Two Opportunities of Beyond Budgeting

BEYOND BUDGETING: ENABLING RADICAL DECENTRALIZATION

Swedish bank Svenska Handelsbanken has annual revenues of around $2 billion, 9,200 employees, and 520 branches. In 1970 it was struggling and losing customers, especially to a smaller rival run by Dr. Jan Wallander. The bank invited him to join as its new chief executive officer. But he came with certain demands, one of which was to radically decentralize operations and (to achieve this effectively) to abandon the budgeting process. Since then, the bank has outperformed its Nordic rivals on return on equity, total shareholder return, earnings per share, cost-to-income ratio, and customer satisfaction.

Handelsbanken has developed a performance and rewards culture based on competitive success at every level (branch to branch, region to region, and bank to bank). These peer comparisons create intense pressure to perform to high levels of expectation (e.g., to achieve an average cost-to-income ratio of around 40 to 45 percent). Two key benefits underline Handelsbanken's sustained success: *fast response to customers and lower costs*. Strategy, action plans, and resource decisions are devolved to regions and branches. With no product targets to reach, managers are free to tailor solutions to customer needs. This is one of the primary reasons why Handelsbanken has the lowest number of complaints in its sector and consistently tops the customer satisfaction charts in Sweden. Handelsbanken is the most cost-efficient bank in Europe. A flat, simple hierarchy, few controllers, no bureaucracy, well-trained and empowered staff, no budgets to act as barriers to cost reduction, cost-based performance rankings, and a few simple-to-understand measures—these are all factors that contribute to maintaining a low cost base.

The delegation of decision-making and spending authority has always been one of the key functions of budgeting. However, this delegation, by and large, is strictly within a regime of compliance and control. It differs significantly from the approach taken by organizations like Handelsbanken. It has gone much further and transferred power from the center to operating managers and their teams, vesting in them the authority to use their judgment and initiative to achieve results *without being constrained by some specific plan or agreement.* Thus the devolution of responsibility is about enabling and encouraging local decisions, not dictating and directing them.

Like Handelsbanken, other organizations have opted for radical decentralization to provide a distinctive competitive advantage. Leaders believe it addresses six key changes in the competitive environment:

1. *Shareholders demand best-in-class performance.* To maintain the loyalty of investors, firms must be at (or near) the top in their industry sectors. Beating the competition rather than some negotiated target is now the way to please investors. Leaders have responded by creating a *high-performance climate* based on relative success at every level.

2. *Talented people are increasingly scarce.* As a McKinsey survey confirmed, people want jobs that emphasize "values," "freedom," and "autonomy" more than anything else.[17] Leaders have responded by providing a *governance framework based on clear principles and boundaries.*

3. *Product and strategy life cycles are shrinking.* Firms must constantly produce new solutions and more imaginative strategies to compete. Leaders have responded by *empowering front-line people to make decisions* that are congruent with strategic goals.

4. *Global competition is driving down prices and driving up quality.* Firms must operate with low-cost business models and accept that high quality is no longer a competitive advantage. It is a prerequisite for global competition. Leaders have responded by giving front-line people the *capability to act by providing them with the ownership of the resources they need.*

5. *Customers are in charge.* Customer loyalty is increasingly fickle. Firms must keep close to customers and respond rapidly to their changing needs. Leaders have responded by *focusing people on customer outcomes.*

6. *Investors and regulators are demanding higher standards of reporting.* They will make life increasingly difficult for those that do not comply. Leaders have responded by *supporting open and ethical information systems.*

How Have Leaders Created a High-Performance Climate?

What They Have Abandoned

Organizations have abandoned the use of the previous year's performance as the basis of the current year's targets—a process that leads to incremental changes. They have abandoned an internal focus on negotiating financial numbers that fails to provide a

---

[17] Elizabeth G. Chambers, Mark Foulon, Helen Handfield-Jones, Steven M. Hankin, and Edward G. Michaels III, "The War for Talent," *McKinsey Quarterly* (1998): 3.

reality check on performance. And they have abandoned the focus on agreeing annual targets for each individual unit and subunit that fails to see them in the context of an integrated value delivery system.

What They Have Promoted

These firms have elevated peer-based performance reviews to a whole performance culture based on relative success. They have set high performance standards based on world-class benchmarks. They have recognized the need to balance internal competition and corporation by clarifying who owns which customer. The result is a virtuous circle of high standards followed by improved performance.

How Have Leaders Built a Clear Governance Framework?

What They Have Abandoned

Organizations have abandoned the notion that employees base their commitment on mission statements and detailed plans prepared by someone else. They have abandoned the command, compliance, and control approach that assumes strategy formulation and execution take place in separate compartments. And they have abandoned the assumption that front-line managers cannot be trusted with the responsibility to think and act on the latest information in the best interests of the firm as a whole.

What They Have Promoted

These organizations have recognized a high-performance culture needs a governance framework that provides clear principles and boundaries to support empowered decisions. They believe it is the challenge, responsibility, clear values, and fairness of shared rewards that drive people to achieve extraordinary results. They have adopted a coach-and-support management style that places performance responsibility on the shoulders of front-line people. It is this continuous involvement in planning and execution that builds motivation and commitments and leads to ambitious strategies and continuous improvement.

How Have Leaders Empowered People to Make Decisions?

What They Have Abandoned

They have abandoned the culture of dependency whereby local managers would always have to go up the line before a decision could be taken. They have abandoned the cautious safety-first approach to strategy that leads to low expectations. And they have abandoned the exclusion of people from the strategy process on the assumption that only people at the center have the experience and wisdom to make good decisions.

What They Have Promoted

They have set high standards, expectations, and benchmarks to stretch ambition and performance. They have challenged local strategies and action plans to ensure they are sufficiently ambitious but at the same time robust and that risks are appropriate. And they have opened up the strategy process to anyone who can make a contribution. The benefits are that local people are more likely to produce imaginative strategies and are more committed to their successful execution.

How Have Leaders Given People the Capability to Act?

What They Have Abandoned

They have abandoned the role of the corporate center as central banker accepting or rejecting plans on the basis of short-term numbers. They have abandoned the entitlement culture as managers seek to improve their own department's position against others. And they have abandoned the use-it-or-lose-it mentality that says that the budget must be spent, come what may.

What They Have Promoted

They have turned the role of the corporate center into that of a venture capitalist supporting a portfolio of existing and new investments. They have provided local units with the freedom to manage their own resources and be accountable for them retrospectively. They have created an internal market within which central services serve and support operating units. The benefits are that local teams have the capability to respond to threats and opportunities as they arise. Moreover, central service providers must satisfy their needs with high-quality, value-for-money products and services and maintain their costs (and prices) as low as possible.

How Have Leaders Focused People on Customer Outcomes?

What They Have Abandoned

They have abandoned the functional hierarchy with its tendency to produce increasingly large business units on the basis of cost savings. They have abandoned the plan-make-and-sell business model with central quotas and fixed sales targets that assumes customers can be persuaded to buy what the firm decides to make. And they have abandoned the not-invented-here syndrome that prevents units sharing knowledge.

What They Have Promoted

They have taken decentralization beyond major business units and down to the front line, enabling a network of small local teams to work within a clear framework of values and boundaries. They have encouraged a can-do and no-blame culture. Managers can do what needs to be done and fix what needs to be fixed, knowing that there will be *someone to support them if it does not work out.* And they have focused teams serving and satisfying customers' needs. The result is greater accountability for outcomes and more satisfied and profitable customers.

How Have Leaders Supported Open and Ethical Information Systems?

What They Have Abandoned

They have abandoned the notion that information can be controlled when networks and e-mail enable it to flow around the globe in nanoseconds. They have abandoned the belief that the primary beneficiaries of information are people at the center. And they have abandoned the culture of treating and spinning information to make it represent a misleading outcome.

What They Have Promoted

They have promoted information flows to new levels of openness and transparency. They have given their people access to the sort of strategic, competitive, and market-based information once the preserve of senior executives. And they have understood that all the numbers within the organization should stick to "one truth" and be transparent. They should be seen by everyone in their raw state without people treating them or painting pictures that are designed to mislead. This gives everyone confidence in the numbers and supports decision making. The outcome is more transparent and reliable information and more ethical reporting.

An Alternative Coherent Performance Management Process Has Emerged.

When fused together, the two opportunities of Beyond Budgeting offer organizations a coherent alternative to the traditional budgeting model. Moreover, giving front-line people more of a strategic voice enables them to be reconnected to the organization's purpose and its strategic goals.

Beyond Budgeting is a guiding set of principles. It is not a model or set of tools. These already exist in the form of shareholder value models, benchmarking models, balanced scorecards, activity-based management, customer relationship management models, and enterprise-wide information systems. The problem is that they disrupt the existing coherence without reestablishing a clear alternative. Thus, for example, the balanced scorecard focuses managers on medium-term strategies (two to five years ahead), but the budgeting counterculture remains rooted in achieving this year's performance target. The philosophy of all these tools is that power can be devolved to front-line decision makers, but, in practice, this power is withheld.

Using these tools within the framework of an adaptive and devolved organization releases their full potential. For example, the balanced scorecard can truly turn an organization into one that is strategy focused with strategy being continuous and "everyone's everyday job." And customer relationship management means that front-line people have the capability to provide solutions and solve customer problems the first time. Utilizing the value of these tools and *integrating them within a coherent framework for the adaptive and devolved organization* is one of the more important potential benefits of abandoning the traditional budgeting process.

Exhibit 8.2 shows how the management tools underpin adaptive processes that in turn enable the devolution of performance responsibility. This creates capable,

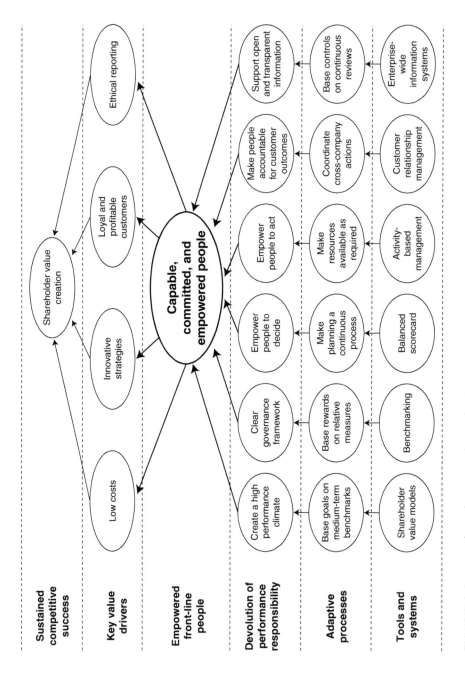

Sustained competitive success

Key value drivers

Empowered front-line people

Devolution of performance responsibility

Adaptive processes

Tools and systems

EXHIBIT 8.2 How the Adaptive and Devolved Organization Reconnects People with Organizational Success

committed, and empowered people at the front line. With the full power of tools and systems to provide them with the capabilities to make fast and effective decisions (unfettered by the budgeting counterculture), they can reduce costs, produce innovative strategies, create loyal and profitable customers, and provide more ethical reporting systems. Finally, these key value drivers lead to shareholder value creation and sustained competitive success. This is, in essence, the story of Handelsbanken over the past 30 years.

Transforming the performance potential of the organization by breaking free from the annual performance trap and releasing the full power of front-line people and the tools at their disposal is the vision of Beyond Budgeting. *Implementing more adaptive performance management processes* does not require project managers to stray too far from their comfort zones. *Devolving performance responsibility to front-line people* is more radical and needs strong and determined leadership from the top of the organization. But the potential benefits are greater and more enduring.

CHAPTER NINE

Moving Beyond Budgeting: An Update

Steve Player

*North American Program Director,
Beyond Budgeting Round Table*

Managing Director, The Player Group

INTRODUCTION

Companies in today's marketplace have been forced, by a variety of factors, to reassess their planning, budgeting, and forecasting processes. These factors include globalization of our economy, increased competition, technological advances and innovations, volatility of the stock market, decreased supply of raw materials, environmental constraints, and political changes. These external factors coupled with the ever-present need to meet Wall Street's expectations can make traditional budgeting a hindrance instead of an asset.

Jack Welch, former chief executive officer of General Electric (GE), wrote in his best-selling book, *Winning*, that the budgeting process at most companies "has to be the most ineffective practice in management. It sucks the energy, time, fun, and big dreams out of an organization. It hides opportunity and stunts growth. It brings out the most unproductive behaviors in an organization, from sandbagging to settling for mediocrity."[1] In fact, while Welch was at GE, the company did away with the term "budgeting" altogether.[2]

The end result is that everyone, from senior executives to front-line managers, commits to overly aggressive targets and fudges the numbers to meet expectations. In extreme cases, such as Enron and WorldCom, this led to outright fraud. But even

---

[1] Jack Welch with Suzy Welch, *Winning* (New York: HarperCollins, 2005), p. 189.
[2] Ibid., p. 190.

in less dramatic cases, the management team begins to spend more and more time on developing and focusing on these fixed-performance targets and less time on achieving added value for the shareholders. This, in turn, greatly detracts from the company's ability to adapt quickly to changes in the marketplace, opportunities for growth/profit, and advances from competitors.

The ability to adapt is the key to beating the competition in modern times. In his book, *Leading Change*, Harvard Business School professor John P. Kotter wrote that in order for a company to compete in the twenty-first century, it must become more precise in targeting windows of opportunity, more creative in how it competes, and more customized in what it delivers.[3] The Beyond Budgeting framework offers companies the ability to adapt, compete, and prosper in these ever-changing and challenging times.

BEYOND BUDGETING ROUND TABLE (BBRT)

The Beyond Budgeting Round Table (BBRT) is a network of member companies with a common interest in improving planning and control practices.[4] The BBRT offers principles in its management model that lead to a more adaptive organization and one in which employees are empowered to succeed. The end result of adopting the BBRT model is that the organization's performance management is based on a *relative performance contract* rather than on fixed performance targets.

The Beyond Budgeting model offers several key principles for enabling an organization to implement a continuous adaptive process in regards to planning and budgeting. We discuss these principles in the sections that follow.

Base Evaluations and Rewards on Relative Improvement

This principle calls for creating a rewards system that fosters employee self-satisfaction for a job well done rather than depending solely on monetary rewards. The desire to continually strive to be the best is cultivated throughout the company under the Beyond Budgeting model.

In a recent case study of one of North America's leading financial service companies, it was found that monetary rewards were a very minor incentive to employees. Instead, the organization found that if its key performance drivers were achieved, then the monetary issues took care of themselves. Thus, the company's focus needed to be centered on job performance and outperforming the competition rather than on bonuses and other monetary rewards. Additionally, this study tends to challenge the very foundation of traditional budgeting (i.e., the use of fixed performance targets).

Coordinate Cross-Company Actions with Prevailing Demands

The Beyond Budgeting model calls for developing a unity of purpose throughout the company. One way to achieve this is by creating internal service agreements with other

---

[3] John P. Kotter, *Leading Change* (Boston: Harvard Business School Press, 1996), p. 171.
[4] For more information on Beyond Budgeting, visit www.bbrt.org.

units within the company. Doing this not only decreases reliance on outside vendors and helps meet customer demands quicker but also instills unity among departments within the organization.

This process also encourages the sharing of customer profitability information with front-line managers so that the customers' needs are identified and responded to. An outgrowth of this action is the ability of operational managers to understand the needs of customers and provide customized solutions as needed. The real-world application of this principle can be seen in the case of Guardian Industries, discussed later in this chapter.

Base Controls on Effective Governance and on Key Performance Indicators

Implement adaptive management by using rolling forecasts, trend analysis, and moving averages to set controls instead of a fixed budget. The company's ability to respond to changes in the marketplace or opportunities is dependent on fast, accurate financials and everyone having access to such information.

A recent case study of a large offshore drilling company showed how vital understanding of key performance indicators can be to achieving long-term success in today's global marketplace. The company implemented a series of rolling forecasts to more effectively manage the company's day-to-day operations and found that by studying historic trends in weather patterns, it could significantly increase profitability because weather could be taken into account more accurately when planning on moving a rig from one hemisphere to the next. The company also created a system whereby every level of management had access to the company's financial data. This, in turn, led to the individual drilling rig managers having more input and responsibility for their rig operations, which in turn increases productivity and profits.

Front-Line Empowerment

The Beyond Budgeting model is more than just a checklist of management processes and procedures—it is a concept that can dramatically change a corporation's entire culture and that empowers it to achieve more than most companies ever thought possible. One of the most significant changes a switch to the Beyond Budgeting model can bring is in the corporation's culture. Companies that have fully embraced and implemented a "budget-less" management approach have prospered and openly state their disdain for traditional budgeting.

 ## GUARDIAN INDUSTRIES CORPORATION

In the case of Guardian Industries Corporation (Guardian), the company has adopted a corporate culture where bureaucracy such as traditional budgeting is not tolerated. Guardian is one of the world's largest float glass manufacturers with annual revenue of $5 billion, over 19,000 employees, and operations in over 50 countries. It operates in highly volatile and competitive markets. Yet after over 45 years of operation, Guardian maintains an A+ credit rating and has achieved sustained strong cash flow and profitability, all without ever using budgets.

Guardian feels that budgets are time consuming and a waste of resources, adding little or no value. It also feels traditional budgets pose the threat of becoming obstacles to responding quickly to changes in the market and/or opportunities for growth or profit. Guardian has listed its primary reasons for not using budgets as:

▪ Budgeting smacks of big company bureaucracy.
▪ It doesn't believe in "crystal balls."
▪ Budgeting is a non–value-added, resource-intensive exercise.
▪ Budgeting takes away from management's freedom and authority, which is counter to Guardian's corporate culture.
▪ Guardian has been highly successful for over 45 years without using budgets.

Guardian's success is attributable to a strong corporate culture, use of adaptive planning and controls, and its workforce's feeling of empowerment. Guardian's president, William Davidson, is responsible for instilling this strong corporate culture. Davidson has led Guardian for over 45 years. He has steadfastly maintained the belief that managing the organization like a "family" would foster creativity and establish a culture of team responsibility. Also, he felt that big business bureaucracy stifled creativity and discouraged action.

Davidson has strong convictions regarding planning and budgeting. He thinks that planning and budgeting based on "prediction and control" is an illusion that can lead organizations into making poor decisions and prevent them from responding to change. Instead, Davidson built Guardian as a company where simplicity, transparency, and accountability mean something. The company uses few job titles and has even fewer formal job descriptions and no organizational chart. Yet it has sustained continual growth and profits since 1957.

Instead of using vast resources to create an annual budget, Guardian uses various tools to manage its financial resources. The company chooses to focus on monitoring its daily cash flows and on its return on capital employed (ROCE). Such forecasting, coupled with its maintaining a relatively constant debt and cash balance, allows the company to identify the activities that show the greatest promise for ROCE. This system allows resources to be channeled into those activities that show the most promise for a greater return on investment. This process also separates any dependency between controls and earnings growth or the creation of wealth.

Guardian's real key to success is the empowerment felt by its workers. The company Web site www.guardian.com tells future employees what to expect: "Make sure you bring your motivation, your creativity and your integrity. Because at Guardian, we expect honesty and ethics to drive everything you do. In return, you'll get more than your share of responsibility and challenge."

Guardian pushes responsibility and decision making down to the lowest levels. Managers are empowered by giving them control and authority over their production areas. This control includes personnel practices, setting customer prices, and setting work schedules and shift changes. Plant managers are encouraged to pass this approach down to their front-line staff. Indeed, most line managers have authority to stop production without seeking higher approval to solve a quality issue. The end result of Guardian's decision to empower its employees is that everyone feels a true sense of ownership in the company. This, in turn, results in higher motivation and production for the company.

Clearly, Guardian is a bright and shining example of how companies can excel when choosing to operate without traditional budgets. As a global manufacturer in a highly competitive industry, Guardian uses the Beyond Budgeting principles in its day-to-day operations and continually ranks as the best-in-class company in its market.

PART TWO

Tools And Techniques

CHAPTER TEN

Implementing Forecasting Best Practices

Terrence B. Hobdy, BBA, MBA
Management Information Specialists, Inc.

INTRODUCTION

The headlines from the past year clearly indicate that Corporate America has failed miserably in regard to reporting accurate and reliable financial results. The mere mention of an accounting irregularity has severely affected the stock prices of major corporations. Additionally, the cozy relationship among Wall Street firms, accounting firms, and Main Street clients have further clouded this issue. Unethical issues aside, the average investor cannot fully understand the financial results presented by corporations to make clear investment decisions.

During an interview on *60 Minutes*, the chief executive officer (CEO) of a multibillion-dollar software corporation stated, "The only way that any company can predict their financial results, earnings per share, to the penny is to cook the books." Instead of reporting true corporate performance, some companies have resorted to unethical approaches to produce unrealistic financial results. Overall, the lack of transparency in financial performance has seriously dampened the trust between corporations and investors.

In response to the growing problems with reporting financial results, several steps have been taken to restore investor confidence.

1. Congress enacted the Sarbanes-Oxley Act, which established a new Public Accounting Oversight Board. In addition, CEOs and chief financial officers of publicly traded

companies are required to certify in every annual report that they have reviewed the report and that it does not contain untrue statements or omissions of material facts.

2. Some corporations have presented a more accurate portrayal of their financial results through such moves as expensing employee stock options, thereby accounting for the full effect on earnings.

3. Companies have provided greater disclosure regarding results by providing greater information about accounting and other management practices, such as loans to key employees.

All of these actions are designed to restore investor confidence and establish more accountability for financial results.

In a study of earnings reports for the fourth-quarter 2000 by Hackett Best Practices, over one-third of the 71 companies examined failed to meet their earnings projections. Additionally, one-quarter issued warnings that they would miss their original earnings targets, lowering earnings forecasts by an average of 42 percent. Not only did these companies suffer the loss in earnings that might have been avoided had problems been foreseen and managed earlier, many also experienced a decrease in investor confidence as well as substantial declines in share price.

BUDGETING VERSUS FORECASTING

In most companies, the annual budgeting process is labor intensive, has a very long cycle time, and is outdated the day the budget is complete. Per research from Hackett Best Practices, the budget process typically takes more than 76 days at the average billion-dollar company. Although the budget is designed to provide management and investors with a fiscal-year view of performance for planning purposes, the nature of the business cycle does not follow a normal 12-month cycle. Because businesses will continue to encounter recessions and experience unexpected events that impact financial performance, they need to adopt better approaches to measure and manage results. Specifically, companies need to move beyond the annual budgeting process and improve their forecasting processes and systems. By implementing better forecasting processes and systems, companies can develop a forward-looking and continuous planning process that is aligned with their strategic goals and objectives. Additionally, companies can improve the accuracy and reliability of financial results and, more important, improve investor confidence in their financial results.

IMPLEMENTING FORECASTING BEST PRACTICES

Although companies will continue using an annual budgeting process to measure and manage fiscal-year performance, the adoption of best practices for forecasting can provide better information for decision-making purposes. The implementation of these best practices should achieve two specific goals.

Process

•Implement rolling forecast

•Leverage driver-based approach

Organization	Technology
•Clearly defined roles and responsibilities	*•Implement integrated technology*

EXHIBIT 10.1   Focus on Three Areas

1. The accuracy and reliability of the forecasted information should improve. Reliability and accuracy can be measured on the basis of the discrepancy between forecasted results and actual results.
2. The implementation of best practices should assist the company in reducing the cycle time required to develop forecasted information. Thereby, management can access timely information regarding business performance.

A best-practices approach to forecasting involves implementing practices along three dimensions: process, organization, and technology (see Exhibit 10.1). This chapter provides the reader with an overview of key best practices for forecasting and, more important, how these best practices can be applied within their company across these three dimensions.

FORECASTING BEST PRACTICES: PROCESS

Over the past few years, many companies have implemented a rolling-forecast process. A rolling forecast is a forward-looking continual update of the company's forecast. For example, if a company develops an 18-month rolling forecast for six quarters, each quarterly update of the forecast includes an additional quarterly view of estimate performance from the last forecasted period. As shown in Exhibit 10.2, the company creates a rolling forecast during the second quarter of the current year through the end of the fourth quarter for the following year (Q4 Y1). During the next update of the forecast for the third quarter of the current year, the company updates the rolling forecast through the first quarter of year 2 (Q1 Y2).

Although this example illustrates the application of a six-quarter rolling forecast, companies should tailor the time horizon for the rolling forecast specifically to their

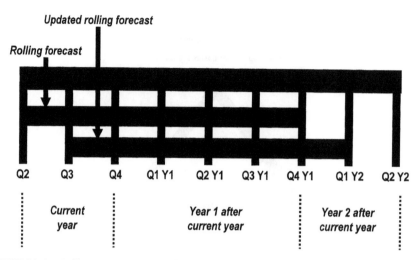

EXHIBIT 10.2   Rolling Forecast Timeline

business cycle. For example, companies in a capital-intensive industry may choose to adopt a longer horizon for the rolling forecast that matches the business cycle required to build new plants or facilities. However, companies in an industry with short product life cycles (e.g., software industry) may choose to adopt a shorter horizon, such as a one-year rolling forecast.

The predictive accuracy, advance warning, and decision-making benefits of rolling forecasts provide management with an updated and more realistic estimation of their business performance based on the existing economy and business environment. As shown in Exhibit 10.3, data from Hackett Best Practices indicate that about 23 percent of companies have adopted this best-practice approach to forecasting. In contrast, the forecast process at 77 percent of companies focuses on the current fiscal year. The primary reason that companies continue to focus their forecasting process on the current

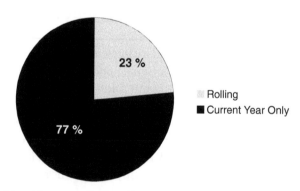

EXHIBIT 10.3   Monthly versus Rolling Forecast

Source: Answerthink's Hackett Best Practices, *Strategic Dicision Making 2002 Book of Numbers,* 2002.

fiscal year can be attributed to the incentive compensation plans. In 60 percent of the cases, incentive compensation plans are aligned with achieving fiscal-year results versus creating long-term value. Companies that leverage the rolling-forecast approach can look beyond the next quarter and, more important, differentiate themselves from their competitors.

Along with the implementation of the rolling-forecast process as a best-practices approach, companies can leverage the use of a driver-based approach to more accurately predict financial performance. A *driver* is a factor that impacts revenues, costs, and for profits. Driver-based forecasting is a technique that incorporates drivers to model or forecast future business performance. A driver-based forecasting approach establishes a relationship between the driver, which can be external (e.g., legislative changes, economic environment) or internal (e.g., number of orders by type) and the resulting financial impact from either a revenue or cost perspective. The driver must be material and volatile to be included in the forecasting model.

To develop a driver-based forecasting process, companies first need to identify their specific revenue and cost drivers. From a revenue perspective, an examination of the sales process can provide a company with examples of revenue drivers. The drivers are often leading indicators of financial performance. For example, in professional service organizations such as consulting or law firms, billable hours are examples of revenue drivers. Billable hours by resource type (e.g., partner, associate, etc.) can be used as a good predictor of future revenues.

As illustrated in Exhibit 10.4, revenues for the professional service organization (e.g., consulting firm) are influenced by a couple of factors. The opportunity to develop proposals for services increases the chances for the professional service organization to bid successfully on client projects. If the organization is successful in winning the proposal and thus starting a project with the client, then the professional service

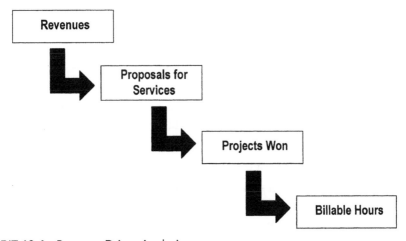

EXHIBIT 10.4   Revenue Driver Analysis

EXHIBIT 10.5   Examples of Revenue Drivers

Driver Name	Driver Quantity	Revenue per Driver	Estimated Revenues
Partner hours	10,000	$200	$200,000
Associate hours	30,000	$150	$450,000

organization can charge the client fees for each billable hour of services performed based on the terms of the proposal. From a driver-based forecasting perspective, the billable hours can be used to estimate future revenues. In Exhibit 10.5, the driver name, estimated driver quantity, estimated revenue per driver, and estimated revenues are listed to provide insight into this approach.

Just as drivers are used as predictors of revenues in a driver-based forecasting approach, companies should also develop drivers as predictors of costs. When identifying cost drivers, companies should also perform cost driver analysis and specifically identify units of measures that are good predictors of resource consumption. Examples include the number of machine hours required to manufacture products and number of new hires required to sell a new product line. These drivers are also operational measures, which are used to estimate costs. In Exhibit 10.6, the driver name, estimated driver quantity, estimated cost per driver, and estimated costs are listed to provide insight into this approach.

Both revenue and cost drivers are often captured in operational systems (e.g., sales ordering, manufacturing, time and attendance systems, etc.). In Exhibit 10.7, other examples of drivers are provided for both revenues and costs.

In summary, implementing a rolling forecast and leveraging a driver-based forecasting approach are two best-practices techniques to improve the forecasting process. By implementing these best practices, companies can develop a more meaningful forward-looking and continuous forecast approach that is more aligned with the true cycle of their business. Additionally, using operational drivers for revenues and costs provides more accurate and timely forecasting information that is based on realistic predictors of financial performance. In this way, the forecasting process establishes a linkage of operational performance to financial results. Clear documentation of the drivers, forecasting process, policies, and procedures is essential to implementing these new approaches.

FORECASTING BEST PRACTICES: ORGANIZATION

As discussed, implementing best practices for forecasting from a process perspective can help organizations to develop more reliable financial results. In addition to

EXHIBIT 10.6   Examples of Cost Drivers

Driver Name	Driver Quantity	Cost per Driver	Estimated Costs
Machine hours	3,000	$500	$15,000
Trips	20	$10,000	$200,000
New hires	10	$ 5,000	$50,000

EXHIBIT 10.7   Other Examples of Revenue and Cost Drivers

Revenue Drivers	Cost Drivers
Number of new customers	Number of machine hours or labor hours
Number of orders by type	Number of full-time equivalents (FTEs) by level
Number of new contracts	Number of trips
Number of renewed contracts	Number of products produced
Number of billable hours by resource type	Number of shipments by type of customer
Number of revenue miles	Gallons of fuel or other raw materials

implementing these best practices along the process dimension, companies should implement best practices from an organization perspective as well.

The tremendous amount of time dedicated to documenting business processes has made companies keenly aware of the benefits of redesigning and reengineering business processes. These benefits have included a reduction in cycle time and costs as well as increases in quality. Along with a well-documented forecasting process, one of the more salient forecasting best practices from an organization perspective is to have clearly defined roles and responsibilities. Although this best practice may sound like a simple and commonsense statement, many organizations do not have clearly defined processes and/or organizational roles and responsibilities specific to the forecasting process.

Although the finance organization may manage the overall forecasting process, such as consolidating results, operational and financial data from the other organizations are very important. Specifically, the forecasting process involves capturing both operational and financial data from many organizations, including sales, operations, manufacturing, finance, and distribution, to name a few. Additionally, the introduction of Web-based budgeting and forecasting applications has greatly expanded the roles of managers from these other organizations as they support the forecasting process. In an April 2002 issue of *Business Finance* magazine, the article "Birth of a New Budgeting Culture"[1] contains several examples of the impact to the organization's culture caused by redesigning budgeting and forecasting processes and implementing enabling systems. Clearly, the introduction of new processes and systems has increased the responsibilities of managers who support the forecasting process.

The expanded responsibilities for managers who support the forecasting process can create other problems. Specifically, these managers may lack the appropriate finance and accounting skills required for the forecasting process. The implementation of new processes and technology will not accomplish the goals of improving the reliability of the forecasted information if the gaps in skills are not addressed. Therefore, after identifying the gaps, companies have to provide appropriate training to the managers to ensure that they possess the proper skills, including training in financial modeling and analytical techniques. Both finance and human resources organizations should play a key role in developing training for the organization.

---

[1]   Tad Leahy, "Birth of a New Budget Culture," *Business Finance* (April 2002): 31–34.

EXHIBIT 10.8 Sample Roles and Responsibilities Matrix

Position/Role	Responsibilities	Key Skills
Sales and Operations Analyst • Support the company's forecasting process to improve the accuracy and reliability of the financial information.	• Gather operational (e.g., orders, machine hours, etc.) and financial data to support the development of the company's forecast. • Input or load operational and financial data into the forecast model. • Analyze revenue and cost results. • Provide a written and oral explanation of results as required. • Produce ad hoc reports and analyses as requested.	• Experienced functional analyst • Good oral and written communication skills • Knowledge of accounting and finance processes, policies, and procedures • Knowledge of company's sales and/or operational processes • Cross-functional process focus • Knowledge of company's accounting, financial, and operational systems • Ability to use MS Office products, including spreadsheets

A high-level description of the roles, key responsibilities, and skills/knowledge requirements is included in Exhibit 10.8. As indicated in the exhibit, the sales and operational analysts are responsible for gathering operational and financial data and then modeling the data to develop the forecast. These analysts should have a working knowledge of the company's processes, policies, and procedures as well as the forecasting application. Additionally, good oral and written communication skills are required for this role.

Exhibit 10.8 provides the reader with a sample of roles, responsibilities, and key skills. The development of roles, responsibilities, and key skills should be tailored to the company's specific organizational and human resource requirements.

In summary, the development of clearly defined roles and responsibilities is imperative to implementing a best-practices forecasting process. The company should assess the new roles and responsibilities required by the people in the organizations who will support the forecasting process. Gaps in skill sets should be addressed through proper training prior to the implementation of new forecasting software.

FORECASTING BEST PRACTICES: TECHNOLOGY

So far, we have covered forecasting best practices from a process and organization dimension. From a process perspective, implementing a rolling forecast and using a driver-based approach are two important practices to improve the forecasting process. From an organization perspective, the company needs to clearly define the roles and responsibilities required to effectively execute the forecasting process. Any gaps in required skill sets should be addressed through proper training. Implementing best practices from both a process and organization dimension should provide the company with more timely, accurate, and reliable forecasting information.

Along with implementing best practices for forecasting from a process and organization perspective, companies should also implement best practices from a technology perspective. A number of companies have implemented new technology without leveraging the full return on investment (ROI) from the new technology. Costly implementations of transaction-based and analytical systems without good returns on ROI are well documented in business literature. Often these companies do not develop a good process and/or an organizational design prior to implementing technology. Some companies have viewed technology as the panacea to what may be just plain-vanilla process and/or organizational problems. According to Hackett Best Practices, approximately 30 percent of benefits are lost without integrating process, organization, and technology improvement efforts.[2] In other words, mere process improvement without organizational or technology changes may not help the company achieve relevant benefits.

In simple terms, technology should be viewed as an enabler of the process. Some companies can effectively forecast using spreadsheets if they have good processes and clearly defined organizational roles and responsibilities. However, implementing more robust integrated technology beyond spreadsheets provides a better forecasting solution for the vast majority of larger companies with diverse products and services, multiple geographic territories, multiple currencies, and numerous financial and nonfinancial systems.

Although the forecasting solution should be tailored to address the specific business and process requirements of the company, a best-practices approach to forecasting should integrate technology. In other words, the data required to support the business requirements for forecasting should be integrated with the forecasting application. Exhibit 10.9 presents a high-level example of an integrated forecasting approach. As indicated in the exhibit, both operational and financial data are loaded into the forecasting application. In Exhibits 10.5, 10.6, and 10.7 examples of operational data were provided to support a driver-based forecasting model. As discussed earlier, the operational data are sourced from various systems throughout the company. For example, sales orders are captured in the ordering system and machine hours are captured in the manufacturing operational systems. Financial data are primarily captured in the company's general ledger (GL) system. Both operational and financial data are loaded into the company's forecasting application, as shown in Exhibit 10.9. The company's forecasting application contains the rules or algorithms for calculating the forecasting results. Finally, users should be able to access the data via Web-enabled robust online analytical processing (OLAP) reporting tools and thereby produce standard, ad hoc, and/or customized reports. It is important to note that information should be placed in the hands of the users.

Several technology choices available in the marketplace provide real-time forecasting solutions for businesses. These solutions range from purchasing package applica-

---

[2] Answerthink's Hackett Best Practices, *Strategic Decision Making 2002 Book of Numbers*, 2002.

tions, which combine data extraction, transformation, and loading (ETL) tools along with data warehousing capabilities, to developing customized business intelligence solutions with best-of-breed software purchased from leading vendors. Additionally, standalone package applications with built-in forecasting functionality are available from leading vendors. A thorough assessment of the company's forecasting business requirements and ability of the vendor's package to meet these requirements is necessary prior to the purchase and implementation of new technology.

CONCLUSION

In summary, businesses will continue to encounter recessions and experience unexpected events that impact financial performance. Therefore, implementing key best practices for forecasting from a process, organization, and technology dimension can improve the accuracy and reliability of forecasted information. A rolling forecast provides management with a forward-looking and continuous planning process that is aligned with the true nature of their business cycle. Additionally, this information is useful for supporting the annual budgeting process. Leveraging a driver-based approach to forecasting provides the linkage of operational measures to financial performance. In this way, the company can focus on the true drivers of revenues and costs rather than merely completing a financial exercise. As noted, some of the driver-based data are available on a real-time basis within the company. Both of these process best practices help align the forecasting process to the strategic goals and objectives of the company. More specifically, these drivers are often leading indicators of future performance. Developing

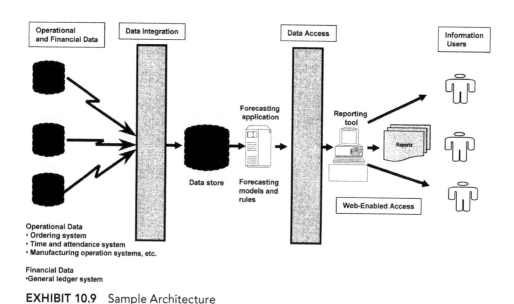

EXHIBIT 10.9 Sample Architecture

clear roles and responsibilities is also a key to effectively executing the forecasting process. As discussed, training should be provided as necessary to ensure managers possess the appropriate skills to support the forecasting process. Finally, technology that integrates both operational and financial systems with the forecasting system should enable the new process. The proliferation of robust analytical systems, especially in the planning and forecasting areas, provides users with several options from leading vendors.

Going forward, the need for greater disclosure of financial information and improvements in forecasting accuracy will continue as a necessary requirement for investors in both privately owned and publicly traded companies. Companies should continue to look at implementing best practices to improve their forecasting processes.

CHAPTER ELEVEN

Calculations and Modeling in Budgeting Software

Paul Barber
President, PROPHIX Software Inc.

 **INTRODUCTION**

Nearly every company that acquires a budgeting software product is doing so because of the limitations of spreadsheets. Most of these limitations are associated with data management, reporting, or workflow. However, there are also major differences between the ways calculations are performed in spreadsheets and in budgeting applications. This chapter discusses how calculations are performed in general ledger systems, spreadsheets, and best-of-breed budgeting products, and explains the benefits of the latter.

WHY COMPANIES USE BUDGETING SOFTWARE

The first uses of computers by accounting and finance departments were associated with automating manual accounting systems. Accounting systems were developed to handle large volumes of transactions, such as accounts payable invoices and sales orders. Later, other applications, such as material requirements planning and human resources were added to automate the other high-volume applications needed by any modern business. Eventually, the whole bundle of applications was renamed the enterprise resource planning (ERP) system.

The general ledger has always been different from the other modules in either an accounting system or an ERP system. Although it was needed to tie together all the other components, it was not just a mechanism for storing and processing large volumes of transactions. The general ledger had to do other things, such as perform calculations and produce analytical reports that were not simply listings of invoices or orders.

In the 1980s, the spreadsheet came along. It was the answer to the accountant's dream; data from the general ledger could be exported to a spreadsheet and massaged, recalculated, and formatted to produce almost any report imaginable.

It was also possible to use a spreadsheet for planning. This was a natural evolution; once the historical data from the general ledger were available, it was easy to use this information as a basis for forecasting the future.

Everything was fine for a while, but three phenomena have made the spreadsheet unsuitable as a platform for planning and budgeting:

1. *Increased volume of information.* Historically, the data volumes and data structure of the general ledger remained fairly simple. However, as ERP and accounting software have become more sophisticated, accountants have needed to plan for more accounts in more cost centers. This means that management of all the budgeted and historical information has become a major issue since spreadsheets are not good at data management. An integral part of this job is the consolidation of data from many (often thousands of) departments or cost centers.

2. *Increased participation of departmental managers in the planning process.* In the past, their involvement in many companies had been quite minimal, with most of the work being done by corporate accountants. However, the downsizing trend in the mid-1990s meant that top-heavy, centralized finance departments became unfashionable—in many companies, the onus of budget preparation has increasingly fallen on departmental management. The finance department is less the source of the numbers in the budget and instead has become more the orchestrator of the budget, responsible for managing workflow in a multiuser environment. Therefore, a need has arisen for multiuser budgeting software.

3. *Increased frequency of planning.* Years ago, the budget was produced annually and, once approved by the board, was cast in stone. All managers had to run their departments based on plans that, by year-end, might have been formulated as much as 18 months previously. Today, many companies create reforecasts throughout the year. An event like 9/11 changed economic expectations worldwide, and every company needed to immediately incorporate this in its plans. Rolling forecasts, concertina planning, and quarterly reforecasts are becoming standard; these techniques all increase the workflow and data management requirements associated with planning. The finance department needs software that is more flexible than spreadsheets and enables it to quickly and easily create new plans and new versions of plans.

This need is met by *budgeting software,* which is nearly always acquired by companies that want to perform multidepartmental, multiuser planning more effectively than they can with spreadsheets. It is not unusual for a budgeting software solution to reduce the effort required for the annual budgeting process (in, say, person-days) by factors of 2, 3, or 4 when compared with spreadsheets. This means that financial professionals will be able to spend more time analyzing the company's plans instead of copying data between worksheets or maintaining complicated spreadsheet-based systems.

Budgeting software occupies a unique niche between the data management world of accounting systems (or ERP systems) and the calculation world of spreadsheets. For a financial professional who is moving from spreadsheets to a best-of-breed budgeting system, it is important to understand the differences in the ways numbers are calculated. Some of the differences between spreadsheets and accounting systems are summarized in Exhibit 11.1.

A budgeting system combines the multiuser data management and consolidation features of a general ledger with the calculation and ease-of-use features of a spreadsheet. It might be argued that ease of use is not important for a budgeting application since it is a corporate multiuser system and therefore should be designed and built like any large computer application. This process typically includes specifications, a development cycle, and a finished application that is developed by information technology (IT) professionals and delivered to the finance department for them to use.

In reality, nothing could be further from the truth. Economic conditions, government legislation, market opportunities, and corporate strategy are constantly changing. It would be totally impractical if every spreadsheet model used in the finance department needed to be developed by IT staff. It is just as essential that a budgeting system can be implemented directly by finance staff, and therefore ease of use is paramount.

CALCULATIONS IN ACCOUNTING SYSTEMS AND SPREADSHEETS

Obviously, not all accounting systems work the same way, but they typically have very basic calculation facilities in the general ledger. Usually calculations are performed as

	Accounting Systems	**Spreadsheets**
# of users	Multiuser	Single User
Strengths	Management of large volumes of data securely and efficiently	Ease-of-use and calculation power
Consolidation capability	Enabling input of many detailed transactions (e.g., invoices) and rolling-up data to total levels	None inherent— implemented with calculation formulas
Complexity of calculations	Very simple roll-up of data	Calculation of almost anything that can be defined using formulas

EXHIBIT 11.1 Comparison of Accounting Systems and Spreadsheets

Account	Account Type	Data Stored	Aggregating Data	Adjusting Signs	Calculating Ratios
Sales	Credit	(200)	(200)	200	200
Costs	Debit	150	150	150	150
Profit	Credit		**(50)**	50	50
% Margin					**25%**

EXHIBIT 11.2   Steps Used in a Typical Accounting System to Produce Reports

part of a report definition. An archetypical general ledger labels each account as a credit account or a debit account. Credits are held as negative numbers and debits as positive. Reporting might consist of the next steps, which are illustrated in Exhibit 11.2:

▪ Aggregating stored account values together (so credits cancel out debits)
▪ Adjusting the sign for credits accounts (so sales appear positive)
▪ Calculating ratios, and so on

The calculations available in most general ledgers are very limited and usually part of the reporting process. Even then, many general ledger vendors depend on bought-in report writers for calculating ratios and formatting. Many companies that own online analytical processing (OLAP)–based budgeting systems use them for monthly variance reporting because of the limited reporting available in their general ledger.

Calculations in spreadsheets are totally different. The cell-based calculation paradigm almost defines what we mean by a spreadsheet and should be familiar to all finance professionals. However, it is important to realize that there is a second way of performing calculations in a spreadsheet: with macros.

From a calculation perspective, macros are a way of manipulating large volumes of data. For example, a macro can be built that copies data from one worksheet to another and then increases the data by a certain percentage. Macros are procedural, which means that the user determines the order of calculation, and they also have the look and feel of a programming language. Most spreadsheet users do not use macros because they can be difficult to use; using spreadsheet macros is a bit like using a low-level programming language.

BUDGETING SOFTWARE

The most basic type of budget is a simple aggregation of expenses, but most companies use their budgeting software for more than this. Even though preparing the annual budgets might be the justification for product acquisition, budgeting software is usually used also for other, more analytical purposes. These include:

▪ Balance sheet and cash flow planning
▪ Depreciation of planned capital additions
▪ Multicurrency planning

- Monthly reforecasting
- Variance reporting and analysis
- Overhead allocations
- Activity-based planning

Many of these uses are analytical in nature and sometimes involve quite sophisticated calculations. We discuss some of these in greater detail later.

It is important to be aware that there are many products available that claim to be budgeting products but which have very limited functionality. For example, some products are little more than a technology for interfacing spreadsheets to a general ledger database; the user (or the budget administrator) can download data for a cost center from the accounting system, calculate plans using the spreadsheet, and upload data into the budget "bucket" in the general ledger. Products like these use spreadsheet calculations for individual cost centers and the general ledger calculations for consolidating data and reporting, but they lack functionality such as workflow and are limited by the data storage capacity of the general ledger—many accounting systems can hold only one budget version instead of, say, multiple forecasts. Such products are little more than a way of transferring data between the accounting system and a spreadsheet. A best-of-breed budgeting product is highly flexible and adds a lot more value.

This chapter describes the functionality of budgeting software with which the author is familiar. However, not all budgeting software products perform calculations in the same way and there is a great deal of variety.

The major calculation differences between budgeting software and spreadsheets are these:

- In a spreadsheet, data and calculations are both entered into a cell. However, a budgeting system separates calculations from data. This means that the same calculations can be used with different data. For example, an original budget and a revised budget can use identical calculations and these calculations will need to be entered only once. A single calculation definition in a budgeting system can apply to a large number of entities—for example, across all months and all cost centers. There is no more laborious copying of calculations between cells and checking to make sure that the generated calculations are what you really want.
- In a budgeting system, calculations can be easily documented and printed. This is a major benefit over spreadsheets, where it is usually impossible to document calculations effectively.
- In a spreadsheet, consolidating data across departments is done using regular cell calculations. Budgeting software typically does this differently, using a different language to define financial consolidations. Ideally, a budgeting system should use an OLAP database for consolidating data (discussed in detail later). OLAP databases are fast at consolidating data and also have major benefits in data management and reporting.

The types of calculations used in a budgeting system can be classified as:

- *Consolidation.* This is where data from multiple cost centers, business units, products, or departments are added together to give a company total. There may be hundreds or thousands of entities that need to be aggregated.
- *Modeling.* Most financial professional professionals have used spreadsheets for creating simple models. Within the scope of a budgeting system, users can create a model that will automatically be applied to multiple entities.
- *Processes.* Processes are used to manipulate large quantities of data. Processes can be used to import data, perform allocations, initialize data values, or copy data between planning versions.

OLAP DATABASES

Because of the consolidation and analytical requirements of budgeting, most high-end budgeting products use an OLAP database; therefore, it is useful to understand how OLAP databases work. Most computer applications store data in relational databases that are optimized for data storage and data-throughput capacity. Nearly all ERP systems use relational databases. OLAP databases are different. OLAP databases have a built-in capability for consolidation and calculation that is much more powerful than the relational model. The data in an OLAP database are stored in structures called *dimensions.*

In a straightforward expense budgeting application, the dimensions are:

- *Time.* Months roll up to quarters that roll up to years.
- *Organization.* Cost centers roll up into departments that roll up to total company.
- *Versions.* There may be multiple versions of the budget. Typically these are not aggregated.
- *Accounts.* Simple account calculations are just cost roll-ups, but more sophisticated examples include calculating ratios, such as % margin.

OLAP databases are designed to perform calculations that, at the most basic level, involve aggregating or consolidating data based on their dimensional structure. That is why OLAP databases are ideal for budgeting applications. OLAP technology originated with large-scale marketing applications, where sales order data was stored in dimensions for products, customers, and sales channel. In these applications, the only calculation requirement is simple aggregation. However, in a budgeting system, the calculations may be more complex; if they involve anything more than simple aggregation, the results may be ambiguous. For example, if we have these two calculations defined:

Total Company = East + West
% Margin = Profit/Sales

the value calculated for % margin at the total company level is ambiguous, because it depends on the order of calculation. As illustrated in Exhibit 11.3, it could be either

First calculation

	West	East	Total Company	
Sales	100	200	300	Second calculation
Profit	50	75	125	
% Margin	50%	38%	???	

EXHIBIT 11.3   Order of Calculation required of % Margin Calculation

the sum of the % margin values for the East and West cost centers (88 percent) or the % margin calculated at the total company level using the sum of the sales and profit figures (125/300 or 42%). Obviously in this case we want to use the latter calculation. We want first to sum the sales and profit figures and then to calculate % margin.

However, there is no single, right way of determining the order of calculations. If the formulas are

Total Company = East + West
Revenue = Price * Volume

then the desired order of calculation is different because we want to first calculate revenues for East and West and then, as illustrated in Exhibit 11.4, add the calculated revenues together (instead of first adding the volumes and prices for East and West and then calculating revenues for the total company by multiplying these together). In fact, in this case, the definition of price for the total company is not simply just the sum of the East and West prices but the average price, which will be calculated to be revenue/volume for the total company (a third calculation).

This illustrates that OLAP databases are not only very powerful and sophisticated; when it comes to performing calculations, they are also complex enough that it is quite easy to use them incorrectly. Because of this, OLAP budgeting software products can demand a great deal of implementation help and customization in order to get them to work effectively. It is therefore very important to purchase software that makes it easy for finance professionals to define calculations like those shown without having to invest a great deal either in training internal staff or in paying external consultants for customization.

First calculation

	West	East	Total Company	
Price	5	6	???	Third calculation
Volume	1,000	500	1,500	
Revenue	5,000	3,000	8,000	

Second calculation

EXHIBIT 11.4   Order of Calculation Required for Revenue and Price Calculations

MODELING AND BUDGETING

To appreciate the differences between modeling and budgeting, it is useful to understand procedural and nonprocedural calculation methods. Spreadsheet cell formulas and spreadsheet macros illustrate the difference between procedural and nonprocedural calculations.

Spreadsheet *formulas* are nonprocedural, which means the user does not need to specify the order in which they are calculated; it does not matter in which order the calculations are entered in the spreadsheet since the spreadsheet program works out the correct order of calculation based on the dependencies between the cells—if cell A1 refers to cell Z99, then Z99 is automatically calculated first.

However, spreadsheet *macros* are procedural—the user specifies not only the calculation formulas but also the order in which they are calculated. For example, copying last year's actual data into this year's plan and then increasing it by 10 percent is very different from increasing this year's plan by 10 percent and then overwriting it with last year's actual data.

Nonprocedural calculations might appear to be a lot easier to use, but they have a downside too. The major drawback is that every value to be calculated must be completely defined in one single formula. For simple formulas, this is quite easy, but for more complex calculations, the formulas can get very complicated and difficult to understand.

To illustrate the difference between procedural and nonprocedural calculations, let us consider the calculation of taxes that are 25 percent of operating profit less depreciation up to a maximum of $1,000. Procedurally, this could be calculated as:

Taxes = (operating profit – depreciation) * 25%
If taxes < 0 then taxes = 0
If taxes > 1000 then taxes = 1000

The procedural version depends on the order of the statements being calculated. However, it contains the expression being calculated only once and is relatively easy to understand. The nonprocedural formula might be:

Taxes = If (operating profit – depreciation) * 25% < 0 then 0
Else if (operating profit – depreciation) * 25% > 1000 then 1000
Else (operating profit – depreciation) * 25%

The expression being calculated is defined in three places and, if any of these is wrong, the results will be unpredictable. The nonprocedural version is like a complex spreadsheet formula with multiple IF functions. Anyone who has used a spreadsheet to create a large model knows that formulas can get very long and, when the formulas need to be copied to many different cells, it can be difficult to understand whether the correct formula is in each cell. In fact, certain calculations cannot be properly defined nonprocedurally. An example is days-of-sales calculations where an accounts receivable balance is expressed in days of historical sales.

The difference between procedural and nonprocedural calculations might not appear to be very important, but it illustrates one difference between financial modeling and budgeting. At its simplest level, a *budget* consists of forecasting every "input" account in company's general ledger. Creating a budget involves forecasting some accounts, perhaps based on prior years' experience, collecting other information from cost center managers, and consolidating the data across accounts and cost centers. Because budgeting is a series of processes, it is inherently procedural; before sales forecasts can be adjusted at the corporate level, individual sales managers will first need to enter them. A *financial model* is a simulation of how the general ledger accounts are related, based on certain assumptions. A simple assumption might be that, for every dollar spent on product sales, customers will spend a dollar on associated services. These assumptions can get quite sophisticated, so that the actual number of accounts for which data need to be entered (input accounts) are quite small and most accounts are calculated. To quickly see the effect of a change in one of the input accounts, financial models are usually nonprocedural. Spreadsheets are ideal for financial modeling.

Another difference between budgeting and financial modeling is the number of people involved. For all companies over a certain size, budgeting is a multiuser process, usually involving managers who submit sales and expense forecasts. Modeling is usually performed by a single person who understands the details of the financial model and who can change the calculations if required.

In practice, budgeting software will include a modeling component. For example, it may be decided that branch managers will enter a forecast of units sold for each product and that both revenues and direct costs will be calculated. Also, a budgeted balance sheet will normally be calculated from the consolidated income statement. However, a budgeting software product is more than just modeling; it is a multiuser system that also manages the collection and consolidation of data.

In the modeling component of a budgeting system, nonprocedural calculations are highly desirable. However, budgeting is a process, so it is also important to perform calculations and other processes procedurally. Therefore, best-of-breed budgeting software will include both a nonprocedural modeling component and a procedural process manager. Both models and processes should be easily created and maintained by financial staff.

PROCESSES

The processes used in budgeting include importing data, performing allocations, copying data between versions, and checking in data supplied by a user into the main model. Not all processes involve calculations. However, even importing data will change the values in the budgeting model and hence has the same effect as a procedural calculation.

Sometimes it may not be clear whether a calculation is a modeling calculation or a process calculation. For example, consider the allocation of overheads. The modeling way of allocating overheads might involve defining the amount to be allocated in the following formula, which will be calculated for all departments:

Allocated IT overhead = IT expenses * # of PCs / total # of PCs

Here, the allocation driver (or cost driver) is the number of personal computers in each department. The "total" figures are the total amounts for the entire company. For a small model, this might be a feasible calculation, and this is the way it would probably be calculated in a spreadsheet.

A procedural approach does not attempt to instantly calculate the allocated values as data change. Instead, it is assumed that the budget administrator knows when data have changed (when, e.g., data have been imported or checked in from a user) and he or she will run a process to perform the allocation. The process might be defined as:

Allocate "IT expenses" from the IT department to all other departments using "# of PCs" as an allocation driver.

This process might be one of a series of processes that are run together. For example, when monthly actual data are read in from the general ledger, a series of allocations can be run, data can be consolidated, and so on.

It might seem that there is not much to choose between the two approaches to performing calculations. However, with the modeling approach, every time the IT expenses change or the number of PCs in any department changes, the formula needs to be recalculated for all cost centers. This might work in a spreadsheet, where all data are held in random access memory, but for a large model, where data are stored on disk, constantly recalculating the formula can be prohibitively slow.

Generally speaking, the process approach is easier to implement, easier to maintain, and easier to modify. This does not mean that modeling is not required, but it should be complemented by a powerful yet easy-to-use process manager.

MORE COMPLEX BUDGETING CALCULATIONS

The issues previously identified are an overview of the different calculation approaches available in modern budgeting software and their associated benefits. In practice, other, more complex calculation capabilities are needed to adequately budget for a company of any size. These include:

▪ *Calculations that vary by data version.* An example might be when, in the budget model, "% costs" is entered in order to calculate "costs," but, when analyzing historical actual data, "% costs" is calculated as a metric to be used in planning (see Exhibit 11.5). This is also a common requirement for when a budgeting model is used for monthly (or quarterly) reforecasting—very often a forecast does not need to be as detailed as an annual budget and so, instead of users entering detailed data, many values will be calculated.

▪ *Balance sheet and cash flow calculations.* These are typically more complex than the types of calculation needed for the income statement. A very common requirement

History Months			Plan Months	
Value	Calculation Method	Account	Value	Calculation Method
1,000	Imported from G/L	Sales	1,500	Input by user
750	Imported from G/L	Costs	1,050	Calculated ("sales" × "% Costs")
75%	Calculated ("costs"/"sales")	% Costs	70%	Input by budget administrator

EXHIBIT 11.5 Illustration of Different Calculations for History Months and Plan Months

is to restrict these calculations to part of the model structure. For example, "personnel expenses" might be calculated for all departments, but a balance sheet account such as "cash in bank" only be calculated (and stored) only for "head office."

▪ *Depreciation.* Most companies will have a fixed assets system that will calculate depreciation for existing assets. However, a budgeting software product will need to plan capital additions and the associated depreciation.

▪ *Allocations.* Allocating data between departments, product lines, or business units is a standard financial analytical method. Activity-based costing and activity-based planning involve performing sophisticated allocations and can be implemented with many budgeting software products. But even if a company does not want to make the investment for true activity-based planning, allocation calculations can be used for fully absorbed costing models, calculating standard costs, and other analytical techniques.

▪ *Time conversion methods.* Budgeting systems will typically hold data for each month. When reporting for a different time period, an annual or quarterly value needs to be calculated. Most data (e.g., "sales," "costs") will be calculated by summation (Q1 is the sum of January, February, and March). Other data (e.g., "cash in bank," "headcount") will be calculated by taking the last value (Q1 "cash in bank" is the same as March "cash in bank"), the average of the months, or simply calculating a formula based on other accounts. Exhibit 11.6 shows a selection of time conversion methods.

Account	Jan. Value	Feb. Value	Mar. Value	Q1 Value	Time Conversion Method
Sales	100	250	375	725	Sum
Cash	1,078	1,903	1,245	1,245	Last
Headcount	12	16	20	16	Average
Sales per employee	8.33	15.62	18.75	45.31	Calculated (= "sales"/"headcount")

EXHIBIT 11.6 Illustration of Time Conversion Methods

- ※ *Currency conversion.* Planning for entities with multiple currencies is a common requirement. Plans can be entered in a variety of different currencies and converted into a single "reporting" currency using different exchange rates for different accounts, and finally, currency conversion adjustments need to be calculated to keep the accounts in balance.
- ※ *Recalculating accounts at consolidated levels.* A common calculation requirement is to have a value such as "price" entered for cost centers and then recalculated at a higher level in the consolidation structure. At higher levels, "price" would be calculated to be the average price across all cost centers.

These more sophisticated types of calculations may make budgeting software appear complicated and difficult to understand. However, best-of-breed budgeting software not only will include all these features but also will be easy to implement. It is precisely because these more complex calculations are built in that companies use budgeting software instead of reinventing the wheel with large spreadsheet models.

CONCLUSION

Compared with spreadsheets, budgeting software has major benefits in the way calculations are performed, and many best-of-breed budgeting systems use OLAP databases for speed and power of calculations. In budgeting software, a single calculation can apply to multiple entities, and the calculations can be easily documented. This means that a companywide budgeting model can be quickly and easily set up and maintained.

Whereas in a spreadsheet all calculations are defined and performed using a cell-based calculation paradigm, budgeting products typically perform calculations in different ways. These include defining dimensional structures to consolidate data across business entities such as departments, product lines, or cost centers; creating business models that apply to multiple entities; and running processes that manipulate potentially large amounts of data within and between entities.

As well as basic income statement calculations, best-of-breed budgeting software will include functionality to perform much more complex calculations. It should be able to address balance sheet and cash flow forecasting as well as consolidating multiple currencies, depreciation on capital additions, calculations that vary by version and also allocations, including fully absorbed costing models and activity-based planning.

CHAPTER TWELVE

Cost-Accounting Systems: Integration with Manufacturing Budgeting

Paul D. Warner, PhD, LLM, CPA
Hofstra University

Edward Mendlowitz, CPA
WithumSmith+Brown

INTRODUCTION

The purpose of this chapter is to identify the basic cost-accounting system options available for accounting for the manufacturing costs of a company. A cost system is necessary for reliable product costing and pricing, the execution of plans and budgets, and timely management reporting of operations that permit cost control and the identification of cost-reduction opportunities. The various cost-accounting systems described in this chapter do not represent discrete alternatives; the cost-accounting system selected by a company frequently combines features of the various options.

A properly designed cost-accounting system should be integrated with the organization's structure and budgeting system. Budgets are structured according to area of responsibility and represent the financial implications of a plan; the cost-accounting system provides a system for reporting against the plan as well as for cost control over manufacturing operations.

Although this chapter does not discuss the other information systems within a manufacturing environment, the cost-accounting system must function in harmony with the systems depicted in Exhibit 12.1. Information needs and data collection required to maintain the cost-accounting system are dependent on and interact with other information systems.

The basic cost-accounting concepts addressed in this chapter relate to the control of costs associated with manufacturing a product. The costs of manufacturing a product are those costs used to measure inventory value on the balance sheet and the costs of

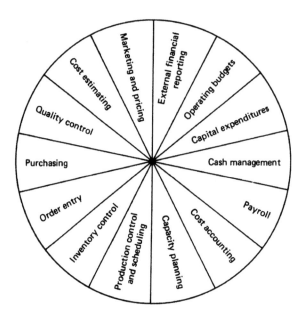

EXHIBIT 12.1   Manufacturing Information Systems

goods sold on the income statement. The total product cost includes the direct material and direct labor, and may include indirect manufacturing overhead costs.

By definition, *direct material* is material that is used directly in the product. *Direct labor* is the labor directly identified with producing a product. *Manufacturing overhead costs* are those indirect manufacturing costs necessary to the manufacturing process but not necessarily directly identified with a specific product or process. The manufacturing overhead costs associated with a product involve different conceptual considerations (variable [direct] versus full [absorption] costing) as well as the nature of the manufacturing process, the organization's structure, and the financial reporting system.

DECISION FACTORS IN THE SELECTION PROCESS

In order to obtain the benefits of the cost-accounting system selected, these factors should be evaluated before the cost system is designed and implemented:

■ Management philosophy and information requirements
■ The organization's structure
■ Control objectives of the company
■ Accounting system and accounting personnel capabilities
■ Detailed information available or required from the shop floor
■ Integration of detailed reporting for budgeting and cost control with other information requirements such as sales, production scheduling, inventory control, and purchasing

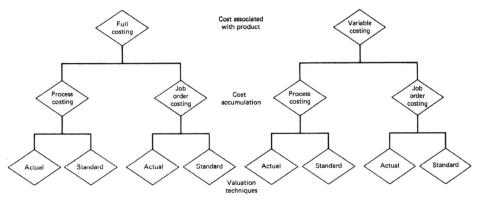

EXHIBIT 12.2 Cost-Accounting System Options

- External financial reporting requirements
- Nature of the manufacturing process
- Type of industry
- Costs/benefits of the various cost-accounting options

COST-ACCOUNTING SYSTEM OPTIONS

A cost-accounting system can be represented as a three-tier option tree, as depicted in Exhibit 12.2.

The first option is to determine the manufacturing costs to be included in product costing (variable versus full).[1] The second option is to determine the system to use in collecting the costs and in monitoring the flow of production (process versus job order). The last option to be selected is the valuation technique selected (actual versus standard). This chapter discusses each component of the cost accounting selection process—the options, purpose, advantages, disadvantages, and interrelationship with the budget process.

COSTS ASSOCIATED WITH A PRODUCT

The distinction between full (absorption) manufacturing costing and variable (direct) manufacturing costing is in the treatment of fixed manufacturing overhead. "Fixed costs" are defined as those costs that do not change over a substantial range of operations and/or for a given time span. For budgeting purposes, items such as property taxes, managers' salaries, and building depreciation normally constitute fixed costs. These items are essential and directly related to manufacturing operations; therefore, proponents of full costing believe that these costs should be included in the cost of the product. They tend to be related to capacity to produce rather than to the products.

---

[1] Internal Revenue Regulation 1.471–11 imposes other rules regarding the accumulation of product costs.

Variable costing is based on the concept that costs identified with a product should be only those costs that vary with the production activity. As in full costing, the cost of product includes direct material, direct manufacturing labor, and variable manufacturing overhead. (Variable manufacturing overhead normally includes employee fringe benefits, payroll taxes, supplies, machine maintenance, and other costs that vary in proportion with the level of operations.) Proponents of variable costing believe that fixed costs should be excluded from the product cost because they interfere with certain decision-making procedures.

LABOR COST

Labor costs include the actual payroll costs as well as taxes and every fringe benefit.

To begin a cost system for a company, you must first obtain a list of all the company's employees categorized by department and function, along with their annual pay or hourly rate, bonus structure, overtime policy, vacation, sick day, time off and holiday policy for that employee, and any other pay factors.

You then need to determine how many hours each employee gets paid for and how many he or she actually works. For example, an hourly paid employee might get paid for 40 hours per week for 52 weeks giving 2,080 hours that the employee is paid for. You should then calculate the days or hours the employee does not work. Taking the company's factors into account, you might come up with 240 of these 2,080 hours are not worked by an employee. Therefore, it will turn out that the employee might only work 1,840 hours while being paid for 2,080 hours.

If you are provided an annual base salary rather than an hourly rate, you can skip the total hours employees are paid for and start with the actual hours worked. This should be done for each employee.

The next step is to group the employees by department or function. This will give you the hourly rate for each department.

Once this is done, you should calculate overtime by department and in some cases individual employee. The overtime rates are determined based on information provided by the company as well as deriving the rates from company-supplied information.

You also should know the total number of hours worked overtime. This can be derived by dividing overtime paid by the premium pay factor. If overtime is paid at time and a half, then your factor is 1.5. Divide the total overtime pay by this factor to determine the hours worked. Now that you know how much overtime was paid and how many overtime hours were worked, you can calculate the total salary paid by adding overtime paid to the annual base.

You now want to find out the average cost per hour worked per department that offers overtime. This falls under the direct labor departments (excludes overhead, administration, and sales departments). First add together the annual base salaries per department to the overtime pay per department to determine the total salaries paid per department. For each department under direct labor, divide the total salary paid by the number of hours worked to determine cost per hour worked per department. For example, the average cost per hour worked of one department could be $28.39, while the average pay for overtime hours for that department could be $35, yielding the average pay per regular hours worked is $26.12.

The next schedule calculates the actual hours worked per year.

Total Hours Not Worked	**240**
Hours Paid Per Year:	2080
Less Hours Not Worked:	240
Equals Paid Hours Worked:	**1840**

Payroll Assumptions

	Widgets
Total Payroll as a % of Total Sales	32.4%
Average Pay Per Employee will be:	35000
Overtime as a % of Payroll	15%
FICA, % of Payroll	6.2%
Medicare, % of Payroll	1.45%
Unemployment Ins./Disability, fixed amount per employee	1000
Worker's Comp, % of Payroll	6%
Liability Insurance, % of Payroll	2%
Federal Unemp. Ins., fixed amount per employee	56

VARIABLE COSTING AND BUDGETING

Full costing and variable costing have a direct impact on the budgeting process. Using variable costing, the budget process must distinguish between fixed and variable costs so that capacity variances do not affect product costs.

The responsibility for control over manufacturing variable costs and fixed costs may rest with different functional areas within an organization. A responsibility budgeting system using variable costing must distinguish among variable costs, discretionary fixed costs, and committed costs.

Manufacturers' *variable costs* may be defined as those costs directly associated with producing an item as well as those costs that vary with the level of production activity. The common components are the direct material and direct labor required to produce an item and those manufacturing overhead costs that vary with the level of activity.

Discretionary fixed costs are costs reflecting periodic appropriations by management as determined during the budgeting process. These costs may include lease commitments and employee training programs.

Committed costs are those costs that are required to maintain the operating facilities of the company. Committed costs normally reflect capital budgeting decisions. For budgeting purposes, these items are represented by depreciation, property taxes, insurance, and top-level management salaries.

Variable costing is a logical extension of a responsibility and flexible budgeting and reporting system. Top management is responsible for profitability and therefore is ultimately responsible for all variable, committed, and discretionary costs incurred. In the short run, the department operating managers must control variable costs based on activity (production) levels.

Variable Overhead Manufacturing Costs and the Accounting Records

To maintain the distinction between variable and fixed costs, the chart of accounts must include two expense classifications—one for variable costs and one for fixed costs. Additionally, a department code is necessary to identify the department responsible for and/or controlling the cost.

Variable overhead manufacturing costs are charged directly to the department and expense classification. The source for the actual postings to the department account may be purchase register, material requisition, labor distribution, or journal entries.

Fixed costs are reallocated from the department, or cost center, that incurred them. Frequently, department activity ledgers are maintained as subsidiary ledgers to a manufacturing overhead control account(s) in the general ledger. The credit to the overhead control account is the application of overhead to work in process, based on a predetermined rate(s). The difference between actual charges and the applied amount represents overapplied or underapplied overhead. The concept of overhead and the procedures for applying overhead to product costing will be discussed later in this chapter. Although there are various alternative procedures for integrating responsibility budgeting with product costing, the basic objectives for accumulating manufacturing overhead are: (1) reporting costs to the appropriate responsibility center; (2) comparing actual cost to budgeted amounts and determining causes, if any, for variations; and (3) assigning manufacturing cost to the product (inventory).

Because fixed manufacturing costs are not charged to a product using a variable-costing system, they are reflected in the income statement as period expenses (i.e., they are charged off fully in the period incurred) during the accounting period. No determination of applied overhead is required.

Variable (Direct) Costing as a Management Tool

Variable (direct) costing is considered by many authorities as most useful for short-range planning. Application areas include short-term profitability planning and break-even analysis. Variable costing provides relevant management data regarding the effect of changes in production or sales mix, the effect of changes in pricing, the impact of volume on profitability, and the impact of variable-cost reductions brought about by increasing capacity costs (fixed) or vice versa.

Management asks such questions as: What happens to profit if we increase the sale of B and this reduces the sale of A? Should we accept the order at a reduced price during a period of less than full capacity operations? At full capacity, management needs variable-costing data in order to determine which product makes the largest contribution to profits. These orders normally should be given sales priority.

Additionally, variable costing can be used to compare actual profits to budgeted profit goals. There are four main conditions that contribute to the overall profitability of a manufacturing organization: sales volume, product mix, pricing level, and expense control.

Illustration of Product Profitability Analysis

The illustrations used in the exhibits in this section of the chapter depict the various profitability evaluation techniques available that use variable budgeting and costing techniques. The amount of detail used in the analysis depends on its intended use. For instance, the accuracy of product cost data necessary for strategic planning would not need to be as accurate or detailed as it would for cost estimating.

The mathematics of these analyses are relatively simple; however, the analytic process should be a continuous effort in which management constantly evaluates the potential for cost reduction or other procedures necessary for improving profitability. Additionally, the cost data should be constantly reviewed for reliability. Changes in the product structure, the manufacturing process, activity levels, costs, and cost relationships must be included in the analysis. Outside factors such as competitive forces and financial, market, production, and manpower constraints must also be considered.

The next analysis should be performed during each phase of the profit-planning and budgeting cycle, as depicted in Exhibit 12.3. During the profit-planning period, top management requires preliminary estimates to determine whether profitability will be in the range of established corporate goals, based on current or expected financial conditions.[2]

During the detailed budgeting process, the product cost information should be a logical and necessary extension of the process. Detailed product cost data developed during this period should provide data required for pricing decisions.

During the budgeting reporting period, actual results should be compared to budgeted product cost data. Any significant variation from budgets should be investigated, and, if necessary, product cost data must be adjusted to reflect current operating and economic conditions.

---

[2] Variable product cost data constitute one component of product cost considered during the profit-planning and budgeting process; however, some additional cost concepts also affect the profit-planning decision. Other costs useful for profit planning include: current or future investments in facilities, machinery, and equipment (out-of-pocket costs); the amount invested in tangible, productive assets or an intangible asset (sunk costs); costs that are directly associated with a product or product line (traceable), which can be variable, semi-variable, or fixed; costs associated with replacing current facilities, machinery, or equipment (replacement cost); the cost of alternative courses of action (opportunity costs); and costs that can be saved by selecting an alternative method (avoided) or postponed.

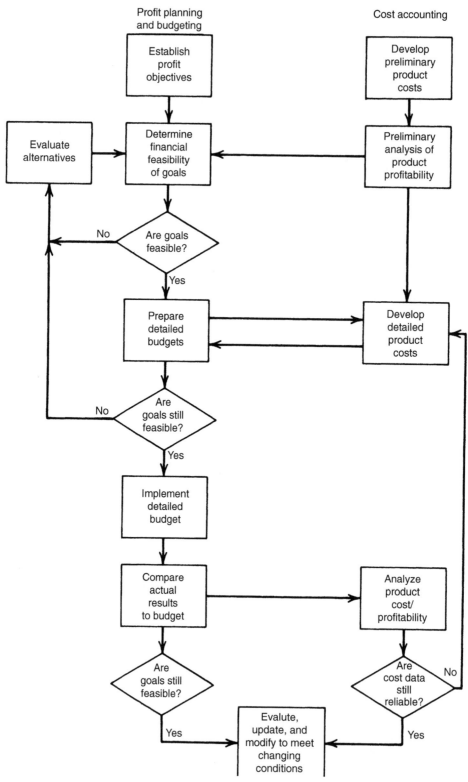

EXHIBIT 12.3   Cost-Accounting, Profit-Planning, and Budget Overview

EXHIBIT 12.4 Budget Data

Evaluation Technique	Product A		Product B
Sales			
Price per unit	$3.50		$8.25
Sales volume (units)	3,500		2,000
Cost per Unit			
Direct material	$0.75		$2.80
Direct labor	0.50		0.85
Variable manufacturing overhead	1.05		1.75
Total cost per unit	$2.30		$5.40
Other Budget Data			
Fixed manufacturing overhead		$3000	
Selling, general and administrative		$2200	
Production Statistics			
Practical capacity (units)	5,000		2,400
Budgeted volume (units)	3,800		2,100

In evaluating the results of operations for the budget period, the cost-accounting system must provide data that will allow comparison of the budget to the actual results of operations. The product cost variances must also be analyzed. The information in Exhibit 12.4 is used to illustrate the various evaluation techniques using variable costing.

Based on the budget data provided in Exhibit 12.4, budgeted income from operations is determined as shown in Exhibit 12.5.

EXHIBIT 12.5 Budgeted Results of Operations

Item	Amount
Sales	$28,750
Variable Manufacturing Costs	
Direct material	8,225
Direct labor	3,450
Variable overhead	7,175
	18,850
Contribution margin	9,900
Period Expenses	
Fixed manufacturing	3,000
Selling, general and administrative	2,200
	5,200
Income from Operations	$4,700

EXHIBIT 12.6 Actual Results of Operations

	Product A	Product B
Sales		
Price per unit	$3.40	$8.50
Sales volume (units)	4,125	1,390
Cost per Unit		
Direct material	$0.80	$3.00
Direct labor	0.50	0.90
Variable manufacturing overhead	1.10	1.60
	$2.40	$5.50
Period Expenses		
Fixed manufacturing	$3,400	
Selling, general and administrative	2,320	

The profit goal, as established during the planning or budgeting period, depends on volume, sales price, product mix, and cost. Any variance from planned operations will have an immediate impact on income from operations.

The original budget, shown in Exhibit 12.5, indicates that, with a sales volume of 3,500 units of product A and 2,000 units of product B, the contribution to period expenses will be approximately $9,900. Exhibit 12.6 shows what the actual results of operations are assumed to be.

EXHIBIT 12.7 Comparative Income Statement

	Budget		Actual		Over (Under) Budget	
	Amount	%	Amount	%	Amount	%
Sales	$28,750	100.0	$25,840	100.0	($2,910)	(10.1)
Cost of Goods Sold						
Direct material	8,225	28.6	7,470	28.9	(755)	(9.2)
Direct labor	3,450	12.0	3,314	12.8	(136)	(3.9)
Variable overhead	7,175	25.0	6,761	26.2	(414)	(5.8)
	18,850	65.6	17,545	67.9	(1,305)	(6.9)
Contribution margin	9,900	34.4	8,295	32.1	(1,605)	(16.2)
Period Expenses						
Manufacturing	3,000	10.4	3,400	13.2	400	13.3
Selling, general, and administrative	2,200	7.6	2,320	8.9	120	5.5
	5,200	18.0	5,720	22.1	520	10.0
Income from Operations	$4,700	16.4	$2,575	10.0	(2,125)	(45.2)

EXHIBIT 12.8   Profitability Analyses

	Product A	Product B	Total
A. *Sales Volume*			
Actual unit sales	4,125	1,390	
Budgeted unit sales	3,500	2,000[a]	
	625	(610)	
× Budgeted unit price	3.50	8.25	
	$2,188	$(5,032)	
B. *Sales Price*			
Actual unit price	$3.40	$8.50	
Budgeted unit price	3.50	8.25	
	(.10)	.25	
× Actual unit sales	4,125	1,390	
	$(413)	$347	
C. *Unit Cost*			
Budgeted unit cost	$2.30	$5.40	
Actual unit cost	2.40	5.50	
	(.10)	(.10)	
× Actual unit sales			
	4,125	1,390	
	$(412)	$(139)	
D. *Product Mix*			
Budgeted unit sales	3,500	2,000	
Actual unit sales	4,125	1,390	
	(625)	(610)	
× Budgeted unit cost	2.30	5.40	
	$(1,438)	$3,294	
E. *Summary*			
Sales volume	$2,188	($5,032)	($2,844)
Sales price	(413)	347	(66)
Unit cost	(412)	(139)	(551)
Product mix	(1,438)	3,294	1,856
Decrease in contribution margin	($75)	($1,530)	($1,605)
Fixed expenses over budget			(520)
Total decrease in income from operations			($2,125)

[a] Decrease in income from operations in parentheses.

A comparative operating statement, as illustrated in Exhibit 12.7, indicates that income from operations has declined, based on volume, price, and cost variances from budget.

The decline in income from operations is composed of the variations from budget, as shown in Exhibit 12.8.

The causes for these variations should be analyzed. Corrective management actions, if appropriate, can be made based on the analyses provided.

Other Uses of Variable Costing

Variable costing is an excellent tool for evaluating results of current operations in terms of comparison of actual results to budgets or plans. In addition, variable costing provides valuable information required for other management decisions. Selected uses for variable costing include:

- *Appraising alternative pricing or marketing strategies.* These decisions require knowledge of the change in the contribution margin as compared to the increase in sales volume.
- *Prioritizing customer orders or product orders when a company is at capacity.* Variable costing can assist in determining the product that makes the greatest contribution to profit. The greatest contribution to profit is determined by the unit contribution margin and the number of units that can be produced based on the available resources (i.e., operating hours).
- *Evaluating plant or production-line expansion or reduction programs.* Variable costing can assist in determining the effect of changes in volume on contribution to fixed operating costs.
- *Establishing market or sales strategies and/or determining sales commission rates.* Variable costing provides contribution margins necessary to ranking products by a profitability index. Those products with the largest unit dollar-contribution margin are normally ranked highest. Limited resources, such as operating capacity or market demand constraints, must also be considered.
- *Make versus buy decisions.* Management must be able to determine the variable and incremental costs associated with producing an item.
- *Short-run cost-control purposes.* Variable costs are considered controllable at the departmental operating levels. Variable-costing budget statements highlight variances from currently controllable costs.

Identifying Fixed Manufacturing Costs

There are problems encountered in determining which expenses are fixed and which are direct. Some expenses are easily recognized as fixed (e.g., real estate taxes); others as direct (e.g., direct materials); many, however, are mixed (e.g., plant heat and power). The simplest solution is to classify those that are product related as direct and those that are capacity dependent as fixed. Techniques are available for segregating the direct and fixed components of an expense. The effort involved is usually unwarranted.

The relationship between fixed and direct costs is best shown by the next problem:

The XYZ Company sells 100 units in April at a price of $10.00 per unit. Unit and total costs for the month are:

	Per Unit	Total for Month
Sales	$10.00	$1,000.00
Direct costs	6.00	600.00
Fixed costs	2.00	200.00
Total costs	8.00	800.00
Operating profit	$2.00	$200.00

How much would profits have increased in April if one additional unit had been sold? It depends on whether the fixed costs have been completely absorbed in the first 100 units sold.

Break-Even Relationship

One of the major benefits of direct costing is its ability to provide break-even analysis data for decision-making purposes. Although break-even data and the information listed are available from absorption costing, the effect of the absorbed fixed costs must be taken into consideration. The use of direct costing avoids this unnecessary work.

- Product decisions relative to sales mix and the establishment of our selling prices
- Procurement decisions relative to make versus buy decisions and plant capacity changes
- Marketing decisions relative to sales efforts, sales commissions, and other marketing matters
- Responsibility reporting based on controllable cost information

The next definitions are required in order to examine how the break-even relationship functions. Break-even analyses are graphically presented in Exhibits 12.9 and 12.10.

- The break-even (BE) point is reached when sales (S) covers just the sum of the direct costs (DC) and fixed costs (FC). Thus, at the BE point, there is no profit (P). The algebraic form is:

$$S = DC + FC + P, \text{ but since } P = 0 \text{ at the break-even point,}$$
$$\text{then } S_{(BE)} = DC + FC$$

- The contribution margin (CM) is defined as:

$$CM = S - DC = FC + P$$

- The profit-volume (P/V) relationship is defined as:

$$P/V = \frac{SP - VC}{SP}, \text{ where SP is defined as the selling price.}$$

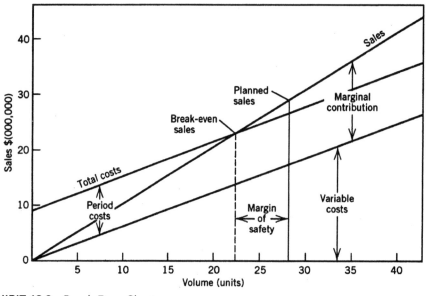

EXHIBIT 12.9   Break-Even Chart

▪ Gross profit (GP) is defined as:

$$GP = \frac{SP - (VC + FC)}{SP}$$

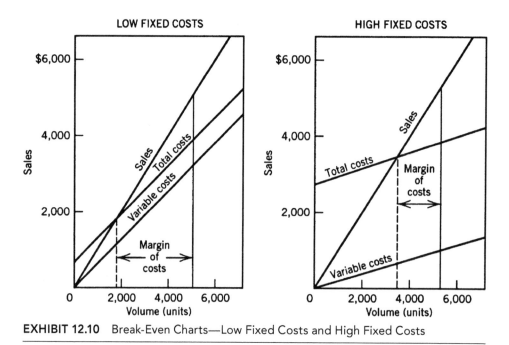

EXHIBIT 12.10   Break-Even Charts—Low Fixed Costs and High Fixed Costs

▪ The margin of safety (MS) is the difference between the average sales and the sales at break-even but only if the average sales is greater than the break-even sales, thus:

$$MS = \frac{\text{Av. Sales} - \text{BEP Sales}}{\text{Av. Sales}}$$

▪ The profit contribution (PC) is defined as:

$$PC = \frac{CM}{\text{Sales}}$$

▪ The profit-contribution ratio (PCR) is defined as:

$$PCR = \frac{PC}{\text{Sales}}$$

▪ Break-even sales in dollars $= \dfrac{FC}{PCR}$

Exhibit 12.10 shows the impact of fixed costs on the break-even point.

▪ Break-even sales in units $= \dfrac{FC}{PC/\text{unit}}$

The following shows the type of information available when direct costing is used. (Refer to Exhibits 12.11 to 12.14.)

A. The tentative profit plan (Exhibit 12.11) shows a proposed P/V of 24.3 percent and a return on investment (ROI) of 15.6 percent. (Operating profit + capital employed − 5,000/32,000 = 15.6%.) Plans are usually set up on this basis.

EXHIBIT 12.11   ABC Company—Tentative Profit Plan

($000 omitted)				
			Product Line	
	Total	A	B	C
Forecast sales	$70,000	$10,000	$20,000	$40,000
Variable cost of sales	53,000	5,000	14,000	34,000
Margin	$17,000	$5,000	$6,000	$6,000
P/V	24.3%	50%	30%	15%
Planned period				
Specific	$5,000	$1,500	$1,000	$2,500
Nonspecific	7,000	1,000	3,000	3,000
Total planned period	$12,000	$2,500	$4,000	$5,500
Operating profit	$5,000	$2,500	$2,000	500
% of Sales	7.4%	25%	10%	1.3%
Capital employed	$32,000	$10,000	$12,000	$10,000
% Return	15.6%	25%	16.7%	5%

EXHIBIT 12.12   ABC Company—Tentative Profit plan (Revision 1)

($000 omitted)

	Total	Product Line A	B	C
Forecast sales	$70,500	$13,500	$17,000	$40,000
Variable cost of sales	52,650	6,750	11,900	34,000
Margin	$17,850	$6,750	$5,100	$6,000
P/V	25%	50%	30%	15%
Planned period expense	$12,000			
Operating profit	$5,850			
% of Sales	8.3%			
Capital employed	$32,000			
% Return	18%			

EXHIBIT 12.13   ABC Company—Tentative Profit Plan (Revision 2)

($000 Omitted)

	Total	Regular A	Product Line DEF A	B	C
Forecast sales	$72,100	$13,500	$1,6000	$17,000	$40,000
Variable cost of sales	53,570	6,750	920	11,900	34,000
Margin	$18,530	$6,750	$680	$5,100	$6,000
P/V	25.7%	50%	42.5%	30%	15%
Planned period expense	$12,000				
Net Operating profit	$6,530				
% of Sales	8.8%				
Capital employed	$32,000				
% Return	20.4%				

B. The tentative profit plan also shows planned period costs (planned fixed costs) broken into specific and nonspecific categories.
   1. Specific planned period costs are fixed costs applicable to a given product line.
   2. Nonspecific planned period costs are fixed costs not applicable to any specific product line (e.g., corporate manufacturing expenses). These are allocated to product lines on some predetermined basis (e.g., estimated sales).
C. There are numerous changes possible once the basic plan is formulated. The basic plan (Exhibit 12.11) shows an ROI of 15.6 percent. Suppose the desired ROI is 20 percent (an operating profit of $6,400,000). What can be done?
   1. One possibility is to shift sales from product lines B and C to product line A. Such shifts would be explored by marketing. Exhibit 12.12 shows the effect of shifting sales from product line B (reduction of $3,000,000) to product line A

EXHIBIT 12.14   ABC Company—Tentative Profit Plan (Revision 3)

($000 Omitted)

	Total	Product Line			
		Regular A	DEF A	B	C
Forecast sales	$72,100	$13,500	$1,6000	$17,000	$40,000
Variable cost of sales	53,570	6,750	920	11,900	34,000
Margin	$18,530	$6,750	$680	$5,100	$6,000
P/V	25.7%	50%	42.5%	30%	15%
Planned period expense	11,722				
Operating profit % of Sales	$6,808				
	9.4%				
Capital employed	$32,000				
% Return	21.3%				

(increase of $3,500,000). The net effect is to increase both the margin and the operating profits by $850,000, thereby increasing the ROI to 18 percent. The improvement results from two factors:

(a) Increased profit margin—
    20% × $3,000,000 = $600,000
(b) Additional sales   250,000
    50% × $500,000 = $850,000

2. When capacity permits, special orders may be appropriate. Suppose customer DEF offered to buy $1,600,000 per annum of product line A if 24-hour delivery could be guaranteed. Suppose this could be achieved, but at an increase in the variable cost of sales. The results of this offer can be seen in Exhibit 12.13. The P/V has decreased to 42.5 percent, but both the margin and the net operating profit have increased by $680,000 with the result that the ROI has now increased to 20.4 percent. The desired ROI of 20 percent has been achieved.

3. Other possibilities for improvement exist. For example, a review of the planned period expense might reveal a potential savings in plant maintenance of $278,000 (Exhibit 12.14). Such an item is included as part of the fixed factory overhead, which is absorbed into the product costs under an absorption system. It tends to be lost unless it is isolated. Direct costing highlights such items by keeping them isolated.

The central issue in the absorption costing versus direct costing controversy is really a question of timing. The central question is: What is the proper timing for the release of fixed factory overhead as an expense: when incurred, or at the time the finished units to which the fixed overhead relates are sold?

The effect of this timing difference can be seen in Exhibit 12.15.

- When sales and production are in balance, direct- and absorption-costing methods yield the same profit. Under both methods, the amount of fixed cost incurred

EXHIBIT 12.15   Comparison of Direct Costing and Absorption Costing

Annual Statements					
Basic production date at standard cost:					
Direct materials		$1.30			
Direct labor		1.50			
Variable overhead		.20	$3.00		
Fixed overhead ($150,000 ÷ 150,000 unit denominator volume)			$1.00		
Total			$4.00		

Sales price, $5.00 per unit

Selling and administrative expense, assumed for simplicity as being all fixed, $100,000 per year

	First Year	Second Year	Third Year	Fourth Year	Four Years
Opening inventory in units	—	—	30,000	10,000	—
Production	150,000	170,000	140,000	150,000	610,000
Sales	150,000	140,000	160,000	160,000	610,000
Closing inventory in units	—	30,000	10,000	—	—
Direct costing:					
Sales	$750,000	$700,000	$800,000	$800,000	$3,050,000
Cost of goods manufactured	$450,000	$510,000	$420,000	$450,000	$1,830,000
Add opening inventory @ $3	—	—	90,000	30,000	—
Available for sale	$450,000	$510,000	$510,000	$480,000	$1,830,000
Deduct ending inventory @ $3	—	$90,000	30,000	—	—
Cost of goods sold	$450,000	$420,000	$480,000	$480,000	$1,830,000
Contribution margin	$300,000	$280,000	$320,000	$320,000	$1,220,000
Fixed factory overhead	(150,000)	(150,000)	(150,000)	(150,000)	(600,000)
Selling and administrative expense	(100,000)	(100,000)	(100,000)	(100,000)	(400,000)
Net operating income	$50,000	$30,000	$70,000	$70,000	$220,000
Absorption costing:					
Sales	$750,000	$700,000	$800,000	$800,000	$3,050,000
Cost of goods manufactured	$600,000	$680,000	$560,000	$600,000	$2,440,000
Add opening inventory @ $4	—	—	$120,000	$40,000	—
Available for sale	$600,000	$680,000	$680,000	$640,000	$2,440,000
Deduct ending inventory @ $4	—	$120,000	40,000	—	—

	First Year	Second Year	Third Year	Fourth Year	Four Years
Cost of goods sold	$600,000	$560,000	$640,000	$640,000	$2,440,000
Volume variance*	—	(20,000)	10,000	—	(10,000)
Adjusted cost of goods sold	$600,000	$540,000	$650,000	$640,000	$2,430,000
Gross margin	$150,000	$160,000	$150,000	$160,000	$620,000
Selling and administrative expense	100,000	100,000	100,000	100,000	$400,000
Net operating income	$50,000	$60,000	$50,000	$60,000	$220,000

* Computation of volume variance based on denominator volume of 150,000 units:
Second year $20,000 overapplied: (170,000 – 150,000) × $1.00
Third year 10,000 underapplied: (150,000 – 140,000) × $1.00
Four years combined $10,000 overapplied: (610,000 – 600,000) × $1.00

during the period is charged against revenue of the period. (See the first year in Exhibit 12.15.)

■ When the production exceeds sales (i.e., when in-process and finished inventories are increasing), absorption costing shows a higher profit than does direct costing. The reason is that, in absorption costing, a portion of the fixed manufacturing cost of the period is charged to inventory and thereby deferred to future periods. The total fixed cost charged against revenue of the period, therefore, is less than the amount of fixed cost incurred during the period. (See the second year in Exhibit 12.15.)

■ When sales exceed production (i.e., when in-process and finished inventories are decreasing), absorption costing shows a lower profit than does direct costing. Under absorption costing, fixed costs previously deferred in inventory are charged against revenue in the period in which the goods are sold. Total fixed costs charged against revenue, therefore, exceed the amount of fixed cost incurred during the period. (See the third and fourth years in Exhibit 12.15.)

■ When sales volume is constant but production volume fluctuates, direct costing yields a constant profit figure, because profit is not affected by inventory changes. Under the same circumstances, absorption costing yields a fluctuating profit figure, which will be directly affected by the direction and amount of the changes in inventories. (See the third and fourth years in Exhibit 12.15.)

■ If production volume is constant, profit moves in harmony with sales under either direct or absorption costing. The profit figures will move in the same direction but will not necessarily be the same in amount, because inventory costs that are carried over from period to period will be greater under absorption costing. (See the first and fourth years in Exhibit 12.15.)

■ The divergence between period profit figures computed by direct- and absorption-costing methods tends to be smaller for long periods than for short periods, because production and sales volume tend to approach equality over a long period. Thus, the difference between total profit figures computed by the two methods is usually smaller for a few years (taken together) than the difference between year-to-year profit figures. Over a period of years, the methods should give substantially the same result, because sales cannot continuously exceed production, nor can production continuously exceed sales.

■ Direct costing excludes fixed factory overhead from inventory. In formula form, the difference between net incomes of absorption and direct costing may be shown:

EXHIBIT 12.16　Managerial Cost Statement

Direct-Absorption Cost Co.			
For the Year Ended December 31, 20XX			
Net sales—at standard (Schedule I)	$32,250,000		
Direct cost of sales—at standard	21,000,000		
Contribution at standard	11,250,000		
Variances—sales (Schedule I)	198,000		
—direct costs (Schedule II)	462,000		
—contractor costs (Schedule II)	74,000		
Total variances	734,000		
Contribution at actual	10,516,000		
	Actual	**Variance**	**Budget**
Period Costs			
Factory overhead (Schedule III)	4,125,000	$(125,000)	$4,000,000
Selling expenses	2,726,000	(26,000)	2,700,000
General and administrative	1,205,000	(55,000)	1,150,000
Total period costs	8,056,000	$(206,000)	$7,850,000
Net profit before allocation of factory overhead to inventories	2,460,000		
Allocation of factory overhead to inventories (Schedule IV)	268,000		
Net profit absorption-cost method	2,728,000		
Other income and expenses	(31,000)		
Net profit before taxes	2,679,000		
Income taxes	1,300,000		
Net profit	$1,379,000		
Net increase in inventories during period (Schedule IV)—at standard	$1,500,000		

EXHIBIT 12.17   Net Sales Schedule

Direct-Absorption Cost Co.			
For the Year Ended December 31, 20XX			
Schedule I			
	Standard	Actual	Variance
Sales—regular merchandise	$40,500,000	$40,300,000	$(200,000)
Less returns and allowances	3,200,000	3,180,000	20,000
Net	37,300,000	37,120,000	(180,000)
—irregular and other	—	—	—
Total sales	37,300,000	37,120,000	(180,000)
Less: trade discounts	2,700,000	2,690,000	10,000
Sales commissions	2,350,000	2,378,000	(28,000)
	5,050,000	5,068,000	18,000
Net sales	$32,250,000	$32,052,000	$(198,000)

EXHIBIT 12.18   Direct-Cost Schedule

Direct-Absorption Cost Co.			
For the Year Ended December 31, 20XX			
Schedule II			
	Total		
	Standard	Actual	Variance
Direct labor			
Cutters	$600,000	$612,000	$12,000
Bundlers	18,000	18,000	—
Operators	2,800,000	2,913,000	113,000
Belt department	48,000	49,000	1,000
Button/slides	15,000	14,000	(1,000)
Pleaters	26,000	27,000	1,000
Examiners	94,000	99,000	5,000
Finishers	15,000	14,000	(1,000)
Pressers	324,000	321,000	(3,000)
Bonus	200,000	200,000	—
Total	4,140,000	4,267,000	(127,000)
Pension and health insurance	190,000	197,000	(7,000)
Payroll taxes	590,000	600,000	(10,000)
Total direct labor	4,920,000	5,064,000	(144,000)
Direct material			
Piece goods and trim—purchases	14,682,000	14,960,000	(278,000)

(Continued)

EXHIBIT 12.18   *(Continued)*

	Standard	Actual	Variance
Freight and trucking	410,000	454,000	(44,000)
Discounts and anticipation	(12,000)	(16,000)	4,000
Total direct materials	15,080,000	15,398,000	(318,000)
Total direct costs	$20,000,000	$20,462,000	$(462,000)
Contractor costs	$2,500,000	$2,574,000	$(74,000)

EXHIBIT 12.19   Factory Overhead Schedule

Direct-Absorption Cost Co.
For the Year Ended December 31, 20XX
Schedule III

	Total		
	Actual	**Variance**	**Budget**
Buildup	$189,000	$6,000	$183,000
Overtime (premium portion)	295,000	22,000	273,000
Holiday and vacation	453,000	4,000	449,000
Truck drivers	39,000	1,000	38,000
Supervisors	977,000	20,000	957,000
Pattern makers	246,000	2,000	244,000
Shippers	309,000	5,000	304,000
Receiving department	159,000	2,000	157,000
Repairs (garments)	46,000	4,000	42,000
Sewing office	7,000	—	7,000
Factory maintenance	146,000	4,000	142,000
Nonproduction	210,000	—	210,000
Vice President Production (partial)	26,000	—	26,000
Pension—salaried persons	97,000	—	97,000
Severance pay	25,000	3,000	22,000
Rent	51,000	—	51,000
Cutting room expenses	74,000	3,000	71,000
Heat, light, and power	86,000	22,000	64,000
General factory expense	129,000	3,000	126,000
General maintenance expense	70,000	6,000	64,000
Depreciation	124,000	—	124,000
General insurance	182,000	2,000	180,000
Vice President Engineering (partial)	15,000	—	15,000
Travel factory	20,000	6,000	14,000
Telephone	4,000	1,000	3,000

	Actual	Variance	Budget
Buying expenses	11,000	1,000	10,000
Trim buyers	24,000	1,000	23,000
Factory office	64,000	3,000	61,000
Machine repairs and parts	47,000	4,000	43,000
Total factory overhead	$4,125,000	$125,000	$4,000,000

$$\begin{matrix} \text{Profit computed} \\ \text{by absorption} \\ \text{costing} \end{matrix} - \begin{matrix} \text{Profit computed} \\ \text{by direct costing} \end{matrix} = \frac{\begin{matrix}\text{Total fixed factory}\\ \text{overhead}\end{matrix}}{\begin{matrix}\text{Volume used for unitizing}\\ \text{fixed overhead}\end{matrix}} \times \begin{matrix}\text{(Volume produced}\\ \text{minus volume sold)}\end{matrix}$$

or

$$\text{Difference in profits} = \text{Fixed factory overhead per unit}$$
$$\times \text{ Change in inventory units}$$

Application of this formula to Exhibit 12.15 is shown as follows:

- Note that the difference in profit between the absorption-costing and the direct-costing methods is due to the changes in inventory position.

EXHIBIT 12.20   Changes In inventories and Proration of Factory Overhead

LIFO Basis

Direct-Absorption Cost Co.

For the Year Ended December 31, 20XX

	Standard Cost	%	Overhead	Totals Absorption
Opening inventory	$6,000,000	(A)	$200,000	$6,200,000
Total direct costs	20,000,000		4,000,000	24,000,000
(Schedule II)				
Contractor costs	2,500,000		—	2,500,000
Total	22,500,000	100.0	4,000,000	26,500,000
Direct cost of sales	21,000,000	93.3	3,732,000(B)	24,732,000
Increase in inventory	1,500,000	6.7	268,000(B)	1,768,000
Closing inventory	$7,500,000		$468,000(C)	$7,968,000

Notes

(A) % computed as: 21,000,000 + 22,500,000 = 93.3%

(B) Computed as: 93.3% and 6.7% of $4,000,000

(C) Opening balance ($200,000) plus increase applicable to increase in inventory ($268,000)

Disadvantages of Variable Costing

In the long run, both variable and fixed costs must be recovered through the pricing structure. No company could stay in business without its sales price covering fixed costs to include a reasonable profit. Any pricing decision must include full recovery of all costs over the expected sales life of the product.

The next six problems are considered by some to be major deterrents to implementing a variable cost-accounting system:

1. The determination of a causal relationship between a cost and a unit of activity is often difficult, and therefore management is reluctant to implement flexible budgeting procedures necessary for an effective variable-costing system.
2. It is believed that variable costing will lead to underpricing of products. However, variable costing is an effective tool for ensuring that long-run profitability is considered in the decision process.
3. The Securities and Exchange Commission, the Internal Revenue Service, and the American Institute of Certified Public Accountants do not recognize variable costing as a generally accepted procedure for inventory valuation.
4. Variable-cost data as used for product profitability analysis are inappropriate whenever capital investment requirements for various products or product lines vary significantly.
5. The use of absorption costing appears to be the preferable method since direct costing excludes fixed factory overhead from the cost of the product. Therefore, sufficient data may not be available with which to properly establish minimum selling prices. That is, the product cost is incomplete.
6. Other problems may result from the use of direct costs, such as:
   - Valuation of inventories for insurance, merger, and so on
   - Seasonal distortions due to changes in inventory levels
   - Inability to compare operating results with other companies
   - The requirement of absorption-cost data in order to comply with the requirements of:
     a. The Robinson-Patman Act
     b. Cost-plus contracts
     c. Government contracts
     d. Litigation

Direct/Absorption Alternative

The solution to these problems is to have a system that provides both direct- and absorption-costing data. Such a cost system would provide direct-cost information for:

- Product decisions
- Procurement decisions
- Plant capacity decisions
- Marketing decisions
- Profit planning

and would provide absorption-cost information for:

- Full-cost inventory
- Full-cost sales price evaluations
- Conventional financial statements
- Income tax reporting purposes
- Comparability with other companies
- Elimination of seasonal distortions

The only mechanical difference between direct and absorption costing is the level at which fixed factory overhead is allocated to the product. Direct costing does not allocate the fixed factory overhead below the product level, and then it does so only on a total level, without adjustment for the amount absorbable into inventory. Absorption costing utilizes the fixed factory overhead into the individual product or job.

Exhibits 12.16 through 12.20 depict a direct/absorption-costing system report.

FULL COSTING AND BUDGETING

For budgeting purposes, full costing is often associated with fixed budgeting. This means that once the level of activity is established during the budget process, the budget remains fixed regardless of the level of activity (volume). This is not always true; a company may use flexible budget techniques that adjust budgeted costs to changes in activity yet may use full costing for inventory valuation and cost of sales determination. Some companies combine flexible budgeting and variable costing for internal management reporting and use full costing for external reporting.

Comparison of Full Costing and Variable Costing

Both full costing and variable costing will provide identical operating income when there is no change in the inventory level of manufactured goods. When production is greater than sales during a period, net income normally will be higher using full costing because fixed manufacturing costs are deferred (included in inventory); using variable costing they are charged against current sales. Net income will normally be lower with full costing in a period when sales are greater than production because fixed costs previously included in inventory are now being charged against current sales via cost of goods sold.

Using the data given in Exhibit 12.21, a comparative income statement using the two cost-accounting options is demonstrated in Exhibit 12.22.

Regardless of the option selected, the cost-accounting concept (variable or full costing) must be fully understood by users of the data. Careful investigation and interpretation by the accountant or budget director are essential to acceptance by operating managers.

A Final Word on Variable and Full Costing

In the long run, a company must sell a product at a price that recovers both variable and fixed costs and that contributes to net income. The system selected must be able not

EXHIBIT 12.21   Variable Versus Full Costing

Budgeted Production (Units)	12,000
Budgeted Sales	11,200
Sales Price per Unit	$25.00
Budgeted Variable Cost per Unit	
Material	$8.00
Labor	2.00
Manufacturing overhead	2.00
	12.00
Fixed Manufacturing Overhead	2.50
	$14.50
Budgeted Fixed (Period) Costs	
Manufacturing	$30,000
Selling	28,600
Administration	32,500
	$91,100
Beginning Finished Goods Inventory	
Units	4,000
Material	$7.50
Labor	1.75
Variable manufacturing overhead	1.50
Fixed manufacturing overhead	2.00
	$12.75

EXHIBIT 12.22   Comparative Income Statement

	Variable Costing	Full Costing
Sales	$280,000	$280,000
Cost of Goods Sold		
Beginning inventory	43,000	51,000
Production	144,000	174,000
Less ending inventory	(57,600)	(69,600)
	129,400	155,400
Contribution margin—gross profit	150,600	124,600
Period Expenses		
Manufacturing	30,000	NA
Selling	28,600	28,600
Administration	32,500	32,500
	91,100	61,100

	Variable Costing	Full Costing
Income from Operations	59,500	63,500
Difference can be reconciled as follows:		
Full costing income from operations	$63,500	
Less fixed manufacturing costs included in ending inventory (4,800 units × $2.50)	(12,000)	
Plus fixed manufacturing costs deferred (inventoried) from the prior period and charged against sales in the current period (4,000 units × $2.00)	8,000	
Variable-costing income from operations	$59,500	

only to provide data required for short-term decisions but also to convey the long-term implications of the decision.

In many industries we are witnessing increased automation, government environmental requirements, and so forth, all of which require increasing investments in plant and equipment. The cost of these assets must be recovered over their useful life.

The key to a properly designed direct-costing system is the inclusion of fixed manufacturing overhead in the product cost. In an absorption-costing system, this is done at the product level; in a variable-costing system, it should be done at the product-line level.

COST-ACCUMULATION PROCEDURES

Regardless of which manufacturing costs are associated with a product, the cost-accounting option selected must be able to accumulate and monitor the selected costs. With a job order-costing system, material, direct labor, and manufacturing overhead are charged to a specific job, shop, or customer order (a discrete order). As a result of this accumulation procedure, work-in-process inventory can be computed as the sum of all open orders at the end of an accounting period. Upon order completion, the cost of the order is transferred to finished goods or to cost of sales, using either standard or actual cost as discussed later in this chapter. With a process-costing system, manufacturing costs are charged to specific work centers or departments. This work-in-process inventory can be computed as the sum of all production costs charged to each department plus transfers in from other departments or finished goods inventory.

A comparison of the production and cost flow of a job costing and a process costing is illustrated in Exhibit 12.23.

Impact on Budgeting

Although the main purpose of job and process cost accounting is in determining product cost, the properly designed cost-accumulation system should be readily integrated with a responsibility budgeting system. Production reports indicating only unit costs would

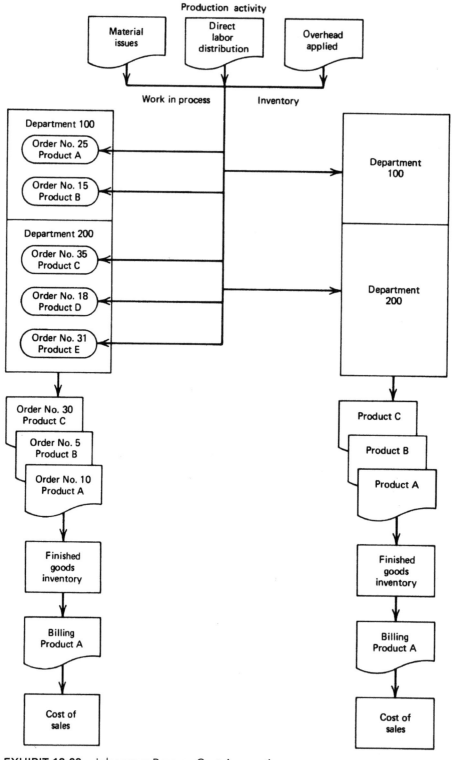

EXHIBIT 12.23 Job versus Process Cost Accounting

not be satisfactory for controlling costs. The system must be able to identify each element of cost (material, labor, and overhead) for each department. The production data, such as direct labor utilization, material usage, scrap, and budget control over manufacturing overhead costs, must also be reported.

Selection of the Cost-Accumulation Procedure

Each cost-accumulation procedure has several advantages and disadvantages. A process-costing system is normally associated with industries requiring mass production or continuous processing operations, and a job order–costing system with companies that control manufacturing operation by issuing specific production orders for defined quantities of a specific product. The production order can be for stock replenishment (finished goods) or for a specific customer order. However, many manufacturing companies have all the requirements necessary for a job order–costing system but select process-accumulation techniques. The reasons vary, but it appears that the major reason for not selecting job-accumulation procedures is the reluctance to implement the detailed shop floor reporting and accounting procedures necessary for a successful job order–costing system.

Although job order–costing procedures require detailed shop floor reporting and detailed postings to the accounting records, the system has some distinct advantages over process costing in that:

- ▪ It provides details of costs incurred on each order.
- ▪ It theoretically provides more reliable product costing because costs are reported against a specific order and product.
- ▪ It facilitates comparison of actual costs with cost estimates or standards. Additionally, product profitability via gross margin analysis can be calculated on each order.
- ▪ It can be readily incorporated into most manufacturing product-cost systems.

A properly designed and installed system also facilitates responsibility budgeting by associating costs (and cost variances) with specific areas of responsibility, such as department, work center, or operation.

Process costing has certain advantages and disadvantages. The main advantage is that it identifies costs by responsibility area. (However, a properly designed job order–costing system can also provide costs by responsibility area.) Additionally, the system does not require the detailed record keeping required for job order costing. The major disadvantages of process costing are that there may be less reliable product costing because of averaging units of production during the accounting period and that gross margins on each customer order are not available.

VALUATION: ACTUAL VERSUS STANDARD

The final cost-accounting system option to be selected is the identification of costs associated with the product, or *valuation*. The selection of variable or full costing was the first valuation option selected; however, within these two options, the cost-accounting system can be either an actual or a standard cost system. The term "actual cost" should not be constructed as the true cost but as the actual quantity required to produce an item times the computed actual unit cost. The key concept is that an actual-cost system uses an actual quantity, such as material and labor, times an actual unit cost. In using actual costs, there is no predetermined material usage or predetermined labor time for each operation in the manufacturing process.

With standard costs, actual costs not only are identified and monitored but also are compared to predetermined standards to determine variances from the standard. The identification of variances is the distinguishing feature of standard costing and is considered indispensable to cost control. The establishment of standard costs is a logical extension of the budgeting system. Standard costs allow management to report against budgets as well as to provide input into the development of budgets.

The various valuation techniques are depicted in Exhibit 12.24.

EXHIBIT 12.24 Valuation Techniques

Actual	Standard
Material cost	
Weighted average	Price of most economical supplier
First-in, first-out (FIFO)	Weighted average of several suppliers
Last-in, first-out (LIFO)	Price for the quantity usually purchased
Specific vendor invoice	Most economical quantity size
Labor Rate	
Employee	Operation
Operation	Work center
Work center	Department
Department	Plant-wide
Plant-wide	
Manufacturing Overhead	
Budget Technique	
Flexible (variable)	Flexible (variable)
Fixed	Fixed
Combined	Combined
Types of Rates	
Plant-wide	Plant-wide
Department	Department
Work center	Work center
Operations	Operations
Overhead Allocation Procedures	
Direct	Direct
Sequential	Sequential

Cross allocation	Cross allocation
Bases for Applying Overhead	
Direct labor hours	Direct labor hours
Direct labor dollars	Direct labor dollars
Machine hours	Machine hours
Material value	Material value
Units produced	Units produced
Other	Other
Activity Level	
Theoretical	Theoretical
Practical	Practical
Normal	Normal
Expected (budgeted)	Expected (budgeted)

 ## ACTUAL COSTING

In considering actual costing, each distinct transaction must be considered. Various transactions of the manufacturing process include:

- Purchase of materials
- Issues of material to production
- Labor operations performed
- Application of manufacturing overhead
- Production completion and transfer to finished goods
- Shipment (sale) of finished goods

Although this is an oversimplified depiction of the manufacturing process, these transactions represent the essential production control points of a cost-accounting system and are useful in analyzing valuation alternatives.

Purchase of Materials

With an actual-cost system, material purchases are recorded at the actual unit cost. The purchase price per unit includes the vendor's invoice price plus freight-in charges. Purchase discounts may be deducted from the computation of unit cost; however, many companies record the material purchase at the gross invoice amount and separately record the discount in a separate account.

As a practical matter, freight-in may be charged to a separate freight-in account. As material is issued to production, freight-in is charged to production at an applied rate. At the end of an accounting period, the balance in the freight-in account (actual less applied) is closed to work-in-process inventory or prorated between work-in-process inventory and materials inventory.

EXHIBIT 12.25   Actual Material Valuation Procedures

	Units	Unit Cost	Weighted Average	FIFO	LIFO
Beginning inventory	5,000	$0.50[a]	$2,500	$2,500	$2,500
Purchases					
First	3,000	0.52	1,560	1,560	1,560
Second	4,000	0.55	2,200	2,200	2,200
Third	7,000	0.60	4,200	4,200	4,200
Total receipts	14,000		7,960	7,960	7,960
Total available	19,000		10,460	10,460	10,460
Issues					
First	(7,000)		(3,850)	(3,540)	(4,200)
Second	(6,000)		(3,300)	(3,320)	(3,240)
Total issues	(13,000)		(7,150)	(6,860)	(7,440)
Ending inventory	6,000		$3,310	$3,600	$3,020

[a] For illustration purposes, all beginning inventory unit costs are assumed to be the same. This would normally not be true in a dynamic environment.

Issues of Material to Production

Three of the four procedures for computing actual material cost are compared in Exhibit 12.25. The specific invoice method is not really practical unless it is material that can be assigned to a specific product and/or customer order. The other three methods of costing material to production can be adopted to most actual-cost systems.

Weighted average actual cost is usually determined at the end of an accounting period where the records are maintained manually.[3] It is determined by adding the beginning inventory value plus receipts during the period to obtain the total available for production. The total available ($10,460) is divided by the total available units (19,000) to determine the weighted average cost per unit ($0.55). All issues to production during the period are charged to production based on the computed average cost. A company using a job order system would charge each job for the actual material issued to the job at the actual computed average cost ($0.55). With a process system, each department (or work center) would be charged at $0.55 per unit.

Using first-in, first-out (FIFO) cost, issues would be charged to production based on the order of receipt. In this example, the first issue of 7,000 units to production is valued as:

Beginning inventory	5,000 × $0.50	= 2,500
First receipt	2,000 × $0.52	= 1,040
	7,000	3,540

Ending inventory is to be composed of the most current receipts valued—in this example, at $0.60/unit, or $3,600.

---

[3] Many systems have options that permit the recomputation of the weighted average cost after each purchase.

Using last-in, first-out (LIFO) costs, the flow of inventory is the last purchased and the first to be issued to production. In this example, the first issue to production of 7,000 units is valued as the third receipt (last purchase) of $7,000 \times \$.060 = \$4,200$.

The ending inventory is composed of the units included in beginning inventory of 5,000 units valued at $2,500 plus the increase in ending inventory of 1,000 units first purchased during the period at $0.52 per unit, or $520.

As a practical matter, LIFO is not used to charge material to production on a day-to-day basis. Computations of LIFO reserves, the adjustment to state FIFO, and weighted-average or standard-cost inventories at FIFO values are normally maintained in a separate LIFO adjustment to the inventory accounts.

Labor Operations Performed

The next component of a product is the direct labor required to fabricate, assemble, machine, and so forth, the product. The *actual cost of labor* is defined as actual hours charged to a job, a product, or a department multiplied by the actual rate. The actual rate, as illustrated in Exhibit 12.24, may be the employee, operation, work center, department, or plant-wide rate. The actual selection of the rate would be based on (1) the variation in skill levels and wage rates, (2) the control objectives of the company, and (3) the budget system used. The greater the variation in skill level and wage rate and the greater the need to identify and measure performance by responsibility center, the greater the need to establish the labor rate by the smallest control unit, such as an operation.

Regardless of the rate selected, the procedure for reporting actual labor must be consistent with the procedures used to develop the budget. If direct labor budgets are prepared by department, then direct labor hours and dollars must be determined based on the department wage rate.

Application of Manufacturing Overhead

In an actual-cost system, predetermined overhead rates are determined during the budgeting process. The amount charged to production (job, product, or department) would be determined as the actual overhead base, such as labor hours, times the predetermined rate. The difference between actual manufacturing costs and the amount applied to production would be considered an overabsorption or underabsorption of overhead costs. The procedures for developing overhead rates and the accounting and budgeting procedures related to the cost-accounting system are discussed in the section on manufacturing overhead in this chapter.

Production Completion and Transfer to Finished Goods

The actual cost of a completed product is the sum of all actual material, labor, and overhead costs rolled up through the final operations performed. The actual product cost is determined in the same manner as the cost of purchased material. However, it is important that the material, labor, and overhead actual costs be separately identified. The data from the actual product cost will provide input into cost estimating, budgeting direct labor and materials, requirements, current cost control, and budget review.

Shipment of Finished Goods

The actual cost of sales or transfer of finished goods is determined in the same manner used to value issues of material to production, as illustrated in Exhibit 12.26. The weighted average, FIFO, and LIFO valuation techniques are acceptable procedures for valuing sale or transfer of finished goods.

ACTUAL COSTING, BUDGETING, AND COST CONTROL

Actual costing has several inherent deficiencies that make it incompatible with budgeting and cost control. The basic requirements of a manufacturing budget include the ability to:

- Determine cost control responsibilities within the manufacturing organization
- Compare actual results of operations to predetermined (budgets) results
- Identify variations from budgets in a timely manner

An actual-cost system provides no predetermined measurement standards. As a result, the actual cost of a product may include excess material usage and labor and machine inefficiencies, which are not easily identifiable. To determine if the "actual" cost represents the real or true cost necessary to produce an item, the actual-cost data must be analyzed. Additionally, the credibility of the cost-accounting system may be impaired because actual costing often means varying cost for the same product within the same business cycle.

Actual costing cannot be used effectively for product profitability analysis if it is out of line with what the product should cost based on engineered standards, production capabilities, and economic purchasing and production quantities.

STANDARD COSTING

Standard costing is considered an indispensable extension of the manufacturing budget process. Standards provide the ability to compare actual to predetermined results and the cost data that identify the variance from budgeted results in a timely manner. The difference between an operating budget and standard costing is that a budget represents a summary of standard costs at the budgeted level of operations and production mix, whereas standard costs represent what product costs should be based on measurement standards (performance objectives).

Definition

Standard costs are defined as the measure of what a product should cost. As with an actual-cost system, the standard-cost system collects the actual-cost data, but it charges the product only for the standard quantity at the standard unit cost. The difference

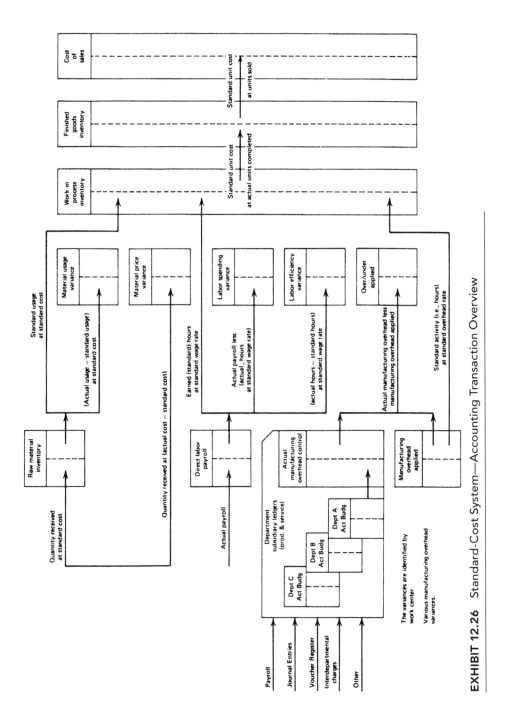

EXHIBIT 12.26 Standard-Cost System—Accounting Transaction Overview

between the amount charged to a product (costs that can be inventoried) and the amount actually incurred is considered a variance.

The standard cost comprises a standard unit of measure (hours, quantity, etc.) and a standard unit cost. With a properly structured standard-cost system, management can make timely evaluations manufacturing options on both a quantitative and a financial basis.

The accounting transaction flow is graphically displayed in Exhibit 12.26.

Standard Costs and Budgets

If standards are based on current operating and business levels as defined during the budget process, then the budget represents the sum of standard costs. In this chapter, we assume that standards represent reasonable performance measurements that are currently attainable and that are accepted by operating managers as being reasonable goals.

Purpose of Standard Costs

Cost Control

The main purpose of a standard-cost system is to control costs. Actual costs can be compared with predetermined standards to determine variance from planned (budgeted) results. Variances from standards represent red flags to management. The properly structured standard-cost system should also provide the ability to identify the operation and the product or products incurring the variance. The variance will indicate a deviation from plans; management analysis of the cause for the variance is necessary to determine why the variance occurred and to identify actions to prevent variances from occurring in the future.

Preparation of Budgets

Raw material, purchased parts, and direct labor requirements to meet budgeted production schedules require predetermined usage and/or operation times as well as procedures to translate production and inventory data into financial terms necessary for the budget. Standard costs, which are composed of two components (a standard measurement unit and a unit cost), can be used in determining the production and inventory quantity requirements and in costing the requirements. The department overhead budgets are essential to the development and evaluation of manufacturing overhead rates, as discussed in the section of this chapter on manufacturing overhead.

Measurement of Production Capabilities

A summary of operation requirements based on standard operating hours can assist in identifying production capabilities and/or constraints. The identification of potential production constraints will directly affect the capital investment budgeting process. The identification of excess capacity may affect management decisions to add a new product or product line or to increase marketing efforts for an existing product line.

Valuing Inventory and Determining the Cost of Sales

Generally accepted accounting principles (GAAP) recognize the acceptance of the FIFO, average, LIFO, and reverse markup procedure (normally associated with retail accounting) of inventory costing. However, the accounting profession recognizes that standard costs are acceptable (for inventory costing) if adjusted at reasonable intervals so that at the balance sheet date, standard costs reasonably approximate costs computed under one of the recognized bases.

Cost Estimating

Standard costs are often used for cost estimating subject to these revisions:

- Standard material costs are adjusted to expected or current purchase price.
- Standard labor costs are adjusted for expected wage increases.
- Manufacturing overhead rates are adjusted to meet the production volume at levels greater or less than budgeted (expected).
- Depreciation included in the overhead rate utilized for cost-estimating purposes may be based on replacement cost.

The standard quantities identified on the bill of material and the operation times (machine or labor) can be used for cost estimating for existing products or for products with slight modifications or enhancements.

Successful Standard-Cost Systems

The major elements of a successful standard-cost system can be judged using these six criteria:

1. Standards must reflect current economic, production, and product-design (structure) considerations.
2. Standards should be attainable.
3. Operating managers should be responsible only for those costs that they control. Managers must believe that the cost-accounting system is providing reliable and relevant data.
4. Significant variances from standards should be reported in a timely manner and properly investigated as to the reason for the variances.
5. The system should not overburden production personnel with cumbersome paperwork.
6. The standard-cost system should be integrated with the manufacturing budget process.

Although these concepts are fairly self-evident, they are presented to stress their importance. The exclusion of any of these elements could make the system ineffective.

EXHIBIT 12.27   Standard-Cost Components

Component	Document	Source
Quantity of material	Bill of material	Engineering specifications
Material unit cost	Purchasing records	Vendor/purchasing analysis
Operation times	Process routings	Industrial engineering studies
Wage rate	Payroll records	Labor agreements
Overhead rate	Overhead rate determination process	Budget system

Setting Standard Costs

Standard costs are composed of two components: a standard measurement unit and a unit cost. The components of a standard cost, the means of documenting the standards, and the source for developing the information are illustrated in Exhibit 12.27.

Material

The bill of material identifying the product structure (quantity requirements) should include acceptable levels of waste, spoilage, shrinkage, and so forth. The standard material unit cost should be the expected purchase price reflecting economic volume purchases from vendors who will fulfill delivery schedules and quality requirements. Normally, the cost includes inbound freight, if significant.

The standard material unit cost is normally set for a prescribed period, such as one year. As such, the price should reflect anticipated price increases or decreases during the period under consideration.

Labor/Machine Operating Times

Operating standards can be determined based on nonengineered or engineered work-measurement techniques. The various alternative procedures are illustrated in Exhibit 12.28.

EXHIBIT 12.28   Procedures for Setting Labor/Machine Time Standards

A. Nonengineered work-measurement techniques

   1. *One-person standard.* A person is timed by wristwatch while performing a job on several occasions. This technique is useful when trying new methods, improvement ideas, and workflow alterations.

   2. *Time ladders.* This method accounts for a person's time during the day and is most useful on long-cycle, relatively low-volume tasks, where interruptions are likely to occur and confuse other methods of establishing standards. This method is frequently used for establishing office clerical standards.

   3. *Historical standard data.* This method bases standards and results previously achieved. It shows how long it actually took to perform specific jobs but not how long it should have taken.

B. Engineered work-measurement techniques

1. *Work sampling.* This is a statistical technique using random sampling of what a person is doing and when he or she is idle. The output is divided by the active time to establish a labor standard. This process is not recommended for specific task elements in which a relatively precise measurement of task elemental time is required.

2. *Time (stopwatch) study.* Time standards applicable to any form of human or mechanical effort may be established by either of two methods using a stopwatch:

   a. *Job study* consists of measuring the time required to perform an operation and using this operation time plus a standard allowance for delays and personal needs as the standard time for that job.

   b. *Elemental standards development* consists of measuring the time required for each work element contained in an operation on a part or a product, collecting and tabulating similar information for other parts and operations, deriving a time value for each element from these data, and establishing an operation or job standard by adding together the element times so developed. Additionally, an allowance for delays and personal needs is provided.

3. *Predetermined time standards.* Methods-time measurement (MTM) is the most widely accepted of the predetermined time systems. It is well suited to measurement of highly repetitive short-cycle operations because it demands close analysis of work motions. The time required to establish standards, however, may be longer and more costly than with time study.

4. Standard data for determining various types of machine cycles are available from published engineering guides and textbooks. Standard data also can be prepared for operations unique to a plant by using time study, MTM, or some other method. This method's advantage is the relative ease of applying standard data.

Wage Rates

Standard wage rates are established during the budget process. The procedures for determining the standard wage rate are identical to the procedures used to determine the actual wage rate, as illustrated in Exhibit 12.27. The rate should include adjustments for any incentive pay based on contracted efficiencies. For effective cost control, the standard wage rate should indicate the skill level required to perform the operation. It would be expected that the greater the fluctuation in skill (and pay) levels within a manufacturing organization, the greater the need to develop wage rates for each specific operation type or work center.

Overhead Rates

Manufacturing overhead rates are predetermined rates usually established during the budget process. The procedures for setting overhead are discussed in the section of this chapter on manufacturing overhead. These rates are applied to product cost based on the standard bases of manufacturing activity, such as labor hours or machine hours.

VARIANCE REPORTING

A key difference between an actual cost-accounting system and a standard cost-accounting system is the recognition of variances from standards. The ability to

EXHIBIT 12.29 Standard-Cost Variances

Variance	Purpose	Recorded
Material		
Price	Impact of price increases or decreases on profitability	Purchase
Usage	Effective direct use of material in production	Issue to production
Substitution	Substitution of alternative material(s)	Issue to production
Labor		
Rate	Skill-level utilization	Operation performed
Efficiency	Relative productivity	Operation completed
Manufacturing Overhead		
Spending	Control over spending level based on actual activity	End of an accounting (budget) period
Variable efficiency	Efficient use of production facilities	End of an accounting (budget) period
Fixed efficiency	Effective employment of available capacity	End of an accounting (budget) period
Idle capacity	Cost of not operating at capacity	End of an accounting (budget) period

distinguish between what should occur (standards) and what actually occurred by way of variance reporting is essential to cost control. There are several major variances; some of the more common ones are illustrated in Exhibit 12.29. The computations of the more common variances are identified in Exhibit 12.30.

Material Variances

The *material price variance* is normally recorded at the time of purchase (alternatively, it may be recorded when the materials are used); all subsequent inventory transactions are recorded at the standard unit cost. If the actual unit price paid for an inventory item is greater than or less than the standard cost, a price variance occurs. Significant price variances should be investigated. (This is why the price variance should be generated at the time of purchase.) Although it is the normal procedure to hold the purchasing department responsible for price variances, the underlying reason for the variance could be attributable to a multitude of factors. For instance, a rush order or abnormal expediting by production scheduling may affect the purchasing function. Purchasing may have to expedite materials delivery, thereby incurring excess freight costs and/or loss of quantity discounts. The price variance may be only a manifestation of problems occurring in other manufacturing departments.

EXHIBIT 12.30   Common Variance Computation Methods

Variance	Computation
Material	
Price	(Actual unit cost less Standard unit cost) × Actual units
Usage	(Actual quantity less Standard quantity) × Standard unit cost
Labor	
Rate	(Actual rate less Standard rate) × Actual hours worked
Efficiency	(Actual hours less Standard hours) × Standard rate
Overhead	
Spending	Actual manufacturing overhead less Budgeted expenses based on actual hours
Variable efficiency	Budgeted overhead (based on actual hours) less Budgeted overhead (based on standard hours)
Fixed efficiency	(Actual hours × Predetermined fixed overhead rate) less (Standard hours × Predetermined fixed overhead rate)
Idle capacity	(Budgeted capacity hours × Predetermined fixed overhead rate) less (Actual hours × Predetermined fixed overhead rate)

The *material usage variance* represents the difference between the actual quantity of material issued to production for a specified product, order, or operation and the standard quantity specified. Often material is issued to a production order or to a work center based on the standard quantity requirements indicated on the bill of material (or prior production records). Any material in excess of the original issue is often requisitioned on a separate requisition card and is specifically identified as "excess" usage. A periodic summary of excess usage provides the total of the usage variance. To be an effective cost-control document, the usage variance should identify the product or process and the area or individual responsible for the variance.

Labor Variances

Direct labor is charged to production based on standard hours multiplied by the standard wage rate. The difference between the actual dollars paid for direct labor operations performed and the amount charged to production is composed of two major variances: wage rate and efficiency (productivity).

Wage Rate Variances

Since wage rates are normally based on contractual or prior agreements, wage rate variances would not be frequent in nature. However, if standard rates have been established for skill levels, such as operation or work center, rate variances would occur under these conditions:

- The operation(s) is performed by an employee with a different skill (and pay) level than required (standard).

- The skill rating is changed for specified operations without a change in the standard rate.
- Wage rate increases made during the period exceed or are less than rates used to establish standards.

Efficiency (Productivity) Variances

The determination of the productivity variance is based on a comparison of actual direct labor hours reported and the standard hours required to perform the operation. An effective standard-cost system records the productivity variance upon operation completion and provides daily and weekly departmental variance reports. The hourly productivity variance is then summarized at the end of the reporting (accounting) period.

The productivity variance indicates the relative efficiency of labor production efforts. The cause of the variance may be the result of actions and/or problems beyond the control of the operator or department incurring the variance. Potential causes of variance could be:

- Expediting activities are interfering with planned operations.
- Defective material is causing unusual manufacturing operations, assembly, and other problems.
- Personnel are being trained, do not have the appropriate skills, and/or are not properly supervised.
- Actual production operations as performed are not as documented (as used to determine standard operating hours).

The productivity variance indicates that production efforts are not being performed efficiently; appropriate investigation is necessary to determine why the variance occurred.

Manufacturing Overhead Variances

Regardless of whether a standard- or actual-cost system is selected, manufacturing overhead is applied to product cost based on a predetermined rate. The predetermined overhead rate times the actual production level is applied to product cost with an actual-cost system; a standard-cost system applies overhead based on earned (standard) production levels.[4]

The next data are used to illustrate the computation techniques for analyzing the difference (variance) between actual manufacturing overhead costs and the amount applied to product cost during an accounting period:

The *overapplied/underapplied manufacturing overhead* is the difference between the total of all costs charged to manufacturing overhead accounts and the amount applied to production, computed as:

---

[4] It should be noted that fixed manufacturing overhead is not applied when direct costing is used. It is charged off as a current period expense.

Total manufacturing overhead (actual)		$20,480
Less manufacturing overhead applied		
(5,000 earned hours × $4.00)		20,000
Overhead variance (debit)		× $480

The accounting entry to apply overhead to production would be:

Work-in-process inventory	20,000	
Manufacturing overhead applied	20,000	

To close out the remaining balance (credit) in the manufacturing overhead control account, a classification and identification of the variance must be made using the techniques described in the next paragraphs. For practical purposes, many companies group all variances in the overapplied/underapplied overhead account. A separate analysis of the types of variances is provided to management as a supplemental report to the operating statements.

The *spending variance* is the difference between the actual overhead costs and the budgeted amount based on the actual hours reported. As a practical matter, the spending variance is composed of differences in the budget variable application rate and the actual application rate. Before any judgment is made regarding the spending variance, a careful review should be made of the reliability of the variable overhead rate.

Spending variance is computed as:

Actual manufacturing overhead		$20,480
Less budgeted at actual hours		
Fixed cost	10,500	
Variable cost (5,200 reported		
hours × $2.25 variable rate)	11,700	22,200
Spending variance (credit)		$1,720

The spending variance can be further identified as a budget that is $2,500 under in fixed cost and $780 over in variable cost. The variable spending variance is normally considered the responsibility of the department supervisor; the fixed spending variance is the responsibility of the supervisor or manager having control over discretionary and committed costs.

The *variable efficiency variance* is a relative indication of the cost of not maintaining efficient operations. It is computed as:

Variable budget allowance based on actual	
reported hours	$11,700
Less variable costs applied to production	
(5,000 earned hours × $2.25 variable rate)	11,250
Variable efficiency variance (debit)	$ 450

The *fixed efficiency variance* is a measure of the effective use of plant and equipment. It is computed as:

5,200 actual hours × $1.75 fixed rate	$9,100
Less 5,000 earned hours × $1.75 fixed rate	8,750
Fixed efficiency variance (debit)	$350

The *idle capacity variance* represents the cost of unused capacity based on the budgeted level of operations. For budgeting and accounting purposes, the idle capacity variance represents the difference between the budgeted activity base used in establishing the fixed rate and the actual hours reported. It is computed as:

6,000 expected hours × $1.75 fixed rate	$10,500
5,200 reported hours × $1.75 fixed rate	9,100
Idle capacity variance (debit)	$1,400

The excess of actual manufacturing overhead to applied overhead can be summarized in this way:

Spending (credit)	$(1,720)
Variable efficiency	$450
Fixed efficiency	350
Idle capacity	1,400
Underapplied manufacturing overhead	$480

VARIANCES AND BUDGETING

Variances represent exceptions from standards and budgeted manufacturing costs. To control manufacturing operations and costs effectively, variances must be analyzed. The computation techniques provided in this chapter identify the type of variance; however, it is necessary to determine why the variance occurred, what functional area or department could have controlled the variance, and what actions are necessary to prevent the variance from occurring in the future.

A properly designed standard-cost system will collect the cost-accounting information from the lowest control level and provide the data required for summary reporting of actual results to budget. Significant variances at the summary level can be investigated by determining the applicable department(s) or product(s) responsible for the variance. If further information is required, the cost-accounting system should be able to provide the specific control point, such as an operation or work center. The depth of the analysis would be contingent on the relative magnitude of the problem as well as the level within the organization responsible for control. A schematic of the variance identification and analysis is depicted in Exhibit 12.31.

MANUFACTURING OVERHEAD

Both standard- and actual-cost systems require the determination of a manufacturing overhead rate to apply to product cost. The key difference is that an actual-cost system

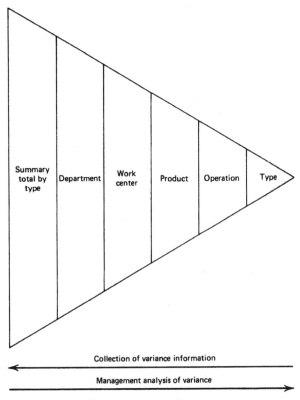

EXHIBIT 12.31 Variance Identification and Analysis

applies the rate to product cost based on actual activity; a standard-cost system applies overhead based on the standard (earned) activity level.

The 14 steps and decisions required in determining and analyzing overhead rates are:

1. Determine variable- and fixed-cost categories.
2. Select departments to include in manufacturing costs. (For discussion purposes, a *department* represents the lowest operating level with budget and operational responsibilities.)
3. Budget controllable expenses by department.
4. Budget indirect expenses.
5. Develop and collect statistics to allocate indirect expenses to departments based on causal relationships.
6. Allocate indirect expenses to manufacturing departments.
7. Redistribute service department costs to production departments.
8. Select appropriate base to assign overhead to product cost.
9. Determine activity level.
10. Calculate overhead rates.
11. Assign overhead to product cost.

12. Compare actual manufacturing overhead to budgets and to manufacturing applied.

13. Analyze overhead variances.

14. Provide variance analyses data to management.

Steps 1 through 6 are normally performed during the budget process; steps 7 through 10 are necessary for converting budget data to predetermined overhead rates. Steps 11 through 14 are completed at the end of each accounting period. The various overhead rate options available are depicted in Exhibit 12.27. The options selected may have a significant impact on overhead rates and therefore on product cost.

The steps necessary to convert department budgets to a manufacturing overhead rate are not necessary for responsibility budgeting; the procedures are necessary only so that (1) indirect manufacturing costs can be charged to a product and (2) the analyses of overhead variances provide management with summary information on the manufacturing operation.

Converting Budgets to Overhead Rates

Steps 1 to 6

The manufacturing overhead budget identifies the expenses that are directly controlled (or influenced) by the appropriate operating level of the organization (steps 1–3), as discussed in other chapters. Costs such as payroll fringe benefits, building depreciation, and utilities cannot be directly assigned to a department; however, they can be assigned to each department based on either benefits received or a causal relationship. The various procedures for allocating indirect expenses are numerous and can be grouped into these general classifications:

- ▪ Payroll/labor
- ▪ Consumption level
- ▪ Space
- ▪ Investment value
- ▪ Activity level

For instance, payroll fringe benefits are normally allocated on the basis of payroll dollars or hours;[5] building depreciation is often allocated on the basis of department size (square feet). In practice, the selection of the appropriate allocation statistic must be based on the ability to obtain the appropriate statistic as well as on the materiality of the expense to be allocated.

Step 7

The manufacturing operation is usually organized along functional lines. Departments responsible for direct production are organized according to similarity and/or location; departments providing service to the direct production departments are normally organized according to functional responsibilities. The actual department classifications do

---

[5] Where payroll fringe benefits are substantial in regard to payroll, they frequently are considered to be part of the direct payroll cost rather than as an overhead item.

not have to adhere to the classifications used for budgeting. The departments used for setting overhead rates may be larger or smaller than the number required for budgeting. The reliability of the overhead rate(s) and the effort required to evaluate actual results of operations should be the determining factors in the final selection process.

Since manufacturing overhead rates are calculated for production departments only, service department costs must be redistributed to production departments based on a causal relationship or on measurable benefits received. There are three redistribution methods available: direct, sequential, and cross-allocation.

Using the direct allocation method, the direct costs of a service department are allocated directly to production departments only, with no allocations made to other service departments. No redistribution of total service department costs are required. This is the simplest method, but it is the least accurate; it does not recognize the interdependence among service departments.

Sequential allocation methods recognize the interdependence of service departments. The sequential allocation begins with the service department's providing the most universally used services being redistributed to all other departments. The total costs (direct and redistributed) of the service department next most widely used are redistributed next and so on. This method is demonstrated in Exhibit 12.32.

The cross-allocation method recognizes the interdependence of service departments. Each service department is charged with a portion of the costs of each of the other service departments from which it receives benefits. The redistributions are determined simultaneously. This is the most accurate method, but it may require the use of special multiple apportionment programs.

Step 8

The selection of the base for activity depends on the activity that determines (measures) production effort and cost relationships.

Several bases may be used by way of supplementary rate procedures. For example, payroll fringe benefits may be computed based on direct labor dollars or hours; indirect material costs on material usage and machine-related costs such as depreciation, machine maintenance, and so forth can be allocated to production based on machine hours. The degree of cost accuracy and the significance of total product cost differences using supplementary rates should be weighed against the cost and time required to develop and monitor the rates. Various alternative bases for applying overhead rates are detailed in Exhibit 12.33.

Step 9

There are four levels that may be used for estimating production activity levels: theoretical, practical, normal, and expected (budgeted).

Theoretical capacity represents maximum efficiency with no allowance for normal downtime. Using this procedure, the applied overhead will always be less than actual overhead. Use of this activity level implies that any production at less than 100 percent utilization represents idle capacity costs and should be charged against current income.

EXHIBIT 12.32 ABC Manufacturing Company Manufacturing Expense Budget (December 31, 20XX)

Description	Fixed (F) or Variable (V)	Total Manufacturing Budget	Production Departments			Manufacturing Administration	Service Departments			Budget Bases
			Special Assembly	General Assembly	Machining		Maintenance	Industrial Engineering	Production/ Inventory Control	
Indirect Labor										
Supervision	F	$317,840	$16,400	$51,350	$47,100	$100,890	$40,700	$18,300	$43,100	Direct charge
Other indirect	F	202,300	19,800	45,600	29,300	—	39,400	53,400	14,800	Direct charge
Rework	V	28,950	6,640	12,450	9,860	—	—	—	—	Direct charge
		549,090	42,840	109,400	86,260	100,890	80,100	71,700	57,900	
Payroll-Related Costs										
Vacation and holiday	V	93,405	19,320	36,240	28,695	—	3,350	4,540	1,260	Direct charge
Overtime premium	V	27,325	5,680	10,655	8,440	—	1,180	1,070	300	Direct charge
Pension plan	V	83,410	14,146	29,175	24,755	7,073	5,304	4,421	3,536	Total salaries and wages
Group insurance	V	142,145	27,008	51,172	41,222	5,686	7,107	5,686	4,264	Number of employees
Workers' compensation	V	34,205	5,473	11,288	9,577	2,736	2,053	1,710	1,368	Total salaries and wages
Payroll taxes	V	127,200	20,352	41,976	35,616	10,176	7,632	6,360	5,088	Total salaries and wages
		$512,690	91,979	180,506	148,305	25,671	26,626	23,787	15,816	

Cost		Total								Allocation basis
Other Variable Costs										
Power	V	78,800	18,124	33,884	26,792	—	—	—	—	Rated machine consumption
Supplies	V	8,930	2,050	3,840	3,040	—	—	—	—	Direct charge
Perishable tools	V	131,370	30,360	56,375	44,635	—	—	—	—	Direct charge
		219,100	50,534	94,099	74,467	—	—	—	—	
Fixed Discretionary Costs										
Employee education	F	12,400	900	250	550	3,400	350	5,150	1,800	Direct charge
Equipment rental	F	6,900	3,820	90	2,120	70	—	800	—	Direct charge
		19,300	4,720	340	2,670	3,470	350	5,950	1,800	
Fixed Committed Costs										
Building depreciation	F	20,330	2,440	5,896	7,929	1,830	1,218	610	407	Building square feet
Machine depreciation	F	46,000	10,000	13,000	23,000	—	—	—	—	Direct charge
Property taxes	F	68,500	15,070	19,865	33,565	—	—	—	—	Material charge
General insurance	F	67,700	8,124	19,633	26,403	6,093	4,062	2,031	1,354	Building square feet
		202,530	35,634	58,394	90,897	7,923	5,280	2,641	1,761	
Total		$1,502,710	$225,707	$442,739	$402,599	$137,954	$112,356	$104,078	$77,277	

EXHIBIT 12.33 ABC Manufacturing Company Calculation of Manufacturing Overhead Rates

	Total Manufacturing Budget	Production			Service				Budget Basis
Description		Special Assembly	General Assembly	Machining	Manufacturing Administration	Maintenance	Industrial Engineering	Production/ Inventory Control	
Total overhead manufacturing budget before redistribution	$1,502,710	$225,707	$442,739	$402,599	$137,954	$112,356	$104,078	$77,277	
Redistributions: Manufacturing administration		26,211	52,423	42,766	$(137,954)	6,897	5,518	4,139	Number of employees
Maintenance		16,695	41,739	54,856		$(119,253)	3,578	2,385	Building square feet
Industrial engineering		26,030	48,665	38,479			$(113,174)	—	Direct labor hours
Production/inventory control		18,436	24,302	41,063				$(83,801)	Material usage
Total service department redistributions		87,372	167,129	177,164					
Total	$1,502,710	313,079	609,868	579,763					
Bases									
Direct labor hours		33,030	61,950						
Machine hours				25,000					
		$9.48	$9.85	$23.19					

242

Practical capacity is a measure of manufacturing activity that includes an allowance for normal machine setup, maintenance, and idle time. Practical capacity is a more realistic appraisal of maximum production capabilities.

Normal capacity considers the utilization of plant and equipment required to meet average production demands over a period long enough to level out the production peaks and valleys. Often normal capacity is used in the determination of the fixed overhead rates.

Expected capacity represents the capacity required to meet current production levels based on budgeted sales and inventory levels. The expected level is used in establishing variable overhead rates.

The capacity level used to set overhead rate(s) must be considered in the analysis of the overapplied/underapplied overhead.

Step 10

The procedure for determining the overhead rates is illustrated in Exhibits 12.32 through 12.34.

Steps 11 to 14

Steps 11 to 14 are completed at the end of the accounting period. Examples of the worksheets required to determine overapplied/underapplied overhead and the accounting entries are provided in the ABC Manufacturing Company. ABC Manufacturing has three production departments—special assembly, general assembly, and machining—and four service departments—manufacturing administration, maintenance, industrial engineering, and production/inventory control. The department classification corresponds to the organization chart of the company. Based on an analysis of indirect costs, the company has decided to allocate these costs to each department based on the data collected during the budget process. ABC Manufacturing Company uses the sequential allocation method of redistributing service department costs to production departments. The company uses full costing for inventory valuation (overhead rates); however, flexible budgeting is used in evaluating department performance. Additionally, variable data are monitored and provided to management. Direct labor hours and machine hours are used to recover overhead costs (and therefore are used to set overhead rates).

Actual Manufacturing Overhead

Direct manufacturing expenses are charged to the department responsible for the expense; indirect expenses such as fringe benefits are initially recorded in a pooled/indirect expense category. At the end of an accounting period, these indirect expenses are allocated to both production and service departments based on the actual statistics accumulated during the period. Additionally, the service department actual expenses are redistributed to the production departments.

For illustration purposes, the ABC Manufacturing Company maintains:

- Subsidiary activity ledgers for each production and service department
- Separate subsidiary ledger for each pooled/indirect expense

EXHIBIT 12.34 ABC Manufacturing Company Budget Statistics (December 31, 201X)

Departments	Direct Labor Hours	%	Direct Labor Dollars	%	Total Salaries and Wages[a] Dollars	%	Employees Number	%	Materials[b] Usage	%	Building Square Feet Feet	%	Rated Machine Consumption[b] Units	%	Machine Hours Hours	%
Production																
Special assembly	33,030	23%	$168,453	21%	$211,293	16%	23	19%	$1,875,000	22%	4,406	12%	9,640	23%	—	—
General assembly	61,950	43	328,335	42	437,735	33	45	36	2,540,000	29	10,885	29	18,085	43	—	—
Machining	49,050	34	291,848	37	378,108	28	36	29	4,290,000	49	14,292	39	14,313	34	25,000	100%
Service																
Manufacturing administration	—	—	—	—	100,890	8	5	4	—	—	3,369	9	—	—	—	—
Maintenance	—	—	—	—	80,100	6	6	5	—	—	2,258	6	—	—	—	—
Industrial engineering	—	—	—	—	71,700	5	5	4	—	—	963	3	—	—	—	—
Production/ inventory control	—	—	—	—	57,900	4	4	3	—	—	852	2	—	—	—	—
Total	144,030	100%	$788,636	100%	$1,337,726	100%	124	100%	$8,705,000	100%	37,025	100%	42,038	100%	25,000	100%

[a] Total of indirect and direct labor.
[b] Based on production budget.

- Control accounts in the pooled/indirect expenses subsidiary ledger for allocations to production and service departments
- Control accounts in the general ledger to post summary totals of production department expenses to include allocations of pooled/indirect and service department reallocations
- Control accounts in the general ledger to apply manufacturing overhead to the cost of production (work-in-process inventory)

Exhibit 12.35 illustrates the procedures for determining the overapplied/underapplied manufacturing overhead. Although not illustrated in this example, a manufacturing expense report comparing year-to-date actual results of operations to operating budgets is prepared for each department. The actual statistics accumulated during the period are illustrated in Exhibit 12.36.

Accounting Procedures

During an accounting period, the manufacturing overhead rate is applied to production (work in process) based on the data supplied by a production report, labor-machine report, or customer-factory order. Regardless of the procedure(s) used to accumulate the base to apply overhead, the amounts must be periodically summarized and entered into the general ledger. The entry to record the applied manufacturing overhead for the ABC Manufacturing Company would be:

Work in process	$133,849
Manufacturing overhead applied—special assembly (3,010 earned hours at $9.48 per hour)	$28,535
Manufacturing overhead applied—general assembly (5,630 earned hours at $9.85 per hour)	$55,456
Manufacturing overhead applied—machining (2,150 machine hours at $23.19 per hour)	$49,858

The control account balances for the manufacturing departments would be:

Special assembly—control	$27,875
General assembly—control	$55,820
Machining—control	$52,375
Total	$136,070

A comparison of actual manufacturing expenses incurred and the amount applied to production results in an underapplied overhead (actual manufacturing overhead in excess of amount applied) of $2,221. The variance between actual and applied should be categorized, using computations illustrated in the section on manufacturing overhead variance in this chapter.

EXHIBIT 12.35 ABC Manufacturing Company Redistributions of Actual Service Department Costs and Calculation of Overapplied/(Underapplied) Manufacturing Overhead (Period Ended January 31, 201X)

Description	Total Manufacturing Expense	Production			Service				Budget Bases
		Special Assembly	General Assembly	Machining	Manufacturing Administration	Maintenance	Industrial Engineering	Production/ Inventory Control	
Total manufacturing expense before redistribution	$136,070	$20,520	$41,400	$36,800	$11,550	$10,300	$9,050	$6,450	Direct and allocated pooled/ indirect expenses
Redistributions									
Manufacturing administration	—	2,030	4,330	3,660	(11,550)	580	580	370	Number of employees
Maintenance	—	1,525	3,770	4,950		(10,880)	330	305	Building square feet
Industrial engineering	—	2,285	4,275	3,400			(9,960)	—	Direct labor hours
Production/inventory control	—	1,515	2,045	3,565				$(7,125)	Material usage
Total service department redistributions		7,335	14,420	15,575					
Total	$136,070	$27,875	$55,820	$52,375					
Total applied manufacturing overhead	$133,849	$28,535	$55,456	$49,858					
Overapplied/(Underapplied) manufacturing overhead	$(2,221)	$660	$(364)	$(32,517)					

246

EXHIBIT 12.36 ABC Manufacturing Company Manufacturing Statistics (January 31, 201X)

	Employees		Building Square Feet		Earned Direct Labor		Standard Material Usage		Machine Hours	
	Number	%	Feet	%	Hours	%	Unit	%	Hours	%
Production										
Special assembly	22	18%	4,406	12%	3,010	23%	170,900	21%	—	—
General assembly	45	36	10,885	29	5,630	43	230,900	29	—	—
Machining	38	30	14,292	39	4,480	34	402,000	50	2,150	100%
Service										
Manufacturing administration	5	4	3,369	9	—	—	—	—	—	—
Maintenance	6	5	2,258	6	—	—	—	—	—	—
Industrial engineering	5	4	963	3	—	—	—	—	—	—
Production/ inventory control	4	3	852	2	—	—	—	—	—	—
	125	100%	37,025	100%	13,120	100%	803,800	100%	2,150	100%

Note: Statistics required for redistribution of support departments only.

MANUFACTURING OVERHEAD, BUDGETING, AND COST CONTROL

Overhead rates are necessary for product costing, product profitability evaluation, and evaluation of gross variances from budgets. An effective cost-accounting system depends on effective budgeting and cost-control systems. Manufacturing overhead variances (spending and efficiency) provide gross measurements of how well manufacturing supervisors are controlling costs. Additionally, the fixed efficiency and idle capacity variances, as discussed previously, provide management with an analytical tool in measuring the effective use of plant and equipment. The activity level of operations as measured by these variances provides management with data necessary for directing marketing efforts, introducing new products or product lines, scheduling existing orders through production, identifying work-center bottlenecks, and so forth.

For instance, underutilized capacity in a certain department or product line, as measured by an idle capacity unfavorable variance, would affect the decision to search for products or additional orders to utilize excess capacity. A favorable idle capacity variance (actual production in excess of normal or practical capacity) may indicate that additional equipment or additional shifts are required.

A well-designed cost-accounting system not only will provide product cost data necessary for inventory valuation and cost of sales determination but also will incorporate responsibility budgeting and reporting and affect profit-planning strategies.

CHAPTER THIRTEEN

Break-Even and Contribution Analysis as a Tool in Budgeting

Jay H. Loevy, CPA, CFE
Edward Mendlowitz, CPA/PFS/ABV/CFF

INTRODUCTION

The budgeting process is the manager's primary tool for dealing with future uncertainty. In developing a period budget, managers must make certain assumptions of cause and effect: "Unit sales will increase 10 percent because of overall demand for the product, assuming that sales prices can be held to a 5 percent increase." "Gross profit percentage can be maintained despite a 6 percent increase in purchase costs." "Sales demand will hold steady unless there is a war in Abyssinia."

Although they cannot do anything about Abyssinian affairs, managers can, to some degree, influence purchase costs, sales volume, and selling prices. How well they understand their relationship and the effect on the enterprise will largely determine the effectiveness of the business plan. This chapter describes the relationship of cost, volume, and price as well as certain techniques for integrating these considerations into the budgeting process.

BREAK-EVEN ANALYSIS

Perhaps the best way to understand the cost–volume–price relationship is to examine the technique commonly referred to as *break-even analysis*. The name is unfortunate. Except for certain situations, such as the start-up of a new business or the determination

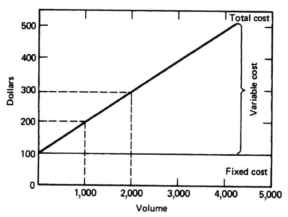

EXHIBIT 13.1   Break-Even Analysis

of when to pull the plug on losing operations, managers are not particularly interested in pinpointing break-even volume. The planning effort is directed toward maximizing profit, and where the break-even point happens to fall is academic. Nevertheless, the techniques used to determine break-even are useful, because they help us understand the interplay of cost, price, and volume.

Fixed cost	$100
Variable cost: 1,000 at $0.10 per unit total cost	100
	$200

There are two cost elements in break-even analysis: fixed costs and variable costs. These are illustrated in Exhibit 13.1. In this example, the fixed cost of $100 remains the same regardless of volume. The minute the doors are opened, $100 is incurred. Thus, at zero volume the chart indicates $100 of cost. The variable cost is $0.10 per unit. At a volume of 1,000 units, the total cost is $200, calculated as shown:

Doubling the volume to 2,000 units will add only $100 to total cost, since the fixed cost remains at $100.

This calculation, simple though it is, illustrates the basic functioning of costs. It lies at the heart of break-even analysis and contribution analysis.

Since the treatment of costs as fixed or variable is critical to the analysis, it will be useful to define and illustrate these terms.

Fixed Costs

Fixed costs are those cost elements that are expected to remain at a constant level regardless of the volume of business. In reality, no cost is fixed forever. It is considered fixed only under a given set of conditions. For example, the fixed cost connected with a one-shift

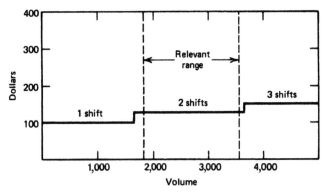

EXHIBIT 13.2   Relevant Range

manufacturing operation would change if the company were to go to a two- or three-shift facility, since there would be added fixed costs for production-control personnel, plant management, foremen, certain utilities, and so forth. A fixed-cost line for each condition might appear as in Exhibit 13.2.

For planning purposes, it is necessary to deal only with those costs that are *relevant* to the planning horizon. In Exhibit 13.2, it is assumed that a two-shift operation will be used and that the expected production would be in the range of 1,850 to 3,500 units. This is termed the *relevant range*. The planner normally can ignore conditions outside that range.

In judging what costs are fixed, the planner must look beyond traditional labels. For example, direct labor is normally considered a variable cost. However, there is a printing plant that operates three shifts, six days per week, with a mandatory crew size on each press. The plant always has sufficient orders to operate at capacity. In this company, direct labor is considered a fixed element. The same could be true of a company that, as a matter of policy, does not lay off employees even if production is down. Within the relevant range, such costs are fixed.

These conditions notwithstanding, costs that are normally considered fixed in a manufacturing company would include rent, property taxes, building maintenance and insurance, administrative and supervisory salaries, depreciation, and so on.

Variable Costs

Variable costs are those cost elements that are expected to vary in direct proportion to a volume indicator (e.g., units produced, service calls made, applicants processed). Variable costs are usually more difficult to identify than fixed costs, because there is often not a true linear relationship between volume and cost. Some costs tend to be variable over long periods but may not vary directly within one year. For example, it is not unusual to find that the cost of hand tools did not change appreciably from the prior year, even though there was a drop in annual production volume. This happened because there was a fixed element in the cost of hand tools: Affected employees needed a full array of tools to do their jobs, regardless of the production volume processed at their station.

That tools did not wear out as fast had less of an impact on the annual cost. Costs of this nature—and there are many of them—are actually *semivariable,* in that they are composed of both fixed and variable elements.

Since these elements usually cannot be identified with any great precision, and since such precision is not usually required in financial planning, it is common to classify as variable those costs that are more variable than fixed over the long term. Costs that are normally considered variable include direct labor, direct materials, sales commissions, freight, packing supplies, and so on.

Break-Even Chart

Exhibit 13.3 illustrates a break-even chart. It is composed of the fixed and variable cost lines shown on Exhibit 13.1 plus a sales line, which represents the linear relationship of units sold and the resulting sales dollars. The point at which the total cost and sales lines intersect (1,800 units/$270) is the break-even point. Additional sales will produce a profit, whereas fewer sales will result in a loss. The difference between the expected sales volume of 2,500 units and the break-even volume of 1,800 units is termed the *margin of safety.* It is that number of units under the expected volume at which a profit could still be expected.

The break-even point can also be calculated by the next equation:

$$\text{Break-even} = \frac{\text{Total fixed costs}}{1 - \dfrac{\text{Total variable costs}}{\text{Total sales}}}$$

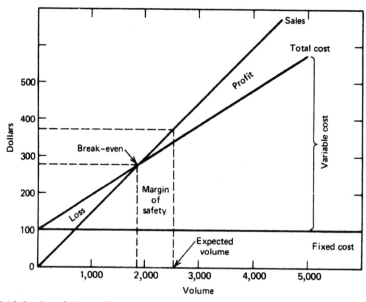

EXHIBIT 13.3   Break-Even Chart

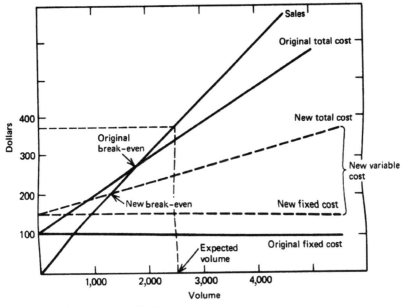

EXHIBIT 13.4   Change in Break-Even

Using the figures from Exhibit 13.3, we have

$$\text{Break-even} = \frac{100}{1 - \dfrac{240}{380}}$$

$$= \frac{100}{0.37}$$

$$= \$270$$

Consider the effect on break-even of a company that wishes to modernize its plant. In so doing, the fixed costs are expected to rise 50 percent% to $150 to cover additional depreciation and amortization of plant improvements. However, production throughput should also rise, causing a 20 percent, or $54, decrease in unit variable costs, primarily attributable to a reduction in direct labor per unit. The change in break-even is illustrated in Exhibit 13.4.

The calculation of the new break-even is:

$$\text{Break-even} = \frac{150}{1 - \dfrac{100}{380}}$$

$$= \frac{150}{0.74}$$

$$= \$202$$

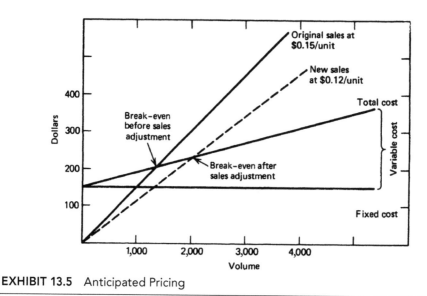

EXHIBIT 13.5   Anticipated Pricing

Further, because of advances in technology, the unit selling price in the company's industry is expected to decrease. Thus, to properly reflect anticipated pricing after the plant modernization, an adjustment is made to the slope of the sales line, as shown in Exhibit 13.5.

PRICE/VOLUME CHART

The manager is primarily interested in profits—the bottom line. In the break-even charts that have been illustrated, profit is indicated by the gap between the sales and cost lines. A clearer presentation of profit is achieved by the price/volume chart, which is illustrated in Exhibit 13.6.

Here the relationship of the fixed and variable cost and the sales lines are combined into a profit line. The starting point on the vertical axis indicates the amount of fixed

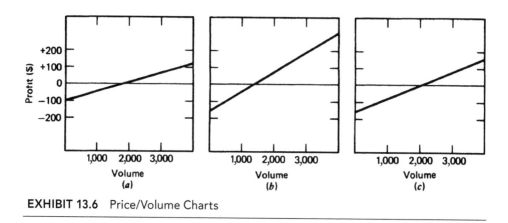

EXHIBIT 13.6   Price/Volume Charts

costs ($100 and $150 in the examples). The slope of the line is determined by the amount of profit per unit of sales. The steeper the slope, the more profitable the sales. The three conditions of the break-even chart example are charted to illustrate the change in slope and profit using the price/volume chart.

CONTRIBUTION ANALYSIS

The preceding charts illustrate that each additional unit of sales reduces the loss until the break-even point is reached. Profits increase thereafter. Another way of looking at it is that the direct, or variable, profit on each unit of sales "contributes" to the payment of fixed expenses. That is, the sales price less the variable cost yields a profit, the cumulative effect of which will, it is hoped, exceed the total fixed cost by a desired amount.

Such an approach is used to present period income in Exhibit 13.7. The "traditional" method presents manufacturing costs as one amount, whereas the contribution method separates fixed and variable components. Further, selling expense, traditionally shown below gross profit, is shown as a variable cost above the line on the contribution statement. Although income before tax remains the same, the effect of the contribution statement can be quite different. The fixed expenses represent a commitment on the part of company management. Operating managers have little control over such costs as depreciation, rent, insurance, and so forth, and thus their performance should usually not be measured by the levels of fixed costs. However, managers do have direct control

EXHIBIT 13.7 Comparison of Methods Presenting Period Income

Traditional Method		
Sales		$ 1,000,000
Cost of sales		500,000
Gross profit		500,000
Selling expense	$ 250,000	
General and administrative expense	100,000	350,000
Income before tax		$ 150,000
Contribution Method		
Sales		$ 1,000,000
Variable costs		
Manufacturing	$ 200,000	
Selling	150,000	350,000
Contribution to fixed cost		650,000
Fixed manufacturing cost		300,000
Operating profit		350,000
Selling, general, and administrative expense		200,000
Income before tax		$ 150,000

over the variable manufacturing costs and should be measured by the effective use of such costs in the manufacture of product. Likewise, sales managers control variable costs, such as commissions and travel expense, and their performance can be evaluated on the basis of cost per unit of sale. The identification of such variable costs as separate statement items permits such evaluation.

The contribution approach has great significance to budget managers as well, because it permits them to derive an optimum plan in which, for instance, alternative pricing policies are possible. It is axiomatic that in a normal market (i.e., one that is not heavily skewed to either buyers or sellers), volume will vary inversely with selling price. Increasing prices above the market level will normally reduce volume. A decrease in price should increase volume. Being able to quantify the effect on profits for alternate pricing policies enables budget managers to reach the optimum level. Contribution analysis is a tool to make this happen.

Consider the examples shown in Exhibit 13.8. Through market analysis or perhaps merely by guesstimate, the budget manager determines the sales volume that would result from four alternative pricing policies. By applying variable costs per unit, the manager finds that lowering prices by 10 percent will yield the greater contribution and thus the greater net income, assuming fixed costs will remain fixed. (If fixed costs must be increased to produce the additional volume, the calculation must be extended to the operating profit line.)

There is always a conflict in trying to determine whether prices should be increased to make more money, or decreased to create a greater demand so the business could make more money. This can be calculated using simple arithmetic based on the break even analysis model and applying it to a guess of how your customers would react versus the potential to gain added business. The calculations also require converting the amounts used from dollars to product units. Exhibits 13.9 and 13.10 show the effect of looking at units rather than dollars. Notice the extreme differences between the results in dollars and units. We measure activities in dollars, but it is the units that are produced and sold. Units determine market share. Also, when comparing companies in similar industries, unit sales are a better

EXHIBIT 13.8 Alternative Pricing Policies

	Current Policy	Raise Price 10%	Lower Price 5%	Lower Price 10%
Sales price per unit	$1.00	$1.10	$0.95	$0.90
Expected volume	1,000,000	900,000	1,100,000	1,250,000
Sales	$1,000,0000	$990,000	$1,045,000	$1,125,000
Variable cost at $0.35	350,000	315,000	385,000	437,500
Contribution to fixed cost	$650,000	$675,000	$660,000	$687,500

measure of comparison since one company could charge premium prices for exceptional service, or training or customer on-site installation, while another ships the product without any extras.

Exhibits 13.9 and 13.10 are models used to determine when to raise or lower prices *solely in order to make more money*. There are a myriad of reasons to change prices, but these exhibits illustrate the break-even points when the focus is to make more money.

There are two models: using 30 and 40 percent gross profits *before* the price changes. In these illustrations, "gross profit" refers to the sales price less the variable cost percents and not the traditional financial statement terminology. Since the gross profit is a function of the sales price less the variable costs, as the sales price changes so will the gross profit percent. Both exhibits show the number of additional physical units that are needed to be sold to make the same money before the price reduction or the number of reduced physical units at the new higher price in order to make what was made before the price increase. The reality is that many businesspeople and managers mistakenly believe that reducing prices will increase volume enough to offset the lower gross profit; these exhibits indicate that you will make less money when you lower prices and more when you increase prices.

A discussion of the 30 percent illustration, 10 percent decrease in price, and 10 percent increase in price is presented next.

The 10 percent decrease makes the $100 regular selling price $90. The cost remains at $70 so the new gross profit is $20 and 22.22 percent. The total sales needed to make the same gross profit amount increased from $1,000 to $1,350, or a 35 percent dollar sales increase. Further, a 50 percent increase in physical units is needed to be sold (an increase from 10 to 15 units) just to make the same dollars as before the decrease. Logically, this does not seem possible in most situations. The manager would have to evaluate the market very carefully before decreasing prices when the goal is just to make more money. Note that there are normal situations when you would reduce prices, such as to reduce excess inventory, clean out obsolete or defective inventory, or make room for new designs. Also, many companies have traditional sales periods. But our discussion is directed at reducing prices in order to make more money. Now let us look at increasing prices to make more money.

Using the 10 percent price increase the new price becomes $110, new gross profit is $40 and 36.36 percent. The dollar sales needed to make the same money drops to $825 and the decrease in units is 2.5, or a 25 percent drop. Now, in reality, a 10 percent price increase, unless you are solely selling a commodity, will not cause you to lose 25 percent of your business. Think about it. Customers have a stake in maintaining the relationship just as the vendor does. Most customers will not leave immediately after the price is increased. With a little marketing, the price increase will further thwart the flight away from your company.

Conclusion: Raising prices usually results in greater profits while reducing prices results in lower profits. The break-even technique clearly illustrates this.

The preceding examples, although illustrative of a basic technique, does not reflect the typical company. Most business enterprises deal in many variations of a product—differing sizes, qualities, packaging—or even entirely different products manufactured

EXHIBIT 13.9 Units versus Dollars: Part 1

Determining whether to raise or lower prices in order to make more money

Regular gross profit before price changes: 30.00%

% decrease in price	new price per unit	$ amount of cost per unit	$ amount of gross profit	new gross profit %	$ sales needed to earn $300 gross profit	increase in total $ sales needed to earn same gross profit $	# physical units that have to be sold to earn $300 gross profit	% increase needed in physical units sold to earn same $ amt. of gross profit as before price decrease
0.00%	$100.00	$70.00	$30.00	30.00%	$1,000.00	0.00%	10.0	0.00%
5.00%	$95.00	$70.00	$25.00	26.32%	$1,140.00	14.00%	12.0	20.00%
10.00%	$90.00	$70.00	$20.00	22.22%	$1,350.00	35.00%	15.0	50.00%
15.00%	$85.00	$70.00	$15.00	17.65%	$1,700.00	70.00%	20.0	100.00%
20.00%	$80.00	$70.00	$10.00	12.50%	$2,400.00	140.00%	30.0	200.00%
25.00%	$75.00	$70.00	$5.00	6.67%	$4,500.00	350.00%	60.0	500.00%

Regular gross profit before price changes: 30.00%

% increase in price	new price per unit	$ amount of cost per unit	$ amount of gross profit	new gross profit %	$ sales needed to earn $300 gross profit	% decrease in total $ sales permitted to earn same gross profit $	# physical units that have to be sold to earn $300 gross profit	% decrease in physical units sold permitted to earn same $ amt. of gross profit as before price increase
0.00%	$100.00	$70.00	$30.00	30.00%	$1,000.00	0.00%	10.0	0.00%
5.00%	$105.00	$70.00	$35.00	33.33%	$900.00	-10.00%	8.6	-14.29%
10.00%	$110.00	$70.00	$40.00	36.36%	$825.00	-17.50%	7.5	-25.00%
15.00%	$115.00	$70.00	$45.00	39.13%	$766.67	-23.33%	6.7	-33.33%
20.00%	$120.00	$70.00	$50.00	41.67%	$720.00	-28.00%	6.0	-40.00%
25.00%	$125.00	$70.00	$55.00	44.00%	$681.82	-31.82%	5.5	-45.45%

EXHIBIT 13.10 Units versus Dollars: Part 2

Determining whether to raise or lower prices
in order to make more money

Regular gross profit before price changes: 40.00%

% decrease in price	new price per unit	$ amount of cost per unit	$ amount of gross profit	new gross profit %	$ sales needed to earn $400 gross profit	increase in total $ sales needed to earn same gross profit $	# physical units that have to be sold to earn $400 gross profit	% increase needed in physical units sold to earn same $ amt. of gross profit as before price decrease
0.00%	$100.00	$60.00	$40.00	40.00%	$1,000.00	0.00%	10.0	0.00%
5.00%	$95.00	$60.00	$35.00	36.84%	$1,085.71	8.57%	11.4	14.29%
10.00%	$90.00	$60.00	$30.00	33.33%	$1,200.00	20.00%	13.3	33.33%
15.00%	$85.00	$60.00	$25.00	29.41%	$1,360.00	36.00%	16.0	60.00%
20.00%	$80.00	$60.00	$20.00	25.00%	$1,600.00	60.00%	20.0	100.00%
25.00%	$75.00	$60.00	$15.00	20.00%	$2,000.00	100.00%	26.7	166.67%

Regular gross profit before price changes: 40.00%

% increase in price	new price per unit	$ amount of cost per unit	$ amount of gross profit	new gross profit %	$ sales needed to earn $400 gross profit	% decrease in total $ sales permitted to earn same gross profit $	# physical units that have to be sold to earn $400 gross profit	% decrease in physical units sold permitted to earn same $ amt. of gross profit as before price increase
0.00%	$100.00	$60.00	40.00%	30.00%	$1,000.00	0.00%	10.0	0.00%
5.00%	$105.00	$60.00	42.86%	33.33%	$933.33	-6.67%	8.9	-11.11%
10.00%	$110.00	$60.00	45.45%	36.36%	$880.00	-12.00%	8.0	-20.00%
15.00%	$115.00	$60.00	47.83%	39.13%	$836.36	-16.36%	7.3	-27.27%
20.00%	$120.00	$60.00	50.00%	41.67%	$800.00	-20.00%	6.7	-33.33%
25.00%	$125.00	$60.00	52.00%	44.00%	$769.23	-23.08%	6.2	-38.46%

at a common site. (One enterprise, for example, manufactures missile parts and furniture in the same plant.) In such situations, the determination of cost by product line and the resulting profitability become more difficult to calculate with accuracy. Normally, variable costs can be determined either through identification of materials and labor specifically used by product line or through the use of engineered assumptions, or standards, to identify the variable costs that should be borne by a product or product line. However, there remains the problem of identifying the portion of fixed cost that a particular product or product line should bear.

Exhibit 13.11 illustrates how a different method of apportionment affects the conceived profit by product. The amounts shown as direct fixed cost are those that are identifiable by product line, such as depreciation on equipment, supervisory salaries, amortization of leasehold improvements, and so forth. All other fixed costs are allocated to product lines on some rational basis.

In method 1, fixed costs were allocated on the basis of square footage occupied by the equipment used in each product line. The rationale for this method was that fixed costs were related primarily to supporting the costs of operating the building and equipment. In method 2, fixed costs were allocated on the basis of variable costs, because it was felt that fixed costs were related more to supporting direct labor and the acquisition, storage, and handling of direct materials. From the standpoint of product profitability, the results are strikingly different. In method 2, for example, hot sauce appears to be a marginally profitable item, whereas in method 1, the profit margin is respectable. The consequences of making decisions regarding the retention, expansion, or elimination of product lines on the basis of such calculations are apparent—such decisions must be made with caution.

Unfortunately, there is no right or wrong method to guide us. Most cost-accounting literature speaks of the doctrine of fairness in the allocation of fixed costs. That is, each product or product line should bear its fair share of fixed costs, allocated on some logical basis. Exhibit 13.12 provides a somewhat conventional approach to allocation. It is a good starting point for determining a fair allocation, but it must, of course, be tailored to fit the circumstances found in a particular business.

An effective test of any allocation method is to develop a pro forma operating cost budget based on the total elimination of a product line from the operation. In so doing, it should be possible to estimate the costs that would not be incurred under such circumstances. For example, the production-control section might be reduced from eight to five employees, or the electricity bill might be lowered by 20 percent, and so on. The total so eliminated should approximate the total being allocated under present methods.

Irrespective of any shortcomings, the break-even analysis technique can be an extremely effective tool. Keep in mind that it is not a scientifically exact calculation but rather a guide to making management decisions. The information provided presents a range and, when used properly, shows the possibilities and ranges of what can occur. It also helps identify product lines with differing gross profits and forces the recognition that traditional classifications are not valid, such as much of direct labor being fixed rather than variable. The conversion of dollars into units can also help put things in perspective.

EXHIBIT 13.11   Impact of Allocating Fixed Costs

	Allocation Method 1				Allocation Method 2			
	Jiffy Spread	Hot Sauce	Chili Mix	Total	Jiffy Spread	Hot Sauce	Chili Mix	Total
Sales	$ 500,000	$ 150,000	$ 350,000	$ 1,000,000	$ 500,000	$ 150,000	$ 350,000	$ 1,000,000
Variable cost	160,000	75,000	115,000	350,000	160,000	75,000	115,000	350,000
Contribution to fixed cost	340,000	75,000	235,000	650,000	340,000	75,000	235,000	650,000
Direct fixed cost	40,000	15,000	40,000	95,000	40,000	15,000	40,000	95,000
Allocated fixed cost	65,000	25,000	115,000	205,000	97,000	49,000	59,000	205,000
Total fixed cost	105,000	40,000	155,000	300,000	137,000	64,000	99,000	300,000
Operating profit	$ 235,000	$ 35,000	$ 80,000	$ 350,000	$ 203,000	$ 11,000	$ 136,000	$ 350,000
Operating profit (%)	47.0	23.3	29.9	35.0	40.6	7.3	38.9	35.0

EXHIBIT 13.12   Some Typical Bases for Allocating Fixed Cost

Cost	Alternatives for Allocation Basis
Building costs—depreciation, maintenance, insurance, taxes, etc.	Square footage occupied
Heat, light, and power	Square footage occupied
Production control department	Number of direct labor employees
	Amount of direct labor
	Total direct cost
Shipping and receiving, purchasing	Number of items
	Cost of material
Stores	Number of requisitions
	Cost of material
Personnel department	Number of employees
	Hours worked

COST–VOLUME–PRICE AND THE BUDGETING PROCESS

In the foregoing sections, the elements of cost, volume, and price were discussed separately so as to illustrate the effects of each on business profits. In actual business situations, however, the three elements coexist. Because they are interrelated, any budgeting effort must consider the total effect on profit of these interrelated variables. Modeling requires the identification and simultaneous input of a number of variables. For example, the marketing manager may wish to test the profit effect of several pricing plans. Each plan could involve a change in volume, sales mix, distribution costs, commissions, cash discounts, and so on. Further, within each plan, it might be necessary to input various distribution cost arrangements or commission structures. Thus, perhaps 20 or 30 different pro forma income statements might be produced before the marketing manager is satisfied with the results.

The chief financial officer, however, would want to determine the effect on cash flow of the various marketing plans, plus certain other variables, such as inventory levels required to support the plans. Thus, any programming should be able to produce cash flow analyses, profit and loss statements, and eventual balance sheets as well as any number of subsidiary schedules. Obviously, the results of this method of budgeting are directly proportional to the validity of the underlying data. The definition of fixed and variable costs, and the interrelationship of cost, volume, and price on which the program's algorithms are based, are critical to the success in using this tool. The more knowledgeable managers are about the effect of these elements on the business, the better they will budget and the more effective the budgets will be.

CHAPTER FOURTEEN

Profitability and the Cost of Capital

Mike Kaufman
Management Advisory Group

INTRODUCTION

Developments over several decades have focused attention on the cost of capital as a management decision factor.

- Our loss of international competitive position, although largely regained, has been partially blamed on a relatively high cost of capital.
- Choices among emerging technologies with different cash flow profiles may depend on the cost of capital used for discounting.
- The rise of multibusiness corporations has led to the need to estimate divisional cost of capital.
- The desire to measure and improve performance has caused many corporations to link costs of capital to executive profit goals and executive compensation plans.

International position and technological choices reflect the quality of new capital investment. However, performance evaluation standards and divisional costs of capital should also consider capital already committed.

This chapter considers that question of how to manage existing investments over a normal planning horizon. In that context, it is important to address the question of determining the cost of capital, at both corporate and division levels.

Traditionally, companies have relied on computations of earnings and earnings growth to gauge the performance of a division and its managers. More recently, firms have realized that price/earnings ratios do not reflect shareholder's required returns. This has led to increased popularity of certain accounting measures (e.g., return on assets employed). Unfortunately, this approach often creates more problems than it solves.

For example, many companies try adding a computation of return on assets employed to the management reports, perhaps on a divisional or group basis. It can be guaranteed that in short order the manager of group A will be complaining that he has newer (or older) capital goods than group B and that therefore his performance is distorted, or he will be making some other seemingly valid objection. The manager of group B will soon follow with similar complaints, but on the other side of the issue.

This sort of situation can quickly convince senior management that return on assets is useless as a guide to action. More insidiously, it can also foster the fallacy of the higher the better, in which good performance is equated with ever higher rates of return. Obviously, what is important is to improve future profits, not percentage returns, and they are emphatically not the same thing. To take an extreme example, a manager can become a hero in a rate environment by converting her $1 million asset division earning $175,000 (17.5 percent return) into a $500,000 division earning $100,000 (20 percent). Excess emphasis on high rates of return is an implicit command to limit the growth of the enterprise and perhaps even endanger its future health by failure to commit capital at more modest, but still attractive, rates.

Most companies say that they avoid such problems by controlling more than just rate of return. One company controls financial performance on 17 key variables, which reminds one of the cartoon showing a harried secretary asking a boss, "Should I rush this job before I rush the rush job I'm rushing now?" Inevitably, the question of priorities among financial objectives arises, prompting some firms to resort to increasingly complex and bizarre bonus systems, wherein profit targets count so much, inventory targets so much, and on and on.

Obviously, no single measure applied in a single year can totally describe a manager's performance. Market position and personnel development are important, and a myriad of other factors can come into play. In the financial area, however, performance factors are too often treated as discrete variables rather than as elements in the accomplishment of the one paramount financial objective: maximizing future economic profit, which is dollar profit after deducting the dollar cost of all the capital employed.

Capital employed can be managed within an integrated system of financial controls focusing on profitability. In fact, such a system is the only sensible way to manage either capital or profits. To appreciate this, it helps to recall that there are only three ways by which to increase profitability:

1. Add new profit-making investment in either fixed or working capital.
2. Improve the rate of return on existing investment either by increasing the amount of profit per dollar of sales or by decreasing the amount of capital needed to produce each sales dollar.
3. Increase the use of debt leverage by escalating the percentage of capital supplied by relatively inexpensive debt.

Only the first method is consistently available to management as a means of improving profitability. Profit margins cannot be infinitely improved, nor can the productivity of capital employed, although there is often more room for improvement in the latter because of a lack of systematic attention to it in the past. Similarly, there is an obvious limit to the increased use of leverage. Investment of capital, however, is a means of profit improvement available to management day in and day out, year after year.

The focus here is not on major new capital projects, which presumably get their fair share of attention, but on managing the employment of working capital and existing fixed assets to ensure that they are being committed wisely. Portions of working capital are being liquidated and reinvested every day. Is the reinvestment truly profitable? Underutilized plant and equipment represent a most costly investment. Operating managers should be made aware that the assets they control are in no sense free, simply because they are already owned by the company. As noted, profit and return on investment are not independent measures of performance but are inextricably intertwined.

If profitability and capital investment are so interrelated, one cannot be managed effectively without the others being so. This chapter discusses a system of capital management and performance control that brings these two together while avoiding some of the horrendous problems that have plagued control systems. No performance control system, however, is any better than its standard of measurement. Let us turn, then, to the problem of developing a standard that can evaluate the ongoing performance of committed capital as well as new capital investments.

A MARKET GAUGE FOR PERFORMANCE

It is a rule of science that any measure can be objective and independent of the thing being measured. Where can one find an objective measure of financial performance? Certainly not by taking last year's performance and aiming to improve on it. How good was last year's performance anyway? We cannot reliably take a comparison with the rest of our industry group. It is a strange definition of performance indeed to equate it with being perhaps the least wretched example in a crowd of ne'er-do-wells.

Look everywhere. The only objective performance evaluator is the market. The product market gives us an objective answer as to the quality of our products. The financial market provides an objective answer as to the quality of our performance. The financial market, however, cannot be as tightly circumscribed as the product market. The buyer in the financial market is not limited to buying the securities of Acme Widgets or Beta Widgets. The whole panoply of financial instruments offers options, from venture capital to treasury bills. It is not that the individual buyers are considering all of these but rather that all buyers are trying to acquire the same thing: a dollar return on the funds they invest. This permits the market to arbitrage among investments, based on the relative risk/return trade-off each one offers.

The price the market will pay for a company's securities is a function of the returns it promises in relation to the risks it offers. Since the cost of anything can be defined as the price one must pay to get it, the cost of capital is the return a company must promise in order to get capital from the market, either debt or equity. A company does not set its own cost of capital; it must go into the market to discover it. Yet meeting this cost is the financial market's one basic yardstick for determining whether a company's performance is adequate.

The cost of debt capital is unmistakable. It is there for all to see in the form of an effective interest rate. The cost of equity capital is another matter entirely. Does equity have a cost? If so, does the company bear sole responsibility for meeting it? How is it determined?

COPING WITH THE COST OF EQUITY

Does equity capital have a cost? Unless one asserts that stock certificates are bought simply as collector's items, equities must be bought in anticipation of a dollar return (yield, if any, plus appreciation), which will be a cost to whomever pays it. The problem is that the consequences of not meeting that cost are unclear. If a customer pays for 12 light bulbs and finds only 10 in the package, there is certain to be some commotion. However, if he or she buys a stock anticipating a 12 percent return and gets only 10 percent, the consequences to the company are not immediately obvious. Of course, in economic substance, an owner of the business is being shortchanged. Moreover, no company can build a viable long-run business by systematically and continually shorting its customers, either product or securities customers. No company of substance would plan to do so.

Is the company solely responsible for meeting the cost of equity capital? Shareholders buy their stock in the market. Should they not have to look to the market for at least a substantial portion of their return? The argument seems persuasive. Unfortunately, on an overall basis, the market itself is unable to provide any return whatsoever. Were it not for company earnings, gains for some shareholders in the market would be precisely offset by the losses of others. Yet, over time, stocks do provide a positive return.

In the most extensive study of this nature, the return (yield plus appreciation) on a portfolio consisting of all the common stocks on the New York Stock Exchange was calculated for 51 years (January 1926 through December 1976). The average return was 9.9 percent for the series of 42 ten-year holding periods beginning in each year from 1926. In a similar study, the same return on the Standard & Poor's (S&P) 500 was reviewed from January 1926 through December 1985. For this series of 51 ten-year holding periods, the average return was 9.8 percent. Returns in recent years have moved higher with the current extended bull market. The 10-year period ending December 1995 shows a shareholder return around 15 percent. Current in-year values approaching 20 percent will likely push future 10-year returns beyond 15 percent. However, so far, these values continue to be close to the aggregate value of corporate returns on equity (ROEs) for the same periods. Thus, over time, what shareholders as a group get is what companies earn.

Cost of Equity

Determining the cost of equity is the hardest question of all. This question cannot be answered with great mathematical precision, which is very disturbing to many people. Executives who are quite willing to stake vast sums based on some readings of the product market can become very tense when told that assessing the cost of equity capital depends on some readings of the securities market. We are all required to make judgments based on limited information, and in judging the cost of equity capital, we can at least be assured that we are asking the right question in developing an objective performance standard.

The outlook for finding a good answer is not all that bleak. We can rather quickly dismiss some approaches that are clearly wrong. First, the cost of common equity does not equal dividends paid. If this were so, we could reduce the cost (i.e., the investors' demand) to zero by eliminating the dividend, which flies in the face of reason. Second, the cost of common equity does not equal the reciprocal price/earnings of the ratio. If a stock earning $5 sells at $100, its cost of capital is not 5 percent. Who would buy a stock expecting to earn 5 percent when treasury bills will pay as much or more?

No amount of lead/lag analysis of historical earnings and stock prices is likely to be productive, because the relevant earnings are expected future earnings, not historical earnings. The relationship between those expected earnings and the market price defines the cost of common equity. The relationship is expressed as a percentage, and the size of that percentage is a function of the perceived risk.

Any reasoned attempt to judge the cost of equity capital must give some consideration to relative risk. A four-step process is suggested.

1. One can observe the strong central tendency of returns in the area of 10 percent over long periods for large groups of equities. In recent periods, that average has drifted up to about 15 percent. Companies, of course, do not have the market value of their stocks to work with in the form of earning assets. However, if we could look instead at returns on book value, studies indicate that ROE also tends to be around 15 percent for the same period.

2. Over a period spanning more than a decade, several hundred senior financial officers were asked to assume the role of manager of their companies' pension funds and to indicate what rate of return on the equity portion of their funds over the next several years would satisfy them. Through the early 1980s, their answers averaged around 12 to 13 percent. Since investors in the aggregate can receive only what companies earn, these demands will be met only if the companies they invest in earn at that rate. As a second step, one can observe the logical bounds for equity costs on either side of the central tendencies that have been mentioned. At the upper end of the scale, the returns sought by venture capitalists for very high-risk deals begin somewhere around 25 percent. No well-managed company with a decent track record should need to offer consistent returns above 20 percent. Common stock, the ultimate residual security, would have to offer more return to the investor than the bonds of investment-grade issuers, which suggests a lower limit of around 10 percent. Thus, we can have a logical range, with an observed strong mean value toward the lower end.

3. One can look at risk directly. What is risk to investors? Basically, it is uncertainty concerning the amount of their return. If corporate earnings followed a smooth, fully predictable trend line, there would be no uncertainty. Thus, risk for the investor can be associated with variability of returns, which can be measured. For example, earlier studies of ROE had coefficients of variation around 0.150. This, or some other standard, can be the basis for estimating relative risk for a sector or industry and thus the premium to be added to a return standard.

4. One can apply a judgmental overlay to these statistics. In what direction are overall market returns moving? What factors would suggest that this industry will become relatively more or less risky in the future? What factors in regard to the particular company being studied would tend to suggest that it will display more or less risk than the industry average?

As mentioned, the process does not produce great mathematical precision. It does, however, permit one to zero in on the probable cost with enough accuracy for the purpose of developing an overall profit standard, derived from objective market information.

Combining Capital Costs

Surveys show that weighted average cost of capital (WACC) is the reigning method among leading corporations. However, variation in the calculation of key elements leads to disparate results. Therefore, in computing the WACC for the firm, these caveats are in order:

- Common equity must include both common stock issues and retained earnings.
- Proportions should be calculated using market-value rather than book-value weights, since market value reflects the true cost of each financing component.
- Logically, marginal weights should be employed in the case of new projects. However, a case can be made for using current or target aggregate weights for capital already committed.
- Marginal costs of debt and equity should be based on forecasts of future market expectations.

 ## BUILDING COMPANY-WIDE PROFIT GOALS

With an informed judgment of the company's cost of debt and equity in hand, there remains the matter of blending these into a WACC, based on the planned use of each:

	Planned Percentage		Cost Rate (%)		Cost of Capital (%)
Long-term debt	25	×	8	=	2
Common equity	75	×	12	=	9
Total capital	100				11%

In this illustration, a WACC of 11 percent has been calculated, assuming a pretax average future debt rate of 8 percent and an after-tax future common equity cost (including all paid-in capital and retained earnings) of 12 percent. If there was an existing or planned use of preferred stock, that would be included on an after-tax basis as well, and all convertible issues would be treated as equity for this purpose. The combining of pretax and after-tax rates is deliberate, since the cost of capital reflects the market's requirements, which are set irrespective of the company's tax position.

Developing a numerical profit goal from the WACC is a simple matter of translating to an after-tax equivalent rate. For example, if the tax rate were 50 percent, the after-tax cost of debt would be reduced to 4 percent, and the profit goal would be 10 percent overall: (25% × 4% = 1%) + (75% × 12% = 9%).

Setting the profit goal equal to the overall after-tax cost of capital permits evaluation of ongoing performance and new investment without regard to the source of the capital being employed. Without it, one would have to read across the balance sheet, appraising each asset investment based on the source of its financing. Doing this can lead to some rather absurd results. For example, one might be able to justify a new plant because it could be debt financed but unable to justify the net investment in receivables and inventory that it would generate, since these might have to be financed out of retained earnings.

In our example, requiring all asset investments to earn 10 percent before consideration of financing charges will provide for meeting the individual costs of both debt and equity. To illustrate, for $100 of capital:

Profit goal	$10
Add back taxes at 50%	10
Pretax equivalent	$20

This pretax equivalent is composed of:

Net income before interest and taxes	$20
Less interest ($25 at 8%)	2
Income before tax	$18
Taxes at 50%	10
Net income ($75 at 12%)	$ 9

A profit goal established in the preceding manner is the most effective way to bring home to operating management the standards of performance being set by the financial markets. New profit-making capital should not be deliberately committed below such a rate; existing capital should be managed so that it achieves or betters that rate.

Three rates of return are of interest in evaluating the performance of a business: (1) the cost of capital, (2) current corporate return on today's stock prices, and (3) management's forecast of the corporate rate of return. A premium, based on market expectations, explains the difference between the cost of capital and current corporate return.

The central question is which standard to use for evaluating managers. Paying managers for returns above the firm's cost of capital justly rewards them for creating shareholder value. However, such a standard falls short of what shareholders need to realize their required return at current share prices.

Using market price return to evaluate managers is an alternative; however, management may not believe that market expectations are reasonable. Using management's forecast of corporate return invokes the problem of using a standard different from that required to create shareholder value.

In making the choice of an appropriate standard, one may again wish to distinguish new projects from capital that is already committed. For example, use cost of capital or market expectations for committed funds and management's forecast for new projects.

BUILDING DIVISIONAL PROFIT GOALS

The appropriate profit goal for the whole company should at least equal the after-tax equivalent of its cost of capital. To illustrate, if a firm determines that (1) its proper capitalization should be 25 percent debt and 75 percent equity; (2) its future cost of debt and equity should be 8 (pretax) and 12 percent respectively; and (3) its future effective tax rate on income should be 50 percent; then its profit goal would be 10 percent as shown next:

(% of debt × cost) + (% of equity × cost) = Cost of debt and equity = Profit goal
(0.25 × (8% × 0.50)) + (0.75 × 12%) = (1% + 9%) = 10%

Let us see what happens when this concept is applied to the multidivisional firm. Suppose there was a large company, half of whose business was manufacturing computer equipment and half commercial financing. (Any resemblance to a company you may think of is purely coincidental.) A well-capitalized manufacturer might well opt for a 25/75 debt/equity mix, whereas a solid commercial finance business could easily carry a 75/25 mix. For simplicity, assume that each division has the same capital investment and that the market cost of debt and equity would be the same for both divisions. We would then have the profit goals that are outlined in Exhibit 14.1.

Consider what would happen if decisions were based strictly on the overall corporate goal rate. Capital would flow easily to the computer division. The required rate for investment is only 8 percent, but they should be able to average 10 percent or more in competition with other computer equipment firms.

EXHIBIT 14.1 Divisional versus Corporate Profit Goals

			Proportion × Cost		
Computer Division					
Debt	25	×	(0.08 × 0.50)	=	1.00
Equity	75	×	0.12		9.00
Capital	100				10.00
Profit goal					10%
Finance Division					
Debt	75	×	(0.08 × 0.50)	=	3.00
Equity	25	×	0.12	=	3.00
Capital	100				6.00
Profit goal					6%
Corporate					
Debt	100	×	(0.08 × 0.50)	=	4.00
Equity	100	×	(0.12)	=	12.00
Capital	200				16.00
Profit goal					8%

However, the finance division management would be hard pressed to justify even its current investment, since 8 percent is still the standard, whereas 6 percent is a legitimate expectation in the business. Of course, management may indeed decide that it wants to emphasize one division at the expense of the others, but this is no way to do it. If, over time, the company became 75 percent manufacturing and 25 percent finance, the corporate profit goal itself would have shifted to 9 percent while investments were still being judged at 8 percent.

Profit goals must be developed and applied to each of the company's identifiable lines of business. It will not do to look at the company overall or to lump the several units, divisions, or subsidiaries together and take an average. What is an identifiable line of business? There is no easy answer. Certainly, 8-ounce cans are not one line and 12-ounce cans another. However, drilling for oil overseas and refining and marketing it in the United States may well be two distinct lines, with different risks and capitalization standards as recognized by the financial markets.

The key is just that: What is the market's perception of the company? Does it view the company as being in one business or several? In general, the market tends to accept management's implicit judgment on the point, as revealed by the extent of divisionalization of the firm.

A universal problem for divisional goal setters is selecting a basis for division standards. One common approach is the so-called pure play, employing an independent proxy corporation as standard. The imputed capital structure model proposed earlier would draw on the structure of such a proxy. The pure-play method has its own shortcomings, a primary one being the frequent failure to identify a public proxy. Of course, this is yet another reason to rely on the logical methodology suggested here, drawing on management's experience and intuition.

A Problem for Divisional Goals: Overhead

Divisional profit goals introduce at least two other sources of complication. The first is what to do with the capital and expenses of central service departments (research and development, purchasing, etc.) and the home office itself. Some of this may be chargeable to the divisions based on their actual use of these departments or units. One convenient solution establishes such departments as internal profit centers, charging user divisions at cost plus a markup percentage designed to produce a return on the internal center's capital equal to the weighted average corporate profit-goal rate.

However this is handled, there will almost always be a block of capital and expense that cannot logically be associated with any division. At this point, one may make a gross allocation of the balance to the divisions (which is a practical answer if the amounts are relatively small) or leave it undistributed, viewing the divisional goal rates as, in effect, contributed and the divisional returns as, in effect, contribution margins—that is, available to cover both overhead and profit. In general, the contribution margin method seems preferable, since profit independence is vital to any good system of evaluation and control, and since it heads off pointless grousing about the fairness of what is definitionally an irrational allocation of corporate overhead.

Another Problem: Portfolio Effect

The second complication concerns the theory of portfolio effect. Portfolio theory says that, by combining two or more businesses within one company, we may decrease (or increase) the cost of capital for the firm overall, beyond what would be the weighted average for the component lines of business. Statistics and logic would both suggest that this is at least a possibility for any multidivisional company. The real issue, however, is whether the benefit of any such portfolio effect should go to reduce the profit goal of the several divisions below the appropriate goal for an independent company in the same line of business. One would think not.

In any event, it must be recognized that any company has but one cost of capital, in that investments in the divisions separately are not available to the market. The company must meet or better that overall cost. If portfolio effects have decreased the indicated overall profit goal below the weighted average of the several divisions, the company should consistently sell at a premium in the market. Potential diversifications should be weighed carefully, lest the premium potential be destroyed by adding other elements to the business mix.

If, however, the company's apparent cost of capital far exceeds what a weighted average of the divisional profit goals can produce, management should consider the composition of the business and possible divestitures.

Use of Hurdle Rates

Why do we spend so much time and effort agonizing over a rather precise profit-goal estimate? Why not just pick a hurdle rate that we know is above any reasonable estimate of our cost of capital? Management could, if necessary, set different hurdle rates for various divisions, to reflect their judgment of relative risk or to force allocations of capital in line with their strategic plans. This approach has particular appeal when the company has traditionally earned a high rate of return. Why let a manager "get away with" a 12 percent standard when the company has consistently earned 18 percent or more on total permanent capital? Perhaps we should even set a stretch target of 20 percent to get division managers really producing.

The hurdle rate approach to goal setting is widely applied, but it has a number of very serious problems. First, the hurdle rate approach constitutes a retreat from objective standards. Lacking a demonstrable anchor in market evidence, hurdles become matters of management fiat, fit subjects for argumentation, dispute, and perhaps even evasion. To operating managers, such hurdles become rules of the game rather than hard tests of performance.

Second, the purpose of market-determined profit goals is to recognize costs, not to soak up all economic value from investments. No imminent ruin looms over managements that refuse to invest in all opportunities down to the point at which costs (including capital costs) and revenues are exactly equal, that is, the profit-goal rate. If a division has traditionally earned 18 percent, and management expects that such performance can continue, it may justifiably require that performance for planning purposes and establish a new investment cutoff at that level through a profitability-index system of evaluation. By using a market-determined profit goal to charge for both existing and new capital, however, management avoids deluding itself into thinking that it cannot afford to accept investments with lower returns.

This is a very important concept, yet it is not widely appreciated. The cost of capital measures the risk of committing funds to a particular line of business. If we insist that all of our investments in that business be at rates appreciably above that cost, sooner or later our risk-adjusted cost will likely rise above the old nominal cost, since we will take only the riskiest investments offered and not make the cost-reduction or other risk-reducing investments that will keep us in line with the general risk parameters of the business.

Finally, if the cost of capital is a reasonable measure of our future financing costs (as it is meant to be), the company is demonstrably better off using the equivalent profit goals for evaluation rather than higher hurdle rates. For example, consider a company with a profit goal derived from market evidence of 10 percent yet showing a consistent ability to earn 14 percent in its business. It is evaluating two investments, A and B, of $1 million each, as described in Exhibit 14.2. If investments A and B were evaluated at a 14 percent hurdle rate, the company would see equal value and be indifferent between the two. Obviously, since $291,000 × 5 is not arithmetically equal to $1,925,000, the equivalence must reflect an implicit assumption that the annual $291,000 can be reinvested at some rate to produce a future value of $1,925,000 in total. It should come as no surprise that the rate is 14 percent.

Stated another way, the problem with investment A is that it throws off no cash until year 5 and thus funds no other interim investments, whereas B is funding such 14 percent return investments in years 1, 2, 3, and 4. That is, using the hurdle rate implies that the interim investments of $291,000 per year would not be made under investment A.

To make a fair comparison, assume that we make the same $291,000 reinvestments under both alternatives. Because investment A provides no interim returns, the reinvestments with new capital will be financed at our cost of capital rate (see Exhibit 14.3). The other investments will add their $470,000 return to the value of investment A, minus the $326,000 cost of the additional capital. Investment A's net worth is now $146,000 more than investment B and is clearly preferable. If this evaluation had used the 10 percent profit-goal rate from the start, the conclusion would have been imme-

EXHIBIT 14.2 Comparison Using a Hurdle Rate: Investment A versus Investment ($ thousands)

	Investment	
Year	A	B
0	$ (1,000)	$ (1,000)
1	—	291
2	—	291
3	—	291
4	—	291
5	1,925	291
Total return	$ 1,925	$ 1,455
Future value, using 14% hurdle rate	$ 1,925	$ 1,925

EXHIBIT 14.3 Revised Comparison of Investment A versus B ($ thousands)

Year	Project	Investment A — Reinvestment at 14%			Investment A — Financing at 10%			Investment B		
		Amount	× Factor (FV[a])	= FV	Amount	× Factor (FV)	= FV	Amount	× Factor (FV)	= FV
Now	($1,000)	—	—	—	—	—	—	($1,000)	—	—
1	—	($291)	1.689	$ 492	$291	1.464	($ 426)	291	1.689	$ 492
2	—	(291)	1.482	431	291	1.331	(388)	291	1.482	431
3	—	(291)	1.300	378	291	1.210	(352)	291	1.300	379
4	—	(291)	1.140	332	291	1.100	(321)	291	1.140	332
5	1,925	—	—	—	—	—	—	291	—	291
	$1,925			$1,633			($1,487)			$1,925

Future value of A $1,633

Future value of B 1,925

$1,925 + $1,633 − ($1,487) = $2,071

Net advantage to A $146

[a] FV = future value

diately apparent. Do profit goals or hurdle rates exert a better influence on managerial behavior? Do profit goals set at the cost of capital discourage managers from seeking outstanding but risky investments? Do hurdle rates above the cost of capital exclude value-creating projects essential to the firm's future? Or do hurdle rates above the cost of capital encourage optimistic forecasts for low-return projects?

For new investments, the answer may depend on the culture of the firm, its competitive standing, and its economic cycle position. For managing committed funds in the form of existing investments, profit goals based on divisional cost of capital appropriately address the needs of the capital market, not the economics of the product market.

There are, of course, other approaches to developing the cost of equity capital. All have their advocates in academic circles and among financial analysts. Some begin with the microeconomic concept of the risk-free rate of return, analyzing its components in terms of a basic cost of deferred consumption, plus a factor for inflation. From these data, one would then attempt to derive a risk premium for various classes of securities, up through the common equities of untried, aggressive new companies. Others implicitly abandon the idea of equity investors' being the true "owners" of a business. Under this approach, one would assent that the only real costs to a business can be measured by the cash that flows out of it. Thus, the "cost" of equity capital is equal to the minimum dividend that it must pay (presumably to keep management incumbent).

By far the most popular variation, however, begins with the idea that the earnings of a stock can be divided by its market price to derive its cost. In other words, the reciprocal of the price/earnings ratio yields a percentage that is the cost of equity capital. Of course, as an abstract principle, this is absolutely correct: The discount rate, which equates the summation of all future earnings to the market price, is mathematically the cost of capital. The difficulty is in deriving an accurate summation of all those future earnings. Even if such an objectively accurate summation could be developed, there is no certainty that the market's subjective opinion would be the same. Furthermore, real-world evidence suggests that there is very little market pricing of stocks being done this way. In fact, there is some evidence to suggest that the market changes its pricing judgments mainly by shortening or lengthening the future period over which it is even willing to consider potential earnings. Thus, in the real world, the discount rate (or cost of capital) stays relatively constant, and the discounting period changes most.

Many companies employing mathematical models for calculating the cost of equity now use a dividend growth model and/or the *capital asset pricing model (CAPM)*. Consider that the first makes intuitive sense only for companies that pay a dividend and are able to forecast growth. Second, the CAPM may provide low-quality results. The well-known beta coefficient yielded by the CAPM is often statistically insignificant, being poorly correlated with market behavior.

Many corporations using these models find themselves forced to introduce subjective preference factors to rationalize their results. Why not eliminate spurious number crunching and adopt the largely intuitive, but logically appealing, model described herein?

Future research may provide financial analysts with a more rigorous mathematical approach to estimating the cost of capital. Such an approach would have to provide a means of developing the utility function (risk profile) of the financial markets and a way of identifying the earnings horizon being evaluated as well as a means of dealing with the statistical noise being generated by current economic conditions and short-term expectations of dividend increases, stock splits, and so on. Until that day, we are left, as we so often are in business dealings, making decisions based on reasonable, but incomplete, information. As always, when one is in that position, it is at least comforting to know that one has asked the right questions.

INFORMATION PROBLEMS AND COST OF CAPITAL

Information quality affects the cost of capital in the form of "agency costs." Since investors have imperfect knowledge of their agent managers' actions and expectations, managers must be motivated to act in investors' interests.

Agency Cost of Debt

Managers can increase shareholder wealth at the expense of lenders by creating a riskier portfolio of assets. This hazard, plus the cost of monitoring and ensuring against it, constitutes the agency cost of debt. Lenders will want an interest rate that includes these costs.

Agency Cost of Equity

Managers may not act responsibly on behalf of shareholders, thereby increasing expenses and reducing investment quality. The smaller the percentage of management ownership, the more likely managers are to act in their own self-interest and the greater the agency cost of equity.

Communicating with the Market

Managers have more information about their firms than do their shareholders; management's credibility in communicating news to the market obviously affects the company's share price. Communication can be enhanced by using changes in capital structure to signal investors about management's expectations: a debt ratio increase is a signal of good prospects, and vice versa. For these signals to be credible, managers must be time-restricted as to buying or selling company shares; they must be seriously penalized in the event of bankruptcy.

SUMMARY

Determining the cost of capital is one of the many controversial issues of corporate finance. Financial authors often disagree among themselves, and more often with corporate practitioners, as to relevant capital structures and cost of capital models. However, the WACC model advocated here continues to be widely accepted among authors and practitioners.

Division-level standards for performance evaluation assume a fair level of homogeneity among project types within a division. If division projects run a gamut of categories, then project specific hurdle rates may be useful.

Also worth consideration is the more generalized concept of opportunity cost, defined as the rate of return on the best alternative investment available. As an investment-standard concept, opportunity cost is quite flexible, allowing for project-specific, divisional, or corporate investment alternatives as a basis. Distinctions may also be made between strategic and tactical opportunities or between monitoring committed capital and evaluating new investments. As with other investment standard methods, care must be taken that weighted average divisional returns recover the corporate cost of capital.

Economic value added (see Chapter 15) is a popular measurement for determining whether a business is earning more than its true cost of capital. It has its own ways of measuring capital employed and linking performance to management compensation; however, its practitioners tend to accept a company's assessment of the true cost of capital.

CHAPTER FIFTEEN

Budgeting Shareholder Value

Serge L. Wind, PhD
Lucent Technologies

 INTRODUCTION

Businesses that want to grow their market shares, or at least to be competitive in their markets, must improve productivity, foster innovation, and strive toward enhanced customer satisfaction. Businesses that want to grow, as manifested by these objectives, must increase investment now for the future.

As the source of much of this required funding, shareholders assess the potential increase in "value" of their investments in a business when deciding whether to invest. This assessment is based on their anticipated return and the risk they associate with it.

It is vital, then, for firms to focus on shareholder satisfaction by understanding what is important to this stakeholder. In this manner, the drivers of intrinsic value (or *shareholder value*) of the firm can be discerned and its value managed.

Purposes

Shareholder value provides the valuation of a business. The principal purposes of implementing (period) performance measurement of shareholder value are to:

- Provide an economic measurement of business performance from the perspective of the shareholder

- Supplement traditional accounting-based measures of business performance with cash flow valuation
- Provide proper vehicles for achieving management objectives and decisions—including the planning process, resource utilization, and employee compensation—that drive creation of value
- Provide a link between period performance metrics and shareholder value

What Is Shareholder Value?

Return to the shareholder is in the form of cash dividends and share price appreciation. Aside from psychic and other nonfinancial attributes of an investment, these are the only returns available to common stockholders.

The value of the shareholder investment emanates from the cash flow generated over the life of the business, assessed with the associated business risk. Thus, shareholder value—the economic measure of the value of a business—is expressed as the sum of future cash flows in today's dollars.

The cash flows are after-tax cash generated each period from the operations of the business, available to all providers of company capital. For a proper analysis of the true worth of cash flows over time, they must be expressed in terms of today's dollars. (See the section later in this chapter called "Time Value of Money.")

Why Focus on Cash Flow?

The concept of shareholder value is expressed in terms of cash flows and is based on current and future cash outflows and inflows from now out to the future. We are adopting an economic perspective in which cash outlays are delineated as the underlying components of an economic model of valuation. This framework was laid out by Rappaport and others.

The emphasis on the discounted cash flow (DCF) approach versus the standard, accounting-based approach also manifests itself in the types of financial measures that are most expressive of economic performance in which investors are interested. Traditional measures, such as earnings per share, returns on equity (ROE) and operating assets, do not capture all aspects of value creation, including:

- Business risk
- Investor expectations
- Time value of money

They also often reflect the effects of leverage or the debt ratio, which is the total debt of the firm divided by total capital. Finally, they are single-period, short-term measures. We need to start concentrating on measures such as the two value-based indicators delineated in the next section, which (unlike accounting earnings) have been found to be highly correlated with stock price, an external indicator of company value.

In their book on valuation, Copeland et al. sum it up accurately: "Managers who use the DCF approach to valuation, focusing on long-term cash flow, ultimately will be rewarded by higher share prices. The evidence from the market is conclusive. Naive attention to accounting earnings will lead to value-destroying decisions."[1]

Two Complementary Value-Based Measures

Two measures of shareholder value are discussed, because they are related in important ways. Both are value-based measures.

Shareholder value, based on DCFs, measures total long-term value. Long-term valuation is used for:

- Evaluation of investment decisions (both capital projects and acquisitions)
- Assessment of long-term plans and projects
- Economic decision making

As we have seen, this measure—the investors' perception of the total worth of a company—is based on all the cash flows to be generated, in order to include all future benefits or returns as well as costs of all current and future investments and added assets.

For both short-term planning and tracking, economic value added (EVA), developed by Stern and Stewart, captures the value created (or depleted) during a period of business activity.[2] (A *period* is a finite time interval, such as a year.) Because of its importance to planning and budgeting, EVA is more fully explained in the section called "Economic Value Added."

Both measures share another key property: They distinguish between operations and financing and measure the effects of only the former in valuation. Inclusion of financing effects (such as interest and number of shares), along with traditional accounting, introduces misleading non–cash-based information in measures like ROE and earnings per share.

The critical assertion to be developed for budgeting purposes is that EVA is particularly useful in tracking a plan's contribution to the total shareholder value. The nature of cash flows and their inherent difficulty for budgeting, coupled with the observation that the period cash-flow component does not reveal the state of incremental value, combine to favor an added role for EVA. Thus, EVA, apparently relegated to a period measure of value added, takes on an important new role: short-term budget tracker of total value.

LONG-TERM VALUATION

In the last section, we introduced two measures: shareholder value and EVA. Shareholder value is the long-term valuation of a company whereas EVA is a measure of

---

[1] Tom Copeland, Tim Koller, and Jack Murrin, *Valuation—Measuring and Managing the Value of Companies* (New York: John Wiley & Sons, 1990), p. 94.

[2] Joel Stern and Bennett Stewart defined a form of residual income or EVA in two publications: G. Bennett Stewart III, *Stern Stewart Corporate Finance Handbook* (New York: Stern Stewart Management Services, 1986); and G. Bennett Stewart III, *The Quest for Value* (New York: HarperCollins, 1990).

EXHIBIT 15.1   Definition of Free Cash Flow

Example of a Statement of Funds Flow		
Operating income (before interest and taxes)	$895	
+ Other income (operating)	112	
– Cash operating taxes paid	(189)	
Income after cash taxes (before interest)	818	$818
– Additions to plant net of depreciation	(98)	
– Additions to operating capital	(34)	
– Additions to investments		
Reinvestment	$(132)	$(132)
Free cash flow		$686
= Income after cash taxes (before interest)		
less Reinvestment		

short-term value creation for a period of business activity. Total value, or shareholder value, is always quantified at a point in time (e.g., as of this year), and value is a function of all future time periods.

Shareholder Value Recapitulation

Long-term valuation is the best approach to linking shareholder value creation to investment decisions. We have defined the term "value" as the summation of all projected free cash flows for a business or project, expressed in the equivalent of today's dollars.

Free cash flow represents the after-tax cash generated each period after reinvestment from the operations—not financing—of the business. Reinvestment, from the firm's perspective, consists of net plant adds (or capital expenditures for plant and equipment), changes in operating capital (or changes in receivables and inventory less payables), and investments (or acquisitions, mergers, etc.).

In Exhibit 15.1, an example is shown of free cash flow, forecasted in terms of future dollars, which must be subsequently "discounted" back to today's dollars.

Time Value of Money

The reference to "today's dollars" in the introduction is to the economic tenet that most people prefer to have cash now rather than later, because the cash can now be invested to produce returns unavailable if the cash flow is delayed. The time value of money derives from the cost of forgone opportunities.[3] With the cash flows forecasted in terms of future dollars, the time-value-of-money concept dictates that they must be discounted to equate them to today's dollars, thus providing an estimate of the present value of

---

[3] Copeland, Koller, and Murrin, *Valuation*, p. 94.

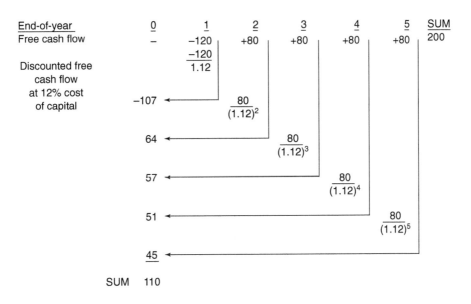

EXHIBIT 15.2　Discounted Free Cash Flow: An Example

the business from each period. We see later that risk as reflected in the cost of capital determines the discount rate.

Cost of Capital

The rate used to discount future cash flows back to the present for valuation is called the *cost of capital*, or *discount rate*. (See Chapter 14 for further discussion.)

The numerical example of discounting assumes negative cash flow of $120 in the first year for an initial project investment and positive cash flows of $80 in each of the next four years. Although the total of the five years added up to $200 in absolute dollars, that $200 is only equivalent to $110 in today's dollars. The $110 is the *present value*. Exhibit 15.2 illustrates the end-of-year free cash flows using discounted cash flow techniques at a 12 percent cost of capital.

The cost of capital is the risk-adjusted opportunity cost for investors, or the minimum required return. The cost of capital represents the average rate of return that investors expect when they decide to invest in a company of a certain risk.

The cost of capital is the weighted average cost of debt capital supplied by bondholders and equity capital supplied by the shareholders.

$$\text{Cost of capital} = (\text{After-tax cost of debt} \times \% \text{ of debt in capital ratio}) \\ + (\text{Cost of equity} \times \% \text{ of equity in capital ratio})$$

For debt, with interest tax deductible, the after-tax cost of debt is based on the prevailing interest rates (and the effective income tax rate). For equity, the more complicated

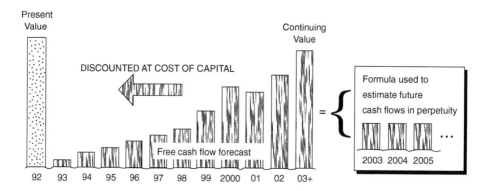

EXHIBIT 15.3   Long-Term Value: An Illustration

methods described in Stewart's book[4] are needed to estimate the cost of equity of different companies. Finally, the weights are determined by the corporate objective (or sometimes the actual) debt ratio, usually determined by the treasurer of the company. The cost of equity, in essence, is an estimate of the return required by shareholders for investing in the company's common stock, based on an assessment of the level of risk in the company and other investment alternatives in the marketplace.

Continuing Value

As shown in Exhibit 15.3, a graphical representation of a long-term value calculation, *shareholder value* is the present value of all future free cash flows. For time beyond the explicit planning period (usually five or ten years), *continuing value* captures the remaining future cash flows forecasted into perpetuity. Formulas for continuing, or residual, value can be found in the valuation book by Copeland, Koller, and Murrin.[5]

Continuing value, absolutely necessary to compute discounted cash flows, often accounts for more than 70 percent, and sometimes more than 100 percent, of total value. Moreover, with even near-term forecasts often hard to estimate, the long-term–based continuing value is often difficult to estimate reliably. However, it does represent the premium that investors are expecting beyond the explicit planning period.

Budgeting Implications

With the most important decisions made by company managers involving value of a pending project or business unit, accountability based on successful implementation is vital. A business plan and budget for the company must reflect the benefits and costs of those projects and business units for which value has been altered.

However, we have seen that valuation is a complex procedure, depending on multiple years' continuing value, which is determined by imprecise parameters and accounts for the majority portion of value, and cash flow projections with start-up problems that

---

[4] Stewart, *The Quest for Value*, pp. 431–475.
[5] Copeland, Koller, and Murrin, *Valuation*, pp. 207–230.

reverberate throughout the DCF. Budget practitioners responsible for cash flow items know that actual end-of-year (or start-up) balance sheet items (known only after the budget has been approved) must be taken into account in reestimating budget-year cash flows (such as payables, receivables, additions to plant, and free cash flow).

The complexity and reliability of budgeting and tracking discounted cash flows for even the first few years leaves us amenable to other budgeting notions.

ECONOMIC VALUE ADDED

We have seen why shareholder value is vital in assessing a company's value over the long term. An ongoing firm must be able to check progress as well, and measure increases in value with a short-term measure. Economic value added, depicted as the most important period measure of value added (or depleted),[6] will also be seen to provide a means for effective budgeting for the DCF measure of shareholder value.

Economic Value-Added Overview

Rather than estimating total value via multiyear cash flows, EVA measures period value added to or depleted from shareholder value. It relates income statement and balance sheet activity to shareholder expectations and uses traditional accounting information as a surrogate for cash flows. It is more highly correlated with stock price than are traditional measures, according to empirical studies by Stern and Stewart.

The EVA formula incorporates earnings, cash income taxes, balance-sheet capital, and the cost of capital so that value created is measured. (Positive value is created when the return on invested capital exceeds the cost of capital.) Operating returns in excess of (or below) the cost of capital are measured by EVA. (Financing impacts, such as the tax deductibility of interest expense, are excluded.)

Example of Value-Added Concept

If you borrow $100 from a bank at a 10 percent rate for one year, and you earn 12 percent return on the money through investment or the racetrack, you have created value for yourself. Your return exceeds the bank's cost to you by two percentage points.

If, however, with the bank cost fixed at 10 percent, you manage only an 8 percent return, you have lost money and value by two percentage points.

In an analogous fashion, if the return on invested capital (ROIC) exceeds the cost of capital, value is added. Value is depleted for the period when ROIC is less than the weighted average cost of capital.

We have already referred to the cost-of-capital component; it is more complex (e.g., two dimensions) than the cost of debt in the example, but plays a role analogous to the hurdle rate. (A *hurdle rate* is a threshold value for determining economic acceptance of a project: The return must exceed the hurdle rate.)

---

[6] Stewart, *Stern Stewart Corporate Finance*, pp. 3–14.

We now need to be a bit more precise in defining the return on capital and an explicit EVA equation.

Economic Value-Added Formula

Building into the formula the feature that EVA is positive only when the return exceeds the cost of capital, the EVA formula[7] can be written in this way:

$$\text{EVA} = (\text{Return on invested capital} - \text{Cost of capital}) \times \text{Average invested capital}$$

Note that EVA is an actual dollar figure, not a percentage. Its sign indeed depends on the sign of the *spread*, the difference between return and cost of capital (both percentages). Its magnitude or size depends, in large part, on average capital, which is also dollar denominated.

Implications for Value Creation

There are three basic means of securing an increase in EVA for the company, as pointed out by Stewart.[8] An increase in EVA will result if:

- Operating efficiency is enhanced (rate of return on existing capital base improves)
- Value-added new investments are undertaken (additional capital invested returns more than cost of capital)
- Capital is withdrawn from uneconomic activities (capital withdrawn where returns are below cost of capital)

Components of Economic Value Added—Return on Invested Capital

Return on invested capital in the EVA formula must exceed the cost of capital (the hurdle rate; defined in the "Cost of Capital" section earlier in this chapter). Also a percentage, ROIC is defined as:

$$\text{ROIC} = \frac{\text{Net operating profit after taxes}}{\text{Average invested capital}}$$

Net operating profit after taxes (NOPAT) represents posttax earnings before payment of capital costs (i.e., interest and dividends). Essentially, NOPAT includes all revenues and sales net of costs and expenses, plus other operational income, less cash income taxes paid (except for the deductibility of financing-related interest). As such, NOPAT is the right measure to compare pre–capital-cost earnings with investors' costs. Cash

---

[7] Joel Stern and Bennett Stewart defined EVA and its concept and are responsible for its development into an important model for creating and managing value; the description of EVA in this chapter is based on the value-based framework they generated. See Stewart, *Stern Stewart Corporate Finance Handbook* and *The Quest for Value*.

[8] Stewart, *The Quest for Value*, p. 138.

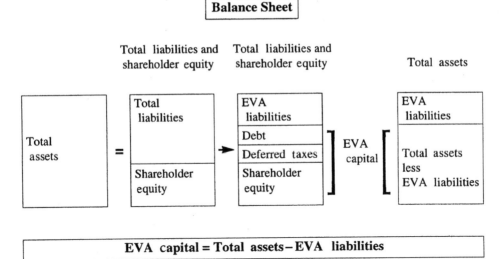

EXHIBIT 15.4   EVA Capital

taxes are more consistent with cash-flow valuation and serve as an appropriate operating driver of EVA, because of comprehensive income taxation employed in accounting.

Components of Economic Value Added—Invested Capital

The third component of the EVA formula is average *invested capital*; it also forms the denominator of ROIC. Invested capital represents the cumulative cash invested in the company over time. Exhibit 15.4 illustrates how EVA is calculated.

Economic value-added capital is defined as the difference between assets and EVA liabilities (excluding debt and deferred taxes), or, equivalently, in terms of the right-hand side of the balance sheet, equity plus equity equivalents (e.g., deferred taxes), plus debt.

In both capital and NOPAT, some corresponding adjustments to each term are required to fit in the EVA formula. Basically, as defined by Stewart,[9] most of these adjustments involve replacing book accounting value with terms that are more cash-flow or economic based. EVA capital, including the adjustments contained in equity equivalents (e.g., deferred taxes), which convert the standard accounting book value to a form of economic book value, is a truer measure of the cash invested.

Operating Drivers of Value

Key value drivers can be used effectively to include a detailed analysis of the EVA sensitivity to changes in input parameters. Operating drivers include revenue growth, NOPAT margin (i.e., NOPAT divided by revenues), capital turnover (revenues divided by average capital), and some of the other variables from the income statement and balance sheet

---

[9] Stewart, *Stern Stewart Corporate Finance Handbook*, pp. 8–13.

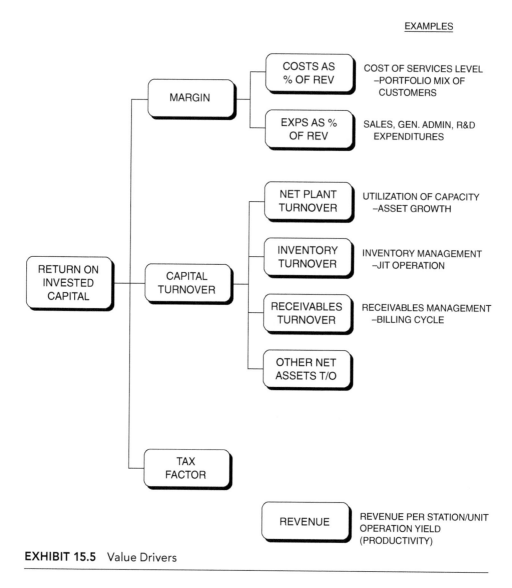

EXHIBIT 15.5   Value Drivers

as depicted in Exhibit 15.5. For example, inventory turnovers and receivables turnover (or days outstanding) are operating drivers of EVA via capital.

Most of these drivers are related to ROIC via duPont decomposition, or *ROIC tree*.[10] For example, NOPAT margin times capital turnover times the tax factor equals ROIC.

Financing drivers, distinct from operating drivers, include debt ratio and amounts and costs of capital but are not controlled by business units or profit centers.

Sensitivity analysis can be applied to valuation and associated decision making once the key drivers with the greatest impact on value are identified. For budgeting,

---

[10] Copeland, Koller, and Murrin, *Valuation*, p. 125.

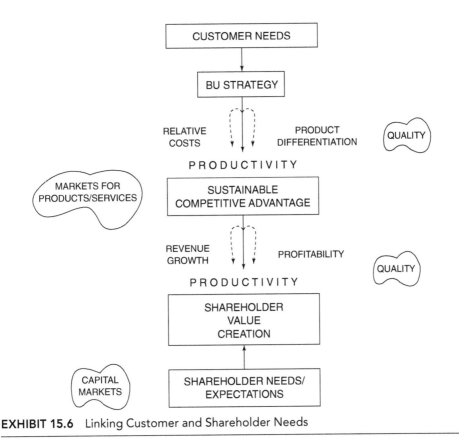

EXHIBIT 15.6 Linking Customer and Shareholder Needs

Source: Adapted and generated from Prakash Deo's unpublished AT&T paper, "Resource Alignment" (1991).

the drivers can identify the source of any variance and can be used for unit trend comparison.

Economic Value-Added Attributes

In describing EVA, its principal attribute in short-term planning is that it is "the single most important indicator of value creation. . . . EVA measures not only management's ability to manage capital efficiently, but takes into account the magnitude of capital investment as well."[11]

In addition, EVA is an indicator of the company's productivity. We usually think of a firm or industry as competing in a market for products and/or services. The conceptual approach of shareholder value suggests that there is another market—the market for investor capital—in which all publicly owned companies must compete simultaneously with their other markets.

As indicated in Exhibit 15.6, the firm strives to attain a sustainable competitive advantage in its markets for its products and services, through product differentiation,

---

[11] *Stewart, Stern Stewart Corporate Finance Handbook*, pp. 3–14.

cost minimization, and so forth, to satisfy its customers. Simultaneously, via profitability and revenue growth drivers, the firm satisfies its shareholders' expectations by value creation emanating from its products and services.

Productivity is foremost a measure of ability to create value (or output) in excess of the cost (input) of generating it. Two complementary productivity measures are suggested:

1. *Operating margin.* For expense productivity and income statement efficiency (pretax NOPAT divided by total revenues)
2. *Capital turnover.* For capital productivity and balance sheet efficiency (revenue per average capital)

Productivity improvement is year-over-year percentage change in either measure.

ROIC is the joint measure of operating margin and capital productivity; it reveals the company's productivity, as determined by the spread between return on capital and cost of capital, in competition for investor capital.[12]

EVA can also be decomposed by disaggregating financial results to delineate the impact of key operating drivers, such as revenue growth; pretax profit margin per sale; cash tax rate; net operating capital (NOC) charge; and plant, property, and equipment (PPE) charge. These last two drivers, proposed by Stern Stewart, represent the normalized variable (NOC/sales and PPE/sales) times the cost of capital (COC) (before taxes), and are derived from viewing EVA as residual income (of earnings in excess of capital charges); that is, EVA = NOPAT − COC × Average invested capital.

In the 1992 AT&T Annual Report, chief financial officer Alex Mandl wrote:

> EVA is truly a system of measurement. It supplements traditional accounting measures of performance, giving us additional insight into our business and helping us to identify the factors that affect our performance. We have made it the centerpiece of our "value-based planning" process. And we are linking a portion of our managers' incentive compensation to performance against EVA targets in 1993.

Moreover, EVA has the important facility of connecting forward-looking valuation to performance evaluation (via actual operating performance) over discrete periods. EVA thereby enables consistent tracking of valuation. However, first, we need to explore in more depth the relationship between the two measures, EVA and shareholder value.

COMPLEMENTARY MEASURES OF VALUATION

Economic Value Added and Valuation

The term "shareholder value" was defined as the multiperiod, long-term valuation of a company (as of a point in time), whereas we have just seen that EVA measures value added to a shareholder's investment for a period (e.g., a year or quarter).

---

[12] Stewart, *Stern Stewart Corporate Finance Handbook*, pp. 3–14.

To determine the economic value of an enterprise, operating unit, or project requires a valuation—or all-period analysis—of all future cash flows. Generally, the entity value is the future expected cash flows discounted at a rate (or cost of capital) that reflects the riskiness of the operating cash flow. In particular:

$$\text{VALUE} = \text{PV(FCF)} = \frac{\text{FCF 1}}{1 + \text{COC}} + \frac{\text{FCF 2}}{(1 + \text{COC})^2} + \cdots$$

where FCF 1 stands for the free cash flow in period 1 and PV denotes present value or discounted sum.

It is, however, true (only under some conditions) that VALUE also equals the present value of the EVAs plus initial capital (CAP):

$$\text{VALUE} = \text{PV(EVA)} + \text{CAP}$$

where

$$\text{PV(EVA)} = \frac{\text{EVA1}}{1} + \text{COC} + \frac{\text{EVA2}}{(1 + \text{COC})} +$$

Here the term "capital" is not equal to the book value of traditional accounting but represents economic book value, where adjustments, such as the deferred tax reserve, are added to book debt and equity to allow capital to reflect a more economic and accurate base on which to earn. Exhibit 15.7 shows an example of valuation.

Although individual-period EVA is usually different from FCF for the same period, under a specific set of assumptions, the two approaches generally yield the same value, that is,

$$\text{PV (FCF)} = \text{PV (EVA)} + \text{CAP} = \text{VALUE}$$

when the amount of initial capital of the firm is added to the discounted EVA (or value-added) sum.

This result is important, because it suggests that VALUE may, under certain assumptions, be calculated using EVA components (in place of cash flow) and that the

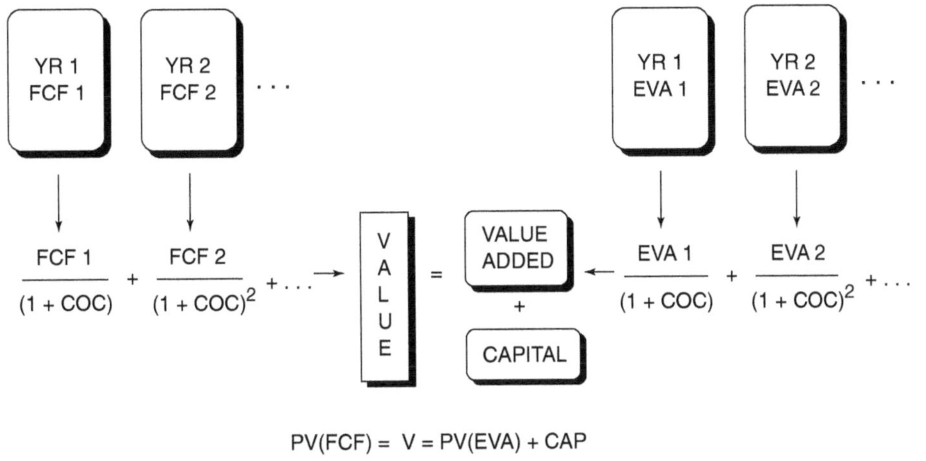

$$\text{PV(FCF)} = \text{V} = \text{PV(EVA)} + \text{CAP}$$

EXHIBIT 15.7 Valuation

definition of EVA as a period measure of value added yields the same VALUE when a discounted sum of EVA terms is taken. Shareholder value can be expressed in terms of EVA components too.

For initial implementation, using VALUE (EVA) for valuation is not always recommended, because the set of assumptions for value equality may not be valid in all cases and FCF-based routines are well established for project valuation in business cases in most firms. The specialized circumstances and assumptions for VALUE equality may not be applicable to the majority of projects and investments of a firm without an adjustment.

Identification and correction of any systematic difference in the VALUE determined by EVA and FCF (usually a function of project timing and start-up assumptions) may be viewed as a transition issue. As implementation takes root, the advantages of consistency—of using EVA as one common measure with a common language and framework, with operating drivers for all planning and budgeting, for both period and total value estimation—may dominate the discomfort of any needed adjustments. In addition, as shown by Worthington,[13] the contribution (as a percentage of total value) from EVA continuing value will be less than the percent value attributed to the FCF continuing value; part of this effect is attributable to the role of initial capital in the EVA net present value (NPV) formulation. Even with reliance on the cash flow approach to calculating value, it would be useful to complement it with the EVA approach to get a different perspective on the components of total value, specifically the value added in the early years and the continuing value.

What is interesting, however, is that the period component of PV (FCF) does not yield any information about value added for the period—but EVA does, by definition. Instead, FCF merely indicates the dependence on parent or external financing.

Tracking by Economic Value Added

We have already touched on some difficulties associated with budgeting and tracking valuation by cash flows: the dependence on an intractable continuing value, the impossibility of tracking all years, the shifts in cash flows in the budget year caused by actual prior year-end balance sheet variances, and the lack of information inherent in component cash flows.

A few years of EVA data, however, indicate how much value has been created by management and thereby evaluate progress toward shareholder value. When all-period valuation is appropriate, it is recommended that EVA period measures be generated for the first three to five years of analysis, along with the multiyear valuation to supplement the FCF valuation approach and to provide a basis for meaningful budgeting and tracking. As a period performance measure, EVA connects forward-looking valuation to performance evaluation. Because EVA is not a cash-flow measure and because its period interpretation is value oriented, it greatly facilitates period tracking of value, thereby adding "memory" to the planning process.

---

[13] Adapted from Mac Worthington's unpublished AT&T presentation, "Terminal Value Computation in Cash Flow Valuation of Business Opportunities" (1994).

Guide to Appropriate Uses of Economic Value Added

EVA is the best internal, single-period measure of value creation. However, single-period values of EVA are not to be used for critical asset or investment and project evaluation decisions, which are based on long-term value creation potential. Instead, discounted cash-flow valuation utilizing NPV is mandated for decisions involving multiperiod benefits, such as business unit evaluation, lease/buy decisions, mergers and acquisitions, and strategic options assessment.

As discussed earlier, EVA, in addition to its primary role, can serve as a complement to discounted cash-flow valuation, particularly to gauge the initial impact of the project or investment, and to track.

 ## BUDGETING SHAREHOLDER VALUE

Critical investment decisions, based on long-term valuation, come in several different forms in a typical corporation. Budgeting of these investments is often spotty, partly because it is difficult to isolate the effects of an investment project embedded in an operating unit's returns.

Business Cases

Business cases are the fundamental support analysis for business decisions involving resource utilization. The business-case process, while dealing with periodic projects and investments, must be an integral part of budgeting and planning.

Business cases for research and development and capital (additions to PPE) also serve as the basis for subsequent measurement and tracking actions.

As part of the financial analysis of the project, business-case output should exhibit the NPV and other standard measures as well as the EVA forecasts for the first three to five years. The latter will be compared to actuals to determine whether initial additions (or depletions) from value are on schedule. Incremental cash-flow effects of investment are represented, along with risks, uncertainty, and alternatives.

Review and approval procedures are usually specified by corporate governance. For example, it is a Lucent corporate requirement that a rigorous business-case process drive business investment decisions. Capital investments are further discussed in Chapter 25.

Capital and Investment Programs

Potential mergers and acquisitions, divestitures, investments, and joint ventures are included in these programs, along with additions to capital and additions to finance assets; the latter two categories are included in the program at a more aggregate level.

Consummated ventures should be tracked quarterly, comparing budget and actual values for revenues, EVA, funding, and the like.

Part of the investment analysis is an evaluation of the expected impact on the parent's reported EVA earnings after the acquisition. This assessment is usually more important than the EVA expected from the new entity itself.

Review of major investments will be based on a comparison of original enabling business-case expectations with actuals. Again, comparison of the first few years' actuals versus plan EVA values is strongly recommended.

A clear understanding should exist as to the circumstances under which a potential acquisition should be included in the company and entity budgets rather than merely covered by a separate investment program or business case. Generally, large magnitudes combined with a high degree of uncertainty result in omission of the investment from the budget or statement of the budget with and without the investment. "Ready for approval" investments are usually reflected in the budget.

Business Plans

As a part of the annual planning process, each business unit is expected to generate a business plan, consisting mainly of a strategic plan and a financial plan. The first year of the financial plan usually becomes next year's budget. Its monitoring and tracking are discussed in the "Operating Budget Review" section later in this chapter.

However, budgeting and tracking should also play a role in subsequent assessments of the business plan. To curtail undue optimism in the late years of the plan (the hockey-stick effect), financial projections, particularly EVA and revenue, should be monitored and compared to actuals, from the second through tenth years. Such an assessment would conceivably contribute to a greater degree of comfort or discomfort for the attainability of the immediate budget year.

Resource Allocation

Based on resource requirements expressed in the business plans to achieve business strategies and long-term economic profits, senior management makes resource allocation decisions as a step in arriving at a budget for next year and beyond. Strategic considerations are paramount, or at least share equal billing with economic considerations in all resource-allocation decisions. A business-case analysis of the life-cycle cash flows indicates the economic value of a project.

Economic considerations generally can be assessed by two broad categories: benefit and efficiency measures.[14] Benefit measures reveal the cash benefit from investing in a particular proposal, expressed in dollar terms; measures include shareholder value, NPV, and discounted cash flows. Efficiency measures, expressed as a percentage, indicate how productive a project is in generating cash, relative to resource costs. A ratio of shareholder value or NPV to the PV of all cash outflows (resource expenditures) is used, as is an internal rate of return. Long-term attractiveness tends to dominate decisions, and capital projects and investments could be ranked by total value (or by value per resource input).

Translation of the consequences of resource allocation must be included in the budget. Economic impact should include impact on EVA and total value. Considerations of cash affordability for the firm must also be evaluated.

---

[14] Adapted from Harish Chandra's unpublished AT&T memo, "Resource Allocation" (1993).

Operating Budget Review

Once major resource allocation decisions are made, attention falls on the commitment budget. Now period measures such as EVA and FCF are more important as indicators of value added and current cash flow than total valuation. The year-to-year change in unit EVA is as important a measure as the current level of EVA (and its sign).

The budget should pose a challenge that is achievable. If each operating unit makes its EVA level, and that EVA level is viewed as a stepping stone toward maximizing shareholder value over time, the enterprise will be successful.

A budget (by year; quarter; and, usually, month) consists of parts or all of an income statement, balance sheet, funds flow, and measures (particularly, the explicit commitment measures to which compensation is tied). In this budgeting mode, EVA is the best measure.

Monthly Actuals Reporting

Key measures compared by unit and month for budget versus actual and budget versus last year's period should include EVA, FCF, and revenue. EVA can be decomposed into its operating drivers—revenue growth, NOPAT margin, and capital turnover—and the respective variances compared, to better understand shortfalls.

Exhibit 15.8 displays useful information for management of budget/actual differences in EVA, underlying data, and drivers. Consolidated EVA is also shown in internal company reports as a sum of entity EVAs for actual and budget, enabling identification of entity shortfalls. A modified tree diagram (see Exhibit 15.5) displays more value drivers, to assess the principal source of actual/budget variance.

EXHIBIT 15.8   EVA Year-to-Date Results

($)	Actual	Budget	Difference
Operating income	133	139	(6)
EVA adjustments	(11)	(9)	(2)
Adjusted operating income	122	130	(8)
Cash taxes paid	(35)	(37)	2
NOPAT	87	93	(6)
Average invested capital	579	599	(20)
EVA	20	24	(4)
EVA Drivers Impact			
Change in NOPAT			(6)
Change in adjusted operating income		(8)	
Change in cash taxes paid		2	
Change in average capital @ 11.5% cost of capital			2
Change in EVA			(4)

SUMMARY

Effectively managing and measuring value calls for different, although complementary, techniques depending on the intended use and the associated time period required. For decisions involving long-term value creation potential, the all-period FCF valuation should be utilized to estimate shareholder value. However, for budgeting purposes, the EVA annual component is particularly valuable in budgeting as a measure of value created in a period. It indicates how much value is to be created from capital by management and thereby evaluates progress toward the all-period shareholder value.

For a single period, EVA is the best measure of value creation, and EVA should be monitored and tracked for budgeting.

Valuation must be closely linked to single-period measures of value created. When all-period valuation is required (e.g., business cases), it is recommended that EVA period measures be generated for the first three to five years of analysis to provide a basis for meaningful budgeting and tracking.

We have seen that EVA is particularly well suited to discern the drivers of EVA budget variances, especially to determine whether the income statement or balance sheet is variance causative.

Adding measures such as EVA to budget and planning processes has some practical consequences, which have been very positive. In particular, attention must be paid to balance sheets, not just income statements.

The use of EVA has also aided the establishment of market-facing business units and strategic business units by prescribing a meaningful sufficient set of financials and an associated measure of value added that enables close scrutiny of the true financial performance of these discrete entities. Thus, adoption of EVA is seen as a boon to driving financials to the smallest revenue-generating units, because cash taxes and capital on the balance sheet, in addition to standard profitability, are required components at a business-unit or strategic–business-unit level (usually characterized by separate markets, customers, products/services, competitors, etc.).

CHAPTER SIXTEEN

Applying the Budget System

R. Layne Weggeland
Malcolm M. Knapp, MBA
Malcolm M. Knapp Inc.

Edward Mendlowitz, CPA
WithumSmith+Brown

INTRODUCTION

This chapter discusses the considerations and techniques involved in the analysis, review, presentation, and approval of the budget.

Earlier chapters have described the need for the budget manager to issue both a comprehensive planning calendar and the statement of the chief executive officer (CEO) of overall corporate and divisional goals and objectives for the next planning period. The budget manager should also prepare a clear and concise planning manual containing completed examples of all forms that must be used by the divisions. Care must be taken to ensure that the forms are simple in format and easy to use.

Recognition needs to be made that there is no one overall budget system but rather a system of many little budgets that are combined to form the comprehensive overall company budget and projection. Further, care must be made to determine that the budgets are not only properly prepared but are providing the right information to establish areas of control, responsibility and accountability for areas where the outcomes can be measured and to effect the proper outcome from each department or subdepartment budget control person. Each department budget has to be integrated in a way that reflects the realistic manageable projected outcomes.

The manager responsible for the review, presentation, and approval process must accomplish three tasks early in the budget planning and review cycle.

1. In establishing an effective budgetary control system, the budget manager of any organization must create a system within his or her department that will provide for the careful analysis and review of the data submitted as part of a budget proposal. The manager must then present the budget, after appropriate review and discussion with lower-level management and departmental groups, in a clear and concise format for senior management review, discussion, and eventual approval.

2. The budget manager should try to convince the CEO of the need for a clear relationship of the line-division executive's performance review, compensation, and career-path development with the budgeting process. When this linkage is established, the divisional operating executives are involved thoroughly in the budgeting process and follow, with great care and commitment, the analysis, review, and approval of their individual budgets.

3. The budget manager should be sure that the budgetary planning system reflects both the artificial time constraints proposed by the need for annual financial reporting and tax filing and the real-world, longer-term business patterns of various corporate projects (i.e., major marketing plans, capital improvements, and research and development activities), which frequently extend over a two- to five-year time span.

Before detailed analyses and reviews are made of individual divisional budget plans, it is important that the budget manager identify and keep clearly in mind the key variables in his or her own corporation, its industry, and the economy. These variables include:

- The rate of new product introduction by the company and its competitors
- Market share and relationship to competitors
- Marketing and sales policies
- Financial ratios
- The degree of capital intensity
- Raw material and manufacturing capacity limitations
- Governmental restrictions
- Economic factors

There might be other key variables that are carefully monitored by senior management and that must be considered by the budget manager in the review.

Budget managers must be very knowledgeable about the degree of accuracy that their organizations have attained in their accounting and reporting systems and sales forecasts and about the organization's historical ability to achieve marketing and cost-control programs and goals.

Before beginning any analysis, the budget manager also must be very clear about the budget-year goals of the company as stated by senior management early in the planning-cycle year. Ideally, the budget officer would have been involved in discussions with senior management in formulating the goals of the company that must be incorporated in the budget period to be reviewed.

Each division or appropriate operating group prepares as part of its budget package (where appropriate and as requested by the budget manager) these items:

- Detailed sales and marketing plans
- Manufacturing and operating expense plans
- Manpower budgets
- Capital expenditure plan
- Financial budgets (balance sheet, profit and loss statement, sources, and application of funds)

The budget manager, depending on the circumstances and the degree of detail that is needed, may request the preparation of a variety of additional budget forms to provide details under the broad categories just listed. Each operating group's budget package could possibly contain a combination of these detailed schedules:

- Gross/net sales by product line
- Analysis of gross sales growth
- Sales forecasts by product line
- Manufacturing expense analysis
- Monthly departmental expense plan
- Personnel compensation analysis
- Summary of operating group net income
- Cost of sales plan
- Operating expense analysis
- General administrative expense analysis
- Capital projects summary
- Capital projects listing of new projects
- Capital projects listing of carryover projects
- Balance sheet
- Cash-flow forecast plan
- Inventory forecast plan

Accompanying each operating group's budget submission should be a general manager's commentary on the plan's assumptions, profit objectives, primary programs, and required investment and profit potential that would result from the acceptance by senior management of the operating group's budget plan.

INITIAL BUDGET DEPARTMENT REVIEW OF DIVISIONAL BUDGET PACKAGES

Following the receipt of the divisional budget packages, the budget-planning group starts a series of reviews of each budget submission, as shown in Exhibits 16.1 and 16.2.

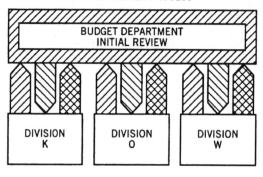

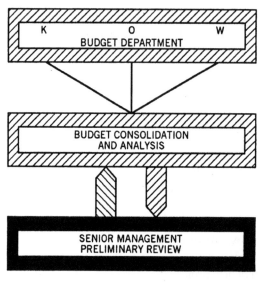

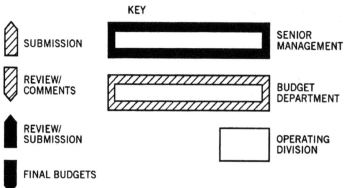

EXHIBIT 16.1   Budget Review Process—Initial Review

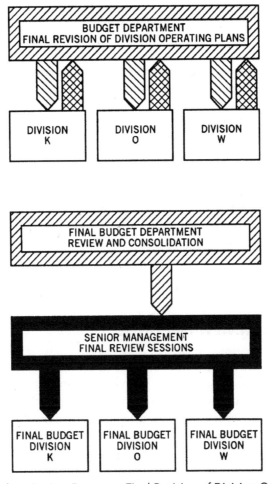

EXHIBIT 16.2 Budget Review Process—Final Revision of Division Operating Plans

The initial review includes three steps:

1. *Data verification*

   a. Review of the mathematical calculations within the plans
   b. Confirmation that the sales and marketing estimates are integrated correctly into all operating budgets within each division

2. *Analysis of previous forecast reliability.* A comparison should be made between the actual results and the forecasts of past years, that of the current year, and the proposed performance in the next planning year. The reasons for the current-year variances should be carefully evaluated, and then a comparison should be made with the proposed budget year to see that corrective action has been built into the plan in order to avoid significant variances in the following year. Variances

should be segregated as much as possible into categories of dollars and units. In some cases dollar variances are beyond the control of the person responsible for the budget, such as sharp rises in commodity prices or company pricing policies as it reflects desire for greater market share without regard to the bottom line profits.

3. *Analysis of divisional budget assumptions and goals.* The assumptions and goals incorporated into each division's budget plans must be tested for validity in these areas:

   a. Correlation to CEO's planning objectives and goals
   b. Relation to general economic conditions and forecasts of possible economic changes within the forthcoming planning year
   c. Impact of specific economic issues affecting that operating division's interest rates, cost of capital, and so forth
   d. Competitive analysis
   e. Technological change
   f. Raw material cost and availability
   g. Other assumptions incorporated into the budget submission, such as sales and marketing goals

DIVISIONAL REVIEW MEETINGS

After the budget department's initial review of each division's budget-plan submissions, the budget manager should hold a series of review meetings at the divisional staff level. These meetings should involve discussion and resolution of the issues that developed from the initial budget department staff review. The outcome of these meetings should be a revised budget that is free from obvious errors and omissions.

Following the divisional group staff-level reviews, the budget manager should hold a private review meeting with the division's general manager. During this meeting, the budget manager should identify and attempt to resolve those items that surfaced during the staff-level review meetings and to be certain that the division's general manager will make a total commitment to the revised budget plan that has resulted from the review meetings at the divisional staff level. Since, ideally, the compensation of the division's general manager would, in part, be related to his or her division's performance in the next planning cycle, it is important that all areas of dispute be clearly resolved and that the general manager and his or her staff be in total agreement and fully accept and support the revised budget plan.

During these review meetings, the budget manager must be very alert to the possibility of reserves being incorporated into the division's plans in order to provide a cushion and to protect performance-oriented compensation payments for the division's general manager and his or her senior management group. This type of reserve must be clearly identified and eliminated at the divisional level prior to the final presentation of each plan to senior management.

BUDGET CONSOLIDATION AND ANALYSIS

Following its review of the divisional plans, the budget department staff prepares a consolidation of the various divisional budgets. Ideally, budget managers and their staffs should have access to the latest budget-control software systems permitting rapid and accurate consolidation of the divisional group budgets; easy intercompany eliminations; and elimination of sunk, fixed, or overhead cost allocations to that department.

At this point, budget managers would have their first indication of the total corporate profit that would result from the consolidation of the individual budget plans. They must then test the total corporate budget against the previously stated senior management goals and objectives for the next planning period. Typical goals might be:

- A certain level of sales for the corporation
- Specific earning targets
- A specific return on asset targets
- Staffing requirements
- Inventory levels

The budget manager should form a comprehensive opinion as to whether the total corporation will be within or will fail to obtain the original objectives that were set forth by the CEO.

 ## PRELIMINARY SENIOR MANAGEMENT REVIEW

After the first corporate consolidated budgets are reviewed and analyzed, the budget manager and his or her staff should prepare a summary written review and analysis for the CEO, the chief financial officer, and the executive vice president. The budget manager then would meet with the senior executive management of the company and review in broad terms the total corporation's consolidated budget summaries, discussing whether each operating division has, in its budget plan, satisfactorily met the CEO's planning objectives.

If, during the planning cycle, external events and internal evaluation provided by the divisional managers create the need for a critical reassessment of the CEO's original goals and objectives, then the budget manager must raise this question with senior management. Possibly, modifications may be required in the corporation's goals and objectives.

If senior management gives a general acceptance of the division's plans and the overall corporate plan, then the budget manager goes back to each division and indicates senior management's acceptance of the division's plans or identifies specific areas that must be changed prior to senior management's final review and approval.

■ FINAL REVISION OF OPERATING GROUP PLANS

The operating division's general manager and his or her management would revise their budget to conform with any comments, suggestions, and criticisms expressed by senior management during its initial review.

■ SECOND BUDGET STAFF REVIEW OF OPERATING GROUP PLANS

Following revisions, the budget manager and his or her staff would again test the revised budgets against the stated objectives and the specific comments raised during the initial senior management review. The divisions would again be contacted, and any further modifications would be discussed and accepted by the operating groups.

A method of testing the validity of the budgets should be developed to maintain process integrity. The tests should be done in real time and at unscheduled times. The procedure does not need to be involved. Auditors should review the underlying documentation that supports the conclusions on the budget. This documentation should then be tested against actual transactions. Many times the budget is seen as a chore by a department manager, and the previous year's budget or the current year's actual results are used as the basis for the budget. This method creates a macro budget for that department but loses all elements of control or specific responsibility and responsiveness to change events. To be an effective tool, the budget needs to have all the minutiae of each control segment. The CEO can apply the macro thinking to the company's comprehensive consolidated budget, but they need to know that each element was deliberately thought out and the right degree of thought was present.

A method of viewing post period events that affect the previous year's budget also need to be developed. This can be done by looking at any of the current year's activities that should be rolled back to the prior year. An example could be where excess inventory is acquired to meet quantity pricing schedules or obtain discounts, or where the inventory is clearly above desired amounts. Another situation is where extra inventory is produced drawing in overhead and fixed costs elements that increase the cost of the inventory and shift such fixed costs into a later period—one where there is inventory reduction.

An example of the detail needed can be shown by the issues to be considered for the sales projections:

- The types of customers
- The number of customers
- The frequency of orders and reorders
- The size of each order
- The dependence on the four or five largest customers and the aggregate concentration of their business
- The reliance on a single customer or group or industry the customer is in
- How the customers will use the product

- Effects on maintaining inventory
- The potential for style becoming stale
- The uniqueness of the product
- The reason the customers will patronize the company
- The existence of contracts with customers and their length
- Whether the business cycle is seasonal (If so, indicate that in the projections of monthly sales.)
- If it is seasonal:

    - A schedule showing each month's percentage of the annual sales
    - Results of a test to determine if this information was used in the purchasing, manufacturing and inventory buildup projections

- Besides dollars, units that will be manufactured, inventoried, and sold
- Schedules for growth in units and sales prices
- An indication of the geographic area the company operates in—whether local, regional, national, or international customer base—and why and what expectations of success the company has
- If not local, the warehousing and distribution facilities the company has and how they are staffed and controlled

REVISED CONSOLIDATED BUDGET PREPARATIONS

When the budget department is satisfied that the divisional revised plans are in accord with the planning goals and that they are prepared properly, the budget department would prepare a new consolidated corporate budget summary. The summary would be prepared in various levels of detail, to reflect the particular interests and needs of senior management and divisional management.

Also, the budget department, where appropriate, could prepare a variety of visual aids to be used during the senior management planning review sessions. The budget manager and his or her staff should be very careful to preview visual aids with the division's general manager and staff prior to using them in the senior management review sessions.

FINAL SENIOR MANAGEMENT BUDGET REVIEW SESSIONS

At least a week before the senior management final budget review meeting, the budget manager should distribute the divisional and consolidated budgets, with appropriate commentary, to all managers scheduled to attend these meetings. It is very important that the commentary and any additional data prepared by the planning department for use during senior management review meetings be reviewed in advance with each divisional manager and his or her staff.

The final senior management review ideally should be scheduled in a location away from the normal work environment. In this way, all levels of management can concentrate totally on the divisional and consolidated budget plans without being distracted by other activities.

During the review meetings, the budget manager should take careful and detailed notes of all decisions and changes made during the review process. In addition, the planning manager should promptly issue minutes of each planning session so that there will be a clear understanding of all agreed-on changes and/or additions within each divisional plan.

OPERATING GROUPS' MONTHLY SUBMISSIONS

Following the final review and revision of group and corporate plans, the budget manager should request monthly divisional budgets. These budgets should then be quickly incorporated into the financial reporting system of the company, and the monthly financial reporting should accurately reflect variances from previously budgeted performance and cost levels. In addition, the budget manager and his or her staff should prepare at least quarterly performance analyses and reviews of all operating groups. Review meetings should be held with all divisional and senior management groups.

The budget manager should be satisfied that the financial reporting system of the company can provide enough detail to permit each operational unit within the divisions to identify promptly the reasons for a variance from previously forecasted budget performance and to take corrective action in order to maintain budgeted performance levels.

EFFECTIVE USE OF GRAPHICS

In many companies, large numbers of departments submit, monitor, and are accountable for budgets. Efforts should be made to have comparisons to actual results done in real time. These results should be presented where the people accountable can readily see how they are doing and where it doesn't become a "career." This process is best accomplished with effective use and delivery of graphics. In some instances, a manager should meet with an accountant and a graphics person to discuss the needs and explore the possibilities of what can be provided, and how and to whom. The use of computer dashboards to deliver quick and easy-to-grasp data in chart, tabular, or graphic format is quite popular.

SUMMARY

The most important element in applying the budget system effectively is the appropriateness of the system to the culture of the company, its internal workings, and the external environment. The CEO must believe in the system and promote its use and must insist on the clear linkage of line-division executives' performance reviews, compensation, and career-path development to the budgeting system. Finally, the system must be mechanically good, clear, easy to use, and well executed.

17

Budgets and Performance Compensation

Graef S. Crystal

INTRODUCTION

"You didn't make your budget, so there's not going to be any bonus this year." Or: "If you exceed your budget by 20 percent%, you will receive twice your normal bonus."

Statements like these reverberate through "mahogany row" as companies come to grips with the difficult issue of rewarding their executive cadre. The top managers of these companies know that before performance can be rewarded, it must first be measured. Therefore, they frequently seize on the company's already established budgeting process as the yardstick by which some people will receive a lot, others a little, and still others nothing. Interestingly, they do this notwithstanding that at other times, and perhaps even on the very same day, they are holding their sides and rolling on the floor after first viewing the ludicrous budget figures submitted by their operating unit managers.

The purpose of this chapter is to view the budget as a tool for measuring and rewarding executive performance. Its uses and abuses are explored first concerning the area of short-term incentive compensation plans and, later, longer-term incentive plans. Short-term incentives are aimed at rewarding performance in a single fiscal year whereas longer-term incentives (e.g., stock options) are geared toward rewarding performance over a series of years.

MEASURES OF EXECUTIVE PERFORMANCE

By definition, incentive plans are supposed to "incent" something. So, before we begin to talk about budgets per se, we must first briefly explore the various profit measures that different companies use for incentive compensation purposes.

Net Income after Everything

Let us start by mentally evoking a picture of a company's income statement and focusing on its bottom line, the one labeled "net income after taxes and after extraordinary items." There is an instinctive appeal for this measure of corporate performance. Shareholders, after all, take their rewards from the bottom line, and, so the argument goes, why should executives not do the same?

Few companies, however, see it this way in practice. They believe that extraordinary items, as the name implies, are truly extraordinary and that executives should not be held accountable for what might be termed the UFOs of the income statement. Besides, changes in accounting rules have made extraordinary items really extraordinary as opposed to the looser interpretations of the past. Also, an extraordinary item might be the result of actions taken years ago and by a different management team.

Exclusion of Taxes

This being the case, let us move up a line on the income statement and look at "net income before extraordinary items." Surely, this ought to be a winner for incentive-compensation purposes. Once again, however, some companies are contrary minded. They note that this measure includes the effects of income taxes, and they point out, seemingly quite properly, that executives have no control over income taxes.

Lately, a growing number of companies have begun to reject this line of reasoning. They note that the government is, most of the time, also in the incentive business, offering reductions in taxes for investing in new capital equipment, drilling for oil, and the like. (To be sure, the comprehensive tax law passed in 1986 was designed to take the government out of the incentive business, but tax incentives nonetheless remain. If history is any guide, more tax incentives will, like barnacles on a ship, attach themselves as time passes.) They reason that executives should not be insulated from these governmental inducements, or else they just might decide not to build a new plant because the pretax return on capital in contrast to the after-tax return looks marginal. These companies are also of the more generalized view that, in the final analysis, many facets of business life (not just taxes) are inherently uncontrollable. Take the case of a supermarket chain in which the supplier of shopping bags raises prices. If you are managing the supermarket chain, what are you going to do? Presumably, you will first ascertain whether you can get a better deal from another supplier; but suppose you cannot. Well, you can stop giving shoppers any bags at all or you can charge them for bags, but in either case, your assumption that you will lose market share will likely be borne out—and quite quickly. Alternatively, you can look for some other costs to cut—for example, paring inventories or decreasing the number of checkers—but these strategies may also prove counterproductive. As a last resort, you may be forced to raise prices to cover the costs of the shopping bags, or you may simply have to live with a lower bottom line. The point here is that income taxes, like shopping bags, are a cost of doing business and cannot be conveniently ignored just because they are uncontrollable.

Exclusion of Incentive-Plan Costs

Nonetheless, for the sake of discussion, let us grant the pretax school its point of view. Do we stop here with net income before income taxes and before extraordinary items? Most likely not, for we have yet to confront a cost that is upstream to this measure of performance; namely, the cost of the incentive plan itself. Consider this hypothetical conversation between a chief executive officer (CEO) and his or her controller.

> *Controller:* Well, Chief, it looks like our pretax profits this year will be an even $1 million.
>
> *CEO:* That's great. Since our incentive plan gives us 20 percent of pretax profits, we'll have a $200,000 bonus fund to play around with.
>
> *Controller:* Well, not quite. If we spend $200,000 on bonuses, our pretax profits will be only $800,000.
>
> *CEO:* Oh, I see. So I guess we'll have to be content with a fund of only $160,000, or 20 percent of the $800,000 of profits.
>
> *Controller:* Well, that's still not quite right, Chief. If we spend only $160,000 on bonuses, our pretax profits will be $840,000!

And so it goes. If the dialogue were carried far enough, the CEO and the controller would finally hit on the correct bonus fund amount; or if they still remembered their algebra, they could have employed simultaneous equations to determine the answer. However, given that most top managers seemingly have little patience and sometimes even less mathematical ability, it usually makes sense to utilize a profit measure for incentive purposes that excludes any accruals already made for the incentive plan itself. Thus, if we are dealing with a pretax profit measure, we simply add back to pretax profits any amounts already charged for the incentive plan. If we are dealing with an after-tax profit measure, we add back a sum equal to the increase in after-tax profits that would have occurred had no bonuses been payable. Doing this involves not only the reversal of the bonus accrual itself but also the related reduction in provision for income taxes.

Thus far, several alternative corporate performance measures have been discussed, all of them drawn from the company's income statements. There are pros and cons for each of these measures, and one cannot axiomatically state that a given measure is better under all circumstances than other measures.

Taking Account of the Cost of Capital

In a sort of pox-on-all-your-houses perspective, one can at least question whether any of these measures is really right for most companies. This is because the cost of raising capital has not yet been taken into full account.

Remember that the philosophical view underlying most incentive plans is that executives will not instinctively do what is right for the company. Rather, they will do what is right for themselves, and if that happens by chance to benefit the company, so much the better. Accordingly, the primary purpose of most incentive plans is to align executives' economic interests with those of the company, permitting them to maximize their income while doing the same for the shareholders.

Let us assume that net income after taxes has been tentatively adopted as the measure of corporate performance that we wish to "incent." How are we going to get into any real trouble? Well, for example, the executive group decides to sell another 1 million shares of stock to the public. At a price of $100 each, the company gains $100 million in cash. For want of a better alternative, this $100 million can be invested in short-term securities to yield another $6 million in pretax profits, another $4 million in after-tax profits, and *voilà*, some extra bonus money as well.

Do we really want to give this executive group extra rewards for earning a paltry 4% after-tax return on incremental capital at a time when the shareholders could earn essentially twice as much by investing their funds in high-grade corporate bonds?

Earnings per Share

We can, of course, remedy this problem by changing our performance measure from net income after taxes to net income per share. That way, our executive group will presumably steer clear of further share issuances unless it can earn a decent return on incremental capital.

However, net income per share still allows the executives a free ride on incremental retained earnings. If the company produces $100 million of after-tax income for the year, and you are the CEO, why not try to keep the dividends as low as possible or, better yet, eliminate them entirely? That way, the entire $100 million will be available for investment. Since there are neither interest costs nor extra share issuances associated with this capital, any positive return, no matter how minuscule, will drop to the bottom line and enhance the company's bonus fund.

Return on Shareholders' Equity

For this reason, many companies adopt as their measure of performance net income after taxes as a percentage of shareholders' equity, or more simply, return on equity (ROE). Now, for the first time, the executives will have to pay the freight on all sources of capital. If they take on extra debt, the numerator of the ROE fraction will be lowered by the interest costs involved. If they sell more shares to the public, the denominator of the fraction—equity—will be increased and ROE will drop unless some productive use can be made of the incremental capital. If some of the earnings are not paid out in dividends but are retained in the business, the denominator of the fraction will rise again and hit executives in their pocketbooks unless that capital can be made to earn its keep.

It can be seen, therefore, that an earnings per share (EPS) performance measure has the implicit effect of disincenting dividends whereas an ROE performance measure sometimes has the opposite effect. Both the EPS and the ROE performance measures, however, have the seeming effect of incenting the creation of debt over equity as the preferred method of financing and business. For example, a company has earned $200 million of pretax profits and has $1 billion of equity. On that basis, it has a pretax ROE of 20 percent. The company wishes to raise $300 million of new capital for purposes of building a plant with a targeted pretax rate of return of 15 percent. One alternative is to sell another $300 million of equity to the public. By so doing, pretax profits will rise $45 million (15 percent of the $300 million of incremental equity) to $245 million, and the equity will rise from $1 billion to $1.3 billion. However, ROE will drop from 20 to 18.8 percent. Alternatively, the executives can visit their friendly bankers and come away with a loan of $300 million at an interest rate of 10 percent. In this case, pretax profits will rise by only $15 million ($45 million return on the new plant less $30 million in interest), but equity will remain unchanged at $1 billion. The result is an increase in ROE from 20 to 21.5 percent. If you were being incented for ROE, which alternative would you take?

Return on Capital Employed

Of course, executives do not have a totally free hand in deciding whether they will finance the business through debt or equity. If they get too piggish regarding the assumption of additional debt, they will find their interest costs rising and eventually may be denied access to the credit markets altogether. Then the board of directors has to give final approval to the proposed course of financing, and outside directors will presumably not accede to unlimited leveraging.

Nonetheless, many boards of directors do not wish to police this area themselves. Rather, they wish to let the incentive plan do it for them. In such a situation, they are likely to reject both EPS and ROE as measures of performance, preferring instead to utilize what is often termed *return on capital employed* (ROCE). Here the numerator of the fraction starts with the company's basic profit measure for incentive purposes. For example, pretax profits plus any charges already accrued against pretax profits for the incentive plan itself. To this basic profit measure are then added interest costs for long-term debt. (If the basic profit measure is stated in after-tax terms, after-tax interest costs rather than pretax interest costs are added.) The denominator of the ROCE equation is the sum of equity and long-term debt.

The ROCE has the effect of making the executive group indifferent as to the utilization of debt or of equity for financing the business. The numerator of the fraction—profits—remains the same in either instance, inasmuch as any interest costs on long-term debt are reversed out of profits. The denominator of the fraction—equity plus debt—also remains the same.

No wonder drug is without its side effects, and this is the case here. Although the executive group has been rendered indifferent as to use of debt or equity, it has also been rendered indifferent as to the costs of debt. In the somewhat unreal world of ROCE, it matters not what the interest rate on long-term debt is, because all interest costs on such debt have been reversed out of profits. Rather, it matters only what the incremental return before interest costs is; if the interest costs turn out to exceed this incremental return, well, no one is perfect.

Highly capital-intensive companies nevertheless tend to prefer an ROCE measure over either an ROE or an EPS measure. Indeed, a few of these companies go even further and use a return-on-assets measure. In this case, they reverse all interest costs out of the numerator of the fraction, including those on both short- and long-term debt. The denominator then becomes the total assets of the company.

It seems appropriate here to introduce the concept of shareholder value. Ultimately, a shareholder benefits only from increased dividends and/or increased stock price appreciation. Any other performance, such as great growth in EPS, is interesting, but it does not put bread on the shareholder's table by itself.

In a sense, anyone designing an incentive plan (unless he or she is out to lunch) is making an implicit but highly critical assumption, namely, that the performance measure being used is somehow linked to shareholder value creation. To put it another way, unless you are being paid off by the competition, why do you want to design an incentive plan that hands out goodly sums of the shareholders' money and yet does not increase shareholder value?

For some years, many experts asserted a strong linkage between EPS and EPS growth on one hand and stock prices on the other. Hence, it was supposed that the higher a company's EPS, the higher its stock price would be. Moreover, it was also thought even more strongly that the higher the growth rate in EPS, the higher the price would be—earnings multiple.

More recent studies have shown that there is some linkage between EPS and shareholder value, but the linkage is nowhere as strong as has been previously asserted. Indeed, the studies show that if you really want to account for what drives stock prices, at least over the longer term, you must pay attention to three factors:

1. The book value per share
2. The growth in book value per share
3. The "true" return on equity

If a company is exhibiting only normal growth and is earning only a normal return, then its stock price is apt to be about equal to its book value. In other words, its market:book ratio is apt to be 1.00. However, if the company is increasing its earnings at a higher-than-average rate and is also earning a higher-than-average ROE, its market:book ratio is apt to be higher than 1.00. (By the same token, lower-than-average growth coupled with lower-than-average returns will likely produce a market:book ratio lower than 1.00.)

The concept of ROE traces from the so-called capital assets pricing model. This model tells us these things:

▪ When the late Maurice Chevalier celebrated his eightieth birthday, a correspondent asked him how he felt to be 80 years old. His reply: Consider the alternative! By the same token, you, as an investor, also have to consider the alternative—or, more correctly, alternatives. One such alternative is to put your money in riskless 90-day treasury bills. The interest rate may only be 5.5%, but you can at least sleep at night secure in the knowledge that your principal is protected.

▪ If you are going to invest in anything more risky than T-bills, you are going to want to earn a higher return to compensate for the risk. Studies show that, over long time periods, an investment in your average stock will earn you a return that is about seven percentage points above the riskless return rate. Therefore, if the riskless return rate is 5.5 percent, then investing in a stock with normal risk characteristics should earn you a return of around 12.5 percent.

▪ Of course, if you invest in a highly risky stock, you are going to want more than just an average return. Here risk is measured by the so-called beta. The beta gauges the degree to which a particular stock's price movements are more or less volatile than the price movements of the market as a whole. Thus, if the entire market changes its price, on average, by 10 percent (up or down), and the price of your company's stock also changes, on average, by 10 percent, we speak of your beta as being 1.00. However, if the entire market changes its prices by 10 percent while your company's prices change by 20 percent, then we consider your beta to be 2.00. In this case, your stock is twice as volatile as the average stock.

In this example, the capital asset pricing model tells us that an investor will demand a return equal to the sum of the riskless return rate and a risk premium, with the latter determined by multiplying the average risk premium (e.g., 7 percent) by the beta of the stock in question. If the riskless return rate is 5.5 percent and if the stock has normal volatility (beta of 1.00), then investors will demand a return of 5.5% + 7.0%, or 12.5%. If the riskless return rate is 5.5 percent and the stock's beta is 2.00, then investors will demand a return of 5.5% + (7.0% × 2.00), or 19.5%.

How does an investor get the return he or she desires? If investors demand a 12.5 percent return and the company obliges by producing a 12.5 percent after-tax ROE level, things are pretty easy. If the stock trades at its book value and continues to trade at its book value, then investors will get the 12.5 percent return they demand. What if the company is not so obliging? What if the return, instead of being 12.5 percent, is half of that, at 6.25 percent? Investors can still get their 12.5 percent return, provided they let the stock price drop until it is worth only half its book value per share. In that case, even though the company is telling its shareholders that they earned only 6.25 percent on book value in a particular year, those shareholders who were wise enough to buy when the stock price was trading at only half its book value are nonetheless receiving their desired 12.5 percent return. By the same token, if our hypothetical company is earning not a 12.5 percent return but a whopping 25.0 percent return, it is not unreasonable to suppose that investors will bid up the price of the stock until it is trading at around 2.00 times its book value per share. In that manner, investors will continue to receive their desired 12.5 percent return.

What the capital asset pricing model tells us is that returns and growth are the stuff out of which smiling shareholders are created. Growth and return alone, however, are not going to do the trick. Moreover, performance cannot be considered in a vacuum but must be evaluated against the many alternatives that are always available to investors. Therefore, if inflation kicks up and that in turn triggers an increase in interest rates, your company had better start finding a way to earn an even greater return on its equity. Otherwise, its "true return on equity," which we now see is the amount by which its actual return on equity exceeds the return level demanded by investors will fall. Does all this mean, then, that ROE is all that matters? No, it does not, and for these reasons:

- ROE is very important in determining shareholder value. In fact, it is the single most important variable, but it is not the only variable.
- ROE can be measured directly or through proxies. Over the long run, there is a very high correlation between ROE levels and levels of ROCE or return on assets. These two measures can be viewed as surrogates, or proxies, for ROE in most instances. After all, like ROE, they too emphasize the maximization of returns on capital resources.
- Years ago, when I directed the compensation programs of General Dynamics Corporation, a senior executive, who was reviewing the return on investment (ROI) levels of the company's various divisions, was brought up short when he discovered that the Fort Worth division (which is appropriately located in Fort Worth, Texas) had suffered a staggering decline in its ROI levels—from 48,000 to 24,000 ROI. A call to the president of that division revealed the source of the problem. It seems that the government owned all the assets in the entire division, except for the furnishings in the office of the division president. It also seems that the division president had recently bought new furniture, thereby doubling General Dynamics' investment in the division from around $5,000 to around $10,000!

In reality, there are some types of business, but not many, where capital is not a major consideration (i.e., advertising agencies and management consulting firms). In such cases, the use of ROE measures makes no sense at all. With this digression behind us, let us continue to scan the various performance measures that can be linked to incentives.

Operating Unit Performance Measures

Until now, we have been discussing corporate-wide measures of performance. But what about the performance of an operating unit (division, group, etc.)?

We must start with all the same thought processes concerning the preferred measure of raw profits—that is, the inclusion or exclusion of extraordinary items, income taxes, and the costs of the incentive plan itself. We must also go a step further and consider what to do with charges for corporate overhead.

Exclusion of Corporate Overhead

Virtually all operating unit managers consider charges for corporate overhead to be anathema. They cannot control such charges and do not see why they should be penalized by the profligacy of the corporate staff. Although it is true that they will, in theory, be the beneficiaries of any economies achieved by the corporate headquarters, they are quick to underscore the phrase "in theory."

However, a number of CEOs see a certain virtue in allocating charges for corporate overhead. They have a hard time controlling the growth of the corporate bureaucracy, and they figure that all the screaming on the part of the operating unit managers, who have to bear the charges, will stiffen their spines in dealing with their own corporate department heads. At the same time, they know that if they do not charge out corporate overhead, their operating unit managers will not only be seemingly indifferent to the costs involved but will try to transfer some of their own staff to the corporate headquarters. Apropos of all this, I am reminded of a conversation some years ago between the head of a major operating unit and his CEO.

> *Operating unit manager:* You give me these ridiculous profit budgets to meet, and at the same time you charge my budget with the actual costs of corporate overhead. I'm having a hard enough time meeting my own part of the budget, but I'm finding it nearly impossible to achieve the bottom line after having to eat all the costs you're incurring in this puzzle palace you're running out of New York.

> *CEO:* Listen, you ought to consider yourself lucky you're not getting all the service you're paying for!

> *Operating unit manager* (upon reflection): You know, you're right. I'll just keep taking those charges as long as you keep your goons in New York!

Use of a Capital Charge

No matter how the question concerning charging out or not charging out corporate overhead is resolved, one must still confront the issue, discussed previously, concerning the fact that raw profits do not fully reflect the costs of capital. This is moreso here, since a few companies do not allocate the costs of debt, much less the costs of equity, to their operating units.

Some companies think they have the problem licked by defining operating unit performance in terms of contribution to EPS. By this, they mean the operating unit's profits divided by the number of shares outstanding. Their reasoning is, of course, fallacious in that the current number of shares outstanding, or accretions to the number of shares outstanding, is not necessarily correlated with the capital utilization patterns of any particular operating unit.

It would be theoretically possible to utilize an ROE measure, but most companies employ only truncated balance sheets for their operating units. These companies have developed the assets side of the balance sheet in full, but they show only current liabilities on the liabilities side. The reason lies in their inability to come up with any rational, defensible rules for determining the allocation between debt and equity with respect to a particular operating unit.

This problem can perhaps be seen more clearly in the case of a true subsidiary as opposed to a division of a company. In this instance, there is a full balance sheet probably containing some debt as well as some equity. What really is "debt" in the context of a wholly owned subsidiary? In the final analysis, debt is whatever the parent wants it to be (and so is equity) given the parent's ability to decree any dividend policy it wishes. Thus, the only thing that really matters in the case of an operating unit—whether that unit is a true subsidiary or a division—is its level of capital employed: its total assets minus its current liabilities.

In working with ROCE for an operating unit, one first has to learn whether the parent allocates to its operating units the costs of debt, particularly long-term debt. (Strangely, some companies do not allocate long-term debt on an operating unit's balance sheet, but they blithely charge the operating unit's profit-and-loss statement with some portion of the parent's long-term debt.) If such costs are allocated, they will have to be reversed out of profits.

In their place is usually levied a "capital charge" for some or all of the capital employed by the operating unit. This capital charge comes in two basic flavors. In some companies, a charge is made for all capital employed by the operating unit, including the capital the unit has had in place for a long time. If this method is utilized, then the operating unit's profit-and-loss budget will have to reflect the contemplated charge. For example, the operating unit starts out the year with $100 million of capital employed (again, total assets less current liabilities), and the parent imposes a 10 percent capital charge. The unit's business plans call for it to utilize a further $10 million of capital during the year. In that case, the unit's budget (at least for incentive purposes) should reflect a capital charge item of $11 million, thereby lowering budgeted profits by a like sum.

Other companies prefer not to use this approach, since the resulting budget figures are perceived to be too low. These companies will establish a targeted level of capital employed for the operating unit for the particular year, but they will make no capital charge for the targeted level itself. Hence, the operating unit's budget does not have to reflect any capital charge. However, actual profits are debited (or credited) by applying the capital charge factor (10 percent in the earlier example) to the amount by which actual capital employed during the year exceeds (or is less than) the targeted level of capital employed. From an incentive compensation standpoint, it really makes no difference which way a company chooses to proceed.

STRUCTURING REWARD OPPORTUNITIES

Before looking at budgets per se, let us consider how companies structure their reward opportunities. Compensation levels can never be set in a vacuum. Rather, they are set relative to what other companies are offering. That being the case, the typical company goes through a number of steps in structuring compensation opportunities for its executive corps.

First, the company selects a number of other companies against which it wishes to test its compensation levels. Sometimes this group of other companies is engaged in the same industry as the company undertaking the examination. Sometimes this group is more or less the same size (e.g., all companies with $1 to $3 billion of sales, regardless of industry). In still other cases, this group of companies consists simply of all the companies participating in some national survey conducted by a third party (e.g., a survey conducted by the Conference Board).

Next, the company attempts to determine the going rates of base salary and total cash compensation being paid to selected executive positions by the group of companies chosen. In this context, the term "going rate" usually means the average or the median rate of pay. Total cash compensation means the sum of base salary and the average or median short-term incentive award being offered. For example, let us assume that a company has determined that the going rate of base salary for one of the company's operating unit heads, taking into account the responsibilities of that executive and the size of the unit, is $200,000. Let us also assume that the going rate of total cash compensation for the same position is $280,000.

The company has to integrate the findings from its survey into its own internal compensation structure. If our hypothetical company is like most companies, it will assign the operating unit head to a base salary range carrying a midpoint of approximately $200,000 and will go on to offer a norm bonus of $80,000, or 40 percent of salary.

What does "norm bonus" mean here? In most cases, a norm bonus is what executives will receive if their corporation performs in an average manner, if the operating unit of which they are a part performs in an average manner, and if they personally perform in an average manner. This definition should be kept in mind because it can present serious problems in trying to link performance against budget to incentive compensation awards.

Finally, our hypothetical company will have to determine how much swing it will permit around the norm bonuses it has structured and the conditions under which the bonuses will in fact swing. For example, the company might decide that bonuses can range all the way from 0 to 200 percent of the norm award, or, in the case of our example, from 0 to $160,000. It might further decide:

- The operating unit head's bonus will be zero in the event that the unit achieves less than 85 percent of its budget for the year ("budget" being the item[s] on the overall budget that conform to the company's definition of profitability for incentive compensation purposes).
- The bonus will be equal to the norm award of $80,000 in the event that actual profits exactly equal budget.
- The bonus will be twice the norm award, $160,000, in the event that actual profits are equal to 120 percent of budget or more.

This is a rather neat arrangement at first glance. However, first glances are often deceptive, and this could well be the case here.

PITFALLS OF LINKING INCENTIVES TO BUDGETS

Corporate-Level Pitfalls

If you were the executive involved, would you not want to submit the lowest budget you thought you could get away with? By so doing, you would minimize the possibilities of receiving anything less than your norm award and you would maximize the possibilities of receiving your maximum award.

This is one fundamental lesson of using budgets to determine incentive awards—namely, if there is already game playing in the budget-setting process, the game playing will be exacerbated; if there was no game playing previously (an unlikely prospect!), there will soon be some as soon as the players get a handle on the new rules.

Of course, one can assume that CEOs are no slouches at playing games themselves, or else they would not have made it that far in the organization. They can spot a phony budget a mile away, or they can at least spot a phony budget submitted by one of their operating unit heads. Perhaps their own corporate budget is another matter, inasmuch as they are also the beneficiaries of a low budget. Let us assume here, however, that the CEO has a board of directors that exercises more than the usual amount of scrutiny over budget figures or that he or she is capable of exhibiting more "Satan, get thee behind me" behavior than the usual CEO. That being the case, let us go on to assume that the CEO prepares a "realistic" corporate budget that is neither terribly demanding nor terribly easy.

If all these good things happen, are we then in good shape? Well, not exactly. Assume our hypothetical company is very high performing. In years past, it has consistently returned 20 percent after taxes on its equity. Given what he or she knows now, there is no reason for the CEO to assume that the company will not pull the rabbit out of the hat yet again this forthcoming year. Therefore, the CEO submits to the board of directors a budget calling for a continued 20 percent ROE.

Under the ground rules discussed previously, the CEO and the other senior executives with corporate-wide responsibilities will receive their norm bonuses if they meet budget—in this case, a 20 percent ROE. On the surface, this looks to be reasonable, inasmuch as a 20 percent ROE is believed to be a realistic budget for that company in that particular year.

How does a 20 percent ROE stack up against the ROE performance of the group of companies on which the base salary, norm bonus, and total cash compensation levels were predicted? For example, suppose an examination of the financial performance of these other companies revealed that the median company's ROE was only 14 percent. In this case, our hypothetical company would be paying only the going rate of total cash compensation for performance that, though usual for the company itself, was considerably above the average of the group used for comparison. In this instance, the concept of pay for performance would have a rather hollow ring.

To make matters worse, many CEOs (acting on the empirical observation that if you put the carrot right next to the horse's nose, it will disappear and the horse will not move) demand that their budgets contain a lot of the elusive term known as stretch. In our example, the CEO might well give the board a budget calling for a 22 percent ROE, thereby demanding even more performance for no more than median pay.

What about a company that has heretofore been performing at median levels in relation to other companies but now believes that the year in question will likely prove a disaster? Carrying its convictions onto paper, it adopts a budget calling for only a 5 percent ROE level. Ironically, that 5 percent ROE level may well contain plenty of stretch, given all the bad things the company expects to happen. Nonetheless, are we to pay out norm bonuses to that company's executives because they achieved a 5 percent ROE level and thereby "made budget"? If we do, we will be offering the same levels of total cash compensation for 5 percent ROE as the median company is offering for 14 percent ROE. Previously, we had a case of no extra pay for high performance; we now have a case of extra pay for nonperformance. In this situation, we are unwittingly rewarding executives for being the first to run in with the news that the sky is falling.

Pitfalls at the Operating-Unit Level

The problems described for the corporate level are often magnified at the operating-unit level. The fundamental question here is: How do we know we have achieved equal stretch among the budgets of the various operating units? For example, some CEOs think they have achieved equal stretch simply by demanding the same absolute performance level from each of their operating units as they have budgeted for the company as a whole. Thus, if the corporate budget calls for a 10 percent after-tax ROCE, they demand the same 10 percent ROCE level from each operating unit. They do this notwithstanding that one operating unit has comfortably achieved a 16 percent ROCE level for years and shows every expectation of continuing to do so while another operating unit is struggling to cut its losses because it is either in the very early or very late stages of its product life cycle.

Other CEOs avoid this pitfall and properly demand "realistic" budgets from each operating unit based on the environment in which the operating unit then finds itself. They assign the first unit an ROCE budget of 16 percent while insisting that the second unit cut its losses to only $5 million the next year. Having done so, however, they may not be able to bring themselves to give norm bonuses to the executives of the second unit.

As if all this were not enough, there are often problems surrounding the swing in bonuses as a function of the swing in actual versus budgeted performance. Earlier we talked about paying no bonus at all if actual performance fell below 85 percent of budget and about doubling the norm bonus if actual performance rose to 120 percent of budget or more. Perhaps that is a good range of performance for incentive compensation purposes as far as the parent corporation is concerned. It does not necessarily follow, however, that the range will prove optimal for each and every one of the corporation's various operating units.

For example, contrast these two units: The first operates from an order backlog that stretches beyond one year. It buys little in the way of raw materials, and what it does buy is not subject to wild price swings. The unit has also signed a recent three-year agreement with its unions and can look forward to identified labor costs for the next several years. In that case, would it not be reasonable to assume that an achievement of even 90 percent against budget would nonetheless represent an abysmal performance? Also, would it not be reasonable to assume that the operating unit was, in retrospect, lying through its teeth if it ended up achieving 120 percent of budget?

The second operating unit has little in the way of order backlog from which to work. A good part of every sales dollar is used to buy highly price-volatile raw materials, and it is just ending a three-year labor agreement with a highly militant union. In that case, would it not be reasonable to assume that an achievement of 80 percent of budget, though not satisfactory, might not be considered abysmal either under the circumstances? Also, would it not be reasonable to assume that an achievement of 120 percent of budget, though reasonably good, might not connote outstanding performance under the same circumstances?

Finally, there is a problem described by the ancient Chinese adage "Victory has a thousand fathers; defeat has none." For example, a particular operating unit badly misses its budget. Just as it is about to be passed over at bonus distribution time, the operating unit head points to the fact that oil price increases, pushed through by a resurgent Organization of Petroleum Exporting Countries (OPEC), were the culprit. Some top managements, besides recalling the preceding Chinese adage, will also recall another adage: "You live by the sword, you die by the sword." On that basis, the operating unit executives would still receive nothing. Others in top management, however, acting from the theory that executives should not be held accountable for things they cannot control, might be inclined to grant the operating unit some bonus relief. They would do so either by decreasing the unit's original budget figures or by constructing a proforma income statement showing what the unit would have earned that year had OPEC not instituted its price rise, and then comparing the pro forma results to the original budget numbers. In either event, the task would be difficult unless the assumptions underlying the original budget had been made explicit.

It should go without saying that a budget document is essentially worthless unless one understands and accepts its major underlying assumptions. All too often, budget figures are based on the inspiration of the operating unit head after heeding the exhortation of the CEO. In truth, there are no underlying assumptions except inchoate desires to please the CEO and, if possible, to save back some profit for a rainy day.

AN OPTIMAL APPROACH

The reader will have to be forgiven if he or she has come to this point with the belief that only the most benighted company would ever try to use its budgeting process as a means of determining the rewards its executives should receive. Clearly, there are many pitfalls involved in linking budgets to pay, but to a large degree, these pitfalls can be avoided by using the budgeting process in an indirect fashion rather than directly.

Most budget experts agree that a truly viable budgeting process is at heart an iterative process. Someone—whether the corporate top manager or an operating unit head—starts the ball rolling with a tentative budget figure. This figure is then responded to with the result that it may be changed. The changed figure is then responded to again, and once again some further change may be made. This continues until all the parties agree on a final budget. This being the case, let us start the iterative process at the bottom of the organization—with the company's various operating units.

Preparation of Operating Unit Budgets

If budgets are going to play an optimal role in the determination of incentive awards, it would be desirable for each operating unit head to submit not a single budget but rather three different budgets.

The first of these budgets might be termed the worst-case budget. Having identified the major variables affecting profits for the operating unit (e.g., raw material prices, wage rates, staffing levels, volume in physical units, product prices, etc.), the operating unit head would start by assuming that things really go wrong during the year under consideration. For example, if economic projections indicate that it is highly unlikely that oil will cost less than $14.50 per barrel or more than $17.00 per barrel, the operating unit head would use $17.00 as the assumption for the price of oil in determining the worst-case budget.

The second budget is termed the best-case budget. Here the operating unit head will assume that things really go right. Thus, in the case of oil, a $14.50 per barrel assumption will be used.

Finally, the operating unit head will prepare a likely budget. In some situations, this may be merely the midpoint of the range between the worst-case and best-case budgets, but in other situations, the likely budget may lie somewhere other than in the exact middle of the range.

Once these three budgets are prepared by each operating unit head, it will be up to top management to ensure that the principle of equal stretch has been achieved among the various operating units. Here we are dealing not with the question of whether the particular operating unit is delivering sufficient profits but rather with the fundamental assumptions underlying each of the three budgets. For example, suppose an operating unit is about to negotiate a new labor agreement with its principal union. Wage rates are currently averaging $8.00 per hour. Given that other recent settlements by the same union have been running around a 10 percent annual increase level, is it reasonable to assume (as the operating manager has assumed in the likely budget) that wage rates during the first year of the new contract will average $9.25, or 15.6 percent higher than the current wage levels? Also, is it reasonable to assume (as the operating manager has assumed in the worst-case budget) that wage rates will average $10.50 per hour during the first year of the new contract? Finally, is it reasonable to assume (as the operating manager has assumed in the best-case budget) that wage rates will rise only about 1 percent to $8.10 per hour?

Setting Corporate Performance Targets

Having critically examined the major assumptions underlying each operating unit's worst-case, likely, and best-case budgets, and having made such changes as are necessary to ensure that the probabilities of attainment are reasonably the same among the operating units, top management will then be in a position to set some incentive compensation targets for the corporation as a whole.

It might seem that the company need only consolidate the likely budgets of its operating units to derive a likely budget for the corporation as a whole. This budget would then trigger the payment of norm awards. Similarly, it might seem that the company need only consolidate the worst- and best-case corporate budgets of the operating units to derive worst- and best-case corporate budgets for the purposes of paying, respectively, no bonuses and maximum bonuses.

However, such thinking could well prove wrong for the reasons discussed previously. Once again, why should a corporation deliver only norm awards when its "likely" performance can be considered superlative in relation to the performance of other companies utilized for pay-determination purposes? Why should a corporation deliver as much as norm awards when its likely performance can be considered poor in relation to the performance of other companies?

The next step involves not the consolidation of the three budgets from each operating unit but rather the determination of corporate incentive compensation performance targets based on the performance of the same companies utilized for pay-determination purposes. Let us assume that our hypothetical company has adopted after-tax ROE as its measure of corporate performance for incentive compensation purposes. It then determines the ROE levels of the companies in its survey group and tentatively picks the median level as the level it will demand for payment of norm bonuses. Since norm bonuses, as used here, are median bonuses, it follows thus far that the company is offering median incentive compensation for median ROE performance.

Next, the company has to decide on a tentative outstanding ROE level. It could, if it wished, peg this level to the highest ROE level attained by any of the survey companies, but to do so would put it at the mercy of the extremes of the ROE distribution. More likely, the company would adopt some percentile criterion—for example, outstanding performance is equal to the eighty-fifth percentile of the ROE distribution.

The next step involves the determination of a tentative minimal ROE level. Our company could use the same reasoning as was used with respect to the determination of an outstanding ROE level; that is, minimum ROE performance is equal to the fifteenth percentile of the ROE distribution of the companies under study. Alternatively, the company might post an "alternative investment" test—one using the tenets of the capital asset pricing model. Here, the minimum ROE performance might be assumed to be a rate 60 percent as high as the rate mandated by the capital assets pricing model. Hence, if the model shows that investors are demanding a 15 percent ROE level, then the minimum ROE level built into the incentive plan would be 15% × 60%, or 9%.

For the sake of discussion, assume that our hypothetical company has tentatively identified these ROE targets:

- Minimal—9 percent (modeled generally after the alternative investment theory)
- Norm—14 percent (equal to the median ROE of the survey group)
- Outstanding—18 percent (equal to the eighty-fifth percentile ROE of the survey group)

Presumably, these tentative targets would be locked in place as final targets for the particular year if our company was already achieving an ROE level of approximately 14 percent or more. However, suppose the company has not been performing well in the past and has been delivering an ROE level of only 10 percent. In such a case, it would likely prove unreasonable to demand a huge surge in ROE—from 10 to 14 percent—before norm bonuses would become payable.

This, in turn, raises a philosophical question as to the reasons for paying bonuses. Clearly, a company that is already delivering median performance (compared to other companies) and continues to deliver median performance should pay bonuses that, when added to base salaries, yield median total cash compensation levels. Obviously, a company that is already delivering median performance and then goes on to deliver outstanding performance should pay bonuses that, when added to base salaries, yield outstanding total cash compensation levels. Does it necessarily follow, however, that a company that is delivering poor performance and still cannot perform up to median levels should pay bonuses that, when added to base salaries, yield something less than median total cash compensation? The answer is yes, except when the company is demonstrating disproportionate progress in raising its performance from its current levels to median levels. It is this exception that must now be addressed.

Assume that our hypothetical company has been achieving only a 10 percent ROE (with equity calculated as of the beginning of the particular year) and that it has a policy of paying out 40 percent of its earnings in dividends. Were the company to increase its after-tax earnings by 6 percent per year, to continue paying out 40 percent of earnings in dividends, and to raise no new equity capital from outside sources, it would continue to produce a steady 10 percent ROE year after year. In this case, a 6 percent growth in earnings would be indicative of continued poor performance. Alternatively, were the company to increase its after-tax earnings by 8.4 percent per year, to continue paying out 40 percent of earnings in dividends, and to raise no new equity capital from outside sources, its ROE level would begin to rise above 10 percent until it reached 14 percent (the median ROE level of the survey group). At that point, the ROE level would remain at 14 percent as long as the preceding assumptions held true.

The only problem here, however, is that it will take 59 years before a 14 percent ROE level is finally achieved! (In year 1, the ROE rises from 10 to 10.2 percent. In year 2, it rises from 10.2 to 10.4 percent. In year 5, it reaches 11 percent. In year 11, it reaches 12 percent; in year 20, 13 percent; and in year 29, 13.5 percent. During the next 30 years, it crawls slowly from 13.5 to 14 percent.)

Therefore, although an 8.4 percent annual growth in earnings represents progress toward a 14 percent ROE level, and will actually maintain a 14 percent ROE level once the company gets there, one can hardly think of such performance as representing "disproportionate progress."

Accordingly, our hypothetical company will probably have to select a time frame shorter than 59 years to reach median levels of ROE performance if it still wishes to pay out norm bonuses. For example, the company decided that "disproportionate progress" would be achieved by reaching a 14 percent ROE level in five years.

Starting with a 10 percent ROE level and continuing to pay out 40 percent of earnings in dividends, the company would have to increase its earnings 15% per year. In such a case, the ROE pattern would be:

Year	ROE (%)
Base	10.0
1	10.8
2	11.7
3	12.6
4	13.5
5	14.3

By way of further illustration, suppose our company decided that it really should reach a 14 percent ROE level in only three years. In that case, the growth in earnings would have to average 20 percent per year, and the ROE pattern would be:

Year	ROE (%)
Base	10.0
1	11.3
2	12.7
3	14.2

Here, the company would adopt an 11.3 percent ROE level as indicative of norm performance for the particular year under discussion. Subsequently, it would have adopted 10.8 percent as the norm ROE level had it decided to reach for a 14 percent ROE level over five years instead of three.

Having adopted an 11.3 percent ROE level as its norm performance level for the particular year, would the company then go on to scale down its tentative outstanding ROE target of 18 percent and its tentative minimal ROE target of 9 percent? Presumably, it would scale down the former target; perhaps in *a pro rata* fashion. (Thus, an 11.3 percent ROE level represents 81 percent of a 14 percent ROE level. Applying this 81 percent factor to the tentative outstanding ROE level of 18 percent yields a 14.6 percent final outstanding ROE level for the particular year.) It is questionable, however, whether the company would touch its minimal ROE target of 9 percent. That minimal target, by definition, is pretty minimal. To pay any bonuses at all for performance below this point would seemingly be a travesty, no matter how much "progress" might or might not have been made in relation to years past.

ADJUSTING OPERATING UNIT TARGETS

For the sake of further discussion, assume that our hypothetical company has finally settled on these ROE targets for the particular year:

- Minimal—9 percent
- Norm—11.3 percent
- Outstanding—14.6 percent

These targets have been modeled not on the corporate budget for the year in question but rather on the ROE level of the survey group and on the past ROE levels of the company itself. Hence, we may well have a discontinuity between these ROE targets and the three consolidated budget figures (worst case, likely, and best case) submitted by the various operating units. This discontinuity will now have to be reconciled.

Initially, the company must restate its after-tax, corporate ROE targets in terms that match the performance measure adopted for the operating units. For example, the operating units are to be judged on net income before taxes, before interest charges on long-term debt, before corporate overhead, and before the costs of the incentive plan itself. In that case, the company would start with its minimal ROE target of 9 percent and would follow these eight steps:

1. Multiply beginning equity by 9 percent to determine the after-tax earnings represented by a 9 percent ROE (e.g., assume that the beginning equity is $1 billion. Therefore, after-tax earnings at a 9 percent ROE level will be $90 million).
2. Reverse out of the figure in step 1 the provision for income taxes to produce net income before taxes. (Assuming that the company anticipates a 36 percent effective tax rate at a $90 million after-tax profit level, the resulting figure for net income before taxes will be $141 million.)
3. Reverse out of the figure in step 2 the anticipated charges for interest on long-term debt to produce net income before taxes and before interest charges on long-term debt. (Assuming that the company has long-term debt of $500 million and is paying an average interest rate of 8 percent, the resulting interest charges will be $40 million. Hence, net income before taxes and before interest charges on long-term debt will be $181 million.)
4. Reverse out of the figure in step 3 the anticipated charges for corporate overhead to produce net income before taxes, before interest charges on long-term debt, and before corporate overhead. (Assuming that the company anticipates corporate overhead of $15 million, the resulting figure will be $196 million.)
5. Reverse out of the figure in step 4 the anticipated charges for incentive compensation payable at a 9 percent ROE level. (Given that a 9 percent ROE level is the minimal target, no bonuses will be payable, and the $196 million figure developed through step 4 will remain unchanged here.)
6. Add together the worst-case budgets of all the operating units. (Assume that the figure is $175 million.)
7. Divide the figure obtained in step 5 by the figure obtained in step 6. ($196 million divided by $175 million equals 1.12.)
8. Multiply the worst-case budget of each operating unit by the factor obtained in step 7 to derive the minimal incentive compensation performance level for that operating unit. (Assuming that operating unit A submitted a worst-case budget of $40 million, the minimal incentive compensation performance level will be increased by 12 percent to $44.8 million.)

These same eight steps will then be repeated twice more, first starting with the norm ROE level of the corporation (11.3 percent) and then with the outstanding ROE level (14.6 percent).

It is possible at this point to end up with two different sets of budgets. The first are the original worst-case, likely, and best-case budgets developed under realistic sets of assumptions. These original budgets will likely remain unchanged for financial-control purposes. The second set consists of the revised budgets developed through integration with the incentive compensation performance targets adopted for the corporation as a whole. This second set of budgets will be used only for incentive compensation purposes.

Advantages of the Suggested Approach

In my view, the approach suggested here has a number of advantages compared to simply predicating bonus awards on actual performance versus budget. First, the company has avoided the trap of always offering median total cash compensation for making budget, whether the budgeted results compare to the achievements of other companies or are abysmal, average, or superior. Hence, the pay-for-performance principle that many companies espouse has been preserved intact.

Second, bonus payments will be in line with those offered by comparable companies and not simply in line with those offered in the past by the company itself. This should be reassuring news for the shareholders who, it may be suspected, are every bit as interested in paying for performance as the executives themselves.

Third, the temptation to play games with budgets will be minimized. If all operating unit managers submit lowball budgets, each will end up having his or her figures increased through the eight-step process. Granted, it is possible for one operating unit manager, or a couple of managers, to lowball their budgets and end up having only a portion of the decrement laid at their doorstep (the remainder being assigned to the other operating unit managers). However, given a critical examination of each operating unit budget on the part of top corporate management and a concomitant striving to achieve roughly equal stretch among all the operating unit budgets, the likelihood of this happening should be fairly remote.

Fourth, the budgeting process can continue to play a useful role in the proceedings. In effect, though every operating unit manager's budget may get changed in the reconciliation of operating unit budgets to corporate incentive compensation performance targets, the relativities will still have been preserved. Presumably, rough justice also will still have been done.

Fifth, the temptation to assume that a given percentage achievement above or below budget represents the same relative performance for each operating unit will be eliminated. The preparation of thoughtful worst-case, likely, and best-case budgets will underscore the volatility of different operating units to changes in key, and often uncontrollable, factors.

Finally, the explicit identification of major assumptions underlying the worst-case, likely, and best-case budgets will go a long way in resolving after-the-fact disputes as to whether a particular operating unit performed poorly because of events outside its control or just simply performed poorly.

BUDGETS AND LONG-TERM INCENTIVE PLANS

The bulk of this chapter has been devoted to the role that budgets can play in the determination of incentive compensation for annual results. Virtually all companies, however, have more than a single incentive plan with which to reward their management teams.

Most readers will likely be aware, if only slightly, that there are numerous strategies for maximizing the annual results of a firm or an operating unit thereof. Some of these strategies are productive (e.g., increasing market share). Others are hardly productive, at least viewed over the longer term. These include cutting expenses for research and development or for management training and equipment maintenance, reducing product quality, and the like. Eventually, these latter strategies will result in lowered profits (and perhaps bankruptcy), and the managers who used them will "get theirs" in the form of zero annual incentive awards—if they are still with the company or the particular operating unit. If they are not, they will have received the best of both worlds: higher bonuses during the good years and an enhanced reputation later. ("When Joe was running the division, the profits were tremendous. Now Joe has left and things are in deplorable shape. I tell you, that Joe is a miracle worker!").

To minimize the adoption of counterproductive long-term strategies, most companies offer their executives an annual incentive opportunity as well as a further incentive opportunity based on results not in a single year but over a series of years. Thus, the executive who neglects the long-term aspects of the business will end up being penalized even if he or she has left the company or moved to another operating unit. (In effect, he or she will receive maximum bonuses under the short-term plan but nothing under the long-term plan.)

Approximately 20 years ago, virtually every long-term incentive plan consisted of a stock option. However, for a number of reasons (e.g., a plunge in the stock market during the 1970s, changes in tax laws, and increases in interest rates), many companies decided to downplay and, in a few cases, even eliminate the role of the market price of their stock in the determination of long-term incentive awards. Instead, they have predicated part, or sometimes all, of their long-term incentive opportunities on such things as growth in EPS over a series of years and/or the achievement of preestablished ROE or ROCE levels.

Having decided to move away from the market price, which is impersonally set, these companies had to face the task of deciding how much growth in earnings per share should be required for a given payout and/or what level of ROE or ROCE should be attained.

At first, there was a tendency to look to the company's long-term business plans as the yardstick of executive long-term performance. However, most companies shortly discovered that their long-term plans could not take much weight. In effect, they began to perceive that the relationship between the long-term forecast for a particular year and reality was inversely proportional to the square of the number of years between the current year and the year under consideration. To put it another way, they began to perceive that their long-term plans, while providing a useful demonstration to the board of directors that professional management was behaving professionally, were basically exercises in extrapolation.

Accordingly, long-term budgets really are not allowed to play much of a role in the establishment of performance targets under the long-term incentive compensation plans of most companies. Rather, the reasoning goes something like this:

- A survey of other companies shows that, on average, the typical chief financial officer (CFO) receives annual options on stock carrying a purchase price of 1.0 times base salary.
- Given that the median competitive base salary for a CFO in a company our size is $200,000, this means an average annual option grant of $200,000 would be in order, or 4,000 shares at our current market price of $50 per share.
- We think it is unlikely that our long-term earnings per share growth will be any greater than 15 percent per year, and, indeed, it may well be somewhat less.
- If EPS growth did turn out to be 15 percent per year and if our stock traded at a constant price/earnings multiple, then the price of our stock would also advance 15 percent per year.

- If the CFO were to exercise his 4,000-share option halfway through its ten-year term (a Solomonic assumption), the market price of the stock would have risen from $50 per share to $100.57 per share, yielding a pretax gain of $50.57 per share, or $202,300 on all 4,000 shares.
- We wish to reward the CFO purely for EPS growth while simultaneously insulating him from the vagaries of the price/earnings multiple.
- Accordingly, under our new long-term incentive plan, we will offer him $202,300 in cash at the end of a five-year performance cycle, provided our EPS has increased an average of 15 percent per year during the period.
- If EPS growth turns out to be less than 15 percent per year, we will, of course, give the CFO a lesser payment, with such payment derived by applying the very same methodology.
- If EPS growth averages less than 6 percent per year, we will give him no payment at all. It is granted that a 6 percent EPS growth rate when combined with a constant price/earnings multiple does produce a 34 percent appreciation in stock over five years. Given an inflation rate that is running around 5 percent, however, we cannot fail to take account of the fact that 6 percent nominal EPS growth really translates into very little real EPS growth. To put it another way, we cannot continue to assume that the price/earnings multiple of our stock would indeed remain constant in the face of a 6 percent nominal EPS growth rate and a 5 percent inflation rate.

SUMMARY

If carefully handled, a company's budgeting process can play a useful role in determining incentive compensation for annual results (while playing little or no role in the determination of incentive compensation for longer-term results). However, unless the handling is indeed careful, there is the risk that executives will end up being either undercompensated or overcompensated for their performance achievements, and there is the even greater risk that the budgeting process will become so subverted as to render it useless for even its traditional financial role.

CHAPTER EIGHTEEN

Predictive Costing, Predictive Accounting

Gary Cokins, CPIM
SAS Institute

INTERNET FORCES THE NEED FOR BETTER COST FORECASTING

Electronic commerce (e-commerce) and business-to-business (B2B) are shifting power to the buyer from the seller. With the emergence of "exchanges and portals" and e-bidding and spot purchasing, suppliers are discovering that they must dynamically quote prices, ideally knowing the profit margin impact. Buyers will not wait days or hours for a quote. It must be at Internet speed. This is bringing pressure to bear on suppliers to have a rule-based predictive cost-estimating engine and modeling to test various assumptions.

Information technology computing power has made it possible for business analysts and planners to apply advanced methods to estimate the costs for alternative decisions. These methods provide more accurate answers than traditional cost-estimating methods that often simply extrapolate historical cost rates. However, these advanced cost-estimating methods come with a price: They require a greater administrative effort.

People who have been exposed to the new methods are asking:

- At what point would I switch to the more advanced method?
- How much of a difference in results is there between methods?
- How much error will I incur if I do not switch?

Adapted from "Predictive Costing, Predictive Accounting," Chapter 8 in *Activity-Based Cost Management: An Executive's Guide* by Gary Cokins. Copyright 2001, John Wiley & Sons. Permission to reprint granted.

In anticipation of debate, which will be fueled by software vendors who are adding stronger predictive functionality, more research is needed that will:

▪ Describe, compare, and contrast the various cost estimating methods.
▪ Define when each is applicable (as well as not justified).
▪ Describe the conditions and circumstances under which one would switch to a higher-cost, higher-accuracy cost-estimating method.

The two cost-estimating methods that are possible, due to computing power, are activity-based planning and budgeting (ABP/B) and process-simulation-based predictive costing.

In this chapter I first address the shortcomings of traditional budgeting. One of the popular solutions advocated to fix traditional budgeting is activity-based budgeting (ABB). However, as you dig deeper into understanding budgeting and planning, you will discover that you have actually entered into a much broader world of forecasting. Forecasting includes cost estimating, presumably linked with projections of demand. ABB and its companion, activity-based planning (ABP), which are now popularly combined as ABP/B, will be combined in this chapter.

TRADITIONAL BUDGETING: AN UNRELIABLE COMPASS

ABP/B is a better approach to forecasting the location and level of resources and budgeted expenditures than traditional budgeting. It recognizes that the need for resources originates with a demand-pull triggered by customers or end users of the organization's services and capabilities. In contrast, the traditional basis for budgeting tends to extrapolate the level of resource spending from the past. Exhibit 18.1 presents a farcical view of spreadsheet budgeting that is not too far from the truth for some organizations.

A problem with spreadsheet budgeting is that the past is not a reliable indicator of the future. This approach simply takes last year's expenses plus a small amount for inflation. This method implies that the budget process starts with the current level of expenses; however, today many managers believe that the budget should flow backward from the outputs. ABB in effect does flow backward. It logically assists in determining what levels of resources are truly required to meet the future demands placed on an organization.

	Current Year	Budget Year
1		
2 Wages	$ 400,000.00	Formula = Column B * 1.05
3 Supplies	$ 50,000.00	
4 Rent	$ 20,000.00	Copy down
5 Computer	$ 40,000.00	
6 Travel	$ 30,000.00	
7 Phone	$ 20,000.00	
8 Total	$ 560,000.00	

Sheet 1

EXHIBIT 18.1 Spreadsheet Budgeting

ACTIVITY-BASED COSTING AS A FOUNDATION FOR ACTIVITY-BASED PLANNING AND BUDGETING

As activity-based costing (ABC) moved into the early 1990s, some companies began leveraging the activity cost data for more operational purposes to change and manage the same ABC-calculated activity costs that were accumulating in their product- and service-line costs. People referred to this use of the data as activity-based management (ABM). As is typical with new management techniques, early trials with ABC and ABM sometimes fell short of expected results or even failed altogether. Some industry leaders in accounting even proclaimed that ABC was an inappropriate method and tool.

But organizations and companies that passionately believed in the ABC data forged ahead because they saw little hope from perpetuating their decision making using their existing traditional data. They discovered that their personal computer-based ABC models were useful for modeling their cost behavior.

In the late 1990s, the more mature and advanced ABC users increasingly began using their activity costs and the ABC-calculated unit cost rates for intermediate work outputs and for products and services as a basis for estimating costs. Popular uses of the ABC data for cost estimating have been calculating customer order quotations and doing make-versus-buy analysis. The ABC data were being recognized as a predictive planning tool. It is now apparent that the data have a tremendous amount of utility for both examining the as-is, current condition of the organization and achieving a desired to-be state. (Note: A more robust version of ABC is called *resource consumption accounting* [RCA]. It is briefly described at the end of this chapter, but more can be learned about RCA at www.rcainstitute.org/.)

 ## BUDGETING: USER DISCONTENT AND REBELLION

Why is there increasing interest in ABP/B? In part the interest is due to increasing problems with the annual budget process, and not just because individuals are not getting the approval for funding they want. They are disturbed by the budgeting process altogether. There is great cynicism about budgeting. The other reason for discontent is that people sense that a better way to budget exists.

Often when there is a substantial change in a management technique, it stems from a combination of dissatisfaction with the current methods and a vision of what a replacement method would look like. With ABP/B we have both conditions present.

Why are managers and employees cynical about the annual budgeting process? They find the process is too long, too detailed, and excessively burdensome. In addition, they view budgeting as a political game that still usually results in some departments being overfunded while others continue laboring as have-nots. This latter group of workers toils without relief. With organizational downsizing, senior management has often removed the bodies but not taken out the work. Across-the-board percentage cuts in staff, some of the slash-and-burn variety, are likely to cut into the muscle in some places while still leaving excess capacity in others.

☐ Is a death march with few benefits.

☐ Takes 14 months from start-to-end.

☐ Requires two or more executive "tweaks" at the end.

☐ Is obsolete in two months due to reorgs or competitor moves.

☐ Starves truly needed spending with excess funding elsewhere.

☐ Caves in to the "loudest voice" and "political muscle."

☐ Rewards veteran sandbaggers who are experts at padding.

☐ Is overstated from the prior year's "use-it-or-lose-it" spending.

☐ Incorporates last year's inefficiencies into this year's budget.

☐ Provides lifetime security for our budget analysts to perform variance analysis with all the subsequent forecast updates.

☐ Focuses much less on "*What* should we be doing?" and much more on "*How much* are we doing what we did?"

☐ De-motivates managers when targets are too easy or too tough.

☐ Could get better results if managers signed fewer POs.

☐ Is a trap for the young and naïve who have yet to learn how to negotiate to pad and "sandbag" for the unexpected.

EXHIBIT 18.2 Quiz—Check the Boxes—Our Budgeting Exercise

Exhibit 18.2 contains some sarcasm about traditional budgeting in the form of a checkbox survey.

Fortunately there is a vision of what a better way of budgeting looks like. But a better way for what purpose, and for whom? Fundamentally we need to understand what purpose a budget serves. The typical impression most people have is that the budget is a set of predetermined spending limits defined in such a way that if everyone roughly spends what was allotted to the department, the estimated total spending for the organization will be reasonably achieved. The purpose of that kind of budget thinking is as a control tool, not an analytical and allocation tool. Do not exceed your spending limit or you will get your hand slapped by the accounting police: "You took two more airline flights than planned. Explain why."

The broader purpose for a budget should be to predetermine the level of resources that will be required, such as people, material, supplies, and equipment, to achieve an expected or desired amount of demand for employee services—meaning demands for their work. ABB advocates are interested in the notion of "resource requirements" as being the result, not the starting point. They want to be able to first estimate oncoming customer and management demands, and then estimate the "supply" of resources, in terms of cost, that will be needed to match that supply with the work demands. In short, ABP/B advocates want to reverse the traditional budget equation and start with the expected outcomes, not with the existing situation.

WEARY ANNUAL BUDGET PARADE

There are many criticisms about the use and development of budgets. Some organizations are saying they want cost management, not budget management. In fact, they believe their organization will never budget manage its way to cost management. Why do organizations bother to budget? What are the origins of budgeting? The simple answer is that business owners and senior managers have always desired some form of control to responsibly match actual spending with planned funding for expenditures.

Historically, the most convenient way to restrict managers from improper spending and to prevent excesses or abuses was to start with the official financial reporting mechanism and structure, the fund accounting system for the public sector or the general ledger for commercial companies. The fund accounting and general ledger systems track spending (and report the profit-and-loss picture for commercial companies). These ledger systems disaggregate the organization's spending accounts into their constituent parts, called *natural cost elements*. These ledger systems are also conveniently structured by the organization's departments, which in turn are usually further hierarchically disaggregated again and again into cost centers. When these two are combined, the accounts and the cost centers are hardened into a coding scheme called the account/cost center. By assigning spending targets using the same classifications as the actual financial reporting, namely the ledger chart of accounts, the budget effectively mirrors total organization-wide financial spending and funding.

With hindsight, we now realize that the fund accounting and general ledger system, as well as their derivative budget, are a mirror of the organization chart, not of business processes. Yet the processes are what actually deliver value to service recipients and customers. Worse yet, the budget has no visibility to the "content of work." The budget also has no provisions to logically determine how external or internal cost drivers govern the natural levels of spending caused by demands on work from those cost drivers. Traditional budgeting is done more by push than by pull.

The next list provides additional observations about traditional budgeting, some of which appeared in the survey quiz:

- Low cost is a dependent variable; low costs are the result of doing other things well. You cannot budget your way into low-cost operations. Budget management and cost management are not synonymous.
- Budgets are useful for organizations that are stable and in which senior management does not trust the organization to intelligently spend money. Both of those conditions are invalid today.
- The budget should reflect strategies. Strategies should be formulated at two levels.

  - The diversification strategy level answers: What should we be doing?
  - The operational strategy level asks: How should we do it?

  Unfortunately, most of the effort is spent on the latter question, and companies become preoccupied with simply finishing the budget, which by that time may be disconnected from the strategy.

In response to rising awareness, leaders will be moving away from silo planning to process-based thinking and enterprise demand planning. Typically organizations spend about three months developing their operational budget—every year! Public-sector organizations are probably similar. The irony is that the budget is typically wrong the day it is "frozen." A better to way to budget will consolidate what is today an extremely fragmented and disjointed exercise.

ABC/M AS A SOLUTION FOR ACTIVITY-BASED PLANNING AND BUDGETING

Although many organizations recognize the problems with traditional budgeting and acknowledge their dissatisfaction, there has been little action taken to mend matters. But activity-based cost management (ABC/M) provides hope.

ABC mechanics effectively models the resource consumption rates and patterns of an enterprise on a cross-functional basis that focuses on work activities. Therefore, ABC/M-type budgets can be regenerated at periodic intervals based on estimates of the quantities of activity drivers in combination with the precomputed historical cost rates for the activity drivers.

The attraction of using ABC/M data to generate ABP/B is a natural. Managers want to plan their resources by examining what future forces are coming at them, which in turn will require calculable levels of people and supplies. These forces come in the form of volumes and quantities of activity drivers that cause work. It is true that activity drivers have their own cost drivers of a higher order; ABC/M relies on the lower-order activity drivers that are the measurable outputs of the work activities. Managers will need to determine how the root cause and higher-order drivers influence the volumetric driver quantities used in their ABP/B projections. But regardless of how they translate the future forces into the level of work and supplies required to match demand, managers want to solve for a valid level of resource expenses using logic, not politics.

In the 1980s, financial planners, particularly in the U.S. federal government, experimented with a precursor to ABP/B, zero-based budgeting (ZBB). Managers' instincts then were similar to what they are today. They suspected it might be better to imagine a budgeting process in which each department begins its budget thinking with a clean slate, as if it were just starting up new and staffing the department from scratch. What resources would the department need next year if it had no idea what it had last year?

However, as with most new programs, timing is everything when it comes to making major changes in management techniques, and the timing was not right in the 1980s for successful ZBB. Cost pressures were not as significant then as they are today. In addition, the software modeling tools and good ready-to-use measured activity driver cost rate data were hard to come by. Those conditions have now changed for the better. Many organizations have had their ABC/M systems implemented and routinely recalculated for several years. The more advanced and mature ABC/M users have already constructed reasonably good ABC models. These models represent their cost structure and cost behavior. The timing and conditions are now suitable for change.

ACTIVITY-BASED COST ESTIMATING

The advanced and mature ABC/M companies are interested in predictive planning and cost estimating for reasons other than just better budgeting. Managers are faced with numerous trade-off decisions. Should I add more warehouse space or ship direct? As previously discussed, the traditional chart-of-accounts costing view makes it difficult to compute how expenses and costs vary with changes in external and internal demands. Costs vary at the level of work activities, not at the department level.

Advanced and mature ABC/M users are now interested in using ABC/M as a superior basis for estimating costs. Cost estimating is the large umbrella under which ABP/B lies along with other reasons to project future costs, such as quoting customer orders, determining to make versus buy, or capital investment justifications. The major factors in categorizing these various predictive uses of ABC data for cost estimating are the planning time horizon and the scope of the enterprise that is affected by decisions resulting from the data. Exhibit 18.3 shows how these various types of predictive uses of forecast input data relate to horizon time and scope. ABB is the portion of the exhibit that covers the 12-month fiscal period and is enterprise-wide.

Cost estimating is often referred to as what-if scenarios. Regardless of what one calls the process, we are talking about the fact that decisions are being made about the future, and managers want to gauge the consequences of those decisions. In these situations, the future is basically coming at us, and in some way the quantity and mix of activity drivers will be placing demands on the work that we as an organization will need to do.

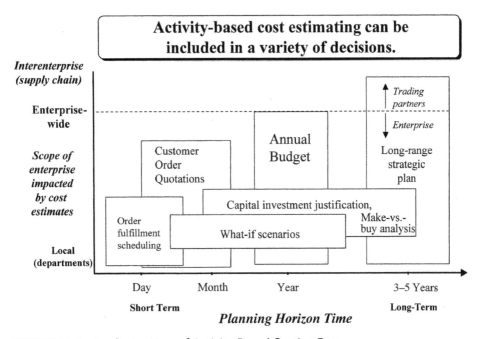

EXHIBIT 18.3   Predictive Uses of Activity-Based Costing Data

The resources required to do the work are the expenses. Assumptions are made about the outputs that are expected. Assumptions should also be made about the intermediate outputs and the labyrinth of interorganizational relationships that will be called on to generate the expected final outcomes.

ACTIVITY-BASED PLANNING AND BUDGETING SOLUTION

ABC management directly relates the consumption costs of work to customer-driven demands. The traditional budgeting method relies on managers to mystically translate all of this into the required number of people needed and their associated materials and equipment needs. That method has no link for how future demands translate into the needed resources. Exhibit 18.4 displays the three major components of an organization's cost structure: direct labor, direct material, and overhead (i.e., indirect expenses). It shows that indirect expenses are displacing direct expenses not simply due to automation but much more as a result that increases in the diversity of products, service lines, types of channels, and types of customers. As diversity broadens, complexity grows, which creates the need for more overhead to manage it. Planners for direct and recurring resource expenses almost always begin with estimates of future demand. Then, by relying on standards and averages (such as routings and bills of material in manufacturing), the planners calculate the future levels of staffing and resources.

All that ABP/B is suggesting is that the same approach for projecting direct labor and direct material should be applied to the indirect and overhead areas as well or to business processes where the organization prior to ABC/M had the misimpression that it had no outputs.

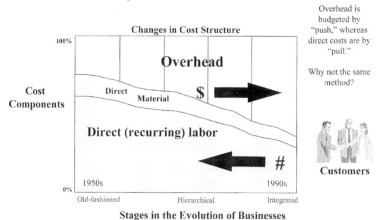

A key to understanding both ABC and ABB is to understand how cost behavior truly varies in relation to other factors.

EXHIBIT 18.4 Need for Activity-Based Costing and Activity-Based Budgeting

EARLY VIEWS OF ACTIVITY-BASED PLANNING AND BUDGETING WERE TOO SIMPLISTIC

Initial thoughts about ABP/B were fairly simplistic. Analysts appreciated the fact that, given an ABC/M model, they were now provided with the truly variable costs in a format and structure that were liberated from the structural deficiencies of the general ledger. Analysts not only had the activity costs cleanly isolated (i.e., translated) from the organization chart, they also now knew the activity driver cost rates, those ratios that related the cost of a work effort to a single unit of output.

Unfortunately, early attempts by the commercial ABC/M software vendors in the late 1990s led to their embarrassment. They released versions of ABC/M software that basically calculated ABC/M backward. That is, these versions simply accepted estimates for quantities of the activity drivers and multiplied them by the activity driver cost rates that had been calibrated from the past representative periods of time. This form of extrapolation can work when the volume and mix of the driver quantities of the future are very similar to those of the past. It can also work when what is being estimated will have only a relatively small impact on the total enterprise's costs, such as a quotation for a new customer order. A single customer order in a sea of thousands of orders may be imperceptible, yet each and every order would, it is hoped, be profitable. In Exhibit 18.4, the cost estimating used for price quotations can fall into a planning horizon from a few days to a year.

However, when the volume and mix of future driver quantities significantly differ from the past, the organization will begin to drift toward not having enough skill sets and resources for what it needs and concurrently having too much of what it does not need. Usually an organization will add the new needed resources (or suffer serious degradation in its service levels) and not remove the excess resources (e.g., lay off employees) it does not need. The net effect is that the "rates" that were calibrated from the past, if applied to the future, will underestimate the true cost. But by how much?

As a result of the recognition that there may be conditions in which ABP/B can be better than traditional budgeting but provide a less-than-perfect answer, we need to broaden the discussion to include general cost estimating, of which budgeting is only a subset.

IMPORTANT ROLE OF RESOURCE CAPACITY CAUSES NEW THINKING

Businesses, not-for-profit organizations, and governments are increasingly scrutinizing how they make managerial decisions. The margin for error continues to narrow. New questions and challenges are surfacing about how financial accounting systems provide a basis for making better managerial decisions.

Most managers and teams rely on internally generated managerial accounting data to support their decision making. They have questions and concerns regarding the accuracy and relevance of various internal accounting data and the usefulness of the data for decisions. Often the managers and teams adjust the accounting data to remove distortions and compensate for the deficiencies in the method being used to calculate the costs; ABC/M resolves most of the accuracy and distortion problems.

A nagging question concerns most organizations—the inability to know the true impact of a change or an improvement from an overall system perspective. That is, when a decision is acted on, how does anyone know with confidence whether the organization will in fact receive net positive benefits?

Managerial accounting substantially relaxes consideration for dependencies among resources and at an extreme ignores them altogether. From a historical perspective of an organization's spending, managerial accounting applies absorption costing that serves to assign the expenses to components, parts, and products served by the system. ABC/M is a refined form of absorption accounting. Exhibit 18.5 illustrates how ABC/M enhances the assignment of resource expenses into "calculated" costs by reflecting activity-to-activity assignments as well as cost object–to–cost object assignments.

In short, ABC/M is a multistage expense-assignment network. The accuracy of the final cost objects is determined much more by the structure of the network—as it reflects the diversity and variation of outputs placing demands on work activities—than by the accuracy of the activity driver and resource driver data. This is often counterintuitive, but the dampening or offsetting of error increases through the closed, zero-sum-error structure of absorption accounting.

The focus of ABP/B is on the future, not the past. Its emphasis is on the whole system, not its parts. It is true that accountants see part of their role as measuring the costs of the outcomes. However, by analyzing the past and using rates from recent past consumption behavior, changes can be made for a better future.

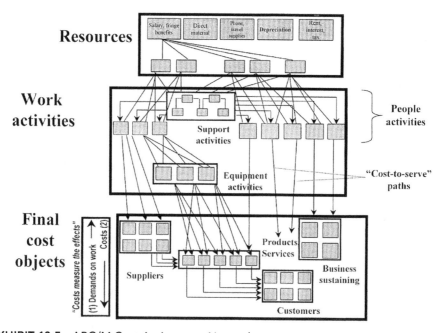

EXHIBIT 18.5 ABC/M Cost Assignment Network

MAJOR CLUE: CAPACITY EXISTS ONLY AS A RESOURCE

As most organizations plan for their next month, quarter, or year, the level of resources supplied is routinely replanned to roughly match the firm customer orders and expected future order demands. In reality, the level of planned resources must always exceed customer demand to allow for some protective, surge, and sprint capacity. This also helps improve customer on-time shipping service performance levels.

However, management accountants will be constantly disturbed if they cannot answer the question: How much unused and spare capacity do I have? because in their minds this excess capacity equates to non-value-added costs. Exhibit 18.6 illustrates how traditional management accountants view resources, expenses, and capacity.

To production planning managers, some level of idle capacity allows for time buffer management—the acceptance that people and equipment must sit temporarily idle and available—to act as the shock absorber of time for uncertainty and volatility. This is in the interest of maximizing the facility's overall throughput. Lessons from lean operations and just-in-time (JIT) manufacturing have been to not overly emphasize utilization rates or else you risk local optimizing, where workers run their equipment regardless of schedule priorities. This simply results in unneeded buildups of in-process inventories—a waste.

This broad topic of unused and idle capacity will likely be a thorny issue for absorption costing. As management accountants better understand operations, they will be constantly improving their ability to segment and isolate the unused capacity (and the nature of its cost) by individual resource. Managerial accountants will be increasingly able to measure unused capacity either empirically or by deductive logic based on projected standard cost rates. Furthermore, accountants will be able to segment and assign this unused capacity expense to various processes, owners, or the sales function or senior management. This will eliminate overcharging (and

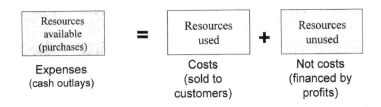

- *Cost* is a measure of *use*, whereas *expense* is a measure of *spending*. They are usually never the same.

- Resource expenses equate to system capacity. Capacity does not exist at the activity level. It exists only as a resource. *Resources supply capacity* for productive use by work, whether of people or equipment.

- Absorption costing measures the first term of the equation, the resource costs of workload performed. Absorption costing assigns these costs to products, services, channels, and customers.

EXHIBIT 18.6 Absorption Costing Recognizes the Importance of Capacity

overstating) product costs resulting from including unused capacity costs that the product did not cause.

MEASURING AND USING COST DATA

The sole focus of this section is managerial accounting, not financial accounting. Financial accounting addresses external reporting used as compliance reporting for banks, owners, publicly owned companies, and government regulators. This information is compulsory. Financial accounting is governed by laws and rules established by regulatory agencies.

In most nations, financial accounting follows generally accepted accounting principles (GAAP). Some people jokingly refer to this as the GAAP trap because focusing on these numbers may distract the organization from more relevant numbers or prevent it from finding more appropriate ways to calculate costs and profit margins. GAAP means something to accountants, but to others it sounds like a blue-jeans retail store or a space between your teeth.

In contrast, managerial accounting is used internally by managers and employee teams for decision making. If you violate financial accounting laws, you may go to jail. You do not risk going to jail if you have poor managerial accounting, but you run the risk of making bad decisions. For all organizations, the margin for error is getting slimmer as the pressure grows for better organizational performance.

At the highest level of managerial accounting, there are two broad elements: measuring the costs and using the cost data. Exhibit 18.7 displays an overarching framework

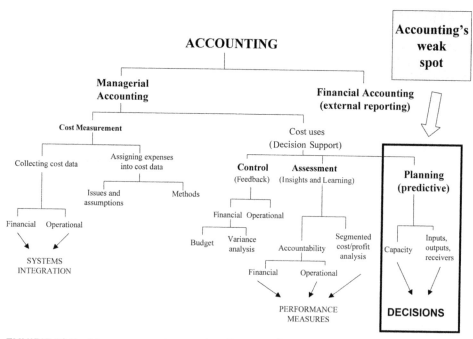

EXHIBIT 18.7   Management Accounting Framework

for managerial accounting with a tree, branch, and leaf structure. In this framework each branch can be further separated into these key components:

- *Cost measurement.* Measuring costs comprises collecting data and assigning the source expenses in a way that is meaningful for the organization.
- *Cost uses.* Chapter 1 of many managerial accounting textbooks usually states that there are three broad purposes for using cost data: operational control, assessment and evaluation, and predictive planning.

The first two uses, operational control and assessment, are less challenging for cost accounting. This is because they are descriptive of history. I refer to them as "cost autopsies.'" The money was spent. There is no debate about that but rather where the money was spent. So the only accounting task is to focus on rules of traceability. But with the third view, predicting future expense, things get much trickier. Now we need to worry about classifying how future resource expanses will vary relative to future changes in volume and mix.

USEFULNESS OF HISTORICAL FINANCIAL DATA

Absorption costing is basically a segmentation calculation related to historical spending. From a historical view, the real problem is that expenses reported in a chart of account as resources are not only structurally deficient, they also encourage fortress politics as some silo managers hoard resources regardless of demand. ABC/M translates chart-of-accounts spending into activity costs, which can reflect variability plus ease tracing to final cost objects, such as products, based on activity drivers. Exhibit 18.8 illustrates how ABC/M performs this translation.

But the organization's resources are ultimately what are being managed. Exhibit 18.9 illustrates this point. It shows that organizations try hard to manage their level and types of resources in the context of present and future demands. But the key is to make better decisions—for the future. Absorption accounting creates visibility about the use of resources.

Exhibit 18.10 illustrates how ABC/M, a refined form of absorption accounting, provides an activity as well as an output view. These are the calculated costs that TOC users fear. ABC/M substantially improves on simplistic and broad-averaging cost allocations to reflect true consumption patterns. In the historical view, absorption costing has added visibility to both "the work" and the "outputs" of the work. (Note that in this view, "the work" costs also belong to the processes, which is a time-based view. Process-simulation software tools are taking advantage of this link to absorption costing tools.)

Exhibit 18.11 completes the series of graphics by pointing out when activity costs are translated into outputs. ABC/M data provide employees and management teams with insights and inferences. Now comes a critical point: This exhibit illustrates that when historical information is applied to the future, it may not be sufficient for that information to merely suggest what actions to take; the information must also be accurate. That is, it must reasonably reveal the impact of those changes on outcomes.

In addition to seeing the "content of work," the activity view gives insights to what drives each activity's cost magnitude to fluctuate.

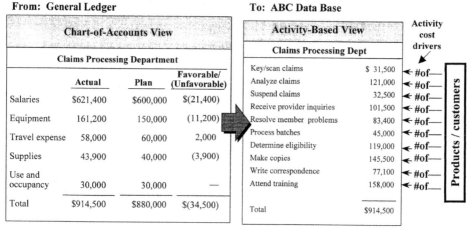

From: **General Ledger**

Chart-of-Accounts View

Claims Processing Department

	Actual	Plan	Favorable/ (Unfavorable)
Salaries	$621,400	$600,000	$(21,400)
Equipment	161,200	150,000	(11,200)
Travel expense	58,000	60,000	2,000
Supplies	43,900	40,000	(3,900)
Use and occupancy	30,000	30,000	—
Total	$914,500	$880,000	$(34,500)

To: **ABC Data Base**

Activity-Based View

Claims Processing Dept

Activity cost drivers

Key/scan claims	$ 31,500	←#of—
Analyze claims	121,000	←#of—
Suspend claims	32,500	←#of—
Receive provider inquiries	101,500	←#of—
Resolve member problems	83,400	←#of—
Process batches	45,000	←#of—
Determine eligibility	119,000	←#of—
Make copies	145,500	←#of—
Write correspondence	77,100	←#of—
Attend training	158,000	←#of—
Total	$914,500	

Products / customers

Fixed versus variable classifications get re-defined with ABC/M.

EXHIBIT 18.8   Each Activity Has Its Own Cost Driver

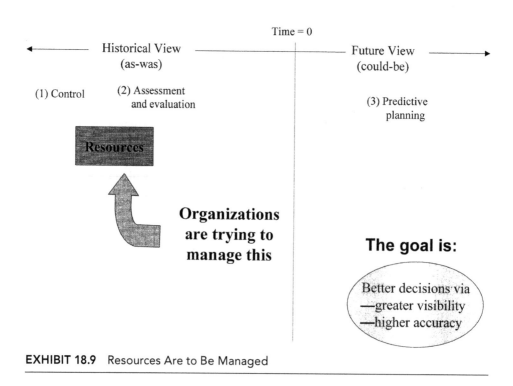

Time = 0

Historical View   Future View
(as-was)   (could-be)

(1) Control   (2) Assessment and evaluation   (3) Predictive planning

Resources

Organizations are trying to manage this

The goal is:

Better decisions via
—greater visibility
—higher accuracy

EXHIBIT 18.9   Resources Are to Be Managed

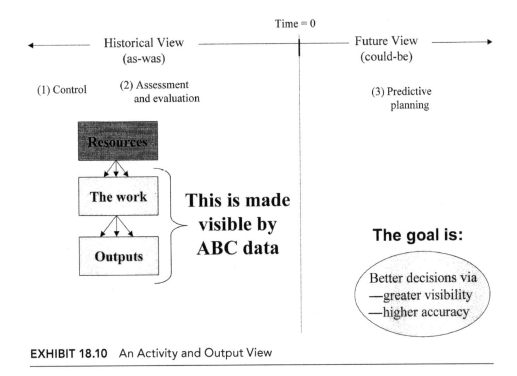

EXHIBIT 18.10   An Activity and Output View

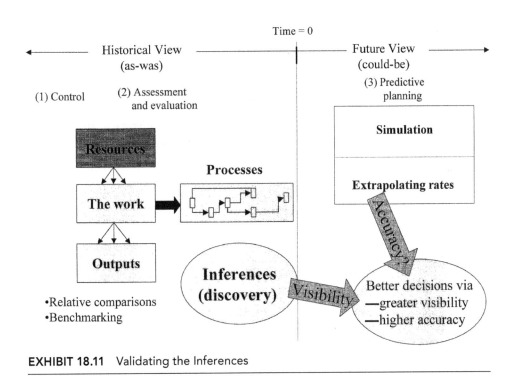

EXHIBIT 18.11   Validating the Inferences

In other words, based on inferences as well as cost estimates that may use the ABC/M activity driver rates and estimates of driver volumes, "extrapolated costs" may require further validation to ensure that the predicted resources are realizable. Under some conditions, the use of simulation technology will improve an ABC/M-derived cost estimate by providing greater accuracy. The key question is: What are those conditions?

Exhibit 18.12 illustrates that the effort level to adjust capacity becomes easier farther out in time. It takes a while to convert in-case resources into as-needed ones. However, committed expenses (in-case) today can be more easily converted into contractual (as-needed) arrangements in a shorter time period than was possible ten years ago. Fixed expenses can become variable expenses. The rapid growth in the temporary staffing industry is evidence. Organizations are replacing full-time employees who are paid regardless of the demand level with contractors who are staffed and paid at the demand level, which may be measured in hours.

Understanding the cost of the resource workload used to produce a product or deliver a service is relevant to making these resource reallocation decisions. Ignoring incremental changes in the actual resources (i.e., expense spending) when making decisions can eventually lead to a cost structure that may become inefficient and ineffective for the organization. There will always be a need to adjust the capacity based on changes in future demand volume and mix. This in turn equates to raising or lowering specific expenses on resources.

WHERE DOES ACTIVITY-BASED PLANNING AND BUDGETING FIT IN?

Costs can be considered from both a descriptive, historical view and a predictive view. There is a difference in time perspective between assigning and tracing costs to products and services in the past and estimating how future resource expenditures (cash outflows) will vary as the volumes and mix of products and service lines, as well as varying service levels to different types of customers, fluctuate. In the descriptive view, the resource expenditures are precisely known, and one solves for the unknown product costs. The

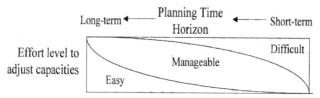

In the very short term, you would not fire employees on Tuesday due to low work load, but hire them back on Wednesday. But in the future you may replace full-time employees with contractors, or lease assets you might have purchased. In this way, so-called fixed costs behave variably.

EXHIBIT 18.12   Capacity Exists Only as Resources

reverse is true in the predictive cost-estimating view. In forecasting, the demand volume and mix of the outputs are estimated, and one then solves for the unknown level of expenditures that will be required to produce and deliver the volume and mix. One is basically determining the capacity requirements of the resources.

The second difference, estimating future levels of resource expense cash outflows, becomes complex because resources come in discontinuous clumps. That is, resource expenses do not immediately vary with each incremental increase or decrease in end-unit volume. Traditional accountants address this with what they refer to as a "step-fixed" category of expenses. Absorption accounting handles this historical versus prospective view of time by applying "demand-pull" absorption costing. This is where ABC/M becomes ABP/B.

Demand-pull absorption costing is ABP/B, which is all about predictive costing—the estimated expenses and costs for a future time period. This method involves extrapolations that use baseline physical and cost consumption rates from prior-period ABC/M calculations. Managerial accountants relate ABP/B to a form of flexible budgeting (which is normally applied annually to a 12-month time span). In contrast to "push" absorption costing, ABP/B recognizes that changes in end-unit volume and product mix can have nonvariable impacts on the usage and expense of the system's various resources. It recognizes only the changes in resource expenditures that will result from a plan or a decision. The terms "demand-pull absorption costing" and "ABP/B" are used interchangeably in this chapter.

Assignments in ABP/B are designed to reflect a fair measure of the usage of consumed resource expenses. The unused expenses represent idle and unused capacity. These unused expenses are usually assigned to management as a business-sustaining cost (i.e., they are the cost of doing business in an ongoing concern).

ABP/B measures the impact of changes in the mix and volume of outputs originating *from* customers and their order requests for varying quantities of specific products and services. Hence the reference to a pull created by the "demands" on the organization's work and resources.

ACTIVITY-BASED PLANNING AND BUDGETING SOLUTION

Traditional planning and budgeting methods carry many unpleasant connotations due to somewhat dysfunctional practices. Plans and budgets may be highly detailed, but they have low user confide nce. The detail may imply accuracy and precision, but the assumptions are questionable. There are often too many iterations based on organizational politics that still arrive at unrealistic projections of expenses.

The use of ABP/B became increasingly popular mainly due to cynicism about traditional budgeting. Traditional budgeting tends to assume that the existing level of resources is already justified. As part of the game, managers then lobby for even more resources. ABP/B computes the level of resources by applying a reverse calculation. This technique is not restricted to a 12-month planning horizon. As a result, this cost-estimating technique can be applied to any planning horizon. ABP/B and ABP are best combined as a single term, but ABP is likely to become the popular application because it provides for what-if analysis, something that managers increasingly want answers for in financial terms.

ABP/B leverages ABC/M's calculated data; ABC/M directly relates the consumption costs of work to customer-driven demands. That is, it translates how customer demand consumes resources. The traditional budgeting and planning methods rely on managers to mystically translate all this into the required number of people needed and their associated materials and equipment need. The traditional budgeting and planning methods have few valid links for how future demands translate into the needed resources.

The ideas in this chapter on activity-based resource planning (ABRP) are based on excellent research from a professional society. The researchers are from the Activity Based Budgeting Project Team of the Consortium of Advanced Manufacturing—International's (CAM-I) Cost Management Systems group. There is more at www.cam-i.org.

Exhibit 18.13 illustrates how capacity planning is the key to the solution. Planners and budgeters initially focus on the direct and recurring resource expenses, not the indirect and overhead support expenses. They almost always begin with estimates of future demand in terms of volumes and mix. Then, by relying on standards and averages (such as the product routings and bills-of-material used in manufacturing systems), planners and budgeters calculate the future required levels of staff and resources. The ABRP method suggests that this same approach can be applied to the indirect and overhead areas as well or to processes where the organization often has a wrong impression that they have no tangible outputs.

The commercial ABC/M software vendors successfully resolved their original problem with simplistic ABP/B, just calculating their ABC/M model in reverse. They recognized that ABP/B begins with the cost objects, such as products. Demand volume drives activity and resource requirements; ABP/B is forward focused, but it uses actual historical performance data to develop baseline consumption rates.

ABP/B assesses the quantities of workload demands that are ultimately placed on resources. In step 1 in Exhibit 18.13, ABP/B first asks: How much activity workload is required for *each* output of cost object? These are the activity requirements. Then ABP/B asks: How much resources are needed to meet that activity workload? In other words, a workload can be measured as the number of units of an activity required to produce a quantity of cost objects.

The determination of expense does not occur until after the activity volume has been translated into resource capacity using the physical resource driver rates from the ABC/M model. These rates are regularly expressed in hours, full-time equivalents, square feet, pounds, gallons, and so forth.

As a result of step 1, there will be a difference between the existing resources available and the resources that will be required to satisfy the plan—the resource requirements. That is, at this stage organizations usually discover they may have too much of what they do not need and not enough of what they do need to meet the customers' expected service levels (e.g., to deliver on time). The consequence of having too much implies a cost of unused capacity. The consequence of having too little is a limiting constraint that if not addressed implies an erosion in customer service levels.

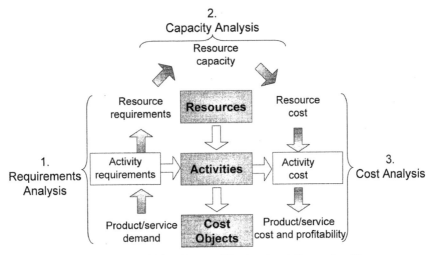

EXHIBIT 18.13 Activity-Based Planning and Budgeting Information Flow

In step 2, a reasonable balance must be achieved between the operational and financial measures. Now capacity must be analyzed. One option is for the budgeters, planners, or management accountants to evaluate how much to adjust the shortage and excess of actual resources to respond to the future demand load. Senior management may or may not allow the changes. There is a maximum expense impact that near-term financial targets (and executive compensation plan bonuses) will tolerate. These capacity adjustments represent real resources with real changes in cash outlay expenses if they were to be enacted.

Assume that management agrees to the new level of resources without further analysis or debate. In step 3 of the flow in Exhibit 18.13, the new level of resource expenditures can be determined and then translated into the costs of the work centers and eventually into the costs of the products, service lines, channels, and customers. Step 3 is classic ABC/M—but for a future period. Some call this a pro forma ABC/M calculation. The quantities of the projected drivers are applied, and new budgeted or planned costs can be calculated for products, service lines, outputs, customers, and service recipients. At this point, however, the financial impact may not be acceptable. It may show too small a financial return.

When the financial result is unacceptable, management has options other than to continue readjusting resource capacity levels. These other options may not have much impact on expenses. Exhibit 18.14 reveals five types of adjustments that planners and budgeters can consider to align their expected demand with resource expenditures to achieve desired financial results. This approach has been called a closed-loop ABP/B framework.

Each of the five numbered options is intended to improve results; however, the relative impact of each adjustment will be unique to each organization and its situation. As previously described, the ABP/B model uses as its source input the estimated demand quantities to determine the degree of imbalance there may be between the required and actual resources.

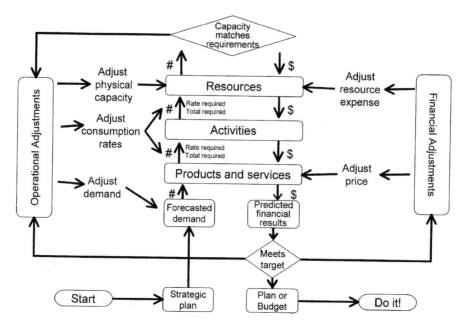

EXHIBIT 18.14   Activity-Based Budgeting and Activity-Based Planning Require Making Adjustments

Assuming that the result will be shortages and excesses of capacity, management can *physically*:

1. *Adjust capacity.* Additional staffing, supplies, overtime, equipment, and the like can be purchased for shortages. There can be scale-backs and removals of people and machines for excesses.
2. *Adjust consumption rates.* If possible, the speed and efficiency of the existing resources can be cranked up or down. If, for example, the increase in staffing makes a decision uneconomical, fewer people can be hired, with an assumed productivity rate increase assumed.
3. *Adjust demand.* If resources remain constrained, demand can be governed or rationed.

The last two options are operational but also affect the level of resource expenses required. After this cycle of adjustments balances capacity of supply with demand, if the financial results are still unsatisfactory, management can make two incremental financial changes:

1. *Adjust pricing.* In commercial for-profit enterprises or full cost recovery operations, pricing can be raised or lowered. This directly affects the top-line revenues. Of course, care is required because the price elasticity could cause changes in volume that more than offset the price changes.

2. *Adjust resource cost.* If possible, wage levels or purchase prices of materials can be renegotiated.

For a more in-depth discussion of ABP/B, see *An ABB Manager's Primer* by Alan J. Stratton and William S. McKinney at www.abctech.com.

Unfortunately, in the area of budgeting, there is one last step that is in its infancy: to integrate the results from the ABP/B system into the traditional and formal budget statement format. Recall that budget reporting format is a mirror image of the general-ledger cost-center reporting that aligns with the hierarchical organization chart and lists expenses according to the chart-of-accounts. Exhibit 18.15 illustrates how ABP/B must be combined with other inputs from the traditional process. The issue is that although ABP/B produces the comprehensive measures of expenses, it does not yet easily track these expenses by the cost centers and their expense account codes. In short, a budget will not appear to managers as complete until it looks very much like what they typically receive as their standard reports and reflects the organizational structure they relate to.

The pioneers in ABP/B are undaunted. They recognize the logic and power of the ABP/B method even though its reported format is one step removed from the formal budget format. My opinion is that the issues involved in this final conversion will be healthy for advancing management methods to human resources management. These issues involve treating people as important assets.

ABP/B acknowledges that there are a substantial amount of expenses that do not vary with a unit volume of final output. These expenses are not variable costs as determined by an incremental new expense for each incremental unit of output. As mentioned, resources often come in discontinuous amounts. Economists refer to these as step-fixed costs. An organization cannot purchase one-third of a machine or hire half of an employee. ABP/B recognizes the step-fixed costs in step 2 where resource capacity is adjusted. It recognizes that as external unit volumes fluctuate, then:

■ Some workload costs do eventually vary based on a batch size of output or on some other discretionary factor.

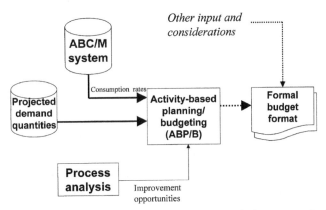

EXHIBIT 18.15 Combining Activity-Based Budgeting and Planning with the Formal Budget Format

▪ Some resources expenditures will be acquired or retired as a whole and indivisible resource, thus creating step-fixed expenses (i.e., adding or removing used and unused capacity expenses).

On the short-term horizon, an organization would not add or reduce employee staff levels to match daily workload requirements, so there is a step-fixed cost function. The effect of varying conditions on the accuracy of cost-estimating methods needs more research.

In summary, absorption costing is descriptive; however, its data may be used for predictive purposes. The data provide inferences. In contrast, ABP/B is predictive; ABP/B strives to monitor the impact of decisions or plans in terms of the external cash funds flow of an organization.

RISK CONDITIONS FOR FORECASTING EXPENSES AND CALCULATED COSTS

When it comes to looking to the future either to use insights gained from historical cost reporting or to forecast costs, how inapplicable might the historically absorbed cost data be? How much from the descriptive patterns of the past can be extrapolated to predict and measure the impact of changes in the future?

If one uses simple cost rates rather than physical consumption rates from ABP/B, how significant will the difference be? The answer is: It depends on the conditions. In addition, if the assumption is that ABP/B does yield a superior answer, what are the relative levels of effort to collect the essential data and analyze the decision?

As illustrated in Exhibit 18.11, some methodology and assumptions are needed to provide accuracy and a sense of confidence for decision makers that the outcomes of their decisions likely will be favorable. Hunches and intuition are not sufficient; a validation may be required. Extrapolation using absorption costing rate data is the default method for estimating costs, but in some cases, the higher forms of cost estimating, like ABP/B and simulation, may be required.

Another way of asking this question is: What are the conditions that exist when projecting cost estimates would inadvertently lead to a poor decision? That is, what are the outside limits of assumptions, such as for planned volumes, and where are their risks from using "extrapolated" costs? How broad is the so-called relevant range in which changes in expenses vary nonlinearly with changes in volume? What are the conditions that exist when an apparently good decision results in a poor one? The conditions that can change include:

1. *Significant mix changes.* The cost rates in absorption costing are calibrated based on recent history reflecting recent output mix. These are commonly referred to as *actual* costs. If the new scenarios contain a substantially different mix of products and services, then the past rates will be less valid. That is, the new scenarios will likely have too much idle and unneeded capacity and not enough of the needed type of capacity. The true pro forma cost rates would rise or fall in the future scenarios due to step-fixed and semivariable cost functions on resource expenses.

2. *Significant volume changes.* When the future scenarios apply substantial changes in volume, the calibrated rates are less applicable because the new volumes are outside the "relevant range": again, step-fixed and not variable costs.

3. *Constraint and near-constraint impact.* When some resources are near full utilization and/or the capacities of the entire system resources are nearly balanced (i.e., the risk of interactive constraints or of shifting constraints), a slight change in demand load could affect the global throughput. The constraint would shift to a new location and possibly delay sales and erode on-time shipping performance. Interdependencies affect the outcome.

4. *Uncertainty and volatility.* Unplanned events and variation in performance disrupt and can invalidate any assumptions about resource usage, throughput, and the recovery efforts to achieve customer-promised due dates. The impact of uncertainty, volatility, and variation of inputs and performance is usually unrecognized (except for a sloppy fudge factor) under conventional cost forecasting. These factors are baked into the historical cost rates as part of the "averages." Delays may cause greater-than-planned idle capacity, but most of the operating expense cash outlay expenses may not change.

5. *Degree of heterogeneity of products and services.* When an organization's outputs are not diverse or varied, extrapolating cost rates based on the past may be directionally reasonable. But when diversity of outputs increases (which is the more normal situation for most organizations), additional complexity results. Consequently, forecasting the cost impact of a decision becomes trickier. Simple extrapolations based on the descriptive past may not produce reasonable expense and cost estimates.

6. *Degree of resource dedication/inflexibility.* When equipment or people are capable of performing specific tasks only, substantial changes in customer demands significantly shift the entire workload. The result can be not having enough of what is needed and having too much of what is not needed—a capacity imbalance. Forecasting the impact on changes to the resource mix is tricky.

These six restrictive conditions can be concurrent, which further increases the possibility of an invalid cost forecast.

The unmet challenge for calculating estimates of future expenses will be to know how far-reaching the conditions are under which traditional cost projections may or may not be valid. How intense must the changes in these conditions be to generate major significant differences between cost projections from absorption costing and from throughput accounting?

Extrapolations and ABP/B cost estimating are acceptable as long as the conditions just described are not severely compromised. That is, when the future conditions are not too restrictive, then future costs can be extrapolated or reverse-calculated based on recent historical physical and cost rates.

Many management accountants accept extrapolations as being very reasonable. They know that the cost rates that were derived from a recent and representative time frame also reflect the capacities of that same period. The cost rates already contain and reflect the variation and uncertainties experienced during that same period.

Therefore, the accountants conclude that unless the future period has substantially greater variation and interdependent congestion than the past period did, the cost rates they are using are acceptable to apply for the future. They reflect real experience. The extra costs caused by the variations are already baked into the cost rates. The question is how different the next few weeks will be compared to the past weeks in these same categories. The use of extrapolated cost rates assumes that there is organizational inertia and that there will be no volatile and punctuated spike, up or down, in the pace at which employees and equipment work.

FRAMEWORK TO COMPARE AND CONTRAST EXPENSE-ESTIMATING METHODS

Exhibit 18.16 presents a framework that describes various methods of predictive cost estimating. This entire framework represents the box that appeared in the upper-right corner of Exhibit 18.16 as "simulation/extrapolating rates." The horizontal axis is the planning horizon, short term to long term, right to left. The vertical axis could represent any of the six restrictive conditions, but the label that was selected is a hybrid of the six, implying the types and magnitudes of change in demands of the future relative to the recent past.

Examine the lower part of Exhibit 18.16, which illustrates the level of effort to adjust capacity across the planning horizon. This is Exhibit 18.12 embedded in this exhibit. It describes expenses as becoming more variable and less committed as the planning horizon lengthens. Historical cost rates can be more easily applied for decisions over longer time frames; there are fewer step-fixed expense issues.

There are no definitions for the boundary lines between the various zones, and there is overlap as one estimating method gives way to another as being superior. But how much do the various conditions need to change before additional decision support is needed to validate the feasibility or completely evaluate a decision? That is a good question. I am investigating the question of just where the zones begin to overlap. So far, it appears that ABP/B has substantial applicability across a wide set of conditions. (Also, now I know why one of my industrial engineering college professors at Cornell University warned us to use simulation only as a last resort. It requires a lot of administration to configure and maintain.)

In Exhibit 18.16, the upper-right corner illustrates that as the time period to adjust capacity shortens and simultaneously the number of changes in conditions from the past substantially increase, it becomes risky to rely exclusively on extrapolation methods for cost forecasting. Discrete-event simulation tools may provide superior and more reliable answers in this zone relative to the other methods. It can evaluate and validate decisions in any zone, but in particular the upper-right corner of Exhibit 18.16.

Caution is required when applying extrapolated costs because they are not sensitive to capacity limits, for a shift in the system constraint to another constraint, or for the impact of changes in uncertainty in the form of delays and schedule slippage. There are

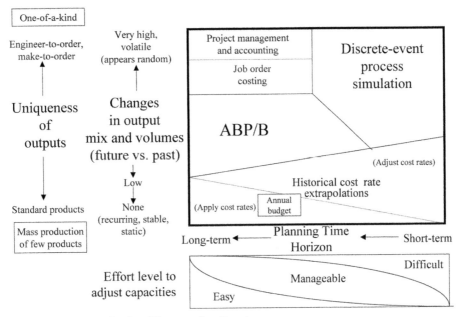

EXHIBIT 18.16 Methods of Forecasting Results

decisions for which extrapolations using "cost rate averages" derived from absorption costing simply will not be useful; ABP/B is a next-best alternative—it is a capacity-aware method. But when the conditions are such that ABP/B might calculate excessive error, an option is to estimate the workloads, delay times, and magnitude of resources required using discrete-event process-simulation software. This class of analytical application software contains rule-based logic that acknowledges capacity limits, time, constraints, and dependencies.

Discrete-event process-simulation software calculates multiple feasible solutions, from which comparisons can be made to select the most preferred. But none of these feasible solutions is necessarily an optimal solution. Discrete-event process-simulation software has the ability to run hundreds to thousands of iterations for a single scenario to show the on-average effect of collective variability. (In this approach, variability can occur in multiple locations and produce interactive effects among constraints and nonconstraints.) The relevant expenses are derived using "net change" comparison logic because full scenarios are generated that can be netted against the existing baseline. With simulation, there is no methodology to manage or time buffers. Instead, there is substantial trial and error to search for a "best" solution.

Finally, Exhibit 18.17 provides a sense of the administrative effort versus the benefits of selecting the expense-forecasting method. It is a tedious task to configure the data and the rule-based relationships for discrete-event process simulation. But under certain conditions, this simulation is applicable. When it comes to cost forecasting, apply this test: Is the climb worth the view?

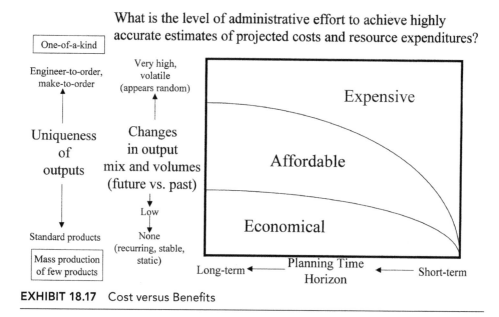

EXHIBIT 18.17   Cost versus Benefits

A commercial organization ultimately manages itself by understanding where it makes and loses money, or whether the impact of a decision produces incremental revenues superior to incremental expenses. Organizations are increasingly achieving a much better understanding of their contribution profit margins using ABC/M data. By leveraging ABC/M with ABP/B and discrete-event process-simulation tools, an organization can produce a fully integrated plan. It can be assured that its plan is more feasible, determine the level of resources and expenditures to execute that plan, then view and compare the projected results of that plan against its current performance to manage its various profit margins.

The combination of these tools allows boardroom-level thinking to begin with the company's complete income statement, generate a feasible operating plan, and restate the results of that plan with an income statement—again for boardroom reporting. Advocates of simulation-planning software believe that the brute-force computing power of personal computers and/or seamless integration with servers now adequately provides simulation information that is comprehensive, finite scheduled, and rule based and allows for various assumptions about uncertainty. Others argue that this is a last resort, and that good modeling provides sufficiently accurate results.

There has been recent exploration by one of CAM-I's interest groups in an advanced form of managerial accounting called RCA, which is based on a German method of marginal cost analysis called GPK. More can be learned at www.rcainstitute.org/. In contrast to ABC/M, RCA places a greater emphasis on modeling resource capacity utilization with a more rigorous level of modeling. In the area of responsibility accounting, RCA provides period feedback to operational managers in the form of flex budgeting and cost-variance reporting.

 **ECONOMICS 101?**

It may feel like this chapter was a revisiting of an economics textbook. You are probably correct. But what is different is this: In the textbooks, marginal cost analysis was easily described but extremely difficult to compute due to all of the complexities. In the past, computing technology was the impediment. Now things have reversed. Technology is no longer the impediment; the thinking is. How one configures the ABP/B model and what assumptions one makes become critical to calculating the appropriate required expenses and their pro forma calculated costs.

CHAPTER NINETEEN

Cost Behavior and the Relationship to the Budgeting Process

Eugene H. Kramer, CPA

 INTRODUCTION

Management is always faced with uncertainty about the future. Unless managers can forecast cost and revenue trends reasonably well, their decisions may yield unfavorable results. Forecasts concerning cost–volume–profit relationships are necessary to make accurate decisions about such matters as how many units should be manufactured, should price be changed, should advertising be increased, or should plant and equipment be expanded.

 COST BEHAVIOR

Cost–volume–profit relationships depend on accurate descriptions of cost behavior. Cost behavior is affected by a number of factors, including volume, price, efficiency, sales mix, and production changes. Therefore, any analysis must be made with regard to its limitations. The benefit of cost–volume–profit relationships is in understanding the interrelationships affecting profits.

To be analyzed, all costs must be broken down into their fixed and variable portions. This is essential in determining what a cost will be at a certain point (usually defined as production or sales volume). Otherwise, management will not be able to regulate the costs properly, which is vital for efficient budgeting or for making any plans or decisions. Various alternatives as to how costs will be allocated may be utilized, and accurate cost estimates should be prepared for each alternative in determining the best decisions.

Fixed Costs

Costs that remain constant over the entire range of output are referred to as *fixed costs*. These costs are incurred simply because of the passage of time and do not change as a direct result of changes in volume. Exhibit 19.1 depicts the relationship of fixed costs on a graph.

Depreciation, property insurance, property taxes, and administrative salaries are all examples of fixed costs.

Variable Costs

Costs that vary directly with changes in volume are referred to as *variable costs*. Exhibit 19.2 depicts the relationship of variable costs on a graph.

Variable cost equals unit cost multiplied by the volume. A good example is the direct materials used in making a product. Every automobile has one steering wheel. If steering wheels cost $10 each, then the steering wheel cost of one automobile is $10, of two automobiles $20, of 100 automobiles $1,000, and so on. Other examples include direct

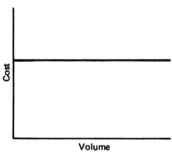

EXHIBIT 19.1　Relationship of Fixed Costs

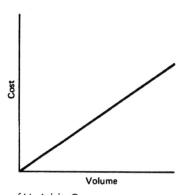

EXHIBIT 19.2　Relationship of Variable Costs

labor in variation with production volume and sales commissions and cost of goods sold in variation with sales volume.

Semivariable Costs

Semivariable costs are those costs that have traits similar to both fixed and variable costs. These types of costs can be seen in various forms. For example, while a manufacturing plant is idle, certain maintenance costs will be incurred. Once production is under way, though, additional maintenance costs vary with production volume. Exhibit 19.3 depicts these costs, separating them into their fixed and variable portions.

Some semivariable costs will not fit into a straight-line pattern. They may begin at a certain point and rise at an increasing or decreasing rate. For cost analysis, however, they are assumed to have straight-line relationships (see Exhibits 19.4 and 19.5).

Sometimes a cost will function as a fixed cost for a segment of the range, jump to a different cost level for another segment of the range, and then jump to yet another level. Clerical costs may fit this pattern. The clerical staff may be able to handle the work at a certain range of production, but once production moves into another range, additional staff will be required. These types of costs may be handled in one of two ways. The first is to assume that a straight-line relationship exists, as depicted in Exhibit 19.6.

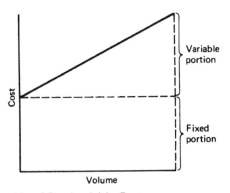

EXHIBIT 19.3　Relationship of Semivariable Costs

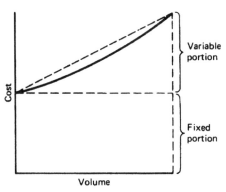

EXHIBIT 19.4　Relationship of Semivariable Costs Not Fitting into a Straight-Line Pattern

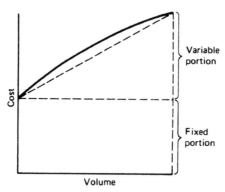

EXHIBIT 19.5   Relationship of Semivariable Costs Not Fitting into a Straight-Line Pattern

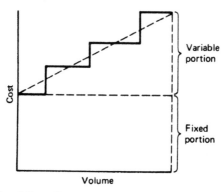

EXHIBIT 19.6   Example of Step Costs

When there are only one or two steps, the costs are sometimes treated solely as fixed costs. Thus, for one step, total fixed costs would change for the two different ranges (see Exhibit 19.7).

BREAK-EVEN ANALYSIS

The effects of cost behavior can be seen quite clearly in cost–volume–profit relationships when using a break-even chart. With break-even analysis, we can see the effect upon net income of various decisions that affect sales and costs (see Exhibit 19.8).

The *break-even point* is that point of output at which total revenues and total costs are equal. The ability of management to control costs accurately can be greatly enhanced by forecasts of the effect on the break-even point. To keep management informed of the effect of major and minor changes in cost and revenue patterns, the management

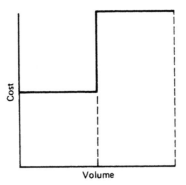

EXHIBIT 19.7   Example of Step Costs, Assuming Only One or Two Steps

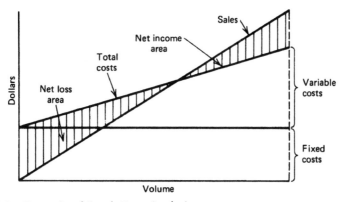

EXHIBIT 19.8   Example of Break-Even Analysis

accountant must continually analyze cost behavior and update break-even points periodically.

Break-even charts enable managers to glance over potential profits. The use of preliminary budget figures as a basis for the break-even chart can give management a chance to make changes in the budget if the forecast is not satisfactory.

Variable Cost and the Contribution Margin

In break-even analysis, variable cost is an important determinant in establishing the optimum level of activity. When the variable cost ratio (total variable costs divided by total sales) is known, the total variable costs at any level of activity can be determined.

The *contribution margin* is that portion of the sales dollar available to cover fixed costs and to attain profits. It is a complement of variable costs and is computed by subtracting variable costs from sales. When using the contribution margin technique, the break-even chart will take the form that is depicted in Exhibit 19.9.

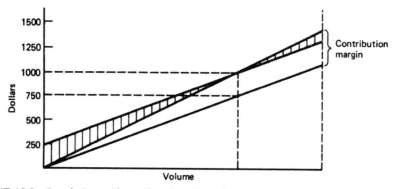

EXHIBIT 19.9   Break-Even Chart Showing Contribution Margin

EXHIBIT 19.10   Example of Computing Contribution Margin Using Changing Volumes

	Given Volume	Percentage	Increase in Volume	Decrease in Volume
Sales	$1000	100	$100	$200
Variable costs	750	75	75	150
Contribution margin	$250	25	$25	$50
Fixed costs	250			
Net income	$0		$25	$50

When the contribution margin is presented as a ratio of sales, the effect on profits is easily computed with respect to prospective changes in volume. Using the data presented in Exhibit 19.9, Exhibit 19.10 gives an example of this computation.

Because the total fixed costs do not change over the volume range, they are not relevant. Thus, the contribution margin ratio will give the results for any contemplated change in activity.

Knowledge of the contribution margin ratio can benefit management in a variety of useful ways. The ratio indicates how much profits will either diminish or increase with each dollar change in volume. A high ratio will cause greater profits as volume increases above the break-even point, whereas it will cause greater losses as volume decreases below the break-even point. A low contribution margin ratio will require greater increases of volume to create noticeable increases in profits. Basically, the greater the ratio, the larger the change in profits as volume changes.

Changes in Fixed Costs

It has been seen that changes in variable costs will affect the contribution margin, which directly influences earnings. Fixed costs are not stable year after year either. They must be budgeted for as accurately as possible because of their long- and short-term effects on the profits of a business.

Fixed costs are not independent of the other two major profit determinants: revenue and variable costs. A manufacturer may decide to create a new department in order to sell directly to retailers instead of selling through intermediaries and thereby create a greater per unit sales price. Management may also be contemplating purchasing more efficient machinery, which would result in lower variable costs per unit. Thus, when a major change in fixed costs is proposed, determining the effects on the break-even point and the contribution margin is vital for wise management decisions.

Relevant Range

Each cost analysis is assumed valid only for a specified relevant range of volumes. Outside of this range, the intrusion of different costs will alter the assumed relationship. In a manufacturing company, variable costs would be quite high if only a few units of a product were produced. However, producing more than the capacity of the plant will permit would require additional fixed costs to cover expansion or additional costs to cover overtime and other inefficiencies not taken into account under normal production.

Exhibit 19.11 depicts on a graph an example of relevant range. In this case, the figures are relevant for output from 500 to 5,000 units. All other data are irrelevant.

Short-Run Budgeting

Although an analysis of cost–volume–profit relationships by itself is insufficient for proper decision making, knowledge of the relationships can be valuable for many short-run budgeting decisions. Such decisions as whether to increase sales promotion costs in order to increase sales volume, whether to make or buy a part, or whether to eliminate a product can be enhanced by the knowledge of how these additional or remaining costs will affect net income. The differences in costs are compared with the differences in revenue for various alternative actions in order to form a sound basis for decision making. Planning, in general, is made easier by careful evaluation of break-even charts.

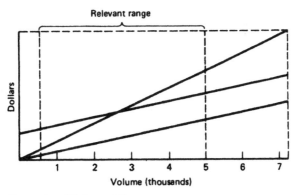

EXHIBIT 19.11   Example of Relevant Range

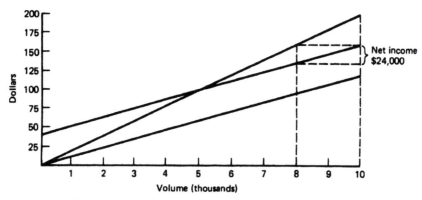

EXHIBIT 19.12 Illustration of Use of Break-Even in Budgeting

Assume that data for a company are:

1. *Sales price.* $20 per unit
2. *Variable costs.* $12 per unit
3. *Fixed costs.* $40,000

If management wished to collect $24,000 net earnings, then that sales volume must be 8,000 units, as shown in Exhibit 15.12.

Management now learns that if it invests $10,000 of fixed costs in sales promotion, it will be able to operate at 100 percent of capacity, or at a sales volume of 10,000 units. By making a new chart, it can be seen whether this investment would be profitable. Exhibit 19.13 shows the effects of the change, with earnings increasing to $30,000, provided the cost and revenue estimates are correct.

The validity of using break-even analysis in decisions such as these depends on the facts in each case. In the preceding example, if peak operating capacity was 8,000 units, then, in order to increase the volume, even more fixed costs would be required, and probably new data computations would be necessary to determine the cost behavior.

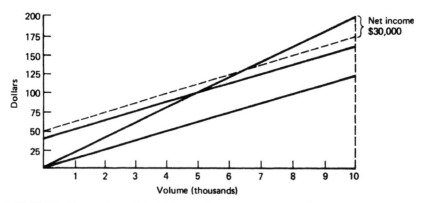

EXHIBIT 19.13 Illustration of the Effects of Investments in Additional Fixed Costs

The size of the contribution margin would also affect decision making. A low percentage margin would require a greater change in volume in order to increase the total contribution margin enough to cover any increases in fixed costs.

Decisions must also take into account any long-term effects. It is possible that profits may increase in a short-run situation, but over the long run, they may suffer because of the disordered use of such a technique.

Long-Run Budgeting

Knowledge of cost behavior patterns is often useful in long-run planning. Studying fixed and variable costs, and relating these costs to prospective sales and profit goals, will give management additional information to use in making an initial budget or in revising plans as deemed necessary.

One method of planning is to determine the profit goal that management would like to attain. This profit goal plus the expected fixed costs will equal the contribution margin needed to cover the fixed costs and the desired profit. By determining the expected operating volume, gross profit per unit can then be computed. Adding expected variable cost per unit to the gross profit will determine the net sales figure that must be attained.

As an example, assume that management requires a $10,000 net income each year and that expected costs are $10,000 of fixed costs and $1 per unit of variable costs at a normal operating level of 5,000 units. Exhibit 19.14 gives the computations for determining the net sales figure per unit that must be attained in order to meet the profit goal.

If the selling price of $5 per unit is not a competitive figure, then managers must revise their plans in order to achieve the profit goal. The break-even point could be lowered, possibly by reducing fixed costs or variable costs. Studies may show that, by increasing volume over the normal level, the necessary profit goal may be attained. Alternatively, managers may decide to alter the products, add or delete products, or improve methods of production in order to increase the contribution margin per unit. Nevertheless, several studies and break-even charts may be necessary for surveying the various alternatives in order to reach the best decision.

ADDITIONAL COST CONCEPTS

To meet the needs of managers, costs are classified in many ways. The behavior patterns of fixed, variable, and semivariable costs, and their importance to the budgeting process,

EXHIBIT 19.14　Using Selling Price to Meet Expected Profit Goals

Profit goal	$10,000
Expected fixed costs	10,000
Contribution margin	$20,000
Gross profit per unit ($20,000/5,000 units)	$4
Variable costs	1
Selling price	$5

have already been discussed. The ability of managers to plan and budget costs also must be taken into account in any analysis of cost–volume–profit relationships. In this regard, a number of questions must be answered: Can costs be controlled? How do costs relate to a certain cost objective? Is an individual department profiting the company? If not, can it be eliminated?

Committed versus Discretionary Costs

Fixed costs can be divided into two types: committed and discretionary. The distinction between these two types is important to managers in their budgeting decisions.

Committed fixed costs are those costs that relate to the basic framework of the company. They are based on top management decisions that will affect the business for several years. Depreciation on buildings, equipment, and salaries to executives are examples of such costs.

Discretionary fixed costs are those costs that fall under management control from one period to another. Managers are not committed to a certain level of expenses and may increase or decrease the level as seems warranted. Advertising, reasearch and development, and training programs fall into this area.

Distinguishing between committed and discretionary costs has relevance to the cost–volume–profit analysis. As an example, in a recessionary period, a company whose fixed costs are almost all committed will have trouble reducing the break-even point and probably will experience some losses, whereas a company with substantial discretionary fixed costs may be able to cut costs enough without disrupting operations so that it can show some earnings.

Controllable versus Noncontrollable Costs

In determining the efficiency of a company or in planning the budget, responsibility reports must be made by the managers. These evaluations of costs are necessary at each level of management, so that in the case of an undesirable situation, corrective action can be taken at the point at which it is necessary. For example, if direct labor is excessively high, the problem area can be seen and proper steps can be taken to alleviate the problem. This type of reporting is essential for controlling costs and for proper budgeting.

In preparing cost evaluations, it is necessary to separate the costs of a segment into controllable and noncontrollable costs, because not all costs in a given segment are controllable at that managerial level, and therefore the manager cannot be held responsible for them. Controllability must be defined with reference to a specific management level for proper evaluation.

A cost is controllable at a given managerial level if the manager has the authority to significantly influence its amount. For example, a supervisor may have control over maintenance, equipment, and overtime costs, but the department's depreciation and overhead, as well as the supervisor's salary, are noncontrollable costs at this managerial level. Exhibit 19.15 illustrates the use of responsibility reporting with regard to controllable costs and the budget.

Direct versus Indirect Costs

Costs are frequently classified as direct or indirect. Such classification has nothing to do with the nature or behavior of these costs; rather it indicates the objective against which the costs are being measured. *Direct costs* are those costs that can be clearly identified with the cost objective. All variable costs therefore are direct costs. *Indirect costs* are

EXHIBIT 19.15 Illustration of Responsibility Reporting Using Controllable Costs

Controllable Expenses	Amount	Over or (Under) Budget
Supervisor, Shop #1		
Maintenance	$200	$10
Supplies	100	20
Tools	50	(30)
Overtime	100	50
Total	$450	$50
Plant Manager		
Office expense	$250	$(10)
Shop #1 costs	450	50
Shop #2 costs	600	20
Supervisor salaries	5,000	0
Total	$6,300	$60
Manufacturing V.P.		
Office expense	$500	$0
Plant costs	6,300	60
Purchasing	500	200
Receiving	700	0
Plant management salaries	7,000	0
Total	$15,000	$260
President		
Office expense	$1,000	$100
V.P., manufacturing	15,000	260
V.P., sales	8,700	400
V.P., finance	4,000	(100)
V.P. salaries	9,000	0
Total	$37,700	$660

costs that cannot be clearly identified with a single cost objective and therefore must be allocated among the various cost objectives to which they apply. For example, the wages of employees working in a single department are direct costs of that department, but the cost of heating the building where they work would have to be allocated among all the departments in the building, and so it would be an indirect cost to the department.

EXHIBIT 19.16   Impact of Costs on Business Segments

	Segment A	Segment B	Segment C	Total
Sales	$20,000	$25,000	$20,000	$65,000
Direct costs	5,000	10,000	10,000	25,000
Indirect costs	5,000	10,000	15,000	30,000
Net income	$10,000	$5,000	($5,000)	$10,000

Direct costs are sometimes defined as those costs that would be dropped if their cost objective were eliminated. Although there are exceptions, this concept can be important in evaluating performance and in deciding whether to keep a segment of a company. Even if the segment were eliminated, many or all of the indirect costs would not be eliminated and would have to be allocated among the remaining segments of the company. This situation can be illustrated as described next.

Suppose that sales, direct costs, indirect costs, and net income are reported for three segments as seen in Exhibit 19.16.

Management is trying to determine whether to eliminate Segment C because of its continuing losses. It can be seen that, if the segment is eliminated, the company will lose a contribution to indirect expenses of $10,000 ($20,000 – $10,000). Segment C's indirect costs will have to be allocated among the remaining segments. Exhibit 19.17 shows the effects of the elimination, assuming these costs are allocated evenly.

DIFFERENTIAL COST CONCEPTS

Many budgeting decisions made by managers are short-run decisions that involve differential analysis. These short-run decisions may involve such matters as whether to change the price of a product, to manufacture a product instead of buying it, to add or drop a product, or to process joint products and by-products.

Relevant Costs

Relevant costs are future costs that differ between alternatives. Past costs, or *sunk costs*, are not relevant because there is nothing management can do about them since they have already been incurred. Future costs that are the same for two alternatives

EXHIBIT 19.17   Impact of Allocating Costs Evenly

	Segment A	Segment B	Total
Sales	$20,000	$25,000	$45,000
Direct costs	5,000	10,000	15,000
Indirect costs	12,500	17,500	30,500
Net income	$2,500	($2,500)	0

EXHIBIT 19.18   Illustration of the Differential Cost Between Two Alternatives

	Project A	Project B	Differential
Revenues	0	0	0
Costs	$20,000	$15,000	$5,000
Net benefit in favor of choosing Project B			$5,000

are not relevant either since they will affect both alternatives equally. The amount by which the relevant costs of two alternatives differ is called the *differential cost*.

To illustrate relevant costs, assume that management has been working on Project A, which has incurred costs of $10,000. To finish the project, it is estimated that $10,000 of fixed costs and $20,000 of variable costs will be incurred. A new proposal, Project B, has been introduced, which would require $10,000 of fixed costs and $15,000 of variable costs. Exhibit 19.18 shows the differential cost between the two alternatives, assuming that total revenues for both projects would be the same and that only one project can be attempted.

The $10,000 already incurred in conducting Project A is a sunk cost, and the future fixed costs of $10,000 do not differ between the alternatives; therefore, the only relevant costs are the future variable costs of $20,000 and $15,000 for Projects A and B, respectively. Thus, Project B should be chosen by management because of the savings of $5,000.

Incremental (Marginal) Costs

Marginal cost is a term used to describe the increase in total cost resulting from the production or sale of one more unit. Decisions usually involve levels of operation of hundreds or thousands of units. The difference of total cost between the levels of operation in this case is called *incremental* (or *differential*) *cost*.

The incremental cost concept can be described in this way: Suppose normal production is set at 10,000 units, with price, fixed costs, and variable costs set at $10 per unit, $50,000, and $4 per unit, respectively. An order has been received for an additional 5,000 units at $5 per unit. This is half the regular selling price and less than the average cost per unit at normal production. An analysis of relevant costs and revenues is seen in Exhibit 19.19.

EXHIBIT 19.19   Analysis of Relevant Costs and Revenues

	Accept Order	Reject Order	Differential
Revenue	$125,000	$100,000	$25,000
Variable costs	$60,000	$40,000	$20,000
Net benefit in favor of accepting order			$5,000

Because the selling price of the additional units was greater than the variable cost per unit, additional net income could be received. Usually it is the variable costs that set a floor for the selling price in marginal and incremental analysis, because a price only slightly higher than variable costs will bring a contribution to earnings. The exception is in the case of semivariable costs when a different level of production will cause an increase in fixed costs. This type of analysis, however, is used only for short-run decisions. In the long run, full costs must be covered, and any incremental analysis should be appraised in light of the long-run effects on the company.

Joint Product and By-Product Costs

Several products are sometimes manufactured from raw materials or from a manufacturing process. These are called *joint products*. Examples are the meat and hide processed from livestock. The costs incurred until the products are separated from each other are called *joint-product costs*. These are sunk costs when determining whether to process or sell a joint product once it is separated. This concept is the same in deciding whether to discard or to further process and sell low-value (or waste) products resulting from the manufacturing process. These low-value products are called *by-products*.

Assume that the data in Exhibit 19.20 concern joint products A and B.

The differential revenues and costs of further processing the two products are seen in Exhibit 19.21.

Based on this joint-product analysis, Product B should be further processed because of a net increase in earnings of $1, whereas Product A should not be further processed because of a decrease in net earnings of $1.

EXHIBIT 19.20 Illustration of Joint Products

Product	Selling Price at Separation	Cost of Processing	Selling Price after Processing
A	$5	$6	$10
B	4	3	8

EXHIBIT 19.21 Impact of Differential Revenues and Costs on Joint Products

Product	Differential Revenue	Differential Cost	Net Advantage (Disadvantage)
A	$5	$6	($1)
B	4	3	1

MAXIMIZING RESOURCES

In budgeting, managers need to determine the most efficient method of allocating costs in order to provide maximum profits. This is most important in a multidepartment or multiproduct company. It has been seen that several cost-analysis techniques can provide management with assistance in deciding whether to eliminate or add products

EXHIBIT 19.22   Relevant Data for the Production of Three Products

	Product A	Product B	Product C
Units produced	2,000	$2,000	2,000
Sales price per unit	$2.00	$1.00	$1.50
Variable cost per unit	1.00	0.50	1.00
Contribution margin per unit	1.00	0.50	0.50
Fixed costs	$1,000	$500	$1,000
Net earnings	1,000	500	0

and departments and whether to increase or decrease production in order to establish profit goals. These techniques usually determine whether an alternative contributes to fixed expenses or whether the incremental revenue is greater than the incremental cost. These methods may be incomplete, though, and may overlook other facts, such as the operating capacity of a firm, when determining production of various products.

Exhibit 19.22 presents relevant data for a company producing three products.

The break-even chart for the company realizing the product mix in Exhibit 19.22 is shown in Exhibit 19.23.

By analyzing the data in Exhibit 19.23, it is seen that all three products should be retained because of positive contribution margins in all departments. This analysis is incomplete, however, because it is possible that the production schedules are being utilized inefficiently for maximum profit.

Suppose that plant operating capacity is 1,700 hours. If the full resources of the plant are devoted to only one product, it is computed that 4 units of Product A can be produced per hour, 3 units of Product B per hour, and 10 units of Product C per hour. Also, maximum production is limited to 6,400 units for Product A, 3,000 units for Product B, and 5,000 units for Product C.

Instead of contribution margin per unit of sales, contribution margin per hour of operating capacity is used to determine maximum rates. Exhibit 19.24 illustrates this point with the three products using the data given.

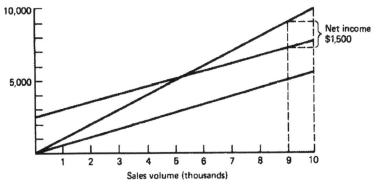

EXHIBIT 19.23   Example of Break-Even

EXHIBIT 19.24 Computation of Contribution Margin Per Hour

Product	Contribution Margin per Unit	Units Produced per Hour	Contribution Margin per Hour
A	$1.00	4	$4.00
B	0.50	2	1.00
C	0.50	10	5.00

EXHIBIT 19.25 Computing Production Rates

Product	Contribution Margin per Hour	Maximum Production	Units to Produce	Time to Produce
A	$4.00	6,400	4,800	200
B	1.00	3,000	0	0
C	5.00	5,000	5,000	500
				1,700

Based on these figures, Product C is the most profitable to produce, and Product A is the next best alternative. Exhibit 19.25 shows the determination of the production rates of the three products, taking into account the limitation on producing the three.

According to this analysis, Product B should be eliminated. Exhibit 19.26 shows the effect of this product mix on the break-even point. It is seen that net earnings have increased over $1,000 by allocating production in this fashion.

This type of analysis should also take into account other factors. Switching to other products may cause an increase in fixed costs. Also, the long-run objectives of a company could prevent the elimination of a product.

Other methods of determining the cost allocation within a company can also be used. These include quantitative decision models such as economic order

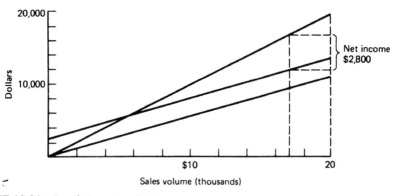

EXHIBIT 19.26 Break-Even Analysis

quantity, which determines ordering cost and carrying cost behavior for inventory control; linear programming, used in various phases of decision making; and statistical analysis, used when decision variables are not deterministic but are probabilistic.

ESTIMATING COSTS

As stated previously, it is necessary to identify costs as fixed or variable. With semivariable costs, it is sometimes difficult to do this, and methods of estimating these costs must be used. The fixed portion represents the cost of having a service available for use. The variable portion is the cost associated with various levels of activity.

Scatter Diagram

One method of estimating semivariable costs is to use a scatter diagram. With this method, actual incurred costs at varying levels of activity are plotted on a graph. A line (called the *regression line*) is then drawn through what appears to be the center of the pattern (see Exhibit 19.27). In Exhibit 19.27, the fixed portion would be $18,000, and the variable portion would be figured as:

$$\frac{\$51,000 - \$18,000}{10,000 \text{ units}} = \$3.30 \text{ per unit}$$

Least Squares Method

A more accurate method of obtaining the regression line is called the *least squares method.* This method makes use of statistical analysis and requires the solving of two simultaneous equations:

$$\Sigma XY = a(\Sigma X) + b(\Sigma X^2)$$

and

$$\Sigma Y = Na + b(\Sigma X)$$

where

$$N = \text{number of observations}$$

$$X = \text{units of volume}$$

$$Y = \text{total costs}$$

$$a = \text{total fixed costs}$$

$$b = \text{variable cost per unit}$$

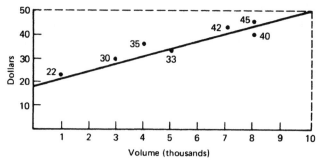

EXHIBIT 19.27   Scatter Diagram

The next data were developed from Exhibit 19.27:

X-axis	Y-axis
1	22
2	30
4	35
5	33
7	42
8	45
8	40

EX	EX2	EY	EXY
1	1	22	22
3	9	30	90
4	16	35	140
5	25	33	165
7	49	42	294
8	64	45	360
8	64	40	320
36	228	247	1391

Using these data and substituting them into the equations, we get

$$\$1,391 = 36a + 228b$$

and

$$\$247 = 7a + 36b$$

Solving the equations, we have fixed costs of \$15,300 and variable cost of \$3.69 per unit.

High–Low Method

Another widely used, but less precise, method of identifying the behavior of semivariable costs is called the *high–low method*. This method uses only the highest and lowest plots on the scatter diagram for the analysis.

Again using the values in Exhibit 19.27, the amount of variable cost is found as:

$$\frac{\text{Change in cost}}{\text{Change in volume}} = \frac{\$45,000 - \$22,000}{8,000 - 1,000 \text{ units}} = \$3.29 \text{ per unit}$$

The amount of fixed costs is then found as shown, using the highest plotted output:

Total cost at 8,000 units	$45,000
Less variable cost (8,000) × $3.29	26,320
Fixed cost at all levels	$18,680

 SUMMARY

For purposes of cost–volume–profit analysis, costs must be divided into their fixed and variable portions. Various techniques, including scatter diagrams and statistical analyses, are used to separate semivariable costs.

Computation of the break-even point is an important aspect of cost–volume–profit analysis. The modern multiproduct company is influenced by so many factors that it would be quite tedious, if not impossible, to portray all of them on a single break-even chart. Therefore, assumptions must be made and several charts must be devised in order to give management full information on the various factors. When properly used, cost–volume–profit analysis offers an overview of costs and sales in relation to profit planning.

In preparing budgets, costs are sometimes classified in different ways in order to determine the effectiveness of different phases of the company. These classifications assist management in determining which costs can be controlled and which costs are influenced by a certain objective and in making various short-run decisions, such as eliminating a department or a product.

It is imperative that managers know the behavior patterns of costs for their company. Proper decision making and budgeting depends on the knowledge of how costs will react in a set of circumstances, how costs will affect profits, and what changes can be made to produce greater profits.

PART THREE

Preparation of Specific Budgets

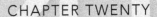
Sales and Marketing Budget

R. Malcolm Schwartz
PricewaterhouseCoopers LLP

INTRODUCTION

The sales and marketing budget is an important link with all other budgets. To make this link effective, the budget system should be based on a sound understanding of the vision, culture, and objectives of the organization; an awareness of the relationships among business processes and with other business functions; the ability to use external information about competitors, customers, suppliers, and public policy; and good judgment.

The importance of these factors suggests that the sales and marketing budget process should be discussed broadly and not merely in terms of how related data should be entered, stored, and printed from a computer system. Therefore, this chapter concentrates on these subjects:

- Overview of the budget process
- Special budgeting problems
- Pertinent tools
- Unique aspects of some industries

OVERVIEW OF THE BUDGET PROCESS

The sales and marketing budget process links to product, channels of distribution, and profit a group of largely discretionary expenses that focus

379

on customers' acceptance—on the downstream components of the value chain. Most firms try to sell profitably what customers want—that is, what the market will bear. As a result, the sales and marketing budget is a means of integrating the functional plans as well as the process capabilities of an organization. It is important that the budget be controlled because marketing expenses, which are not only largely discretionary but also can be changed dramatically as to priorities and mix, can be misdirected quite easily.

As a result, a budget process should be in place that can be integrated with other plans and that can provide useful analyses to support the judgments of marketing planners.

Link between Strategic and Other Functional Plans

The sales and marketing budget provides a link between the business strategy and other functional plans. The sales budget defines the level and mix of projected product and service offerings as well as such support costs as sales organization expense, trade promotion, and education programs. This information generally is developed to be consistent with the organization's overall strategic plan and to provide more detailed information for the planning period covered by the overall budget.

Much sales information traditionally is "top line" (i.e., it is presented at the top of a profit and loss statement): The identification of short-term activity that it provides links the strategic plan to the budgets of other functions that support achieving the intended operating level. These other budgets include:

- *Operations (sourcing, conversion, and physical distribution)*. Factors that are affected include inventory and service levels, replenishment techniques, production mix, and lengths of production runs.
- *Research and development (R&D)*. Replacing products over their life cycles, anticipating customers' wants and needs and competitors' actions, and taking advantage of technological developments should help to identify priorities for development projects as well as the funding levels.
- *Administration*. A number of these support functions—ranging from clerical activities, such as order entry and customer service, to legal specialists—can be influenced by the sales budget.
- *Capital investment*. The needs for facilities, tooling, and equipment should be coordinated with sales activity.
- *Cash*. Inventory, accounts receivable, and accounts payable all can be affected by the sales budget.

The marketing budget in turn relates in two ways to sales plans: (1) It can be driven by sales plans, as when higher volumes can cause greater expenditures for cooperative advertising; and (2) it can be used to drive sales plans, as when promotional activities are planned to support sales growth or mix. The overall sales and marketing budget is therefore a means of integrating a number of plans to the strategy of the organization.

Today, many organizations think of this integration in process rather than functional terms. In such cases, plans and budgets may be process focused rather than function focused. A typical framework of processes and the business cycles they encompass might include:

- *Customer management.* From offering to selling products and services
- *Product management.* From planning through discontinuing product offerings
- *Supply chain.* From receiving demand signals through delivering products and services, including sourcing and conversion activities
- *Development.* From considering innovations through applying them
- *Support.* All infrastructure activities

Whether a company takes a functional or a process view, the sales and marketing (or customer and product) planning is an important link between strategy and business activities.

Discretionary Expenses

In addition to consideration of product, price, promotion, and volume, the sales and marketing budget deals with a number of expenses that are largely discretionary. Sales budgeting deals with issues such as what products are to be sold, what prices are to be charged, how customer loyalty can be encouraged, and how much volume should result.

The marketing portion of the budget considers what resources are to be used, and in what mix, to move products from the organization to its customers. Major elements of the marketing budget include:

- *Selling.* May involve direct selling through various media, an employed sales force, sales representatives, or some combination.
- *Sales promotion.* Often includes a combination of price and premium programs, trade shows, store fixtures, coupons, sponsorship, and the like.
- *Advertising.* May concentrate on the image of the firm, a product line, or a brand; may be national, regional, local, or customer specific; can use various media.
- *Product development.* Some organizations consider this a marketing expense, particularly for short-term efforts; can include new features, packaging changes, new products, and the like.
- *Customer service.* Includes both warranty and out-of-warranty support, education, training, complaint handling, and a variety of other services.
- *Physical distribution.* Some organizations treat as a marketing expense; might be handled centrally or might be spread through the regions served; other discretionary factors include how goods are shipped and whether the firm elects to use its own resources, distributors, or public warehouses.

The marketing budget considers what mix and levels of these elements will be used. Therefore, the budget process should enable analyses that consider trade-offs, priorities, and contingent actions in support of the eventual agreed plan.

Operating Factors

The budgeting process should consider a number of operating factors that shape the expenses planned for sales and marketing.

There are several different ways in which the levels of the various elements of marketing expense can be analyzed and targeted; these include historical trends, standards or benchmarks, and operating factors.

Historical trends can be applied rather simply; for example, if sales are planned to increase by 10 percent, then advertising can be increased by the same percentage. This approach takes little effort, but it assumes that prior levels of expenses were effective, that there are no benefits from growth, and that similar levels of expense will be needed in the future.

Standards—usually in the form of typical levels of expenses for certain industries—might be available, but because most firms have different objectives and operations, they can be hard to apply. Furthermore, an industry-wide benchmark can be too broad to have useful application. At the least, if benchmarks are used, the underlying practices should be understood and applicable. Standards for marketing expenses are usually more effective for checking if the plan varies from industry practice—and for being able to understand why and the associated risks—than as a means of developing the budget.

When developing the marketing budget, it is probably more useful to analyze the underlying operating factors that drive market performance than to rely on history or on benchmarks. Examples of such drivers include:

- Market share
- New account and customer retention rates
- Customer ordering patterns (size, frequency, and mix)
- Value of the customer and value to the customer
- Competitive position
- Impacts of past promotions
- Costs to acquire an account
- Sales call patterns

Exhibit 20.1 shows the impact of these and other factors on sales and marketing costs. By reviewing the factors that are important to the organization and how they relate to performance, the marketing planner likely will be able to make better recommendations regarding the amount and mix of marketing expense elements. Therefore, the budgeting system should include operating information as well as cost information.

Culture and Management Style

The organizational architecture and the priorities that underlie the sales and marketing budget should fit with management style as well as with other processes. When constructing the sale and marketing budget, and because it is a means of integrating plans throughout the organization and the actions that result, it is important to consider issues of culture and management style. These issues deal with responsibility, authority, accountability, and empowerment; the importance of sole contributors or teams; how

	Impact on Cost	
Factor	Consumer Product	Industrial Product
Increased size of sales force	⬆	⬆
Product purchased more frequently than once per year	⬆	⬇
Higher market share or sales volume	⬇	⬇
Broader geographical coverage	⬇	⬇
Greater number of accounts	⬆	⬆
Marketing effort focused on end user	⬆	⬆
Higher product price	⬆	—
Increased customer service or technical support	—	⬆
Greater amount of distribution through others	⬆	⬆
Greater proportion of orders filled from inventory	⬆	⬆
More competitors	⬆	⬇
Increased importance of the product to the firm	—	⬇

⬆ Tends to increase ratio of marketing cost to sales

⬇ Tends to decrease ratio of marketing cost to sales

— Not significant

EXHIBIT 20.1   Impact of Selected Factors on Sales and Marketing Cost

decisions get made; and the like. Culture issues also must consider information management—efficiency, cost, integrity, and the like—so that actions can focus on what should be done and not on whose information is correct.

An important culture issue is goal setting. Some executives prefer to hold managers responsible for the actions that they directly control whereas others want managers to be aware also of the indirect consequences. For example, promotional activity directly affects prices and volumes and might indirectly affect the costs of order entry, credit, and accounts receivable, among other activities. In dealing with these different styles of relating responsibility to the budget structure, two approaches are used, the direct- and the full-cost methods, the concepts of which were discussed in Part Two of this volume.

The direct-cost method relates to products only those costs that are expressly associated with them; in addition to product costs, these may include elements of the sales and marketing budget, such as promotional expense, cooperative advertising programs, and the like. The full-cost method relates all costs to products by allocating indirect cost elements; as a result, product profitability can be measured in the same way that business profitability is measured. The direct-cost method is often supported today by activity-based costing principles.

In the direct-cost method, which is simpler from a performance management viewpoint, product performance is measured in terms of contribution to business overhead and profit.

Whichever costing method is used, the sales and marketing budget system should be coordinated with other systems. For example, the chart of accounts should be used effectively. With proper planning, subaccounts can be established for products, salespersons, customer classifications, promotional programs, and other categories that are useful for planning and control. Just as expenses can be related to the accounting system, operating factors can be related to other parts of the management information system.

Incremental Planning and Analysis

Assuming that the sales and marketing budget is used to integrate other plans and budgets, and that the revenue and expense information is built up from operating factors, another major system feature is to allow for incremental planning. Depending on the business and industry, planning increments might include geographic regions, channels of distribution, classes of customers, and product lines.

When plans are developed incrementally, adjustments can be more focused during the review process. Key steps in budgeting incrementally include:

- Identify the increments.
- Analyze the related operating factors.
- Develop the sales and marketing plan for each increment.
- Extend each increment to revenues and expense.
- Sum the increments to form a base budget.
- Review the base budget for consistency with the organization's strategy, for profit, for an assessment of competitive actions, and for overall affordability.
- Adjust the base budget as needed and at the level of the individual increments.
- Test the adjusted base budget for profit sensitivity to different levels of expense.

Finally, when the optimal incremental programs have been budgeted, and at levels that should generate desired profits, the budget can be approved and a road map will have been provided for sales and marketing efforts. This approach enables the linking of "top-down" and "bottom-up" budgeting, focused at the sales and marketing decisions. Exhibit 20.2 provides an overview of this process.

SPECIAL BUDGETING PROBLEMS

Because marketing expenditures are so discretionary and can be combined in so many different ways, it can be difficult to develop meaningful levels of expense for each element

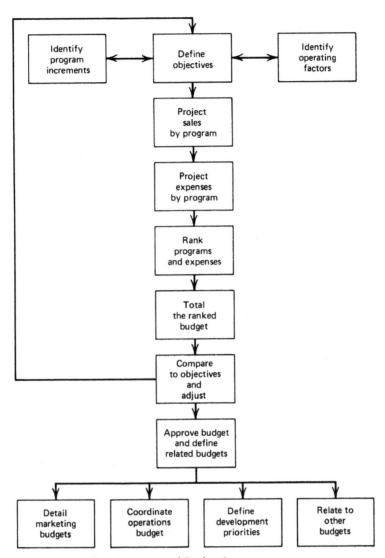

EXHIBIT 20.2   Approach to Incremental Budgeting

of cost. During the budgeted period, it can also be difficult to control expense levels and to adapt them to changing circumstances. This section reviews some of the more general aspects of these problems as they relate to the major cost elements.

Pricing Adjustments

Planned pricing and any adjustments need to be budgeted if future revenues are to be attained and controlled.

Prices are usually developed both in relationship to costs and in response to competition. For products that have leading positions in the market, prices might be based on value to the customer.

New products can be difficult to price. At the time of initial market entry, prices are sometimes set close to cost to achieve desired volume and market share. After these goals are attained, prices might be adjusted. During the same period—as volume is growing—product costs could be declining; as a result, prices could be kept stable and profits would increase.

When prices are declining, it may be necessary to plan additional discounts. In the systems of many companies, these usually can be better controlled than outright price reductions because they can be recorded and tracked as expenses. Some companies overcome this limitation by tracking both standard and realized prices.

For any product for which a price change is planned, it is useful to control this by budgeting at the base price and then showing for each period in the budget the pricing adjustments that are to be made.

Selling Expense

Selling expense includes a number of cost elements, such as salary, commissions, training, and salespersons' expenses. These costs often are associated with different sales forces for regions, classes of customers, or groups of products. Selling expense should be budgeted incrementally in ways that enable future analyses, for example:

- Organizations with large in-store sales forces might want to budget and report selling expense by department, by transaction, by day, and by time of day; data such as these enable correlating store staffing with service levels.
- Organizations whose sales forces cover wide geographical areas might want to compare the times to call on customers in urban and rural areas.
- Mail-order firms usually want to evaluate selling expense geographically (zip codes are often used) and by the source of the sale (which could be from a specific list of names, from particular advertising copy, or from a media placement).

The kinds of monitoring analyses that will be used should be identified as the budget is being assembled so that techniques for reporting and control can be established.

Sales Promotion Expense

Too often, sales promotions are undertaken to increase sales without sufficient attention to planning and controls. Lack of control can be found with sales personnel as well as with customers, as seen in the next examples:

- The internal auditor for a household products firm found that some promotional fixtures never had been placed in stores, yet sales representatives were receiving commissions approved by the sales manager.
- When a mail-order firm revised its customer list programs, it found that one customer had made a number of minor changes in her name and address to obtain more than $10,000 worth of free promotional merchandise.

Because there are few industry standards for sales promotion expense, each firm needs to use its own track record to determine what is effective. Records should be kept and incorporated into budgets and controls for the relationships among volume, product, media, and promotional devices. Later promotions can be correlated to benchmarks that are developed, and variances can be analyzed, as misredemption or promotional losses, as examples.

In addition to incremental planning and control of merchandise, the expenses for premiums and coupons and other elements of sales promotion also should be planned and controlled incrementally, for example:

- Trade shows and exhibits often are planned and controlled for each instance and analyzed in relationship to sales activity generated.
- Samples and giveaways are usually controlled by salespersons, to evaluate any unusual rates of usage.
- Fixtures often are controlled as if they were inventory and might need accountability by both salesperson and customer.

Advertising Budget

Advertising often appears to be discretionary to management and can become one of the first elements of expense to be reduced in bad times. Therefore, it is important to be able to assess the effectiveness of advertising. Copy, timing, media, and placement can be important factors. The budget should be assembled so that advertising expense and sales activity can be correlated. Similarly, tests of geographical coverage, copy, and the like need to be controlled.

Control can be exercised by having the advertising organization develop standards (examples can include recall, impact, or sales percentages) for effectiveness, and then conduct tests regularly to measure that impact. Advertising expenditures by product are often published (e.g., in *Advertising Age*), so that an organization's expenditures can also be compared to these external benchmarks.

Dealer cooperative advertising presents another problem in planning and control that can influence both the design of a budget system and the process of budgeting. Cooperative claims should be verified by tear sheets for print advertising and by invoices for television and radio. As a consequence, a subsystem is needed, by dealer, in regard to claimable amounts, claims pending, and claims approved and paid. The claimable amounts, which are usually based on purchases of a given product or products for a specified period, should be tracked to establish the potential expense, although actual claims paid might be less.

Even with the use of benchmarks and analyses to explain what advertising is important and why, it still remains a discretionary expense. Occasionally, when management attempts to reduce advertising expense, it finds that commitments already have been made for future expenditures. Therefore, the budget system and the resulting controls should incorporate plans for the timing and amount of commitments as well as expenditures.

Product Development Costs

Marketing management uses product development to procure new styles of packaging, new features, and the like. Such procurements can be internal, or items might be purchased from suppliers. In any case, development efforts and their associated costs are best controlled by project. A product-development project subsystem can be used to link the R&D budget with the marketing expense budget.

Customer Service Expenses

The influence of consumer price and value sensitivities, and the needs for differentiation in the marketplace, have caused warranty and other service programs to be expanded. Recalls and replacements have become more common. More staff is being used to answer consumers' questions, and more information is available, in return, to shape product and marketing plans.

As a result, new methods are being used to plan and control customer service expenses. Warranty expenses have usually been planned as a percentage of sales, but today more attention is being given to relating warranty expense to particular products and their sources. Recall expenses can be projected from total quality management programs and from the statistical process control activities that tend to follow. Replacement expenses can be estimated from failure rate percentages related to the product and developed in the quality control laboratory.

Comparative trends of expenses on these elements of cost should be monitored and should be used to:

- Adjust the budget
- Provide reserves on actual performance
- Focus development activities
- Direct quality assurance actions

Physical Distribution

Physical distribution involves market-responsive trade-offs between service and cost. Service levels should be planned and performance monitored. Often service can provide an important competitive advantage when price, product features, and the like are not highly differentiable among competitors.

Higher levels of inventory usually accompany better service, and with the annual costs to carry inventory sometimes approaching 25 percent of inventory value, it is important to ensure that service is worth the cost. In many cases, service can be improved with the same or a reduced inventory level by planning and controlling where the inventory is located across the overall supply chain and for what product, by improving demand communications (using point-of-sale information, e.g.), and by synchronizing the sourcing, conversion, and delivery activities.

As a consequence, the sales and marketing system should be linked to the inventory-control system and, through it, to manufacturing and purchasing. Marketing information is needed by product and location; service as well as cost data should be planned, reported, and analyzed. A system of this sort provides the performance benchmarks related to objectives that can help to resolve the usual conflicts about inventory among marketing, finance, and operating managers.

 **PERTINENT TOOLS**

A number of techniques are helpful in budgeting and controlling sales and marketing expense, including:

- Product life-cycle analysis
- Marginal analysis
- Break-even analysis
- Forecasting techniques
- Sensitivity techniques
- Bracket budgeting
- Pricing techniques
- Performance tests

This section discusses some of the key features of these techniques.

Analysis of Product Life Cycles

Each phase of a product's life cycle presents different budgeting concerns, ranging from early investment requirements and inventory to fill the pipeline to later issues of price and of product discontinuance. Methods must be established in advance to determine when a product is moving from one phase to another so that:

- Strategies and budgets can be adjusted.
- Agreement can be reached on whether to extend the product's life.
- Planning guidelines can be set on removing the product from the market.

A product life cycle is usually longer than the budget period, so a product plan should be developed that relates to a series of budgets. The product plan should include information on the competitive environment because:

- Little competition might relate to the introductory phase.
- New competitors might indicate the beginning of the growth phase.
- A variety of differentiated products often shows the maturity phase.
- Identical competitive products may point to the decline phase.

The technique of monitoring product life cycles can help to direct development efforts for differentiating and improving products and thus for extending their lives.

Marginal Analysis

Marginal analysis, which has been discussed previously, can be helpful for cost allocation. Different geographical or sales categories can be tested so that incremental revenue less incremental cost derived from the last unit sold in each area is equal. To illustrate marginal analysis, an advertising budget can be assigned to two categories, and then $1.00 can be transferred from the first to the second; if profit increases, then the transfer is worthwhile and should be continued until no change in profit occurs.

Break-Even Analysis

Break-even analysis, which is discussed in Chapters 13 and 19, requires knowledge of fixed and variable costs and of contributions for individual products. With these data, the break-even point can be calculated. The result of such an analysis might indicate that increasing the sales of selected products will help to cover fixed costs; if so, the sales and marketing budget should focus on efforts to support that objective.

Forecasting Techniques

Most firms forecast by extending historical data for themselves, for competitors, and/or for the overall industry. Some companies incorporate economic data, or have determined that there are leading indicators that help in forecasting sales, such as new home starts for heavy appliances or marriage rates for tableware. Economic data can be obtained from government publications, trade journals, industry associations, consulting firms, and banks; computer programs can be used to test historical correlations.

Many firms rely heavily on internal data for forecasting sales. By using regression analysis or other statistical techniques, a series of internal and external factors can be selected and tested to determine if they help to predict sales. Often firms rely on simpler statistical techniques, such as moving averages.

Of course, because forecasts are never precise, it is best to rely on actual demand signals for operational and tactical actions. For planning, however, some form of forecasting usually will be needed. To deal with the uncertainty of forecasts, it is useful to consider a range of possible outcomes, with related assumptions, impacts, and probabilities of occurrence.

Sensitivity Analysis

Sensitivity analysis can be used, for example, to simulate best, likely, and worst cases before they occur. Relationships must first be understood between the conditions that are to be tested and their effects on sales, costs, and profits; these conditions could include changes in:

- The market, such as overall demand or competitive share
- The economy, such as monetary or fiscal policies or local business conditions
- The environment, including changes in life style or demographic shifts

Sensitivity analysis is often coupled with probability techniques to answer what-if questions. A firm might want to know the impact of interest rates on cash flow—for example, at 5 percent interest a particular project is profitable but at 12 percent interest it is not. The project can be analyzed for a series of interest rates, and a probability can be assigned to each one. An overall expected benefit thus can be determined, as illustrated in Exhibit 20.3.

Bracket Budgeting

Bracket budgeting is a form of built-in contingency planning. Expenses are developed at higher and lower levels (e.g., plus or minus 10 percent) than the base budget, and

EXHIBIT 20.3 Example of Sensitivity Analysis

Sensitivity Analysis[a]

Year	Cash Flow	5%	6%	8%	10%
1	$10,000	$9,524	$9,434	$9,259	$9,091
2	10,000	9,070	8,900	8,573	8,264
3	8,000	6,910	6,717	6,350	6,010
4	7,000	5,759	5,545	5,145	4,781
5	5,000	3,918	3,737	3,403	3,105
Total cash in		$35,181	$34,333	$32,730	$31,251
Cash out		(33,000)	(33,000)	(33,000)	(33,000)
Net present value		$2,181	$1,333	$ (270)	$ 1,749

Conclusion: If interest rates approach 8%, do not do the project. What is management's judgment on the likelihood?

[a]Using present value technique.

The Expected Benefit Analysis

Year	5%	6%	8%	10%	Adjusted Net Present Value
		Probability by Interest Rate			
1	80%	20%	—	—	$9,506
2	80%	20%	—	—	9,036
3	—	50%	30%	20%	6,466
4	—	50%	30%	20%	5,272
5	—	50%	30%	20%	3,511
Estimated cash in					$33,791
Cash out					(33,000)
Net present value					$791

Conclusion: If management's judgment about interest rates is correct, do the project.

sales that are likely to result are then forecast. At a later date, if sales were to rise and management should act to maintain the higher level, the likely impact on expenses would already be understood.

If the sales budget were not achieved, the bracket budget gives management a sense of the profit impact, and a contingency plan can be installed quickly. A more detailed discussion of this subject is found in Chapter 31.

Tactical and Strategic Pricing Techniques

Various techniques are used for tactical pricing, which is usually practiced in times of static market conditions and growing demand. These include cost-based pricing, reaction to competitors, and penetration pricing.

Cost-based pricing rests on sound knowledge of all costs as well as effective management of costs that are allocated among products. Reaction to competitive moves has been used by smaller firms that must respond—often by charging less—to industry leaders. Penetration pricing occurs when a firm consciously reduces its usual profit objective to increase market share or to emphasize profitable aftermarket sales (e.g., selling razors to sell blades).

Strategic pricing is appropriate with slow-growing economies, changing demand levels, and stiff competition. This technique often relates to value as perceived by the customer. For example, reformulating a product by removing an additive that did not have broad appeal could enable a price reduction with a concomitant sales gain. Strategic pricing can also relate to the pace of technological change or to the uniqueness of the product.

- For a market in which technology is expected to change in five years, product durability could be designed to that period and price reduced accordingly.
- Unique product or service features—or the level of technical support—might enable product differentiation and value-added pricing; alternatively, store-branded products can be priced lower because they use available capacity and require less marketing expense.

In any regard, the pricing techniques that are used can influence the structure of the sales and marketing budget as well as the related systems and reports. Emphasis on cost-based pricing, for example, requires more complete cost portrayals, more emphasis of cost differentiation by product, and sensible rules for allocating fixed costs; activity-based costing is a useful supportive approach.

Testing Actual Performance

Whatever specialized techniques are used for planning and evaluation, the system should have the ability to provide feedback. Plans to increase or decrease expense should be tested in controlled situations to measure the impact on sales.

For example, results of a market test should be compared to plan, and the budget system should be adapted accordingly. The capability of analyzing controlled changes will enable the extrapolating of results to later budget periods.

UNIQUE ASPECTS OF SOME INDUSTRIES

Just as each firm is distinctive, so many industries have different characteristics that cause different approaches to sales and marketing budgeting. This section identifies some features of selected industries—namely, consumer packaged goods, industrial products, retailing, and banking—to illustrate some of the differences. These four industries were selected to illustrate differences resulting from products or services, from customers, and from method of distribution.

Consumer Packaged-Goods Firms

Budgets for this type of firm often begin with stated goals for market share. Strategies for product, distribution, price, copy, media, promotion, special programs, and volume are formed to reach these goals. Costs are assigned to each strategy and, along with expected volume, are compared to profit objectives. Expense levels are generally determined by a combination of experience and test marketing; external standards are rarely used to determine expense levels, but benchmarks are often used to test the reality and risk in the plan.

The budget usually links other functional plans. Marketing efforts are geared to the profit objective. The manufacturing plan provides cost information that must be assumed by marketing management. The product manager (in the marketing organization) often controls the R&D budget. Because plans are linked and the overall effort is market driven, the marketing plan often includes a section that identifies where and how the budget should be changed if conditions warrant.

Selling efforts are often important and the sales force can be large. Pressure therefore can be created to price low, to provide substantial promotional activity, and to structure large incentive compensation programs. The trade (the direct customer) also can come to expect continuing promotions, cooperative allowances, and the like. The budget system enables management to plan and evaluate these activities and to make sure that they really are productive.

Industrial Products Firms

The sales force is the key element in the selling of industrial products; hence, the budget should be geared to provide the mix of expenses that will best support that selling effort. Underlying policies are important, such as warranty, prepaid freight, and trade-in allowance. These are often developed more to fit the company objectives than to imitate competitors' policies. Costs generally are influenced by the policies that are set. This individualized approach precludes the use of external standards to set expense levels, so an internal data base is important. Again, benchmarking and analyzing best practices are increasing in use.

Sales forecasts also are usually based on internal data. Firms with long order lead-in times can analyze their backlogs or, in some cases, the progress against completion of large jobs. Share of market information is seldom used because share tends to remain stable or is less meaningful. Most sales projections involve collecting and interpreting historical and competitive data.

The budget is usually linked with the purchasing and manufacturing plans. Occasionally, too little attention is given to linkages with service and applications engineering budgets. Sales personnel can overpromise service or product adaptability, and the support functions have difficulty in delivering what was promised; effective planning and control, coupled with procedural guidelines, can prevent problems of this sort.

Retailing

Whereas the focus for consumer packaged goods is on the market and for industrial products is on the selling effort, for retail the budgeting focuses on the merchandise—

what to sell and how it is to be sold. Key factors include fashion trends, the cycle of selling seasons, and the pressure to move inventory.

Forecasts are often quite detailed, in some cases down to item by store. Forecasts are coordinated between buyers of merchandise and store managers—the first reflects fashion trends and the second relates the merchandise to local conditions. Expenses are usually projected by store and sometimes by department. Various trade associations publish extensive data on expenses by merchandise category, by store size, and by volume. Pricing involves target and historic markups by product line, adjusted for inventory movement and promotional activity.

The budget is closely linked to buying activities. Usually a buyer can commit only up to an inventory limit (called an "open to buy"), so merchandise must be sold to enable future merchandise to be bought. Open to buy is carefully planned and monitored. The expense budget is controlled by store management; if sales are low, steps usually are taken to reduce advertising expense or the sales force.

Banking

Bank budgeting focuses on budgeting the differential between the costs to obtain and the costs to lend funds. Key elements of the budget include projecting availability of funds, interest rates, loan demand, deposit demand, and operating expenses.

Economics information and knowledge of the business environment are important factors in budgeting. In banking, sales information is in terms of the amount and types of loans, the interest rates that pertain, the timing of repayment, and likely loan losses.

Sophisticated forecasting and control techniques are used in regard to economic conditions, interest rates, loan demand, and consumer needs. Banks' marketing departments use research techniques (those that are traditionally used by consumer products firms) to evaluate new financial services products.

▪ SUMMARY

The sales and marketing budget is a key integrative device in many industries. It relates the firm's strategy to operating plans for various functions. It is a means with which to deal with a mass of external and internal data. It should link a number of subsystems for controlling elements of marketing expense and for evaluating the strategy for a product over its life cycle. Therefore, developing and maintaining a sales and marketing budget system requires a broad understanding of the overall business and its strategy and needs.

CHAPTER TWENTY-ONE

Manufacturing Budget

C. Eugene Moore
C. Eugene Moore & Associates

INTRODUCTION

Our objective in this chapter is to review the concepts used in preparing the operations/
manufacturing budget, to discuss some of the problems encountered in preparation,
and to suggest techniques that the manager should employ in building that budget into
a full business plan and profit program pro forma. Nothing that exists when you start
this process should be the same when you finish it. You must plan deliberate change
unrelated to history to be successful.

In consulting specialized reference material, readers normally assume that the
information is technical and therefore free of an author's bias. This assumption is false.
The dynamics of a manufacturing organization make preparation of budgets much more
than a sterile planning exercise as the concepts and techniques set forth, all founded in
personal experience, are the basis of the recommended approach.

Other aspects of budgeting have been reviewed in previous chapters, but their successful assimilation into a total budget depends on the decisions made by managers in
the manufacturing organization. The planned action budget methods that will build on
management decisions for planned, deliberate change constitute the general assumption throughout this entire chapter, if you have the will to manage.

Does it work? Yes! In fact, you cannot accomplish the expectations of your associates
if you do not follow this concept. The Association for Manufacturing Excellence (AME)
has held more than 50 seminars, describing that as many companies engaging in such

deliberate changes produced total reductions of more than 30 percent of total cost of goods sold. It is the approach that is different, as explained in this chapter.

Peter Drucker stated: "What distinguishes the truly productive [manager] from the merely competent one is rarely knowledge or effort, let alone talent. The men who are truly productive are men who focus their knowledge, their intelligence, and their efforts on a big, truly worthwhile goal—men who set out to create something [different]."

In their acceptance speeches, Nobel Prize winners usually say: "What started me on the work that led to this achievement was a chance remark by a teacher who said: 'Why don't you try something where the results would really make a difference?' . . . This is a very different question from the ones asked in the managerial organization when it does 'long-range planning' or allocates resources. There, one tries to minimize the possible loss. In innovation, one has to maximize the possible results."

If you believe that your job as a manager is to sit in judgment, you will inevitably veto change. It is always "impractical." You must be a participant in the changes, and when you are, you will see that it takes as much energy and ingenuity to do what we already do just a little better, as it takes to do something entirely different.

A large container manufacturer had elaborate modern accounting systems and monthly budget reports. These had been installed by a major public accounting firm. The manufacturer suffered losses in one division, while the second division, having the major market share in its product line, was steadily declining in annual profit. By virtue of its major market share, the profitable division had held an umbrella over its competitors' costs for years by raising prices to cover the changes in its own operating costs. Suddenly, the second division's declining profit margin slipped, and the total result became a loss.

Management demanded changes, and we decided that none of the existing practices in the better division was sacred and that change was required immediately. We were determined that no activity or element of cost would continue without an organized effort to improve both it and the profits. Deliberate changes were made in the next two years in the more profitable division. These provided sustenance to the crippled division and "saved the company." (These are the words of the company chairman.) The results of the deliberate changes are described next.

- Fixed costs were reduced in six months by reducing floor space by 750,000 square feet for the same volume of production.
- Nonproductive assets were retired and unused property sold.
- The production process was physically rearranged to provide efficient direct in-line feeding during the process, and indirect costs of transportation were reduced by 50 percent in an eight-month period on 73 million metal package caps per day.
- Specifications for quality were reviewed and quantified along with the introduction of statistical methods for inspection, thus eliminating 500 employees engaged in visual and manual inspections.
- Manufacturing staff functions were reorganized to reduce personnel by 30 percent.
- Maintenance organization changes improved "up" time in major processes; output increased.

- The company went from loss to profit in the first year of these changes—and onward to phenomenal growth and profitability.
- The costs to achieve these goals aggregated $2.5 million. These were committed in two increments. The first million was recovered in eight months and the balance within six months of completion (a 14-month process).

Usually management relates each new budget to those of prior years, without considering the assumptions or real opportunities for changes in plant, methods, personnel, and so on. Some opportunities to do this had existed for years prior to the program, but sliding into the loss column was the event that triggered the change.

Must such drastic events occur before managers reexamine their current practices?

This chapter highlights that all present practices must be reviewed and become the subject of intense scrutiny during budget preparation and that significant changes in margins between revenue and costs can be deliberately changed by management actions.

In another situation—that of a major New England machinery builder—we engaged all members of the manufacturing organization, all functions and departments, in the preparation of new budgets for the following year. We examined the actual requirements of all departments. Some received larger allowances for necessary services to be performed, functions were transferred for lower-cost delivery of the same service, and many items of non–value-added costs and services were discontinued. The first year an 18 percent reduction in all manufacturing expenses occurred. This was followed in the second year by an additional 15 percent reduction. These reductions occurred while the output increased 25 percent, new products were introduced, and delivery service to customers improved. The managers learned to manage costs where they are caused.

Thus, we can see that building the manufacturing budget is the most exciting and creative manufacturing management task. During this period, there are fewer side glances from your peers or your boss that imply "Why are you tampering with a going operation?" Budget building seems to be the one time when it is proper to take off the wraps and consider some change.

Having completed such rigorous planning in the past would have signaled the organization to settle down—to carry on with the work and breathe a sigh of relief that we could now get back to normal. We have all done this. However, this cannot be the approach, not now in the world of Kaizen.

We must become aware of the competitive forces throughout the world that requires *continuous improvement*: quarterly, monthly, and daily. This concept was originally introduced to Japan by Dr. Edwards Deming, in his 14 points. It was also used by Taiichi Ohno of Toyota and adopted by the Japanese Industrial Engineering Society, as explained by Masaaki Imai in his book *Kaizen: The Key to Japan's Competitive Success*.[1] Imai has helped manufacturing firms transfer technology between the United States and Japan for 40 years.

The annual rhythmic plan for programming changes in U.S. industrial organizations is a thing of the past. It is well, then, that at the outset of this process, we recognize that it will always be a continuous, never-ending policy, not a program. To get started in this new process, we should be aware of new realities in our environment.

---

[1] Masaaki Imai, *Kaizen: The Key to Japan's Competitive Success* (New York: McGraw-Hill, 1987).

There is a complete discontinuity with past in objectives, techniques, and considerations of direct labor, materials supply, inventories, product design, and process planning, as well as how we want to account for those activities we direct.

First, a budget with regular performance reports does not guarantee a profit. Profit can occur only when actual operating management decisions accomplish beneficial change, not budgets. Many billion-dollar companies regularly go to bankruptcy proceedings with budgets in hand.

Second, most "staff" groups have elaborate mission statements and promise benefits. Seventeen layers of such management at the Ford Motor Company were undone when Mr. Peterson decided to become profitable and he removed them to produce the vigorous successfully competitive company of today (1992).

Third, the direct labor content is usually less than 10 percent of the price the user pays for the product, with most companies now employing three to four people in various non–value-added jobs for everyone labeled as a direct worker. The real problem here is that, as evidenced from personnel evaluation system failures, most managers do not know and/or do not tell salaried people what the real work task is and what performance will constitute success or failure. The failure of salaried employees to be productive is that managers do not intend, or do not know how, to have them be gainfully employed or become value-added employees.

Fourth, doing what we are now produces poor results. It may be wise to forget "our way."

Fifth, current results in return on investment, profits, and the consumption of net worth (undistributed surplus) justify a complete review of our operational and organizational styles that have become so traditional.

Sixth, in the 50-plus years since World War II, all international trade and commerce was influenced by the Cold War—East versus West—and we missed the actual growth and development of new trading areas, partners, and opportunities being thrust on the United States by rapid communication and spread of knowledge and information. We are less the masters of the directions of that commerce than we were earlier. We have to earn our way in competitive situations today.

In addition to those enumerated environmental changes, significant techniques have developed in major functional program areas of industrial organizations, which have major impact on the amounts and kinds of expenditures to be budgeted.

A company receives revenue/income from sales of the product and spends money to buy processing equipment, materials to use, and labor to perform conversion activities. Accountants decided at the turn of the century that industrial engineers could identify the value-added work in micromotions; and they decided that all other manufacturing activities should therefore be related to the purest value-creating activities—those micromotions. They lump all the capital and overhead expense costs and then distribute them proportionately to each micromotion to account for and develop cost/pricing programs and management control reports.

Concepts of Direct Labor Have Changed

The transfer of most cut, shape, form, and other conversion operations to mechanical and electronically controlled multiperation equipment, along with the increasing assignment of people to groups of tasks rather than to a series of a few (or one) micromotions, has changed the traditional measurement and control of people and tasks and of capital equipment use.

Economic Criteria about Purchased Materials Have Changed

The important differences between cost-management systems (CMS) and traditional practices include:

- Continual improvement and the elimination of non–value-added costs
- Activity-based accounting (cost drivers selected)
- Externally driven targets including target cost
- Improved traceability of information to management reporting objectives

We now know that accounting techniques influence behavior. Studies by the U.S. Air Force have shown that 75 percent of the cost-reduction programs submitted focus on direct labor (touch labor) rather than the many other larger potential areas, such as making knowledge workers more productive, improving supplier costs and performance, design for manufacture, improved processes, and so forth, as illustrated in Exhibit 21.1.

Expressed another way, management must learn where costs are caused or occur and then arrange the accounting to reflect those places and activities, so that the management reports and control relate directly to them. The ineffective activities and employees performing non–value-added tasks or duties must be identified.

Following is a formula for manufacturing-cycle efficiency (MCE), which clearly shows non–value-added operations.

$$\text{MCE} = \frac{\text{Processing time}}{\text{Processing time} + \text{Wait} + \text{Move} + \text{Handle} + \text{Waste} + \text{Set-up}}$$

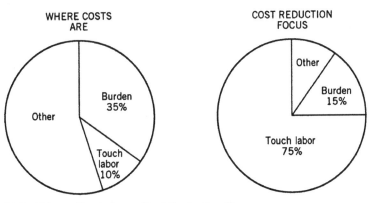

EXHIBIT 21.1   Where Costs Are—Cost Reduction Focus

The MCE should equal 1.00 (processing time only). It now equals approximately 0.20 (20 percent).

To prepare a budget or financial plan in this competitive era without attacks on such basic functional areas is to ignore the real management task of a manager. There are usually conflicts in planning and implementing the programs on which the budget is based.

The different functions necessarily compete for a portion of the existing gross margin above direct costs, to expand or aggrandize their services. The request for growth of each is rationalized as being in the highest interest of either improving the revenue or lowering costs. These conflicting suborganizational goals require that the manufacturing manager make many trade-off decisions in preparing the complete operating plan and budget, as the container manufacturer did in the earlier example. The idea of trade-offs and techniques will be discussed throughout the chapter.

The manufacturing budget is the most significant part of the total business plan because:

- The cost of goods manufactured ranges from 50% to 75 percent and up of the corporate revenue dollars.
- It establishes the planned production rate that governs the expected revenue and deals with the problem of capacity.
- It establishes the level of services that the functional specialists will supply to the factory-direct conversion operations, thereby setting the overhead costs and rates.
- It contains the plans for acquiring the materials to supply the planned production rates for conversion to your product. Therefore, it acts as a throttle for the level of working capital required in raw-materials, work-in-process, and finished-goods inventories.
- A company must develop a pricing strategy independent of cost. At the outset, some business plans call for operations for a period without absorbing the total cost.

New products or plants anticipate learning curves, increasing sales, high initial development costs, and the like, recognizing that the marketplace could not support pricing at full absorption. In competitive periods, this also occurs with a going operation. This situation usually requires the kind of changes being discussed earlier.

Frequently, though, there are many products in the same factory, most of which in reality have quite different needs but draw disproportionate or averaged allocated overhead amounts. Standard line products get upgraded and volume shifts occur. Just-in-time (JIT), quality, and automated processes also skew uniform overhead applications in price planning. Your budgeting process should include exhaustive reviews of across-the-board allocations made for easier accounting and so on. More accurate product cost information will lead to better strategic market decisions as well as decisions in investments for hardware and software.

CONCEPTS

In preparing the manufacturing budget, many decisions have to be made: why each activity is necessary and when, and by what means the various costs are to be met.

It is here that the intention of the manager is stated, the action plan is outlined, and the control points selected to monitor those action plans. Scheduled deliveries, dependability, and vendors' product innovation are all currently more important than current price or ritualistic requests for periodic quotations on price and delivery in former times. For example, IBM recently reduced the number of suppliers to its Lexington, Kentucky, location from 5,000 to approximately 500 in a period of two years.

Many times, such programs to reduce the number of vendors raise the invoice price of materials. However, more precision in quality, deliveries, inventory policy, and arrangements mean a lowered net cost to the purchaser. These factors are nowhere to be seen in any current operations statements without extensive deductive accounting research outside the normal report routines. However, these arrangements have been adopted as amazing profit improvers, as evidenced by many published reports of improvements by many companies, for example, members of the AME.

Most concepts of inventory have changed since the performance of the Toyota production system was described by Shigeo Shingo, Ohno's protégé, and discovered in the United States on Japanese/English bookshelves by C. Eugene Moore, Romeyn Everdall, the Association for Operations Management (APICS), *American Management Association* (AME), and major consulting firms. The initial program thrust by APICS, however, was a false start in that everyone conceived the program was a material supply program called "kanban" (Japanese for "ticket"), now called JIT.

Instead, careful analysis showed that it was a complete analysis; a program of mechanical and industrial engineering to precisely orchestrate supplier delivery, quality, process equipment, materials handling, and a trained employee program to eliminate every waste activity in the conversion of the processing of material into the product. Taiichi Ohno listed seven wastes to be eliminated:

1. Waste of overproduction
2. Waste of waiting and setup
3. Waste of transportation and storage
4. Waste of excess processing itself
5. Waste of stocks (inventories)
6. Waste of motion
7. Waste of making defective products

It is obvious from this list that every existing expense account would be affected by changes under the programs to eliminate these seven wastes using current allocation accounting systems. Under the circumstances, budgeting specific plans would be difficult for operation management. This was becoming a significant management communication problem. Frequently, financial investments in hardware or software were disallowed because of the confusion in tracking results using traditional accounting reports.

Similar problems exist in identifying changes when using more complicated automated processes that make many similar cost changes in processing.

▦ CHANGING TO A COST-MANAGEMENT SYSTEM

These phenomena demonstrated an increasing need for a systematic study to define the role of cost management in such an advanced manufacturing environment.

In early 1986, Computer-Aided Manufacturing-International, Inc. (CAM-I) Consortium of Advanced Management, International, formed a consortium of progressive industrial organizations, professional accounting firms, and government agencies to define the role of cost management in the new environment. The goal of the coalition was to provide an international forum in which cost-management experts could share ideas and experiences and provide a mechanism for consolidating the knowledge of practices that have proven successful in this new environment. In 1987, the outlines of the new cost-management systems concept were presented, and activity-based accounting and activity-based management programs were outlined.

The initial report, written by James A. Brimson, project director, outlined failures of the existing cost-accounting systems as described next. (These are obviously explanations as to why existing accounting systems have failed to support changes you may have already tried.) Reviewing them may point out management areas for improvement.

- They are plagued by high overhead rates due to inadequately traced costs.
- They do not isolate the costs of unnecessary activities, which add unnecessary cost, rather than customer-perceived value, to product.
- They do not penalize overproduction; the philosophy of overhead absorption through allocation of overhead cost based on production volumes, in fact, encourages excess inventories.
- They do not adequately identify and report the cost of quality deficiencies in products or processes.
- They focus on controlling the production process while significant costs that determine the design and development phases of a product's life cycle are inadequately identified.
- They do not support the justification of new investments in advanced manufacturing technology and fail to monitor the benefits identified.
- They employ performance measurements that often conflict with strategic manufacturing objectives.
- They cannot adequately evaluate the importance of nonfinancial measures such as quality, throughput, flexibility, and so forth.

Collaboration: A Key Concept

The manufacturing budget should present a plan for the coordination of a specified amount of direct production activity and of the specialized services to be supplied in the conversion operation. The next functions should be provided for regardless of whether each function has a manager:

- Product engineering or design for manufacturing
- Materials management (production and inventory control)

- Manufacturing engineering (processes)
- Industrial engineering (fitting people, accessories, and plant layout)
- Plant engineering (maintenance of physical plant and equipment)
- Quality control (training, support to achieve production design and performance expectation)
- Stores and shipping
- Physical distribution

During the planning for such changes, these groups must be led into an intense collaboration with highly mutual goals. In order to meet the organizational requirements:

- Each member must know his or her accountability and yet assume the responsibility for the whole task.
- Each member must recognize the effect of trade-offs in value-added costs and beneficial services for the several activities planned. Do the service at the least net cost.
- There must be open and direct communication and a freedom from fear of being "wrong" or "difficult" within the group during the preparation and planning.

Budget Does Not Guarantee Profit

A second concept has importance in the preparation of the manufacturing budget: A budget does not a profit make. Simultaneous functional changes must occur (i.e., in tooling, training, vendors, design engineering, planning, and scheduling). A company typically has the budget performance it deserves. That remains true despite capable, conscientious individual or group efforts that could change the results with more innovative planning.

Manufacturing managers tend to think of auto manufacturers as successful and well managed, but serious challenges to their management skills appeared in the mid-1980s and remain in 1998. Their management styles and strategies require continuous change and eternal vigilance to stay competitive. Design for manufacturing, research in new materials, and more efficient processes are the constant concerns to maintain and regain market share. Of the 20 firms listed in the Fortune 500 (1998), their ten-year (1987–1997) median earnings per share was 6 percent while the median for all listed companies was 8 percent for the same period.

Managers explain failure to meet budgeted goals with these reasons:

- Sales forecasts too high
- Bad cash management
- Expanded too quickly
- Not enough capital
- Good product design, but it did not sell
- Unexpected quality problems
- Too much competition
- Obsolete production methods
- Fell behind in technology

These reasons are the same answers given annually to explain poor budget performance in many companies today.

No matter how successful or certain a company seems, most companies to regroup and seriously adjust their internal management. Worldwide industrial activity spurred by such extensive communication is too dynamic for companies to rest. Richard Foster, managing director of McKinsey and Company, demonstrates this in *Innovation: The Attacker's Advantage.*[2] His studies caused him to observe that

> [C]ompanies that were leaders in their field see their fortunes suddenly disappear. Do leading companies in fact not have the natural advantages they are supposed to, or are their natural advantages outweighed by other inherent disadvantages? I think the latter is the case . . . and that these disadvantages result from technological change.
>
> Technological change is the reason why only one company out of three manages to cover its cost of raising money most of the time. It is why most companies manage to achieve what Bob Waterman and Tom Peters have defined as "excellent" financial performance in any one year out of twenty, and then immediately drop back into the great middle ground of average financial performance; why even the best companies, by anyone's definition of excellence, retain their superior competitive performance for only three to four years.

You may not assume that tomorrow will be like today. Even so, managements feel that innovation is more risky than defending their position, when they find they are behind.

Successful companies make the opposite assumptions; they assume change is going to occur; there are patterns that are discernible and will come more swiftly than is desired. This is because they understand the dynamics of their competition.

Who is responsible when conditions such as these or those of our container manufacturers arise? Neither the customers nor the work force that carried out the orders is. *Management* has to accept responsibility for poor understanding, poor decisions in these areas, and a lack of good action plans.

In his book *ROI—Practical Theory and Innovative Applications*, Robert Peters notes rather poor performance for many companies in terms of constant dollars.[3] Because budgets are usually synonymous with profit plans in management's thinking, we should review this idea.

Peters states in the preface of his book:

> The Income and Expense statements which attempt to match costs against revenues have been the traditional measures of financial performance. In recent decades, however, two evolutionary changes in the environment of business have eroded their value. First, a combination of technical and social advances has increasingly substituted capital for labor in manufacturing. Second, profit itself, as normally reported has become a product of many artificial and transient influences due to latitude in the areas of depreciation, taxes, and capital share values manipulations.

---

2 Richard Foster, *Innovation: The Attacker's Advantage* (New York: Summit Books, 1988), 29ff.
3 Robert Peters, *ROI—Practical Theory and Innovative Applications* (New York: AMACom, 1979).

Peters suggests that a better standard should be devised for measuring financial results: "The increasing dominance of capital or cash flows in terms of both investment and a return can provide a more incisive basis for metering business progress, giving support for cost management system (CMS) (activity-based accounting)." [4]

There are also some external factors involved in tracing budgets to earnings statements, as all assumptions are not clearly stated in budget documents.

Frequently, inflation and deflation in the economy are not accounted for. We have controlled inflation (1996–present) along with long-term interest rates but short-term rates minus inflation have been rising sharply over the past year (1997–1998). However, Bob Norton of *Fortune* shows in the Fortune 500 (April 1998) that "real rates are higher than they have been since the recession, meaning that the Fed has in effect been tightening monetary policy even as it appeared to sit tight."

Second, many changes have occurred in general asset and balance sheet accounting practices and in the disposition of the profits from the budgeting processes. Ben C. Ball, a former vice president of corporate planning, a professor at Massachusetts Institute of Technology (MIT) and now a consultant, prepared an analysis and expressed concern for these manipulations. He believes that the executives assume they are using shareholders' resources (equity) efficiently if the company's performance (return on equity) and earnings are good and shareholders do not rebel. They assume the stock market automatically penalizes those that invest resources poorly. In short, the stock market performance and company performance are inexorably linked.

A close examination Ball did initially of 50 of the largest, mature, publicly held U.S. companies from 1970 to 1984 shows just that.[5] He continued:

> Many profits never found their way to shareholders either as dividends or as higher stock value. Over time, in half the companies a large portion of retained earnings simply disappeared. Traditionally, systems are not designed to track the profits to Wall Street or to see whether it arrives there.

Ball's article "states that the shareholders are deprived of their share of this important wealth of the company. Remembering that the budget is a management tool and is actually a plan for the micromanagement of the uses of resources to produce a gain or profit, we should be aware of what and where they are. This will be important, as the rapid growth of technology will be increasingly classified as intellectual capital. It could easily become the largest part of future assets.

With capital tools being substituted for manual labor as an operating policy, the concomitant need to use technology and to modernize facilities demands more reinvestment capital. Internally generated capital can come only from an excess of revenues over costs. Thus, new cost-management systems must prevail.

Although budgets are a familiar management technique, they must be developed and applied in a more creative way than they have in the past in our large, too-well-bureaucratized institutions, in which plans are usually a substitute for decisions and actions.

---

[4] Ibid., pp. v–vi.
[5] Ben C. Ball, "The Mysterious Disappearance of Retained Earnings," *Harvard Business Review* (July–August 1987). In June 1998, Ball stated that there has been "little change in practice."

During a recent visit with a client, the chief executive officer (CEO) recounted the current malaise of rising costs of materials, labor contracts, and so on. He said, "Well, the others have the same problems; they'll be facing it the same way, we'll raise prices to cover those changes in costs."

Global competition and rising real productivity in Asian/Pacific Rim countries now remove this alternative management course of action. The United States cannot assume minimum competition. Since inflation is not acceptable, it increases the need to reconsider the cost of existing functions and style of management when preparing the budget.

It is well to remember that pricing is a marketing responsibility, not a cost pass-through.

George Sorter, professor of accounting at the Graduate School of Business, New York University, believes that the emphasis on accounting practice is misplaced. In the *New York Times*, he criticized the new second edition of *Handbook of Modern Accounting*[6] because it placed primary emphasis on only one line of the statement: profit. "Can anyone seriously believe," he asked, "that all that has happened to a complex company during an eventful year can adequately be captured by a single bottom line figure?"

Although activity-based accounting/management has yet to be accepted, it is the better tool/information.

Bold Analysis Crucial

When approached on the basis of a bold analysis of things as they are, the process of preparing the manufacturing budget assumes a third critical conceptual dimension. The preparation process becomes an opportunity to create new common objectives among the various manufacturing functions. Analysis may also help eliminate the intense concentration on minute aspects of your problem and the current emphasis on specialists' tasks. Marshall McLuhan calls this the "strength of western man." He remarks that "the specialist is one who never makes small mistakes while moving towards the grand fallacy." Little did he know that he was describing most budgeting processes today. Changing emphasis and finding higher mutual interest for value added to all products from all the specialists' functional programs is of prime importance in putting the manufacturing budget together.

The rewarding fact is that the presence of a budget process is evidence that someone is at least thinking about what is expected to be, which may appear to be good management. However, the wiser planners have identified and outlined the proper balance of interaction and services, calling for the simultaneous developments of production, tooling, acquiring capital tools, work pace, plant layout, and so forth. They recognize that trade-offs are required to ensure more margin. They also recognize that they can organize their manufacturing for lower costs in four key areas: (1) product design; (2) conversion process design (methods); (3) scheduling (to control throughput rate); and (4) utilization of managers, specialists, and supervisors.

---

[6] Sidney Davidson and Roman Weil, eds., *Handbook of Modern Accounting*, 2nd ed. (New York: McGraw-Hill, 1984).

Current management programs that encourage highly developed department objectives should be abandoned in favor of a more collective operations program. This could change "what is expected" to "what ought to be."

A good manufacturing budget depends on the quality of management imagination and bold plans for breakthrough change based on dissatisfaction with things as they are. This means that managers should acquire new knowledge and improve forecast accuracy. This would create a more proper balance of relationships, better levels of service, and an efficacious budget. The technique is to apply a value-added test to all the factors in the MCE formula discussed earlier and review management decisions regarding all elements in the capacity-planning chart.

PROBLEMS IN PREPARING THE MANUFACTURING BUDGET

Usually the approach in preparing the manufacturing budget is to avoid any changes from the recent past. Change is viewed as creating risk. In addition, if there may be some windfalls to be realized in the next periods, changes are minimized to provide a little insurance in the future period. A third reason is that a new approach may promise changes that managers believe they cannot control. It seems safer not to change. That approach too often keeps the organization in most factories trapped in programs of diminishing total productivity, as was our container manufacturer and the machinery builder.

There is evidence in business circles of a style called "new management." Harold Wolf, professor of the Sloan Institute at MIT, said in one interview with me earlier:

> While old management concerns itself with efficiency in the production process and the direct workforce, the "new management" seeks the optimum use of all resources along with flexibility rather than rigidity in job descriptions and lines of authority.

This implies more collaboration among managers. He continued:

> Recognize that new management doesn't have anything to do with age, education, or technology. Success will depend on the manager's comfort in the presence of risk and his tolerance for ambiguity and uncertainty in the pursuit of high mutual interest in common output and cost objectives.

Innovation and higher risk in new budget plans can provide more planned profit.

What Ought to Be

A significant challenge in the budgeting process is to make that process entrepreneurial in character as it moves from what is expected, which relates to the present, to describing what ought to be when innovation occurs.

The assessment of what ought to be should come from (1) more analysis, (2) more planning, (3) more frequent injections of what-if questions, and (4) ongoing discussions among the functional managers about what further coordinated programs will increase revenue and lower costs. And decisions to throw off non–value-added activities.

"The operating executive who is forever looking for a single accounting formula or approach on which to base all his decisions should recognize this is futile," notes Robert

Peters. Instead, investigative effort must be concentrated on areas in which costs are caused or found.

In practice, more than one resource (capacity, manpower, or machinery) will probably be a limitation, so managers must combine and weigh the results and make trade-offs as their judgment dictates. As George Sorter asked when criticizing most accountants' approach during his lectures at the University of Chicago, "Is profit now more important than other strategic goals—the longer product life expected, expanded markets, new facilities, or shorter delivery cycles?"

Few of these goals can be accomplished in a single budget year; thus, a proper time frame should be established for any changes. This is suggested by Banks and Wheelwright in the *Harvard Business Review* and is more correct in the 1990s.

> Pressure for shorter term profits can seriously impede the achievement of long range goals. . . . S/L trade-offs are now more obvious than they used to be. Through the expansion and development of formal strategic planning process during the past decade, top managers have become more aware of where the corporations could be going, deviations . . . are more noticeable and the consequences . . . can be more significant as companies continue to grow in size and complexity. Managers receive greater authority and responsibility, and [their] decisions made to favor the short run over strategic goals . . . may have some serious financial consequences.[7]

Faster-paced securities markets, public relations programs, and necessary reassurances to old stockholders in newly conglomerated corporations all increase demands for short-term results. These are not usually expressed in terms of constant dollars or with considerations of the effect of inflation. This is coupled with the realization, too, that short-range forecasts are frequently less accurate than long-range trends.

Banks and Wheelwright indicate the next areas in which these trade-offs occur and in which substantial progress may be deterred by management decision. They suggest that we reconsider during the budget preparation:

- The postponement of capital investment (prolonging lower productivity or higher cost methods)
- Deferring operating expenses in product development or capital facility maintenance
- Reducing operating expenses by reductions in the work force affecting customer service or labor relations
- Reducing inventories with more elegant scheduling to enhance deliveries and service to markets
- Reducing training of employees, impairing quality service or output efficiency
- Other operating changes affecting product mix, delivery, pricing policies, and so forth

---

[7] R. L. Banks and S. C. Wheelwright, "Operations vs. Strategy: Trading Tomorrow for Today," *Harvard Business Review* (May–June 1979).

Why do such things happen? Unfortunately, when division or plant managers decide to favor short-term profits over long-term strategic goals, they have likely been influenced by two considerations. The first, and perhaps more influential, is the manner in which their performance is measured by the corporation. The second is a combination of the lack of balance between the short- and long-range plans as emphasized in corporate communications on one hand and the general management culture of the company on the other.

These trade-offs can be properly balanced when the procedure of recording what is expected is changed to detailed budget building, which outlines the programs, actions, and organizational changes, along with objectives that are realistic and attainable and yet reflect a change to what ought to be.

The company's philosophy of operations, its style of management, and the culture of the management group all limit the specific budget programs to whatever extent the management culture in any company limits realism in planning changes. To the extent that realism is limited, a budget becomes less meaningful.

As Thomas Pallante, comptroller of Owens–Illinois Company in Toledo, suggests, "The budgeting process becomes the use of activities-based planning rather than one of applying measurements and yardsticks. [The question to be asked is] What activity is necessary to produce these goods efficiently?" Programs that become budget-approved items or that are eliminated as trade-offs to achieve higher mutual benefit among functions are examples of what he calls "activities-based planning."

When time has run out and some or any numbers have to be supplied, it is too late to "make the budget" (meaning achieve a planned result). In such a situation, random events, poor forecasts, and overlooked problems will conspire against good performance.

Dennis Hiese, corporate operations comptroller of Texas Instruments, said in a seminar discussion that "the budget preparation process" [referring primarily to zero-based budgeting] "should be a mechanism to facilitate trading off operating expenses against strategic expenses."

Each manufacturing budget assumes a level of output; each usually sets the revenue. These output data become the basic multiplier for the direct unit costs and require some minimum levels of services from the direct specialists. Beyond that, we cannot overlook the fact that unavoidable cost levels result from such factors as the specific process design (the technology of the conversion processes), machinery layout, handling, and product performance specifications. Further, a level of employment is required to man those processes. Costs can change only when management decides these elements change.

To give a more entrepreneurial character to the budget, the manager must step back and look realistically at the present situation. The current difficulties and crises seem to leave an imprint, making it impossible to perceive how different the general relationships of processes and costs could be.

Three probable reasons for this effect may be noted:

1. The manufacturing manager may feel that approval for change sizable enough to affect costs rests with someone "up there."

2. He or she may also say "If I change much of this operation, I admit that I haven't been right up until now."
3. There may be a lack of top management perspective about who creates costs and how and where the costs functionally occur.

Unfortunately, feeling justified in the present mode of operation, the manager sees the future as a continuation of the exact same matrix of events. He or she has difficulty perceiving a mechanism to develop the future as anything except a straight-line extrapolation of the present, which forecasts disaster.

THREE SOLUTIONS

There are three ways to avoid such straitjacket thinking: (1) zero-based budgeting, which is usually initiated by corporate dictum; (2) simple, forceful orders to reduce cost by X percent; and (3) a "planned action" budget to ensure revenue levels and manage costs, describing what ought to be in detailed programs for improvements in product design, process or method designs, scheduling operations, and utilizing people.

Zero-based budgeting is discussed in detail in Chapter 30 and represents an approach to breaking away from this "imprint," or cause-and-effect chain. Specifically, zero-based budgeting assumes as this author does that no present cost is approved and that every item and dollar of cost must be justified as it enters the spending plan of the budget. Usually this is not possible because of mixed responsibility for several fixed costs buried and allocated along with administrative items, and the CEO will not participate in starting from ground zero. Most adaptations of the zero-based budgeting programs start with the executive targeting a percentage of current costs—usually 50 percent or more—as a basic starting point. The challenge is to determine whether current practices offer opportunities for significant changes. Many such "closed or untouchable areas" present the largest amounts of cost available and amenable to change.

That program has some advantage over the second format, in which top management dictates a cut of some percentage and refuses to participate in any of the strategic decision making necessary to accomplish this order.

The third program, which seems more beneficial to the company, is to reconsider the necessity for existing activities, to support management programs for such activities as manufacturing research, and to determine the possibility of abandoning many of the expenses currently being incurred. This method describes the planned action budget. It can establish more realistic goals; it necessarily produces more planned, deliberate change and demonstrates more professional management.

What is the technique for preparing a planned action budget? The technique requires explanation in some detail.

TECHNIQUE

As noted, a manufacturing budget should not be an accounting document. It should be a management control tool that outlines future action and estimates the expected costs that will be incurred in producing a product at some assumed level of output. It must reflect both strategies and tactics.

A planned action budget, the preferred type, describes what ought to be by outlining and establishing standards for:

- What will be shipped?
- When that will happen?
- What materials, labor, and supplies are needed?
- How much time will be used by whom and when?
- Who does what and what is expected of each person?

Most budgets are compiled by accounting after a CEO says, "Next year will be ____ percent of this year." He may add that "sales will be up (or down)." Then present ratios are applied by accountants and the extrapolated budget is published.

The budget should be a map for making a profit that balances expected output from the factory (which is revenue) with:

- The levels of services mandated by management (all value-added service).
- The amount of inventory changes planned. (Consider JIT work-in-process scheduled time by product and "common to all design concepts.")
- The levels of employment (direct, indirect, salaried, and management). (Does everyone have "real work" to do?)
- Capital acquisitions to be made in the period (usually one year)

The first management decisions to be made go to manufacturing basics. They include concrete judgments on:

- The design of the product to be shipped and the quality specifications for it
- The arrangement of production facilities
- The schedule for all parts manufacturing and continuous processes
- How to organize and utilize employees

Costs could be substantially changed as those very decisions are changed.

The ideal technique is to practice planning and decision making, not to improve on accounting technology. The budget should be conceived realistically, based on dissatisfaction with the status quo. Finally, it should include specific plans, not hoped-for change.

DETERMINING PRODUCTION REQUIREMENTS

An initial task faces managers who are trying to determine production requirements to set the activity level. They should first develop a master schedule of confirmed, month-by-month revenues. The schedule should be set down in terms of the units the company sells, not in dollar terms. Only the U.S. Treasury manufactures dollar bills. Your plant makes assemblies, kits, or product units from specific materials, with trained labor and allocated other costs per unit.

When expressed as shipped units, the master schedule becomes a confirmed total operating plan. It may not be exactly as the sales force stated if inventory usage or building are considered or your plant capacity is overutilized or underutilized. The most common mistake is for company management to be unaware that there are these other considerations.

Capacity, too much optimism, limitations in working capital, and late or incomplete product development are frequent limitations; therefore, manufacturing managers should learn how to review sales forecasts when starting a budget.

The budgets require consideration of many of these elements:

- The market requirements as perceived by marketing and programs planned on a timely basis to fill that need.
- The availability of product design, time phased to support shipments in that period (this includes tool-up, test, and market). (Time should be shorter with simultaneous design, process, and tool planning.)
- The availability of material to be acquired for that shipment plan. (Use JIT, stock-where-used, etc.)
- Establishment of a parts or materials replenishment plan to continue the shipping revenue plan materials requirement planning (MRP) and elegant shop-floor control.
- A distribution plan to meet the sales demand, including transport mode and time required; schedule and plan to capacity that has been demonstrated.
- Capacity to manufacture products in terms of tools, people, and process time.
- Control of facilities programs that support the changes in capacity called for by the new schedule.
- A program balancing receivables, payables, and JIT inventory levels to set the working capital levels.

If you cannot identify the preceding items or be assured of reasonable control, the projected shipments and revenue may not occur. Then the levels of expense and employment planned and the programs started would be excessive for the lower rate of shipments. Also, planned profit could not occur even if managers remained cost conscious.

The way to reconcile these various factors in a shipping rate and revenue plan is to adopt a master scheduling routine for the core of your production items that can be planned. The master schedule routine should contain the next sequence of events:

Step 1. Determine the core of product offerings that can be planned.
Step 2. Obtain sales history and forecast.
Step 3. Schedule new and/or revised product appearance in revenue schedule.
Step 4. Determine inventory changes necessary to accomplish schedules.
Step 5. Establish "real" shop capacity.
Step 6. Publish master schedule and report progress.

STEP 1: DEVELOPING THE PLANNABLE CORE

Such intense interest in planning to make specific shipments of specific products could possibly produce a malaise in the reader. Managers might comment: "Our business is so different, we cannot project or forecast around this." Under these circumstances, managers will have the tendency to gloss over or generalize the revenue program into dollars too early in budget preparation.

All companies are faced with this phenomenon. Experience shows, however, that every company can develop a "plannable core." The best evidence is that some companies' revenues may vary more than 10 to 15 percent a year without identifying where the sales changes occurred. Identifying those items leads to finding constant and variable products that constitute the plannable core.

In most companies, inventories at strategic points in the process or as finished goods provide hedges against planning or forecasting errors. An increase in inventory, however, increases direct-cost factory activity and working-capital requirements.

The materials-management section and manufacturing or industrial engineering departments should be able to supply information about and identify the plannable core. Do not be deceived into creating too general a program for future shipments. The shipments are made up of specific products and selected and customer options. A few examples are given next.

In one case, a major replacement auto battery manufacturer had 12 geographically distributed facilities with a number of stock-keeping units in inventory equal to the unshippable unit orders on hand. One million units were mismatched with demand. With a manufacturing list of 9,958 items, it was soon determined that 200 or fewer were the equivalent of more than 90 percent of sales. These were most frequently on the stock-out list. Inventory-planning profiles of this plannable core for seasonal and geographic distributions reduced inventories by several million dollars, and immeasurably improved service came when management considered this information, which had been there all the time.

A similar example involved a major truck manufacturer. The total finished inventory in house, plus dealers' stocks, which they financed, and major subassembly parts in process were examined and found to be equivalent to more than one and one-half years of sales. Analysis of actual purchased truck configurations by major features, which helped to identify the plannable core, reduced all inventories by approximately $25 million and improved factory efficiency and planning.

In both instances, a new approach to existing information produced a better understanding of the plannable core, smoothed production, and improved budget performance. A portable oil derrick manufacturer accepted this same challenge to find a plannable portion of his business. He discovered that approximately 76 percent could be predicted. Many more examples exist.

STEP 2: OBTAINING SALES HISTORY AND FORECAST

The plannable core is a basis for a master schedule (in units) that merges and time-phases the mutual interests of sales, product-design program, and actual shop capacity into a budget revenue program. The sales information to be supplied should include both history and forecasts. Since marketing expectations drive the whole budgeting process, the forecast should undergo constant scrutiny by operations people too.

Customer (sales) orders are all converted into shop manufacturing orders. The best information available about actual sales history by product configuration is usually in the production-planning (materials-management) section. When materials management analyzes these data for the sales function, a more accurate story of anticipated sales will emerge. Field sales personnel provide their superior information on product trends, customers, new product needs, product problems, competitive products, quantity, and so forth. In this manner, a superior forecast of sales is accomplished, and "extra" safety stock used to cover low forecast accuracy can be reduced.

The manufacturing department can accept only the marketing or sales functions' final estimates of market demands and the sales program established to meet them. However, manufacturing should be aware of the problems of forecasting sales.

Operating sections require more information than forecasts usually provide if the operating people do not participate in incorporating that forecast into a master schedule. Problems occur or are created for budget performance if the operating department fails to ask sufficiently detailed questions during the forecasting process to get the information it needs to plan production levels of various factory processes or departments.

Forecasting accuracy is a basic ingredient in manufacturing budget preparation. The attitudes of manufacturers about and during the process of forecast development are important; all available techniques should be explored to select those most suitable for use.

Copulsky's *Practical Sales Forecasting* (now out of print) approaches the problems of managerial attitude in a humorous way.[8] Some paraphrased questions and answers from the book are given next.

Question: Who should not forecast?

Answer: Anyone who believes the future is only a straight-line extrapolation of the past. Recognize that changes occurring are an important element in forecasting. Remember, it is never possible to step twice into the same river.

Question: Who else should not forecast?

Answer: The man who substitutes arithmetic for sense. Alfred North Whitehead, a philosopher, said there is no more common error than to assume that because prolonged and accurate calculations have been made, the applicability of the result of some fact of nature is absolutely certain.

Question: Who else should not forecast?

Answer: The man who thinks he has the only magic formula. Inventories are provided in anticipation of that forecast of use or demand

---

[8] William Copulsky, *Practical Sales Forecasting* (New York: AMACom, 1987).

The various techniques of forecasting are described adequately in the July–August 1971 *Harvard Business Review*.[9] The best uses of each, the kinds of data required, and their dependability are charted for easy review. The list of techniques included follows as a reminder of how wide the range of possible approaches is.

Qualitative Methods

1. Delphi
2. Market research
3. Panel consensus
4. Visionary forecast
5. Historic analogy

Times-Series Analysis and Projection

6. Moving average
7. Exponential smoothing
8. Box-Jenkins
9. X-11
10. Trend projection

Causal Methods

11. Regression model
12. Econometric model
13. Intention-to-buy survey
14. Input–output model
15. Economic input–output
16. Diffusion index
17. Leading indicator
18. Life-cycle analysis

A multimethod index approach has recently been tried with excellent results in consumer goods forecasting. It was developed by Bernard T. Smith and is described in his book *Focus Forecasting*.[10]

STEP 3: SCHEDULING NEW AND REVISED PRODUCT APPEARANCE

The next step in preparation of the master schedule is time-phasing the new product design or revisions program. Some companies have many of their major items in a state of flux or design change at a given time, thus limiting shipments. Manufacturing budget planning should provide answers to such questions as: What kind of an effect is this

---

[9] *Harvard Business Review* (July–August 1971): 45–47.
[10] Bernard T. Smith, *Focus Forecasting: Computer Technique for Inventory Control* (New York: Van Nostrand Reinhold, 1978).

product design going to have on schedules, output, and revenue? When does the new product come on? Does it have an impact?

The master schedule requires a definition of the product represented by the plannable core and forecast items in the form of complete bills of material or parts lists. This is a primary requirement from the product-design section. These lists must be maintained in up-to-date form to avoid continuation of the manufacture of obsolete items. These bills of material describe what the factory will make.

Many good budget revenue plans fail because product designs are not available on time. Frequently, management's control of the product design program is so minimal that safety time factors are not included to cover the premature and infant design failures for the new product that is to be shipped in a given period. The production of revenue is also delayed. Operations management has the principal responsibility for delivery of these designs—or proof of concepts, preliminary production runs, and initial production output—in time to accomplish the sales forecast and marketing program and to fulfill revenue budgets.

Obviously, operations managers have to keep product-design managers in the same master schedule relating to the budget if the income plans are to be realized. Techniques used for project control or design include the critical-path method, program evaluation and review technique, and others.

STEP 4: DETERMINING REQUIRED INVENTORY LEVELS

The fourth step in the master schedule routine is the determination of required inventory levels for the budget plan. Once the shipping rate has been established from the forecast, the actual production plan and shop manufacturing orders should be planned to accomplish levels of inventory that support the expected level of shipments. If the forecast, as edited, represents an increase in the rate of shipment, time may be required for the appearance of additional raw or purchased materials and for higher levels of manufacturing to occur. Such change would be supported by consumption of present inventories at a faster-than-normal rate, which would produce a stock-out, or a time of increased levels of work in process could be planned.

Companies invest in inventory when anticipating the receipt of customer orders to shorten delivery offerings or to enhance sales by providing instant availability to satisfy consumer requirements.

Care must be taken in the scheduling of raw materials' arrivals and in managing in-process manufacturing time. Further, there must be ample time for finished goods to reach distribution points and for matching the regular, programmed supply to customers if budgeted revenue is to accumulate at the point of distribution.

In preparing the budget, the operations manager must require that the materials management function develop plans that allow time for the manufacturing to take place by the standard methods on which the expense levels are to be predicated.

Definitions and General Information

A review of inventory definitions and general information is presented next.

Manufacturing inventories are of three kinds: raw materials, work in process, and finished goods.

1. *Raw materials* include all purchased materials to be used in manufacturing but on which no conversion labor has been expended. No distinction is made in the raw materials inventory between direct materials and indirect materials. In many instances, the same materials may be used for either purpose. A distinction is made between direct materials and indirect materials only when they are requisitioned from the raw materials storeroom.
2. *Work in process* includes all costs—material, labor, and burden—that have been expended in the manufacturing process on products not yet complete. The work-in-process inventory is usually broken down into material in process, labor in process, and burden in process. Refer to MCE, discussed earlier in this chapter.
3. *Finished goods* include all manufactured products that are complete and ready for shipment to the customer. No distinction is made in the finished goods inventory as to material cost, labor cost, and burden cost.

Finished goods inventories transferred to sales control and not used by manufacturing to create revenue are excluded in these manufacturing budget considerations. However, if the manufacturing manager is responsible for the total logistics function, these inventories are also considered in the planning activities.

In many companies, no distinction is made among raw materials, work in process and finished goods. In their place, the general ledger carries three different inventory accounts: materials inventory, labor inventory, and burden inventory. The triple inventory is known as a four-wall inventory system. All materials are charged to materials inventory upon receipt. Direct labor expended is charged to labor inventory. Burden applied is charged to burden inventory. When shipment is made, each inventory is relieved of its pro rata share of the product cost. This is the poorest cost control.

Setting Inventory Level

Setting a company's inventory level is very difficult because sales, operations, and finance all have different goals and interests in that inventory. This occurs because the top manager judges the performance of each functional head by different criteria. These are the wastes as identified earlier by Ohno.

A basic conflict occurs when operations managers want to build and use inventory as a way of carrying them over an excessive number of changeovers. Finance managers want to operate with the least investment. They know that every plan for an increase in inventory to handle the irregular sales demands has a negative aspect as far as maximizing the return on investment is concerned. Sales expects all sizes, colors, and models in order to make dollar sales and quotas competitive.

There exists a plannable core that satisfies the best interests of these three functions. We have demonstrated how such a core can be identified. The "important few" (basics) and popular optional add-ons can be immediately distinguished from the "trivial many" in terms of frequency and quantity of orders when the actual sales are examined more objectively and in detail, using a classic A-B-C analysis.

Finally, the phasing out of present product designs and preliminary buildup to ship new models requires special attention. Temporary growth in inventory *and* shop activity accompanies these changes.

Understanding that this basic conflict is present in establishing inventory levels enhances the development of higher mutual interests in the preparation of master schedules for shipping product and setting inventory levels.

When most firms put budgets together in dollars, they lose all opportunity for meaningful materials control and management. The final dollar extension is appropriate, but backing into specific material needs from dollars rather than from identifiable product units is the reason top management is frequently not in control of inventory.

STEP 5: ESTABLISHING REAL DEMONSTRATED SHOP CAPACITY

Two questions should be answered here: Have you identified the level of resources required for the master schedule, the basis of your planned-action budget? Is there capacity available, or can it be made available?

The final element required to prepare the master schedule is the consideration of actual shop capacity. In planning for an output, historical reality should supersede standard figures or theoretical capacities in estimating shipment of product, which produces the revenue.

Let us first dispose of the accounting and cost-allocation concerns and then return to the problems that operations people have in ensuring the expected shipments of goods.

The accounting manager must select a basis for allocating a wide variety of ongoing time-committed costs and costs associated with depletion of asset values such as depreciation. Those allocations are policy decisions on how to spread all indirect costs back into production units for pricing and so forth.

The manufacturing manager is concerned with actually producing the units. In the budget-planning process, other questions relate to how much we can produce now, whether it is enough, and what is required to increase output. A variety of alternative combinations of capacity and operating patterns is usually possible. However, to quote Horngren's *Cost Accounting: A Managerial Emphasis*: "To most people the term 'capacity' implies a constraint in upper limit. This view is commonly held in industry."[11] This suggests that the manager who is planning the budget must test the realism of currently held views of upper limits on capacity.

Horngren also states that "although the term capacity is usually applied to plant and equipment, it is equally applicable to all other resources . . . [such as] . . . manpower, material supply level, [and] executive time or working capital for a higher operating level." He notes further that subcontracting, overtime premiums, or premiums for material may ease these limitations but with an uneconomical result: "Then the upper limit [must be] specified by management for current [budget] planning and control purposes."

---

[11] Charles T. Horngren, *Cost Accounting: A Managerial Emphasis* (Paramus, NJ: Practice Hall, 1967).

There are three general conditions to be noted in considering capacity versus demand. First, where there is a variable demand but the average level is always lower than the maximum capacity, it becomes relatively easy to plan. The second condition would exist when the variable average requirement is about equal to the average capacity. There will be peak periods when the demand will be greater than capacity and periods when it will be lower. This situation needs very close planning to avoid delivery problems.

The third situation, one frequently not recognized by management, occurs when the demand is variable but the average requirements are always greater than the total capacity. It must be recognized that even good planning cannot prevent the delivery problems in this situation.

If there is a constant backlog, the lack of capacity may be limiting actual sales. However, if the backlog has continued to grow, you are making an unconscious decision to limit sales. The failure to increase capacity by improving the use of present resources or additions to plant and equipment should be at least a conscious choice of top management. It is the manufacturing manager's responsibility to define his or her position in this matter in each budget period.

Real Factory Capacity (Demonstrated)

Recognizing real factory capacity requires the broadest possible analysis of current demands as defined in the early steps of master scheduling. Also crucial is the utilization of existing plant equipment and human resources in satisfying that demand.

In the planned-action budget, it is important to consider capacity as representing practical, attainable output capacity. Such capacity may be further defined as the maximum level at which the plant or department would operate efficiently from year to year.

It is assumed that there is an existing capacity with historical records of output or a projected statement of proposed output in the pro forma program for a new or infant plant. Capacity should be reviewed and expressed in relation to the plannable core units of output being forecast—or in appropriate subsets of items or parts used in the final configuration of the predicted product shipments (assemblies, kits, or sets).

One must also distinguish between two other basic elements: (1) continuous-process operations, in which distillation, refinement of basic materials, or automatic processing of materials or parts takes place; and (2) batch processing, batch machining, or assemblies in which other human-controlled operations take place.

It should be noted that many operations managers, when they have some of each type of operation, set some capacities in line with expected output from the continuous operations and some from their batch processes. Although it is slightly more complicated to consider utilization of the factory or several production units, control points are more appropriate and control reports more meaningful if both batch and continuous operations are recognized at planning time. In either instance, the standard volume should be established.

Having suggested that realism in assessing capacity requires a review of several years' historic performance and engineering projection, the current budget year's expected output is computed as a percentage of the long-term level for convenience. This percentage is sometimes called the *index volume.* This technique assists in maintaining a reference point when longer-range capital additions and expansion programs are tied with annual tactical planning.

Realism and the assessment of attainability are both value judgments and provide the keys to successful budget programs. In assessing capacity, operating managers have rates of activities in mind. Too frequently, they apply these to the total lapsed time of the budget period, assuming that they should plan for *ideal* conditions. This is not the best way to plan, since ideal and controlled standard conditions seldom prevail for a whole year.

The average situation is not usually ideal. Manufacturing processes are not going on a full 100 percent of the lapsed calendar period for which we plan. Anything less than 100 percent continuous conversion activity is a limitation on the capacity of the enterprise.

Benjamin W. Niebel's charted savings from methods engineering and time studies,[12] examining the disposition of each worker's total time, has been adapted as a tool to consider how capacity is affected by unmanaged situations and events. The chart, which is shown in Exhibit 21.2, describes total lapsed (available) clock or calendar time and the uses thereof.

In assessing capacity, the total elapsed time of the budget period contains a minimum-work-time content. This is work created by management-directed specifications, designs, technology, processes, and so on. The remainder is the portion of total lapsed time that is ineffective. This time reduces capacity. We find that this ineffective time is actually prescribed by the design of ineffective methods and/or management shortcomings, such as weak supervision, failure to train operators, scheduling errors, and nonstandard materials. This ineffective time is management's opportunity to affect capacity directly by improving methods or overcoming management shortcomings. Further, the manager can introduce processes of leadership that address the problems of employee shortcomings in lack of training or job disinterest.

Ideal and Controlled Standard Performance

The charts shown in Exhibit 21.3 may be used as a map to guide planning for those conditions that preclude ideal or controlled standard performance. They may also stimulate review of those conditions under which added cost in one circumstance could provide a benefit in another. Such a trade-off can either contribute to revenue or change costs beneficially.

The formula for budgeting successful operations is simple: revenue minus cost equals profits. Either increase revenues at the same cost level or lower costs to improve unit profits.

In considering capacity on a realistic basis, we should start by reviewing the activities that affect capacity in order to determine what ought to be and what can be planned for the budget period.

---

[12] Benjamin W. Niebel, *Motion and Time Study* (Homewood, IL: Richard D. Irwin, 1972), p. 5.

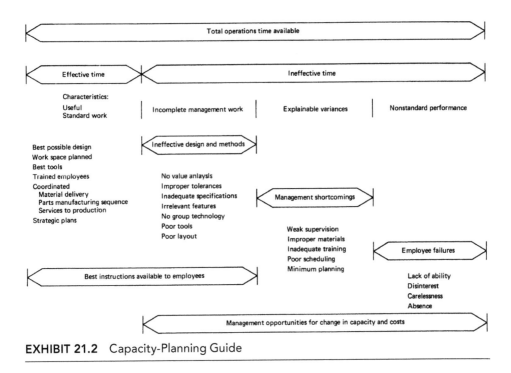

EXHIBIT 21.2   Capacity-Planning Guide

The graphs of lapsed-time utilization in Exhibit 21.3 show an example of changes in actual capacity created by a new capital tooling in a machinery builders' plant. The graphs also demonstrate the effect of current ineffective time used, as shown in Exhibit 21.2.

In considering a family of parts to be manufactured by a numeric-controlled (NC) lathe, a machinery company reported the current total time (Exhibit 21.3a). It became apparent that true comparisons of current methods with the new machine would be erroneous unless slack or ineffective time relative to management practices were removed in the comparison. Note the possible recovery from management actions without the new machine, a reduction from 644 minutes to 417 minutes, or 167 minutes. The new method contributes additional time and therefore more capacity, as shown in Exhibit 21.3c.

Reducing Ineffective Time

Most failures in budget performance come about because assumptions made during the budget-preparation process were not valid or clear. Very commonly, estimates of overall capacity will be faulty.

For such reasons, manufacturing managements are required to plan for support of efforts to reduce ineffective time. Methods of approach to the problem include value analysis, tolerance control, master scheduling (previously discussed), and employee training. These trade-offs add to costs temporarily but lead to major improvements in the amount of effective time spent. They are briefly described next. Each technique deserves additional study.

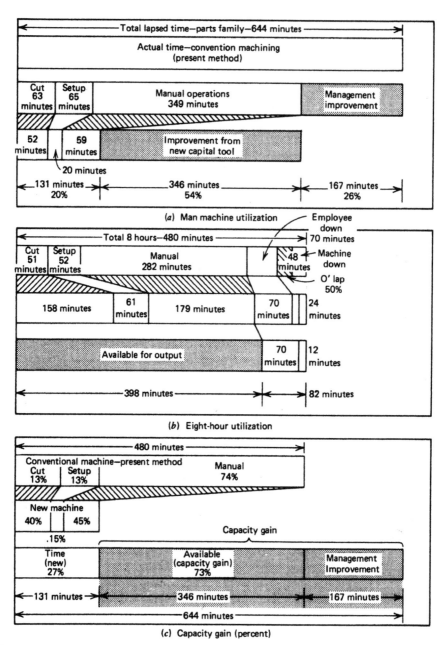

(a) Man machine utilization

(b) Eight-hour utilization

(c) Capacity gain (percent)

EXHIBIT 21.3 Lapsed-Time Utilization

Value Analysis Reduces Minimum Work Content

The impact on value analysis as a management-directed program to reduce standard materials or manufacturing time and/or programs to improve ineffective methods cannot be minimized in considering budget capacity and costs. A few comments here about each should sharpen budget planning in your operating group.

Value analysis and value engineering are important because the design of a product commits the productive system to specific processing methods. Therefore, the greatest opportunity for cost savings or impact on output capacity occurs during the initial design phase. Once the manufacturing process is under way, however, cost reductions may be possible through *redesign* or changes in the processing methods, selection of components, and materials. Value engineering and value analysis are useful techniques because engineering changes affect adaptations of materials (raw, in-process, and finished), manufacturing processes, time-phase plan, and operation sequence. All of these factors have broad economic impact and define in detail what is to be made.

Value Engineering Defined

Briefly, *value engineering* is the systematic identification of the function of a part or a product, the establishment of a value for that function, and the testing of it to ensure that the required function is provided at the lowest total alternative cost method. Its purpose is to make certain that every element of cost—such as labor, materials, supplies, styling, service, repair, and warranty—contribute proportionately to the function of the product. The fundamental objectives are (1) to provide better value in delivered products and (2) to improve the company's competitive position.

In practice, value engineering includes a series of trade-off decisions intended to improve the product for a given cost and to provide the same or better performance at lower cost without reducing quality or reliability. Value analysis and value engineering must be considered the most effective tools of management because they are planned, deliberate change. Arthur Spinanger, in "Increasing Profit through Deliberate Methods Change,"stated that deliberate change is quite different from cost improvement. Improvement techniques frequently resemble efficiency or budget-cutting strategies that encounter psychological resistance from management and labor alike. This is particularly true if the operation is well run and the improvements are difficult to achieve. However, the "How can the methods of work be changed?" approach is often much better received, and its advocates claim it has greater potential savings. This approach takes the next point of view:

- *Perfection is no barrier to change.* This implies that if further improvement to an existing work method is nearly impossible, there is probably a different and superior method that may be feasible.
- *Every dollar of cost should contribute its share of the profit.* Because each dollar that is invested in anything is done so with the idea of making a profit, the investment should not be made if it does not have this result.
- *The savings potential is the full existing cost.* This attitude does not consider any item of cost as necessary. An example is the procedure of using a liner in a carton to package shampoo. The liner was omitted first, and next the carton. The shampoo sold better unpackaged. In another example, a storage tank roof involved high maintenance costs, but on examination it was determined that neither evaporation into

the air nor dilution through rainfall significantly affected the tank's contents; thus there was no need for a roof, and it was eliminated.

Many value-engineering programs can be adapted to individual needs.

STEP 6: PUBLISHING THE MASTER SCHEDULE

The sixth and final step in the scenario that ends in a master schedule is to publish the end product. Subsequently, that involves measuring progress. In this phase, the work that went into the earlier steps reaches the payoff stage.

In the program thus far, you have reviewed a number of items and considered/made a number of changes. For example, you have:

- Made performance improvements in the shop
- Set forth significant changes in ineffective time spent
- Clarified product specifications and processes for quality/cost changes
- Considered value analysis opportunities
- Summarized the changes in "demonstrated capacity" forecasted by those changes

New schedules can now be planned to meet the forecasted customer demands as interpreted by the sales/marketing function. The materials supply function should assess, advise, and set up the master schedule as the categorical imperative for the whole economic enterprise.

If the estimate of the new "demonstrated capacity" is not equal to the needs as determined by the sales/marketing program, subcontracting or outright purchase of finished goods must be undertaken. The program, for alternative manufacturing sources, is not part of a manufacturing budget being discussed here.

The next question can be asked as your planned-action budget takes final form for publication to your managers: Do you really have a master schedule? If you can answer these subsidiary questions logically and sensibly, you are ready for publication of the planned-action budget:

- Are the short- and long-range objectives of the sales operations and of finance the same, and are the same criteria used for judging the performance of each in your division?
- On what criteria is each function judged?
- Can order and mutual interest be developed into a single master schedule?
- Do you know why a master schedule should be expressed in units?
- Is sales information required? What is the difference in need between actual and forecast sales information? What is the value of 10 percent improvement in forecast accuracy? Does it affect inventory? Does it affect working capital requirements?
- Do schedules for new and revised products affect the master schedules and therefore the revenue?
- Can you define explicitly by parts, lists, or bills of material the units in the master schedule?

- Do engineering changes alter the product defined in the master schedule?
- Do you have control of the changes, their quality, quantity, timing, and urgency?
- Do such changes affect actual product output? How?
- What is the real capacity of the plant? Can you track this with daily booking and shipping reports? (This is discussed later in the chapter.)
- Where do you get standard hour content for guidelines?

A TOTAL QUALITY PROGRAM—THE OTHER ALTERNATIVE

We have demonstrated the way in which the initial product concept (design) management can impact total cost before (frequently called "inept") manufacturing operations even start making the product. We have in most instances "designed in" or failed to manage the details of design, processes, and training that cause the costs before manufacturing takes over.

Deming said at the outset that 85 to 90 percent of the problems in quality were caused by management. In going through endless quality circle group programs, statistical quality control, and employee training exercises, we realize what it takes to correct that management problem. Management of each functional group must—at the start of manufacturing one, some, or all products—control the designs, processes, training of employees, purchases, and plan for quality of the end product at a part and detail level.

In thousands of daily forays into shop problems with incorrect materials, configuration conformity, or product performance, we find it was uncertainty, error, or lack of vision before the manufacture that were the roots of the quality problems being reviewed. This most significant array of costs can be planned out of the operation. That is what Deming means. A total quality control program produces those savings. They never appear in accounts because they are avoided by management.

Other areas for review in restructuring the ineffective time are tolerance control, process control, and quality specifications. These management alternatives all have concomitant costs that should be considered when preparing manufacturing budgets and outlining what ought to be.

In any manufacturing company, three separate groups are constantly concerned with the problems of determining the magnitude of the tolerances—in dimensions, appearance, or performance—and ultimately what is to be done about manufacturing situations in which the shop does not meet the prescribed specifications and/or tolerances. They are the product-design group, the manufacturing engineering group, and quality control. These three groups do not usually use the same techniques for analyzing tolerance relationships, for example, particularly product design and manufacturing engineering; when problems develop in which the three groups must join forces, communication is usually poor and bureaucracy and "turf protection" set in.

In considering mechanical tolerances, for example, managers argue over the correctness of tolerance buildup and calculation. If the calculations from one design engineer are fairly involved, it becomes almost impossible for that person to take another through the maze without losing contact if the second party is not familiar with this whole series of calculations.

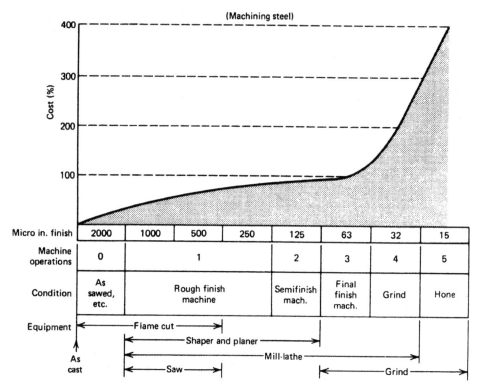

EXHIBIT 21.4   Relative Cost of Manufacturing Due to Tolerance: Machine Finish Tolerances

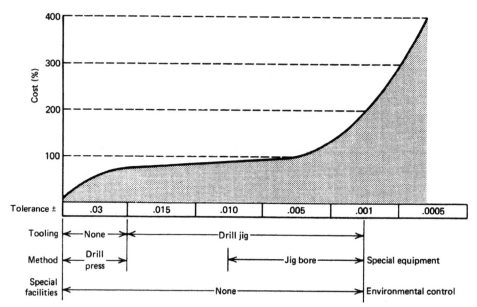

EXHIBIT 21.5   Relative Cost of Manufacturing Due to Tolerance: Hole-Location Tolerances

What is the problem? In this instance, the techniques of tolerance analysis constitute the problem. Therefore, a common language and communication skills must be developed if these three groups are to talk about tolerances and configurations.

There are well-developed systems for the consideration of mechanical tolerances. One such program was developed by Oliver R. Wade and is explained in a book called *Tolerance Control in Design and Manufacturing.* A second system was described in a section of the U.S.A. Standard Drafting Practices, *Dimensioning and Tolerancing for Engineering Drawings,* published by the American Society of Mechanical Engineers.[13] A third computerized program has been developed and is available from General Motors Production Engineering Center, Detroit, Michigan. This program provides optimum tolerance plans for each component involved in an assembly, thereby forecasting successful combination of fits.

When tolerances change, costs and capacity also change. The effect is demonstrated in Exhibits 21.4 and 21.5, prepared by Dorian Shanin of V. P. Rath and Strong, Boston, a noted authority in quality, and reliability.

It should be clear from the graphs in Exhibits 21.4 and 21.5 that unnecessary requirements build in total cost of greater magnitude in percentage than efficiency and employee attention can possibly recover for any given design.

All of the next 17 costs are associated with tighter-than-necessary specifications and tolerances that affect capacity and are not easily identified in allocated costs and charts and forecasts:

1. Better-than-necessary manufacturing equipment (higher capital cost)
2. Better-than-necessary tool tolerances (more frequent changes and setups)
3. Better-than-necessary gauges and/or test equipment (more initial cost)
4. Better-than-necessary gauge-checking equipment (higher capital cost)
5. More frequent calibration checking (lost time)
6. Shorter-than-possible tool life (more changes in setup)
7. More inspection planning than needed (more nonproduction time)
8. More frequent process-control checks (more nonproductive time)
9. More frequent process shutdowns (more nonproductive time-loss capacity)
10. More expensive components (higher-cost product as standard)
11. Larger sample sizes for product acceptance (more nonproductive labor)
12. Complete inspection in place of sampling (more nonproductive labor)
13. More internal scrap, rework, and extra processing
14. More material review time consumed (more nonproductive management time)
15. More corrective-action time consumed (more nonproductive management time)
16. More written corrective-action reports for customers (potential loss of sales)
17. More less-than-effective specification changes made (more confusion in future)

In considering making changes in manufacturing costs during budget preparation, one should review any recent major manufacturing losses attributable to quality

---

[13] *Dimensioning and Tolerancing for Engineering Drawings* (New York: American Society of Mechanical Engineers, 1980).

problems. Questions may arise. Is there a common ground of understanding between your design engineers and your manufacturing people? Do you understand how the absence of direction to accomplish uniform thinking in product design, manufacturing, and quality control could generate significant cost and/or delivery problems and surprises for you at some time in the future?

Cost Changes and Capacity Increase

Further opportunities for planning cost changes and capacity increases on a slightly longer-range basis rest in the instructions to product-design engineers and manufacturing engineers to develop multiple uses for the same part, or groups of parts with the same processes, which differ only in size. Have you given every opportunity to the development of parts grouping for maximum application of more productive tools and machinery?

"Group technology" is the term applied to planning for clusters of parts that are similar in configuration and that use the same general process flow. Frequently, opportunities may exist to arrange factories within factories for such groups of parts that increase machine and manpower utilization and that add capacity in output terms.

The heart of every problem for operations management is the number of items to be manufactured. The capacity of a plant for one part, one size, one shape, and one color is quite different if the same plant has to process 65,000 different parts with varying configurations. Capacity, then, is directly related to the breadth of the product line, which can be altered to some degree by operations managers by their directing product design into simplifications and by applying group technology.

Factory supervisors play a major role in capacity planning by the daily direction of the work force in job assignment. During budget planning, consider programs that improve their job instruction and assignment practices.

The setup or get-ready time required to make products in all factory processes is accompanied by lost time. There are probably records at your company that document the lost time that has occurred in the past. They should be reviewed to indicate how or to what extent the theoretical capacity was reduced by this non–value-added activity.

Ohno developed a program called "SMED" (single minute exchange die). Using the concept, American manufacturers have reduced setups by 75 percent. With current budgets at 25 to 30 percent of total direct labor in most companies, this is a real cost reducer. One hundred or more companies have reported to AME 70 to 90 percent reductions of set-up actual times.

In the production setup time, which is controlled by line managers, the items of lost time or ineffective time include:

▪ Maintenance/repair requirements that shut down machines
▪ Rework time spent on the productive machine because of either employee errors or engineering changes
▪ Cleanup operations to maintain the equipment
▪ Extra time caused by nonstandard methods, parts shortages, materials shortages, nonstandard materials, and so forth

- Experimental and developmental parts manufacturing
- Vendor error rework
- Training time for operator improvement

Capacity is reduced by all of the preceding items. However, even with perfect planning for every movement of material and with superb motivation of the workforce, you still should consider two basic pieces of data for capacity planning. First, although the employee has an attendance requirement of 1,900 to 2,000 hours per year, under the most favorable circumstances, he or she will produce not much more than 1,340 to 1,400 standard hours per year that can go into inventory because the employee is not expected to be, nor is he or she able to be, productive during that entire clock time. The reasons for such lost time will be discussed in a later section on determining direct labor costs.

Second, it is commonly agreed that machines can be loaded or expected to perform, or have an uptime, of not more than 90 percent. It is reasonable that 50 percent of the employee's downtime will not occur during the downtime of the machine in the same scheduled period.

Further, total capacity for shipments may be seriously limited by only one obscure process or machine. An intensive search must be made for such bottlenecks, in which additional equipment, a new machine, or a new plant may be the solution.

It might seem that all of these considerations for changing capacity through better management of existing plant and equipment are minor and subordinate to purchasing new capital equipment. The concern is not justified. Universally, opportunities exist for the application of existing modern machinery for increased output and for the further development of "undreamed-of" machinery. However, the capacity of each newly acquired machine is subject to the same reductions by poor management in actual output capacity, as has been outlined in the time chart and highlighted by the charted examples on the purchase of an NC lathe shown previously in lapsed-time utilization (Exhibit 21.3). The effective utilization of such capital acquisition still remains an operating problem that cannot be bought off.

Capital Tools

Capital budgeting is discussed in Chapter 25. These comments may help during budget planning when considering capital acquisitions.

Comprehensive analyses of productivity in the United States suggest that the correlation is highest between productivity figures and the level of capital tool investment. In America, the consideration of processes is synonymous in management's mind with productivity. Whereas the only current measure of productivity is person-hours per unit of output, we recognize that very few products are made entirely by the hands of workers. It is a combination of the workers' hands, their minds, their energy, the management of the employers, and the wise selection of tools or machinery that will reduce the man-hour content and improve productivity. Carl H. Madden, chief economist of the U.S. Chamber of Commerce, said that "people ought to know that productivity has less to do with working harder or longer than it has with working smarter." He continued:

Productivity comes from know-how. It's surprising enough that people don't know this. It's even more surprising that some government officials and business executives make productivity sound like a repressive campaign for law and order.

Direct labor is not the problem of productivity today. Poor specifications, unnecessary operations, and non–value-added tasks, all authorized or directed to workers to occur by management, subtract from true productivity.

The capacity of your plant or plants is limited only by the thoroughness of your investigation of these several opportunities for change and the development of programs to reduce ineffective time and improve the selection of capital equipment.

Frequently, special-purpose machinery or groups of machines that serve a majority of parts or products and their historical output level are not properly identified with regard to their effect on total output capacity in the plant. Activity-based accounting will greatly assist.

Capacity in Continuous Processes

The capacity of a continuous process may be affected at several points. The process-improvement opportunities chart shown in Exhibit 21.6 illustrates an imaginary composite process and suggests points in the process for control and/or cost change. These points also indicate where capacity is limited or could be altered for the budget's planned output.

Finally, it is also important in assessing capacity in either continuous or batch process to consider idle facilities that cannot be used for the sales level forecasted or that may be too costly to use in production. The continuing fixed costs for these facilities must be accounted for in budgets, while the capacity is not to be used in assessing capacity versus master schedule.

Incoming material	Primary process	Inspect	Secondary process	Inspect	Unitize	Package unit identify	Shipping package	Distribution
Control Quantity Contamination Losses	Control Input Handling Additional material	Measure	Control Correction Additional material Handling		Control Cut Fold Mold Cure Portion	Materials		First package Storage Shipping
Meter in	Ambiance Time Temperature Pressure Atmosphere		Ambiance Time Temperature Pressure Atmosphere					

EXHIBIT 21.6 Process-Improvement Opportunities

A special note: These expenses for idle plant facilities should never be included in overhead costs that are listed as inventory expense.

INVENTORY AND REPLENISHMENT

Two final, yet basically important, factors remain to be reviewed: inventory and replenishment. The two have elements in common, but they should not be confused. *Inventory* is normally considered as the level of raw, work-in-process, and finished goods, whereas *replenishment* is the scheme used to maintain that level.

Again, a series of questions represents the shortest road to determining the actual role of inventory and replenishment in your planned-action budget—and of course in its predecessor, the master schedule:

- Do you understand the *need* as opposed to the rationale for any given level of inventory as distinguished from a replenishment or maintenance of level program?
- Have you adopted MRP, or do you maintain a reorder point system? What manpower planning program do you use in relation to the master schedule? How have you directly related the machinery and equipment or plant capacity with the master schedule?
- Assuming that a computer is available, do you conceive reorder points systems as average requirements planning? Can adjustments in order-point levels change the availability for all parts in the list for assembly use?
- If economic order quantities are applied to reorder points, do shortages in assembly of all the different items improve? Why or why not?
- What is the product structure approach to establishing the discrete requirements for a master schedule?
- Does your inventory management program net out the requirements? The diagram shown in Exhibit 21.7 outlines this question.

In connection with Exhibit 21.7, two subquestions should be asked. The first is: What are the planning requirements for part number 1 from the diagram?

From demand for product A	2
From demand for assembly C	1
From demand for part 1	1

The second is: What are the inventory requirements for part number 1 from Exhibit 21.7? Review the differences between planning requirements and inventory requirements. Do your inventory control personnel distinguish between the planning requirements and the numbers they would have in inventory? Review your processes for netting out. The key to this technique is deciding units you really need to store as stock-keeping units. Those that you do not need as stock-keeping units are not required to be kept in inventory as both subassemblies and parts.

It may be sufficient to advise operations or manufacturing managers that there is currently a struggle in materials management about how to handle changes in

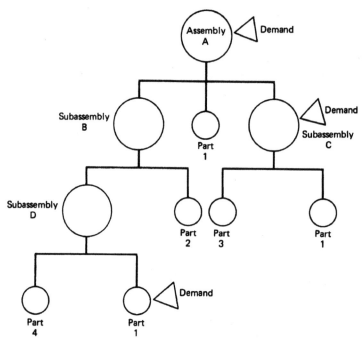

EXHIBIT 21.7 Product Structure Approach to Material Requirements

requirements. The reader would do well to investigate the two schools of thought regarding the handling of such changes. Briefly explained, there are two ways to handle changes in demand. One is to compute only the total net change in demand for parts or materials quantity. The earlier approach was to totally regenerate the new demand, using it as the requirement and abandoning the first forecast. Inventory planning is more immediately satisfied without interpretation when a net change system is used. Materials managers are primarily responsible for this, but in a frequently changing demand, inventory levels could rise faster with regeneration than with the net change program.

Some additional questions on inventory management, recognizing that orders to make parts change factory activity, are given next.

- Do product structure and discrete planning and scheduling require a structured bill of material (BOM)? Can your computer manipulate a BOM?
- What activities do engineering changes affect in your factory? Materials (raw, in process, and finished), manufacturing specifications, time-phase plan, operations sequence, direct labor performance, direct material usage—whose job is it to control the changes?
- Who knows most about the changes to complete the revision?
- Who should control the introduction of an accepted engineering change?
- Are changes up to date in your plant? How far do they lag behind the planning schedule?
- Do engineering changes affect inventory and replenishment?

- Have you identified the gross annual usage of the parts and classified them into A, B, and C for economic value? (There is a further classification for each part or material into 30-, 60-, and 90-days average process time required.)
- Must all items be replenished in your program or ordered for use on the same procedural basis? Why not?
- Who does the service parts planning and provisions?

Still other questions should be asked as you move toward publication of the budget. Some that can be used in considering the planned output level and the capacity to produce that level are given next.

- Do you have to expend "nonstandard" hours and activities to achieve the projected levels? This affects all overhead allocations, usually equivalent to 60 percent of total cost of goods sold.
- Are supplies of materials available at the projected levels? What effect will these requirements have on prices paid, or what is the cost impact?
- Where is the bottleneck in the output?
- Are there changes in capacity required for the budget level? Are they labor or capital tool intensive?
- Is the planned level of sufficiently long-range duration to invest in capital-intensive solutions to the problems?
- Can you list the five indirect cost changes most important in the achievement of the budget level of output?
- What is the situation in your plant regarding the expected production per direct labor worker and machine uptime?
- What is the interference factor between the two? Is it the same in each department and on each type of machine?
- What limitations are created by the levels of job skills in the work force? Have you identified these areas in your plant? When assemblymen or skilled persons in smaller special classifications are required, and training is long term or impossible, they could be computed to be capacity limitations, as are machines.
- In addition, can you inquire of your operating people if there are any special building facilities, such as pits, high-ceiling requirements, space, ventilation, and dust-free or environmental spaces, that have a maximum throughput capacity and therefore become limiting in any way? Have you identified these areas in your plant?
- Have you identified families of parts or specific parts whose volume has grown so large or so small that the original equipment or tooling is inappropriate?
- Have you identified specific parts for which a specific patented or special process has been developed that makes your process outmoded?
- Have you considered acquiring the new technology or abandoning the manufacture of your parts by your outmoded process to make that same capacity available for some other items?
- Have you identified the appropriate limits for more vertical integration in your processes?
- Have you identified the areas to reduce your vertical integration?

- What kinds of parts or processes could most economically be subcontracted to expand your plant capacity?
- Have you decided consciously to maintain your division as a cash cow?
- Does your 18-month capital-budget program provide an increase of capacity or simply a reduction in cost? Are you thereby reducing the operation rather than growing?
- What special organization skills are required for growth?
- Have you identified the single unit process change or the investment required to increase capacity?
- Have you ever considered a complete rearrangement and/or minor building modifications as solutions to your plant-capacity problems?

MORE ON THE MANUFACTURING BUDGET

The topics that remain to be discussed in this chapter are determining raw materials, determining other (indirect) materials, determining direct labor, and determining manufacturing overhead costs.

These topics imply that "what ought to be" in these areas can be defined with some assurance as predictable standard amounts of raw materials, other indirect materials, and direct-labor costs of conversion. The manufacturing overhead costs are a conglomeration of all the administrative activities that assist that conversion to shippable product. The principal questions in each of the four areas are how much is necessary, and how can that be decided?

DETERMINING RAW-MATERIAL REQUIREMENTS

Raw materials are defined herein as those materials acquired for conversion into the product. They could be finished goods, purchased for subsequent assembly, or materials used in vertically integrated manufacturing from refinement of minerals and ores into secondary fabrication and product sales.

The kinds of materials are those selected by the product-design engineer during the design or description of the product. He or she may also authorize substitutes at the time of design.

Manufacturing engineering should indicate the standard materials and their quality and should estimate the usable or sellable yield from the quantity of materials purchased. Every process has some loss in the conversion activity, either by chemical or physical change or by unavoidable production of unusable items.

In addition, during many processes, the unit of control may be changed from pounds to formed units. For example, billets are changed to skelp and then to cut and threaded pipe lengths. The factors used for such conversions in units of measure must be carefully selected to ensure that management has control. The addition of extra amounts of ground particles or fines of materials into mixtures may change the yield; if their inclusion is at all discretionary, then management is not setting proper raw-materials standards.

Historical records may be a clue to usage per unit; however, they should be reviewed to match current technology and process-control capabilities in order to issue valid standards.

The amount provided over the standard direct quantity used for each unit in the schedule is determined by the consumption quantity expected, the amount to cover the usage during the standard replenishment time, plus the safety stock, per policy. This quantity total should then be adjusted by two considerations: (1) forecast accuracy and (2) the commodity character of the materials and the company policy regarding its ownership and costing.

Let us review each of these items and their impact on the budget.

Forecast Accuracy

Most schedules call for a safety-stock base, which should preclude the inventory's reaching the zero balance available. Most managers think that this is all the safety stock that they have. They are frequently puzzled in trying to reconcile inventory turns with this level of safety stock.

Manufacturing companies, as differentiated from packers, distributors, and so on, have to time phase the receipt of raw materials to include queuing time for batch processing and for several levels of the process into assemblies, kits, or apparatuses.

Most items have some minimum process times. Frequently, subsection managers respond to exacting requirements for "on-time" completion by using inventories as a hedge, to avoid criticism. For example, purchasing has material arrive some time before actual requisitions, for withdrawal will show up vendor failures, and each successive factory operation will plan for their anticipated failures by requesting early delivery— "just to be sure." Their fudge factors in many different activities throughout the company create impossible scheduling plans, build in work-in-process time, and increase materials for that time period.

The inventory categories affected by policies that are set by managers but usually not evaluated as management-authorized investment levels include:

- *Finished goods.* Safety stock, cycle stock, "leveling" stock.
- *Assembly.* Work-in-process time.
- *Component or parts inventory.* Cycle stock (lot sizing).
- *Fabrication.* Work-in-process time.
- *Raw material.* Safety stock or time, cycle stock (lot sizing), commodity "leveling" stock.

Experiment with your own figures—compute 15 percent of the value of all those fudge factors just outlined. What percentage improvement in the forecast accuracy would eliminate some of these? What amount of your present inventory would it be?

The focus of such necessary and uncharted acquisitions of material are suggested in the next questions:

- Do you stock finished goods or assemble to order?
- Is there a distribution network that you supply and own?

- Do you have short or long assembly cycles? Are they timed?
- Have you identified the length of fabrication or machining or, in the case of food products, bacterial incubation waiting periods?
- What is your raw material and purchased parts stocking policy?
- Does the number of product lines change raw-material requirements?
- Is there a significant amount of spare part sales for which you inventory? Has the service level policy changed?

A target level for your inventory in all these areas should be set at the time of budget preparation, to ensure that anticipated direct and indirect costs of ownership are included.

Special Commodity Characteristics

The commodity characteristics of the materials you use and the policies that you have consciously or unknowingly authorized affect the levels of inventory, the production rates, and the indirect costs for those inventories.

You should first determine if the volume of materials that your firm uses is a significant factor in the supply–demand curve for that commodity. If you estimate that your demand affects the market, you must next decide if you are going to time the purchases to "even" the price fluctuation or not.

If you have sufficient volume, you could plan and maneuver your purchases to increase values on those materials you already own. If your quantities are not significant, you could select a policy to hedge against price increases. In some instances, doing this increases earnings on inventories as differentiated from standard-cost values used in budgets and pricing.

Manufacturing engineering sets standards for the production units, using master schedule requirements and prior usage experience as a basis. Purchasing responsibility is to set the standard prices to be paid in the budget period. Wise managers expect and budget for both price and usage variances from standard. At the conclusion of this chapter, a few ideas are advanced to assist manufacturing managers with the problems of variances from planned cost.

DETERMINING OTHER INDIRECT-MATERIAL COSTS

Indirect or other materials are the materials used and consumed during the manufacturing operations that do not become part of the product. They are also items that are difficult to identify with a specific unit of shipped product.

The chart of accounts furnished by your accountant or suggested in other sections of this book provides more specific definitions of the items.

The budgets for and the control of the usage of these items depend mostly on the exercise of judgment, based on historical consumption and specific control procedures.

These indirect costs are usually proportionally lower than other costs, although some materials are very expensive while others are uncontrolled in their use because of their lower value.

The surest way to tackle the level of total cost for this type item is to apply Pareto's law (80 percent of the expense is in 20 percent of the items).

Costs for all materials of this nature should be arranged in descending value based on an annual consumption and reviewed to find the closest association between the highest dollar items and some specific direct production process or operation.

The simulated continuous process shown in Exhibit 21.6 suggests areas in which control of indirect materials and labor could also be applied.

If some other materials are identified with specific parts of the process, the consumption allowance should be related to that specific activity. If this correlation cannot be made, the larger expenditures in this category should be identified by the manufacturing engineer for the process or by the industrial engineer in measuring and describing the employee's job and his or her performance.

In either the continuous-process operations or the employee-paced and managed tasks, the manufacturing engineering staff should set standards for usage of most other materials consumed and describe the limits of expected yield of the process.

Consumable tools in metal working and items, such as catalytic materials in a chemical process, may either be measured against units produced or be distributed by time period, for the total units produced in that time. Frequently, tools in the perishable class are a significant expense, which requires subclassification for suitable control. In planning for metal-cutting tools, the consumption pattern must be coordinated among tool engineers, quality-control personnel, and industrial engineers.

To explain, the metal-cutting tool is set in relation to a solid object to be cut. Its location is required to be accurate within a few thousandths of an inch. As the tool wears, the final dimension of the piece being cut would change. At the point at which such change would be in excess of allowable shape and size, the tool must be changed. Improved durability of that tool is the responsibility of the manufacturing engineer; quality control could predict, by statistical method, the optimum point in that process at which to change the tools for uniform parts manufacturing, and the industrial engineer will identify the additional amount of direct labor costs for the operations of making such regular changes. In this manner, trade-offs will occur throughout the manufacturing process between the initial costs of tools, the expected levels of quality, and the standard direct labor for employees.

Annual reviews of consumption patterns should suggest manufacturing research projects for improvement. However, elaborate controls that are more costly than the controllable or recoverable amount of the expense should be noticed and abandoned.

DETERMINING DIRECT-LABOR COSTS

Direct labor is defined as labor used directly in the conversion process.

Standard amounts of such labor for budgeting purposes are set by industrial engineers and can be one of the following:

- Historical amounts by part, by product, or by period, considered by the management as a suitable basis for future control and comparison

- Estimated engineered standards by part or by product from time standards data, such as motion time measurement (MTM) (Maynard), work factor (Wolfac), time measurement units (John Schwab), and average elements from internal time studies
- Explicit time studies setting the employee's performance by job, by part, or by product unit

If incentive wages are paid for "extra" performance, please remember that it is impossible to produce more than clock or calendar time allows. The incentive, or extra, performance occurs for only an identifiable portion of the total clock or calendar time. Capacity in the plant is frequently miscalculated because of the assumption that incentive performance will occur for all the calendar or clock time. It cannot be so sustained because of shortcomings of both managers and employees, as was discussed previously.

Considering the several allowances that are usually part of the employee relations policy in nonunion shops or the specific allowances for nonproduction time granted in most union contracts, the budget plan should estimate that the workers' outputs would be approximately 1,350 to 1,400 standard hours per year into inventory, as stated previously.

We have already observed that actual work of direct labor or production from a continuous process is reduced by planning for the minimum labor by designing the product or selecting the most efficient methods or tools and workplace layout that supports a well-trained employee.

Wishing or hoping for such ideal conditions to exist at the time of budget preparation cannot be translated into budgets showing lower costs, unless the specific plans that change current practices are implemented.

We have indicated that budget time is when the most experimental or new, unfettered thinking can take place. The various experiences of your own staff and their bias in favor of one or another approach to defining this standard and fundamental unit of cost can be best resolved by exploration, learning, and conferring to find the highest level of mutual interest in one approach. There are as many good programs as there are good managers.

In the discussion of capacity, the chart on effective and ineffective time shown in Exhibit 21.2 showed good and useful or standard production time spent by the work force, along with its characteristics. The characteristics of ineffective time spent were also shown.

Aside from the potential for lowered planned costs through the redesign of the product, we all look toward the performance of employees in the system. The desirability of their being motivated to be attentive and efficient, and the techniques to achieve such a climate in your company, are for other authors to discuss. However, there are many popular ideas currently in use. They include incentive wage payment plans and profit-sharing schemes; zero defect programs and quality circles for peer pressure; and suggestion systems, which have minor success.

Daniel Yankelovich, president of a well-known public opinion research firm, says in *Industry Week* that traditional incentives are not well matched to today's workforce.[14]

---

[14] Daniel Yankelovich, *Industry Week*, August 6, 1979, p. 1*ff.*

He finds that fear, money, work organizations, and reliance on work ethic are being blunted as tools of management and are less effective today. He explains that these are to be replaced (on a trend basis, it appears) by flex-time schedules, health improvement, educational opportunities, and other amenities. The forecast he makes is for developing a sort of cafeteria concept of incentives that provide programs tailored for each individual.

To provide a basis for proceeding to establish direct-labor standards, I provide a series of questions that touch on most of the major points on work measurement. I recommend that you proceed by planning a series of meetings, well in advance of budget planning time, to begin the dialogues and select a program that meets the capabilities of your personnel and company circumstance.

The questions are those that the reader can ask his or her staff. They will reveal the depths of understanding of the subject and the new knowledge required to establish a program to be used as a basis of a budget. The effect of teams, usually synergistic, is not measurable (specific) at this time.

Getting Realism into Direct-Labor Work Standards

- Do you use machine-operating hours or person-hours as a standard? Which control is most important? Which control produces the most improved cost?
- Do you consider standards absolute? How much variation is expected? What kinds of variation are predictable and therefore explainable?
- Are current standards for performance *attainable* in either machine hours or person-hours in your company?
- Do you recognize that maximum time available for useful work is clock time and/ or calendar time minus the established nonproductive periods, such as holidays, nonoperating shifts, lunch periods, and specific contracted employee release time?
- What is the maximum uptime for standards expected in your operations?

Measurement

- How do you establish a physical effort for work-standards purposes? What are rating films? What is the objective of time study?
- If you do time study, how does it compare with MTM or work-factor time values? Do the many studies provide equity from job to job?
- What is an adjusted time-study time? Why omit high and low observations?
- What are allowances for personal time and fatigue? Should they be used?
- Is there a difference between work-measurement and incentive-payment plans?
- Is measured day work a superior management tool?
- Is measurement improper if incentive plans are not used?

Wage Incentives

- Are there actual jobs available in your plant in which the additional physical effort that is possible for a person, without injury to his or her health, can make a contribution in the output level?

- Can these operations be carefully identified, and are they consistent enough that they may be measured and wage payment bonus be paid in a meaningful way for increased output?
- Have you examined the places in which individual performance plans cannot be set up or group plans may be applicable? Is the incentive to be paid only for increased pace in highly repetitive direct-labor operations, or do you intend to pay it for improved performance in other indirect output such as quality, reduced waste, reduced machine downtime, and so forth?
- Is the financial incentive an indirect incentive applied on a company-wide or plant-wide basis, or is it directly related to that small group of employees? If such an opportunity exists, can it be monitored and maintained so that, if changes in the work content occur, the program can change?
- Does an incentive-payment plan maintain a sustained physical output for several years?
- Do incentive programs contain restrictions on management?
- Do hourly incentive-payment plans contain seeds of mistrust between employers and employees?
- What are elements of the total cost of an incentive-payment plan for hourly employees? Do they include excess tool consumption, extra quality costs for policing, costs of lower-quality output, excess machine-maintenance costs, extra expense tool cost, inventory write-offs due to improper counts, shop clerical personnel, additional time-standards personnel, extra record costs related to information-systems requirements, loss of absentee control, and loss of employee interest in interpersonal relationships with the members of management and technical staff?

ESTABLISHING THE MANUFACTURING OVERHEAD FUNCTIONS AND SERVICES

Having determined from the master schedule the operating range of various processes in your company, and having considered the programs affecting the effective and ineffective time used, it is necessary to relate the fixed, variable, and other incremental costs associated with the product. We review here the definition of fixed, or burden, costs, along with some other terminology.

Definitions

Variable Costs

Variable costs are production and distribution costs required to place an additional unit of product in the hands of the customer. These include all costs that vary in direct proportion to sales volume—for example, direct labor and material.

Most manufacturing managers do not understand allocated costs (overhead distribution), in order to glean information about changes occurring: how, where, why? Activity-based accounting was developed because current accounting methods do not relate a cost to the reason or locus of the occurrence. You must understand it now to use and adapt the new way successfully.

Fixed Costs

Period costs are those costs incurred as a function of time rather than volume—for example, administrative salaries.

Programmed costs are those incurred as a result of specific decisions, without direct relation to either sales volume or the passage of time. Examples include research and development expenditures, advertising, and the company picnic.

Normal burden rate denotes an average or expected burden rate that is determined in a number of ways. The method is predominant in industry today. It provides for a consistent application of manufacturing burden to the inventory. The rate is based on studies that are made periodically by accounting and manufacturing personnel. It can be based on history and judgment if the historic capacity method is used, or it can result from a more scientific analysis from an industrial engineering study outlining the practical capacity.

The use of the normal rate has the effect of leveling the peaks and valleys of spending and production volume. As such, it is the most acceptable means of arriving at a proper inventory valuation and hence the estimated profits from month to month. Usually it permits a more prompt method of preparing financial statements and is the most inexpensive clerical method to use.

Unabsorbed burden denotes the difference between the amount of manufacturing expense carried to inventory with product manufactured in the period (by use of normal burden rates) and the actual amount spent for manufacturing expenses during that same period. Unabsorbed burden may consist of *underabsorbed burden* if production is below normal expectations in the period or of *overabsorbed burden* if production into inventory is greater than expectations used as a basis for "normal."

Underabsorbed burden occurs when the actual amount of manufacturing burden expense is in excess of the amount carried to inventory by the normal burden rates. This generally occurs when:

- A company experiences considerable fluctuation during a year in its production because of seasonal variations in product demand.
- Unusual expenses are incurred that were not anticipated when normal burden rates were established.
- A manufacturing plant is geared to produce much more than the sales demand.
- Even in instances where the production level is equal, differences in spending will fluctuate. This, in turn, will distort the inventory valuation and produce entirely unacceptable valuations.
- No provisions are made for the expensing of unused plant capacity during low productive periods. Instead, these costs are carried to inventory by means of overstated manufacturing burden rates. This is not accepted accounting practice, nor is it economically sound. Profits are considerably distorted (overstated), and both potential and active investors are misled.

Levels of Overhead

The levels of overhead that should be budgeted are the most significant part of costs. The levels of these costs on the budget are the most direct reflection of the experience, expectations, and "style" of top management. They are all nontechnical and nonscientific management terms. This is because the levels of these costs are influenced the most by a series of value judgments made by the managers about the level of services the direct conversion activity requires to optimize its performance.

A review was made of the functional basis for costs in many companies relating to the price paid by the consumer for the product. It is shown in Exhibit 21.8. These data were collected by interview and participation in 50 company-management programs and were extrapolated from published statements of an equal or greater number.

If your technical staff has been effective, the 10 percent standard direct labor represents the probable minimum conversion labor content for present products and/or processes in hours. (This has been converted into dollars for budget purposes.)

Since the owners have invested capital, they are certainly entitled to some rent on their money (profit). As these two elements are each approximately 10 percent, the remaining 80 percent of costs are incurred as a result of decisions about how operations people run the company.

Examples of typical questions frequently asked about these functional cost areas are provided next.

- What product design review has taken place to reflect the cost benefit of each element of the product or the features offered to the customers?
- What are we doing to be assured that we are using the most effective tools and methods?
- What new beneficially planned quality and maintenance programs are in process of installation?

In answering these questions, managers create and mandate the cost levels. Therefore, they can do away with costs just as easily, recognizing that the costs are a

EXHIBIT 21.8   Concept of Managed Costs (from Approximately 100 Corporate Statements)

	Average Grocery and Household Products	Average Fork Truck Manufacturing	Estimated Drugs
Director labor[a]	$0.09	$0.10	$0.09
Direct material[a]	0.25	0.30	0.3175
Plant overhead expense[a]	0.25	0.30	
Work cost and distribution[a]	$0.59	$0.70	$0.4025
Selling expense			
General expense	$0.26	$0.21	$0.4225
Administrative			
Subtotal	$0.90	$0.91	$0.825
Taxes and profit	$0.10	$0.09	$0.175
	$1.00	$1.00	$1.00

[a.] Per sales dollar.

result of their style of management and determining what they want to control and how.

As the process starts, it must be realized that there should also be a continuity of the top management objective all the way down to the bottom. Integrity is required at every level, because the fudging and hedging that normally alter those top management objectives expressed on the way down reduce the credibility of the budget as a real management working plan. Each manager, without control, includes some protection against the "real" expectation, and such actions dilute the realism of subsequent performance reports. It is important, therefore, to start from the right point in order to plan for and achieve better levels of cost.

All overhead of staff departments is based on the workload or volume of items the departments expect to handle. This workload is usually related to the current levels, altered by indications that the future is up or down. This is a sound rationalization, but the planned work expands as the specialization's technology grows.

The manufacturing manager's principal objective to meet or achieve planned costs places the responsibility to forestall such proliferation on his or her own shoulders. These specialists would have a lower workload if the number of items they handle were reduced. A corrective goal for manufacturing managers and their staffs therefore is to simplify the number and variety of items to consider, thereby reducing the number of overhead transactions required per sales dollar.

Maintenance of fixed assets, long-range contracts, capital borrowings, and so forth preclude an opportunity to start over from ground zero. I am reminded of earlier training in planning fixed and semivariable expenses, which had been overlooked in decisions to expand at all costs and/or raise prices to cover inflationary costs.

A suggested approach is simply to recognize that your company's future could be very seriously upset by a variety of random events. Assume, therefore, what some dire circumstance might be; for example, a process failure upsets a whole product line's sales, a prolonged labor dispute occurs, or an interruption in the supplies of vital materials. Assume that the extent of that major interruption in revenue will require a six-month shutdown, with an expectation of the resumption of minimum production at the end of six to eight months. Since some kinds of contracted and fixed expenses would continue, identify them. What basic management activities and operations or maintenance programs would have to be continued?

Obviously, such a dramatic change would forecast for some managers that the company would cease to exist, but with reasonably good management, it should not be so. (If the purpose of your enterprise is perpetual, as provided for in its charter, is the management less capable in its own life span?)

In this exercise, wisdom dictates that managers faced with planning would be able to proceed without prejudice in four major steps:

1. Identify those continuing, fixed, and sunk costs for taxes, insurance, depreciation, maintenance of assets, and so forth.
2. Identify incremental expenses required and timing for the first or minimum unit(s) of output.

3. Plan the direct-cost elements—materials and conversion labor.
4. Determine when and how many additional units of output would require additional management support and overhead costs. It would be well here to try to determine the sensitivity of production rates to various overhead activities or programs.

Inquisitive managers engaging in this process probably now perceive the emergence of management style and sense levels of costs associated with that style—the things they feel they would want to do or are now doing.

The most graphic example of such a complicated concept of style may be seen in the costs of having five daily reports containing information that is considered basic to all operating managers. The example indicates the information required and the ways to get it. The five reports are listed next.

1. Manufacturing managers must know the demand for their output related to their current active production. This is usually available from a daily booking and shipping report, which shows the value of orders received and the value of orders shipped. It usually includes a running total, showing a sales and shipments balance due or indicating backlog that is growing or diminishing. This tells manufacturing managers that they are running ahead or behind the current demand.
2. The operating manager usually has some force report or personnel report showing the direct labor or indicating that the workforce is present and equal to, greater than, or less than the requirements of the order board.
3. Daily production usually posts actual output to the schedule. Note: Two kinds of interruption affect production after the proper number of people are present: machine breakdown and quality problems.
4. A maintenance report of production equipment should be available every morning, showing the continuing, chronic production-equipment problems not yet solved and any new, acute, or unusual equipment failure in the past 24 hours.
5. Quality failures in production are usually reported to satisfy accounting procedures, but manufacturing managers should also know daily the continuing chronic failures of materials and parts or production operations and any acute failures that reduced production in the last 24 hours.

These five reports are basic operations management information. These reports can be compiled on a daily basis, even in a larger plant, from telephone calls to a secretary or clerk. Yet they can consist of thousands of details manipulated by the most extensive computers with concomitant costs incurred in all of these areas:

▪ Computer rental
▪ Data collection (leased wire, if any)
▪ Data-processing personnel
▪ Program rental costs
▪ Program personnel
▪ Program maintenance
▪ Direct labor reporting collection time allowed or consumed

- Indirect labor reporting collection time allowed or consumed
- Timekeepers
- Production-control information programs
- Scheduling and dispatching time used for information and work-in-process reporting
- Administration analysis time
- Report-preparation time
- Printing and paper costs

Computer costs are soaring in most companies, along with administrative costs that are incurred indirectly in support of computer uses. The next questions can be used as guides in your discussion to determine the appropriate levels for the direct associated costs and those administrative cost elements indirectly associated with your management style.

- Do you know the total management information cost per dollar of sales? Note: Since the information requirements determine the administrative transactions, does the information available have a potential recovery greater than the cost to get it?
- Could you establish what would be a desirable level of per sales dollar for information cost? For how much of this information requirement are government regulations responsible?
- Is the preparation of that information organized for your own administrative and control use?
- Since most budgets start with a sales figure or are related to dollars of revenue, what items of cost are hidden in the change from gross to net sales? Is this discounting of the sales value of goods produced budgeted?
- Do you maintain control reports on the elements of this discounting of gross sales, which include warranty, replacement, service, and sales policy adjustment of factory losses, errors, and defects? What is the percentage of gross sales?

These items are examples of the kinds of costs incurred as a result of management style and of several directives issued to the manufacturing staff, which incur cost because "the boss says he needs this." The vast distance from minimum production in earlier times to present levels in most companies has allowed for these costs of style to become permanent costs in planning budgets.

In proposing a budget of revenue and cost, the presentation fosters the assumption that all of the expenses listed are in appropriate balance. The presentation also represents hundreds of decisions that have been made by the operations managers about the efficacy of existing or authorized personnel programs, relationships, and output plans. (They are therefore minimum levels of expected cost, although they appear to be upper limits.)

Without an edict to start from scratch in implementing zero-based budgeting programs or without the understanding that the manufacturing budget is presenting a suitable total program with its parts having been tested against this total production requirement with all costs at their developed minimum level, we are simply setting up a series of traffic lights, advising stop, caution, or go for various existing activities. Under these circumstances, we have not presented a plan for optimum long- and short-range operating results.

Manufacturing Research

There are many times and circumstances when good planning and forecasting cannot be done with the information available. New knowledge and an understanding of new, untried techniques or machinery are frequently necessary to improve the quality of planning. For these reasons, manufacturing research is every bit as valuable to a company as research for a new product. It is urged that manufacturing managers support at least one manufacturing research project in each budget year.

Review Questions for Overhead Budgets

The next questions are included to guide the reader in conferring with functional heads of industrial engineering, quality control, plant engineering, and production control in developing the new action plans for change that will point the way to lowered levels of expected cost:

- Have you established work simplification as a technique in your industrial engineering programs?
- Does the industrial engineering department maintain a running record of the net effect of standards changes versus or related to the current year's master schedules of parts requirements?
- What is the three-year trend of your products' standard hour content?
- Do you receive quarterly reports? Does the industrial engineering department furnish cost–benefit summaries of their operations?
- Does the industrial engineering department use a total cost concept, including indirect labor, scrap, lost time, and so forth, in developing methods and establishing standards?
- Does the industrial engineer participate in the consideration of new parts or product designs and engineering changes? Are they supported in making suggestions to change the design?
- Does the industrial engineering department regularly engage in the control of tolerances for manufacturing and engineering?
- Does the industrial engineering department ensure that tolerances in "form" are used for flatness, roundness, straightness, and so forth, as defined in the terms of the American National Standards Institute Standards?
- Does the industrial engineer propagate the selection of the most economical tolerance plans with design engineering?
- Has the industrial engineering department eliminated unnecessary extra paperwork by using standard operating descriptions in preparing routines for manufacture of similar parts?
- Are the industrial engineers aware of working capital requirements being established when they select an economic lot size for setup purposes?

- Is the lot size determination more appropriate if done by materials control and scheduling? Does the industrial engineering department conceive its job as being one of the economists for the company?
- Do industrial engineers participate in the quality-control planning of the parts manufacture? Do they understand the full implication of cost for quality-control activities, or has the professionalism of quality control superseded real economic considerations?
- Do the industrial engineers constantly review what place layouts are needed to maintain motion-efficient and safe conditions?
- Do industrial engineers consider the time and cost implications of working safely, or is there a conflict of interest between prescribed methods and employee welfare for the benefit of the lowest standard time?
- Does the incentive payment plan work at cross-purposes with employee safety?
- Has the industrial engineering department developed clear job descriptions that outline the specific skill requirements for each job?
- Have they provided training outlines to enable the personnel in shop departments to train employees in the specific skills that they have allocated?
- Is there a tendency to create too many classifications? How frequently do you use "all-around" machinists' classifications or "all-around" assembly people? Have you considered the advantages that fewer classifications can bring? Is there a significant cost savings in having many job descriptions, or does this tend to limit assignments, increase conflict, and encumber promotions, transfers, and development of employees?
- Do industrial engineering personnel get opportunities to become shop supervisors and managers?
- Do industrial engineers participate in variance analysis and in regular operations meetings?
- Do industrial engineering standards provide adequate programs for machine maintenance? Has the maintenance department been advised of the requirements in standards for service to machinery and equipment? Does this affect capacity?
- Has the industrial engineering department identified all routine maintenance jobs and established work measurement data for the elements of those routine maintenance jobs, along with the elements of the work in both routine and special repair work?
- Have the chronic variances been identified and basic process changes planned to avoid them?

QUALITY CONTROL ECONOMICS REVIEW QUESTIONS

Quality control enters the productive system at levels in every function—at the executive level in determining what the product-line general configuration and quality should be; at the operating level in ensuring product conformance to specifications; and at the customer-contact level in quality assurance, so that they get what they thought they were buying.

Perhaps you should ask yourself these questions: Is the quality level of the product accurately evoking the desired corporate image? Are the existing products consistent with the long-range plans and with research? Have you recently decided, as a high-cost manufacturer, to enter a low-cost, competitive quality market with another product? Has this had any impact on your company's reputation? Has it changed the customers who have been buying the higher-quality products from you? Has the reverse been true? Have you been a manufacturer of lower-quality competitive goods, moving into a high-quality prestige market? Have you programmed the market learning trend in this change in your image? Have you established the right atmosphere for quality?

You should recognize that these items can affect attitudes of the employees regarding quality:

- Are your restrooms and locker rooms clean, well lighted, well painted, and equipped with soap, towels, and so forth, or are they dirty and poorly lit and badly in need of painting?
- Is your shop area clean, well lighted, painted and neat, with an orderly flow of material, or do you permit a dirty shop, poor lighting, and confusion in material flow? Is your maintenance of equipment excellent, average, or nonexistent?
- Are your drawings clear and concise, well dimensioned, and most usually not the cause for quality problems, or are they vague, poorly dimensioned, incomplete in detail, and frequently the cause for quality problems? Do your quality and inspection personnel have final approval? Are they respected, well paid, and adequate, or do they have virtually no say, are poorly trained, or are practically nonexistent? Are the next work elements part of your total quality control system?
- Do you have a plan and administration program for the total quality control system?
- Do you appraise the total quality control system to relate its adequacy to the customer's reliability needs?
- Are the quality data available and sufficient to be included in bid proposals?
- Have you compared the implied customer reliability and quality requirements with the available physical program and with your product?
- Have you considered reliability?
- Have you established appearance standards by both quantitative and qualitative means?
- Have you determined in your industrial engineering measurement programs the location of quality changes, the kind and amount of change possible, procedures to be followed, characteristics to be measured, equipment to be used, and forms and records to be kept?
- Have you planned for testing of your product performance?
- Do you have any program for the design of measurement or test equipment?
- Do you have a program for maintaining the calibration of inspection in test equipment?
- Do you train inspection and test personnel?
- Do you distribute quality information to vendors and subcontractors?
- Do you inspect incoming and subcontracted material?
- Do you conduct vendor evaluation?

▪ Do you frequently instruct workers to use questionable material or frequently require that the shop remanufacture products from the outside from subcontractors?

In summary, does your environment indicate that you are really interested in quality or that it is a temporary campaign program, not worthy of long-range intentions?

PLANT ENGINEERING BUILDINGS AND EQUIPMENT MAINTENANCE REVIEW QUESTIONS

A further way to improve cost performance is to improve the maintenance function. Maintenance has historically been viewed as low-level work, trailing most other operating functions in importance—a necessary evil to be tolerated. This downgrading is unfortunate, since the maintenance function, if properly run, can greatly enhance the operation of the production system. Nevertheless, an efficient maintenance operation is the exception rather than the rule. As a result, maintenance problems abound.

These questions indicate symptoms of maintenance neglect:

▪ Do you have excessive machine breakdowns?
▪ Do you have frequent emergency work?
▪ Is there a domination of the maintenance operations by production personnel?
▪ Is there a lack of equipment-replacement programs?
▪ Is there sufficient spare equipment for sensitive operations?
▪ Do you have sufficient preventive maintenance outlined?
▪ Do you have a planned selection for maintenance supervisors and managers, and have you maintained training courses necessary to keep them at a level commensurate with the skill requirements of new machinery and equipment that you have been purchasing?
▪ Are there regular training programs for personnel going into the maintenance department? Are they as adequate as those for personnel going into the production operation?
▪ Does the maintenance department have appropriate shop facilities in which to complete its work?
▪ Do you recognize that there is an opportunity for reducing unnecessary work through preventive action, better methods, and improved tools in maintenance?
▪ Have you any correlation, recently developed, that gives you an indication of the labor productivity changes when better planning, scheduling, and performance evaluation of maintenance programs occurs?
▪ Have you drawn any correlation recently between excess costs, such as overtime, machine downtime, and materials and supplies wasted, and poor maintenance of machinery and equipment?
▪ Have you ever received a report that an operator's performance or an industrial engineering standard will have an impact on the continued good operation of the machine? Have you ever noted or been asked to referee any conflict between a

method or tooling job sequence outline and the plant engineer because of its impact on the machinery and equipment?

▪ Have you ever considered the probabilities of component breakdown in any of your machines based on your maintenance records so that you could establish a preventive maintenance program?

FLOOR AND WORK-IN-PROCESS CONTROL REVIEW QUESTIONS

These measures of scheduling performance on the shop floor should be checked:

▪ Has the mean production order completion rate been improving?
▪ Has the average number of days a job is finished behind schedule increased or decreased?
▪ Has the percentage utilization of men and machines increased or decreased in recent history?
▪ Have the characteristics of the process waiting or queuing increased? Do you know what caused them?

Improvements in the scheduling system would be reflected in any or all of these measures:

▪ How many jobs, shop orders, or work orders are in the shop now?
▪ How many do you finish per day, per week, per month, by department?
▪ Does any product part require more than 30 days of continuous actual manufacturing time?
▪ Why should a product be in manufacturing in the shop for longer than three months?
▪ Do you believe that less work and process on the floor improves efficiency more than a complicated scheduling apparatus?
▪ When dispatching work in the shop, is it related to specific demand for scheduled periods? Could materials requirement planning help?
▪ Why not use a time period and level of part in the BOM as the schedule priority and thus eliminate factory dates, complicated schemes, and so forth?
▪ How would a plant-within-a-plant help improve scheduling?[15]
▪ What is short-interval scheduling? How can it help in a job shop? What is the proper application? (As a scheduling approach, it is severe but has some benefit. As a cost reducer, its effect is temporary [6 to 12 months] and disastrous to morale. Study long-range effects carefully.)
▪ What are all of the transactions required to get a part order? These activities cause work in the production-control department. You, as a manager, can affect the volume by managing other areas.

---

[15] See Wickham Skinner, "The Focused Factory," *Harvard Business Review* (May–June 1974): 113–121.

In measuring performance as suggested in the preceding questions, the results could be summarized with these questions:

- Have the trends minimized inventories in all classes?
- Has factory utilization actually increased?
- Have we accomplished more uptime for machines?
- Have we more standard hours per direct-labor worker per year?
- Has customer service really improved? How?
- Is direct-labor performance stable, or do we have many production crises?
- Do we have high performance against standard costs?
- What percentage variance do we have to costs—not to direct labor?
- Is it easy to change schedules to accommodate customer requirements, engineering changes, and so forth, or is it difficult?
- Do we have control of our standard methods?
- Do inventory levels provide response to customers' delivery requirements?
- Have backlogs grown? What is our prediction ability? *Note:* You are in trouble when the actual total inventory exceeds the target by more than 15 percent, when A items are over the target at all, and when B items are more than 10 percent over the target.

You are in trouble when the percentage of the parts delivered to the shop for assembly have more than a 7 to 8 percent shortage. You are in trouble when any percentage of short list items is a surprise. You are in double trouble when surprises are the direct responsibility of production control and inventory control. You are in trouble when scheduled changes are more than a minor inconvenience for shortages of parts and materials.

You are in trouble when you cannot identify a problem as an A, B, or C part and cannot correct the chronic poor supply performance. You are in trouble when the obsolete inventory is greater than one-tenth of 1 percent of the total. You are in trouble when credit balances appear on the inventory records. You are in trouble when you have not identified decontrol items and have used the three-bin system plan.

It should be noted that many decisions in material and inventory control affect various standard performance indexes and measures. Do you know which ones they are? Are you satisfied with the decisions and the methods in making the decisions?

SUMMARY

This discourse has suggested the early, middle, and final steps in considering what costs should be in preparing a planned action budget. Any form for the budget that satisfies the user and is capable of reporting progress is acceptable.

When the manager has outlined programs and has investigated their expected change in various cost, planned revenue, and inventory accounts, there is the final reality that variances from that plan will occur. They will occur both in prices paid above standard and in labor, materials, and supplies used in achieving the budget shipments.

The major elements of the planned-action budget presented are not new when considered individually, since many techniques discussed have been used for years. The key impact will come from the simultaneous consideration by all operating sections of the company and their probable combined effect on the company statements.

The budget must contain these elements in order to monitor or report variances from the plan:

- Proper cost standards and flexible budget system construction, so that manufacturing line supervisors will be able to understand the expectation and the actual variance. (It should include necessary operating formulas as well as written definitions required for understanding.)
- Placement of each variance in an appropriate group according to type or technical category that is understood by the manufacturing management group.
- Variance and account codes related directly to the proper organizational function or unit that is accountable for the results, in line with the concepts of the basic organizational structure of the company.

James Wall, consultant, Union Special Machine Company, discussed variance reporting in this way:

> Cost variances relating to standard cost and flexible budget systems can be separated and reported in four groups so that they will be more understandable to supervision and top management: processing product, conversion costs, price of material, and cost adjustment. Variances so grouped can be generally described as follows:
>
> - *Processing product.* This group is concerned with the yield, gains, and losses resulting directly from processing products through in-process inventory in the various forms of product, at standard unit value and eventually at standard cost value. This group is sometimes called *operating variances.*
> - *Conversion costs.* This group, composed of producers' (direct) labor and all other manufacturing overhead, is concerned with those variations which result in gains or losses from standard conversion cost and should never enter inventory but are written off currently or in line with existing accounting practices.
> - *Price material.* This group is concerned with the price variation resulting from the comparison of actual to standard prices for raw and related materials, purchased parts, etc.
> - *Cost adjustments.* This group is concerned with those variations which are the result of management policy or accounting decisions and, for the most part, are not the result of operations.
>
> For purposes of definition and for assignment of accountability to management, the first two groups of variances are the result of plant operations and can be related to the processing of products and the general activity of production. The last two groups are the responsibility of functional and top management, rather than plant operations.

The pyramid principle of reporting requires the following:

- Reporting of costs to the level of management that is responsible for cost control and is accountable for taking management action to either improve costs or maintain a continuing performance level.
- The condensing of operation information so that only essential data are presented to each higher level of management (in line with the former organization structure).
- Issuance of one series of control reports for each level of management; additional copies may be provided to others for information purposes, but only one should be directed to each level for purposes of control.

Planned-action budgets are merely management tools and not *management* itself. A successful plan for control of operations requires certain actions and support by management. This means describing what performance ought to be, supporting changes, and providing the proper "climate" for improvement in the continuous struggle to achieve a reasonable level of proficiency.

This is not an impossible task, but one-shot programs and constant directions for erratic short-term changes tend to undermine effective operating control. Continuous improvement is required to compete.

A program of intense study has been recommended for determining what your plant is now doing in order to measure the distance it must move to achieve what ought to be. The effort may appear to be too much for preparation of a budget. The justification for such a complete analysis rests in the disappearing margins of profitability and the growing shortage of internally generated capital for the rejuvenation of our aging manufacturing plants.

It has always been surprising, however, to realize that most companies faced with actual losses can find the organization, energy, and reasons to suddenly take the steps to change from loss to profit. The same opportunities have been available during all of the declining margin years.

The attitudes of the manager have changed. That is all it takes—a real dissatisfaction with things as they are and a willingness to regroup, to question openly what is going on, and to tackle the problem. Such programs usually contain the same elements of review inherent in the planned-action budget approach that has been outlined. I have used these programs in several companies with success, as indicated at the beginning of this chapter. Without use of such programs, margins will continue to decline or prices will be raised to cover these management-created costs.

Finally, when considering new plans, new products, and new approaches, we frequently gamble on the person who is doing the job. We cannot rely solely on statistics, which may be against a proposal, nor can we use them only in defense of the status quo. We put our reputations on the block in committing to proceed with a plan that we have recommended. When we have done a good job of planning and forecasting, we want the boss to take our word. The final test for you now is, was your plan that well prepared? Did it have the winning combination for competition?

CHAPTER TWENTY-TWO

Research and Development Budget

Maurice I. Zeldman

Emzee Associates

RELATIONSHIP OF RESEARCH AND DEVELOPMENT AND ENGINEERING TO THE TOTAL BUDGETING PROCESS

To understand the relationship of research and development (R&D) and engineering to the total budgeting process, the difference between those functions and other corporate functions will be examined.

R&D, unlike any other department, deals in the company's future profits and growth. Corporate growth can be internal, obtained from the products or processes produced by R&D and refined by engineering, or can be attained through acquisition. Strong modern companies involved in high- or medium-technology areas look toward both of these routes for growth.

Other departments of the company—marketing, manufacturing, service, quality assurance, quality control, electronic data processing, purchasing, and so forth—are involved in *today's* profit. These groups produce, test, and sell yesterday's R&D or engineering products or processes. This fact is often overlooked by financial people concerned with today's profit. R&D is an investment in the future. Statistical data gathered from many sources show an interesting relationship between profits and sales. The data assume a free market. Monopoly situations or government-regulated industries fall into a different category. Typical sales and profit curves for industrial products and some consumer products are shown in Exhibit 22.1.

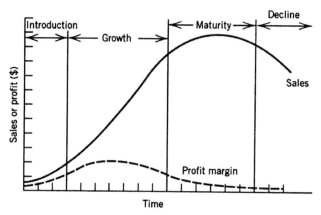

EXHIBIT 22.1 Typical Product or Process Life-Cycle Curves

The relationship between profits and sales may vary from industry to industry, but generally the profit margin peaks in the middle of the growth period and decreases past this point even though sales continue to grow.

It is obvious from Exhibit 22.1 that a corporation will go out of business without new product sales when current products become obsolete. In industries in which life cycles are short, this phenomenon is more easily observed (i.e., electronics and other high-technology industries). The question that a corporation must ask is: What is the right level of R&D funding for healthy corporate growth?

This question is part of the corporate strategic budget plan. The answer is based on:

- Product life cycles
- Level of technology in the industry
- Position that the company wants to attain in its industry segment—what the competition is doing
- Risk involved in development
- Marketing risk

Every industry has characteristic life cycles. For example, in electronics, life cycles range from 1 to 3 years; in chemicals, they range from 10 years to many decades; in pharmaceuticals, they range from several years to 40 years; in mining machinery, the product is often used in the field for up to 40 years; in the iron and steel industry, the life cycle of an alloy can be hundreds of years. Each industry involved in profitable product sales can determine when a product is at the end of its useful life. This occurs when the profit margin can no longer support the investment. When a company can use the funds more efficiently elsewhere, the product is no longer viable.

Level of Technology in Industry

Each industry has technological leaders. The innovative companies set an industry's technological pace. Those companies that do not keep pace lose market share. In old industries, or under conditions in which a company is the last remaining producer of an obsolete product line (e.g., the only buggy-whip manufacturer left in the business), the need for technological innovation does not exist. For all other corporations, not keeping pace with competition technologically can put the company out of business. One method for establishing the technical level for an industry in question is to examine relevant industry statistics.

Statistics for each industry can be obtained by reviewing 10-K reports[1] of specific companies. By doing this, a company can determine which of the competitors it wants to use as models. Occasionally, a specific set of statistical data is obscured by conglomerate corporations. If this is the case, the data can be projected from known data.

To show the variation in R&D spending from industry to industry, review the information presented in Exhibit 22.2. Keep in mind that these data are *average* for an industry. A specific company will have variations from the average, and as a matter of fact, these variations are often the result of the corporation's strategy.

Position that a Company Wants to Attain

From the information shown in Exhibit 22.2, it is obvious that each corporation can use statistical data as budgetary guides for scaling its R&D. Combining these guides with corporate strategic considerations and based on its competitive position in an industry, a corporation can form an R&D policy. In some industries, being second in the marketplace with a superior product makes sense. In others, being second is a guarantee of failure. Product life cycles and technological level combine in some industries (e.g., electronics) to force self-imposed product obsolescence. In other industries (e.g., construction equipment), these factors are less important, and production and service factors weigh more heavily.

Corporate strategic considerations are generally not based on industry averages but on specific competitors. By assembling data from 10-K reports and stockholder reports for specific competitors, a company can determine what investment competition is making in technology. Then, based on the company's long-range internal growth goals, the level of technological spending can be set. This level considers all or some of the next areas:

▪ Long-range company position in the industry
▪ Overtaking specific competitors
▪ Maintaining market share
▪ Lead or lag position technologically
▪ Growth in specific market segments
▪ Quality or value relative to competition
▪ Technological diversification plans
▪ New markets for existing technology

The concept is to set or find the existing corporate R&D datum, to reference it against specific competitors, and then to determine the effect of technological spending on corporate growth relative to these competitors.

---

[1] 10-K reports for a company are obtained from a stockbroker or by writing the company directly.

EXHIBIT 22.2   Examples of R&D Spending

Industry	1988 Average R&D Budget (% of Sales)	R&D Spending R&D Budget (% of Profit)	Average R&D Budget ($/Employee)
Aerospace	4.4	86.7	4,354.3
Appliances	2.0	35.0	1,642.1
Automotive	3.5	54.6	4,919.7
Building materials and construction	1.8	18.6	2,232.4
Chemicals	3.7	31.8	6,208.8
Computers	11.1	93.7	10,987.8
Conglomerates	3.0	36.0	3,382.3
Containers and packaging	1.1	23.2	1,045.2
Drugs and medical products	9.5	46.7	11,766.2
Electrical	2.4	24.6	2,134.0
Electronics	4.4	57.7	3,561.6
Food and beverages	0.7	9.4	852.4
General manufacturing	1.9	20	1,796.6
Instruments	6.0	122.5	5,129.1
Leisure products	5.0	50.9	5,247.4
Microelectronics	9.6	123.6	7,080.1
Metals and mining	1.2	31.7	1,644.9
Office equipment	1.9	22.3	1,779.4
Oil and gas	0.6	10.7	3,151.6
Paper	1.0	10.3	1,604.0
Personal care products	2.7	38.2	4,154.8
Service industries	1.3	31.8	1,049.9
Special machinery[a]	3.0	76.1	3,276.6
Steel	0.7	56.0	981.0
Telecommunications	5.5	55.9	5,794.5
Textiles	0.8	26.2	651.5
Tools (machine and hand)	2.0	37.6	1,875.5
Software services	9.3	72.3	10,771.6
All-industry average	3.4	41.7	4,465.1

[a] Farm machinery and material handling.

In companies that are conglomerates, setting the technological policy is difficult. It must be a multilevel policy, segmented by different markets and technologies. Most conglomerate companies divide themselves internally by industry groupings. These groupings are generally divisions of the large company. Each division will have different technological goals based on its competitors; a single "coherent" technological growth policy is not possible for a conglomerate.

Risk Involved in Development

Risk is a double-edged sword. There are financial risks involved in every new technological venture, but there are also risks in not pursuing technology. Companies have gone out of business by not keeping level with their competition.

Risk analysis requires sound input data. The data are gathered by the major departments of a company and include:

- Development costs (technological)
- Sales projections (marketing)
- Fabrication costs (manufacturing)
- Capital-equipment costs (manufacturing)
- Cash-flow requirements (finance)

Based on the industry's product life cycles, annual forecasts must be made for each of the items cited. These forecasts can range from three years for one full life cycle to ten years or more. Optimistic, pessimistic, and likely cash flows for all balance sheet items are then developed, and probability factors are assigned to each. Technological risk, when integrated with market risk, requires a corporate policy for screening and evaluating ideas. Our goal is to minimize this risk without stifling internal growth.

PROBLEMS IN ESTABLISHING RESEARCH AND DEVELOPMENT AND ENGINEERING OBJECTIVES

Before technical objectives can be established, corporate objectives must be set. Corporate or group objectives set a clear path for business development. If the path is not defined, technological developments can run counter to desired company growth. Large companies have recognized this need for many years. Small companies, unfortunately, often leave the objectives unspecified. Unspecified objectives can result in technological failure. Without a clear company position and direction, a company defeats itself. Thus, the first step in technical planning is to obtain or set, if need be, the company's objectives. The chief executive officer (CEO) should be consulted in this matter. The second step is development of coherent technological objectives for:

- Basic research (if any)
- Development of new products or processes
- Maintenance of existing products, processes, or activities
- Defensive activities in response to competitive thrusts or regulatory requirements

Long-range and short-range objectives can be developed. Long-range objectives are generally in the R&D domain, and short-range objectives in the engineering department's domain.

Basic Requirements of an Objective

All objectives, corporate or technological, have basic requirements. These requirements are discussed next.

▪ *Objectives should be realistic; that is, they should be achievable and understandable.* A little stretch in a corporate position is within the realm of possibility. Too much stretch in attempting to get a corporation from one level to another in too short a time can be demoralizing or outright defeating. Understanding the corporate position, its finances, its technological level, and its ability to withstand adverse conditions leads to setting realistic objectives. Once set, objectives must be clearly communicated. Tasks, goals, or activities that are not understood cannot be achieved.

▪ *Objectives should be measurable in one or all of these categories:*

   ▪ *Schedule.* The accomplishment of given tasks in a given period. The closer a task is to the state of the art, the more difficult a schedule projection becomes. This is one of the areas of technological risk.

   ▪ *Fiscal.* A budget is a special fiscal measurement of finances versus time and accomplishments. Other fiscal measurements include sales, profits, and expenditures.

   ▪ *Quantity.* This is an easy measurement if the initial planning is realistic. Quantity measurements include volume, product mix, market share, growth, and productivity. Some quantity measurements are easy to measure, and others are difficult.

   ▪ *Quality.* This is a more difficult measurement. It may take years to determine the quality of a new technology or the effect on customers. Of course, quality control go–no-go measurements are easier to specify and measure.

▪ *Objectives should be desirable.* Corporations and technological groups can set objectives that are not worth achieving—the tendency to reinvent the wheel. Yesterday's projects recur often in industry, because they are easily scheduled and because the results and timing are clearly predictable. Of course, the funds expended on these projects will not be returned. Each project or corporate goal should be able to stand on its own merits.

▪ *Objectives must be assignable.* Activities, tasks, or specified results are accomplished by an individual or a group. If an objective is specified, but it is not possible to say *who* will do the work or be responsible for getting the work done, it is clear that the work will not get done. Corporate objectives relating to new product or process internal growth requirements are in the R&D or engineering departments' domain. Naturally, the entire corporate structure is required to accomplish a successful objective, but one individual or department must have clear responsibility and authority if the objective is to be successful.

Many modern corporations use management by objectives (MBO) to control corporate growth and accomplishments. If MBO is used, the objectives should be negotiated. This negotiation is accomplished among senior managers and the people responsible for the work. Without the negotiation process, used to retain realism in the MBO process, management by edict results. Unfortunately, edicts are not necessarily realistic.

Using Corporate Objectives to Develop Research and Development Budgets

Many corporations are apprehensive about internal growth. The reasons are clear: The mortality of new product or process ideas is high. For this reason, most large and some small corporations have a screening system designed to lessen the risk. Prescreening and business analysis, outlined in another part of the chapter, remove the ideas that do not meet corporate objectives. The remaining ideas that enter technological departments have these statistical mortality ratios:

- On an average (all-industry average), one out of every three ideas that enters technology will be successful. The funding associated with development of successful products is an average of 28 percent of the total cost associated with getting products into the marketplace. This 28 percent covers the cost for all developments and their subsequent elimination in favor of the successful product.
- On an average (all-industry average), one out of every two ideas that enters the marketplace is successful. The funding associated with commercializing the successful product is 60 percent of the total cost. This cost covers all product entries. Thus, although marketing risks are lower, commercialization costs are higher.
- The remaining 12 percent of the costs associated with a successful product is used to do the screening and business analysis. This analysis eliminates 90 percent of the raw ideas evaluated by a company.
- Companies that do not screen their products have a small chance of financial success. Screening concepts are outlined in a succeeding section of the chapter.

Long- and Short-Range Technological Objectives

Long-range corporate technological objectives are based on the position that a company wants to achieve in three to ten years. In the food industry, three years is generally considered a long-range plan. In power generation and energy-related industries, ten-year and longer-range plans are often developed.

Long-range plans of an industry segment look forward to problems and advantages to be faced by that industry. Competitive threats, incursions from other technologies, material shortages, market shifts, growth of existing technologies and markets, internal growth, acquisitions, profitability, inflation, and sales growth are examples of long-range planning considerations. R&D uses the corporate long-range plan to screen ideas. Ideas that pass through screening and business analysis become development projects or areas for basic research. These projects eventually lead to future sales, profits, and internal growth.

The preceding outline does not imply that R&D cannot contribute to ongoing current products or processes. Of course it does. However, the primary thrust of R&D is the future. Too many industries dissipate their R&D funds on product maintenance. By so doing, these industries block the progress of their company.

The mechanical watch and clock industry, an old industry, did not invest in basic research or new product development to the extent that it should have. When the electronics industry replaced the pendulum with an accurate quartz crystal oscillator and the escapement and gear train with electronic counters, it was able to build a more accurate, more rugged watch at a lower cost. The development of liquid crystal readouts clinched the future. The mechanical watch, except to collectors and antique dealers, was doomed. If the watch industry had invested in true development, it might have made its own product obsolete and remained a competitive force in the business world.

Engineering departments work on shorter-range projects. Their efforts are generally concentrated on new developments slated for production and on product line maintenance. In some companies, R&D and engineering are combined. These companies are in intermediate- to low-technology areas. In high-technology areas, R&D and engineering are separate departments. Engineering does the bulk of the product maintenance, which keeps products or processes current, and application activities. Some engineering departments work on long-range activities, but the primary thrust of engineering is short range.

Historically, the total annual technical budget for most U.S. companies is divided into three major segments: research and exploration, development (applied research), and technological sustaining funds (product or process).

Research and Exploration

This segment is used to do exploratory investigations, assorted studies, and basic research. Basic research is generally a funded activity performed outside the company by special research organizations. There are exceptions to this rule, but most U.S. companies are uncomfortable with in-company research.

In basic research, unlike applied research or development, the technology is not known; thus, the studies cannot be scheduled. These studies can be likened to chartering an explorer to go into unknown territory. The explorer may have a mission to find land suitable for a farm community in the wilderness. Setting off on the mission, he does not know what type of terrain or hostile environment he will face. Basic research is similar. It can be controlled financially in a staircase manner, but not with a schedule, or, by definition, it would not be basic research. Staircase control issues a given quantity of money for a given period. If the researcher and the company feel that progress is being made, additional funds and time are allotted to the problem. This process continues until either a successful technology is developed or agreement is reached that the task must be abandoned.

Because basic research cannot be scheduled and results cannot be predicted, most corporations minimize the budget for this function. History shows that the technological growth of an industry is directly related to basic research. Without a continuing investment in this area by the government and corporations, the United States has fallen behind other industrial countries. Historically, funds allocated to basic research in the United States have been gradually reduced each year since the end of World War II. This is not true for other industrial countries and evolving Third World countries.

Development

In development, the technologies are known. Some technologies are in rapid flux, and the state of the art is shifting rapidly. In others, the technology is stable and often old art. Product and process development uses a mixture of these technologies, but all projects can be scheduled using the normal planning tools (program evaluation and review technique [PERT], Gantt, critical-path method, etc.).

When the development activity is close to the state of the art, the scheduled time and budget are more risky. When the development activity is a combination of new and old art, the risks are reduced.

An example of a project with old and new technology is the development of the atomic submarine. The nuclear energy system was new technology, which at that time was the leading edge of the state of the art. Hull design and the crew's quarters were older art. The new art faced the question of how small an atomic pile could be made and still operate, or how much shielding was necessary for the safety of the crew. When these areas were estimated, statistics and probability theory were applied to the time estimates. For other areas, routine estimating techniques were acceptable. Combinations of old and new technology in product or process developments account for the development risks. These risks are the potential cause of developmental failures.

In any event, when the technology is known, development costs and time are estimable. Schedules and budgets can be prepared, and project-control techniques can be applied. It is for this reason that industry concentrates its resources on development. The ratio of development to research is approximately 6:1. New products and processes are the output of development. These developments are the generators of future profit and internal corporate growth.

Development funds can be used defensively to react to competitive threats that might affect a company's market share. Analysis of competitive products or processes, shifts in technology, and monitoring the technological aspects of the marketplace are areas that use parts of the development budget.

Technological Sustaining Funds

Funds expended in this segment are used to keep existing products from becoming obsolete or for product or process application activities. The bulk of these funds is spent in engineering. The activities include:

- Minor modification of the product or process through improvements and/or correction
- Scrap reduction
- Productivity improvement
- Value analysis and cost improvement
- Application studies for interface with other products
- Liaison with production
- Documentation
- Liaison with marketing
- Analysis of technological customer needs

Technological Budget-Segmentation Ratios

In most companies in the United States, budgetary funds are segmented among the technological areas as shown next.

Research and exploration	0%–10%
Development	20%–35%
Sustaining	55%–80%

When a company is close to the edge of the state of the art in its technology, it will, as a result of the environment, spend more money in new technology areas. R&D departments will be large, and engineering departments either completely submerged in R&D or of equal status.

Companies with older technology will spend small percentages of their funds in R&D and major percentages in engineering. In those companies, R&D is either a non-existent department or it is submerged in the engineering department.

Three budget segmentations are shown in Exhibit 22.3. One is for high-technology companies involved in such industries as electronics, instruments, pharmaceuticals, and specialty chemicals; another is for low-technology companies involved in such industries as heavy machinery and paper; and the third is for average-technology companies involved in such industries as leisure products and automotive products.

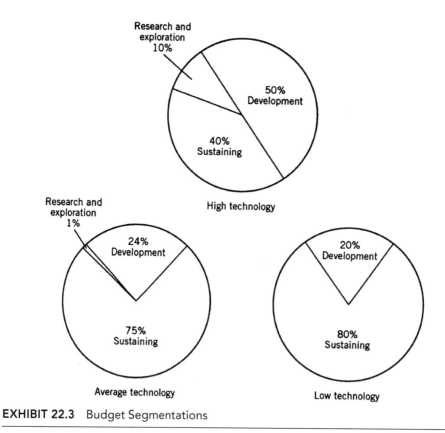

EXHIBIT 22.3   Budget Segmentations

DEVELOPING A TECHNOLOGICAL BUDGET

To develop the technological budget for either R&D or engineering, it is necessary to use a selectivity principle. Scarcity of technical personnel, equipment, and facilities requires some approach to optimization of these rare and costly areas. Improved engineering and R&D productivity will result.

The general concepts required for project selection include:

* Project screening
* Setting project priorities and evaluating finances
* Risk analysis and final project selection

Once these steps have been taken, a budget can be assembled using zero-based concepts. The technique is to assign a priority 1 first, 2 next, and so on, until a predetermined level is reached. This predetermined level can be obtained historically from head count and other considerations or by analysis of successful competitors' funding.

A word of caution—it is impossible or inefficient to attempt to control 100 percent of all development project budgets and schedules. One hundred percent control is a poor use of management time; it eventually throttles creativity. A degree of technical freedom is essential to morale and productivity in technical departments. This does not mean that 100 percent of the budget cannot be accounted for. Hundreds of little projects and intermediate-size projects can be funded and accounted for. It is desirable and good management to control 20 percent of the projects that account for 80 percent of the budget. This selectivity principle, the 80/20 rule, was developed by Vilfredo Pareto. In studying the wealth distribution of Europeans, Pareto discovered that 80 percent of the wealth of a country was vested in the hands of 20 percent of the population. Understanding this truncated or skewed distribution permits its application to many activities. It leads to effective management by exception.

Pareto's law can be applied to cost reduction. It is senseless to worry about a large number of such low-cost items as nuts, screws, and bolts in an assembly. Good cost-reduction efforts concentrate on the 20 percent of the parts that accounts for 80 percent of the cost. (We are using 80/20 as an example; 90/10 or 70/30 is possible.)

A budget based on screening and funding the few large projects that account for approximately 80 percent of the total development costs can be well planned. The remaining 20 percent is spread over studies, small projects, fire-fighting activities, and so forth. At the end of the year, all costs are accounted for. Small and intermediate projects can be used for manpower leveling. The peaks and valleys associated with manpower needs can be minimized. Exploratory studies can lead to future large development projects. It is a good idea to perform a Pareto analysis in your company to find the distribution.

Project Screening

Once corporate objectives have been outlined, a clear technological path can be established. A project, process, or product can then be subjected to a screen. The screen must

EXHIBIT 22.4   Factors Used to Screen Products

Technical

Regulatory requirements (Occupational Safety and Health Administration, Food and Drug Administration, Environmental Protection Agency, etc.)

Likelihood of technical success, risk

Customer's requirements

Development cost

Development time

In-house skills, availability, and capability

Resources and facilities required for development

Patent potential

Historic technological corporate strengths

Project fit with ongoing projects

Cost reduction

Manufacturing or Operations

Capital requirements

Existing facility, availability, capability, and needs

Raw-material availability

Regulatory influences resulting from new manufacturing processes

Manufacturing safety

Manufacturability of the new product

Quality considerations

Productivity variance of the new product

Financial

Profitability and return on investment

Net present worth

Internal rate of return

Profitability index (capital considerations)

Payback period

Risk

Asset utilization

Cash flow

Marketing and Sales

Customer needs

Compatibility with other products or processes

Size of potential market

Corporate image leverage in the marketplace

Ability to market the product

Market trends and product growth potential

Market share and trends

Market risk

Pricing strategy and competitors' pricing

Product-line fit

Domestic and international markets

Stocking attractiveness

Effect on current customers

Sales force, increases or decreases

Legal

Warranties

Liabilities

Regulatory compliance

Patents/trademarks/copyrights

Unified commercial code considerations

Contractual commitments

Strategic

Meets long-range objectives

Meets short-range objectives

Timing needs, seasonal/contract/competitive considerations

Overall corporate image

include technological, manufacturing, marketing, financial, and other considerations needed to keep the company in a healthy condition relative to its competition. In some industries, one or more of these areas may be overriding. It is therefore necessary to develop a screen that is peculiar to your company. This is accomplished by variable weight for the critical factors. Some of the factors used by companies are shown in Exhibit 22.4.

A screening sheet developed for the preliminary assessment of a power transmission company's raw product ideas is shown in Exhibit 22.5. In this sheet, the factors of importance to the company have been given greater weight factors. These factors were developed by each department head through negotiation with the CEO of the company. They emphasize corporate objectives in the screening process. Not all of the factors outlined in Exhibit 22.4 were considered important for this company. When the projects are screened, each department considers the agreed-to factors and decides whether they represent an excellent (2×) weight, a good (1×) weight, or a poor (0) weight. By multiplying the opportunity assessment by the importance factor, the department can arrive at a relative score. When all departments have acted, the total scores are compared and negotiated, and a minimum level is agreed on.

In this screening activity, each department has a veto right if the product is deemed to be unacceptable. For example, if finance cannot show sufficient profitability in initial considerations, legal is convinced that there are liability problems, manufacturing is sure of construction safety difficulties, or technology is concerned about product safety, the product will not be pursued even if the screening score is very high. Naturally, these

EXHIBIT 22.5   Project-Screening Sheet

Project: Departmental Considerations	Importance Multiplier	Opinion Factor[a]			Total Score
		E 2 ×	G 1 ×	P 0	
Financial					
Profitability[b]	3				b
Burden absorption	2				
Payback period	1				
Risk	2				
Cash flow requirements	3				
Technical					
Regulatory requirements[b]	3				b
Likelihood of success	3				
Development cost	2				
Effect on corporate projects	1				
In-house skills utilization	2				
Manufacturing					
Manufacturing safety[b]	3				b
Capital requirements	3				
Facility utilization	2				
Raw material availability	2				
Manufacturability	1				
Marketing and Sales					
Market risk[b]	3				b
Customer needs	2				
Marketability	2				
Market size	2				
Effects on customers	2				
Legal and Strategic					
Warranties and liabilities[b]	3				b
Patent potential	2				
Contractual commitment	3				
Corporate image	2				
Seasonal requirements	1				
Total[c]					

[a] E = excellent, G = good, P = poor.
[b] Zero score in these factors vetoes the project.
[c] Minimum acceptable score without veto is 70.

objections must be verified in order to keep the screening activity from becoming a political process.

On the screening sheet, veto factors are asterisked. Zero score for those factors automatically eliminates the project from development consideration. Thus, to pass through the screen, a product must attain a score above minimum and must not have zero for any of the veto factors.

A word of caution: The screening sheet is a preliminary estimate. Any product that passes through the initial screen will be subjected to a more detailed financial study. This financial study requires sales forecasts, production-cost estimates, and all of the data associated with the preparation of a product or process for the marketplace. The effort to truly evaluate a candidate project is time consuming. It requires a large amount of input data. Getting the data is the problem. The evaluation, although mildly complicated, can be computerized or organized in a way that reduces the evaluation to a set of predetermined calculations. A typical filled-out screening sheet is shown in Exhibit 22.6. In that exhibit, the corporate level of 70, negotiated with the CEO, has been met. When scores are close to 70, the project should be reviewed critically. The score itself is not a priority-ranking system.

Once the financial analysis is complete, additional concepts will be screened out. The few survivors represent real opportunities for future corporate technological development.

Setting Project Priorities and Evaluating Finances

After projects have been screened, the high-cost projects are subjected to financial analysis. This is an intelligent use of Pareto's law. It is too costly and inefficient to subject all projects to a financial screen, but 20 percent of the projects that account for 80 percent of the technical budget must be evaluated. The only exception to this rule are projects involving the Environmental Protection Agency, Occupational Safety and Health Administration, Food and Drug Administration, or other government agency requirements that are mandated by law. These projects must be done if a company is to remain in business. Other mandated projects may develop from competitive threats.

The basic theory that is followed in setting priorities is, in order:

1. *All mandated projects.*
2. *The most financially sound projects.* These projects are judged on the basis of one of these calculations: net present value (NPV), also known as net present worth; internal rate of return (IRR); or profitability index (PI). These indexes are described in greater detail in this section and are discussed in later chapters. Simple payback period considerations, once used exclusively by industry, are no longer considered valid, since they do not take into account the time value of money.
3. *Research and exploration projects.* These projects cannot be planned or scheduled, but they represent technological opportunities for future growth potential. Many corporations simply set a fixed percentage of the budget for this function. These projects can be used as fill-in work for scientists or engineers. They tend to level

EXHIBIT 22.6 Completed Project-Screening Sheet

Project: Copier Departmental Consideration	Importance Multiplier	Opinion Factor[a]			
		E 2 ×	G 1 ×	P 0	Total Score
Financial					
Profitability[b]	3	√			6[b]
Burden absorption	2	√			4
Payback period	1		√		1
Risk	2		√		2
Cash flow requirements	3		√		3
Technical					
Regulatory requirements[b]	3	√			6[b]
Likelihood of success	3	√			6
Development cost	2		√		2
Effect on corporate projects	1			√	0
In-house skills utilization	2		√		2
Manufacturing					
Manufacturing safety[b]	3	√			6[b]
Capital requirements	3		√		3
Facility utilization	2		√		2
Raw material availability	2			√	0
Manufacturability	1	√			2
Marketing and Sales					
Market risk[b]	3		√		3[b]
Customer needs	2	√			4
Marketability	2		√		2
Market size	2	√			4
Effects on customers	2	√			4
Legal and Strategic					
Warranties and liabilities[b]	3		√		3[b]
Patent potential	2		√	√	0
Contractual commitment	3		√		3
Corporate image	2	√			4
Seasonal requirements	1	√			2
Total[c]					74

[a] E = excellent, G = good, P = poor.
[b] Zero score in these factors vetoes the project.
[c] Minimum acceptable score without veto is 70.

manpower and create an atmosphere of technological freedom for the staff. In so doing, the gain in motivational involvement often carries into the other projects.

4. *Sustaining projects.* Although this is the largest segment of the engineering and R&D budget, it is the easiest to fund. Based on current products, processes, and technological interfaces, a fixed percentage of sales can be set aside for this function.

Financial decisions are based on the time value of money and on risk analysis. Older techniques involving payback period are not currently used. Definitions of payback period, NPV, IRR, and PI are given in the next section.

Definitions

Payback period is the number of years it takes a firm to recover its original investment from net returns before depreciation but after taxes. Unfortunately, the time value of money is not considered.

Net present value is a discounted cash-flow technique. The technique is implemented by finding the present value (PV) of the cash in any period and discounting it at the cost of capital. Each period's PV is summed for the investment, and then the initial cost outlay of the investment is subtracted. If the NPV is positive, the project should be accepted. If projects are mutually exclusive—that is, only one can be funded—then the one with the highest NPV is accepted.

$$NPV = \left[\frac{R_1}{(1+k)^1} + \frac{R_2}{(1+k)^2} + \cdots \frac{R_n}{(1+k)^n} \right] - C$$

where

R = cash flow for the period
C = cost outlay
k = cost of capital

In *internal rate of return,* the interest rate is found for the specific condition in which the sum of the PV is equal to the cost outlay for the project. An interest rate, sometimes referred to as the *hurdle rate,* is used. Corporations often use a hurdle rate that reflects the cost of capital and historic criteria. In this method, which involves trial-and-error procedures or a computer program, all projects should be selected above the hurdle rate. If projects are mutually exclusive, select the project with the highest IRR.

$$C = \left[\frac{R_1}{(1+r)^1} + \frac{R_2}{(1+r)^2} + \cdots \frac{R_n}{(1+r)^n} \right]$$

where r = IRR.

The *profitability index,* sometimes referred to as the *benefit–cost ratio,* is calculated by dividing the sum of the PV for the project or investment by the required investment outlay. If projects are mutually exclusive, choose the highest PI.

$$PI = \left[\frac{R_1}{(1+k)^1} + \frac{R_2}{(1+k)^2} + \cdots \frac{R_n}{(1+k)^n} \right]$$

where cost = investment outlay. When the outlay occurs over more than one year, the cost includes the present value of future outlays.

Consider this graphic example of NPV: Assume that a series of investments in all aspects of a product development have been outlined for seven years. These include R&D, engineering, plant equipment tooling, cost of sales, and other expenses. Also assume that sales, amortization, royalties, and cash inflows are estimated for the same period. Then, after income tax and nontax capital inflows and outflows for the period have been established, all cash flows for the product can be calculated and annualized. These data can be organized by filling out the worksheet provided in Exhibit 22.7.

EXHIBIT 22.7 Emzee Associates Worksheet

Client:							
Project:	**Amount (in $1,000s)**						
	Fiscal Year						
IRR: %	1	2	3	4	5	6	7
Cash Outflow							
1. R&D expense							
2. Market introduction and launching costs							
3. Plant equipment and tooling expense							
4. Cost of sales							
5. Incremental operating expenses							
6. Other							
7. Cash-outflow total (1 through 6)							
Cash Inflow							
8. Sales							
9. Amortized expenses and royalties							
10. Other							
11. Cash inflow total (8 through 10)							
Before-Tax Cash Flow (No Capital)							
12. Line 11 minus line 7							
After-Tax Cash Flow (No Capital)							
13. Income tax at 48%							
14. Line 12 minus line 13							
Capital Expenditures Outflow							
15. Changes in capital							
16. Plant equipment and tools capital changes							
17. Working-capital increases							

Project:	Amount (in $1,000s)						
	Fiscal Year						
IRR: %	1	2	3	4	5	6	7
18. Total capital (15 through 17)							
19. Line 14 minus line 18							
Capital and Other Inflow							
20. Working-capital decreases							
21. Residual net assets at end of project							
22. Depreciation							
23. Income tax credit							
24. Sum lines 20 to 23							
Net Cash Flow In-Out							
25. Line 19 plus line 24							

The PV of cash flows in the future can be obtained by applying a compound interest factor appropriate to the period to each of the annualized results calculated in line 25 of Exhibit 22.7. These factors are obtained from the next equation:

$$PV_{factor} = \frac{1}{(1+i)^n}$$

where i = interest rate based on the company's cost of capital and n = the time period in future years when the investment cash flow is being examined.

EXHIBIT 22.8 $1/(1 + i)^n$ Present-Value Factor

n (years)	5%	10%	15%	20%	30%	40%
1	0.9524	0.9091	0.8696	0.8333	0.7692	0.7143
2	0.9070	0.8264	0.7561	0.6944	0.5917	0.5102
3	0.8638	0.7513	0.6575	0.5787	0.4552	0.3644
4	0.8227	0.6830	0.5718	0.4823	0.3501	0.2603
5	0.7835	0.6209	0.4972	0.4019	0.2693	0.1859
6	0.7462	0.5645	0.4323	0.3349	0.2072	0.1328
7	0.7106	0.5132	0.3759	0.2791	0.1594	0.0949
8	0.6768	0.4665	0.3269	0.2326	0.1226	0.0678

Applying this equation to n time periods at various interest rates generates Exhibit 22.8.

For example, $1 million of income eight years from today at an interest rate of 20 percent is worth $232,600 today. This figure is obtained by multiplying $1 million by the PV factor for 20 percent in eight years ($1,000,000 0.2326 $232,600). The interest rate is based on your company's cost of capital and some risk factors. The techniques for evaluating cost of capital are discussed in a later section.

If we assume that a product was evaluated using the annualized worksheet in Exhibit 28.8 and that the data start one year from today, then the possible cash flows that might show on line 25 are:

$$\frac{\text{Dollars (in } 1,000s)}{(400)(250)\,100\,300\,600\,1,000\,400}$$

The values shown in parentheses are negative values. Is this project sound if the cost of capital is 20 percent?

The vector diagram shown in Exhibit 22.9 is used to describe the calculation. It is, of course, possible to get special-purpose calculators or computer programs to do this calculation today, but our purpose is understanding. Once you are familiar with the process, the actual calculation of net present worth (NPW), or NPV, is very easy. The problem is getting the background data. These data involve forecasts of R&D, engineering, manufacturing, marketing, and finance in order to evaluate the project realistically.

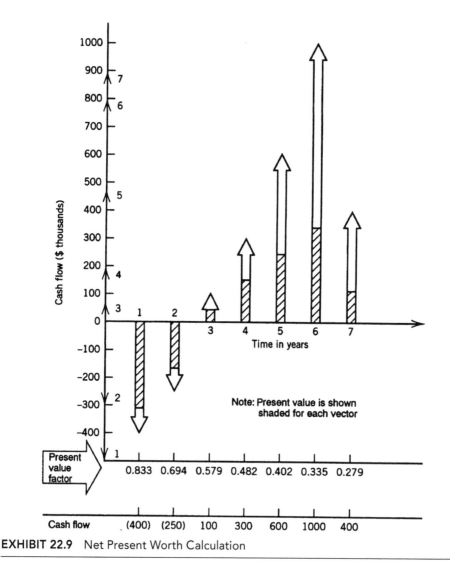

EXHIBIT 22.9   Net Present Worth Calculation

The investments in Exhibit 22.9 are laid out at their appropriate time interval and are shown as vectors. All cash outflows are plotted negatively; all cash inflows are plotted positively. Simple addition of these vectors assumes that the interest rate cost of capital is zero. In this example, we have assumed an interest rate of 20 percent. For 20 percent, the PV factors are obtained from Exhibit 22.8. They are shown at the bottom of the graph. Multiplying the money for the period by its PV factor yields the PV or discounted cash flow of the period. If these vectors are added, the result is called NPW or NPV. This is done on the origin of the graph. In our example, the NPW is $383,320 positive; thus, the investment is excellent. If the NPW were negative, the return would be less than 20 percent. Since it is positive, the return is more than 20 percent.

If a higher cost of capital were used in the example, the NPW would be smaller. Eventually, a point would be reached at which NPW 0. At this point, the cost of capital is given a special name, internal rate of return. For this example, the IRR 38.53 percent.

All of the time-value-of-money methods (NPW, IRR, and PI) are useful for ranking projects. Assuming that the project has passed through the screen, financial analysis can be used to rank projects of first priority, then second, and so forth. Where projects are mutually exclusive, these rankings can be used to select the optimum use of funds.

Risk Analysis and Final Project Selection

Before final project selection, it is often important to determine the project risk. Risk analysis can be done scientifically, or it can be based on experience. When experience is used to evaluate risk, a variable cost-of-capital technique is common. When scientific methods are used, either Monte Carlo or sensitivity analysis can be employed. It is obvious, however, that a single calculation of NPW is only as good as the input data. These data involve projections of all cash flows into the future. It must be obvious that the chance of accuracy in a single calculation is small. Risk analysis brings credibility to the evaluation.

When experience is used to assess the project risk, different cost-of-capital rates are employed. The *cost of capital* is normally the discount rate used in capital budgeting. This rate varies from industry to industry. Average cost of capital includes a debt-to-equity ratio. For example, assume a 20 percent debt, a 16.5 percent cost of equity (net worth), and a 9 percent cost of debt. The average cost of capital is (20% × 9%) + (80% × 16.5%) = 15%.

One method for normalizing risk is to apply different discount rates to different projects. Higher-risk projects are given a higher discount rate. Conversely, lower-risk projects are given a lower discount rate. These data can be obtained historically by product line or by industry segment.

Thus, low-risk projects might use a 15 percent cost of capital, intermediate-risk projects might use 18 percent and high-risk projects might use 25 percent. These factors must be determined by experienced analysts. Even so, the technique has limited appeal.

A more scientific risk analysis is based on a multiple estimate—Monte Carlo analysis, which uses statistical information—or on a sensitivity analysis.

Monte Carlo Analysis

The principles are simple. For each cash flow of Exhibit 22.7, three or more estimates are obtained. These cost estimates shape the annual characteristic curve of the cash flow for that activity. Optimistic, pessimistic, and most likely estimates are normal input data. The problem is bounded by these estimates, some of which are cross-coupled (e.g., sales and manufacturing cost). When one is specified, the other is also specified within some known relationship.

It is possible to do an NPW calculation for all optimistic and all pessimistic conditions, but these data would not be valuable since they are unlikely events. An alternate approach is to divide the data into regions, say 1 to 5, and then to use random number generators for each cash-flow curve. This is shown symbolically in Exhibit 22.10. Cross-coupling is also shown. Once the curves are specified and the data have been zoned, it is possible to generate random numbers for each activity by year and then to calculate

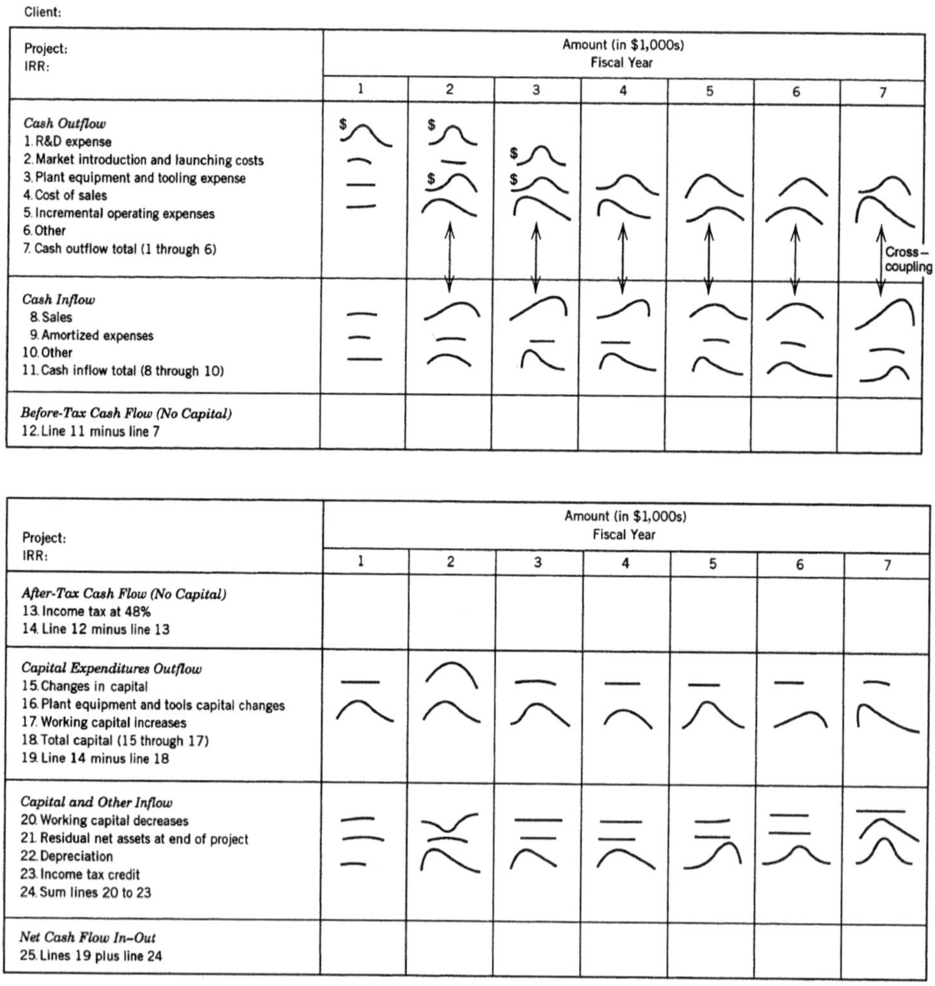

EXHIBIT 22.10 Emzee Associates Worksheet

NPW for that data. Repeating the process 100 or 1,000 times will yield a range of NPW values that are likely to occur. Computer programs for this process are available. Again, the problem is in getting the input data, not in the actual calculation. The calculation, although cumbersome, is reduced to a routine.

An alternative approach is to do the single NPW calculation with the best data available. Then perturbations or shifts of the data are impressed on the calculation. Some of these data shifts will be insignificant to the NPW; others will alter the NPW significantly. This is a sensitivity analysis. It helps a financial analyst determine areas that should be carefully re-estimated or controlled during project evolution.

Monte Carlo and sensitivity analysis can be applied to all of the financial analysis tools (IRR, NPW, and PI). They demonstrate the strength or weakness in a project. Obviously, projects that run into the poor category easily should be avoided. Final project selection can be guided by profit impact and risk.

Relationship of Budget and Schedule

Technical budgets, both engineering and R&D, are developed from project manpower and material needs. When these needs are correlated with the scheduled activities on a time base, a dollar-versus-time project budget can be developed. The normal techniques involved in scheduling are PERT and a newer form of bar chart called mechanized Gantt. In both methods, a critical path is developed for the project. If PERT is used, a bar chart still must be developed to display the project's real-time manpower and material needs.

To illustrate the budgeting process, we examine a simple project for the design development fabrication assembly and test of a developmental unit. Budget for this project is constructed using mechanized Gantt planning concepts. The concepts of PERT can be directly converted to mechanized Gantt charts. These concepts involve critical path, slack time, and interface data applied to a time base.

Realistic planning and scheduling concepts require negotiated estimates. We assume that the data shown in Exhibit 22.11, the input data for planning, were negotiated with the task leader assigned to each of the coded tasks. This method of getting input data from the people responsible for the work produces commitment and realism in the estimates. If an estimate is too high, the manager can negotiate it downward. If the task timing or manpower demands are unrealistic, the task leader can negotiate for more time or manpower. With both parties attempting to develop honest input data, the likelihood of a realistic schedule is higher. Schedules that have been established by edict lack commitment and ultimately will fall short of the mark. The manager cannot lose by this negotiation—he or she will gain in the likelihood of project success.

Referring to the data in Exhibit 22.11, task leaders estimated the manpower, span time, and raw materials required to accomplish their task. The project manager developed the interface requirements based on his or her knowledge of the project. Where no interface is shown, activities can be started immediately. Where interfaces are shown, they constrain the dependent activities. The data in this exhibit are used to develop mechanized Gantt schedules, manpower time histograms, and baseline project budgets.

The listed symbols are used to develop the mechanized GANTT chart shown in Exhibit 22.12:

EXHIBIT 22.11 Task Table

Code	Task	Activity Interface	Span Time (Months)	Manpower Estimate (Person-Months)	Activity Cost	Cost of Materials
A	Design concept	None	3	3E 6D	$ 15,000	$ 500
B	Design calculations	None	2	4E	$ 8,000	—
C	Design component tests	None	1	2T 1D 1E	$ 6,000	$ 250
D	Design layouts	100% A	3	6D	$ 9,000	—
		100% B				
		100% C				
E	Detail parts	50% D 75%	2	4D	$ 4,000	—
F	Check layout and parts	100% D	1	1 E	$ 2,000	—
		50% E 50%				
		50% F 25%				
G	Purchase components	100% A	3	—		$ 10,500
H	Fabricate parts	100% E	2	8M	$ 10,000	$ 3,500
I	Assemble unit	100% G	2	4T 2M	$ 7,500	$ 1,000
		50% H 50%				
J	Test unit	100% I	1	1T 1E	$ 3,250	$ 1,000
Total					$ 64,750	$ 16,750
Total project						$ 81,500

- The arrow pointing upward points to the interface constraint.
- The "X" locates a possible constrained activity start. If several X's are located on an activity's plan line, the last X constrains the start of the dependent activity.
- The "O" is used as a start or stop milestone for each activity.
- The line connecting milestones uses real project span time. Thus, a three-month span-time activity would have a milestone at the initial start and another milestone at a location three months away. The connecting line joins the milestones for the activity's planned duration.
- When 100 percent is used as an interface, the constrained activity requires that *all* of the constraining activity's work be completed *before* the planned start of that activity (see Exhibit 22.11). When several X constraints exist on a constrained activity line, the last constraining activity dominates. Thus, "100% A" on activity G means that activity G cannot start until activity A is completed. Activity D has three constraints, and the dominant activity in this case is activity A. Thus, activity D cannot start before activity A is completed.

- Where partial constraints are used, they must be followed by a completion constraint requirement. Thus, in activity E, the partial constraint "50% D 75%" means that part drawings can be started when half of the design layouts have been completed. Activity E cannot go beyond its 75 percent point until *all* of the layouts have been completed. Partial constraints always involve some form of synchronous work between the constraining and constrained activities.
- The arrow pointing downward shows the completion requirement for partial constraints. In Exhibit 22.12, it shows where the end of activity D must meet activity E. Synchronous activities occur between D and E, between E and F, and between H and I.
- The solid triangle denotes the latest time an activity can be completed. It is the same as T_L in a PERT chart. If the triangle is directly over the end milestone, the activity is critical; it has zero slack. If the triangle is displaced from the end milestone, the activity has slack. Slack is developed by multiple constraints. Where several X constraints exist on an activity line, the last one controls the constrained activity start. The other X containing activities have slack equal to the space between this dominant X and the X being considered.

It is possible to use other symbols for the mechanized Gantt chart development, but these were chosen for specific reasons. For example, the "O" is used as a planned milestone start and stop. A solid "O" is used for actual historic start and stop activity milestones. In this way, project control and historic data can be obtained from the same graph. (The solid "O" symbol is developed further when budget management is discussed.)

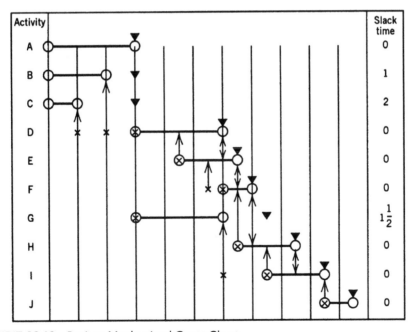

EXHIBIT 22.12   Project Mechanized Gantt Chart

The data of Exhibit 22.11 are used to develop the project schedule. This mechanized Gantt chart (Exhibit 22.12) shows the interface, span time, critical path, and slack path activities. It is generated using the symbols just described. Once the activities are charted, slack is developed from bottom-up assessment of the multiple interface constraints. If slack cannot be established, the activity is critical. The critical path is A, D, E, F, H, I, S.

A manpower histogram, shown in Exhibit 22.13, is developed by placing the Exhibit 22.11 manpower estimates in time synchronization with the activities displayed in Exhibit 22.12. The histogram developed assumes linear manpower loading. Thus, the designers and the engineer are displayed linearly over the three-month time span of activity A. The high peak in the first week of the program can be eased by using some of the slack associated with activity C. Activities E, H, I, and J start in midmonth. The people assigned to these tasks are shown phased in the manpower histograms in their proper time slots.

To develop the project budget, costs for the skills shown in Exhibit 22.14 are added vertically for each month of the manpower histogram (Exhibit 22.13). In the first week of the project, manpower utilization costs are $15,000. In the next week, they are $9,000, and so forth. Incremental weekly costs are added in this manner to develop the information shown in the incremental row. These costs are then added cumulatively to form the next row of Exhibit 22.15. The project baseline budget is a plot of the labor costs. Material costs from Exhibit 22.11 are synchronized in the correct time frame. When the material and labor budgets are added together, a total budget is obtained. This budget is shown in Exhibit 22.15.

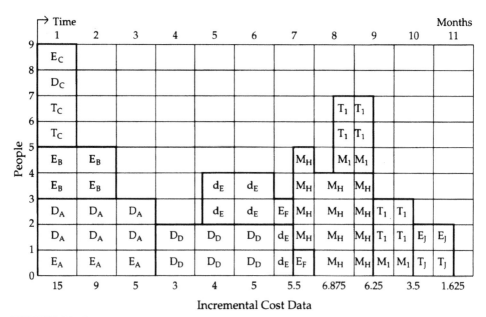

EXHIBIT 22.13   Manpower Histogram

EXHIBIT 22.14   Skill Cost table

Skill	Code	Cost per Week
Engineer	E	$2,000
Machinist	M	$1,250
Technician	T	$1,250
Designer	D	$1,500
Draftsman	d	$1,000

PREPARING A DEPARTMENTAL BUDGET

Technical departmental budgets are the summation of all of the project budgets, all R&D allocations, all sustaining engineering, and all contract R&D on engineering activity. The corporation provides all of the funding, with the exception of contract funds.

The total technical department budget reflects an assortment of factors that are used to develop burden rates. These factors include all direct project charges, administrative charges, holidays, vacations, sick leave, positive or negative allocations, fixed expenses, controllable supplies, travel, reproduction, materials, and miscellaneous services.

To calculate the direct departmental costs, simply add all of the chargeable project-activity expenses and divide by the chargeable hours. To calculate the burden rate, add administrative overhead, allocations, and service charges to project activity costs and divide by the chargeable hours.

Incremental cost (in $1000s)	15	9	5	3	4	5	5.5	6.875	6.25	3.5	1.625	
Cumulative cost (in $1000s)	15	24	29	32	36	41	46.5	53.375	59.625	63.125	64.75	

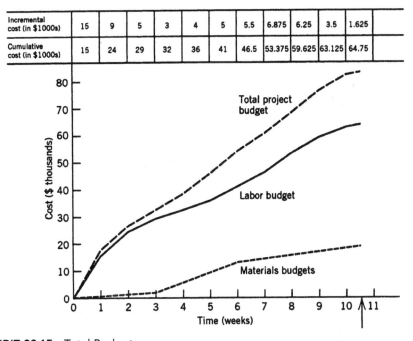

EXHIBIT 22.15   Total Budget

Gross Expenses

Direct chargeable departmental expenses (gross expenses) include:

- Labor expenses
    - Salaries
    - Benefits
- Controllable expenses
    - Supplies
    - Travel
    - Reproduction
    - Services
    - Miscellaneous project expenses

Once these expenses have been tabulated for the department, the chargeable hours are calculated.

Chargeable hours generally are assumed to be 2,080 hours per year per person minus:

- Holidays
- Sick leave
- Vacations (variable, based on length of service)
- Special, nonchargeable projects or meetings
- Administrative duties for working supervisors

When the chargeable hours have been calculated for each individual, the total departmental hours are calculated—dividing direct departmental expenses by chargeable hours will yield the direct rate.

Burden Rate

Burden is based on nondirect charges. The burdens include:

- Interdepartmental allocation costs
- Development overhead costs
- Project administrative expenses
- Secretarial expenses (department)
- Department administrative expenses
- Miscellaneous services and administration expenses for the department

When the burdens have been calculated for the department, they are added to the direct departmental chargeable expenses. This new total is divided by the chargeable hours to determine the burden rate.

These calculations are illustrated in Exhibits 22.16 through 22.18.

There is a major flaw in the concept of burden rate. The flaw develops because the rate is an average for the department. If several major projects are pursued each year,

EXHIBIT 22.16 Electrical Laboratory Annual Direct Chargeable Expenses

Direct Expense	Amount
Salaries	$1,359,990
Employee benefits	$ 339,998
Total labor expense	$1,699,988
Department supplies	$ 58,500
Travel	94,500
Reproduction	27,000
Consultant services	202,500
Project materials	94,500
Miscellaneous expenses	$ 18,000
Total controllable expense	$ 495,000
Total laboratory expense	$2,194,988

and if *all* of the high-salaried people work on the first-priority project and all of the lower-salaried people on the third-priority project, the actual project costs are masked. In contract engineering or contract R&D work, the customer for the first project is getting a bargain, but the customer for the third project is obviously overpaying.

Because of this flaw, many departments build project budgets directly from manpower histograms. Actual manpower costs are used in this concept. Burden rates are added to these project budgets to determine the project's "real" cost.

EXHIBIT 22.17 Electrical Laboratory Chargeable Hours

Name	Available Hours[a]	Vacation Hours	Special[b] Meetings	Project Administration	Chargeable Project Hours
Walker	1920	120	80	60	1,660
Smith	1920	40	40	—	1,840
Badistella	1920	80	40	—	1,800
Jones	1920	120	80	—	1,720
Pocratsky	1920	160	24	—	1,736
Delmastro	1920	80	24	—	1,816
Hermone	1920	160	120	400	1,240
VanDerBokke	1920	120	60	120	1,620
Devine	1920	80	80	60	1,700
McCarten	1920	120	120	120	1,560
Gupta	1920	120	60	60	1,680
Goldstein	1920	120	24	—	1,776
Total					20,148

[a] 52 weeks × 40 hours/week = 2,080 hours annually, minus holidays (10 days/year × 8 hours = 80 hours/year), minus sick leave (10 days/year = 80 hours/year). Total annual hours = 1,920.
[b] Company divisional meetings and training meetings (seminars).

EXHIBIT 22.18 Burden-Rate Calculation for Technical Development Department

Laboratory	(1) Chargeable Expenses	(2) Administration and Overhead	(3) Allocated Costs	(4) Total Lab Expenses	(5) Chargeable Hours	(6) Burden Rate[a]	(7) Direct Rate[b]
Electrical	2,194,988	247,500	112,500	2,554,988	20,148	126.8	108.9
Mechanical	2,364,188	202,500	135,000	2,701,688	22,705	119.0	104.1
Model shop	563,625	112,500	67,500	743,625	5,200	143.0	108.4
Chemical and material	1,238,940	180,000	157,500	1,576,440	12,000	131.4	103.2
General engineering	1,464,525	270,000	112,500	1,847,025	13,578	136.0	107.9
Totals for department	7,826,266			9,423,766	73,631	128.0	106.3

Note: All values are in dollars unless specified.
[a] Burden rate is item 4 divided by item 5.
[b] Direct rate is item 1 divided by item 5.

Both of these budgeting methods are in use today. If all projects are paid for by the company, burden rate can be a useful tool, and the actual project cost flaw is of no consequence. However, if development or research contracts are being paid for by a customer, the manpower histogram cost plus burden rate is the most equitable system. At one time, calculating project costs using actual salaries for an entire department was a difficult task. With the advent of the computer, this refinement is easily factored into the budget.

MANAGING A BUDGET

Traditionally, businesses are managed from budgeted versus actual data, both monthly and cumulative. A typical technical budget is shown in Exhibit 22.19. In this exhibit, the cost centers are individual laboratories or departments that contain the functional skill area. The annual budget column represents each functional laboratory's total for the year. The exhibit also shows the November data. In this budget summary report, each laboratory or department is tracked by comparing its financial performance for

EXHIBIT 22.19 Technical Center Budget Summary Report for the Period Ending November 30, 201X

	Amount (in $1,000s)				
	November		Year-to-Date		Annual
Laboratory or Department	Budget	Actual	Budget	Actual	Budget
Electrical laboratory	212	216	2,295	2,354	2,556
Mechanical laboratory	225	207	2,475	2,457	2,700
Model shop	63	68	675	711	738
Chemical and material	158	185	1,710	1,643	1,575
General engineering	135	171	1,620	1,715	1,845
Total	793	847	8,775	8,880	9,414

the month against the incremental and cumulative year-to-date plan. Some companies plot this data on a chart that shows the total departmental history. Plots of variance are also common.

An individual laboratory's data (electrical laboratory) are broken out in Exhibit 22.20. Salaries, benefits, and so forth, are tracked incrementally and cumulatively for the month and year-to-date.

These monthly reports assist management in controlling a department's expenditures. Most of the traditional tools for tracking technology or construction projects fall short of showing true accomplishment. Overall departmental expenditures can be made on schedule with little or no accomplishment. A more modern technique for tracking projects uses "earned value," a true accomplishment cost. The traditional tools, however, are useful for controlling head count, travel, and supplies. These monthly budgets show potential problem areas. In Exhibit 22.20, the electrical laboratory has used more than its allotted travel allowance. By inspecting the November report, one can see that travel is being carefully monitored by the department head.

Earned Value

Earned-value reporting makes use of three pieces of financial data: the two traditional ones, budget and actual costs, and an accomplishment cost, called *earned value*. Inherent in the concept are "work packages," which are used to build the budget. Value is earned when these work packages are completed. The system can work only if the work packages are increments of the total budget that are sufficiently small to be tracked well. If the work packages are 3 percent of the total budget or smaller, tracking errors will not be significant. If large work packages are used, someone must make an estimate of their percentage complete. This becomes a variable, based on who does the estimate. A poor

EXHIBIT 22.20 Electrical Laboratory Budget Report for the Period Ending November 30, 201X

| Expense | Amount (in $1,000s) | | | | |
| | November | | Year-to-Date | | Annual Budget |
	Budget	Actual	Budget	Actual	
Salaries	126	122	1,206	1,211	1,359
Benefits	32	32	315	333	342
Supplies	5	9	54	68	59
Travel	9	—	81	95	95
Reproduction	5	5	23	18	27
Project materials	5	14	90	113	95
Consultant services	9	5	180	158	203
Miscellaneous expenses	—	—	14	18	18
Total controllable costs	191	187	1,963	2,014	2,198
Fixed costs	32	32	333	342	360
Total expenses	223	219	2,296	2,356	2,558

estimator can destroy the usefulness of the concept. The use of small work packages eliminates the problem.

By counting the completed small work packages and totaling their value, it is possible to obtain the earned value. If one compares earned value with plan or budget, the schedule status can be obtained. By comparing earned value with actual cost, the budgetary status can be developed. Using earned-value reporting for a project, midpoint corrections can be made to keep the project on target. An example and the next definitions will help to clarify the process:

- *Earned value* is the budgeted cost of work performed. It is the summation of completed work packages.
- *Plan* or *budget* is the budgeted cost of work scheduled. It is initially developed by adding all of the work package costs to time intervals based on planned completion dates.
- *Actual cost of work performed* tracks the actual expenditures of project work packages.
- *Work packages* are the building blocks for establishing earned value. A work package can take many forms. The next categories can be applied:

  - A physical assembly of components—for example, mechanism, electronic printed circuit boards, the foundation for a building
  - A design and development activity—for example, layout of a foundation, a vehicle suspension design, an experiment, a bacterial culture growth
  - A study—for example, evaluation of an overall project or part of a project, an environmental analysis

- *Selection of natural break points* in a project, and defining these points as work packages, is the standard procedure.

As an example of the earned-value process, let us assume that the contractor has the responsibility for installing individual wall air-conditioning units in a 50-story building. One two-ton unit will cool each floor. The building is under construction; elevators have not been installed. Installation difficulties become more severe as the elevation increases. To simplify the estimate, the contractor has grouped the units into ten-story value categories. These estimates are given:

Floors	Unit Installation Cost per Floor
1–10	$500
11–20	$550
21–30	$600
31–40	$650
41–50	$700

The contractor has defined a work package as a complete installation consisting of the unit, all electric wires, and the necessary plumbing. There are 50 work packages in the project. (Other definitions could have been used. If 10 installations were defined as a work package, their value would be too big for accurate tracking. Conversely, if lifting the unit was a work package, wiring per floor another, and plumbing another, the total work packages would be too small for efficient reporting.) The contractor's intention is to install five units per week for a total of ten weeks. We require the completed project in the ten-week time span.

This baseline budget can be developed using the contractor's data:

Week	Installation Value
1	$ 2,500
2	2,500
3	2,750
4	2,750
5	3,000
6	3,000
7	3,250
8	3,250
9	3,500
10	3,500
Total value	$30,000

The baseline budget is plotted in Exhibit 22.21.

Let us assume that the project has been in operation for five weeks with these data:

Week	Actual Installation	Earned Value	Actual Cost
1	6	$ 3,000	$ 2,950
2	5	2,550	2,500
3	5	2,750	2,750
4	4[a]	2,200	2,450
5	4	2,400	2,400
Total	14	$12,900	$13,050

[a] A teamster strike delayed shipments; overtime was scheduled.

Exhibit 22.22 shows the budget status, which is obtained by plotting the data against the baseline.

At present, this project is one-fifth of a week late and $60 over budget. These data are obtained by comparing earned value against plan for the schedule and earned value against actual for the budget.

Earned value is a powerful tool. It permits a finance or technical group to monitor accomplishment. In development activities, work packages are defined as tasks or subtasks. The estimate, obtained from manpower histograms and materials, is developed at the beginning of the program. Work packages are then defined as subtasks or groups of

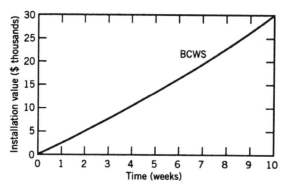

EXHIBIT 22.21 Baseline Budget

tasks, and the baseline budget is generated. As tasks are completed, the value is earned and the development program is tracked.

Budget Tracking

The major advantage of an earned-value tracking system is an outsider's ability to assess real progress without getting involved in the details of day-to-day project management. Project managers can, therefore, evaluate deliveries when the supplier is on a critical

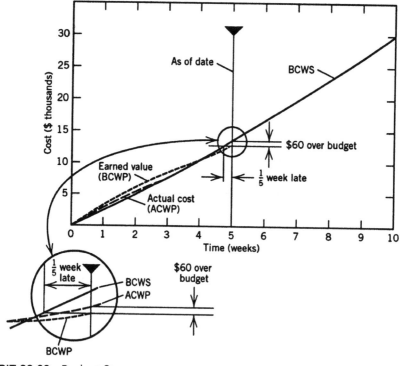

EXHIBIT 22.22 Budget Status

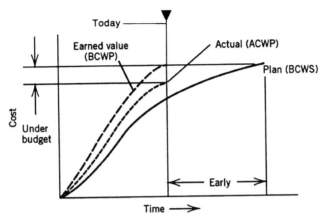

EXHIBIT 22.23   Traditional Reporting of Plan versus Actual

path. Department managers can monitor projects without getting into the day-to-day planning and control charts. The earned-value system permits budget management with the knowledge of real accomplishment. Exhibits 22.23 through 22.25 are used as examples.

In Exhibit 22.23, traditional reporting of plan versus actual would assume that this project is in severe difficulty because actual expenditures have been consistently over budget. In reality, the project is in excellent condition. It is ahead of schedule and under budget. In Exhibit 22.24, traditional reporting of plan versus actual would assume that this project is in excellent condition since actual expenditures are below budget. In reality, there is nothing good about this project. It is behind schedule and over budget.

Exhibit 22.25 represents a mixed project. The project is behind schedule, but more value has been earned than money spent. The project manager can schedule overtime with the surplus funds to get this project back on schedule.

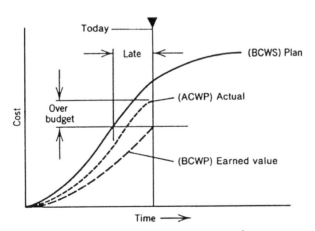

EXHIBIT 22.24   Traditional Reporting of Plan versus Actual

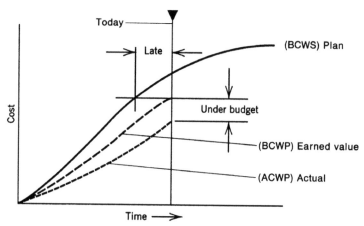

EXHIBIT 22.25   Mixed Project

COORDINATING PROJECT BUDGETS

Projects often involve activities for several functional departments. Coordinating the budget across departmental lines is the responsibility of the project manager. In functional organizations, this can be a difficult task, since people assigned to the project do not necessarily report to the project manager. Data can be slow in transmission. The project manager may not be able to get the functional people to work a sufficient amount of time for project success. Some departments may overcharge; others may be too busy to work on the project.

For this reason, companies have gone to other organizational forms. In the project organization, all people who work on a project report to the project manager. In a matrix organization, the project personnel report to two bosses. Responsibility for schedule and budget are the domain of the project manager; responsibility for technology is the domain of the functional manager. Dual reporting gives the project manager the control needed to get the job done, and it gives the functional manager the pooled specialists needed to ensure quality developments.

Organizational Effects on Data Reports

Exhibit 22.26 outlines the department's major project budgets. The laboratory assigned the development task is coded by number. For example, the electrical laboratory is assigned project number 101, the development of an optoelectronic screen for safeguarding punch press operators' hands. Part of the work will be carried out by the mechanical laboratory, which is responsible for structure, and part by the general engineering laboratory, which is responsible for automation. The model shop will build the physical unit. The electrical laboratory will carry the major burden of design of optics, electronics, and fail-safe circuitry.

In a functional organization, one of the electrical laboratory's engineers would be assigned the project engineering task. In a project organization, people would be pulled

EXHIBIT 22.26   Major Project Budgets for 201X

| | Projects and Code | | | |
Department	Optoelectronics #101	Forming Machine #309	Cable Maker #207	Automation #406
Electrical laboratory	$427,500	$85,500	$139,500	$180,000
Mechanical laboratory	22,500	292,500	427,500	157,500
Model shop	67,500	247,500	202,500	112,500
Chemical and materials	—	922,500	67,500	9,000
General engineering	90,000	382,500	112,500	562,500
Total project budget	$607,500	$1,930,500	$949,500	$1,021,500

Assignment Code		Annual Summary	
Electrical laboratory	100	Major projects total	$4,509,000
Mechanical laboratory	200	Allocated projects	1,822,500
Chemical and materials	300	Sustaining projects	1,206,000
General engineering	400	Miscellaneous projects	1,885,500
Department total			$9,423,000

out of their individual laboratories for the project duration. A project manager would lead the task until it is completed, and all people would work for him or her. In a matrix organization, a project manager assigned from a project-management group would be responsible for the budget and the schedule. The R&D laboratory manager would supply people to work on the project from their normal work area and would be responsible for technology and quality. The people working on the project would have two bosses, each controlling different aspects of their work.

Financial data reporting is most difficult in the functional organization. If projects are to succeed, synchronous data reports from all of the laboratories, from purchasing, and from the model shop are essential. As organizations become larger, this requirement becomes harder to achieve.

The matrix organization requires accurate data, but the demands for reporting are more easily met, since the project manager has a proper balance of authority and responsibility. He or she can cut across all lines to get the data.

The project organization has the easiest reporting system, since all personnel, supplies, and equipment are in the domain of the project manager.

CHAPTER TWENTY-THREE

Administrative-Expense Budget

R. Malcolm Schwartz
Maria Theresa Mateo, MBA
PricewaterhouseCoopers LLP

 ## INTRODUCTION

The administrative-expense budget is an important link with all other budgets, because it comprises activities that support other budgeted activities and at the same time provides some elements of control, and of independent perspective, on those other activities. Therefore, how management views administrative expenses says much about how management governs and leads the overall organization. In this sense, it is important to deal with what administrative expense includes and why it is important, before even beginning to address how it is budgeted. As a consequence, this chapter concentrates on these subjects:

- The role and scope of the administrative-expense budget
- Methods used for preparing the administrative-expense budget
- Factors that impact the administrative-expense budget
- Unique issues impacting the administrative-expense budget
- Tools and techniques for managing the administrative-expense budget

 ## ROLE AND SCOPE OF THE ADMINISTRATIVE-EXPENSE BUDGET

The surge of reengineering and other efforts to improve performance and productivity have increased management focus on administrative expenses. Administrative expenses are somewhat straightforward, but the value of the activities for which administrative expenses are incurred—that is, why administrative expenses are consumed by administrative activities—is not as straightforward. Therefore, the administrative-expense budget is one of the more difficult budgets to manage because it is hard for many people to understand and agree to the value and purpose of administrative expenses. When a company can plan and conduct the activities that consume administrative expenses better than its competitors are able to, the company that is successful in doing so might develop a competitive advantage through such competencies.

Allocating Administrative Expenses from Those Who Incur Them to Those Who Use Them

The difficulty of preparing and managing the administrative-expense budget stems from two factors: (1) the difficulty of allocation, and (2) the discretionary nature of the expenses. A "fashionable" company—which has hired the best people, read all the right books, and implemented the academics' and consultants' recommendations—might have empowered its people, established self-directed teams, and pushed accountability into the organization, hence creating many departments, control units, budget units, strategic business units, service centers, and/or profit centers—each having a separate plan, budget, and/or profit and loss—of the overall administrative-expense budget. Yet it also might have selectively centralized some core functions that provide economies of scale for the overall organization. To hold individual revenue-producing units—the strategic business units (SBUs) or profit centers—accountable for all activities, however, the organization then might have attempted to assign or allocate these central service organizations (or overheads, as viewed by some SBU leaders). But how should the company allocate the costs, for example, of its corporate-image marketing? Should the largest-revenue SBU shoulder most of the burden? That might be inappropriate if that SBU relies less on the corporate image for achieving its mission than other, smaller units. If that is so, then should the smaller SBUs be assigned a larger share of this cost? If so, the economic effect might be larger than can be tolerated, and steps might have to be taken to affect the corporate-image program, to change the way that costs are assigned, or to discourage new businesses. As can be seen, the dilemma of allocating the costs of the administrative-expense budget can lead management into a vicious circle.

Identifying the Value of Administrative Expenses

The discretionary nature of many of the activities that incur administrative expenses also can bedevil managers, because it is difficult for these activities to ascribe a quantitative value (an output) for the explicitly determined (input) cost budgeted. Managers are not always confident that the correct amounts are being spent. Is a larger legal department, for example, a good thing? For an organization that has incurred large regulatory penalties, or that has been sued for patent infringement, increasing legal expenses might be a good thing, but it might be too late. Therefore, it is often difficult to measure the value of corporate services and the right period of time for budgeting the expenditure compared to the period of time when the benefits will be realized.

The difficulty of measuring value might be attributed to, among other factors, the problem of measuring risk, which often is associated with low-probability occurrences but which can have very high costs per occurrence. Administrative organizations that monitor compliance with governmental or corporate policies on safety, environment, and labor issues are constantly battling for funding and for recognition of their value. Their value becomes apparent only when, for example, companies are faced with lawsuits or a loss of goodwill from their handling of a compliance matter, such as happened with the *Exxon Valdez* oil spill. Even in hindsight, it still might not be clear what level of additional investment—and, for that matter, what type of additional expenditure—might have mitigated or prevented problems such as this.

One way to deal with this value issue as it relates to the administrative-expense budget is to categorize administrative activities, and the costs that they incur, as serving one of two purposes—efficiency or effectiveness. For example, the purpose of a payroll department is to be efficient. The payroll department strives to process employee paychecks in the most cost-efficient manner. For an area focused on efficiency, the question is: How much does it cost the company to do what needs to be done? Answering this question is relatively straightforward: Management can conduct a market test, develop unit standards, or purchase available benchmark data to estimate the appropriate cost.

Alternatively, the purpose of another human resources activity—recruiting—is to be effective, not efficient. "Effectiveness" can be defined as the extent to which an activity supports or enables a predetermined objective or target to be met. The recruiting activity strives to identify, hire, and retain high-quality individuals. For an area focused on effectiveness, the question is: How do its activities benefit the organization? Answering this question is much more difficult than answering the efficiency question because areas that focus on effectiveness usually do not produce a tangible product; thus there is less relevancy in performing external benchmarks, and there are few external data available. Rather, these areas tend to focus on the company's well-being related to its analysis of risks and objectives, and these areas are not as easily quantifiable. Value can be ascertained by assessing a company's tolerance for risk and how much it is willing to spend to be at a comfortable level of risk.

What Functions Are Included in the Administrative-Expense Budget?

The administrative-expense budget can be described by what it does not include: In some ways, this is easier to describe than by starting with what it does include. Typically, activities that touch either the organization's product or the organization's customer usually are considered part of core operations, and their expenses fall into operating, not administrative, expense budgets. These activities typically include customer service, distribution, manufacturing, research and development, and sales. Marketing and purchasing are usually considered operating expenses but can be found in some organization's administrative-expense budgets.

Thus, everything else (activities not part of the core operations) falls in the administrative-expense budget. These activities often are shared by a number of internal user organizations. Although organizations more frequently have been taking a process view of their businesses, few companies prepare budgets by process. In most cases, the administrative-expense budget is still prepared on a functional or departmental basis. Exhibit 23.1 lists those areas that are most often part of the administrative-expense budget and identifies whether their purpose is primarily efficiency or effectiveness.

Exhibit 23.1, however, only shows the primary purpose at a high level; for example, within the purchasing function, ordering activities tend to be oriented toward efficiency,

EXHIBIT 23.1   Primary Purposes of Typical Administrative Departments Found in the Administrative-Expense Budget

Department	Type of Focus	
	Efficiency	Effectiveness
Finance		
• Accounting	X	
• Fixed assets	X	
• Internal audit		X
• Tax		X
• Treasury		X
General administration		
• Corporate executives		X
• Internal business development/strategy		X
• Internal consulting		X
• Policies and procedures		X
• Publication services and internal communications	X	
• Risk management		X
• Real estate and facility services	X	
• Secretaries, reproduction, and mailroom	X	
Human resources		
• Benefits	X	
• Employee-retiree administration	X	
• Payroll	X	
• Recruitment		X
• Training		X
Insurance and risk management		X
• Information technology (IT)		
• IT development		X
• IT operations	X	
• Telecommunications		X

Department	Type of Focus	
	Efficiency	Effectiveness
Legal		X
Public relations		
• Community and charitable activities		X
• Government and regulatory relations		X
• Industry, professional, and trade relations		X
• Investor relations	X	
• Media relations		X
Purchasing	X	

but vendor management activities tend to be oriented toward effectiveness. Furthermore, the purpose of an administrative activity can vary from one organization to another, and even for different relationships within an organization. A fast-food company, for example, might want to centralize the purchase of ingredients, to ensure uniformity and to take advantage of scale, and thus might categorize the purchasing department as an administrative expense and might define its purpose as efficiency focused. Conversely, a chain of higher-priced restaurants might purchase locally, to emphasize freshness as well as regional tastes, and therefore might classify the purchasing department as an administrative expense focused more on effectiveness than on efficiency. Organizations also could have the same sizes of administrative-expense budgets, but these budgets might include quite different levels of efficiency and effectiveness. Organizations might have similar levels of performance but a very different levels of administrative costs, as shown in Exhibit 23.2.

What Types of Expenses Are Included in the Administrative-Expense Budget?

The majority of the administrative expenses typically include costs associated closely with human resources (namely, salary and benefits). There often is a large external-service component, as many administrative activities (such as legal, business development, strategy, audit, and data-processing operations and development) are often outsourced. There also might be some capital-asset costs—in the form of depreciation expense, leasehold amortization, and the like—included in the administrative-expense budget, particularly associated with information technology and real estate. Administrative expenses also can be associated with activities that are not easily understood or that might occur infrequently (such as expenses associated with litigation), and they often cannot be linked to specific products or services. Inasmuch as some administrative costs tend to be discretionary, their value and quality tend to be difficult to measure.

In contrast, operating budgets include both physical and human resources costs. Most operating costs are associated with specified and repetitive processes (such as production, sales, and distribution) and can be related to specific products or services. Examples of such operating expenses are raw materials, plant and equipment, and direct labor.

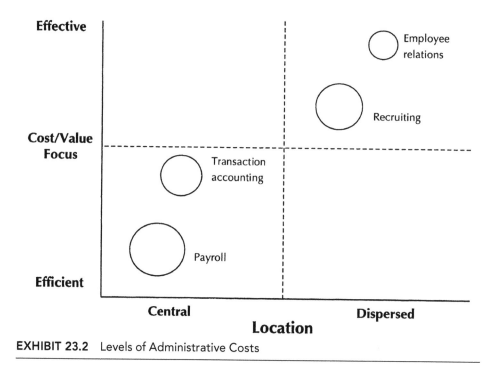

EXHIBIT 23.2   Levels of Administrative Costs

A typical administrative-expense budget, structured for an administrative department, is illustrated in Exhibit 23.3.

METHODS USED FOR PREPARING THE ADMINISTRATIVE-EXPENSE BUDGET

After there is agreement on the roles and purposes of the administrative activities, as discussed in the previous section, there are three basic steps to preparing the administrative-expense budget: (1) projecting the level of activity, (2) projecting the level of resources expected to be consumed to support that level of activity, and (3) projecting the factor costs of those resources. Each is discussed in the next sections. Also important in preparing the administrative-expense budget is how to gain buy-in while maintaining a clear sense of direction. This means combining what are often identified, respectively, as the bottom-up and top-down approaches.

Projecting the Level of Activity

Typically, a first step in preparing the administrative-expense budget is to project the level of services to be provided and hence to project the level of expenses expected to be incurred to provide that level of services. Companies use a number of different methods to project administrative expenses and hence to develop a basis for applying costs to administrative activities. This section briefly discusses the applicability of these methods to the administrative expense budget.

- *Historical basis (or ordinary incremental).* Historical-basis budgeting takes into account the previous year's budget and the actual results. Budgeted levels of activity for the projected period are adjusted, depending on the previous year's results and on the expectations for the projected period. Historical-basis budgeting does not usually consider the nonpeople costs; instead, it drives the budget to the number of people and the rates they are paid and then adds other costs through ratios.
- *Expense/revenue basis.* This method of budgeting determines the amount to be budgeted for the projected period based on some defined relationship between the particular administrative expense under consideration and revenue. For example, human resource departmental expenses, when using this method, might be considered to be equal to about 1 percent of sales: this ratio might be considered to be valid for future periods. Similar to historical-basis budgeting, this method also is driven by people cost.

EXHIBIT 23.3   Typical Administrative Department Expense Budget

Budget Year:	20XX	
Company Code:	19	
Plant:	QU	
Owner:	Alec Mundy	
Cost Center:	421 Mail services	
Cost Element	**Description**	**Annual**
620000	Salaries and wages	$1,956,000
623000	Employee allowances	$11,000
624000	Relocation	$85,000
630000	Other materials and supplies	$504,000
631000	Travel and entertainment	$69,700
634000	Postage	$8,000
640000	Purchased services	$82,000
640015	Maintenance services	$0
641000	Contract labor	$40,000
642000	Professional fees and consult	$6,000
644000	Software	$3,000
	Controllable totals	**$2,764,700**
621000	Fringe benefits	$731,544
622000	Incentive compensation	$220,050
660000	Depreciation	$400,633
661000	L/T operate lease-equipment	$220,000
670900	Act-office building and overtime	$1,154,687
671803	R&D overhead (admin.)	$402,356
672300	General services	$91,468
	Noncontrollable totals	**$3,200,738**
	Cost center totals	**$5,965,438**

▪ *Zero basis.* Zero-based budgeting is budgeting from the ground up, as though the budget were being prepared for the first time. When using this method, every proposed expenditure comes under review. Although zero-based budgeting requires more work than other forms of budgeting, it forces managers to better justify their outlays. Few firms adopt zero-based budgeting on an annual basis for all departments. When zero-based budgeting is undertaken, it typically is on a less regular basis, and only for a subset of responsibility centers at any one time.

▪ *Activity basis.* Activity-based budgeting focuses on the activities that are projected to be used to support the production and sale of projected products and services and then on estimating the costs of those activities. Activity-based budgeting can be valuable in the case of indirect—and administrative—costs. There are several ways to develop activity-based costs. In the accounting approach, for example, activity-based budgeting partitions indirect costs into separate but homogeneous activity cost pools. Management then uses cause- and-effect criteria to identify the cost drivers for the separate cost pools. An organization then can apply these drivers to the costs of the services being provided (and, eventually, to the products themselves) in proportion to the volume of activity that a given service consumes. By assigning all resources to an activity, this method is more precise in that it considers more than just people-related costs.

Exhibit 23.4 compares the different methods.

The trade-offs among the various budgeting methods are between effort and value. Clearly, for organizations in which administrative expenses are not very important, simpler methods should be used. However, in many organizations, decisions about administrative expenses are visible and important, so more care might be taken with—and about—the methods used for budgeting such expenses.

In making its choice, an organization also should consider selecting a method that will provide a means to track performance in comparison to the desired outcomes on operational measures. Good budgeting techniques provide an ability to measure value received and to track performance. Performance measures will vary by activity and by the importance of any activity to the organization, but most organizations will at

EXHIBIT 23.4   Comparison of Budgeting Methods

Comparative Factor	Historical Basis	Expense-Revenue Basis	Zero Basis	Activity Basis
Simplicity	Yes	Yes	No	No
Level of effort	No	No	Yes	Yes
Takes a long time	No	No	Yes	Yes
Enables cost management	Yes	Yes	Yes	Yes
Enables cost–benefit analysis	No	Yes	No	Yes
Links cost drivers	No	No	No	Yes
Supports decision making	No	No	Yes	Yes

the least track: (1) profitability; (2) customer satisfaction; (3) innovation; and (4) other internal measures relating to efficiency, quality, and time.

Projecting the Level of Resources Expected to Be Consumed to Support that Level of Activity

A second step in budgeting administrative expenses, once the level of activities is estimated, is to relate resources to activities. For example, processing payroll checks might lead to an estimate of the clerical and supervisory time that is required. The same might be done for each of the administrative activities. Relating resources to be consumed to the level of activity can be accomplished by using any of the methods described in the previous section. The reason for separating the steps in this description of the budgeting process is to suggest that separate analyses of activity levels and of resources consumed should be undertaken. For example, the level of activity might be the same as in the prior year, but the level of resources projected might be less due to the success of reengineering efforts.

Projecting the Factor Costs of Those Resources

The third step is to project the factor costs that are the unit costs of the resources to be consumed. For example, an increase in the costs of healthcare benefits would lead to a higher factor cost for benefits. However, better procedures and training might lead to a lower set of skills to support some activities than in the prior year. Again, this step can be combined with the previous ones, but it is useful to consider it separately; in this way, the budget can be developed separately for the level of activity, for the level of resources consumed by the activity, and for the factor costs (or unit costs) of those resources. Also, projecting factor costs might use other techniques, such as review of economic indicators (e.g., projected rates of inflation) or review of changed business circumstances (e.g., the effects of changes in purchased-service contracts).

Gaining Agreement, Top-Down and Bottom-Up

The process for any of these methods could be top-down, bottom-up, or a hybrid. A typical hybrid approach entails guidelines provided from the top, numbers generated bottom-up and subject to top-level modification, and several iterations before a final budget is submitted. A blending of the top-down and bottom-up approaches is shown in Exhibit 23.5.

The optimal approach for an organization depends on such characteristics as its governance and management styles, the extent of similarity—and of autonomy— among its business units, the competencies in its business units, and so forth. For highly diversified organizations, the optimal approach might be to have limited direction from the top. However, for less diversified organizations, or for organizations that are more operationally oriented (e.g., with a number of operating units that are not freestanding), the optimal approach might be to have more direction from the top with regard to budgeting.

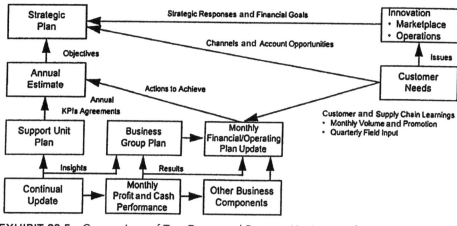

EXHIBIT 23.5   Comparison of Top-Down and Bottom-Up Approaches

FACTORS THAT IMPACT THE ADMINISTRATIVE-EXPENSE BUDGET

The characteristics of an organization and its industry not only affect the approach it takes to preparing the administrative-expense budget and the classification of the expenses (efficiency versus effectiveness) but also can affect the size of the administrative-expense budget relative to other costs. Some of the key factors are listed next.

▪ Characteristics of the industry

  ▪ *Service or product focus.* Service companies tend to have higher administrative expenses, due to such factors as higher turnover and higher training costs; also, labor reporting tends to be relatively more expensive than production reporting, but the costs tend to be less obvious.

  ▪ *Diversified or simple organization structure.* The diversified structure tends to have higher administrative expenses due to greater needs for coordination.

  ▪ *Cyclical or level volumes.* Uneven flows of work tend to lead to higher administrative expenses, to have in place the resources for the peak periods of activity.

  ▪ *Public or private.* A public organization tends to have higher administrative expenses due to a variety of regulatory and reporting requirements.

  ▪ *Regulated or unregulated.* Regulated industries tend to have higher administrative expenses due to regulatory agency requirements.

▪ Maturity of the organization and the industry

  ▪ *Start-up.* A start-up organization can have higher administrative expenses until it learns how to be efficient and until it becomes stable enough to satisfy investors.

  ▪ *Growing.* A growing organization can have higher administrative expenses because it might not be focused on profits, and it might lose a sense of control on administrative expenses.

- *Mature.* Mature organizations can have lower administrative expenses, if they have developed a profit focus.

- Organizational structure of company and operating philosophy

  - *Centralized or decentralized.* Decentralized companies tend to have higher administrative expenses because a cost of decentralization often is to have redundant activities.
  - *Level of technology.* The administrative expenses associated with less automated organizations tend to be higher.

UNIQUE ISSUES IMPACTING THE ADMINISTRATIVE-EXPENSE BUDGET

Unique issues impact the administrative expense budget. Specifically, how does one quantify the value associated with administrative activities?

Budgeting efficiency-oriented costs is relatively straightforward. One can develop cost—and in some cases, time—standards for such process-oriented activities as payroll, purchasing, and accounts payable, and might choose to use staffing ratios for other activities such as secretarial, investor relations, and telecommunications. These standards can be compared and validated with available benchmarks.

Effectiveness-oriented costs, as discussed earlier, are much more difficult to quantify for such reasons as these:

- Activities that are oriented toward effectiveness often do not produce a tangible result and often do not produce any result in the same period in which the costs are incurred. For example, legal expenses are best spent to prevent legal problems; if problems do occur, it might be years after the legal effort (e.g., to conduct a patent search) was expended. In sum, these activities tend to focus on the company's well-being, which is not easily quantifiable.
- The degree of specialization of these effectiveness-oriented activities tends to be higher than for those administrative activities that are more oriented toward efficiency. It might be difficult for an executive who might have come from a sales background, for example, to assess the needs and performance of the public affairs department; yet those activities can help to influence legislators and regulators to understand the organization's point of view and thus to prevent undesirable regulatory rulings. In the more extreme cases, a lack of understanding can lead to a lack of trust, which can cause inappropriate levels of support for these types of activities over time. Finally, the performance and effectiveness of these types of administrative activities depend much more on the quality of people in place than on the process that is followed.
- The factor costs of the kind of people who support these activities often is much higher than for the more efficiency-oriented activities. Legal, treasury, and business development/strategy personnel are often among the highest-paid staff categories in a company. While the internal costs might be high, the costs of outsourcing these activities by using external groups that provide these services can be even higher.

▪ These roles often are shaped to, among other factors, prevent—or, if necessary, respond to—high-cost problems that have a low probability of occurring, yet management might fail to assess the value of these risks in a way that supports the budgeting of these activities correctly.

▪ The environment that drives these effectiveness-oriented costs is not the same as that which drives the other administrative areas or operations areas, and they might be driven by external (technological, governmental, and/or competitive) issues. For example, the costs of recruiting and of corporate advertising might be driven more by how much competitors spend than by the organization's strategy as such.

As noted earlier, the effectiveness orientation can be viewed as the degree to which a predetermined objective or target is to be met, so the value of an activity's effectiveness can be estimated by assessing an organization's tolerance for risk and determining how much it is willing to spend to be at a comfortable level of risk to meet the predetermined objective or target. For example, when considering the legal department, does the organization want to avoid litigation at all costs due to potential damage to its image? Or will some litigation be acceptable, so long as the organization's position is clear and sustainable? Does the organization want all contracts written in an explicit, thorough, and detailed manner because contracting parties are perceived as untrustworthy? Or might the organization accept broader contracts that rely on trust between the contracting parties?

TOOLS AND TECHNIQUES FOR MANAGING THE ADMINISTRATIVE-EXPENSE BUDGET

A number of tools and techniques are useful in managing and controlling administrative expenses. These include:

▪ Budget variance analysis
▪ Administrative charge-back to the operating units
▪ Hybrid transfer costing
▪ Outsourcing alternatives
▪ Performance measures
▪ Activity-based costing
▪ Benchmarking

Budget Variance Analysis

Variance analysis provides useful information for making decisions because it helps to provide insights into why the actual results differ from the planned performance. A variance is a performance gap between a benchmark—generally, the budgeted amount—and the actual results, typically as reported in the accounting system for financial information or in operating systems for nonfinancial information. The most important task in variance analysis is to understand why variances have occurred and then to use that knowledge to promote learning and continuous improvement and to enable better planning and better cost management. It is equally important to focus on positive variances as well as negative variances.

Administrative Charge-Back to the Operating Units

Operating groups often are charged for the administrative services to remind profit-center managers that indirect costs exist and that profit-center earnings must be adequate to cover some share of these costs, as well as to provide for a return on invested capital and a fair return to creditors and investors. Organizations who do this believe that it will stimulate profit-center managers to put pressure on administrative managers to control the costs of the services that they provide.

Hybrid Transfer Costing

Operating groups might be charged the budgeted expense instead of the actual expense, with the difference absorbed by the unit incurring the cost. Organizations that use budgeted costs as the basis for charging believe that this helps to motivate the manager of the support department to improve efficiency. During the budget period, the support departments, not the user departments, bear the risk of any unfavorable cost variances because the user departments do not pay for any costs that exceed the budgeted costs.

The decision of whether to allocate budgeted or actual costs affects the level of uncertainty that user departments face. Budgeted costs let the user departments know the costs in advance. Users then are better equipped to determine the amount of the service to request and, if the option exists, whether to use the internal department source or an external vendor.

Some organizations choose to recognize that it might not always be best to impose all of the risks of variances from budgeted amounts completely on the support departments or completely on the user departments.

Outsourcing Alternatives

Exposing administrative-cost centers to competitive forces of the marketplace is another way that some organizations use to force administrative areas to control their expenses. If operating units have a choice of buying services from an external party, then administrative units have the incentive of self-preservation to contain costs. This does, however, pose some risk of suboptimization of the centralized services if some operating units decide to outsource, leaving the remaining operating units with higher costs for these services.

Performance Measures

Performance measures that are linked to compensation help motivate management in the right direction. However, it is critical that an organization's goals are aligned with how its incentive plan is designed. When this technique is used, performance measures that are both financial and nonfinancial measures of effectiveness or efficiency should be considered; they should be monitored on an ongoing and systematic basis.

Activity-Based Costing

Activity-based costing can provide a mechanism for managing administrative expenses. If the administrative and user departments agree to a framework and agree to the level of work, it can provide an actual per-unit basis for charging back the costs with the associated services. However, if the actual usage level is either above or below the targeted level, the actual per-unit charge-back might be different, and management will have to decide how any efficiency gains or losses will be treated.

Benchmarking

Benchmark studies can provide information on the comparative cost efficiency of an organization. Benchmarking is the continual process of comparing products, services, and activities to objective indicators of performance. Benchmarks can be found inside or outside the organization.

 ## SUMMARY

The administrative-expense budget is an important link with all other budgets because it comprises activities that support other budgeted activities, and at the same time, it provides some elements of control, and of independent perspective, on those other activities. The size of the administrative-expense budget, what it includes, and how it is prepared can be unique to each organization for many reasons. However, the administrative-expense budget primarily reflects how management views its support functions.

CHAPTER TWENTY-FOUR

Budgeting the Purchasing Department and the Purchasing Process

Carl Benner

John N. Trush

Thomas F. Norris

PricewaterhouseCoopers LLP

DESCRIPTION AND DEFINITION OF THE PROCESS APPROACH

Traditionally, management has used the budget as a tool to track, control, and forecast the financial effectiveness of the business. Typically, budgets are prepared in some hierarchical manner by departments and then aggregated along organizational lines to create the business unit's budget. Today, as a result of the use of such techniques as reengineering and right-sizing, and the use of cross-functional teams, there is an increased emphasis and need to manage and optimize along a process perspective as well as to use budgeting for control of the individual responsibilities, departments, and functions within the process. (To distinguish the purchasing department from the purchasing process, the term "procurement" is be used herein to identify the process perspective.) To be effective, an organization must control the spending of both the function and the process; in other words, the organization must consider:

- Purchasing as defined by the activities of the purchasing department
- Purchasing as defined by the activities of the procurement process

Purchasing Department

The control of the purchasing departmental budget is a very important piece of the procurement process. The purchasing budget, to begin, will be influenced by the manner in which the business is organized. Many purchasing departments function both centrally and locally. For example, companies might buy key commodities or services centrally through long-term purchasing agreements, but the actual ordering and releasing might be executed locally, at the operating site. Additionally, there might be local purchasing departments that buy items and services such as capital equipment and maintenance for that particular site. Purchasing activities are sometimes intentionally delegated and distributed to other departments. This normally is a function of size, efficiency, and mission, and the level of special competencies required. Some examples include:

- Advertising, purchased by the marketing department
- Research and development, purchased by medical doctors or scientific specialists
- Transportation, purchased by the logistics arm of the organization
- Outsourcing of information technology activities
- Travel and entertainment, purchased by authorized managers

Another common technique used by the purchasing department to delegate authority to the organization is via the procurement card, usually used for low-dollar and high-volume item purchases. This tool has enabled significant cost reductions through the elimination of several activities, such as the requisition, the purchase order, the invoice, the check request, and the check itself. Some leading-edge companies, in support of programs called Just In Time (JIT) II Purchasing, further delegate purchasing by bringing key suppliers on-site and hooking them up to the company's information system. The suppliers then actually do the buying/planning of the material or service provided to the company. Whenever purchasing delegates responsibility, it is still responsible for oversight, as well as appropriate purchasing training and education.

The purchasing department also has an important role in providing both strategic and operating assistance to the organization. Strategically, purchasing is an integral partner in all make/buy decisions. Purchasing is involved in developing the budget for materials and services. This is a consistent role among the various business sectors, whether private, public, or nonprofit. A 1990 study by the National Association of Purchasing Managers (NAPM) concluded that the tasks or duties that purchasing managers perform are fairly similar in the private, public, and nonprofit sectors: Purchasers across these sectors appear to "speak the same language" and approach their jobs with reasonably the same duties and goals in mind. An article in the December 1996 issue of *Purchasing Today* concluded that manufacturing and service industries faced similar struggles: "In many cases, service industry purchasers find themselves dealing with issues that manufacturing sector companies have already confronted, such as supplier reduction strategies and cost-price analysis."[1]

---

[1] Carolyn Pye, "Service-Industry Speaks Out," *Purchasing Today* 12, No. 12 (December 1996); 24–26.

Purchasing is the department most involved in the selection and control of suppliers. Purchasing typically establishes the policies and procedures that govern the review, selection, and certification of suppliers. Many purchasing departments have focused on cost elimination through strategic partnerships. Successful partnerships have individually yielded cost reductions of 15 to 45 percent of the purchasing bill. Because only a handful of partnerships can be resourced and managed, each partnership is highly leverageable and could be worth 3 to 5 percent of the total annual buy dollars. Advanced organizations are building these targets into their purchasing budgets. A critical mass needs to be developed and dedicated to expand improvement efforts internally and, as appropriate, to extend them to the supplier's suppliers. Care must be taken that reductions are properly resourced and budgeted for implementation.

The purchasing department is well positioned to strongly influence the entire procurement process by its involvement in various supply-chain activities. Purchasing typically is involved in both product and process development as well as in other technical activities within the organization. In most organizations, purchasing has continual involvement with operational activities, such as stores, materials handling, production, quality, receiving, and shipping, as well as with administrative activities, such as accounts payable and accounts receivable.

Whether purchasing departments function centrally, locally, or in a distributed model, or are in the private, public, or nonprofit sectors, departmental expenses can be identified and budgets combined or separated as needed to manage and control departmental spending.

The Procurement Process

It is more difficult to identify and control the expenses of the procurement process. In many organizations, procurement is not recognized as a process, and therefore the complete set of its elements has not been identified. Additionally, expenses are more difficult to track because they are spread throughout the organization. However, there is a value in expanding the departmental focus of the typical budget process to include the entire procurement process. In particular, this is responsive to management's need for continuous improvement.

To begin, it is useful to identify the elements of a process and determine the definition of a process. A *process* is a set of linked activities that take an input, transform it, and create an output. Ideally, the transformation that occurs in a process should add value to the input and should create an output that is more useful to, and effective for, the recipient. Exhibit 24.1 describes a process and illustrates the movement from supplier to customer. How does a process add value? Value can be created or added through improved product quality and/or service, reduced cycle time, and reduced cost to the customer. Exhibit 24.2 describes these value metrics in greater detail. The procurement process not only encompasses the internal organization but also includes external customers and suppliers. This process will vary by industry, by business unit, and by the nature of the product or service provided.

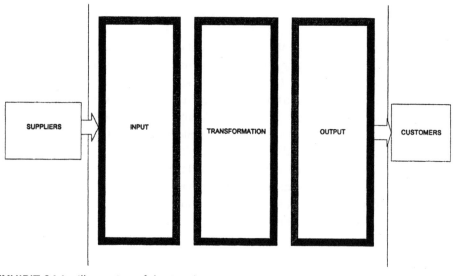

EXHIBIT 24.1   Illustration of the Purchasing Process

Source: David K. Carr and Henry J. Johansson, *Best Practices in Reengineering* (New York: McGraw-Hill, 1995). Reprinted with permission.

For most companies, there are two major components of the procurement process:

1. The product development subprocess, which encompasses the make/buy selection and includes:

   ▫ Marketing
   ▫ Design
   ▫ Manufacturing
   ▫ Costing
   ▫ Engineering
   ▫ Supplier
   ▫ Customer
   ▫ Purchasing
   ▫ Accounting

2. The ordering subprocess, which encompasses ordering, delivery, receipt, and payment of the requested goods or services, including:

   ▫ Customer or requisitioner
   ▫ Purchasing
   ▫ Supplier
   ▫ Receiving
   ▫ Quality
   ▫ Materials handling

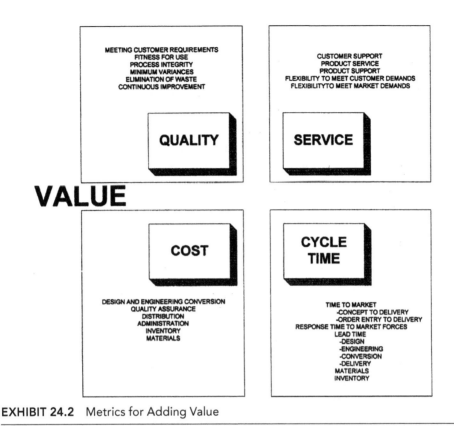

EXHIBIT 24.2　Metrics for Adding Value

Source: Henry J. Johansson, Patrick McHugh, John A. Pendlebury, and William A. Wheeler III, *Business Process Engineering* (New York: John Wiley & Sons, 1993). Reprinted with permission.

- Production
- Customer
- Accounts payable

Implications of the Process Approach

The primary benefits of a process approach are that it is more holistic, reduces departmental suboptimization, and provides a better identification of the total cost and benefit to the business unit.

The evolution of such techniques as benchmarking, and the use of best practices, has facilitated the ability to establish goals for continuous process improvement. Activity-based costing (ABC) provides the information to understand what is spent, what is done, and what resources are required; it also is a useful tool for segregating value-adding from non–value-adding activities rather than having to rely only on control through variances based on estimates and averages. Companies are just starting to recognize that the application of ABC to the procurement process is the next tool required.

ROLE OF PROCESS MEASURES

A key to managing the procurement process is establishing key performance indicators (KPIs), or process measures. Key performance measures will support the enterprise in meeting its objectives. KPIs establish the visibility to monitor and control the process. Each company will have to establish the appropriate measures for its business. Measures should be both strategic and tactical, and should be focused on the goals of the business.

The importance of this focus is reinforced in the book called *Reinventing the CFO*. The authors stress that "best practices derive appropriate business measures from business objectives rather than merely from financial reporting line items. These measures ask: Is what we want to achieve good enough? What key performance indicators must we focus on to meet our goals?"[2]

To be effective, measures must be timely and should result in value-added and integrated support of the process. In the case of the procurement process, measures inevitably will involve each supplier's ability to meet the needs of the process and will be established as part of the budget process when the company typically sets business-specific improvement goals.

Supplier Capabilities and Process Requirements

One of the most strategic aspects of the procurement process is the supplier base. The management of this critical asset requires some very difficult decisions both during the budget process and during operations. There are three very different classes of suppliers:

1. *Strategic.* A provider with whom an open partnership has been established and who provides goods or services that are critical to operations, of high value, and essential for competitive advantage
2. *Collaborative.* A provider with whom dealings are continual and trustworthy and who provides goods or services that are important to operations, of high value, and required but not essential for competitive advantage
3. *Arm's-length.* A provider with whom dealings are under market conditions and from whom purchases are typically at spot or catalog prices, and who provides goods or services that are not of high value and are not essential to the core business

The number of suppliers needed for each class is dependent on a very specific understanding of procurement requirements and on the supplier's ability to meet these requirements. A supplier's classification should be based on its ability to meet specific performance expectations in categories such as:

- Production
- Product development
- Cost reduction

---

[2] Thomas Walther, Henry J. Johansson, John Dunleavy, and Elizabeth Hjelm, *Reinventing the CFO* (New York: McGraw-Hill, 1997).

The individual category measures will vary by industry and the specific needs of the business. However, the number of suppliers per category should be reevaluated during the budget process and, once established, be continually reviewed and realigned based on the supplier's performance.

PROCESS MEASURES

With an understanding of the industry, the business, process requirements, and suppliers' capabilities, specific process improvement goals and process improvement metrics can be established within each of these categories:

- Production capabilities
- Product development capabilities
- Cost-reduction capabilities

By addressing these measures at the time of budgeting the procurement process, the focus is on both planning and improvement.

Production Capabilities

Measures also can be established during the budget process to plan and monitor—in other words, to control—each supplier's production capabilities. Such measures include:

- *Supplier process reliability.* The ability of the process to constantly produce high-quality product. (The processes must run when they are required, at the capable rate, and produce a quality product.)
- *Supplier certification capability and potential.* The ability of the supplier to produce quality output at start-up and throughout the production run, without rework.
- *Supplier capacity utilization.* The time the process is actually in operation compared to the total available time the process is available for operation.
- *Commodity management.* The right-size supplier base as measured by the number of suppliers per materials category.
- *Inventory management capability.* The ability to control and manage the days of inventory on hand for the total supply chain based on seasonally adjusted sales.
- *Technology.* Measured by the systems used to control production, develop products, and communicate and share information.
- *Leveraging purchasing power.* Can be measured as the ability of the customer and the supplier to combine requirements resulting in preferential treatment.
- *Reserve capacity.* The amount of production capacity in excess of baseline capacity that is available to support incremental demand for promotions.
- *Supplier lead times.* The elapsed time from order placement to actual delivery.
- *Service requirements (quantity and timeliness).* Can be measured by the ability to deliver the requested quantities, on time, and as requested, with the required accurate paperwork.

- *Quality levels.* Measured internally as incoming and production defects in parts per million and externally by amount of product returns, reclaims, and recalls.
- *Continuous improvement capability.* The ability to make improvements year to year based on mutually agreed targets and criteria.

These measures provide the necessary information for evaluating suppliers' capabilities, identifying areas for improvement, providing the data for measuring performance, and establishing targets for continuous improvement.

Product Development Capabilities

Product development capability is an area that many companies do not formally measure for either budgeting or monitoring purposes. This capability can be a critical part of the overall business process, and selected measurement often can lead to substantial improvements. Depending on the business needs and goals, some possible areas in which useful measures can be developed are discussed next.

- *Renewal of specifications.* The review and updating of all specifications could identify major opportunities. Cross-functional development teams are useful in this area and should include suppliers.
- *Qualified materials.* It is important to review the requirements for materials specifications and establish performance-based specifications. Overspecifying can limit the supplier's ability to take full advantage of the commodity market because it can create the need for specialty materials or their equivalents.
- *Development process and budgets.* Reviewing opportunities to increase collaborative efforts by sharing technology and best practices could both improve time to market and reduce costs. When these areas are considered, it might lead to the development of a set of mutually agreed measures that will drive the desired cooperative behavior, such as joint

  - Specification development and review, early in the product development cycle
  - Process improvement
  - Product development
  - Cost reduction

- *Number of varieties.* Reevaluating the need for the number of varieties (such as flavors, widths, sizes, colors, and the like) might lead to highlighting products or supplies that are very close to each other and hence might offer opportunities for rationalization.
- *Testing requirements.* Reviewing the need and value of the various customer-specified quality tests might identify areas for cost reduction.
- *Lot-control requirements.* Reviewing the extent to which suppliers are requested to maintain lot control and identification can identify improvement opportunities.
- *Labeling and identification requirements.* Reviewing the extent to which the supplier is required to label, mark, and identify specified information is another possible improvement area.

In summary, it can be seen that procurement budgeting is much more oriented toward operations improvement and control than it is to merely estimating the amount of goods to be procured.

Cost-Reduction Capabilities

Many of the factors that impact product development also impact operational costs and vice versa. Both areas should be reviewed as part of budgeting as both potential cost drivers and appropriate measures should be established. Some possibilities are:

- *Customer requirements and procedures for loading and identification information.* Review all of the requested loading information, such as bills of lading, packing lists, advance shipping notices, bar codes, labels, load reports, and the like, and evaluate costs and benefits.
- *Procedures for establishing and communicating forecast information, orders, and changes to the supplier.* Frequent changes to quantities, varieties, and delivery dates ultimately create the need for excess capacity, and supplier inventories, and are a source of hidden costs. Reexamine the need and the costs avoided by the customer compared to the costs incurred and passed along by the supplier.
- *Communications.* Communications and the supporting technologies are enablers of all improvement opportunities. This is especially true in the area of information technology. Explore opportunities to jointly develop approaches to systems such as the following:

  - Management of total supply inventory at the supplier, in-transit, and at the customer, considering:
    - Consignment
    - Automatic replenishment
    - Direct vendor shipments to customers
  - Administrative systems, including:
    - Procurement cards
    - Monthly or consolidated invoicing
    - Electronic data interchange to share forecasts and transmit orders
    - Electronic funds transfer/automated clearinghouse for payment
    - Bar coding, to record receipts and track inventories
    - Advance shipping notice, to schedule receiving
    - Pay-on-receipt, eliminating invoices

- *Quality information.* Are there opportunities to share certificates of analysis and other quality information?
- *Sharing business plans.* Synchronize business plans, including business development, product development, and process development, with an emphasis on capital expenditures and cost reduction.
- *Sharing technology.* Share both the plans and the current application of various technologies, such as process automation, information automation, and communications automation.

- *Materials and capacity utilization.* Assess opportunities to favorably impact a supplier's cost of underutilized capacity or to share/leverage energy.
- *Sourcing arrangements.* Realign the supplier's shipping locations with the customer's producing plants.
- *Buffer stock requirements.* Variations between the standard and actual plant efficiency and scrap factors have an impact on run-out and replenishment orders placed by the plants. These variations should be mitigated by the plant's run strategy, plant safety stocks, and supplier buffer stocks. There might be an opportunity to improve the effectiveness and cost of how these factors are being used and balanced.
- *Various ways trucks are used, and how material is loaded and unloaded.* Review common routes and evaluate whether there are opportunities for cross-docking, mixed truckloads, or joint scheduling of back hauls. Review the quality and materials-handling characteristics to determine cost-effective ways to load and unload trucks, such as the use of dunnage, reusable pallets, disposable pallets, and so forth. Evaluate the use of requested containers and their usefulness in production.
- *Purchasing leverage with the suppliers of the supplier.* There might be opportunities to combine volume and increase leverage for commodities, for energy, and for shared capacity with suppliers, or by commonly using such items as maintenance materials and spare parts.
- *Physical assets.* Review and compare the locations, equipment, and information used by both companies. There might be opportunities to share facilities, equipment, offices, communications systems, and/or information systems.
- *Best-practice initiatives.* Evaluate each supplier's (and its supplier's) process improvement initiatives and such enablers as statistical process control, supplier certification production certification, and International Standards Organization certification.

Finally, the sharing and accuracy of cost information should be reviewed and confirmed during the budget process. Understanding costs will have an important bearing on each supplier's cost reduction capabilities. These are some of the elements required to understand a supplier's costs:

- Breakdown of costs (labor, materials, and overhead)
- Service requirements (quantity and timeliness)
- Cycle times
- Quality levels
- Continuous improvement capabilities

As with product development, cost-reduction capabilities being reviewed at the budget cycle can lead to substantial improvements beyond simply estimating future procurement expenditures.

CREATING THE PROCUREMENT PROCESS BUDGET

Today, many companies use a series of performance measures to manage and control the budget processes for procurement. These performance measures either supplement or replace traditional budgets. The steps involved include:

- Defining the process
- Establishing appropriate business goals
- Identifying the requirements of the process
- Relating business goals to the process
- Establishing goals for the process
- Establishing metrics for the process
- Organizing those metrics into a meaningful process budget

Many techniques that support process management are available and in use today, such as:

- Business process reengineering is a widely accepted and proven technique to define process and identify requirements.
- Benchmarking and best-practice techniques can identify opportunities for improvement.
- ABC and performance metrics can be used to identify and track causes and results.
- Management reporting can be used to organize and present the results.

All of these techniques are directly applicable to procurement. In addition, there are professional organizations that specialize in procurement. Two of the best are NAPM and the Center for Advanced Purchasing Studies (CAPS), which is jointly sponsored by Arizona State University and the NAPM. Both are important sources for purchasing benchmarking and performance data, and for the cost of the process, providing data such as:

- Purchasing expense per purchasing dollar
- Annual purchasing dollar per purchasing employee (as full-time equivalents)
- Average invoices per employee in the accounts payable function
- Average receipts and inspections per employee involved
- Active suppliers per purchasing employee
- Company purchase dollars per active supplier

CAPS provides substantive research data; according to its mission statement: "Its mission is to help organizations achieve competitive advantage by providing them with leading-edge research and benchmarking information to support the evolution of strategic purchasing and supply management."[3] This includes research that

---

[3] CAPS Research, mission statement, www.ism.ws/CAPS/content.cfm?ItemNumber=7179.

- Identifies the leading edge of current practice and application
- Identifies the current state of procurement practice
- Benchmarks the current state of the practice

Local experience together with sources like CAPS and NAPM can be used to establish metrics to be used in budgeting. These metrics can be prioritized and further integrated with the strategic and tactical goals of the business units as well as with the key activities of the procurement process. Business process reengineering supported with benchmarking and ABC can be used to identify areas for improvement. The goals of the business unit can be used to establish priorities. With an understanding of the process and with the availability and the skill sets of resources and of performance categories, specific targets can be established. These measures, when organized into a process framework, can be used to predict the impact of planned continual improvement and can provide for the management and control of a process-oriented purchasing/procurement budget.

CHAPTER TWENTY-FIVE

Capital Investment Review: Toward a New Process

Bryan Crawford
Bonneville Power Administration

INTRODUCTION

A well-managed enterprise has a strong alignment between its core mission and daily operations. Unless key strategic business objectives permeate the managerial decisions at every level, the firm will not thrive. Few managerial decisions are more important for the long-term viability of a firm than the selection and management of physical assets. In many ways, the choice of which investments to make, as outlined in the investment strategy, is the clearest embodiment of the firm's overall strategy. This is especially true in an industry as capital intensive as the electric power industry.

Although private-sector firms may be in very different businesses, they share the common purpose of increasing shareholder value. Successful private-sector firms have adopted capital strategies that seek the best return on their assets consistent with their overall business direction. This return on assets is measured by cash flows. New capital investment, disinvestment, and divestiture opportunities are selected based on their ability to add to the net present value of cash flows on the asset base.

The Bonneville Power Administration (BPA) is one of four Federal Power Marketing Administrations. Bonneville, headquartered in Portland, Oregon, transmits and markets the power from the Bureau of Reclamation and U.S. Army Corps of Engineers hydroelectric projects located in the Columbia River Basin of Montana, Idaho, Washington, and Oregon, as well as one nonfederal nuclear plant (collectively known as the Federal Columbia River Power System, or FCRPS). Bonneville provides over 40 percent of the region's firm energy and operates about three-fourths of the bulk transmission capacity in the Pacific Northwest.

As a government enterprise in a competitive market, Bonneville has three objectives that must be carefully balanced:

1. Providing competitive rates for power and transmission products and services
2. Assuring full cost recovery, including timely and complete repayment to the U.S. Treasury and other creditors for investments in hydroelectric and other generating, transmission, and public benefit facilities
3. Providing an appropriate level of public benefits

As part of the FCRPS, Bonneville invests in both revenue-producing and non–revenue-producing (public-benefit) assets. Bonneville and its partners in the FCRPS must chose and manage assets so that the revenue-producing investments recover their own costs as well as the costs of non–revenue-producing investments. BPA's competitiveness and ability to recover its costs, including timely repayment of the federal investment, is fundamentally a function of financial returns on investments in revenue-producing assets and on effective, low-cost non–revenue-producing assets. To achieve the key objectives listed, Bonneville must manage existing assets to maximize the potential for financial returns and acquire new assets that enhance the ability to earn returns. The selection of new investments that provide the greatest possible returns commensurate with market risks will maximize the funds available to provide public benefits, whether they come in the form of direct programs (investments and/or annual expenses) or long-term rates below market.

This chapter outlines the process whereby Bonneville developed a new capital-investment review process aimed at rigorously identifying and evaluating new investment opportunities. It begins with a brief overview of the context in which the new capital budgeting process was developed. The chapter then discusses the use of a cross-business team and benchmarking to develop the new method, with an emphasis on lessons learned through benchmarking. This is followed by an outline of Bonneville's new process. The chapter concludes with a discussion of experiences from implementing the new process over the past three years.

CONTEXT OF THE REVISED CAPITAL-INVESTMENT REVIEW PROCESS

The electric utility industry has undergone a large amount of both technological and regulatory change in recent years. As recently as 10 years ago, Bonneville, through its abundance of low-cost hydropower, was in the comfortable position of selling energy at well below prevailing market rates. Investments were proposed based on Bonneville's energy and public-benefit goals, with financial analysis taking a secondary role to programmatic analysis. Northwest ratepayers were a part of overall reviews of Bonneville activities through public-involvement processes, but these reviews again focused on Bonneville's role in providing low-cost energy and public benefits, rather than Bonneville's finances. As Bonneville's annual expenses and investment requirements increased, the fact that our costs remained well below market made raising rates a rather straightforward solution.

These conditions changed, starting with the Energy Policy Act of 1992, which sought to create deregulated wholesale power markets through reregulation of wholesale transmission. This was followed by Orders 888 and 889 from the Federal Energy Regulatory Commission (FERC), which further opened bulk transmission markets by requiring utilities to functionally separate transmission from power marketing activities and to allow nondiscriminatory access to their transmission lines. FERC's current requirements, as outlined in Order 2000 and the Standard Market Design Notice of Proposed Rulemaking, take this direction to its logical conclusion in calling for the formation of regional transmission organizations that will erase traditional company lines and join all of a region's transmission into a single electricity transportation system.

In addition to these regulatory changes, technological advances have been making an impact on the utility industry. The past 15 years have seen dramatic improvements in the efficiency of gas-fired turbine generation. This increased efficiency, coupled with increased natural gas pipeline capacity and lower natural gas prices, has lowered the cost of new generation, allowing independent power producers to compete with existing coal, nuclear, and even hydro-generation.

These regulatory and technological changes came to Bonneville forcibly when it set rates in 1996. For the first time, the price of alternative power was at, or slightly below, Bonneville's projected rates. To retain customers, Bonneville was thus required to set rates based on what the market would allow rather than by the previous practice of determining program levels and then setting rates to recover their costs. In anticipation of this, Bonneville in 1993 launched its Competitiveness Project geared at transitioning BPA from a governmental model to a more private-industry model of doing business. This led to a business plan in 1995, and competitive rates, new contracts, and functional separation into a power business line and a transmission business line in 1996.

Bonneville's customers and constituents in the Northwest, including ratepayers, environmental and conservation advocates, and state and tribal governments, reacted to the increased competition in the power industry and its effect on Bonneville by convening the Comprehensive Review of the Northwest Energy System. This broad public process sought to address Bonneville's near-term financial concerns, the long-term desire to retain the benefits of the hydropower system in the Northwest, and the role of federal government in a competitive market. An outcome of that public policy debate was an increased focus on costs and investment decisions, with a call for a subsequent review of Bonneville and Federal Columbia River Power System costs. This cost review, chaired by a regional board that included five nonpower executives with experience in managing large organizations undergoing competitive transitions, was conducted starting in 1997.

One of the principal recommendations of the cost review, completed in March 1998, called for a consolidated, integrated capital asset strategy for the FCRPS. The capital strategy envisioned a coordinated investment process to rigorously analyze investment opportunities that maximize asset value and the establishment of FCRPS-wide performance targets and accountabilities. Bonneville had addressed the topic of capital budgeting several times, with mixed success. This recommendation provided the impetus for another review of the process BPA should use to determine which capital investments to make.

As a result, a cross-agency capital budgeting team was created to develop a new method of analyzing and selecting capital investments for BPA and the other FCRPS entities whose investments BPA funds. A cross-agency team was needed because, in compliance with FERC direction, BPA had functionally separated its power generation and marketing functions from its transmission activities. This resulted in a company structure of two separate business lines and a joint corporate group overseen by a single administrator/chief executive officer. In spite of their independence, the two business lines and corporate rely on the same sources of capital, and Bonneville's obligation to cover operating costs and repay the federal investment remains a combined responsibility of its single administrator.

To balance the need for independence and common responsibility, the capital-investment review process Bonneville designed had to be flexible enough to apply to the wide variety of investments made by each business line yet uniform and consistent enough to assure that the investments being chosen maximized the value delivered by Bonneville as a combined agency. To achieve such a balance, a diverse team was assembled, combining staff from both the financial and technical sides of each business line as well as corporate staff.

The first activity of the team was to establish the next key objectives. Throughout the design and implementation of the revised capital-investment review process, these objectives were constantly reviewed to make sure the team kept on track. Its objectives were:

- The new capital-investment review process should employ a framework using multiattribute decision making for approving long-term commitments of scarce capital resources (borrowing and future revenues).
- The revised process should have clearly defined roles, responsibilities, and timelines.
- The analytical framework and guidelines employed by the process should result in consistent and comparable reviews of alternative capital investments or long-term expense commitments across the agency while recognizing the unique character and requirements of the separate business lines.
- The process must emphasize performance measurement, monitoring, and accountability, with an understanding of how results will be compared to forecasts.
- The capital budget process development team should provide clear guidance on the essential top management direction and commitment necessary to assure a successful capital-investment review process.

To determine long-term success or failure, the team created the next performance measures. The work would be considered successful to the extent that:

- Business lines adopted the methodology and used it as outlined for FY 2001 capital budget decisions.
- The process, with any necessary improvements, was also used for subsequent capital decisions; it was deemed useful for long-term adoption.

BENCHMARKING CAPITAL-INVESTMENT REVIEW BEST PRACTICES

Once objectives had been developed and received approval from top management, the capital budgeting team started active discussions on the current review procedures, what improvements were needed, and possible revisions to achieve those improvements. It was quickly discovered that there was a need to see how others faced the challenges in making good capital-investment decisions, and what could be considered industry best practices. This led to a series of benchmarking trips, where face-to-face meetings with counterparts from other companies were held.

This type of benchmarking was especially important because one goal was to change from a governmental model of budgeting and decision making to a more private-sector approach. Most of the members of the team had spent the majority of their careers with Bonneville or other federal agencies. A better understanding of private-sector practices such as use of market discount rates, net present value financial analysis, and especially performance measurement was needed.

In the benchmarking effort, the capital budgeting team visited four utilities and one nonutility to gain insights into capital-investment practices currently used by companies known for their success. In choosing which firms to approach for benchmarking, the relationships that members of the team had already developed and the advice of expert financial management and analysis consultants Bonneville was working with were used. Members of the BPA capital budgeting team met face to face with staff from the benchmarked forms, at those firms' sites.

The benchmarking trips also served to energize the team. One challenge in taking on this redesign project was overcoming a certain degree of cynicism. BPA had made numerous prior attempts at improving capital-investment decision making, with only mixed results. Several of the members of the team had been involved in those prior attempts and were not convinced that this attempt would be any more successful. The benchmarking trips helped the team to overcome this cynicism and get behind the objectives, both through sharing the good and bad experiences of their peers in other firms and in the time spent traveling together.

From the benchmarking, valuable insights were gained into four key areas of capital-investment review:

1. Need for clear vision and strategy
2. Top management commitment and discipline
3. Clear authority, roles, and responsibilities
4. Performance measurement

As the next observations on these four areas indicate, there was a great deal of commonality among the firms visited on many aspects of capital-investment review. As an indication of both the importance of a good capital-investment decision process and the difficulties in achieving one, it was learned that within the prior three years all of the firms visited had made substantial changes to their decision processes. Also discussed were both their new and prior processes as well as the lessons learned in implementing major changes. The common traits and techniques gathered from these firms served to define the current industry best practices that Bonneville sought to apply to its redesigned capital-investment review process.

Benchmarking Lesson One: Need for Clear Vision and Strategy

Perhaps the most common point each firm made was the need to forge a clear link between company strategy and the capital-investment process. In many ways, the investment portfolio is the most visible and the clearest manifestation of the company's overall strategic direction, especially long-term direction. This is due both to common time span (strategic direction implies a long-term process of change, matching the long-term nature of significant capital investments) and to the old adage that you "put your money where your mouth is." The nature and direction of a company's investments tell both the business community and its own employees what the company really cares about and which direction it is going. If investments are not consistent with the stated company strategies and goals, the company will have a hard time convincing others that the strategies are valid.

A clear sense of strategic direction and vision is also important because the capital-investment decision process can be seen as a two-step process. When one thinks of capital-investment review, what usually comes to mind is a process that focuses on the most effective and efficient ways to make an investment. This is the *second* step in the process, answering the question of "how" an investment should be made. A clear sense of strategic direction and vision is key to the *first* step, addressing the more important question of "what" investments to make. In the experience of one firm benchmarked, not linking your capital-investment review process to a clear sense of vision and strategy can lead to what can be called "industrial tourism." Prior to changes in its process to accomplish this link, it had problems with managers actively seeking and putting a great deal of effort into developing investment opportunities that penciled out well but were not consistent with the overall direction of where the company wanted to go. By clearly conveying this direction and strategy at the start of the capital-investment review process, this firm found it was more successful in focusing its resources and directing its efforts toward investments that made both economic *and* strategic sense.

Benchmarking Lesson Two: Top Management Commitment and Discipline

After stressing the need for a clear vision and strategy to guide and focus the capital-investment review process, the next strong message from the companies benchmarked was that top management commitment and discipline are essential for successful implementation. Two of the firms listed establishing order and consistency in how capital projects were developed, proposed, and approved as a principal goal of their revised processes.

A successful and effective review process will require considerable effort in developing accurate financial and strategic (nonfinancial) estimates and analysis. It will also necessarily lead to some projects being rejected as either not consistent with the company strategy or not economical (insufficient returns for level of risk). Both the work required and the possibility of rejection will tempt project sponsors to take investments straight to top management for approval, sidestepping the new investment decision process. Top management must have the discipline and commitment to resist these back-door routes to approval. If they do not, and it becomes known that projects have been approved without proper review—or, even worse, have been preapproved—it will be almost impossible to successfully implement a meaningful capital-investment review process. In short, the new tool you develop will be effective only if it is the only tool available for gaining project support and financing.

Top management commitment is also important because an improved review process will likely require a company to develop new skills and partnerships between project sponsors and finance. A common goal of several of the companies visited was to shift both corporate ("headquarters") and business-line finance staff from the traditional gatekeeper role to a more collaborative approach, where finance people get involved early in project development and work with project sponsor and technical experts throughout the process of proposing and evaluating projects. These firms experienced increased efficiency and effectiveness when partnerships were created in which financial staff were perceived as problem-solvers, not as green-eyeshade bean counters. This change in roles and the resulting change in corporate culture cannot occur without active top management direction and support.

Finally, top management commitment and discipline needs to be demonstrated by personal involvement, modeling the patience and perseverance required to implement an improved capital-investment review process. When the redesign process at Bonneville was started, the team's expectation, and the expectation of its management, was that the project could be completed and a new process implemented in less than a year. The benchmarking experience, as borne out during the implementation, made it clear that it would not be that easy. All five of the companies talked to reported that cultural and analytical changes required by their revised processes were taking two to three years to implement, with considerable growing pains. Successful navigation of these implementation challenges requires that top managers be directly and personally involved, continually emphasizing the importance of the new process and demonstrating management patience through a willingness to make and reward incremental improvements and not give up if results are not immediately forthcoming. A successful process requires time commitment on the part of management. It is not something that can be delegated down, ignored, and then expected to work.

Benchmarking Lesson Three: Clear Authority, Roles, and Responsibilities

In addition to clear strategic vision and top management commitment and discipline, the benchmarking showed that an efficient and effective capital-investment review process requires clarity in decision-making authority, including key roles and responsibilities. Several firms talked to indicated that part of the inadequacy of their past processes was confusion as to when, by whom, and how capital-investment decisions would be made. Their redesigned processes all focused on giving one person or group a clear call to decide at each stage of a project within a clear decision structure. This is especially important when it comes to improving performance measurement. Clear responsibility and accountability are essential for effective performance measurement.

The benchmarked firms were seeking to clearly link decision-making authority with accountability for results. Thus, they were moving from the traditional approach of decision-making delegation by the dollar magnitude of the investment to more strategic delegation, depending on the importance of the investment the firms' experience with similar investments, and responsibility for the investment. As an example, several of the firms talked to had become particularly concerned about their investments in information management resources. Even though, in aggregate, the dollar magnitude of many of these investments was small compared to the companies' total investments, these firms established high-ranking teams that met as often as weekly to review and approve information resources investments.

Benchmarking Lesson Four: Performance Measurement a Challenge

One of the primary goals in redesigning the capital-investment review process at Bonneville was to improve its ability to measure both the short- and long-term performance of its capital investments. As a regulated monopoly utility, BPA's ability to assure investment recovery through inclusion in the rate base encourages a primary focus on analysis and review of investments before they are made. This preinvestment analysis seeks to assure that investments are reasonable and prudent, and thus can be recovered through ratepayers. If investments are subsequently challenged and upheld as imprudent before the appropriate regulatory commission, they are not allowed in the rate base and cannot be recovered from ratepayers. This fixation on the front end of investments can lead to a lack of focus on the actual performance of an investment once it is made. As long as making the investment was prudent, its performance after the fact will generally not impair cost recovery through rates.

During the benchmarking efforts, Bonneville hoped to improve its performance measurement by learning how other firms approached this challenge. What it heard gave Bonneville comfort that it was not alone in its struggles but unfortunately did not yield much in the way of new insights or approaches. None of the benchmarked firms was pleased with its ability to measure either short- or long-term investment performance. The difficulties cited included:

▪ *Determining effective performance measures.* The challenges ranged from developing a relevant measure, such as how to measure productivity improvements for an information resources investment, to getting a performance indicator that is measurable, such as for safety and reliability in transmission investments.
▪ *Difficulty determining who is accountable.* Even after a review process that incorporates a clear decision and accountability structure has been established, long-term performance measurement can be difficult if the responsible managers have been promoted or transferred since the investment was made. Often their successors are left with either the benefits of successful investments or the fallout if performance is not what was expected.

▪ *Isolating the impact of investment from previous and subsequent investments and changes in conditions.* This area of performance measurement difficulties presents one of the biggest challenges for a utility. On the generation side, the output of a hydroelectric facility is extremely dependent on the availability of water. The value of that output is dependent on when the water is available, the market at the time, and the ability to shape the output. Separating the impact of the new investment from the impacts of all the other factors influencing performance can be very tricky and subjective.

On the transmission side, once an investment is made for safety, reliability, or increased transmission capacity, it is very difficult to isolate that investment from the overall transmission grid. Once the new investment is in place, it will carry both incremental power and power that would have gone elsewhere in its absence. Although measuring the impact of the investment can be very difficult when the investment is new, it becomes even harder once other investments are made.

In response to these challenges, a common idea that emerged from the benchmarking discussions was to address performance measurement by requiring that the business cases developed to analyze and approve each new investment include both proposed performance measures and the methodology used to calculate them. It was hoped that this would result in greater attention both to the analysis of the investment and to the subsequent performance once the investment was made.

REVISED CAPITAL-INVESTMENT REVIEW PROCESS: OVERVIEW

In keeping with the objectives and the insights gained in benchmarking, a plan was created to design a new capital-investment review process that results in capital investments that maximize financial and strategic returns. Exhibit 25.1 graphically displays the new process Bonneville is currently implementing.

As the timeline indicates, the process focuses on an annual review of potential capital investments. Although capital-investment opportunities arise throughout the year, Bonneville decided to use an annual review process, for several reasons. First, Bonneville invests in a wide variety of assets, including transmission facilities, hydro- and nonhydro-generation assets, renewable generation, fish and wildlife facilities, and information technology. These represent a mix of revenue and non–revenue-producing investments. Financial viability depends in part on Bonneville's ability to maintain a balance of investments such that its revenue-producing assets are able to pay both for themselves and for the non–revenue-producing assets. Using an annual review process permits Bonneville to evaluate and analyze the majority of its investments simultaneously, allowing trade-offs between investments to maintain this balance.

Although Bonneville seeks to review as many potential investments as possible during the annual process, it recognizes that not all investment opportunities are known and quantifiable at one time during the year. As is pointed out later, the process also provides the opportunity to review investments that arise during the year.

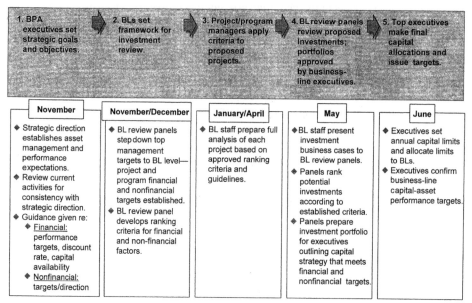

November	November/December	January/April	May	June

◆ Strategic direction establishes asset management and performance expectations.
◆ Review current activities for consistency with strategic direction.
◆ Guidance given re:
  ◆ Financial: performance targets, discount rate, capital availability
  ◆ Nonfinancial: targets/direction
	◆ BL review panels step down top management targets to BL level—project and program financial and nonfinancial targets established.
	◆ BL review panel develops ranking criteria for financial and non-financial factors.
		◆ BL staff prepare full analysis of each project based on approved ranking criteria and guidelines.	◆ BL staff present investment business cases to BL review panels.
			◆ Panels rank potential investments according to established criteria.
			◆ Panels prepare investment portfolio for executives outlining capital strategy that meets financial and nonfinancial targets.
				◆ Executives set annual capital limits and allocate limits to BLs.
				◆ Executives confirm business-line capital-asset performance targets.

EXHIBIT 25.1   Overview of Bonneville Power Administration Revised Capital-Investment Review Process

---

In addition to fostering trade-offs between potential investments, a second reason Bonneville chose an annual process was to dovetail with its practice of setting annual performance targets. In the past, its primary capital target was a cap on total capital spending during the year. Its new review process is working toward setting a more meaningful long-range capital-investment productivity target. In the near term, Bonneville is using the new review process to develop and propose an asset productivity target. Once a target has been picked, one of the objectives of the capital review process will be meeting that target.

An annual capital-investment review process will also build a link between approval of capital projects and development of the organizational budgets necessary to implement the investments. Prior to this revised review process, organizational capital budgets were developed independently of project capital budgets. This resulted in cases where organizational capital spending budgets were approved for which no projects were authorized. More often, capital projects were approved that managers could not implement because they did not have capital funding in their organizational budgets. The revised review process results in approval of capital projects on an annual basis before organizational budgets are set. These budgets can then be developed to implement the approved projects.

Finally, Bonneville is using an annual capital review process to comply with its annual federal budget requirements. As its "board of directors," congressional committees review Bonneville's spending plans on an annual basis. The revised annual capital review process will provide the information needed for that review.

As indicated in Exhibit 25.1, the revised process is scheduled to start in November and end with approved capital-investment portfolios in June. Although the exhibit outlines a five-step process, the five steps can be combined into two major groups, centered on the level at which activities are occurring. The first group, comprised of steps 1 and 5, details activities that occur at the top management level, including setting strategic goals and objectives in step 1 and making final capital allocations and establishing performance targets in step 5. The second group, comprised of steps 2, 3, and 4, details activities that occur within the business lines. These activities include establishing guidelines for the review, developing analysis, and proposing a business-line capital-investment portfolio.

The need for these two groupings arises, in part, from current efforts to deregulate and introduce competition to the electric utility industry. Ideally, when deciding on the final portfolio of capital investments, one would evaluate and weigh all potential investments simultaneously. For Bonneville, this would mean placing on the table transmission, generation, and corporate investments, with trade-offs between individual investments in each business line. The functional separation called for by FERC to foster competitive electricity markets makes this impossible for Bonneville.

Bonneville has committed to clearly separating its transmission and generation business, such that the generation marketing business has no preferential access to transmission information, including potential transmission investments. As a result, Bonneville's power business-line executives cannot review and approve transmission investments without it resulting in transmission investment information being released equally to all other power marketers in the region. At Bonneville, this restriction has led to the two-stage process outlined in Exhibit 25.1, in which top executives discuss strategy and the underlying gross capital requirement first, and then make final decisions on a business-line portfolio basis only.

A brief listing of the key elements and requirements of the proposed capital-investment review process as outlined in Exhibit 25.1 and elaborated on in the remainder of this chapter is presented next.

- The review process is applicable to—and practiced collaboratively by—all members of the FCRPS. This is important to Bonneville because, unlike most other utilities, its generating assets are owned by other entities, such as the U.S. Army Corps of Engineers, the Bureau of Reclamation, and Energy Northwest (operates the Northwest's only active nuclear generating facility), while Bonneville pays the operating and debt services costs. Effective control of Bonneville's costs and effective investment decisions require that Bonneville use a consistent investment review process for all investments it will repay, regardless of which FCRPS partner is making the investment.
- The proposed process applies to any activity that relies on capital funding (U.S. Treasury, appropriations, third party), or represents a long-term commitment of funds resulting in assets with an effective life of more than two years. The goal here is to effectively separate the decision of *whether* to make a capital investment from the *means* used to finance the investment.

If Bonneville were to subject to review only those investments that use traditional capital sources, such as borrowing from the markets or the U.S. Treasury, it would miss investments that are funded by annual revenues or other sources. These "noncapital" investments may be just as large and have just as great a long-term impact as traditionally funded investments.

Focusing on traditionally funded investments would also bias it toward non-investment options, the best example being long-term power supply contracts instead of new generation resources. To avoid this, Bonneville's process separates the investment itself from the means used to pay for it. All long-term commitments of funds are reviewed first using a discount rate that is independent of the financing source to assure that the investment is financially sound. Then the potential means of financing to find the best balance of low cost and other strategic objectives is reviewed.

- All investments will be reviewed under a common set of standards and assumptions. Even "mandatory" or noneconomic investments should undergo financial and strategic analysis. In the utility business, a number of investments can be viewed as "mandatory," such as those required by regulation (Nuclear Regulatory Commission, environmental, etc.), or necessary for safety or reliability. These investments are generally not intended to produce revenues. For these mandatory investments, there is a temptation not to require the same level of analysis and evaluation as for more discretionary investments. By using a uniform investment review method, Bonneville will, at a minimum, better understand the costs of these investments. This will also, it is hoped, lead to better exploration of both capital and noncapital solutions to these mandatory investment needs.

- Multiyear capital projects will be reviewed each year. The revised process requires an annual review of both funding levels and timing of major capital investments. One of the issues we are addressing is "budget creep," which occurs when a capital project is approved at a certain funding level and project schedule, only to have both increase steadily at each reassessment. Reviewing each year's portion of a large capital project assures that management will be aware of changes to scope or costs. Significant changes to either can result in an annual reassessment of the viability and desirability of the project. Because the past investments in a project are treated as sunk costs, ongoing projects are rarely canceled, but the annual review does allow for cancellation if major changes in the market or the project warrant it.

- The appropriate discount rates are used for capital-investment analysis. The foundation of the analytical standards proposed here is *investment-level* net annual cash flow estimation. Cash flow uncertainties are evaluated at the investment level and thus do not include market and other risk factors. These are embodied in the discount rate and are specific to the level of risk in the particular markets in which Bonneville operates.

Two sets of factors are considered in setting discount rates: market factors and risk factors. The two sets are somewhat interrelated. Market factors reflect the price (or rate) constraints that a competitor in an industry faces. For example, market factors in Bonneville's businesses depend on the exposure to price competition. The transmission market is relatively inelastic (transmission rates can be raised without loss of customers) up to some level, at which a "build-around" or regulatory challenges become a threat. In contrast, the deregulated power market is more elastic, with a much higher customer loss exposure to changes in rates.

The risk factors reflect the type of industry under evaluation. From an industry perspective, risk determines the rate of return that an investor would require for making the investment. Clearly, an investor would expect a higher rate of return when investing in an industry that does not have regulated prices or rates. Thus, a deregulated power business will have a higher rate of return than the transmission business.

An appropriate discount rate is important, because, as used in the net present value analysis, it essentially normalizes potential investments for the risk that is generic to that particular industry. It puts all Bonneville investments on a level playing field. Looking at the discount rates from another perspective, the discount rate effectively acts as a hurdle rate above which an investment is anticipated to add positive cash flow to Bonneville. Bonneville aims to exceed the hurdle rates for its revenue-producing investment portfolio in order to increase the value of the FCRPS. If Bonneville's revenue-producing programs fail to generate enough revenues, consistent with industry-standard hurdle-rate-implied performance, it receives an insufficient return on its assets. Eventually, it fails to compete.

In developing discount rates, Bonneville relied on its judgment and the best empirical data available. Professional judgment was particularly important when setting the discount rate for the power business-line investments. The historical information reflects the utility industry as it has been—a vertically integrated, regulated monopoly—not as it is now in moving toward deregulation and business-line separation. Several of the utilities benchmarked indicated that they were also forced to rely more on judgment than on history in setting appropriate discount rates for new investments.

With these general points in mind, we review each step of the proposed process outlined in Exhibit 25.1, starting with establishing the link between corporate strategy and the capital-investment review process through top management guidance.

Top Management Guidance for the Capital-Investment Review Process

Bonneville's benchmarking reaffirmed that one of the most important factors in a successful capital-investment strategy is clear top management guidance and direction throughout the investment-development process. This top management direction forges the essential link between the company's vision and strategic direction and its capital investments, answering the first question of what type and magnitude of investments the company should pursue.

As stated, a primary goal of Bonneville's capital budget process is to maximize the value of the FCRPS through strategic management of FCRPS assets. The purpose of strategic asset management is to create and deliver value by managing assets toward a common destination. Broadly speaking, this requires:

- *Developing a vision.* A vision is a destination, an accurate description of where each of the business lines in the FCRPS wants to be; where stakeholders receive the value the FCRPS is in business to deliver. It helps to clarify how each business line positions itself within the industry and how benefits are defined, produced, and delivered. It should accurately describe:

- Where does Bonneville want to be in XX years?
- How will it know when it is there?
- What will success look like?

The overall FCRPS and business-line visions must be clear enough to provide practical guidance to decision makers. Bonneville's managers need a clear understanding of the role each business line is to play in the region and how that role affects the investments to be made. This vision provides the basis on which FCRPS executives manage the trade-offs among competing interests.

- *Developing strategy.* Strategy is the course of action that enables each business line and its FCRPS partners to achieve the vision. Developing a robust strategy means evaluating strategic alternatives and choosing the alternative that best achieves the vision. An integral part of the strategy should be an assessment of the resources and assets necessary to achieve the vision. When deciding on a strategy, top management needs to understand that it is committing the company to the level of investments and assets needed to achieve the chosen strategy.

For the capital budget process to be successful, the vision and strategies must be as specific and measurable as possible. It then becomes possible to develop criteria that measure how well capital investments contribute to: (1) meeting the business line and FCRPS's strategic goals and objectives; and (2) reaching the destination(s) described by the business line and FCRPS visions. An effective capital budget process that employs these criteria improves the quality of a company's strategic and operating decisions.

The process for developing top management guidance Bonneville's implementing outlines the key parameters and assumptions that the business lines need to effectively develop and propose capital investments. It is divided into two phases in order to create the opportunity for feedback between initial top management guidance and final capital decisions, including overall capital allocations by business lines, approval of specific major investments, and the establishment of key capital-investment financial and strategic performance measures. The decision on how to allocate scarce capital among Bonneville's various activities is of critical interest to the business lines. The proposed process allows the portfolios of available capital investments, and their resulting financial and strategic returns, to influence the final allocation of capital.

Exhibits 25.2 and 25.3 outline the elements necessary for effective top management guidance. Exhibit 25.2 corresponds to step 1 of the capital-investment review process in Exhibit 25.1. Exhibit 25.3 corresponds to step 5 in Exhibit 25.1.

Business-Line Capital-Investment Evaluation Methodology

As confirmed by Bonneville's benchmarking, two of the key objectives it set for its revised capital-investment review process were to clearly define roles, responsibilities, and timelines and to clearly link performance measurement and accountability to the investment review process. Underlying these goals is the requirement that top management establish clear agency strategic direction and performance expectations, with accompanying performance measures and targets. The business lines are then empowered to make

EXHIBIT 25.2 Capital-Investment Review Process: Phase One

Substance/Purpose	Decision Needed	Policy Implications	Inputs to Decision
1. Adoption/approval of business-line strategic plans: Approval includes understanding and acceptance of underlying capital investment needs. Directs BLs as to type of investments to analyze and propose. Also addresses issues of Bonneville's public responsibilities/benefits.	Approval of business-line strategic plans. Answers questions such as: • What is the impact of regulatory changes? • What is the position within the industry? • What products, services, public benefits, and to whom? • Which markets will they operate in? • What is the need for public responsibilities/benefits, such as reliability, economic development, etc.?	Ties directly to Bonneville mission statement and agency strategic goals and objectives.	• Transmission business line strategic business plan • Power business line strategic business plan • Renewables/conservation strategy • Capital asset management strategic plan • Customer/constituent input
2. Capital availability: Determines level of available capital for potential investments. This will help BLs understand the level of potential funding.	Multiyear targets for total capital availability, including both Bonneville and non-Bonneville sources	• How Bonneville will manage U.S. Treasury borrowing (limited by Congress) • What additional sources of capital should be pursued? • Revenue financing?	• Financial strategy • Analysis by CFO staff • Customer input through rate case proceedings (revenue financing)
3. Capital allocation: Preliminary allocation of capital availability to business lines	Multiyear targets (point estimate averages) for capital funding by business lines (including corporate)	• FCPRS vision for each business line • Estimated returns of each business line	• Transmission BL strategic business plan • Power BL strategic business plan • Renewables/conservation strategy • Capital asset management strategic plan • Customer/constituent input

(Continued)

EXHIBIT 25.2 *(Continued)*

Substance/Purpose	Decision Needed	Policy Implications	Inputs to Decision
4. What financial returns will be required from (a) BLs as a whole, and (b) new capital investments?	BL and/or capital asset portfolio targets	• Sustainable level of public benefit investments • Implications for performance measurement/ rewards	• Returns of existing assets • Market-based discount rates
5. Discount rate for capital-investment analysis: (a) sets standard for selection of new investments, and ensure assure risks are adequately accounted for.	Approval of the discount rate methodology and discount rates to be used for analysis Note: Rates will be recalculated annually or to meet sudden market changes.	Potential of revenue-producing assets to fund non–revenue-producing investments and activities	• Financial strategy • Methodology and resulting discount rates prepared for executive approval by CFO staff
6. Guidance/limits on noneconomic investments: How much capital needs to be set aside for these, and therefore, how much is available for economic investments?	Annual capital funding amounts set aside for known noneconomic investments. Direction on planning for unknown investments	• Fish and wildlife mitigation policy • Environmental compliance policy • Other public benefits (support for conservation/ renewables economic development, etc.)	• Integrated fish funding plan • Environmental abatement and cleanup strategies • BL staff analysis

EXHIBIT 25.3 Capital-Investment Review Process: Phase Two

Substance/Purpose	Decision Needed	Policy Implications	Inputs to Decision
1. Capital allocations by business lines and corporate	Final allocation of capital for upcoming operating-year budgets Planning capital amounts by major category within business lines for federal budgets	Approval of overall capital investment levels by Congress	• Capital portfolios proposed by business lines • Regulatory/public benefit investment requirements • Risk preference • Availability of funds under current or proposed rates • Analysis by CFO staff • Customer/constituent input

Substance/Purpose	Decision Needed	Policy Implications	Inputs to Decision
2. Approval of major capital investments	Business-line managing committees individually review and approve major capital investments.	Consistency with Bonneville vision and strategic goals/objectives	Business-line staff who prepared business case
3. Capital investment performance targets: Front office reviews and approves asset portfolio performance measures.	Capital investment performance targets set	Connection to business-line financial and strategic targets	• Performance measures proposed in business cases • Review of past performance measures: performance results and effectiveness of the measures

Timing: This phase occurs after the business lines and corporate have developed proposed capital investment portfolios. This phase represents the opportunity for top management to approve overall portfolios and set performance targets. For Bonneville, these activities occur in June and July.

the operational and investment decisions needed to implement the agency strategy and achieve performance targets within generally accepted parameters. This business-line implementation of top management direction through development, evaluation, and recommendation of capital investments is outlined in steps 2 through 4 of Exhibit 25.1.

The capital-investment review process Bonneville is implementing seeks to balance a uniformly rigorous investment review with flexibility for each business line. This is accomplished through establishing agency-wide analytical standards with accompanying procedures and policies that assure top management that capital-investment analysis is being conducted in a professional and consistent manner across the company. With this assurance, top management can focus their efforts on developing strategy, setting effective targets, and establishing a culture where performance measurement and rewards are effective means of furthering the company's strategic direction.

An important aspect of empowering the business lines is the creation of business-line capital-investment review panels that will oversee the process of capital-investment business plan development within the business lines. Bonneville, has approached this from two different directions. In its power business line, the panel is composed of senior business-line managers who both approve and are held accountable for the performance of capital investments.

Its transmission business line opted for a review panel composed of knowledgeable representatives from each functional area (e.g., operations, maintenance, planning, marketing, design, environment, etc.) who are not direct sponsors of any specific projects, and thus do not have a vested interest in what is approved or disapproved for funding. The managers responsible for both project execution and performance present their business cases to the capital-investment review panels for objective and independent review and appraisal. Projects recommended by the review panel are then submitted to top management for final approval.

As shown in step 2 of Exhibit 25.1, in the annual process, the business-line capital-investment review panels begin their work as soon as top management guidance is available in November. During November and December, the review panels launch the business-line capital-investment review process by performing these tasks:

- Developing and implementing a multiattribute decision-making process

  - Translating strategic direction and performance targets into financial and strategic (nonfinancial) criteria
  - Determining the weighting scheme or other methodology used to prioritize and rank individual projects

- Implementing the company capital-investment review process through developing business-line-specific guidance and issuing the annual call for capital budget development, including establishing necessary timelines and responsibilities
- Translating company and business-line performance measures and targets to the project level, establishing performance measures and targets for each project.

Once the review panel has set the stage for the annual review process by establishing the review criteria and timeline, the project/program managers apply the criteria and methodology to their proposed projects, as shown in step 3 of Exhibit 25.1. During this time, the supporting staff for the business-line capital-investment review panels are actively working with project/program managers to answer questions and facilitate the required analysis.

The project-development phase provides the opportunity for corporate and business-line financial staff to develop a close working relationship with project/program managers, as advocated by the benchmarked firms. By being actively engaged from the start in both the development and evaluation of potential investments, financial staff become problem solvers and expert advisors rather than just gatekeepers. In Bonneville's first couple of years of implementation, this was especially important since it were requiring a greater level of financial and strategic analysis than it had previously. There was the potential for considerable confusion as project/program managers struggled with new investment analysis formats and requirements. Close partnership with the design team members and the review panel staffs helped to reduce confusion by dealing in a timely manner with problems or questions as they arose.

The second major part of the business-line capital-investment review panel's work occurs when the business cases for individual capital investments are prepared and submitted to the review panel in May, as outlined in step 4 of Exhibit 25.1. At this point, the review panel's responsibilities include:

- Reviewing proposed capital investments, and, through application of the criteria and weightings established earlier, developing a capital portfolio for submittal to business-line top management
- Presenting the proposed capital portfolio to business-line top management, resolving issues raised by management, and overseeing any revisions requested

- Developing the proposed level of business-line funds for emerging projects or emergencies
- Working with project/program managers to set performance targets for each individual capital investment.

Once the business-line capital-investment portfolio is approved by business-line top management and company top management, the business-line capital-investment review panel's work is not complete. On an ongoing basis, the review panels are also responsible for:

- Periodically reviewing progress on capital investments, including review of performance results; approving, or forwarding to business-line top management, significant changes in timelines or project scope during the year; developing updated capital spending estimates for business-line or company financial reporting requirements
- Reviewing capital-investment proposals that occur outside the annual process due to emerging opportunities or emergencies
- Working actively with chief financial officer (CFO) financial staff to review and modify the company capital budgeting process and guidelines to foster continual process improvement.

Multiattribute Decision Making: Weighing Evaluation Criteria

One of the greatest challenges in capital-investment decision making is balancing the financial aspects of an investment, such as net present value, with nonfinancial aspects, such as strategic direction, safety, reliability, and the provision of public benefits. To facilitate comparison of projects, Bonneville's review process imposes certain financial criteria and analytical requirements on all capital investments, regardless of their purpose. The financial criteria, including use of market-based discount rates, sensitivity analysis, and calculation of net present value and internal rate of return, provide valuable information for making capital-investment decisions. Decisions, however, are not based solely on financial results. BPA, and any other company, must balance the financial desirability of investments with other decision factors that may be of equal or greater importance. This balancing of financial and strategic criteria is at the heart of multiattribute decision making.

As indicated earlier, under Bonneville's revised capital-investment review process, developing and implementing a multiattribute decision-making process is one of the key responsibilities of the business-line capital-investment review panels. Following the provision of top management strategic guidance and objectives in November, the business-line review panels have the responsibility of translating this guidance and these objectives into financial and strategic criteria. In many ways, the resulting criteria will be the most visible and concrete manifestation of what the strategic guidance and objectives mean to the business lines, through influence on business-line actions.

In addition to developing the criteria, the panels are also responsible for using them in ranking capital-investment opportunities. The appropriate criteria and the accompanying weighting scheme are then given to those within the business who are responsible for developing capital-investment proposals—effectively communicating to staff how agency and business-line strategic guidance/objectives are to be implemented.

These criteria and their weighting are also important tools for verifying that top management and business-line management are interpreting the strategic guidance/objectives consistently. In Bonneville's benchmarking, it learned that one firm uses this approach by dedicating the first part of every capital budget review meeting between the CFO and program manager to a discussion of the criteria and weighting used to rank projects. At Bonneville, the business lines are required to include, in the presentation of their recommended capital-investment portfolio, an outline of the criteria they developed and how the criteria were used to determine which projects to include in the portfolio.

In Bonneville's transmission business line, a multiattribute decision process was implemented in the form of an investment matrix that scores each investment on a series of key criteria, including safety, reliability, customer service, environment, and high-performing organization (an efficiency and human resources measure). These criteria were derived from the business line and the company's strategic plans. At a business-line top management meeting early in the capital-investment review process (step 2 in Exhibit 25.1), the review panel presented the criteria and sought top management assistance and approval in setting the weighting scheme. With the criteria and their respective weights in hand, the review panel then had the means to objectively evaluate each investment and give it a score based on strategic criteria. This strategic evaluation was then combined with the financial analysis to determine which investments should be included in the proposed investment portfolio. Furthermore, these criteria formed the basis for strategic performance measures.

Capital-Investment Performance Measurement

As stated in the objectives, one of the most important advances Bonneville hopes to achieve with its revised capital-investment review process is improved performance measurement. Its benchmarking made it apparent that Bonneville is not alone in its difficulties with effective performance measurement. Every firm it talked to expressed dissatisfaction with its current attempts to measure the effectiveness of specific investments. As mentioned, the common impediments cited included the difficulty of tying incremental revenues to incremental investments and establishing accountability when managers responsible for projects have moved on before the investment's long-term effectiveness is measured.

To enable better performance measurement, our revised process includes performance measurement as an integral part of the entire investment planning and implementation process. As investment business cases are developed, project sponsors are responsible for also developing both the performance measures they intend to use and the methodology needed to measure them. These measures should include traditional cost-control targets, revenue or other performance targets, and strategic measures, as appropriate. These proposed measures are actively discussed and confirmed by the business-line capital-investment review panels when investments are approved for inclusion into capital portfolios.

Whenever possible, output/results performance targets, such as revenues earned, power generated or transmitted, and the like, are drawn directly from the cash flow analysis. This both encourages accurate and reasonable cash flow forecasts and creates an audit process whereby forecasting techniques can be improved for subsequent investment analyses.

Establishing effective performance measures poses a significant challenge for many of Bonneville's investments. Many are not discrete, with discrete revenue or cost-savings streams. Rather, they become integral parts of larger existing assets, so it is difficult to isolate the impact of the new investments on the performance of the larger existing assets. In such cases, it is even more important that performance measurement be addressed with the development of the business case, so that relevant and effective surrogate targets can be created. When more straightforward output/results targets are not possible, the business case should outline the surrogate target and the means by which it will be calculated and measured.

In Bonneville's first three years of implementation, activating the more aggressive financial and strategic analysis required by the new process occupied most of its efforts: Hence, it is just getting a start at establishing performance targets as part of the development of capital-investment business cases. That said, project/program managers have been very receptive to setting targets in this manner and are working toward having performance measures in place for each investment approved this year. It anticipates that the business-line capital-investment review panels will devote more time and effort to performance setting in the subsequent years of implementation. Bonneville is going to focus especially on deriving business-line-wide measures of capital-investment efficiency and performance from the individual investment performance measures.

Business Case Format: Capital-Investment Review Analytical Standards

As part of the effort to develop a uniform methodology and standards for individual investment analysis and review, the capital budgeting team developed a business case format for proposed capital investments. This format represents the company-wide standard for the review of all capital investments. Each business line was given the option of requiring additional information/analysis for its internal review, if it so desired.

Using this common format, one of the first responsibilities of the business lines in implementing the revised review process was to group investments into projects and programs. As an example, reviewing each separate capacitor or transformer as an individual investment would quickly result in an unmanageable workload. Clearly defined and understood projects and programs are essential to creating an efficient capital-investment review process.

The division of investments into manageable units has long been a challenge for Bonneville and other utilities. During the implementation phase of this process, business-line financial staff worked closely with their technical contemporaries to define programs in ways that made sense. As an example, the transmission business line chose to group together as a program the replacement and upgrade of capacitors. Within this program, they established physical and operational criteria that would be used to determine the priority for capacitor investments. This priority ranking results in a list of capacitor projects recommended for a given year. The annual capacitor program's funding request then becomes an output of the priority ranking. During the year, if a capacitor replacement or upgrade is needed that is not on the list, the review panel looks at the capacitor portfolio to make sure all preapproved projects are still on schedule and will be completed. If not, the panel may recommend canceling or deferring an existing project and adding the new one. If everything in the portfolio is necessary and on schedule, the panel can call on resources from an unallocated funds portfolio to add the new investment to the capacitor portfolio. As a result, the actual capacitors that are worked on during the year may not be the same ones included in the original request, allowing for flexibility to deal with operational needs as they arise.

Once a manageable number of investment projects or programs is determined, the recommended format and standards are used to develop business cases. As mentioned, two of the primary objectives of the revised capital-investment review process are to:

1. Create a framework using multiattribute decision making for approving long-term commitments of scarce capital resources (borrowing and future revenues)
2. Foster consistent and comparable reviews of alternative capital investments or long-term expense commitments while retaining reasonable flexibility for the business lines.

To foster consistent review, Bonneville has adopted the following outline for capital-investment business cases. This outline represents the minimum level of analysis and documentation required for investment proposals. Adoption of a common format helped ensure that:

▪ Critical information on each investment, such as net present value, internal rate of return, cash flows, and strategic criteria are located in the same place for each business case, allowing quick comparisons.
▪ All required information and analysis were completed, using the format as an indicator of what is required.
▪ The level of analysis was correctly understood and all assumptions were clearly documented.

The key elements of the recommended standard format for business cases are:

▪ *Financial/economic analysis.* All capital investments are be evaluated for net present value or net present cost (if there are no revenues or explicit cost savings), using a market discount rate. Business lines and project managers are also encouraged to use other measures of prospective financial performance, such as internal rate of return, when they are appropriate and informative. All of these measures use as a foundation the net annual cash flow documented in a detailed cash flow analysis, which, in addition to the point estimates, also includes a probability distribution of net present values based on sensitivity analysis.
▪ *Key assumptions/treatment of uncertainty.* Perhaps the most important and valuable element of the recommended business case format is the requirement that all key

assumptions affecting financial and strategic indicators be carefully and clearly documented. Such documentation is vital to uncertainty analysis, allowing the reviewer to quickly grasp the set of circumstances that will make the project successful, as well as what could drive the project into failure. Difficulties with past Bonneville investments have almost always been due to assumptions that did not work out as planned, the variability of which was not adequately captured in the uncertainty analysis.

Once the key assumptions are outlined, Bonneville uses sensitivity analysis to test the impact of varying those assumptions. The complexity of the sensitivity analysis depends on the investment amount and the uncertainties inherent in the assumptions. For larger investments Bonneville runs a Monte Carlo simulation using all cash flow elements that have significant variance. Simpler sensitivity runs are made for smaller or less complex investments.

- *Strategic (nonfinancial) criteria.* The essence of multiattribute decision making is incorporating financial and strategic (often nonfinancial) criteria into the analysis of investment options. An important element of the business case format is an analysis of the strategic criteria established by the business-line capital-investment review panels at the start of the formal review process. As mentioned, these criteria are used, in conjunction with financial results, to rank investments and develop the annual capital portfolios.

- *Recommended performance measures: financial/performance measures.* As stated, performance measurement is an integral part of the capital allocation and budgeting process. To enable more effective measurement, each business case must include proposed performance measures, together with the methodology for calculating them. Where possible, financial/performance measures (which could include measures of revenue generation, capacity addition, cost reduction, or cost control) should be drawn directly from the cash flow analysis. When it proves difficult to target and measure typical financial results such as revenue generation, the business case should recommend surrogate measures, such as use of pro forma financial statements, to measure before-and-after financial results.

- *Other strategic (nonfinancial) measures.* In addition to financial/performance measures, each business case should include relevant strategic measures. These will be especially important for non–revenue-producing investments for which financial measures are difficult to develop. Strategic measures should tie to the strategic criteria used in the multiattribute decision-making process outlined here.

IMPLEMENTATION: WHAT BONNEVILLE LEARNED IN THE FIRST THREE YEARS

As indicated, Bonneville began the redesign of its capital-investment review process in the fall of 1998. After benchmarking and numerous meetings, the Bonneville capital budgeting team prepared its proposal for the redesigned review process and presented it to top management in May 1999. After their approval, implementation was set for the fall of 1999. Bonneville has now completed the first three years of implementation, starting with the release of top management guidance for the fiscal year 2000 process in November 1999 and guidance for FY 2001 and FY 2002 in November 2000 and 2001, respectively. In these first three years, major efforts have included developing the top management guidance, empanelling and empowering the business-line capital-review panels, working with project/program managers to implement the recommended business case format, and conducting the first three rounds of business review panel decision meetings.

As its benchmarking anticipated, it has found that implementing an improved capital-investment review process is not necessarily a straightforward and simple process. Even after three years, Bonneville is by no means finished, but it has made substantial progress. Its primary successes include:

▪ *A better grasp of the effect of strategy on capital decisions.* One of the key concepts Bonneville is trying to engrain in its organization through the revised process is the critical link between strategy and capital investments. In the new process, before detailed budgets are developed, company and business-line strategies are reviewed and debated, with aggregate estimates of the capital investments required to achieve each strategy. When management decides to embark on a specific strategy, it does so with a clear understanding of the gross capital requirements of that strategy. To adopt a strategy is to also approve, at least in aggregate, the rough estimate of the capital investments needed to make it work. If, after more detailed capital-investment budgets are developed, the result totals more than management anticipated, or if market or financial changes have subsequently occurred that make the proposed capital-investment level untenable, management needs to go back to the drawing board and reassess the strategy.

An outcome of the tremendous upheaval in the electricity industry in 2001 was a clear indication that both the generation and transmission infrastructure in the Northwest was in serious need of reinforcement and enhancement. Years of generation surpluses and tight competitive markets had resulted in reduced investments. As Bonneville reviewed its transmission system, it became clear that it needed to begin an aggressive campaign of new investments to both increase reliability and relieve congestion. An examination of Bonneville-managed generation assets also pointed to a need for accelerated and increased investments. These increased capital needs were not anticipated at the time the FY 2001 top management guidance was released. Rather than working outside the process outlined in that guidance, Bonneville made the necessary adjustments to strategy and the underlying investment needs through convening a top-management capital committee to resolve issues of capital availability and reprioritization.

▪ *Better sense of teamwork/partnership between corporate finance and business lines.* As Bonneville worked through each new investment using the revised business case format, it has had more success than anticipated in these early years in building new relationships of trust and cooperation between financial and project technical staff. Especially for transmission, a lot of the financial analysis it is now requiring is new to the engineers who are developing projects. Although there was resistance at first, enthusiasm, persistence, and patience on the part of both sides have helped Bonneville overcome obstacles and make a good deal of progress in working cooperatively. This is creating the platform from which it can start to tackle more challenging issues such as performance measurement.

- *Adoption of market-based discount rate for analysis.* Prior to the revised process, Bonneville relied on its own borrowing rate as the discount rate to use in financial analysis. One of the major successes of the new strategy has been to educate and persuade management and analysts to move to a market-based discount rate. For Bonneville, this will lead to analysis that better captures uncertainty and result in asset returns more commensurate with those of its competitors.
- *Greater management attention.* As mentioned in its benchmarking results, implementing a new capital-investment review process will not be successful without top management commitment and discipline. A primary success in these early years of implementation has been the commitment and attention shown by top management in overcoming obstacles and making the process work. As its executive sponsor, the chief executive officer's continued and expressed interest has been invaluable in keeping the implementation process moving forward.

Along with the successes, Bonneville has faced a number of significant challenges in these early years of implementation. These include:

- *Getting a clear sense of strategy.* Given the changes occurring in the utility business, and the incredible volatility and unpredictability of power markets, it is not surprising that Bonneville has struggled with developing a clear long-term strategy. Bonneville is currently engaged in discussions with the other regional transmission utilities to form a western regional transmission organization that will control and operate the region's bulk transmission facilities. Participation in this organization will have major impacts on Bonneville. These uncertainties have made keeping a consistent and coherent strategy difficult at best.
- *Developing the appropriate capital performance targets.* As Bonneville continues implementation, one of its primary foci will be developing effective capital performance targets. As mentioned earlier, it faces significant challenges in this area. It has made a good start with investment-specific targets, and is now actively developing meaningful overall asset-performance measures that will lead to both investment and operating decisions that maximize asset value.
- *Changing mindsets and ways of doing things.* Finally, one of Bonneville's challenges has been to change the mind-sets and methodologies of both its technical and financial staff to support the new review process. There has been considerable resistance to the level of economic analysis now required, especially for transmission investments. As mentioned, Bonneville has made progress in developing the partnerships necessary to bring about the changes it needs, but this must be an ongoing focus of implementation.

SUMMARY

As Bonneville has worked over the past three years to develop and implement a more effective methodology for evaluating capital investments, the accelerating pace of deregulation and competition has made its efforts all the more important. The redesign project has been a continuing learning process for all involved, with both successes and ongoing challenges. Bonneville is confident that it has developed a methodology that recognizes its unique needs while employing industry best practices. As stated earlier, perhaps the most important—albeit cynical—objective it set for itself at the beginning of the redesign effort was to develop a process that was effective enough that it would last through implementation and into its second and third years.

26

Leasing

Robert Dale Apgood, PhD, MBA, CPA
Canterbury Group

INTRODUCTION

The budgetary process in today's business environment requires a dutiful coordination of a business strategic plan carefully supported by a capital budget (primarily a balance-sheet–planning tool) and an operating budget (typically an income-statement–planning tool) (see Exhibit 26.1).

Typically, top management envisions a strategy, and subsequently subordinates are required to project a capital plan (assets, liabilities, and equity) that will enable the company to march toward fulfillment of the strategy vision. Accordingly, a capital budget is prepared, complete with all necessary asset, liability, and equity elements. Frequently, however, the company prefers to avoid balance-sheet implications by electing to

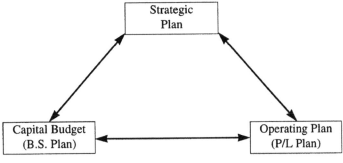

EXHIBIT 26.1 Coordination of Planning Tools

EXHIBIT 26.2 Impact of Leasing in Financial Statements

	Operating Lease		Capital Lease	
	Balance Sheet	P/L	Balance Sheet	P/L
Lessee	-0-	Rent expense	Fixed asset	Depreciation expense
			Accumulated depreciation	Interest expense
			Debt:	
			Current	
			Long-term	
Lessor	Fixed asset	Depreciation expense		
	Accumulated depreciation		-0-	Income
	Debt:	Interest expense		
	Current	Rental income	(Simplest of several	
	Long-term		possible structures)	

lease assets. Thus, off–balance-sheet financing is selected, the balance-sheet impact is minimized, and the operating budget is impacted. To graphically illustrate the financial statement impact, let us examine Exhibit 26.2.

From a budgetary viewpoint, it thus becomes evident that leases must be analyzed carefully, in order that the proper budgets become impacted. Occasionally, leasing transactions may be immaterial for a company, but since the mid-1980s, nearly 33 percent of all property, plant, and equipment acquired by U.S. companies have been acquired through operating and capital leases.[1]

Thus, the case is made: Budgeting is important and leasing is an increasingly material part thereof.

OVERVIEW OF THE LEASING PROCESS

A typical lease (usually called a single-inventor lease) involves four parties (see Exhibit 26.3).

Simple analysis suggests that, if the lessor retains title to the asset in question, the transaction is a rental or lease. If, however, the lessee eventually ends up with the asset, the lease in question begins to look like some kind of sale from the lessor to the lessee. In budgetary parlance, the transaction is either analyzed as part of the operating budget (if an operating lease) or the capital budget (if a capital lease). Because these two

---

[1] Annual statistics available from Equipment Leasing Association of America (ELA), Arlington, Virginia.

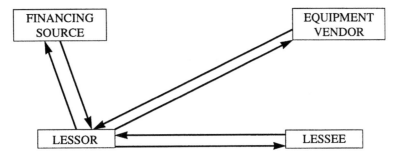

EXHIBIT 26.3 Typical Lease

budgets are frequently prepared by different persons, require vastly differing analytical approaches, and dramatically alter balance-sheet and income statement presentation, we must become skilled captains of the leasing ship as it sails the financial waters. Exhibit 26.4 shows the four typical lease analyses.

Internationally, two different approaches have been taken to properly classify leases on financial statements. The first and simplest approach is observed in the geographical region roughly approximated by southern Europe and is called the "form" approach to leasing. In these countries, if the lease contract stipulates or labels a lease as an operating lease, all analysis is finished. It *is* a rental. Lessor has balance-sheet ownership and lessee is a renter. If, in contrast, the lease agreement calls the transaction a capital lease, it *is*. Lessor then accounts for the transaction as a sale and the lessee has balance-sheet ownership. How simple and consistent! One party is always an owner and the other a nonowner.

In the United States, however, as in many other countries, it matters not what a lease is called or labeled. Evidence must be gathered, measurements taken, and then the lease classified as either on or off balance sheet for both lessee and lessor. In other words, the substance of a lease dictates its financial statement classification. A short list of countries using each system is displayed in Exhibit 26.5.

As long as both parties to the lease, lessee and lessor, are in the same country, lease treatment will normally be uniform. In the event, however, that a lease becomes binational, intriguing cross-border financial results are possible.

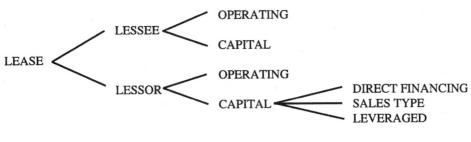

EXHIBIT 26.4 Lease Analysis

EXHIBIT 26.5   International Lease Typology

Countries Utilizing Form	Countries Utilizing Substance	Rules of Substance Found in:
France	United States	FASB 13, 91, 98, and IAS 17
Italy	United Kingdom	SSAP 21 and IAS 17
Spain	Canada	CICA 3065 and IAS 17
Portugal	Australia	ASAP 21 and IAS 17
Malta	New Zealand	IAS 17
Holland		IAS 17
Approximately 50 other countries		IAS 17

Case One

1. Both the lessee and lessor are in France.
2. The lease document stipulates that the lease is an operating lease—therefore, it is.
3. Lessor assumes balance-sheet ownership and is, therefore, entitled to the related income-statement deductions for depreciation and interest expenses. Lessor also has balance-sheet ramifications.
4. Lessee may not assume balance-sheet ownership but rather must account for the lease as a rental.
5. There is one owner and one nonowner.

	Balance Sheet	Income Statement
Lessor	Fixed asset	Depreciation expense
	Accumulated depreciation	Interest expense
	Debt:	Rental income
	Current portion	
	Long-term portion	
Lessee	No impact	Rental expense

Case Two

1. Lessor is an Italian corporation, and lessee is in the United States.
2. The lease document stipulates that the lease is an operating lease. For this lessor, it is.
3. Lessor assumes balance-sheet ownership and takes the related income statement deductions for depreciation and interest expenses as well as all balance-sheet ramifications.
4. Lessee must follow Financial Account Standards Board (FASB) rule 13 (U.S. rules). Let us assume that the present value of the minimum lease payments is greater than 90 percent of the fair value of the leased asset. According to U.S. rules, the lease is a capital lease, the lessee assumes balance-sheet ownership also (not necessarily legal ownership), and we have a double-dip lease, or, as it is frequently called, a *cross-border tax transfer*.

5. Both lessee and lessor must follow the accounting rules of their countries. Thus, each claims accounting ownership.

	Balance Sheet	Income Statement
Lessor	Fixed asset	Depreciation expense
	Accumulated depreciation	Interest expense
	Debt:	Rental income
	Current portion	
	Long-term portion	
Lessee	Fixed asset	Depreciation expense
	Accumulated depreciation	Interest expense
	Debt:	
	Current portion	
	Long-term portion	

Case Three

1. Lessor is a Spanish corporation, and lessee is in the United States.
2. The lease document stipulates that the lease is a capital lease. For this lessor, it is.
3. Lessor accounts for the lease as a sale. It is no longer on the balance sheet.
4. Lessee must follow FASB 13. Let us assume that the present value of the minimum lease payments is less than 90 percent of the fair market value of the asset. According to U.S. rules, the lease is an operating lease. The lessee does not have balance-sheet ownership and accounts for the transaction as a rental. In this case, neither lessee nor lessor claims balance-sheet ownership. It is off the books for each and rightfully so. Lessee and lessor *must* each follow the generally accepted accounting principles of its own country. In the parlance of the leasing community, this is sometimes called a skinny-dip lease, since neither party has balance-sheet coverage.

	Balance Sheet	Income Statement
Lessor	Nothing. This assumes the asset was sold and the resulting note receivable was also sold.	Income
Lessee	Nothing	Rental expense

POSSIBLE ADVANTAGES OF LEASING

1. Shifts risk of obsolescence to lessor.
2. Shifts legal ownership and responsibility to lessor.
3. Provides off–balance-sheet financing.
4. Typically paid for from operating budget rather than capital budget.
5. Profitability ratios appear improved.

6. Liquidity ratios appear improved.
7. Solvency ratios appear improved.
8. Tax benefits (depreciation and interest expense) can be shifted to a party better able to utilize them.
9. Lower cash flow up front to obtain asset.
10. Flexibility increases (swaps, upgrades, roll-overs, take-outs, etc.).
11. Inflation hedge (can negotiate longer term and pay with cheaper dollars).
12. Approval can be accelerated.
13. Circumventing capital budget constraints.
14. Delaying sales tax payments (as high as 33 percent in some European countries).
15. Government reimbursement policies (overhead is frequently a limited or prescribed element for reimbursement; lease payments are not overhead and qualify for reimbursement).
16. Alternative minimum tax may dictate no additional purchases.
17. Ownership may be unavailable (satellite usage).
18. Bundling (full-service leases) is facilitated.
19. Excessive usage of equipment by lessee would make ownership unwise.
20. Vendor control (nonperformance of equipment).
21. Finance source diversification.
22. Fewer restrictions (bank covenants).
23. Lower cost (lessor may obtain economies of scale and pass through to lessee).

POSSIBLE DISADVANTAGES OF LEASING

1. Opportunity to gain from residual value is shifted to lessor.
2. Balance-sheet analysis is hindered, as both asset and liability are disclosed only in footnotes.
3. Capital budgeting decisions are disguised and frequently not analyzed.
4. Tax benefits of ownership: Depreciation and interest expense are not normally available to minimize cash flows.
5. Reimbursement policies may be hindered (utilities, for example, are often given a targeted return on assets (ROA) approval figure for rates. If leased, the assets are less and the targeted profitability can be reduced—rates lowered).
6. Higher cost (if lessee is not sophisticated in lease negotiations).
7. Lease versus buy analytical techniques are not universally known and applied.
8. Trends or fads may suggest that leasing is wise when it is only current.

TYPES OF LEASE SOURCES

Lessors

- Financial institutions (banks, savings and loans, finance companies, etc.)
- Captives (vendors and banks)
- Independents

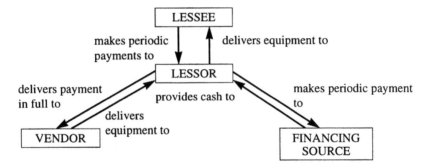

EXHIBIT 26.6 Typical Independent Lease Company Transaction (Third-Party Lease)

In the United States, independent leasing companies have traditionally held the biggest share of the leasing business.[2] Banks entered the game in a big way in the late 1970s and early 1980s and built large portfolios, many of which were liquidated in the late 1980s and early 1990s as they experienced operating and regulatory difficulties. The current trend in the industry is the awakening and substantial growth of the "vendor" sector, with vendors discovering that leasing can be a tremendous marketing tool for expansion as well as a profit center. Exhibit 26.6 illustrates a third-party lease for a typical independent lease company.

Many entities have joined the leasing game. They include:

- *Independent leasing companies.* This is the traditional type of lease provider that originally would lease anything to anyone (Exhibit 22.4). Increased competitive pressure has forced many of these companies to concentrate in niches, such as telecommunications or automobiles. The largest such player is Comdisco, an international participant in Chicago that specialized originally in the used IBM market. Exhibit 26.7 illustrates a typical captive-lease transaction
- *Captives.* This was the hot market of the early 1990s. Because captives operate under the scrutiny of a parent, they are usually not as nimble and flexible as an independent, but they have tremendous clout because of this same parent relationship (Exhibit 22.5). Examples include GECC (General Electric) and ICC (IBM).
- *Brokers.* During the frothy and profitable "go-go" years of the 1980s, many experienced leasing professionals discovered that they could function as financial intermediaries, bringing together the necessary participants, thus functioning as a manager. Brokers come and go but typically prefer to manage bigger deals, such as jumbo jets and large computer mainframes.
- *Banks.* In the United States, banks entered the leasing game after it was somewhat mature. By way of contrast, banks in Europe and the Middle East were primary developers, and hence currently enjoy a much larger market presence in those geographical regions. Banks in the United States dramatically altered their position

---

[2] ELA statistics.

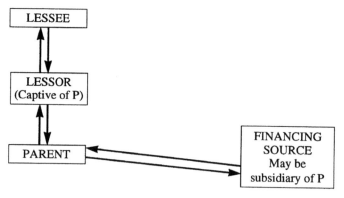

EXHIBIT 26.7   Typical Captive-Lease Transaction

in the leasing arena during the last few years because of large credit losses and subsequent government tightening of regulations.

▪ *Insurance companies.* Two approaches have been taken in this industry. Several large firms, such as Metropolitan Life Insurance, formed leasing subsidiaries and aggressively funded deals. Others are content to purchase large individual leases or portfolios on the secondary market, much like the home mortgage market.

▪ *Finance companies.* Many of these players jumped into the arena, especially in the area of consumer leasing. Because they already were active here, they expanded their horizon to include operating leases and thereby assumed a risk they were not experienced in—residual risk!

▪ *Pension funds.* Usually, these funds serve as a reservoir of lease portfolios and purchased leases from others. Needless to say, many questionable and some worthless paper found its way into the hands of these typically inexperienced participants.

▪ *Lease pools.* Functioning much like a mutual fund, many lease pools sold "shares" in future expected values to wealthy individuals and companies.

LEASE REPORTING

▪ FASB 13, 91, 98—Provide criteria for accrual (income statement, balance sheet) reporting
▪ Internal Revenue Service (IRS) Revenue Ruling 55-540, Revenue Procedure 75-21—Provide criteria for tax analysis of a lease
▪ International Accounting Standard (IAS)—Provides criteria for international lease reporting to the approximately 55 member nations who have adopted it
▪ Internal reporting

  ▪ Lease versus buy
  ▪ Internal rate of return
  ▪ Net present value
  ▪ Break-even
  ▪ Pricing

- Asset tracking
- Accounting
- Tax
- Billing and collections
- Portfolio management

Software providers have developed an abundance of software application packages to assist in lease analysis and reporting.[3]

Basic Terminology

The leasing industry is exceedingly creative, and accordingly a host of synonyms or near synonyms has been created to describe operating and capital leases. These include the ones listed in Exhibit 26.8.

Technical Analysis

Various national and international bodies have labored extensively to codify leasing rules. In the United States, the IRS and FASB have provided mandatory models.

The IRS was the first group in the United States to codify leasing rules, and these still exist. In 1955, Revenue Ruling 55-540 provided initial but very weak "nonguidelines" for lease classifications as either operating or capital. The IRS followed up this initial attempt with an improved but still-weak definition of operating and capital in 1975 with Revenue Procedure 75-21. Since then, the IRS has given the lease definition and measurement process little additional attention. Because what it has produced is impractical and insufficient for satisfactory application, the IRS tends to rely on the subsequent and much superior FASB 13 in its deliberations.

The FASB in 1975 issued FASB 13, which became effective in 1977. This is a much tighter document, which provides definitions and measurements for operating and capital lease classifications.

FASB 13

FASB 13 contains the four criteria that must be observed if a lease is to be classified as a capital lease.

Four Tests of Substance

1. Will title pass from lessor to lessee?
2. Does the lease contain a bargain purchase option?
3. Is the lease life greater than or equal to 75% of the economic life?
4. Is the present value of the minimum lease payments greater than or equal to 90% of the fair market value of the equipment?

---

[3] Some of the major software dealers are: Decision Systems, Inc., Minneapolis, Minnesota; SSI, Norcross, Georgia; Better Programs, Denver, Colorado; McCue Systems, Inc., Burlingame, California; The LeMans Group, King of Prussia, Pennsylvania.

EXHIBIT 26.8　Basic Terminology to Describe Operating and Capital Leases

Operating Lease Synonyms	Capital Lease Synonyms
Operating	Capital
Real	Direct finance
True	Finance
Rental	Installment sales contract
Off balance sheet	Deferred sales contract
Off the books	Open-end lease with a bargain purchase option
Closed-end	$1.00 purchase option
Open-end lease with fair market value purchase option	Nominal purchase option
Tax	Peppercorn (British)
Guideline	Full payout
Nonguideline	Full payoff
Walk away	Sales type
	Nontax
	Secured transaction

If the answer to any of these questions is affirmative, the lease is a capital lease. If all four are negative, the lease is an operating lease.

Internationally, all of the previously mentioned lease codification numbers (CICA 3065 in Canada, FASB 13 in the United States, SSAP 21 in England, etc.) are substantially identical and are also substantially identical to IAS 17, issued by the International Accounting Standards Board in London. In other words, once the intricacies of FASB 13 are mastered, all others are virtually identical.

Therefore, these four tests must be carefully examined and mastered if the financial statements are to be properly stated *and* if the budgeting classifications of operating and capital assets are to be proper. An operating lease will be included in the operating "budget" and is usually approved by a department head. A capital lease, however, is in the capital budget and is typically approved by someone at a higher corporate level.

Analysis of the Four Tests

The first test is simple to control. If an operating lease is desired, do not provide for the transfer of title in the lease document. Simply state that the lease is a closed-end lease or a walk-away lease (i.e., no purchase option is available to the lessee). Conversely, if a capital lease is desired, stipulate how and when title will pass (i.e., after 24 payments, after 60 months, etc.).

The second test is equally easy to control. If an operating lease is desired, avoid the inclusion of a bargain purchase option (BPO) in the lease agreement. If the parties to the lease desire a capital lease, a BPO provision automatically qualifies the lease as a purchase.

The third test is easy to control once one term is mastered—*economic life.* As used in the leasing industry, and in contrast to accounting and tax usage, life of an asset in its "economic" sense is defined as the expected useful life. Fully deciphered, FASB and the leasing industry define *economic life* as the length of time the asset has usefulness to multiple, subsequent users, not just the present user. Thus, economic life assumes a measure much longer than book life and considerably longer than tax life—a long, long life. Thus, cars usually are given an economic life of 10 to 15 years, mainframe computers 12 to 15 years, and ordinary desks and chairs 15 to 20 years. The budget analyst who is trying to convert a lease into a capital variety is probably wise not to try to qualify it with this third test. Lease lives are virtually always much less than 75 percent of the economic life. This third test will normally result in a rental situation.

Understanding and manipulating (not meant in its derogatory connotation) the budgetary journey of a lease from operating to capital usually involves a very mundane control of the fourth test—the present value (PV) of cash flows. This can easily be the point of departure at which the budget novice errs, concluding that a lease is operating when in fact it should be capital and vice versa. In short, the forecasted balance sheet and income statement are in danger of being misbudgeted and malforecasted.

To shorten the fourth test, we observe the technical language of FASB 13.

$$(PV)(MLPs) \geq (90\%)(FMV)$$

If the present value of the minimum lease payments (MLPs) is greater than or equal to 90 percent of the fair market value (FMV), a capital lease exists. Of course, the result is an operating lease if the 90 percent line of demarcation is not reached now to understand the implications of the formula.

Present Value—How?

FASB 13 dictates the alternative discounting rates to be utilized by the lessor and lessee.

Discount Rate to Be Utilized by Lessor	Lower of Discount Rate to Be Utilized by Lessee
The lessor must present-value the cash flows using the implicit rate in the lease.	The lessee must use the lower of: 1. The lessor's implicit rate in the lease, if known by the lessee. or 2. The incremental borrowing rate of the lessee.

Let us examine why FASB directed that the implicit rate is the only acceptable rate for the lessor. In order to establish its logic, let us pictorially examine the cash flows of the lessor in a leasing transaction (see Exhibits 26.9 and 26.10).

Possible cash flows out for the lessor include:

1. Equipment cost (broadly defined as historical cost of the equipment plus freight-in, installation, debugging, etc.)

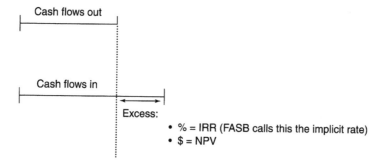

EXHIBIT 26.9 In–Out Cash Flow in a Leasing Transaction

2. Initial direct costs (referred to in FASB 13 and FASB 91 as IDCs)

    A. Commissions paid by lessor to sales representative to obtain lease
    B. Lawyers' fees paid by lessor to structure document
    C. Credit investigation fees paid by lessor to ascertain creditworthiness of lessee
    D. Other costs

Possible cash flows in for the lessor include:

1. Initial (at inception date of lease)

    A. Advance payments
    B. Refundable fees
    C. Nonrefundable fees

2. Periodic (typically occur monthly in U.S. lease transactions but frequently quarterly or semiannually in European deals)
3. Terminal (at the end of the lease term)
    A. Fees (nonrefundable fees, pickup fees, refurbishing fees, etc.)
    B. Sale (could either be to the lessee or to a third party)
    C. Re-lease (could either be to the lessee or to a third party)
    D. Lessee-guaranteed residual value (which automatically makes the lease a capital lease, as all risk has effectively been removed for the lessor)

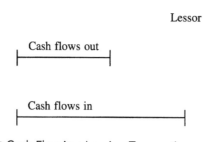

EXHIBIT 26.10 In–Out Cash Flow in a Leasing Transaction

E. Third-party residual insurance (the lessor could buy an insurance policy at lease inception date providing for a stipulated terminal value)

Now let us look again at the top of Exhibit 26.10, keeping in mind that we are examining it from the viewpoint of the lessor. It becomes clear that the lessor knows with precision each and every cash flow assumption (interpret this to mean budget or forecast) in the exhibit. Thus, the lessor can indeed calculate the implicit rate in the lease because the lessor knows all the data.

Next let us remove our lessor hat and replace it with that of the lessee—think like a lessee. Look again at Exhibit 26.10. The lessee rarely knows the equipment cost, never knows the commissions paid, the lawyers' fees, the credit investigation charges, and so on. In other words, the lessee does not know all cash flows out. Likewise, the lessee does not know all cash flows in. Some budgeted (estimated) flows in are known, such as the initial and the periodic flows, but the lessee would know the terminal budgeted flows only if the lessee holds a purchase or renewal option. In conclusion, the lessee would virtually never know all cash flows forecasted in a lease transaction. Thus, the lessee could not possibly calculate the implicit rate inherent in the lease. The only other way for the lessee to know (notice FASB 13 did not use the words "estimate the implicit rate"—it says "know it") the implicit rate would be to ask the lessor for it. Because the implicit rate is also the profitability rate inherent in the lease transaction, no lessor would or could divulge such detail to an outside party. In other words, the lessee normally cannot know the implicit rate. This brings us to the alternative discount rate posited by FASB for use by the lessee—the incremental, pretax, installment, secured, co-terminus borrowing rate—what rate would the lessee have to pay to borrow a like sum for a like period for a like transaction? A strong lessee might, therefore, select prime, whereas a weaker lessee would add several percentage points to the rate.

Lessor and lessee will each present value the budgeted cash flows, but each will use a different rate. If each uses a different rate, one set of cash flows could be above the magic 90 percent and the other below. Conclusion: It is possible, and indeed desirable, that the sophisticated lessor and lessee may structure the budgeted lease so that each gets the desired result, which could be:

- ▪ Single-dip lease—on one set of books only
- ▪ Double-dip lease—on both sets of books
- ▪ Skinny-dip lease—on neither set of books

Enough of rates. Let us move on to MLPs, the second element in the formula of test number four.

Minimum Lease Payments

FASB 13 directs lessors and lessees to present-value the MLPs. Minimum lease payments are not all but just some of the cash flows in the lease—the flows that can be predicted or budgeted with certainty.

Lessor	Lessee
1. Periodic payment in lease (usually monthly payment)	1. Periodic payment in lease (usually monthly payment)
2. Guaranteed residual payment	2. Lessee-guaranteed residual payments
3. Nonrenewal penalties	3. Nonrenewal penalties
4. BUT Fees, per FASB 91, are to be capitalized by lessor and amortized over the lease life, thus impacting future budget periods	4. Fees
5. Bargain purchase option	5. Bargain purchase option
6. *But not* executory costs	6. *But not* executory costs
7. Third-party residual insurance on the terminal value of the equipment	

Let us take a brief detour to discuss executory costs, after which we return to MLPs. Executory costs are defined in FASB 13 and 91 as cash flows out—operating costs paid by the lessee once a lease is in place. A logical way to picture these appears in Exhibit 26.11; Exhibit 26.12 illustrates how lessee executory costs are calculated.

Now assume:

$$(PV)(\$500) = 92\% \text{ of FV} = \text{Capital lease}$$

Lessee may not desire a budgeted capital transaction, so the two parties negotiate a bundled lease resulting in the $800 monthly budgeted payment being allocated as shown in Exhibit 26.13.

Thus, the (PV)($450) < 90% FMV, and the lessee gets an operating lease. Real-world evidence of this exists in the normal lease proposals of Xerox, IBM, and many other companies, wherein they push bundling. They want to provide a machine plus supplies, maintenance, insurance, training, and any other products and/or services.

If the lessee desires a budgeted capital lease, the agreement can bundle more cash flow into the monthly payment. If, however, the capital budget is all used up, bundle a lease so that less of the cash flow is attributed to the monthly payment and an operating lease is created.

Now let us return from our detour to the MLP discussion. Notice that FASB directed that executory costs not be included in the MLP to be present-valued. Also, notice that the minimum lease payments listed under lessor and lessee are *not* the same.

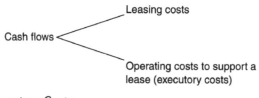

EXHIBIT 26.11 Executory Costs

EXHIBIT 26.12 Lessee Executory Costs

Net Lease	Full-Service Lease or Bundled Lease
Lease pays only:	Lessee pays a higher monthly payment to lessor, who, in turn, pays executory costs.
1. Low net monthly payment (assume $500)	
PLUS	New monthly payment would be approximately
2. Executory (operating) costs (assume $300 per month)	$500 + $300 = $800.

The result? If different budgeted cash flows are present-valued, it is possible to:

- Single-dip a lease
- Double-dip a lease
- Skinny-dip a lease

Ninety Percent Rule

In all countries of the world that follow the rules of substance (not form countries), there is general agreement on the 90 percent rule. However, the lessee and lessor each must measure according to "known" information. Thus, the lessor and lessee end up with different comparison bases (90 percent of the fair market value).

Lessor	Lessee
90% of "the" FMV	90% of "an" FMV

Because the exact cost of the equipment is known to the lessor, the lessor can indeed make this calculation. The lessee, however, normally will not "know with precision" the FMV. Thus, an estimate must suffice. Conceptually, this means that the lessee will rely on one of these for the FMV:

- Written bid
- Telephone quotation
- Newspaper advertisement
- Price list—wholesale
- Price list—retail

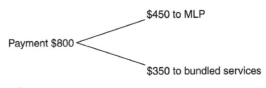

EXHIBIT 26.13 Bundles Lease

- Estimated cost
- Other

Conclusion: Rarely would the lessor and the lessee take 90 percent of the same cost.

Retrospect

Once again, let us examine the fourth test of substance.

$$(PV)(MLPs) \geq 90\% \text{ of the FMV}$$

As we have seen, lessor and lessee will utilize different variables for three of the four test components. It is not only possible but probable that each can control the variables to obtain the desired type of lease and thereby shift impact from the operating budget to the capital budget or vice versa.

LEASE VERSUS PURCHASE ANALYSIS

Lease versus purchase analysis begins with the assumption that the investment analysis (capital budgeting) decision has been made in favor of acquiring a piece of equipment. The next step requires a financing decision: lease versus purchase analysis. Exhibit 26.14 illustrates the analysis between lease-versus-purchase lease arrangements.

Mega Corporation recently decided to obtain a computer with a retail value of $400,000. The company can either obtain a loan and purchase the computer, or it can be leased. Mega Corporation is in the 40 percent tax bracket.

Relevant Information for Purchase Alternative

A bank loan must be obtained for the purchase price of $400,000 less a down payment of $100,000. The balance ($300,000) is to be financed over 36 months with monthly payments in arrears of $9,680, an implicit borrowing rate of about 10 percent. Sales tax is 6 percent and will be paid at the time of purchase. The bank requires a loan origination fee of 2 percent of the loan proceeds. Each monthly payment is composed of both principal and interest, the latter being tax deductible as shown:

Year 1	$25,939
Year 2	$16,492
Year 3	$ 6,055

Depreciation expense on the computer will be straight line for book purposes and Modified Accelerated Cost Recovery System (MACRS) with a five-year life for tax. The sales tax of $24,000 will be capitalized as part of the computer's depreciable base.

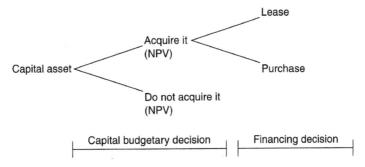

EXHIBIT 26.14 Lease versus Purchase Analysis

Depreciation Calculation

Weighted average after-tax cost of capital of 12 percent.

Equipment cost	$400,000	
Sales tax	24,000	
Depreciable basis	$424,000	
Year 1	$84,800	(20%)(424,000)
Year 2	135,680	(32%)(424,000)
Year 3	81,408	(19.2%)(424,000)
Year 4	48,760	(11.5%)(424,000)
Year 5	48,760	(11.5%)(424,000)
Year 6	24,592	(5.8%)(424,000)
	$424,000	

Operating costs (executory cost):

- Repairs and maintenance = $1,000 per month for 72 months
- Insurance = $400 per month for 72 months
- Supplies = $700 per month for 72 months

Preset Value Factors			
Type of Flow	**Rate**	**N**	**Factor**
PV annuity	.83%	36 months	31.0093
PV annuity	1%	72 months	51.1504
PV annuity	1%	70 months	50.1685
PV annuity	.83%	72 months	54.0375
PV of 1	12%	3 years	0.7118
PV of 1	12%	2 years	0.7972
PV of 1	12%	1 year	0.8929
PV of 1	12%	4 years	0.6355
PV of 1	12%	5 years	0.5674
PV of 1	12%	6 years	0.5066

HP 12 C Keystrokes for Loan Amortization

300,000 CHS PV
g end
9,680 PMT
10 g 12 ÷
0 n

12 f amort	25,939	
X ≷ Y	90,221	
RCL PV	209,779	
12 f amort	16,492	
X ≷ Y	99,668	
RCL PV	110,111	
12 f amort	6,055	
X ≷ Y	110,105	
RCL PV	7	(Rounding error)

Leasing Information

The lease would be for six years with monthly payments of $8,250 in advance. The first and last two payments are due at the lease inception date. A lease origination fee of $4,000 must be paid in advance. The lease contains an FMV purchase option, but Mega Corporation does not plan on exercising the option.

Operating costs (executory costs) are:

▪ Use tax of 6 percent on each monthly payment = $495
▪ Insurance = $425 per month
▪ Repairs and maintenance = $1,000 per month
▪ Supplies = $600 per month

Present Value of Purchase Alternative

	Cash Flow	× PV Factor	× Tax Factor	= Amount
Initial flows:				
Down payment	$100,000	1	N/A	$100,000
Sales tax	24,000	1	N/A	24,000
	6,000	1	1-0.4	3,600
Periodic flows:	9,680	31.0	N/A	300,080
Terminal flows:				
Repairs and maintenance	1,000	54.04	1-0.4	32,424
Insurance	400	54.04	1-0.4	12,970
Supplies	700	54.04	1-0.4	22,697
Tax shielded by:				
Interest expense				(16,247)

Depreciation expense			(125,176)
Net present value of aftertax cash flows to purchase			$354,348

Present Value of Leasing Alternative

	Cash Flow	× PV Factor	× Tax Factor	= Amount
Initial flows:				
Advance payments (2)	$16,500	1	1-0.4	$9,900
	4,000	1	1-0.4	2,400
Periodic flows:				
Monthly payments (70)	8,250	50.17	1-0.4	248,342
Terminal flows:				
Use tax in advance (2)	990	1	1-0.4	594
Use tax	495	50.17	1-0.4	14,900
Insurance	425	50.17	1-0.4	12,793
Repairs and maintenance	1,000	50.17	1-0.4	30,102
Supplies	600	50.17	1-0.4	18,061
Net present value of aftertax cash flows to lease				$310,001

Calculation of Tax Shielded by Interest Expense

Year	Interest Expense	PV Factor	Tax Factor	Income Tax Shielded
1	$25,939	0.8929	0.4	$9,264
2	16,492	0.7972	0.4	15,259
3	6,055	0.7118	0.4	1,724
	$48,486			$16,247

Calculation of Tax Shielded by Depreciation Expense

Year	Interest Expense	PV Factor	Tax Factor	Income Tax Shielded
1	$84,800	0.8929	0.4	$30,287
2	135,680	0.7972	0.4	43,266
3	81,408	0.7118	0.4	3,178
4	48,760	0.6355	0.4	12,395
5	48,760	0.5674	0.4	11,067
6	24,592	0.5066	0.4	4,983
	$424,000			$125,176

FINANCIAL ACCOUNTING STANDARDS BOARD RULE 13 CASE ILLUSTRATION

Lease Provisions

- Lease term: 60 months
- List price of equipment: $140,000
- Discount to lessor from vendor: $14,000
- First and last two payments due at inception date
- Nonrenewal penalty: $1,500
- Estimated residual value: $19,000
- Monthly payment, net of executory costs: $2,600

Lessor Solution

Step 1: Calculation of Implicit Rate

Keystrokes	Display	Explanation
f REG	0.00	Clears all registers
118,200 CHS g CFo	118,200	Enters initial cash flow
2,600 g CFj	2,600	Enters first cash flow
57 g Nj	57.00	Enters number of times first flow occurs
0 g CFj	0.00	Enters second cash flow
2 g Nj	2.00	Enters number of times second flow occurs
20,500 g CFj	20,500	Enters third cash flow
f IRR	1.16	Answer (the calculated monthly yield)
12X	13.94	IRR (the implicit rate)

Step 2: PV of MLPs

Keystrokes	Display	Explanation
f REG	0.00	Clears all registers
1.16 i	1.16	Enters monthly discount rate
7,800 g CFo	7,800.00	Enters initial cash flow
2,600 g CFj	2,600.00	Enters first cash flow
57 g Nj	57.00	Enters number of times first flow occurs
0 g CFj	0.00	Enters second cash flow
2 g Nj	2.00	Enters number of times second flow occurs
1,500 g CFj	1,500.00	Enters third cash flow
f NPV	116,540.57	Answer (the calculated net present value)

Step 2: Calculation of a Comparison Base

$140,000

× 0.9

$126,000

Conclusion: Capital lease, because the PV of the MLPs is more than 90 percent of the FMV.

Lessee Solution

Step 1: PV of MLPs

Keystrokes	Display	Explanation
f REG	0.00	Clears all registers
10 g 12 ÷	0.83	Enters monthly discount rate
7,800 g CFo	7,800	Enters initial cash flow
2,600 g CFj	2,600	Enters first cash flow
57 g Nj	57.00	Enters number of times first flow occurs
0 g CFj	0.00	Enters second cash flow
2 g Nj	2.00	Enters number of times second flow occurs
1,500 g CFj	1,500	Enters third cash flow
f NPV	126,301.28	Answer (the calculated present value)

Step 3: Calculation of a Comparison Base

$$\begin{array}{r} \$126,000 \\ \underline{\times\ 0.9} \\ \$113,400 \end{array}$$

Conclusion: Capital lease, because the PV of the MLPs is more than 90 percent of the FMV.

Conclusion

For the lessor, the lease would be classified as a capital lease because (PV)(MLP) ≥ (90%) (FMV). But for the lessee, the lease could be either operating or capital, depending on the choice of the PV rate. If the lease is being analyzed near the end of the year and if the lessee has extra cash available in the operating budget, an operating lease could be structured, keeping the deal off the books. If, however, the lessee has cash left in the capital budget, a direct finance lease could be structured, thereby putting the equipment on the books.

It is imperative that budget experts, both operating and capital, understand the principles dictated by FASB 13 in order to optimize plans and results.

 ## NEGOTIATION OF LEASES

How do you negotiate a lease? Many factors must be considered, including, but not limited to:

▪ Number of periodic payments
▪ Number of advance payments

- Stub payments (partial initial payments)
- Nonrenewal penalties
- Lease origination fees
- Contingent payments
- Excess usage or "beat up" fees
- Deposits
- Step up, step down, skip payment provisions
- COLA or other escalation provisions
- Tax indemnifications
- Equipment subleasing rights
- Usage restrictions
- Late payment penalties
- Leasehold improvement ownership rights
- Lease assignment rights
- Lessor subrogation rights
- Executory cost provisions (insurance, supplies, repairs, taxes, etc.)
- Warranties on equipment by vendor and/or lessor
- Rollovers, upgrades, early outs, swaps
- Renewal options
- Purchase options
- Residual value insurance
- Equipment inspection provisions
- Equipment maintenance provisions

SELECTING A LESSOR

Lessor selection demands that the lessee consider:

- Financial condition of leasing company
- Flexibility
- Services offered
- Rate commitment
- Turnaround time
- Prior experience with similar equipment
- Geographic presence
- Financing sources
- Ultimate disposition of lease paper

LEASE-ANALYSIS TECHNIQUES

Many types of returns can be calculated for any lease transaction. These measures of performance are usually stated in some form of return on investment. Typical returns would be stated as the internal rate of return for a particular transaction or the "return" on a portfolio. The return on a portfolio would be some type of weighted-average calculation. However, all quoted returns are based on cash flows, or, in other words, when cash changes hands. Some of the different titles for types of returns include:

- Internal rate of return
- External rate of return
- Modified rate of return
- Street sate or stream rate
- Return on assets
- Return on equity
- Average return on assets
- Yield

Because so many different names may be used, it would be easier to take a particular transaction and view the different types of return calculations from the lessee and lessor perspectives. For this example, the next 11 assumptions will be utilized in developing different yield calculations:

1. Lease term: Four years with the first rental payment due at the end of the first year of the lease. For tax purposes, the lease is considered a true or guideline lease; that is, the lessor will be entitled to the tax benefits of tax depreciation, and the lessee will be entitled to expense the full amount of the payments made to the lessor.
2. At the conclusion of the lease term, the lessee will have the option of purchasing the equipment for its then FMV, renewing the lease for the equipment at its then FMV, or returning the equipment to the lessor and having no further involvement with the particular piece of equipment.
3. The lessor is a calendar year taxpayer in the 35 percent tax bracket.
4. The annual rental shall be $60,000, and the inception date of the lease transaction is December 31.
5. The purchase price or FMV of the equipment is $200,000.
6. The expected FMV of the equipment at the end of the lease term is $30,000, as estimated by the lessor at the inception of the lease arrangement.
7. The lessor will require a $5,000 refundable security deposit from the lessee. This amount will be held by the lessor throughout the term of the lease and returned to the lessee at the end of the lease term if there is no reason to use it for default reasons. The lessor will not pay the lessee any monies for the use of these funds.
8. A $1,000 nonrefundable commitment fee is to be received by the lessor from the lessee.
9. A $2,500 brokerage fee is to be paid by the lessor to a third party as compensation for its bringing this transaction to the lessor.
10. General and administrative costs have been allocated to the lease along with the initial direct costs of $4,000. First-year general and administrative costs are $3,000 and have a 5 percent inflation factor built in.
11. Tax benefits are assumed to result fully in tax savings.

The "interest" cost to the lessee is the first type of yield calculation to be performed. The lessee "cost" is calculated because a lease transaction does not contain a stated interest rate or cost of money, as a lease is a usage transaction and not a money-financing transaction. The lessor is providing the use of equipment and not lending money to the lessee to be used for whatever purpose it desires.

From the lessee's perspective, it is gaining the use of $200,000 of equipment for four years, and at the end of four years it has a number of options that may be exercised at its discretion. If the lessee returns the equipment to the lessor at the end of the initial lease term, then it would have the use of $200,000 for four years at a cost of $60,000, payments in arrears for the four-year period. The "interest" cost of money would be 7.71 percent. If the lessee were to purchase the equipment at the end of the four-year term for the lessor's estimated FMV of $30,000, the "interest" cost of money would be 12.29 percent. If the lessee were to renew the equipment lease at the end of the four-year term, it would not be possible to calculate an "interest" cost of money to the lessor, because the terms of the renewal are not yet known, even if the renewal amount of $30,000 were to be known.

Both the 7.71 and 12.29 percent calculations are pretax. From the perspective of the lessee, any after-tax calculations would be based on a number of assumptions and are really not relevant to an understanding of this transaction.

The remainder of the calculations in this chapter are from the lessor perspective and are done from both a pretax and after-tax perspective. The calculations are numerous, and it can readily be seen why confusion often reigns when trying to compare yields in lease transactions. One must understand what elements of cash flow are included when arriving at a particular stated yield and whether the calculation is pretax or after tax. To fully understand after-tax calculations, one must also understand the leverage or gearing of the lessor and whether the transactions have been funded on a pooled or match-funded basis, the pretax cost of debt to the lessor, and whether the rate is fixed throughout the transaction or is adjusted at times throughout the lease term in accordance with some borrowing agreement in place for the lessor. The corporate tax rate and the timing of when taxes are remitted enter into a fine-tuning of any calculation, and the desired return on equity contributed funds plays perhaps the most important role of all these variables.

Pretax lessor calculations would be:

1. *Stream or street rate.* This calculation takes into account only the cost of the equipment to the lessor and any noncancellable payment amounts. Because the residual amount is anticipated but not absolutely known (unknown to the lessee), it would be the same as making a $200,000 investment and receiving $60,000 per year in arrears for the use of this invested amount. This would be a return of 7.71 percent and compares with the same amount as calculated by the lessee previously.

2. *Stream rate including residual.* This calculation includes the expected, but unguaranteed, residual amount of $30,000. When the residual is included in the calculation, then the lessor yield would be 12.29 percent and would be equivalent to the similar calculation of the lessee as performed previously.

3. *Pretax payback.* Both the stream rate and stream rate with residual calculations would indicate a payback period of 3.33 years. This does not take into account any

adjustment for the time value of money. A time-adjusted payback period could be calculated if one were to assume some hurdle rate or cost of funds to the lessor. For purposes of this chapter, this calculation is not performed, but it could be accomplished readily if some hurdle rate were to be brought into focus.

4. *An all-inclusive pretax ROA yield.* This amount would include all of the pretax cash flows and would be based on when the cash is expected to change hands. This would take into account all known and expected cash flows to be received by the lessor, but does not take into account the tax benefits to be received and utilized by the lessor. In our example, the cash flows would occur in this way:

Initial or inception:

($200,000)	Equipment cost
(2,500)	Brokerage fee
(4,000)	Initial direct costs
1,000	Nonrefundable fee
5,000	Refundable security deposit
($200,500)	Net outflow at inception

During the term of the transaction:

Three payments of $60,000 per year

At termination:

$60,000	Final payment amount
30,000	Purchase option amount
(5,000)	Security deposit refund
$85,000	Net termination inflow

When taking into account all of these cash flows and the timing of when they would occur, the yield to the lessor is 11.47 percent. This is close to the 12.29 percent amount previously calculated, but includes all cash flows. As must be noted, this is a lower value than the stream rate including the residual.

5. *Net pretax yield.* This calculation takes into account all of the cash flows as shown in item 4 with the addition of the general and administrative costs. The next illustration shows the timing of the cash flows and results in a pretax yield to the lessor of 9.25 percent. The 9.25 percent value is calculated by determining the internal rate of return for the cash flow amounts for each year of the transaction.

	0	1	2	3	4
Rental payments	0	60,000	60,000	60,000	60,000
Commitment fee	1,000				
Initial direct costs	(4,000)	0	0	0	0

(continued)

	0	1	2	3	4
Brokerage fee	(2,500)				
General and administrative (G&A)	0	(3,000)	(3,150)	(3,308)	(3,473)
Residual	0	0	0	0	30,000
Security deposit	(5,000)	0	0	0	(5,000)
Deduct: cost of equipment	(200,000)	0	0	0	0
TOTAL	(200,500)	57,000	56,850	56,692	81,527
	fIRR = 9.25				

6. *Net after-tax yield.* This calculation takes into account the cash flows included in the previous calculations and then includes the impact of recovering the lessor's investment through tax depreciation. It is seen that this net after-tax yield is 7.00 percent. Some analysts will arrive at the after-tax yield by multiplying the pretax yield of 9.25 percent by the reciprocal of the tax rate, or 65 percent. If this were done (9.25 × 0.65), the resultant yield would be 6.01 percent. As can be seen when calculating the internal rate of return for the final cash flows, the yield is 7.00 percent. The difference is due to the timing of the cash flows, which is not taken into account when performing the 6.01 percent calculation.

	0	1	2	3	4
Rental payments	0	60,000	60,000	60,000	60,000
Commitment fee	1,000	0	0	0	0
Initial direct costs	(4,000)	0	0	0	0
Brokerage fee	(2,500)	0	0	0	0
G&A	0	(3,000)	(3,150)	(3,308)	(3,473)
Depreciation	(40,000)	(64,000)	(38,400)	(23,040)	(34,560)
Residual	0	0	0	0	30,000
Pretax income	(45,500)	(7,000)	18,450	33,652	51,967
Taxes CA 35%	15,925	2,450	(6,458)	(11,778)	(18,188)
A-T income	(29,575)	(4,550)	11,993	21,874	33,779
Add: depreciation	40,000	64,000	38,400	23,040	34,560
Security deposit	5,000	0	0	0	0
Deduct: cost of equipment	(200,000)	0	0	0	0
TOTAL	(184,575)	59,450	50,393	44,914	63,339

7. *Return on equity (ROE).* This final calculation is found by making assumptions as to the method of funding employed by the lessor, which, in this example, assumes that the lessor wishes the lease. Also, the leverage employed by the lessor is 80 percent debt and 20 percent equity. The pretax interest cost on borrowed funds is 9 percent, and the tax rate of the lessor throughout the life of the transaction will be 35 percent. The ROE for the lessor based on the cash flows calculated in item 6 and adjusted for

the cost of debt and including the repayment of borrowed funds is 11.60 percent. This amount is found by deducting the after-tax cost of debt from the after-tax cost of capital as calculated in 6.00 or 7.00 percent The after-tax cost of debt to the lessor is found by multiplying the pretax cost of debt times the quantity (one minus the tax rate, or 0.65) times the 0.8 debt leverage factor. This is found to be 4.68 percent.

Net Aftertax Cash Flows				
0	**1**	**2**	**3**	**4**
(184,575)	59,450	50,393	44,914	63,339

80% Debt = 147,660

20% Equity = 36,915

Year One

147,660 × 0.09 = 13,289 × 0.65 =	8,638	A-T Return on Debt
36,915 × 11.60 =	4,282	A-T Return on Equity
	12,920	
.8 × 9(.65) = 4.68	(59,450)	CF
.2 × 11.60 = 2.32	46,530	
7.00	×.8	
	37,224	Debt
	9,306	Equity

Year Two

147,660 − 37,224 = 110,436 × 0.09		A-T Return on
= 9.939 × 0.65 =	6,461	Debt
36,915 − 9,306 = 27,609 × 0.1160 =	3,203	A-T Return on Equity
	9,664	
	(50,393)	CF
	40,729	
	×.8	
	32,583	Debt
	8,146	Equity

Year Three

110,436 − 32,583 = 77,853 × 0.09 =	4,554	A-T ROD
7,007 × 0.65 =		
27,609 − 8,246 = 19,463 × 0.1160 =	2,258	A-T ROE
	6,812	
	(44,914)	CF
	38,102	
	×.8	
	30,482	Debt
	7,620	Equity

(continued)

Net Aftertax Cash Flows

0	1	2	3	4
(184,575)	59,450	50,393	44,914	63,339

Year Four

77,853 − 30,482 = 47,371 × 0.09		
= 4,263 × 0.65 =	2,771	ROD
[x]		
19,463 − 7,620 = 11,843 × 0.1160 =	1,374	ROE
[y]	4,145	
	(63,339)	CF
	59,194	
	×.8	
[x] 16 Δ due to rounding.	[x] 47,355	Debt
[y] 4 Δ due to rounding.	[y] 11,839	Equity

When this amount is deducted from after-tax cost of capital of 7.00 percent, the cost of equity is determined to be 2.32 percent. When this is divided by the 0.2 equity leverage factor, the ROE to the lessor is determined to be 11.60 percent.

LEASE FORM

AGREEMENT NO. _____

EQUIPMENT LEASE

LESSOR: _____   LESSEE: _____

_____   _____

_____   _____

(STREET ADDRESS)   (STREET ADDRESS)

_____   _____

(CITY, STATE, AND ZIP)   (CITY, STATE, AND ZIP)

Description of Leased Equipment

NEW/USED	QUANTITY	MAKE and DESCRIPTION	SERIAL NO.

EQUIPMENT LOCATION: ☐ SAME AS ABOVE ☐ OTHER: (address) _____

LEASE PAYMENT TERMS

MONTHS	AMOUNTS
TOTAL LEASE TERM # ____ MONTHS	MONTHLY RENTAL AMOUNT: ____
	PLUS USE TAX, IF ANY
ADVANCE RENTALS PAID # ____	TOTAL RENTALS PAID

MONTHS   IN ADVANCE: _____
                                          RENTAL × # PAID

TERMS AND CONDITIONS OF LEASE

LESSEE HEREBY WARRANTS AND REPRESENTS THAT THE EQUIPMENT WILL BE USED FOR BUSINESS PURPOSES, AND NOT FOR PERSONAL, FAMILY, HOUSEHOLD, OR AGRICULTURAL PURPOSES. LESSEE ACKNOWLEDGES THAT LESSOR AND ITS ASSIGNS HAVE RELIED UPON THIS REPRESENTATION IN ENTERING INTO THIS LEASE.

1. LESSEE ACKNOWLEDGES THAT LESSOR IS NOT THE MANUFACTURER OF THE EQUIPMENT, NOR MANUFACTURER'S AGENT AND LESSEE REPRESENTS THAT LESSEE HAS SELECTED THE EQUIPMENT LEASED HEREUNDER BASED UPON LESSEE'S JUDGMENT

THE UNDERSIGNED AGREE TO ALL THE TERMS AND CONDITIONS SET FORTH ABOVE AND ON THE REVERSE SIDE HEREOF, AND IN WITNESS WHEREOF, HEREBY EXECUTES THIS LEASE AND CERTIFIES THAT THE UNDERSIGNED IS DULY AUTHORIZED TO EXECUTE SAME, ON BEHALF OF OR AS THE LESSEE AND THAT HE HAS RECEIVED AN EXECUTED COPY OF THIS LEASE.

Executed this _____ day _____ of, 20____.

LESSOR: _____   LESSEE: _____

BY: _____   BY: _____
                                       TITLE

TITLE: _____   BY: _____
                                       TITLE

PRIOR TO HAVING REQUESTED THE LEASE. THE EQUIPMENT LEASED HEREUNDER IS OF A DESIGN, SIZE, FITNESS, AND CAPACITY SELECTED BY LESSEE AND LESSEE IS SATISFIED THAT THE SAME IS SUITABLE AND FIT FOR ITS INTENDED PURPOSES. LESSEE FURTHER <u>AGREES THAT LESSOR HAS MADE AND MAKES NO REPRESENTATIONS OR WARRANTIES OF WHATSOEVER NATURE, DIRECTLY OR INDIRECTLY, EXPRESSED OR IMPLIED, INCLUDING BUT NOT LIMITED TO ANY REPRESENTATIONS OR WARRANTIES WITH RESPECT TO SUITABILITY, DURABILITY, FITNESS FOR USE AND MECHANTABILITY OF ANY SUCH EQUIPMENT, THE PURPOSES AND USES OF THE LESSEE, OR OTHERWISE.</u> LESSEE SPECIFICALLY WAIVES ALL RIGHTS TO MAKE CLAIM AGAINST LESSOR HEREIN FOR BREACH OF ANY WARRANTY OF ANY KIND WHATSOEVER. LESSOR HEREBY PASSES TO LESSEE ALL WARRANTIES, IF ANY, RECEIVED BY LESSOR BY VIRTUE OF ITS OWNERSHIP OF THE EQUIPMENT. LESSOR SHALL NOT BE LIABLE TO LESSEE FOR ANY LOSS, DAMAGE, OR EXPENSE OF ANY KIND OR NATURE CAUSED DIRECTLY OR INDIRECTLY BY ANY EQUIPMENT LEASED HEREUNDER FOR THE USE OF MAINTENANCE THEREOF, OR FOR THE FAILURE OF OPERATIONS THEREOF, OR BY ANY INTERRUPTION OF SERVICE OR LOSS OF USE THEREOF OR FOR ANY LOSS OF BUSINESS OR ANY OTHER DAMAGE WHATSOEVER AND HOWSOEVER CAUSED. NO DEFECT OR UNFITNESS OF THE EQUIPMENT SHALL RELIEVE LESSEE OF THE OBLIGATION TO PAY RENT, OR ANY OTHER OBLIGATION UNDER THIS AGREEMENT OR ITS ASSIGNEE.

1. LEASE: Lessor hereby leases to Lessee and Lessee hereby hires and takes from Lessor the personal property described above and on any attached supplemental "schedule A" (hereinafter, with all replacement parts, additions, repairs, and accessories incorporated therein and/or affixed thereto, referred to as "Equipment").

2. TERM AND RENT: This Lease is non-cancellable for the term stated above and shall commence upon the Date of Acceptance of the equipment and shall continue for the period specified as the "term" stated above. If one or more advance rentals are payable, the total amount of such advance rentals shall be set forth in the Advance Rental Payment(s) section above and shall be due upon acceptance by the Lessor of this lease. Advance rentals, when received by Lessor, shall be applied to the first rent payment for the Equipment and the balance of the advance rental shall be applied to the final rental payment or payments for said Equipment. In no event shall any advance rent or any other rent payments be refunded to Lessee.

3. Equipment is and shall at all times remain, the property of Lessor, and Lessee shall have no right, title, or interest therein, except as herein set forth, and no right to purchase or otherwise acquire title to or ownership of any of the equipment. If Lessor supplies Lessee with labels indicating that the equipment is owned by Lessor, Lessee shall affix such labels to and keep them in a prominent place on the equipment. Lessee hereby authorizes Lessor to insert in this lease the serial numbers and other identification data of equipment when determined by Lessor. Lessor is hereby appointed by Lessee as its true and lawful attorney in respect to being hereby authorized by Lessee, at Lessee's expense, to cause this lease, or any statement or other instrument in respect of this lease showing the interest of Lessor in the equipment, including Uniform Commercial Code Financing Statements, to be filed or recorded and refiled and re-recorded, and grants Lessor the right to execute Lessee's name thereto. Lessee agrees to execute and deliver any statement or instrument requested by Lessor for such purpose, and agrees to pay or reimburse Lessor for any searches, filings, recordings, or stamp fees or taxes arising from the filing or recording any such instrument or statement.

4. Lessee, at Lessee's own cost and expense, shall keep the equipment in good repair, condition, and working order and shall furnish all parts, mechanism, devices, and servicing required therefor and shall not materially alter the equipment without the consent of Lessor.

5. Lessee hereby assumes and shall bear the entire risk of loss for the theft, loss, damage, or destruction of the equipment, from any and every cause whatsoever. No such loss or damage shall impair any obligation of Lessee under this Agreement which shall continue in full force and effect. In the event of such loss or damage and irrespective of, but applying full credit for payment from any insurance coverage, Lessee shall, at its own cost and expense at the option of Lessor: (a) place the same in good repair, condition, and working order; or (b) replace the same with similar equipment of equal value; or (c) pay all the sums due and owing under this Agreement, computed from the date of such loss or damage, in which case this Agreement shall terminate, except for Lessee's duties under paragraph 9, as of the date such payment is received by Lessor.

6. Lessor shall have no tort liability to Lessee related to the equipment, and Lessee shall indemnify, defend, and hold Lessor harmless against any liabilities, claims, actions, and expenses, including court costs and legal expenses incurred by or asserted

against Lessor in any way relating to the manufacture, purchase, ownership, delivery, lease, possession, use, operation, condition, return, or other disposition of the equipment by Lessor or Lessee or otherwise related to this lease, including any claim alleging latent or other defect under the doctrine of strict liability or otherwise; any other claim under the doctrine of strict liability; and any claim for patent, trademark, service mark, or copyright infringement. Each party shall give the other notice of any event covered hereby promptly following learning thereof.

7. Lessee shall keep the equipment insured against all risks of loss or damage from every cause whatsoever. Lessee shall maintain (a) actual cash value all risk insurance on the equipment, naming Lessor as *LOSS PAYEE* and (b) single limit public liability and property damage insurance of not less than $300,000 per occurrence, or such greater or lesser amount as Lessor may from time to time request on notice to Lessee, naming Lessee as Named Insured and Lessor as *ADDITIONAL INSURED* and Lessee shall be liable for all deductible portions of all required insurance. All said insurance shall be in form and amount and with companies satisfactory to Lessor. All insurance for loss or damage shall provide that losses, if any, shall be payable to Lessor, and all such liability insurance shall be in the joint names of Lessor and Lessee. Lessee shall pay the premiums therefor and deliver to Lessor the policies of insurance or duplicates thereof, or other evidence satisfactory to Lessor of such insurance coverage. Each insurer shall agree, by endorsement upon the policy or policies issued by it or by independent instrument furnished to Lessor, that it will give Lessor *10 DAYS* written notice prior to the effective date of any alteration or cancellation of such policy. The proceeds of such insurance payable as a result of loss of or damage to the equipment shall be applied at the option of Lessor, as set out in paragraph 6. Lessee hereby irrevocably appoints Lessor as Lessee's attorney-in-fact to make claim for, receive payment of, and execute and endorse all documents, checks, or drafts received in payment for loss or damage under any said insurance policies. In case of the failure of Lessee to procure or maintain said insurance or to comply with any other provision of this Agreement, Lessor shall have the right but shall not be obligated, to effect such insurance or compliance on behalf of Lessee. In that event, all money spent by and expenses of Lessor shall have the right but shall not be obligated, to effect such insurance or compliance on behalf of Lessee. In that event, all money spent by and expenses of Lessor in effecting such insurance or compliance shall be deemed to be additional rent, and shall be paid by Lessee to Lessor with the next monthly payment of rent.

8. Lessee shall pay directly, or to Lessor, all license fees, registration fees, assessments, and taxes which may now or hereafter be imposed upon the ownership, sale (if authorized), possession, or use of the equipment, excepting only those based on Lessor's income, and shall keep the equipment free and clear of all levies, liens, or encumbrances arising therefrom. Lessee shall make all filings as to and pay when due all property taxes on the equipment, on behalf of Lessor, with all appropriate governmental agencies, except where Lessor is notified by the taxing jurisdiction that Lessor must pay the tax direct, and within not more than 60 days after the due date of such filing to send Lessor a confirmation of such filing. If Lessee fails to pay any said fees, assessments, or taxes, Lessor shall have the right, but not the obligation, to pay the same and such amount, including penalties and costs, which shall be repayable to

Lessor with the next installment of rent and if not so paid shall be the same as failure to pay any installment of rent due hereunder. Lessor shall not be responsible for contesting any valuation of or tax imposed on the equipment, but may do so strictly as an accommodation to Lessee and shall not be liable or accountable to Lessee therefor.

9. Time is of the essence in this agreement and no waiver by Lessor of any breach or default shall constitute a waiver of any additional or subsequent breach or default by Lessor nor shall it be a waiver of any of Lessor's rights. If any rental payment shall be unpaid for more than TEN (10) DAYS after the due date thereof. Lessor shall have the right to add and collect a reasonable late charge of *five percent (5%)* or a lesser amount if established by any state or federal statute applicable thereto, plus interest at the maximum rate permitted by law together with any other expense necessarily incurred by reason of such non-payment and Lessor may exercise any one or more of the remedies set forth in paragraph 12.

10. An event of default shall occur if: (a) Lessee fails to pay when due any installment of rent; (b) Lessee shall fail to perform or observe any covenant, condition, or agreement to be performed or observed by it hereunder; (c) Lessee ceases doing business as a going concern, makes an assignment for the benefit of creditors, admits in writing its inability to pay its debts as they become due, files a voluntary petition in bankruptcy, is adjudicated a bankrupt or an insolvent, files a petition seeking for itself any reorganization, arrangement, composition readjustment, liquidation, dissolution, or similar arrangement under any present or future statute, law, or regulation or files an answer admitting the material allegations of a petition filed against it in any such proceeding, consents to or acquiesces in the appointment of a trustee, receiver, or liquidator of it or all or any substantial part of its assets or properties, or if it or its shareholders shall take any action looking to its dissolution or liquidation; (d) within 60 days after the appointment without Lessee's consent or acquiescence of any trustee, receiver, or liquidator of it or of all or any substantial part of its assets and properties, such appointment shall not be vacated, or (e) Lessee attempts to remove, sell, transfer, encumber, part with possession, or sublet the equipment or any item thereof.

11. Upon Lessee's default, the rights and duties of the parties shall be as set forth in this paragraph: (a) Acceleration: Lessor may revoke Lessee's privilege of paying the total rent installments and, upon Lessor's demand, the portion of the total rent then remaining unpaid plus all other sums due and unpaid shall promptly be paid to Lessor. (b) Retaking: at Lessor's option, Lessor may demand and Lessee must promptly deliver the equipment to Lessor. If Lessee does not so deliver, Lessee shall make the equipment available for retaking and authorizes Lessor, its employees, and nominees to enter the premises of the Lessee and other premises (insofar as Lessee can permit) for the purpose of retaking. Lessor shall not be obligated to give notice or to obtain legal process for retaking. In the event of retaking, Lessee expressly waives all rights to possession and all claims of injuries suffered through or loss caused by retaking. (c) Disposition: Lessor may sell or release the equipment and Lessee agrees to pay any deficiency resulting from the sale or releasing of the equipment. To the extent of Lessee's liability, all proceeds of the sale or releasing, or both, less all expenses incurred in retaking the goods, all expenses incurred in the enforcement of this lease, all damages that Lessor shall have sustained by reason of Lessee's default, including those incurred

by obtaining a deficiency judgment and a reasonable attorney fee, shall be credited to Lessee as and when received by Lessor. Sums in excess of Lessee's liability shall belong to Lessor. (d) Unpaid Rent: The provisions of this paragraph shall not prejudice Lessor's right to recover or prove damages for unpaid rent accrued prior to default. Lessor may seek to enforce the terms of this Agreement through any court of competent jurisdiction and Lessor may seek relief other than as specified in this Agreement to the extent such relief is not inconsistent with the terms of this Agreement. Lessee agrees to pay reasonable attorney's fees and court costs incurred by Lessor in the enforcement of the terms of this Agreement. In any instance where Lessee and Lessor have entered into more than one contract, Lessee's default under any one contract shall be a default under all contracts and Lessor shall be entitled to enforce appropriate remedies for Lessee's default under each such contract.

12. Lessee shall not sell, assign, sublet, pledge, mortgage, or otherwise encumber or suffer a lien upon or against any interest in this agreement or the equipment or remove the equipment from the place of installation set forth herein, unless Lessee obtains the written consent of Lessor which consent shall not be unreasonably withheld. Lessee's interest herein is not assignable or transferable by operation of the law. Lessee agrees not to waive its right to use and possess the equipment in favor of any party other than Lessor and further agrees not to abandon the equipment to any party other than Lessor. Lessor may inspect the equipment during normal business hours and enter the premises where the equipment may be located for such purpose. Lessee shall comply with all laws, regulations, and orders relating to this Agreement and the use, operation, or maintenance of the equipment.

13. All rights of Lessor hereunder and to the equipment may be assigned, pledged, or otherwise disposed of, in whole or in part, without notice to Lessee, but subject to the rights of Lessee hereunder. Lessee shall acknowledge receipt of any notice of assignment in writing and shall thereafter pay any amounts designated in such notice as directed therein. If Lessor assigns this lease or any interest herein, no default by Lessor hereunder or under any other agreement between Lessor and Lessee shall excuse performance by Lessee of any provision hereof. In the event of such default by Lessor, Lessee shall pursue any rights on account thereof solely against Lessor and shall pay the full amount of the assigned rental payments to the assignee. No such assignee shall be obligated to perform any duty, covenant, or condition required to be performed by Lessor under the terms of this lease.

14. This Agreement cannot be canceled or terminated by Lessee on or after the date the equipment is delivered to and accepted by Lessee. If Lessee cancels or terminates this Agreement prior to delivery or acceptance of the equipment, Lessee shall pay to Lessor (a) the value (at cost) of all equipment ordered or purchased by Lessor prior to Lessee's termination or cancellation, (b) all of Lessor's out-of-pocket expenses, and (c) a sum equal to 1% of the total rents for the lease term as liquidated damages, the exact sum of which would be extremely difficult to determine, to reasonably compensate Lessor for credit review, document preparation, ordering equipment, and other administrative expenses.

15. Upon expiration of the lease term, Lessee will immediately return the equipment in as good a condition as received, less normal wear, tear, and depreciation, to Lessor's

branch office which is nearest to the place of installation or to such other reasonable place as is designated by Lessor. The equipment shall be carefully crated, shipped freight prepaid, and properly insured. Should Lessee not return the equipment at the end of the lease term, Lessee shall continue to pay rent to Lessor in the sum and on the due dates set out in this Agreement as a month-to-month lease term until returned by Lessee or demand therefor is made by Lessor.

16. This Lease Agreement consisting of the foregoing and the reverse side hereof, correctly sets forth the entire agreement between Lessor and Lessee. No agreements or understandings shall be binding on either of the parties hereto unless set forth in writing signed by the parties. The term "Lessee" as used herein shall mean and include any and all Lessees who sign hereunder, each of whom shall be jointly and severally bound thereby. No representations, warranties, or promises, guarantees, or agreements, oral or written, express or implied, have been made by either party hereto with respect to this lease or the equipment other than set forth herein. No agent or employee of the supplier is authorized to bind Lessor to this or to waive or alter any terms or conditions printed herein or add any provision hereto. This Lease Agreement is binding upon the legal representatives and successors in interest of the Lessee. Lessee shall provide Lessor with such interim or annual financial statements as Lessor may reasonably request. In addition, Lessee warrants that the application, statements, and financial reports submitted by it to the Lessor are material inducements to the granting of this lease and that any material misrepresentations shall constitute a default hereunder. If any portion of this contract is deemed invalid, it shall not affect the balance of this Agreement.

DELIVERY AND ACCEPTANCE NOTICE

The undersigned Lessee hereby acknowledges receipt of the equipment described below or on any attached schedule (the "Equipment") fully installed and in good working condition, and Lessee hereby accepts the Equipment after full inspection thereof as satisfactory for all purposes of the above-referenced lease executed by Lessee with the Lessor. Lessee certifies that Lessor has fully and satisfactorily performed all covenants and conditions to be performed by Lessor under the Lease and has delivered the Equipment selected solely by Lessee in accordance with Lessee's directions.

LESSEE AGREES THAT THE LESSOR HAS MADE AND MAKES NO REPRESENTATIONS OR WARRANTIES OF ANY KIND OR NATURE, DIRECTLY OR INDIRECTLY, EXPRESS OR IMPLIED, AS TO ANY MATTER WHATSOEVER, INCLUDING THE SUITABILITY OF SUCH EQUIPMENT, ITS DURABILITY, ITS FITNESS FOR ANY PARTICULAR PURPOSE, ITS MERCHANTABILITY, ITS CONDITION, AND/OR ITS QUALITY, AND AS BETWEEN LESSEE AND LESSOR OR LESSOR'S ASSIGNEE, LESSEE LEASES THE EQUIPMENT "AS IS" AND LESSEE AFFIRMS THAT IT HAS NO DEFENSES OR COUNTECLAIMS AGAINST LESSOR IN CONNECTION WITH THE LEASE.

_____
(Lessee)

Date Equipment Accepted: _____ By: _____

SUMMARY

Over the past several decades, leasing has become a very complicated topic, one that affects the budgetary process in a multitude of ways. The FASB has specified the treatment of leases on balance sheets, income statements, and cash-flow statements. Additionally, internal analysis, such as lease versus purchase, pushes the treatment of leasing well beyond considerations of generally accepted accounting principles. In today's international financial milieu, the managerial expert must cross the financial Rubicon and extend the frontiers of leasing, budgeting, and finance well into heretofore uncharted domains.

CHAPTER TWENTY-SEVEN

Balance-Sheet Budget

James E. Kristy

 INTRODUCTION

Budgeting is most often thought of as having to do with the planning and control of revenues and expenses—that is, managing the day-to-day operations of a business or other organization. The primary goal of a business, as Peter Drucker says, is "to create customers" with the right product and price and to skillfully manage costs so as to make a profit. Profit and loss budgets, therefore, get the most attention because that is where the action is.

As a consequence, in many businesses, the balance sheet is like a stepchild left to his own devices on the theory that, if the household is run efficiently, he will somehow grow straight and strong. Also, if I may stretch the simile a bit further, he only gets attention when he gets sick or fails to do his chores.

Thus, many firms that are dedicated to an operating budget pay scant attention to the balance sheet and more or less let the assets and liabilities fall where they may. Many a neglected balance sheet grows strong anyway, but it is always at the cost of some profit and of the incurring of extra risk. The balance-sheet budget is a logical supplement to an operating budget, and its benefits, though less apparent, are more profound and lasting.

PURPOSE OF THE BALANCE-SHEET BUDGET

The purpose of the balance-sheet budget is to help management plan a mix of assets, liabilities, and equity that will:

- Permit an uninhibited operation of the business with the least investment
- Maintain enough reserve strength to cushion economic shocks
- Provide a capability for exploiting unforeseen opportunities

The key word in balance-sheet budgeting is *proportion.* The same quality that provides grace in art and strength in architecture lends effectiveness to the balance sheet. The size of a balance sheet account only has meaning when it is related to some other balance sheet or income account—or group of accounts. Unlike the profit and loss statement, where more means better, the best balance sheet is one with optimum ratios rather than numbers.

 ## DEFINITION

A *balance-sheet budget* is a systematic plan or forecast of future assets, liabilities, and equity. A typical arrangement of these balance-sheet accounts are shown in Exhibit 27.1. The need for such a plan arises because of the timing differences between business expenditures and income. Like an architect's plan for the construction of a building, it lays out in financial terms the resources (assets) needed to establish or carry on the business. The budget goes further, however, in that it also specifies where the money comes from (liabilities and equity) to acquire the necessary assets.

EXHIBIT 27.1 Typical Arrangement of Balance Sheet Accounts

Assets	Liabilities and Equity
Current assets	Current liabilities
Cash and short-term investments	Notes payable
Accounts receivable	Accounts payable
Inventories	Income tax payable
Prepaid expenses	Accrued liabilities
Investments	Current portion of long-term debt
Property, plant, and equipment	Long-term debt
Less accumulated depreciation	Deferred credits and other liabilities
Intangible and miscellaneous assets	Minority interest
	Stockholders' equity
	Preferred and common stock
	Capital surplus
	Retained earnings

RESPONSIBILITY FOR THE BUDGET

Used most effectively, the balance-sheet budget is a method not only for estimating and planning but also for controlling a company's various resources. Once the budget is agreed to, it becomes a standard against which future performance can be measured. For the budget to be fully effective, the responsibility for managing each item on the balance sheet should be assigned to a specific person or department, as shown in Exhibit 27.2.

Financial Assets

The financial assets—cash, short-term investments, and receivables—are normally the province of the chief financial officer (CFO). Because the purpose of accounts receivable is to help market the company's products, it follows that the marketing department has a special interest in the firm's credit policy. The interest may be a little too special to permit complete control by the marketing people, but the best budget will allow them some say-so over receivables policy and hold them partly responsible for credit costs—the cost of money, credit administration, and bad debts.

There are many ways of handling this dual (finance and marketing) control over accounts receivable. Some considerations are:

- Salespeople should know the rudiments of credit approval, enough so that they can prescreen their prospective customers and be aware of those who are not likely to be approved.
- Credit investigation and approval is a specialty best done by credit professionals. In approving credit today, there is much less stress on "character" than there was in J. P. Morgan's day—people have not changed much, but it is harder, given modern communications, to deceive. The emphasis has shifted to "capacity," which is measured by an analysis of a company's financial strength.

EXHIBIT 27.2 Balance-Sheet Budget Responsibility

	Board of Directors	CEO	Finance	Marketing	Production	Administration
Assets						
Cash			Ⓟ a			
Short-term investments			Ⓟ			
Accounts receivable			Ⓟ	○		
Inventory			○	○	Ⓟ	
Fixed assets	○	Ⓟ	○	○	○	○
Liabilities						
Notes payable		Ⓟ	○			
Accounts payable			Ⓟ		○	
Taxes payable		○	Ⓟ			
Long-term debt	○	Ⓟ	○			
Equity	Ⓟ	○	○			

a Ⓟ indicates primary responsibility.

- The collection of past-due accounts works well as a joint effort of marketing and finance. These steps should be taken:

  - The initial step in collection should be a friendly but impersonal notice that payment has not been received. A good many past-due payments are the result of misunderstandings, errors, and disputes that could be the fault of either party.
  - The second stage of collection—from, say, 10 to 30 days past due—is often best left to the salesperson handling the account. The advantages are that it provides a friendly approach that can often be combined with a further sales effort; it offers a more direct means (than working through the credit department) of resolving disputes and adjustments; and, should his or her efforts fail, it softens the salesperson to a harder collection effort by the credit department.
  - If stronger means of collection are required, marketing should leave the field to finance. Salespeople would only be in the way, and there is no point in associating salespeople with disagreeable but necessary pressures on the customer.

Inventory Levels

Inventory levels are usually managed by the chief production officer in a manufacturing company or the purchasing officer in a retail organization. However, there is often an important influence, it not authority, from the marketing managers.

Moreover, the CFO has an implied responsibility to see that the cash tied up in inventory is yielding the highest return. The purpose of inventory is to uncouple production and sales so that temporary stops and spurts of activity in one will not affect the other.[1] Production is most efficient when it is a smooth and continuous flow. Customers, however, could not care less. They want their goods when they want them, and delivery delays very often jeopardize a sale.

Decision models for inventory control, such as the economic order quantity model,[2] are in fairly widespread use. Generally, their purpose is to find the right balance between the costs of carrying inventory—tied-up money, storage, insurance, and obsolescence—and the cost of replenishing stock.

Fixed Assets

The fixed assets of a firm are usually controlled at the point of purchase by a capital-expenditures policy. Typically, the manager or department that will use the asset proposes its purchase, and a capital-investment committee consisting of the chief executive officer (CEO), the CFO, and other executives or directors passes on the proposal.

Liabilities

The management of a company's liabilities is concentrated in the general staff nucleus. As expected, the CFO plays an important role—sometimes primary, sometimes secondary—in the day-to-day management of all liabilities and shareholder affairs. The CEO is

---

[1] John D. Martin et al., *Basic Financial Management* (Englewood Cliffs, NJ: Prentice-Hall, 1979), p. 231.
[2] Roger D. Eck, *Operations Research for Business* (Belmont, CA: Wadsworth Publishing, 1976), p. 347.

also active in nearly all debt equity management. Even if he or she has little training or interest in finance, the company's commercial and investment bankers generally insist on considerable personal involvement.

Accounts Payable

Accounts payable are usually handled automatically by the controller's department. The purchase of goods on credit carries an implicit promise to pay on a particular day. Although trade credit is notoriously flexible, the complacence of suppliers should not be taken as a sign that they are uncaring about prompt payment. Occasionally, there are stories of companies that deliberately pay their accounts late so as to earn more interest on their cash balances. Such policies are, in a word, unwise. The monetary gains—measured in hundredths of a percentage point per day—are so far from the potential cost attending a loss of trust as to brand such policies as misguided, at best.

When a company is unable, as opposed to unwilling, to pay trade creditors on time, the finance department may be aided by the purchasing department in obtaining extensions or in setting priorities of payment. There may be 100 items of supply, the lack of any one of which being enough to shut down a production line. The more nearly that condition exists, the more influence the production department should have in managing accounts payable.

Notes Payable

Notes payable to banks and any long-term credit arrangements are frequently covered by loan agreements that, among other things, require the maintenance of certain balance-sheet ratios. Typical examples of requirements are a debt–equity ratio less than 1.00 or a current ratio greater than 1.50. The management of such ratios—an unwieldy job at best—falls to the CFO. Lenders of large sums, however, will insist on the close involvement of the CEO, and although they may listen to the explanations of the CFO, they like to talk right into the horse's ear.

Corporate Taxes

The management of corporate taxes increases in importance and complexity with each passing year. One may now obtain a master's degree in taxation (e.g., from the fully accredited Golden Gate University, San Francisco) and the title vice president, taxes is no longer rare. Such a post is normally under the CFO; however, the expectation today is that the CEO will be actively ratifying taxation strategies, if not actually directing them. The switch, for example, from a first-in, first-out (FIFO) to a last-in, first-out (LIFO) valuation of inventory can have far-reaching effects not only on the cash flow of a corporation but also on the reported earnings, which in turn affects the cost of equity capital.

Capital Structure

The management of a corporation's capital structure (long-term debt plus equity) generally requires the personal direction of the CEO. The task of finding the optimal mix of semipermanent funds—that is, the combination that will maximize stockholders' return—is very difficult. (Perhaps the classic, and still pertinent, book on this subject is Solomon's *The Theory of Financial Management*.[3]) It requires the aid, on one hand, of a CFO familiar with the concepts of leverage and the cost of capital, and the mature judgment, on the other hand, of a board of directors as to the outlook for the economy, interest rates, and equity financing. In smaller firms, in which the deeply personal and hidden motives of shareholders have more sway, it requires a CEO who not only knows the right thing to do but is able to persuade others to it.

The American economy in the 1970s, 1980s, and 1990s witnessed the usual cycles of high growth and recession that are endemic to capitalism (or "market economy," if you prefer).

When times are good, investors are enthused, and as stories of success follow one another, capital flows into new investments. Unfortunately, we have no way of knowing when the amount of new investment is sufficient—we only know when there is too much. Overinvestment drives down dollar profits and devastates percentage returns, setting the stage for recession. This cycle is about as predictable as the flu and at least as unpleasant.

When a recession does occur, those firms with the weakest demand for their products or services and/or the weakest balance sheets are unsentimentally weeded out until supply and demand are once again in harmony and the seeds of new growth can once again take root.

Perhaps the only thing surprising about the business cycle is the way people tend to ignore it—stretching themselves too thin in times of prosperity and deploring the lack of bank support just when the economy turns sour and they need borrowed money the most. The renascent timidity of investors and bankers is foreseeable even if the economic downturns to which they respond are not.

Two principles should guide senior executives in their capital-structure decisions. The first principle is that the more debt a company has, the more dependent it is on future cash flows. The requirement to pay interest and principal is implacable while the stream of future profits ebbs and flows. Adjust the debt–equity mix, therefore, to the uncertainty of future earnings, and keep a liquidity reserve to see you through the dry spells that are almost certain to come.

That great teacher, *experience*, which likes to give the test first and the lesson afterward, repeats this instruction for business newcomers every five to ten years or so: The way you make money with borrowed funds is the same way you lose it; borrowed money multiplies both profits and losses.

Compounding the "normal" business cycle is a new era of manufacturing ushered in by the Japanese who have leapfrogged the mass-production system with their "lean-production" methods. While these revolutionary changes have been going on for a decade, many U.S. firms have been slow to react. That company of companies, General Motors, sailed into the rough seas and dropped $2 billion before noticing the water crashing over the deck.[4]

A second guideline is to earn an adequate return on assets (ROA). The penalty for having a skimpy ROA is not limited to the agitated reaction of a faceless horde of

---

[3] Ezra Solomon, *The Theory of Financial Management* (New York: Columbia University Press, 1963).
[4] Donald Woutat, *Los Angeles Times*, May 30, 1992, p. 1.

shareholders. Their annoyance can unsettle a shareholders' meeting, but they rarely act in concert enough to do something really disgusting, such as getting rid of senior executives. A worse problem is that we have entered an era of leveraged buyouts and unfriendly takeovers. Those companies whose assets are earning less than they would if sold to somebody else are enticing corporate raiders. A low ROA betokens change—in managers, products, and marketing. It is true that many business problems resolve themselves while waiting for us to act, but not this one.

TYPES OF FINANCIAL BUDGETS

There are three principal categories of budgets, sometimes referred to as *financial budgets* or *financial plans* to distinguish them from the more detailed operating budgets. These are the profit, cash, and balance-sheet budgets.

Profit Budget

If we accept the premise that the primary purpose of a business enterprise is to create customers and thereby earn a profit, then it is clear that the profit budget is the compass by which it steers. In its simplest form, business has two functions: (1) make a product or provide a service and (2) sell it. All employees and all activities of a firm support one or the other or both of these functions. The profit budget sets forth the anticipated revenues (a self-set goal within a frame of reasonable expectations) and the expense of producing the products, selling them, managing the business, and financing it.

The profit budget is compiled from estimates by each of the several operating departments. Once approved by management, it returns to those departments in the form of an operating budget—a detailed plan for their activities.

Cash Budget

The cash budget is a schedule of cash receipts and disbursements. Its initial objective is to take a weekly or monthly reading of expected cash balances so as to determine the amount and timing of any new financing that may be needed.

Final approval of a cash budget may depend in part on the company's bank or other financing source. In the typical business, there is a rhythm to the ebb and flow of cash and a gradual accumulation from profits. However, the development of the profit budget—particularly those parts dealing with long-range goals, product mix strategies, and the economic outlook—will also give rise to cash needs for new capital assets. Perhaps a larger manufacturing plant will be necessary to meet production goals, special equipment may be needed to produce a new product, or plans might include opening a sales and service center in Europe.

Such capital investments likewise affect the balance sheet, sometimes profoundly. Moreover, once begun, they may be difficult or impossible to stop and in ways large and small forever alter the company's circumstances.

For example, the Singer (sewing machine) Company's capital budgeting decision to manufacture computer systems was found later to have been a serious mistake. Undoing it in the mid-1970s wiped out in one fell swoop three quarters of the retained earnings patiently accumulated by the company over 125 years.

Decisions, therefore, regarding such crucial proposals are usually made with the careful consideration of a capital investment committee, which normally includes representatives from general management, finance, the board of directors, and, when appropriate, marketing, production, and other specialties.

Balance-Sheet Budget

The balance-sheet budget has a format similar to the other two—major balance-sheet items are listed month by month. This budget will reflect the levels of current and fixed assets needed to support the expected sales. Most current and long-term liabilities will also be affected over time by changes in the sales volume, and the line showing retained earnings will change each month by the amount of the profit or loss and dividends declared. The object of this budget is to ensure that month-by-month liquidity is adequate and that the leverage is controlled. It helps to include as supplementary line items the basic ratios that measure these important financial characteristics.

PREPARING FINANCIAL BUDGETS

The budget process is now widely established in the large public corporations, most medium-size firms, and a good many smaller ones. Companies whose own volition may not incline them to a budget system are often persuaded to it by their bankers, who find budgeting to be a valuable passageway leading from the art of lending to the science of lending.

Bringing a budget to a point at which the time and effort spent in creating it is matched by its usefulness requires seasoning. It will take the typical firm from two to five years to make all of the parts fit, to accustom employees to the disciplined thought process and paperwork required, to condition senior management to using a budget as the basis of a reward system, and to harden by exposure the determination needed to make any complex system of rules work. When first seen by middle managers, a budget may seem to be another way of tightening control over their activities. In fact, it more sharply defines the goals to be achieved but expands the influence of middle managers in setting the goals and finding the best means to reach them. The steps in preparing financial budgets are shown in Exhibit 27.3.

It is one thing to work for a company with a budget in place and quite another to be involved in creating a budget system from the ground up. Here are some guidelines for the latter task.

Budget System Checklist

Information Needed

1. Past sales figures in dollars *and* units by
   a. Product

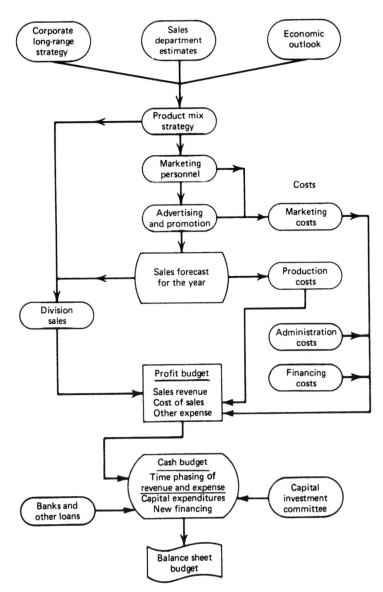

EXHIBIT 27.3 Steps in Preparing the Financial Budget

---

    b. Territory
    c. Distribution (such as dealer sales and direct sales)
  2. Industry sales figures
    a. Domestic production
    b. Imports
    c. Generic competitors[5] (that satisfy the same needs with other types of products, as, e.g., makers of mopeds or jogging equipment might for bicycle customers)
  3. Economic forecasts

---

[5] Philip Kotler, *Marketing Management* (Englewood Cliffs, NJ: Prentice-Hall, 1976), p. 25.

4. Estimates of the potential market for any new product or new group of customers
5. Expenses
   a. Cost of goods sold
   b. Marketing, administration, and other expense
6. New capital equipment needs
   a. Production equipment
   b. Data processing, communications, and general office equipment
   c. Warehouse space, materials handling equipment, and vehicles
7. External financing requirements

Chronology

1. Set corporate sales and profit goals.
2. Prepare standard forms and write instructions for the various budgets.
3. Get ground-floor estimates of
   a. Future sales to existing customers
   b. Personnel requirements, by department throughout the company
   c. Lists of new equipment needed
   d. Existing lines of credit
4. Prepare the required budgets.
   a. Sales and profit budget
   b. Production budget

   - Materials budget
   - Direct labor budget
   - Manufacturing overhead budget

   c. Marketing expense budget

   - Sales personnel budget (salespeople and their managers)
   - Sales administration budget
   - Advertising and promotion budget
   - Distribution budget (including warehousing and delivery equipment expense)
   - Service and parts budget

   d. Research and development budget
   e. Administration budget (including the CEOs and the finance department)
   f. Capital-investment budget
   g. Cash budget (including financing costs)
   h. Balance-sheet budget

   - Accounts receivable budget
   - Inventory budgets: raw materials, work in process, finished goods (units and dollars), and manufacturing supplies
   - Fixed-asset budget

5. Assemble the subbudgets and prepare the financial plan or master budget.
6. Review the master budget and negotiate necessary changes with affected departments.

7. Redo the subbudgets based on the final version of the master budget.
8. Reproduce and distribute the master and subsidiary budgets.
9. Each ensuing month, get actual performance figures and identify variances.
10. Conduct monthly management reviews of performance compared to budget.

As time passes, the need may arise to change the master budget. Most companies will redo their fiscal year's budget at least once during the period. Some firms—and it helps to have automated the budgeting process—prepare a full year's budget each month, continuously inputting current information. There is a danger, however, in overbudgeting—in amassing such a quantity of detail that the chain linking the effect and cause of problems becomes too long for use in day-to-day management.[6]

PREPARING THE BALANCE-SHEET BUDGET

The only way to learn to prepare a balance-sheet budget is to do it. A handbook such as this will remind you of the information needed and the steps to take and thus save you a great deal of time. However, our minds are not accustomed to thinking in the slow plodding way that budgets are built. Mistakes are reducible but inevitable. The personal computer (PC) with electronic spreadsheet (such as Lotus 1-2-3or Excel) is a near-perfect tool for this task.

Throughout this chapter, examples are used from a fictional manufacturing firm, the American Skate Company, a maker of roller skates. All three of its financial budgets—income, cash, and balance sheet—are shown complete in Exhibit 27.4. In addition to a discussion of the balance-sheet budget in general terms, a step-by-step explanation is given of how the cash budget and balance-sheet budget were constructed.

(The derivation of the income budget is not discussed, as it has been covered in earlier chapters.) There are also chapters on cash budgeting, but that activity is so closely linked with balance-sheet budgeting that an explanation of one without the other would be like a treatise on effective parenting without mention of the child.

The years cited present a logical order, and the fact that they have passed has no bearing on the examples used.

A stock printed form will be used for this example. It can be reproduced on Lotus by someone with moderate skill. There are also several software programs for the PC that offer ready-made formats for budgeting. The complexity, sophistication, ease of use, and price of these programs varies widely. The best way to find a good one is the way you would find a dentist in a new town—referral by someone who likes you.

If your budgeting is a prelude to applying for a bank loan, ask your banker's opinion of planning formats. Most commercial loan officers are well engaged in computer forecasting, and using their format might add to your convenience and lessen their resistance.

---

[6] J. Fred Weston and Eugene F. Brigham, *Managerial Finance* (Hinsdale, IL: Dryden Press, 1978), p. 121.

EXHIBIT 27.4 American Skate Company—Projection of Financial Statements

SUBMITTED BY _____ American Skate Company _____

				ACTUAL	**PROJECTIONS**				
SPREAD IN HUNDREDS ☐		DATE		12-31-79	Jan	Feb	Mar	Apr	
SPREAD IN THOUSANDS ☑		PERIOD		Year					
	1 NET SALES			4358	437	479	523	501	1
P	2 Less: Materials Used			1651	186	204	223	214	2
R	3 Direct Labor			507	51	56	61	59	3
O	4 Other Manufacturing Expense			595	60	66	72	69	4
F	5 Depreciation			32	3	3	4	3	5
I	6 COST OF GOODS SOLD			2985	300	329	360	345	6
T	7 GROSS PROFIT			1373	137	150	163	156	7
a	8 Less: Sales Expense			436	37	41	42	42	8
n	9 General Administrative Expense			606	57	58	59	59	9
d	10								10
	11 OPERATING PROFIT			331	43	51	62	55	11
L	12 Less: Other Expense or Income (Net)								12
O	13 Income Tax Provision			133	17	20	25	22	13
S	14								14
S	15 NET PROFIT			198	26	31	37	33	15
C	16 CASH BALANCE (Opening) (Incl securities)				138	157	43	46	16
A	17 Plus RECEIPTS: Receivable Collections				421	246	450	492	17
S	18								18
H	19 Fixed Asset Financing					24			19
	20 Bank Loan Proceeds				24	10	22		20
P	21 Total				583	528	515	538	21
R	22 Less: DISBURSEMENTS: Trade Payables–Mtls				191	213	202	188	22
O	23 Direct Labor				61	59	54	50	23
J	24 Other M'fg Expense				69	69	66	61	24
E	25 Sales Gen'l and Adm. Exp.				94	99	101	101	25
C	26 Fixed Asset Additions				5	39	5	5	26
T	27 Income Taxes						26	33	27
I	28								28
O	29 Dividends or Withdrawals						8		29
N	30 Payments on long-term debt				6	6	7	7	30
S	31 Bank Loan Repayment							10	31
	32 Total				426	485	469	455	32
	33 CASH BALANCE (Closing)				157	43	46	83	33

			ACTUAL		PROJECTIONS			
SPREAD IN HUNDREDS ☐	**DATE**	**12-31-79**	**Jan**	**Feb**	**Mar**	**Apr**		
SPREAD IN THOUSANDS ☑	**PERIOD**	**Year**						
34 ASSETS: Cash		48	57	43	46	83	34
35 Marketable Securities		90	100				35
36 Receivables (Net)		536	552	785	858	867	36
37 Inventory (Net)		875	916	914	856	786	37
38 Prepaid Expenses		49	50	51	51	52	38
39 CURRENT ASSETS		1598	1675	1793	1811	1788	39
40 Fixed Assets (Net)		372	374	410	411	413	40
41							41
42 Other Tangible Assets		128	128	128	128	128	42
43							43
44 Deferred Charges		38	38	38	38	38	44
45 TOTAL ASSETS		2136	2215	2369	2388	2367	45
46 LIABILITIES: Notes Payable–Banks		312	336	437	459	449	46
47 Trade Payables		304	322	305	280	254	47
48 Income Tax		26	42	61	58	46	48
49							49
50 Current Portion-LTD		72	72	84	84	84	50
51 Accruals and Other		41	41	42	43	43	51
52 CURRENT LIABILITIES		755	813	929	924	876	52
53 Long-Term Debt		217	211	217	210	203	53
54 Deferred Taxes		71	72	73	75	76	54
55							55
56 CAPITAL STOCK ⎤ Net Worth for		245	245	245	245	245	56
57 SURPLUS ⎦ Partnership or Individual		848	874	905	934	967	57
58 TOTAL LIABILITIES AND NET WORTH		2136	2215	2369	2388	2367	58
59 WORKING CAPITAL		843	862	864	887	912	59

The left margin is labeled vertically **BALANCE SHEET**.

	May	Jun	Jul	Aug	Sept	Oct	Nov	Dec	Year	
1	458	414	370	425	468	512	447	196	5230	1
2	196	177	159	183	201	221	193	85	2242	2
3	54	49	44	50	55	60	53	23	615	3
4	63	56	50	59	65	72	61	25	718	4
5	3	4	3	3	4	3	4	4	41	5
6	316	286	256	295	325	356	311	137	3616	6
7	142	128	114	130	143	156	136	59	1614	7
8	44	43	43	45	45	46	48	47	523	8
9	60	60	61	62	62	63	63	64	728	9
10										10

(continued)

	May	Jun	Jul	Aug	Sept	Oct	Nov	Dec	Year	
11	38	25	10	23	36	47	25	(52)	363	11
12										12
13	15	10	4	9	14	19	10	(20)	145	13
14										14
15	23	15	6	14	22	28	15	(32)	218	15
16	83	175	191	189	158	87	179	247	138	16
17	516	488	445	401	386	438	482	492	5257	17
18										18
19						96			120	19
20				8	21	21			197	20
21	599	663	636	598	565	642	661	739	5712	21
22	172	175	188	200	196	138	183	226	2272	22
23	45	47	54	56	56	36	44	66	628	23
24	56	53	58	65	66	53	45	62	723	24
25	104	103	104	107	107	109	111	111	1251	25
26	5	6	5	5	5	120	5	6	211	26
27		33			33			33	158	27
28										28
29		12			8			12	40	29
30	7	7	7	7	7	7	11	11	90	30
31	35	36	31				15	123	250	31
32	424	472	447	440	478	463	414	650	5623	32
33	175	191	189	158	87	179	247	89	89	33
34	85	61	49	58	57	59	57	39		34
35	90	130	140	100	30	120	190	50		35
36	809	735	660	684	766	840	805	509		36
37	757	765	836	851	744	742	704	965		37
38	53	54	55	55	56	57	58	59		38
39	1794	1745	1740	1748	1653	1818	1814	1622		39
40	415	417	419	421	422	539	540	542		40
41										41
42	128	128	128	128	128	128	128	128		42
43										43
44	38	38	38	38	2241	38	38	38		44
45	2375	2328	2325	2335		2523	2520	2330		45
46	414	378	347	2355	376	397	382	259		46

(continued)

	May	Jun	Jul	Aug	Sept	Oct	Nov	Dec	Year	
47	265	280	306	291	187	311	310	352		47
48	60	36	40	48	28	46	55	3		48
49										49
50	84	84	84	84	84	132	132	132		50
51	44	45	44	45	46	47	46	45		51
52	867	823	821	823	721	933	925	791		52
53	196	189	182	175	168	209	198	187		53
54	77	78	78	79	80	81	82	81		54
55										55
56	245	245	245	245	245	245	245	245		56
57	990	993	999	1013	1027	1055	1070	1026		57
58	2375	2328	2325	2335	2241	2523	2520	2330		58
59	927	922	919	925	932	885	889	831		59

One feature to look for in a budget package is the simultaneous development of all three financial budgets—income, balance sheet, and cash flow. For example, when a number on the cash budget is changed, the cash line on the balance sheet should be automatically adjusted also. It helps to have a complete view of the financial consequences of the budgeting process in a single format.

Cash and Short-Term Investments

If the balance-sheet budget is prepared without an accompanying cash budget, cash— the first item on the balance sheet—is the last line item to be completed. It becomes, in effect, the "plug" figure that makes the balance sheet balance. The usual procedure is to work out all the other items (as will be discussed) and then to drop in the balancing cash figures. Excesses and shortfalls of cash that are revealed are interplayed with the short-term investment or bank loan accounts to adjust the cash balances to the desirable figure.

If the cash budget is prepared beforehand, the cash balances are already known and are simply transferred to the balance-sheet budget.

Accounts Receivable

Accounts receivable balances are highly correlated to the company's sales, rising and falling in unison with these revenues at some time later. One of the simplest ways of forecasting accounts receivable is to begin by calculating the company's average collection period from the most recent balance sheet:

$$\text{Average collection period} = \frac{\text{Accounts receivable}}{\text{Sales for the year}} \times 365$$

The average collection period (also referred to as day's sales outstanding) is then applied to each month's forecasted sales to determine the receivable balance.

Where there is a pronounced seasonality to sales, as in the case of the American Skate Company (notice the low point in December in Exhibit 27.4), a more accurate average is obtained using just the fourth-quarter (Q4) 1979 sales figures:

Q4–1979	Sales (thousands)
October	$427
November	372
December	164
Total	$963

Because we are using the sales of only one quarter, the multiplier in our formula is the number of days in the quarter:

$$\text{Average collection period} = \frac{\$536}{\$963} = 51 \text{ days}$$

Therefore, the accounts receivable forecast each month were the current month's sales plus 21/30ths of the previous month's sales. The method is illustrated in Exhibit 27.5. Once the receivable balances are known, the receivable collections can be computed. They will equal the current sales (minus an increase or plus a decrease) in the receivable balance. The resulting balances, line 3, and collections, line 7, are then transferred to Exhibit 27.4, lines 36 and 17.

EXHIBIT 27.5   American Skate Company—Projection of Accounts Receivable

1980 →	JAN	FEB	MAR	APR	MAY	JUN	JUL	AUG	SEP	OCT	NOV	DEC	TOTAL
							$000s						
1 Sales[a]	437	479	523	501	458	414	370	425	468	512	447	196	5230
2 21/30 of prev mo	115	306	335	366	351	321	290	259	298	328	358	313	
3 Total[b]	552	785	858	867	809	735	660	684	766	840	805	509	
4													
5 Change in A/R balance	16	233	73	9	(58)	(74)	(75)	24	82	74	(35)	(296)	(27)
6 Collections:													
7 Line 1 – Line 5[c]	421	246	450	492	516	488	445	401	386	438	482	492	5257

[a] From Exh. 27.4, line 1
[b] To Exh. 27.4, line 36
[c] To Exh. 27.4, line 17

Another popular method of estimating accounts receivable balances is to note what percentage of a month's sales is collected in each subsequent month and to forecast the uncollected balances on the same basis. The American Skate Company found this pattern:

	Accounts Receivable	
Typical Month	Paid During Month	Owing at End of Month
Current month	5%	95%
One month later	45	50
Two months later	25	25
Three months later	25	0

Now, to forecast the accounts receivable balance on, say, March 31, 1980, the percentages are applied to March and previous months' sales:

Month	Sales (thousands)
March	$523 × 0.95 = $497
February	479 × 0.50 = 240
January	437 × 0.25 = 109
Total	$846

The two methods of forecasting produce slightly different results. The second method is more reflective of the way money really is collected, but it requires more estimates (the percentages) and additional work. To reflect the real world, the collection percentages would spread out more like nine months than three, tripling the work but improving the results very little. My own preference is the first method (using the average collection period) because it is a little easier and faster. Besides, the more refinements one makes of estimates, the less chance one leaves for errors to cancel out one another.

That is not as facetious as it sounds. Many factors influence customers to pay their bills: their cash on hand; the pressure from other creditors; opportunities to earn a discount by paying promptly or to earn interest by not; and their attitude toward the creditor company, its representatives, and its products. Most important is the way *their* cash flows and that of *their* customers and their customers' customers, and so on. Like the images reflected in interfacing mirrors, the influences on the collection of receivables are an endless series of circumstances that can never be fully known, much less foretold.

Inventories

In general, five factors influence the amount of inventory a company will seek to have on hand:

1. Level of sales
2. Length of the production process
3. Availability of raw materials

4. Durability of finished goods
5. Distribution methods

Level of Sales

In most companies, the relationship of inventory to sales is relatively constant. The number of times inventory is turned over in a year may vary widely from one industry to another and moderately between firms in the same industry, but in the same company over time the variance is usually slight. A useful measure of inventory turnover is the day's sales in inventory (DSI) ratio:

$$DSI = \frac{Inventory}{Period\ cost\ sales} \times Days\ in\ the\ period$$

An example of the calculation using figures from the American Skate Company December 31, 1979, balance sheet (Exhibit 27.4) is shown next (dollars are in thousands):

$$\frac{(Line\ 37)\quad \$875}{(Line\ 6)\quad \$2,985} \times 365 = days$$

Because of seasonal fluctuations, a more accurate figure is obtained using figures from only the fourth quarter of the year:

Month	Cost of Sales (thousands)
October 1979	$290
November	255
December	113
Total	$658

$$DSI = \frac{\$875}{\$658} \times 9 = 122\ days$$

As this figure is approximately four months, one simple method of planning inventory levels is to add the latest four months' cost of sales. Thus, the inventory for January 1980 would be planned at $958 ($658 + $300).

Unlike accounts receivable, however, which relate to *past* sales, inventory is there to service *future* sales. So a better planning technique is the calculation of future DSI. Using the beginning inventory and the cost of sales for Q1–1980, we find (dollars in thousands)

$$Future\ DSI = \frac{\$875}{\$300 + 329 + 360} \times 91 = 81\ days$$

If this method were to be used, the assumption that 81 days' inventory is adequate should be tested by computing the future DSI for known periods in the past, particularly those that included unforeseen sales fluctuations or for which inventory shortages are remembered. A future DSI of 81 days means that inventory at the end of each month is equal to the next two months' cost of sales plus 20/30ths of the third month's. Using our example:

Month	Cost of Sales (thousands)
February 1980	$329
March	360
April × 2/3	230
Desired inventory at 1-31-80	$919

As mentioned previously, the main function of inventory is to uncouple production activities from sales activities, so that if someone in manufacturing catches a cold, it will not cause a sneeze in marketing. The trade-offs for having an abundance of inventory are the people, space, and money thus used and the increased risk of loss from obsolescence. Moreover, every dollar in inventory is one less dollar in the checking account, one less dollar available to pay expenses or make other profitable investments.

Length of Production Process

A company that manufactures electronic testing equipment is apt to require an average DSI of 120 days or more because of the complexity of the production process and the many tests needed for quality control. A meat packer, however, would need a gas mask to count inventory if the DSI went much beyond two weeks.[7] The inventory budgeting of wholesalers or retailers who want to uncouple their purchasing and sales activities is much less complicated than that of manufacturers, who must maintain slack between their raw material purchasing and production process as well as the sales of finished goods.

Availability of Raw Materials

By definition, all manufacturers have a raw material inventory. The term "raw" refers to the fact that it has not yet entered the production process. A completely finished and tested cathode ray tube may be the raw material of a computer equipment manufacturer.[8] Determining the size of this inventory is a study unique to each individual firm. Some of the factors to be considered are listed next.

- Purchase period—order processing and delivery time
- Future demand in relation to the suppliers' capacity
- Payment requirements—terms of sale and availability of credit
- Outlook for prices
- Possible labor disruptions
- Other, nonbusiness, hindrance to supply lines

Just-in-time (JIT) inventory management has gained a respectable audience in the United States after being pioneered by the Japanese industrial juggernaut. As the name implies, its purpose is to reduce manufacturers' stocks or raw materials

---

[7] Composite financial data on more than 300 lines of business can be found in *Annual Statement Studies,* published by Robert Morris Associates.

[8] Martin et al., *Basic Financial* Management, p. 232.

by having suppliers make more timely deliveries, thereby making the whole process more efficient.

The demand by large manufacturers for delivery times and quantities that suit *their* convenience rather than the suppliers' seems to have stimulated some efficiency, such as shortening setup times for manufacturing runs and forcing greater coordination between production and shipping.

If, however, we look behind the apparent benefits of JIT, we see the same old struggle that characterizes virtually all chains of distribution: the effort to place the burden and expense of inventory with someone else. It appears that in many cases, the benefits of JIT to the customer simply become a greater burden to the supplier, which must increase its own inventories to ensure the prompt deliveries now required. Moreover, the closer we tie the customer and supplier, the more each shares the other's mistakes and misfortunes if and when they occur.

Durability of Finished Goods

With respect to finished goods, "durability" means not only resistance to wear and decay but also the whims of fashion, style changes, and technical innovations. The manufacturer of hammers, saws, and screwdrivers has few problems with durability.[9] The same could be said for makers of wristwatches until the electronic model was developed.

Distribution Methods

There is an axiom in marketing management that the best location for inventory is the one nearest the final customer. Typically, that would mean with the dealer or retailer who sells to the end user. However, the financial burden and risks attending inventories are not welcomed with open arms. The automobile industry employs floor-plan financing and enthusiastic persuasion to keep dealer lots choked with new models. Magazine and book publishers practice a form of consignment with their liberal "returns" policies. It is perhaps fitting that the principal inventory burden is usually borne by the manufacturers, for they have the most to gain of all members of the distribution chain. With some notable exceptions, middlemen exist at the sufferance of the manufacturer; if the middle ground gets fertile enough, a vertical marketing system soon emerges.

Illustration of a Comprehensive Inventory Budget

A comprehensive inventory budget would take into account the five factors that have been enumerated. This can be illustrated with the American Skate Company case.

Studies by the company's engineers showed that the average length of the production process was 15 days, including the averaging in of weekends and a factor for holidays. The average value of goods in the production cycle was 81 percent of their final total cost. No dramatic changes were anticipated for the coming year, although the firm was constantly on the lookout for new production equipment that would increase efficiency.

---

[9] Weston and Brigham, *Managerial Finance*, p. 190.

There were some concerns about the availability of raw materials. The bulk of the purchases were of raw polyurethane, steel and nylon bearings, and leather. Although these items, except for some of the metal bearings, were available locally and on relatively short notice, the company made it a practice to keep a month's supply on hand. The raw materials used were normally about 62 percent of total cost of sales. No changes in the supply pattern were foreseen for 1980. In the forecast of sales and cost of goods sold, an assumption was made that inflation would account for an 8 percent increase in dollar sales and a slightly higher increase in the cost of sales.

As to the durability of the finished goods, American Skate had few problems, of course, with breakage and spoilage. But the public's fancy for skating products was another matter. The demand for skateboards had reached its peak in the mid-1970s and had declined slowly but steadily for the remainder of the decade. The sales lost in that area, however, were more than offset by a spurt in the sales of shoe skates with the new polyurethane wheels. In fact, 1978 witnessed a modest fad for shoe skates, with much of the demand coming from new, adult customers who favored the high end of the line. (It is one thing to buy skates for your nephew but another when they are for yourself.)

Sales to this new market segment held steady in 1979, which was taken by some members of American Skate's management to mean that the honeymoon for expensive shoe skates was now or soon to be ended. Moreover, there were a number of new competitor manufacturers gearing up for this uncertain market. (Some of these became original equipment manufacturers customers of American Skate.) During 1979, the finished goods inventory had averaged 50 days' sales, and the consensus of management was that it should be targeted for 45 days in 1980.

Then, too, there had been discussions about the state of the economy. Most economists had branded 1979 a recession year, and when subsequent statistics failed to ratify their opinion, many of them said we had had a small dip and would soon have another—and later some even said three dips—in the year's economy (a tactic that *Barron's* promptly labeled the "ice cream cone" method of forecasting). To compound the confusion, the company's senior managers had not themselves seen any signs of the elusive recession other than what the media said. It was decided that the company should have a prompt budget review if and when there was a verified change in the economy but for the present make no adjustments for that possibility. The discussion ended with a quote attributed to G. B. Shaw that if all the economists were laid end to end, they would not reach a conclusion.[10]

As to methods of distribution, American Skate used a variety of marketing channels.[11] Sales were made to wholesalers, direct to large retailers, original equipment manufacturers, and, if the order were large enough, to skating rinks. This diversity of distribution channels resulted in a strong resistance by the wholesalers to stocking large inventories, and there seemed to be little the company could do to shift some of its finished goods closer to the end user.

After all factors were considered, the company set these three standards as a basis for its 1980 inventory budget:

---

[10] *Modern Quotations* (New York: Penguin Books, 1971), p. 211:73.
[11] Kotler, *Marketing Management*, p. 276.

1. Finished goods inventory at the end of January should equal the next 50 days' sales and gradually decline to 45 days' sales by December 31.
2. Work-in-process inventory represented the goods in the production pipeline. That figure stood at $133,000 and varied little. Although production would be sped up or slowed according to the pattern of sales, the amount of goods in a semi-finished state remained the same. The company was operating at 75 percent of capacity and would need no major additional facilities to handle 1980 production.
3. Raw materials inventory at month's end should be sufficient to produce the goods expected to be sold in the third month forward.

Once the standards were agreed to, the final inventory budget was constructed, as illustrated in Exhibit 27.6.

EXHIBIT 27.6   American Skate Company—Inventory Budget

	$000s												
1980 →	JAN	FEB	MAR	APR	MAY	JUN	JUL	AUG	SEP	OCT	NOV	DEC	TOTAL
1 Sales[a]	437	479	523	501	458	414	370	425	468	512	447	196	5230
2 Cost of Sales[b]	300	329	360	345	316	286	256	295	325	356	311	137	3616
3 Finished Goods Inv:													
4 COS 1 mo forward	329	360	345	316	286	256	295	325	356	311	137	363	
5 COS 2/3 of 2nd mo fwd[c]	240	225	201	178	155	174	187	200	170	73	187	199	
6 FG Inventory at EOM	569	585	546	494	441	430	482	525	526	384	324	562	
7													
8 WIP Inventory													
9	133	133	133	133	133	133	133	133	133	133	133	133	
10 Raw Mtls Inventory[d]													
11	214	196	177	159	183	202	221	193	85	225	247	270	
12 Total, Line 6, 8 & 10[e]													
13	916	914	856	786	757	765	836	851	744	742	704	965	

[a] From Exh. 27.4, line 1
[b] From Exh. 27.4, line 6
[c] Begins at 20/30 and ends at 15/30 of the 2nd month forward.
[d] .62 x COS, 3rd mo fwd
[e] To Exh. 27.4, line 37

Having made an inventory budget, the company was able to schedule production. The production in any given month will be

Goods sold ± Change in finished goods inventory = Goods manufactured

In some companies, the management of production is more critical than the management of inventory, and the formula becomes

Goods manufactured – Goods sold = Finished goods inventory change

Almost every situation requires some trade-offs between manufacturing control and inventory control. The advantages of large-scale purchases, steady production flows, and well-stocked shelves are obvious and, unfortunately, often beguiling. What is not so obvious are the great risks and costs that accompany excessive inventory. There is more truth, perhaps, than style in the grim proverb that "inventory is the graveyard of business." Losses may arise from obsolescence, fashion changes, or the lowering of prices by competitors. The costs of carrying inventory include the expense of storage, insurance, shrinkage, and lost opportunity on the money that is tied up.

At American Skate, the supply of raw materials was plentiful, the production process uncomplicated, and the labor market—for the time being—stable and adequate. However, there was concern over the fad factor in current sales. It seemed a time for the company to hold its manufacturing department to strict inventory levels. The resulting production schedule is summarized on line 5 of Exhibit 27.7. On line 3 is the cost of goods delivered that month—in other words, the cost of sales. Added to or subtracted from that figure is the budgeted change in finished goods inventory (line 4). For example, the $16,000 increase in February is the difference between the February and January inventories ($585,000 – $569,000), as shown in Exhibit 27.6, line 6.

By using known averages, it was possible to split the cost of goods manufactured (Exhibit 27.7, line 5) into component parts:

Cost	Percentage	Line
Direct labor	17	7
Other manufacturing expense	20	9
Raw materials	62	14
Depreciation	1	

Remember, these are the costs of goods *manufactured*, not *sold*, during the month. The difference between the two is the change in the level of the finished goods inventory (line 4).

With the breakdown in manufacturing activity, a forecast can be made of the cash payment flows. Most of the goods and services purchased by American Skate called for payment in 30 days, but a few larger suppliers were content to wait 60 days. The average payment period—calculated the same way as the average collection period but using accounts payable and purchases—was 50 days. However, management felt that there had been ill will because of the slow payment of a few bills, and it was decided to shorten

EXHIBIT 27.7 American Skate Company—Schedule of Goods Manufactured

$000s													
1980 →	JAN	FEB	MAR	APR	MAY	JUN	JUL	AUG	SEP	OCT	NOV	DEC	TOTAL
1 Sales[a]	437	479	523	501	458	414	370	425	468	512	447	196	5230
2 Production:													
3 Goods Sold[b]	300	329	360	345	316	286	256	295	325	356	311	137	3616
4 Change in FG Inv[c]	50	16	(39)	(52)	(53)	(11)	52	43	1	(142)	(60)	238	43
5 Goods manufactured	350	345	321	293	263	275	308	338	326	214	251	375	3659
6													
7 Dir Labor: .17 × Line 5[d]	61	59	54	50	45	47	54	56	56	36	44	66	628
8													
9 Oth mfg exp: .2 × Line 5	70	69	63	59	52	54	62	68	64	42	49	75	727
10 Pmt: .5 of prev mo	34	35	35	32	30	26	27	31	34	32	21	25	
11 .5 of cur mo	35	34	31	29	26	27	31	34	32	21	24	37	
12 Total Line 10 & 11e	69	69	66	61	56	53	58	65	66	53	45	62	723
13													
14 Mtls used: .62 × Line 5	217	214	199	182	163	170	191	210	202	133	156	232	2269
15 Add change in RM Inv[f]	(9)	(18)	(19)	(18)	24	19	19	(28)	(108)	140	22	23	47
16 Raw mtls purchased	208	196	180	164	187	189	210	182	94	273	178	255	2316
17 Pmts for mtls purch'd:													
18 .5 x Line 16, 1 mo prev	108	104	98	90	82	93	94	105	91	47	136	89	
19 .5 x Line 16, 2 mos prev	83	109	104	98	90	82	94	95	105	91	47	137	
20 Total[g]	191	213	202	188	172	175	188	200	196	138	183	226	2272

[a] From Exh. 27.4, line 1
[b] From Exh. 27.4, line 6
[c] Calculated from Exh. 27.6, line 6
[d] To Exh. 27.4, line 23
[e] To Exh. 27.4, line 24
[f] Calculated from Exh. 27.6, line 10
[g] To Exh. 27.4, line 22

the average payment period to 45 days in 1980. There are only two "legitimate" reasons for not paying your debts on time: (1) an honest dispute about what is owed and (2) lack of money. Any other delay is purchased with reputation to character; character flaws, once discovered, are not forgotten within the lifetime of the witness.

A schedule for raw material payments is shown in Exhibit 27.7, lines 17 to 20, and the totals also in Exhibit 27.4, line 22.

With respect to direct-labor costs, it was assumed that all payments would be made in the same month they were incurred. Thus, the amounts on line 7 of Exhibit 27.7 were transferred directly to the cash budget (Exhibit 27.4, line 23). Other manufacturing expense (line 9, Exhibit 27.7) would be paid half in the same month, half in the next. The cash effect is shown on line 12, which amounts were transferred to Exhibit 27.4, line 24. Depreciation, a noncash expense, is excluded from the cash budget.

Prepaid Expenses

Prepaid rent, interest, insurance, and various supplies are usually budgeted at a constant amount or increased as sales increase. In the example in Exhibit 27.4, the amounts on line 38 grew 20 percent during the year, the same as those on line 1.

Fixed Assets

The budgeting of capital expenditures is the subject of other chapters of this handbook and forms a part of every standard work on financial management. There are, besides, a number of books devoted entirely to the topic. In these works, the emphasis typically is on techniques for maximizing return on investment—comparing the costs and benefits of various investment proposals in terms of the time value of money flowing out and in.[12] Here we are concerned with an additional aspect of capital assets—their relation to other accounts on the balance sheet and their effect on a firm's liquidity and leverage positions.

Fixed assets, with one or two exceptions—most notably land—can be viewed as long-term prepaid expenses. They are, in effect, lost costs whose value lies only in their use in producing products that can be sold at a profit. Unlike the fixed assets of an individual—a car and a house, which may be of value to thousands of other persons—the vast majority of business fixed assets have little value beyond their intended first use. The fate of fixed assets is to eat away net worth, either through the orderly process of depreciation or—if a mistake is recognized—through a peremptory write off.

That is not to say that fixed assets should be avoided at all costs. A company needs resources to produce the goods or services it sells. Those resources are a mix of people and capital goods—both are expenses, both are vital. The two have an important difference, however. To a large extent, the number of people employed on a job can be varied with the amount of sales. As sales increase, more people are added, and the expense is

---

[12] Martin et al., *Basic Financial Management* 1, pp. 261–340; Weston and Brigham, *Managerial Finance*, pp. 283–340; and Robert Rachlin, *Return on Investment—Strategies for Profit* (Plainview, NY: Marr Publications, 1976).

a *variable* cost. However, when a machine is substituted for labor, this variable cost is exchanged for the *fixed* cost of depreciation. The extent to which capital assets are used in place of labor is referred to as the degree of *operating leverage*. Once the fixed costs have been covered, a high level of operating leverage will produce proportionally higher profits; likewise, proportionally greater losses will occur when revenues drop below the total of fixed costs.[13]

The decision making centers on the best mix and on whether it is good (profitable) enough. There are certain capital investments, such as office furniture, that "do not require a return on investment justification, since they are investments essential or necessary to the existence of the business."[14] In fact, it is the failure to understand the *continuing* requirement for new capital goods that causes most errors in fixed asset budgeting.

In the 1950s, the concept of cash flow came into prominence. Businesspeople quickly fell in love with the idea of adding depreciation to profits in order to see how much cash there was to play with. If profit was vanilla ice cream, cash flow was a chocolate sundae. What many people overlooked was that the cash generated from depreciation would have to be plowed right back into fixed assets. I wrote about the misleading nature of cash flow in an earlier book:

> In what I call the "non-cash illusion," we are led to think that depreciation (the source of cash) is an act independent of adding fixed assets (a use of cash). In fact, it is easily observed that 90% of the time a typical business will add more in fixed assets than the amount of depreciation in any given year.
>
> Plants and equipment must be replenished, just as inventory is. To say that funds from depreciation do not have to be spent on new fixed assets is as deceptive as saying that cash received from a sale does not have to be spent to buy new merchandise.[15]

As a general rule, net fixed assets will increase as much as or more than sales do. Many of the capital asset expenditures are foreseen and planned, but some—like a suddenly leaking roof—are not. The balance-sheet budget, therefore, should make allowance for the unforeseen requirements.

Meanwhile, back at American Skate, the capital-investment committee approved two large expenditures for 1980. One was for automotive equipment at an expected cost of $34,000. Delivery was scheduled for February. The other was for some plastic injection and transfer molding equipment to be installed in October at a cost of $115,000. There were no other large investments anticipated, but the committee budgeted an amount (unallocated to any specific operating department) for contingencies based on the levels of unplanned expenses in the past three years, adjusted for inflation and growth. The results appear in Exhibit 27.8. The financing of the new additions—whether it be from internally generated funds, borrowed money, or lease financing—are covered in a discussion on liability budgeting.

---

[13] Leopold A. Bernstein, *Financial Statement Analysis* (Homewood, IL: Richard D. Irwin, 1974), p. 526.
[14] *See* footnote 14, p. 40.
[15] James E. Kristy, *Analyzing Financial Statements: Quick and Clean,* 5th ed. (Buena Park, CA: Books on Business, 1991), p. 44.

EXHIBIT 27.8 American Skate Company—Budget of Fixed assets

1980 →	JAN	FEB	MAR	APR	MAY	JUN	JUL	AUG	SEP	OCT	NOV	DEC	TOTAL
					$000s								
1 Net Fixed Assets, EOM[a]	372	374	410	411	413	415	417	419	421	422	539	540	372
2													
3 Additions: Known[b]		34								115			149
4 Unknown[b]	5	5	5	5	5	6	5	5	5	5	5	6	62
5 Less: Depreciation[c]	3	3	4	3	3	4	3	3	4	3	4	4	41
6													
7 Net Fixed Assets, EOM[d]	374	410	411	413	415	417	419	421	422	539	540	542	542

[a] From Exh. 27.4, line 40, 12–31–79
[b] To Exh. 27.4, line 26
[c] From Exh. 27.4, line 5
[d] To Exh. 27.4, line 40

The company uses accelerated methods of depreciation for most of its capitalized assets. The average estimated useful lives are:

Buildings and related equipment	30 years
Machinery and equipment	15 years
Furniture and fixtures	10 years
Automotive equipment	5 years

Ordinary maintenance and repair costs are charged to earnings, but major renewals or improvements are capitalized. The net fixed assets shown on line 7 of Exhibit 27.8 were transferred to Exhibit 27.4, line 40, while the additions on lines 3 and 4 were reflected also on line 26, Exhibit 27.4.

Inflation and Replacement Costs of Fixed Assets

The problem of replacing capital equipment in an era of moderate inflation has been honored in hundreds of articles and speeches. I hesitate to add to the rhetoric, except for the undue pessimism that characterizes most of the talk. We all know that inflation is a terrible blight because that message is drilled into us daily. Yet the history of the world is inflation. Whether it has been the effect of human progress, a contributory cause, or neither is not all that clear. What is clear is that today's average American bears this economic cross in a comfort and security known only to the upper class back when a dollar was really a dollar.

The principal effect of inflation is a shifting of wealth—generally from lenders to borrowers—and the trouble is that it is a disorderly shift and, in the minds of many, an unjust one. It is the scramble to be on the winning side of inflation that causes dislocations and risks.

It is these dislocations—a quick rise in interest rates, the rapid movement of capital into and out of gold, and so forth—that are the main concerns for business, not the fact that capital equipment will cost more dollars. Businesses seldom have trouble raising their own prices in a general inflation unless they have boxed themselves in with long-term contracts. What is more, it is not uncommon to see a business use the everything-costs-more mentality as an excuse to gain a little ground on the field of profit. (To use a homely example, I recently bought a replacement part for a major appliance. I had previously replaced the same part five years before to the month. In that time the price of the part had exactly doubled. That is a compounded rate increase of 15 percent per year, far greater than the five-year inflation rate.)

The task of someday replacing equipment at inflated prices is not unlike that of an individual planning to buy a house at some future date. The new house will probably cost more, the mortgage company will probably lend more, and the buyer will probably be earning more. If the business manages its leverage and liquidity so that equity and cash keep pace with the inflation (and the company's growth), the problem of replacing equipment will not be any greater than if there were no inflation.

The other concern for business under inflation is that the return on shareholders' equity be increased to compensate for the lost purchasing power of their investment. Lenders of money anticipate inflation with higher interest charges. Investors must be given the same relief or they will give up being investors in favor of being lenders. Also, the company that earns more for its investors will be able to retain more earnings and thus help satisfy the need for increased equity to finance fixed asset replacements.

Other Assets

The budgeting of assets other than current and fixed is almost entirely a matter for each particular company. Whether the assets are investments, long-term receivables, goodwill, deposits, or deferred charges, the circumstances surrounding them are so varied that generalizations are useless. In our American Skate example, the other tangible assets and deferred charges (Exhibit 27.4, lines 42 and 44) were carried unchanged through 1980.

Notes Payable—Banks and Others

The budgeting of notes payable will depend largely on the terms of the credits. The purpose of short-term notes is to finance temporary needs—seasonal increases in receivables and inventory are the classic ones. Nowadays, many "short-term" loans are really revolving, or "evergreen," credits, sometimes supported with an assignment of receivables or other viable assets and with repayment planned from profits, a new issue of stock, or a long-term debt issue. Perhaps the ideal arrangement is a working capital line of credit, which means that within the limits of the line the company borrows and repays to suit itself, so long as specified indicators of liquidity (e.g., current ratio), leverage (debt–equity), and profit (return on investment) are satisfactory. Such loans are interfaced with the cash account, and the two are budgeted to traverse the peaks and valleys of cash needs with the least inconvenience and cost.

A company should strive to keep some loan availability in reserve for life's little surprises. In addition, the expanding firm will have ever increasing needs for debt, so that while loans in particular are being paid off, loans in general are usually expanding. The prime prerequisites to obtaining new financing are (1) an outlook for profits and (2) a satisfactory leverage position.

Outlook for Profits

The outlook for profits comprises far fewer elements than the resulting profits. That is, there are so many factors that influence resulting profits, we are unable—even with the most powerful computers—to reckon them all. That is just the tip of the iceberg. Identifying all of the influencing factors is an even greater challenge. Thus, a bank or insurance company faced with a decision to lend its money to a particular company will generally concentrate on six elements. These are listed in the most common order of importance:

1. *Past earnings.* A steady upward trend is ideal, but caution: Points are deducted for "creative accounting."
2. *Past sales and present marketing position.* Lenders feel (or are) helpless in advising how to move the stuff out of the warehouse, so they attach much importance to marketing ability.
3. *Demand for the product.* Again, steadiness is the key; anything dependent on the public's whim or fashion arouses doubt.
4. *Foreseeable changes in competition.* New companies or products entering the field also create uncertainty.
5. *Outlook for the economy.*
6. *Company's ability to control costs and pass along price increases.*

Leverage

The term "leverage" refers to the mix of debt and equity used by a company to acquire its assets. As the term is defined, more leverage means more debt. Business professionals love leverage because if they can borrow money at 15 percent and earn a return of 20 percent on the way they invest it, they get to keep the excess—and the more the better. Lenders, however, hate leverage because more leverage means greater risk. Leverage multiplies losses as well as profits, and creditors who never share in a company's profits *do* share—or, rather, bear—its losses, once they have eaten away all of the equity.

Since there are always more people willing to borrow money than to lend it, companies must be mindful, in their balance-sheet budgeting, of maintaining a leverage position agreeable to present and future lenders. Exactly where that position lies cannot be said with certainty because it is a matter of each lender's judgment. Of course, if a company goes bankrupt, we can say it should have had a little less leverage than it had. Later, in discussing balance-sheet ratios, a guideline is given for an acceptable amount of leverage.

EXHIBIT 27.9 American Skate Company—Loan Budget

$000s													
1980 →	JAN	FEB	MAR	APR	MAY	JUN	JUL	AUG	SEP	OCT	NOV	DEC	TOTAL
1 Notes Payable—Banks													
2 Availability:													
3 .7 × Accts Rec[a]	386	550	601	607	566	514	462	479	536	588	564	356	
4 .15 × Inventory[b]	139	138	128	115	109	113	125	129	111	100	108	135	
5 Total	525	688	729	722	675	627	587	608	647	688	672	491	
6													
7 Loan balance													
8 .65 × Line 5[c]	341	447	474	469	439	408	382	395	421	447	437	319	
9 Less: planned reduct	5	10	15	20	25	30	35	40	45	50	55	60	
10 Adj balance[d]	336	437	459	449	414	378	347	355	376	397	382	259	
11 Net loan or (pymts)[e]	24	101	22	(10)	(35)	(36)	(31)	8	21	21	(15)	(123)	(53)
12													
13 Long-term debt													
14 Bal BOM, Current[f]	72	72	84	84	84	84	84	84	84	84	132	132	72
15 Noncurrent[g]	217	211	217	210	203	196	189	182	175	168	209	198	217
16 Total	289	283	301	294	287	280	273	266	259	252	341	330	289
17 Plus: New financing[h]		24								96			120
18 Less: Payments[i]	6	6	7	7	7	7	7	7	7	7	11	11	90
19 EOM Balance:													
20 Current[j]	72	84	84	84	84	84	84	84	84	132	132	132	132
21 Noncurrent[k]	211	217	210	203	196	189	182	175	168	209	198	187	187
22 Total	283	301	294	287	280	273	266	259	252	341	330	319	319

[a] Calculated from Exh. 27.4, line 36
[b] Calculated from Exh. 27.4, line 37
[c] Avg loan/availability in 1979
[d] To Exh. 27.4, line 46
[e] To Exh. 27.4, line 20 & 31
[f] From Exh. 27.4, line 50 at 12-31-79
[g] Exh. 27.4, line 53 at 12-31-79
[h] To Exh. 27.4, line 19
[i] To Exh. 27.4, line 30
[j] To Exh. 27.4, line 50
[k] To Exh. 27.4, line 53

The American Skate Company had a $750,000 line of credit with its bank, whereby the company could borrow up to 70 percent of its accounts receivable plus 15 percent of the total inventories. No assignment of these assets was made to the bank, but the company did execute a negative pledge, agreeing not to assign them to anyone else, and each month an aging of receivables and description of the inventories—certified by two company officers—was given the bank. The line of credit was renewed each year on April 30. The company agreed to maintain compensating balances equal to 15 percent of the average outstanding loan.

The company's budget strategy was to minimize this revolving loan because of the high interest cost (prime + 3%), while stretching out existing long-term debt, which then had more favorable rates. The first step in budgeting the bank loan was to calculate availability and budget a decline that seemed feasible in the loan balance. The existing long-term debt was budgeted according to terms, and new financing was planned only for the new capital investments, using the cheapest financing known to be available. The results are depicted in Exhibit 27.9.

The amounts for long-term debt (lines 20 and 21) were transferred to Exhibit 27.4, lines 50 and 53. At the same time, the cash effect of new financing and monthly payments (lines 17 and 18) were likewise reflected in Exhibit 27.4, lines 19 and 30.

After all of the other balance sheet items are budgeted, the monthly cash position is computed as well as the leverage ratio. Adjustments to financing, if any, are then considered. This interactive process is one of the things computers do best. Given the desired and minimum levels of cash and the desired and maximum levels of leverage, a computer can be programmed to provide the optimal loan position. Optimal, that is, from the standpoint of the borrowing company. There are still the lenders to be convinced, but if the right guidelines are used, the resulting budget will satisfy them too.

Trade Payables

One can hardly exaggerate the usefulness of trade credit, both to the buyer and to the seller. The convenience alone is enough to recommend it. But there is much more. To the buyer, it is the cheapest and most easily obtained credit—the first and sometimes the only form of credit to the fledgling business; a prime source of funds to the rapidly growing firm; and a significant form of financing for most established businesses (e.g., nearly $4 billion for Sears Roebuck and Company).[16] Trade credit can be overdone, and when that happens, it makes news. For every overextended firm that declares bankruptcy, however, there are hundreds that have been saved from that fate by pliant trade creditors. For the sellers, trade credit multiplies the customers and gives them a host of outlets. In addition, it often serves to smooth out the production cycle and to shift inventory nearer the consumer.

Some business professionals, sad to say, take advantage of creditor complacence by deliberately withholding payment beyond terms or paying a supplier in Miami with a check drawn on a bank in Yakima. Those who are so tempted are risking something

---

[16] See Sears, December 31, 1989, annual report.

dear to gain something cheap. To the chiseler, such little gains are soon forgotten in the sweep of daily events, but the "chiselee," like the mild-mannered elephant that has been kicked, always remembers.

In managing trade payables, my advice would be to pay all bills about a week early. Such prepayment is unusual and quite likely to earn you a favored spot in your supplier's heart, if not on his or her customer list. There are many unspoken ways that the supplier can return the favor: with prompt deliveries when suppliers are short, with the freshest merchandise, with customer referrals, with advance notice of price increases, and so on. In a contrary manner, the deadbeat can be disfavored.

Of course, if you do not have the money to pay promptly, you do not have the money. If you are caught in that situation, that is the most effective thing to tell a bill collector— "I don't have the money." It will at least shorten those time-consuming and fretful collection calls. If your delinquency is due to the pressures of expansion, you might point out to your supplier that he or she will deservedly share in the increased business. If it is due to losses, try to avoid the collection calls and concentrate on the cause of the problem. Silence buys a little time.

The budgeting and management of accounts payable are tricky because payables cut horizontally through all of the operating income budgets. Every major department will generate payables—including sales and administration—yet their purchases are governed by an expense budget, not a cash budget. If a cash shortfall arises, it may be necessary to impose additional restrictions on expenditures. Allocating cash to operating departments is a difficult task, for the pressures on department managers are already great, and their appeals for more money can be touching (e.g., "If I don't get that wire, the line will shut down!"). It is good practice to disclose company cash problems to department managers, at least the upper levels. Such confidence brings out the best in people, in terms of both loyalty and resourcefulness. Besides, they will learn of the problem from suppliers soon enough, anyway, and the rumors that spring up are likely to be far worse than the truth.

To obtain payables figures for the balance-sheet budget, it is necessary to estimate a normal payment cycle. Even a modest-size company can have 1,000 vendors with a couple of dozen different payment terms. An average payment period can be calculated using the next formula:

$$\text{Average payment period} = \frac{\text{Accounts payable}}{\text{Annual credit expenses}} \times 365$$

However, getting a figure for the total expenses put through the accounts payable account is not always easy. Expenses are often mixed in with payments for hard assets and prepaid expenses.

What we are trying to do here is synchronize the three financial budgets—income, cash, and balance sheet. All items of expense on the income budget (except depreciation and other noncash expenses) must be time-phased to the cash budget. Any purchases or expenses not paid in the same month must necessarily be added to the accounts payable balance. Thus, every expense must be reflected either in the cash payments or accounts payable for that month.

Another method of estimating payables is to divide them into broad categories and estimate payment cycles for each. An example of this is given in the American Skate Company case.

You will recall that in 1979 American Skate paid for its purchases in an average of 50 days and decided to bring that figure down to 45 days by the end of 1980. The schedule for raw materials payments is summarized in Exhibit 27.7, line 20. It was assumed that direct labor would be paid the same month; the schedule for other manufacturing expense is shown in Exhibit 27.7, line 12. The sales expenses and general and administrative expenses (Exhibit 27.4, lines 8 and 9), which include salaries, were estimated to be paid one half in the same month they are incurred and one half the following month. The payment schedule for those expenses is shown in Exhibit 27.10.

After comparing the payment schedule on line 9 with the expense schedule on line 4, the CFO decided that the difference was too slight to bother with. So the figures on line 4 were transferred to the cash budget (Exhibit 27.4, line 25), thus saving one step in the process of calculating the accounts payable balances.

That process was to take the accounts payable at the beginning of January, add to it the credit expenses incurred for raw materials purchased and other manufacturing expenses, and subtract the payments on accounts payable during the month. The expenses of sales, administration, and direct labor were excluded from the calculation because they were expected to be incurred and paid in the same month. Here is how it worked.

EXHIBIT 27.10 American Skate Company—Schedule of Payments for Sales and General and Administrative Expenses

	$000s												
1980 →	JAN	FEB	MAR	APR	MAY	JUN	JUL	AUG	SEP	OCT	NOV	DEC	TOTAL
1 Expenses from Exh. 27.4:													
2 Line 8, Sales	37	41	42	42	44	43	43	45	45	46	48	47	523
3 Line 9, G&A	57	58	59	59	60	60	61	62	62	63	63	64	728
4 Total[a]	94	99	101	101	104	103	104	107	107	109	111	111	1251
5													
6 Payment													
7 .53 Line 4, prev mo	48	47	50	51	51	52	52	52	54	54	55	56	
8 .53 Line 4, curr mo	47	49	50	50	52	51	52	53	53	54	55	55	
9 Total[a]	95	96	100	101	103	103	104	105	107	108	110	111	

[a] Line 9 is too close to line 4 to bother with, transfer line 4 to Exh. 27.4, line 25.

EXHIBIT 27.11   American Skate Company—Accounts Payable Budget

							$000s							
1980 →	JAN	FEB	MAR	APR	MAY	JUN	JUL	AUG	SEP	OCT	NOV	DEC	TOTAL
1 Accounts Payable BOM[a]	304	322	305	280	254	265	280	306	291	187	311	310	304
2 Add: Mtls purchased[b]	208	196	180	164	187	189	210	182	94	273	178	255	2316
3 Oth Mfg Expens[c]	70	69	63	59	52	54	62	68	64	42	49	75	727
4 Deduct payments for:													
5 Raw Materials[d]	(191)	(213)	(202)	(188)	(172)	(175)	(188)	(200)	(196)	(138)	(183)	(226)	(2272)
6 Other Mfg Expense[e]	(69)	(69)	(66)	(61)	(56)	(53)	(58)	(65)	(66)	(53)	(45)	(62)	(723)
8 Accounts Payable EOM[f]	322	305	280	254	265	280	306	291	187	311	310	352	352

[a] From Exh. 27.4, line 47 at 2-31
[b] From Exh. 27.4, Exh. 27.7, line 16
[c] From Exh. 27.4, Exh. 27.7, line 9
[d] From Exh. 27.4, Exh. 27.7, line 20
[e] From Exh. 27.4, Exh. 27.7, line 12
[f] To Exh. 27.4, line 47

The figures for the rest of the year are computed in the same fashion—month by month—as shown in the accounts payable budget, Exhibit 27.11.

January 1980	Amount (thousands)	Location
Beginning accounts payable	$304	From Exhibit 27.4 (line 47, at 12-79)
Add: Materials purchased	208	From Exhibit 27.7 (line 16)
Other manufacturing expenses	70	From Exhibit 27.7 (line 9)
Deduct: Payments for materials	(191)	From Exhibit 27.7 (line 20)
Payments for other manufacturing expenses	(69)	From Exhibit 27.7 (line 12)
Ending accounts payable	$322	To Exhibit 27.4 (line 47)

Income Tax Payable

Companies reporting a calendar year must make estimated tax payments on the fifteenth of April, June, September, and December. To avoid penalties, the payments must total 80 percent of the actual tax liability or be equal to the tax paid the previous year. Payment of the difference between estimated and actual tax is due March 15 of the year following.[17]

Legislation passed in 1997 fixed the corporate tax (effective 5/7/97) as:

1997

Taxable Income		Pay	% on Excess	Not the Amount Over—
Over	But Not Over			
$ 0— $	50,000 $	0	15% $	0
50,000—	75,000	7,500	25	50,000
75,000—	100,000	13,750	34	75,000
100,000—	335,000	22,250	39	100,000
335,000—	10,000,000	113,900	34	335,000
10,000,000—	15,000,000	3,400,000	35	10,000,000
15,000,000—	18,333,333	5,150,000	38	15,000,000
18,333,333—	....	6,416,667	35	18,333,333

Taxable income of certain personal service corporations is taxed at a flat rate of 35%.

In preparing their income budget, companies that expect pretax earnings over $100,000 may allocate the savings from the early rates to each month of the year. Alternatively, they may compute the tax on budgeted income, calculate the effective rate, and apply that rate to each month's earnings. American Skate chose to do the latter. Here is the calculation (dollars are in thousands):

1980 operating profit (Exhibit 27.4, line 11)	
Less nontaxable income	$363
	(9)
Tax on first $100	$354
$\dfrac{0.9}{100} \times 254$	
	$22.25
	60.06
Tax	$82.31

$$\text{Tax Rate} = \frac{\$82.31}{6} = 22.7\%$$

A rate of 22.7 percent was then applied to each month's operating profit. Thus, January's tax provision on pretax earnings of $43,000 was $9,761 (Exhibit 27.4, lines 11 and 13).

Most corporations defer part of their income tax liability through the use of accelerated depreciation methods, LIFO valuation of inventory, installment sales, or other

---

[17] Tax laws occasionally change. Consult the current regulations before acting on any specific matter.

EXHIBIT 27.12   American Skate Company—Income Tax Budget

$000s													
1980 →	JAN	FEB	MAR	APR	MAY	JUN	JUL	AUG	SEP	OCT	NOV	DEC	TOTAL
1 Sales[a]	437	479	523	501	458	414	370	425	468	512	447	196	5230
2 21/30 of prev mo	115	306	335	366	351	321	290	259	298	328	358	313	
3 Total[b]	552	785	858	867	809	735	660	684	766	840	805	509	
4													
5 Change in A/R balance	16	233	73	9	(58)	(74)	(75)	24	82	74	(35)	(296)	(27)
6 Collections:													
7 Line 1 – line 5[c]	421	246	450	492	516	488	445	401	386	438	482	492	5257

[a] From Exh. 27.4, line 1
[b] To Exh. 27.4, line 36
[c] To Exh. 27.4, line 17

strategies that result in timing differences between accounting income and taxable income. The result is a savings in immediate tax payments but not (theoretically) in tax expense. Accountants compute the tax liability as if there were no tax-saving devices, and the resulting figure constitutes the firm's income tax expense. The expense is then allocated between income tax payable and deferred taxes.[18]

In its income budget for 1980, American Skate estimated that of the $145,000 tax liability (Exhibit 27.4, line 13), about 7 percent, or $10,000, would be deferred. Each month when the tax liability was computed, 93 percent was allocated to income tax payable and the remaining 7 percent to other deferred liabilities. In January 1980, for example, the income tax provision was $17,000 (Exhibit 27.4, line 13). Of that, $16,000 was added to income tax payable (line 48) and $1,000 to deferred taxes (line 54). An income tax budget illustrating the interplay between provision, payment, current liability, and deferred liability is given in Exhibit 27.12. From this schedule the amounts are obtained for Exhibit 27.4, the balance-sheet budget (lines 48 and 54), and the cash budget (line 27).

Accruals and Other Liabilities

Accrued liabilities—also known as accrued expenses—arise because costs that are incurred in one period are not paid until a later period or entered in a payable account. For example, most companies at the end of a month will owe employees some part of their wages. Besides, there is vacation pay, real and personal property taxes, and

---

[18] Paul H. Walgenbach, Norman E. Dittrich, and Ernest I. Hanson, *Principles of Accounting* (New York: Harcourt Brace Jovanovich, 1976), p. 470.

possible warranty expenses that are best spread throughout the year.[19] The total of these accounting liabilities is generally not significant, nor will it vary much in the typical company. Here are ways in which these amounts may be budgeted:

- Unchanged throughout the year
- As a percentage of sales or total operating expense
- As a percentage of the number of employees or total payroll expense

Other liabilities—for example, customer deposits, dividends payable, and deferred income—are allocated between current and long-term liabilities and budgeted according to their nature. The result for American Skate is shown in Exhibit 27.4, line 51.

Equity Accounts

The long-range strategies of most businesses are based on the objective of increasing sales in order to increase profits—in a word, *growth*, both in revenues and in earnings. As a company expands, it needs more equity to (1) finance the additional receivables, inventory, and other assets, and (2) to provide a leverage base on which additional borrowed money can be obtained, also for expansion. Nearly all companies meet some of their increased equity needs with earnings retained in the business. At times the growth in retained earnings will match that of sales, assets, and debt, and expansion proceeds almost unnoticed. More often the elements grow disproportionately and adjustments become necessary. Just how these adjustments are made will affect the stability and strength of the company.[20]

A firm whose growth in sales and assets is outpacing that of equity can choose among a number of tactics to avoid an imbalance:

- *Limit sales growth.* This tactic has a strong following among outside lenders and inside managers whose position or personality causes them to see the risks accompanying growth more sharply than the rewards. In theory, it works fine. When demand for the company's products is excessive, the firm can raise prices, cheapen quality, tighten credit standards, cut sales expense, and so on, until just the right growth level is reached. In practice, it works very poorly. Product demand is as elusive as it is precious, and in most companies, the money, effort, pressure, and prayers expended to get sales is so great that the idea of deliberately limiting them will not even be comprehended.
- *Keep dividends low.* This works very well when the growth rate is high. If investors understand anything at all, it is making hay while the sun shines. Of course, shareholders who forgo dividends expect to be rewarded with higher market prices for their shares, and every time shares trade hands, it introduces a stockholder to whom past market price increases mean nothing—one who is concerned only with performance from this time forward.

---

[19] Ibid., p. 333.
[20] Jules I. Bogen, ed., *Financial Handbook*, 4th ed. (New York: Ronald Press, 1964), p. 15.30.

- *Sell more stock.* It is unusual if a successful company does not resort to this tactic sooner or later—more often than not, unwillingly, for shareholders do not like their pie cut into more pieces, even when promised a larger pie. Besides, the process is made tedious by regulatory agencies and expensive by underwriters. These drawbacks will be lessened or magnified by a high or low price-earnings multiple on the stock in question. Nevertheless, most companies do—and all should—prepare for the eventuality by setting a limit to the financial leverage they will permit[21]— beyond which they will seek more equity money.
- *Increase financial leverage.* There are two critical elements in determining the amount of leverage a company will employ: the attitude of management and the attitude of creditors. Management may be reluctant to sell more stock because of how that might affect its control or influence in the business. Yet to borrow instead means to incur greater risk. In larger corporations, management control is little affected by increasing the outstanding stock. The ownership is so widespread and diffused that adding a few more shareholders will not shift the balance of control. Then, too, salaried managers tend to place more value on stability than on high growth. The result is that the strongest companies—ones that have the most say-so about their leverage—are usually more conservative in that regard than the smaller firms. Those companies with one, two, or a handful of stockholders usually have less access to additional equity money and, besides, are often more willing to risk higher leverage because of their direct benefit from the rewards.

Nevertheless, the attitude of lenders and other creditors is often the decisive factor. They see leverage as risk, and each places in the file—or in a corner of his or her mind—a leverage point beyond which they will begin to shy away from a particular company. Usually a firm will have to guess where that point is, for lenders who complain ominously when leverage is too high generally say nothing when it is too low.[22] Guidelines for the best level of leverage are discussed in the section on financial ratios.

In the case of the American Skate Company, ownership was spread among 20 shareholders, but majority control resided in 5 persons, all related. There had been no stock issued for several years, and the dividend policy tended to be influenced more by the personal needs of the family owners than by anything else. With the recent revival in demand for roller skate products, the need for more equity was recognized; a dividend totaling $40,000 had remained unchanged for the past three years, even though a greater amount was permitted by existing loan agreements. Management felt that leverage, although moderate in relation to most other companies in the industry, was still too high, and it was decided to continue the same dividend rate in 1980. The cash payments are shown in Exhibit 27.4, line 29.

The equity budget summarizing the effect of profits and dividends on retained earnings ("surplus" on the form used here) is shown in Exhibit 27.13. With the transferring of retained earnings (EOM, line 4) to Exhibit 27.4, line 57, the balance-sheet budget was complete except for the balancing cash (and marketable securities) figures.

---

[21] Martin et al., *Basic Financial Management*, p. 468.
[22] Weston and Brigham, *Managerial Finance*, p. 687.

EXHIBIT 27.13   American Skate Company—Equity Budget

$000s													
1980 →	JAN	FEB	MAR	APR	MAY	JUN	JUL	AUG	SEP	OCT	NOV	DEC	TOTAL
1 Retained Earnings— BOM[a]	848	874	905	934	967	990	993	999	1013	1027	1055	1070	848
2 Plus: Net Profit[b]	26	31	37	33	23	15	6	14	22	28	15	(32)	218
3 Less: Dividends[c]			(8)			(12)			(8)			(12)	(40)
4 Retained Earn—EOM[d]	874	905	934	967	990	993	999	1013	1027	1055	1070	1026	1026
5													
6 Plus: Capital Stock[e]	245	245	245	245	245	245	245	245	245	245	245	245	245
7 Total Equity	1119	1150	1179	1212	1235	1238	1244	1258	1272	1300	1315	1271	1271

[a] From Exh. 27.4, line 57 at 12-31-79
[b] From Exh. 27.4, line 15
[c] To Exh. 27.4, line 29
[d] To Exh. 27.4, line 57
[e] From Exh. 27.4, line 56

Balancing Cash Figure

The final steps proceeded in this way:

1. The total of cash and marketable securities at December 31, 1979, was $138. (All dollars in this section are in thousands.) That became the cash balance—opening (Exhibit 27.4, line 16) for January; it was added to receipts and totaled on line 21: $583.
2. The disbursements added up to $426 (line 32).
3. $583 – $426 = $157, the cash balance—closing on line 33 and the cash balance— opening for February.
4. The $157 was apportioned between cash (line 34) and marketable securities (line 35) by calculating the compensating balance required by the bank and rounding the marketable securities portion down to even $10s. 15% × $336 (line 46) = $50.40.

	First Cut	Adjusted
Cash	$ 50.40	$ 57
Marketable securities	106.60	100
Total	$157.00	$157

5. The last step was to foot the balance sheet and try to figure out why it did not balance. Actually, the reader has been spared that last agony by having the balanced

version. Of the hundreds of budgets I have prepared or reviewed, however, I cannot recall one that was done without some error the first time. Of course, those budgets done by computer are often errorless, because all the dues are paid in the programming and debugging process.

6. This form C117 also has a line (59) for working capital, which is current assets (line 39) minus current liabilities (line 52).

7. The process is then repeated month by month throughout the year.

ADEQUATE CASH

The first test of a balance-sheet budget and/or cash budget is the sufficiency of cash. Businesses are operated for profit, but they are operated on cash. The income budget is not complete unless it is supported by a feasible balance-sheet budget. It is possible for a company to go bankrupt while making a profit—a legitimate profit. (It happened to an appliance dealer whose trade-in sale was so successful that all of his cash became tied up in slow-moving used appliances.) Short of that problem, there is a lot of mischief and costly inconvenience that a firm can bring on itself by running out of cash.

If a cash shortfall appears in any part of the budget, this is the time to plan a remedy for it. Ways to consider include:

- *Borrowing from the bank.* If it can be repaid within the annual cycle, the bank loan is an ideal arrangement for both parties, and the balance-sheet budget will go a long way in selling the bank on the idea.
- *Reducing receivables, inventory, or other assets.* These items seem to have a natural propensity to expand—even when everything else is static—so an occasional trimming is beneficial.
- *Cutting costs.* There are always some expenses that can be deferred without great impairment to the business. How often, do you suppose, is lengthy deliberation about the replacement of departing employees used to save a few dollars under the guise of personnel prudence?
- *Raising prices.* Where this fits—if it fits at all—in a firm's list of options depends pretty much on the competition, both direct and indirect (from substitute products) and sometimes on government and social factors.
- *Leaning on trade creditors and others.* This should be done only reluctantly, for it is impossible to foresee the harm it may cause. Other obligations that might be deferred are management bonuses or major stockholder loans. Even utility bills, tax payments, and bank payments have some "give" in them, but this is last-resort stuff.

FINANCIAL RATIOS

Once the cash shortfalls are provided for, the financial budgets should be further tested for liquidity, leverage, and profitability. At least five ratios should be employed. Ratio analysis adds dimension to the budgets, for it is the harmony among assets, liabilities, and equity, the proportion of the accounts one to another, and the balance of cash flows that determine the financial capabilities of a firm.

There are two problems connected with the use of ratios. One is their proliferation. In my research, I have uncovered more than 150 different financial ratios in use today. The good ones you can count on the fingers of both hands. Most of the others are deficient in some way; that is, they tell you the same story as the good ratios but in a roundabout manner, or they give you a figure that is of no practical use. An example is the ratio of current liabilities to net worth. It says nothing about liquidity because it omits current assets; it gives a misleading picture of leverage because it leaves out the long-term liabilities. Using it to measure financial condition gives haphazard results, at best. It is a little like gauging the gas in your car's tank by counting the miles since the last fill-up.

The second problem is finding standards by which you can judge whether a ratio is good or bad. The way that most financial authors solve this problem—assuming they do not just announce that there are no standards—is to cite industry averages as the standards of acceptance:

> Each year a considerable effort is mounted to compile financial statistics and classify them according to industry. Robert Morris Associates gathers financial data from their member banks on over 300 lines of business, and has published "Annual Statement Studies" for nearly sixty years. Dun & Bradstreet computes "14 Key Business Ratios" annually for each of 124 industries. And many industry associations do likewise for their own groups.
>
> Industry averages can be instructive and sometimes heartening to a firm in much the same way as average salary studies are to individuals. But they must be used with discretion. If the average ROI [return on investment] for department stores is 7%, it does not mean that a store earning 9% is doing well. It means, rather, that department stores taken together are not doing so hot.
>
> A company should never model itself on industry averages or the ratios of other firms. The differences in assets and liabilities, management skills and location, product appeal and price, reputation and luck . . . and a hundred other variables . . . severely limit a comparison. Besides, success in a competitive marketplace is the prize of those who best turn their *unique* capabilities to useful account. Banks illustrate the point. They are virtually alike in products, services, safety, and interest charged and paid. They compete best with their unique resources—people and locations.[23]

There is, I think, a better solution than industry averages: arbitrary standards. While working in financial management nearly three decades, and teaching the subject to college and postgraduate students as well as thousands of executives in public and private seminars, I developed a set of standards, which are presented here, that have served me well in business and, if I can trust the comments of my readers, hundreds of other companies throughout the industry list. Some of the standards are well known—they are established in the literature of finance, and their importance has been verified by statistical studies. Other standards may be unfamiliar, for having found none in my research, I supplied them from my own empirical observations. The standards presented

---

[23] Kristy, *Analyzing Financial Statements*, p. 15.

are universal and apply to most types of commercial enterprises. (Exceptions are banks and other lenders, utilities, and transportation companies.)

The ratios and standards are presented along with a description of the financial characteristics that they measure: liquidity, leverage, and profitability.

Liquidity

The term "liquidity" refers to a firm's ability to pay its debts on time. The sale of its products and the collection of receivables bring cash into a firm each day, while the payment of salaries, expenses, and accounts payable take it out. The amount to be paid out is known more or less in advance, but the cash inflow is less predictable. Thus, the need arises for a reservoir of cash, so that obligations may be met despite the daily ebb and flow of receipts. A company's liquidity position bears a closer watch than its leverage or even its profitability because the dynamics of liquidity are more urgent and pressing. Although a firm can operate with losses for months or even years, the missing of one payroll is apt to close it down forever. The amount of cash flowing in and out of a typical company each year will be 3 to 4 times its total equity and may be 20 times the amount of cash normally kept on hand. Unless that rapid flow is minded and regulated, liquidity can go to the dogs while you are off on a two-week vacation.

To avoid problems, a company should measure its liquidity with three different ratios. The first is the relationship of current assets to current liabilities, known as the *current ratio*. It has been widely used as a measure of liquidity for about 100 years and is the oldest of the financial ratios.

Ratio 1	Formula	American Skate (12-31-79)
Current ratio	$\dfrac{\text{Current Assets}}{\text{Current Liabilities}}$	$\dfrac{\$1,598}{\$755} = 2.12$
Standard: 2.00 to 1		

"Standard" here means standard of excellence. Thus, we would say that American Skate, with a 2.12 to 1, has an excellent current ratio.

This is one measure of liquidity, but we should look at two others to get a complete picture. Current assets comprise three principal elements—cash, accounts receivable, and inventory. Each has a different proximity to cash and therefore lends a different weight to liquidity. Shortly after the current ratio was conceived, it was found that when a company's current assets are composed primarily of inventory, its liquidity position is not as good as one with a more even spread of the three elements. After the current ratio was developed, the *quick ratio*—known also as the *acid test*—came into use as a second test of liquidity.

Ratio 2	Formula	American Skate (12-31-79)
Quick ratio	$\dfrac{\text{Cash + mkt. sec. + accts. rec.}}{\text{Current Liabilities}}$	$\dfrac{\$674}{\$755} = 0.9$
Standard: 1.00 to 1		

At 0.99, I would characterize American Skate's quick ratio as good, which gives one "excellent" and one "good" indicator of liquidity.

The third ratio is one that is still not in widespread use. When I first began applying it in the late 1960s, there was no established name for it. I called it the *liquidity ratio*, but as it has gradually come into use, another name—better, I think—is emerging: *cash ratio*. The cash ratio is a refinement of the quick ratio, as the latter is of the current ratio.

Ratio 3	Formula	American Skate (12-31-79)
Cash ratio	$\dfrac{\text{Cash} + \text{marketable securities}}{\text{Current liabilities}}$	$\dfrac{\$138}{\$755} = 0.8$
Standard: 0.40 to 1		

I would call American Skate's cash ratio "fair minus" or "poor plus." Although the standards given for the current and quick ratios are well established among financial analysts, the standard for the cash ratio is my own—one that I have used for more than 10 years and have found well-serving:

> The cash ratio deserves special attention in marginal cases, for it is perhaps the single best leading indicator of business failure. A company approaching insolvency finds it all but impossible to maintain good cash balances. Occasionally a strong company will post a low cash ratio, relying on available bank lines to meet current needs rather than an inventory of cash; however, the inherent strength of such a firm should be evident in the other ratios.
>
> The cash ratio has also a close correlation to promptness in making trade payments. The typical firm will begin to show some trade delinquency when the cash ratio declines to about the 0.20 level.[24]

Taking the three ratios together, we might describe the American Skate Company's liquidity position as "good." The cash ratio needs improving, but there is no great urgency about it. The company has an established bank line going into 1980, and its current ratio reveals excellent support among the less liquid, but still current, assets. Not to correct the cash ratio, however, would be shortsighted. The humor in the epigram that "banks only lend to those with no need to borrow" hides the truth that banks draw a sharp distinction between "growth" loans and "bail-out" loans. Lenders have little desire to hand their money to a company that cannot manage its own.

Leverage

The term "financial leverage" refers to the relationship between a company's debt and its equity funds—the funds contributed to the business by creditors as compared

---

[24] Kristy, *Analyzing Financial Statements*, p. 9.

to shareholders. The British refer to it as gearing.[25] By leveraging its equity (i.e., borrowing on it), a company can multiply its return (both positive and negative) on investment.

Entrepreneurs concentrate on the extra profits that leverage brings and creditors on the extra risks, and the two often pretend not to understand each other's position. An interesting study made of the 1975 financial statements of more than 2,000 industrial firms revealed almost no correlation at all between leverage and profitability. (The Spearman rank correlation coefficient of the profit-equity and debt-equity ratios was $-.12$.)[26] This would seem to indicate that the chances of leverage—as used in business today—helping or hurting a company are pretty evenly matched.

Several ratios are used to measure a company's leverage position. The one I prefer, the *asset ratio*, shows the dollars of assets for each dollar of creditor money.

Ratio 4	Formula	American Skate (12-31-79)
Asset ratio	$\dfrac{\text{Total assets}}{\text{Total liabilities}}$	$\dfrac{\$2,136}{\$1,043} = 2.05$
Standard: 2.75 to 1		

When talking leverage with bankers, you will more often find them referring to the debt to worth (equity) or the worth to debt ratios rather than to the asset ratio. However, the three ratios all tell the same story and are mathematically linked. The next table shows the equivalent standards:

Ratio	Standard	As the Ratio Decreases Leverage	Risk/Return
Asset ratio	2.75 to 1	Increases	Increases
Debt to worth	0.57 to 1	Decreases	Decreases
Worth to debt	1.75 to 1	Increases	Increases

The standard for the asset ratio, like that for the cash ratio, is my own, although most people concerned with business borrowing or lending will recognize its appropriateness. The amount of leverage a creditor will tolerate is not only an individual opinion but one blown this way and that by the winds of confidence and fear. Since World War II, business conditions within and among developed countries have stabilized, and we find more and more leverage employed. International conflict, recession, inflation, and other destabilizing forces tend to make creditors tighten their standards.

As for American Skate Company, its leverage position is "good minus." Should its asset ratio drop below 2.00 (the limit prescribed in its bank loan agreement), it can

---

[25] *Dictionary of Economics* (New York: Penguin Books, 1972), s.v. "gearing."
[26] George Foster, *Financial Statement Analysis* (Englewood Cliffs, NJ: Prentice-Hall, 1978), p. 182.

expect its bank to nick it for another point over prime or perhaps tighten the borrowing formula. If the ratio got in the vicinity of 1.50, the bank would likely introduce American Skate to a commercial finance company and politely suggest that the loan be transferred out of the bank.

Profitability

Profit in business is the result of many factors. We do not even know them all. Of those we know, we can measure only a small percentage. Of those we can measure, we can control but a minority. Moreover, the influence of each factor is constantly shifting, as with the most important element: demand for the company's products or services. Another important profit factor is the effectiveness of management. Yet each manager differs from another, and each one changes in a small way every day.

Nevertheless, although we have much to learn about predicting future profits, we have pretty good information about evaluating current earnings. Also, all of the many factors involved can be combined and measured in a single scale, the fifth ratio.

Ratio 5	Formula	American Skate (12-31-79)
Return on equity	$\dfrac{\text{Profit}}{\text{Equity}}$	$\dfrac{\$198}{\$1,093} = 18.1\%$
Standard: 14%*		

*For convenience, the ending equity is used in this calculation.

Although I do not find it worth the trouble, a truer return on equity (ROE) would use an average equity: (beginning equity + ending equity)/2. A corresponding standard would be 15 percent.

The standard proposed here is higher than those I have published in the past (10 percent in 1970, 12 percent in 1977) because of the double-digit inflation accompanying us into the 1980s. Inflation affects ROE in two ways:

1. Investors ask for higher yields to compensate for the loss of purchasing power.
2. Inflation means a higher replacement cost for capital assets, which requires a faster accumulation of profits just to stay at the same production levels.

The ROE that an individual company strives for is determined by both theoretical and practical factors. Theoretical factors influencing expected ROE are:

- The basic rent for money, which is the investor's reward for postponing the use of his or her money and letting someone else use it. Historically, this has been about 3 percent.
- The expected rate of inflation, which is difficult to judge if we observe that the inflation rate during much of this century was between 1 and 2 percent, whereas in 1979 it reached 13 percent. The average inflation rate in the 1990s is expected to be 5 to 6 percent.

▪ The risk of loss, the premium for which, among established companies, has averaged about 6 percent as measured by the difference in the yields of AAA corporate bonds and the respective company's common stock.[27]

The ROE goal a company sets for itself will also be influenced by *practical considerations* unique to it. These include:

▪ *How difficult it is for competitors to enter the same business.* Companies requiring heavy capital investment, long lead times, or limited natural resources will be able to achieve higher returns than those in industries that are easy to enter.
▪ *How unique its products or services are.* If competitors can be held at bay with patients, licenses, copyrights, or trademarks, or outdistanced with new products, new models, or new features, a firm can aim for a higher-than-average yield.
▪ *Unexpected changes in demand or supply.* These often affect a company's ROE temporarily. Since shortages tend to be followed by gluts, a company should be wary of making long-term commitments to grasp short-lived opportunities.

In the case of American Skate, the 18.1 percent ROE was rather pleasing to its stockholders, and they recognized that the public's current fancy for roller skates might lessen in the near future. This, plus increased production and marketing aggressiveness by competitors, led management to think that the current rate of return could not be sustained.

A summary of the ratios discussed appears in Exhibit 27.14. In addition, American Skate's ratios were calculated for each month's end of 1980 from the financial budgets, and those results are shown in Exhibit 27.15.

The projection of financial ratios revealed a general weakening in the balance sheet in the first quarter, especially February. Although Q1 profits account for 43 percent of the year's total, they are accompanied by a distinct drop in the liquidity and leverage positions. Liquidity dips again in December but not to the same extent. That these declines are seasonal does not mean they should be ignored, any more than you would ignore dressing warmly in winter just because the cold weather was seasonal.

Among the steps the company might take to improve its interim financial condition is to postpone the February acquisition of automotive equipment (Exhibit 27.4, lines 19 and 26) until, say, April. Of course, there may be compelling reasons for making the

EXHIBIT 27.14 Summary of Financial Ratios

Ratio	Standard	What It Measures
Current ratio (CUR)	2.00	Liquidity
Quick ratio (QR)	1.00	Liquidity
Cash ratio (CAR)	0.40	Liquidity
Asset ratio (AR)	2.75	Leverage
Return on equity (ROE)	0.14	Profitability

---

[27] Douglas A. Hayes and W. Scott Bauman, *Investments*, 3rd ed. (New York: Collier MacMillan, 1976), pp. 343–347.

EXHIBIT 27.15   American Skate Company—Projected Financial Ratios for 1980

	CUR[a]	QR	CAR	AR	ROE[b]
Month End	**(2.00)**	**(1.00)**	**(0.40)**	**(2.75)**	**(0.14)**
December 1979	2.12	0.89	0.18	2.05	0.18
January 1980	2.06	0.87	0.19	2.02	
February	1.93	0.89	0.05	1.94	
March	1.96	0.98	0.05	1.98	
April	2.04	1.08	0.09	2.05	
May	2.07	1.13	0.20	2.08	
June	2.12	1.13	0.23	2.14	
July	2.12	1.03	0.23	2.15	
August	2.12	1.02	0.19	2.17	
September	2.29	1.18	0.12	2.31	
October	1.96	1.09	0.19	2.06	
November	1.96	1.14	0.27	2.09	
December	2.05	0.76	0.11	2.20	0.17

[a] Standards are in parentheses.

[b] $\dfrac{\text{Net profit for the year}}{\text{Year-end equity}}$

purchase in February, but probably not. That small action alone would raise the February ratios a few percentage points:

- CUR from 1.93 to 1.97
- QR from 0.89 to 0.91
- CAR from 0.05 to 0.06
- AR from 1.94 to 1.96

Another reconsideration should be the planned reduction in the bank loan, a total of $60,000 (Exhibit 27.9, line 9). While the attempt to reduce costly borrowing is understandable, it is more important to avoid weak liquidity positions. As Murphy's Law warns us, it is often when we are most vulnerable that fate chooses to trifle with us. Leaving out the reduction would change December 1980 ratios in this way:

- CUR from 2.05 to 1.98
- CAR from 0.11 to 0.18
- AR from 2.20 to 2.14
- ROE from 0.17 to 0.17

Even greater improvement can be made, however, in overall bank loan tactics. The company has regularly borrowed 65 percent of its available bank line, in effect ignoring seasonal cash needs in favor of a consistent and conservative borrowing pattern. This is a mistake. The purpose of the revolving credit is to meet seasonal as well as growth needs, and the company should smooth out its liquidity position by varying the percentage of available credit it uses each month. A month-end cash level equal to 20 percent of current liabilities is necessary in most companies to avoid any slowness in payment to creditors or drawing on uncollected funds during the month.

There is also a psychology of cash. People and companies with too little cash often speak of others as having too much cash, while those they thus accuse say nothing. Large cash holdings seem to command a certain respect and a reputation for power, strength, and brains. That this reputation is not deserved is not as important as the advantages one may make of it. Operating with a zero bank balance is no crime, but it is no great honor either. To be in that position as a result of chance or inadequate planning is understandable. To get into it deliberately may be a sign of extravagant cleverness.

ANALYZING CHANGES IN THE BALANCE SHEET

The balance sheet gives us a picture of the physical assets and financial resources a company has on a particular day. It is these that create the products for future sales and profits. When we speak of a company's financial strength or financial capabilities, we mean its potential for generating future income. Most physical assets are like prepaid expenses—their value lies only in their ability to produce a stream of revenues. By looking at past profits and a current balance sheet, we can impute future earnings.

In addition to the picture drawn from a balance sheet, we can gain knowledge by analyzing the changes in the balance sheet from one period to another. The income statement is, in effect, an analysis of a single balance-sheet account—retained earnings.

Changes in the other accounts are revealed in the *statement of cash flows*, formerly called by other names: statement of changes; sources and uses of funds; source and application of cash; and, in pre-MBA days, when simplicity was still a virtue, the "where-got, where-gone" statement.

Balance sheets are changed, of course, by the dynamics, or activities, of a business. Cash flows out in all directions—for raw materials, salaries, equipment, and so forth—and flows in as a result of sales, loans, and shareholder investments. This flow of cash is subject to a thousand changing forces, but it does acquire a certain inertia, which results in trends, or at least tendencies. The revelation and the control of these trends constitute the basis of balance-sheet budgeting.

The analysis of cash flows gained prominence in the prosperous 1960s. In 1988, the Financial Accounting Standards Board—the policy-making arm of the American Institute of Certified Public Accountants—prescribed its current form and use. The balance sheet, income statement, and statement of cash flows make up the three major financial statements.

Exhibits 27.16 and 27.17 are from the September 30, 1979, annual report of Rockwell International. The changes in the balance sheet from September 30, 1978, to September 30, 1979, are reflected in the statement of changes in the column headed "1979."

Unfortunately, the format adopted by the accounting profession is unnecessarily complicated and unwieldy. It is difficult for an accountant to prepare and more difficult for the nonaccountant to read and understand. As a result, what was once hailed as a breakthrough in financial analysis has, by its convoluted form, given little comfort to investors or use to managers.

As an illustration, we might wonder how the net fixed assets (property) of Rockwell have changed during the year. Given the two years' figures in Exhibit 27.16, we can compute the change: $1,044.3 – $910.4 = $133.9 (millions) increase. But to obtain that amount from Exhibit 27.17 is all but impossible.

Property additions	$275.8 (millions)
Less: Depreciation of property	(125.7)
Depreciation from discontinued operations	(5.2)
Proceeds from disposition of property and businesses	(63.9) 68.9
Plus: Acquisition of business	$149.9

This is about as close as we can come. We can see from the balance sheet that long-term debt declined $32 million ($431.0 – $463.0) during the year, which is a significant change in view of the $592.1 increase in total assets. Yet it is impossible to find that figure on the statement of changes or even to compute it from the information given. A solution to the problem is already apparent: Simply compute the changes between the two balance sheets.

An example of that simpler approach is shown in Exhibit 27.18. The *Delta Flow Statement* was created a few years ago as a tool to highlight the changes in major balance sheet items. This format groups the balance sheet changes so that the relation of long- and short-term sources and uses of cash can be seen at a glance.

> The *Delta Flow Statement* shows the changes between one year-end and the next. It begins with the profits and dividends (Lines 1 and 2) for the year, which together amount to the change in the Retained Earnings account. The rest of the items are simply the present balance sheet amounts minus the same figures from the year before. Normally a company that is growing, or at least keeping pace with inflation, will have positive changes in all of the Delta Flow items.
>
> The things to look for are (1) negative changes, (2) large changes plus or minus, and (3) the change in the mix of long term sources and uses of cash (summarized on Lines 10 and 19, and netted on Line 26).[28]

The Delta Flow Statement for the 1979 Rockwell figures is shown in Exhibit 27.18. It can be seen that there was a good buildup of equity during the year (line 4) but only a negligible increase in deferred obligations (line 9). There was an unusual rise in current liabilities (line 14). A more complete breakdown of that increase can be found in

---

[28] Kristy, *Analyzing Financial Statements*, p. 20.

EXHIBIT 27.16 Consolidated Balance Sheet

Assets September 30	1979	1978
Current assets	**(In millions)**	
Cash (including time deposits and certificates of deposit: 1979, $584.2 million; 1978, $371.4 million)	**$ 633.6**	$ 452.2
Receivables	**1,060.1**	986.4
Inventories	**1,092.6**	937.5
Prepaid expenses and other current assets	**31.8**	34.0
Total current assets	**2,818.1**	2,410.1
Investments	**156.9**	111.3
Property—At cost		
Land	**58.2**	56.6
Improvements to land and leaseholds	**72.2**	63.4
Buildings	**441.0**	403.5
Machinery and equipment	**1,200.0**	1,094.0
Furniture, fixtures and office equipment	**126.6**	117.2
Construction in progress	**132.5**	106.8
Total	**2,030.5**	1,841.5
Less accumulated depreciation	**986.2**	931.1
Net property	**1,044.3**	910.4
Other assets	**108.3**	103.7
Total	**$4,127.6**	$3,535.5

Liabilities		
Current liabilities		
Short-term debt	**$ 132.7**	$ 51.5
Accounts payable-trade	**447.9**	389.7
Advance payments from customers	**228.5**	177.2
Accrued payroll	**167.6**	131.6
Accrued retirement plan costs	**169.0**	144.2
Accrued income taxes	**114.3**	81.9
Deferred income taxes	**434.0**	329.9
Other current liabilities	**338.3**	333.1
Total current liabilities	**2,032.3**	1,639.1
Long-term debt	**431.0**	463.0
Other liabilities		
Deferred income taxes	**107.4**	63.6
Minority interests in subsidiaries	**17.7**	15.2
Total other liabilities	**125.1**	78.8
Stockholders' equity		
Capital stock:		
Preferred stock, without par value:		
Series A (entitled in liquidation to $53.0 million)	**1.3**	1.9
Series B (entitled in liquidation to $36.9 million)	**0.9**	1.1
Common stock, $1 par value	**35.8**	34.5
Additional capital	**266.3**	251.0
Retained earnings	**1,234.9**	1,066.1
Total stockholders' equity	**1,539.2**	1,354.6
Total	**$4,127.6**	$3.535.5

EXHIBIT 27.17   Statement of Consolidated Changes in Financial Position

Years ended September 30	1979	1978
Resources provided	(In millions)	
Income from continuing operations	$261.1	$212.8
Add (deduct) items not requiring use of working capital:		
Depreciation of property	125.7	116.3
Gain on dispositions of property and businesses	(24.8)	(11.9)
Deferred income taxes	40.6	(4.7)
Equity in income of unconsolidated subsidiaries and affiliates	(4.1)	(5.6)
Other	7.1	(3.1)
Total from continuing operations	405.6	303.8
Loss from discontinued operations	—	(36.2)
Add items not requiring use of working capital:		
Loss on dispositions	20.0	
Other, including depreciation of property	5.2	9.4
Total from (applied to) discontinued operations	25.2	(26.8)
Total from operations	430.8	277.0
Proceeds from dispositions of discontinued businesses	101.9	
Proceeds from dispositions of property and businesses	63.9	63.0
Issuance of common stock	21.0	10.7
Working capital of businesses purchased	14.8	
Decreases in investments	2.4	55.6
Long-term borrowings	1.5	12.0
Other	9.0	6.1
Resources provided	645.3	424.4
Resources applied		
Property additions	275.8	218.9
Cash dividends	92.3	80.9
Working capital of businesses sold	77.6	
Acquisition of businesses	68.9	
Increases in investments	45.8	5.4
Reduction in long-term debt	42.1	78.3
Other	28.0	22.8
Resources applied	630.5	406.3
Increase in working capital	$ 14.8	$ 18.1
Changes within working capital		
Increases (decreases) in current assets:		
Cash	$181.4	$ (24.5)
Receivables	73.7	69.2
Inventories	155.1	74.3
Prepaid expenses and other current assets	(2.2)	2.7
Increase in current assets	408.0	121.7
Increases (decreases) in current liabilities:		
Short-term debt	81.2	71.0
Accounts payable-trade	58.2	5.4
Advance payments from customers	51.3	37.5
Accrued payroll	36.0	9.3
Accrued retirement plan costs	24.8	38.3
Accrued income taxes	32.4	(7.5)
Deferred income taxes	104.1	132.4
Other current liabilities	5.2	(40.8)
Increase in current liabilities	393.2	103.6
Increase in working capital	$ 14.8	$ 18.1

EXHIBIT 27.18 Delta Flow Statement

	By	**JEK**
Company <u>Rockwell International Corporation</u>	Date	<u>2-20-80</u>

Instructions: Show changes in the balance sheet from one period to the next. Increases are shown as (+) amounts, decreases as ( ) or in brackets ( ).

☐ Thousands

☑ Millions

Date 9-30-79

Period Year

SOURCES OF CASH

1	Net Income	$ 2611
2	Less Dividends	(923)
3	Other Capital Accounts	158
4	**NET WORTH**	1846
5	Long Term Debt	(320)
6	Deferred Liabilities	438
7	Minority Interest	25
8	Other	
9	**DEFERRED OBLIGATIONS**	143
10	**LONG TERM SOURCES** Lines 4 plus 9	1989
11	Accounts Payable	528
12	Notes Payable	812
13	Other	2592
14	**CURRENT LIABILITIES**	3932
15	**TOTAL SOURCES OF CASH** Lines 10 plus 14	5921

USES OF CASH

16	Net Fixed Assets	1339
17	Intangibles	
18	Other Slow Assets	502
19	**NON-CURRENT ASSETS**	1841
20	Accounts Receivable	737
21	Inventories	1551
22	Other	(22)
23	**CURRENT ASSETS**	2266
24	**TOTAL USES OF CASH** Lines 19 plus 23	4107
25	Cash Increase (Decrease) Lines 15 minus 24	1814
26	Working Capital Increase Lines 10 minus 19	148

The items listed as Sources or Uses of Cash normally increase as a company grows. If an item is a negative amount (i.e., the balance sheet amount declined from one year to the next), instead of being a source of cash, it will be a use of cash; likewise, if an item is a positive amount, it will be a source of cash

Exhibit 27.17, the bottom section. There was a normal increase in current assets other than cash (line 23), and cash itself took a significant leap, as shown on line 25.

As a guideline, the long-term sources (line 10) should cover the change in noncurrent assets (line 19) plus about half of the change in current assets (line 23). In the case of Rockwell it does not, and the result is a drop in liquidity as measured by the current and quick ratios. It is offset, however, by the big increase in cash balances. The maintenance of a good cash ratio to mitigate an only fair current ratio shows good balance sheet management. Nearly all of the cash—except that needed to meet compensating balance requirements—is in short-term investments, earning interest. When you read in the Rockwell annual report that the "weighted average interest rates for all short-term borrowings were 21.1 percent in both 1979 and 1978,"[29] you begin to appreciate the degree of management and care employed. The temptation to apply, say, $500 million of that cash to outstanding loans must be very great. If we assume about a 5 percent differential between what is earned on short-term investments and what is paid on the most expensive loans, the company could save nearly $3,000 an hour in interest costs—days, nights, and holidays! Prudence has its price, but the lessons of experience tell us to pay it.

There is one remaining element in balance-sheet budgeting that is critical yet difficult to cover in a handbook such as this. That is an awareness of each item of the balance sheet—the meaning behind what the figures say. You cannot take the measure of an asset by its accounting value any more than you can take the measure of a person by weighing him or her. The accounts receivable include amounts that will never be paid; inventories list items that do not exist or that lie broken in the corner of a warehouse; machinery with a zero book value hums away, still producing goods. It is only when assets are observed "in action" that the full value of balance-sheet budgeting can be realized.

---

[29] See Rockwell's September 30, 1979, annual report.

CHAPTER TWENTY-EIGHT

Budgeting Property and Liability Insurance Requirements

Ronald K. Tucker, BBA, CPCU, ARM
Hagedorn & Company

Vicki L. Tucker, MS, ARM
Good Samaritan Hospital

INTRODUCTION

Very often, budgeting property and liability insurance expenditures is thought of as a simple purchase with little or few variables. Basically, one buys a policy to protect against an unpredictable loss and, should it occur, the firm will be made whole. Largely, this is true, but there are many variables. Understanding the role of property and liability insurance in the budgeting process requires attention and management of these variables. Unpredictable expenses can ruin the collective efforts of the entire firm in the accomplishment of their financial plan or mission objectives. Inappropriate attention to detail may also ruin the careers of those responsible for understanding the implications of the property and liability protection.

The purpose of this chapter is to assist the budget process through a brief and elementary discussion of financial plans. Usually the purchase of property and liability insurance is relegated to the financial manager. Often the person responsible for this program is not trained in all or some of the aspects necessary to purchase insurance such as:

- The risk management process
- Types of insurance available

- Insurance mechanisms
- Roles of insurance/risk consultants
- Role of insurance brokers/agents
- Role of other service providers
- Quantitative models for informed decisions
- How to identify risks and values
- Property and casualty coverages
- Managing insurer insolvencies

Obviously, a full discussion of each of these subjects requires more space than allocated in this chapter. A brief discussion, however, is possible to assist in forming a decision format with some basis of understanding. Any person responsible for the financial well-being of the assets and revenues of a firm will need much technical and professional assistance in order to maximize the decision-making process. This assistance is usually found through counsel with insurance brokers, agents and consultants, accountants, and attorneys. Each brings a unique perspective to the problem, and the energy created by this team is critical to the proper allocation of limited resources for each firm.

A discussion with leading financial executives suggested that this chapter emphasize the choices, processes, and variables present in the purchase of property and casualty coverages. Almost all these executives had a strong accounting background and focused on the inadequacy of their accounting experience to help understand the demands of the risk management elements of their jobs. This chapter renders assistance to persons in similar situations.

This analysis summarizes the principal insurance coverages and programs available and purchased by most middle-market buyers as the center of their risk-management program. Self-insurance alternatives are not usually considered until the firm accumulates earnings that are large enough to sustain significant losses and still not seriously diminish the value or performance of the enterprise.

Common terms are defined next.

Middle-market firms. Generally, firms under $500 million in gross sales producing net incomes of $10 million or less.

Self-insurance. Absorption of some risk on behalf of the firm. Insurance above a retention (deductible) is purchased. There is a finance plan, which also involves risk financing and loss prevention/reduction, in the risk retention/deductible area.

Twenty-four-hour coverage. A concept of combined efforts in various areas of medical reimbursement. The three most common casualty coverages are workers' compensation (medical component), no-fault automobile coverage, and employee health plan (sickness and accident). Twenty-four-hour coverage attempts to manage medical exposures more economically. As of this writing, this coverage is available in a few states.

Third-party administrator (TPA). An outside vendor (usually a claims administrator) hired to help administer the self-insurance portion (retention/deductible) of a risk-management program.

What does this mean to effective budgeting? Budgeting of property and liability losses, coverages, and ultimate costs are not static. Many premiums are not flat charges but variable costs depending on sales, payroll, units, employees, values, or other fluctuating variables. A budgeter must be aware of these variables in order to plan effectively.

In addition, property and casualty losses cost much more than the actual loss and involve asset replacement or indemnification of injured third parties. This hidden cost of loss resembles an iceberg: The cost of the actual loss is the visible iceberg, and the less identifiable costs are buried beneath the water. The hidden costs are usually three to four times the actual loss cost—a truly significant amount.

ROLE RISK MANAGEMENT PLAYS IN THE BUDGETING PROCESS

The overall purpose of any risk-transfer system is the preservation of physical assets from their value reduction due to fortuitous physical losses. Any decrease in asset value reduces equity or net worth and organizational value for the owners.

All business ventures expect some accidental physical losses. The role of risk management in the budgeting process is to identify the risk possibility of losses and treat them in the most economical and desirable way to minimize adverse effects on the organization. Simply put, losses diminish the organization's worth and ability to produce positive revenues.

Identification of risk exposures is the first step in the risk-management process. The risk-management process can be outlined as:

- *Identification of exposure.* What and where could it happen?
- *Evaluation of risk.* If it happens, how much could it hurt?
- *Risk control.* What can I do to prevent, eliminate, reduce, or transfer losses?
- *Risk financing.* We expect some losses. How should we pay for them?

Usually, most firms use insurance as a risk treatment solution (transfer). Risk transfer trades the cost of premium for the assumption of risk by an insurance carrier. Firms that are large enough to absorb the majority of their losses from current revenues are candidates for sophisticated financing techniques, such as captive insurance companies, pooling arrangements, or self-funded programs. Because most firms purchase insurance to transfer their risk, we focus primarily on insurance and its importance to the budget process.

Projecting insurance cost and the effect of losses on profits is a most important element. Insurance costs are not always "flat" charges but vary depending on fluctuations in exposure bases. Examples are workers' compensation cost, which varies directly with changes in payroll; or product and general liability cost, which varies directly with net sales and other variables.

Understanding these charges will prevent embarrassment with superiors or further diminution of profits from operations. The more important issue is the purchasing of insurance and understanding premium variables so that accurate costs may be anticipated and budgeted.

TYPES OF INSURANCE MECHANISMS

In order to understand the purchase of insurance, we present a brief introduction to the types of property and casualty organizations that exist principally in the United States. These are direct writers; agency/brokerage carriers; and self-funded arrangements, such as: captives, risk retention groups, and self-insurance.

Direct Writers

Direct writers are insurance carriers evidenced principally by their distribution system. Their product is offered directly by company sales persons who can only offer *their* employer's products and services. Examples of such carriers are Nationwide and Allstate.

Agency/Brokerage Carriers

Agency/brokerage carriers are also principally identified by their distribution system. These insurance companies distribute their product through independent agents or brokers who usually represent several companies in their local offices. These insurance companies can take several different forms, such as stock, mutual, or reciprocal. We do not discuss these companies, as doing so would carry us beyond the purpose of this chapter.

An agent is differentiated from a broker in several ways. An agent is a legal representative of an insurance carrier and functions under contract on behalf of the insurance company. A broker has no legal authority to act on behalf of the carrier. Practically, brokers and agents act as advisors and counselors to their insured. There may be no apparent difference to the buyer, but specific checking with your representative is always advisable.

Self-Funded Plans

Self-funded plans are modified self-insurance financing techniques usually most appropriate to very large buyers. Statistically, as a firm grows, the predictability of its actual losses gets more accurate. Specifically, some casualty losses with high frequency and small cost per claim are excellent candidates for self-funding. Examples are workers' compensation, general liability, and automobile losses for large clients.

As the firm grows and its casualty losses become predictable, its smaller losses can be more effectively paid as a direct expense rather than an insurance premium. The reason is that a property or casualty insurance premium, at best, will return only 70 to 75 percent in claims benefits to policyholders. Therefore, payment of these types of losses is really a financing issue rather than a transfer issue.

There are a myriad of plans to better finance losses for larger firms, such as retrospective rating plans, deductible plans, captive insurance companies, and fronted programs. Computing these alternatives requires estimating the largest individual loss or the total amount of accumulated losses that can be absorbed by the firm's "worst case" and form the basis of a modified self-insurance or self-funding finance plan.

ROLE OF INSURANCE/RISK CONSULTANTS

An insurance or risk consultant can be a very valuable asset to a buyer. Insurance agents/brokers generally perform consulting functions to some extent during their brokering process. If the agent/broker is going to perform these functions, usually there will be no charge for the services as an agent/broker is rewarded by commissions built into the price of the insurance premium. If a consultant is used, a fee is generally negotiated depending on the services to be performed.

The benefit of a consultant is to have a completely disinterested third party provide advice and counsel. Generally, consultants will pay greater attention to details, as their credentials may be superior to those of most agent/brokers. Reviewing credentials should be an important element in most buyers' decision processes.

Whichever decision is reached, unless the buyer is trained in risk management, he or she needs assistance in planning and executing a risk-management program. Competent advice is available to assist individuals and firms in maximizing their risk-management budgets.

USE OF AGENTS/BROKERS

As mentioned, agents and brokers usually perform the consulting function as part of their brokering process. It is important to be aware of the differences when selecting an agent/broker. A buyer is wise to compare these characteristics:

- Credentials of salespersons or account executives: Bachelor of Business Administration, Juris Doctor, Master's of Business Administration degrees, and Chartered Property and Casualty Underwriter, Chartered Life Underwriter, Associate in Risk Management designations
- Depth of technical support persons and their backgrounds
- Services provided: consulting, actuarial, loss control, claims management, risk management, loss modeling
- Extent of branch office network (i.e., domestic and international)
- Areas of particular expertise: manufacturing, aviation, medical construction, banking, international
- Types of clients: size, industry group, location
- Marketing focus: *Fortune* 500, 100, middle market
- Carriers represented
- Security committee to evaluate carrier's financial stability
- Corporate vision and mission statement

Very often, the choice of a broker is made for some nonbusiness reasons (i.e., friend, relative, college roommate, or golfing acquaintance). Since the product is very complicated, some buyers feel more comfortable with someone they know and trust. All too often, however, they exchange comfort for poor risk management programs at higher costs. A buyer should be aware of a firm's past decisions and the underlying reasons for making them.

SELF-INSURANCE ALTERNATIVES

As a firm grows, the likelihood of fortuitous losses becomes more certain. This factor is due to the increase of similar exposure units. Obviously, the larger the pool of similar exposure units, the smaller the outcome variations. This statistical concept has been called the *law of large numbers* and forms the basis for the insurance industry's rate structure and outcome predictability. By combining large groups of similar exposure units, an insurer, with the aid of an actuary, can readily predict the losses for this group.

Large firms begin to accumulate group status and predictability as they grow. This predictability becomes the basis for self-insurance plans. As discussed in the introduction to this chapter, self-insurance suggests a plan of risk financing based on risk/reward scenarios and other factors. Largely, a self-insurance program evolves in several ways beginning with small retentions (deductibles).

Good exposure candidates for self-funding are small predictable losses high in frequency but low in severity. Workers' compensation exposures are excellent candidates, as the most frequent losses tend to be small medical claims with no lost time. A catastrophe exposure exists, but severe large losses are rare in most industries. An industry- and individual-loss assessment is urgent before considering even the most basic self-insurance plan.

A key element for any level of self-insurance is the separation of losses from administrative services. An insurance premium contains two elements: losses and expenses (sales, administrative, profit, claims adjustment, taxes licenses, and fees). Generally, a premium allocates approximately 70 to 75 percent for losses and 30 to 25 percent for expenses. By separating these elements, the insured controls them and can improve ultimate costs.

The most basic self-insurance plans are known as *retro plans*. Here, the ultimate premium is a result of ultimate losses plus expenses. The firm's worst-case scenario is capped at a prenegotiated threshold, with the majority of self-funding in the most predictable small loss area. Often it takes five to seven years before all losses are paid and ultimate costs are determined. This fact is critical to the budget process; proper forecasts of ultimate costs are a must. Retro plans are the more efficient net cost plans but represent significant challenges to budgeters. A list of plans from the least aggressive to the most aggressive self-insurance programs is presented next.

- Retention, sliding-scale dividend
- Incurred loss retro
- Paid–loss retro/deductible plan

- Fronted program
- Captive or self-insurance program

These plans are a function of two variables:

1. The amount of risk an insured is willing to take
2. Who retains the investment income from the loss reserves until paid in settlements

The first group of plans is one-way retros, meaning the insured assumes the least risk of additional premiums. The incurred losses in one year are then cut off and compared to a schedule of premiums and losses to determine a dividend. A dividend is then declared to the policyholder based on its individual experience. The plan is then closed, and any additional loss development on these claims in subsequent years is not charged back to the policyholder. The dividend schedule is the least aggressive and progresses rapidly with the plans mentioned as risk is taken and the insured retains the investment income on loss reserves.

In hard markets, carriers are very reluctant to price plans aggressively, and the insured may be relegated to guaranteed cost plans that allow no flexibility. The only loss is the premium payment regardless of the positive or negative loss experience of the policyholder. The plans outlined are relevant only to casualty policies such as workers' compensation, general or professional liability, and auto liability; the most popular clearly is workers' compensation.

A brief outline of the services needed to administer an aggressive self-insurance program is presented next. The intent of this analysis is to help management become familiar with the terms and functions of TPAs available to assist in the administration of a self-funded plan.

Actuarial Services

An actuary is a very sophisticated statistician who will predict future losses and their impact. Within certain confidence intervals, an actuary can predict future losses by both frequency and severity for years to come. These predictions are based on the analysis of past losses and other key factors pertinent to that particular business environment. This computation is largely the first step in any self-insurance analysis and forms the basis of the financial model to help management make a self-insurance decision.

Claims Administration and Reserving

Any self-insurance program requires an individually administered claims program. The function of a claims administrator is to assess the ultimate liability of a casualty claim (liability or workers' compensation) once it has occurred. The administrator uses the details of the claim and individual experience in the appropriate jurisdiction to estimate the ultimate costs for each claim. It is important to recognize the full extent of an obligation as soon as possible after its occurrence. These claim "reserves," or estimates of obligation to be paid in the future, form the basis for many elements of a self-insurance program, the actuarial analysis, the financial analysis, and the budget allocation for future obligations.

Information-Reporting Systems

Providing decision makers with claims and exposure information is a basic element in any risk-management program. If you do not know a problem exists, how can you deal with it? A good information-reporting system is a critical element in managing losses and controlling long-term costs.

Loss Control

Of equal importance to a risk manager, chief financial officer (CFO), or comptroller is the loss-control function. Simply stated, loss control is the process of pre- and postevent procedures to prevent, eliminate, or reduce losses and their financial impact on the firm.

Good loss-control services are a must for both insured *and* self-insured programs. Generally, an insurance company will provide limited loss control services, which clients often consider to be myopic and punitive in nature. Buyers need positive assistance to control loss costs and usually are more interested in these services offered by TPAs or agents/brokers. The reason for this perception appears to be a focus on loss control from the client's and not the insurance carriers' viewpoint. Although not always the case, TPAs or agent/broker loss-control services should be considered in the risk-management decision process.

Legal Representation

Choosing a competent defense firm is unquestionably important for a self-insurance program. In liability litigation, a competent defense firm can save a business many thousands of unnecessary dollars in defense costs as well as damage awards. "Without proper legal assistance, the success of our self-insured trust may not be as certain," says Ed Vanderloop, director of risk management and quality assurance, Ellis Hospital, Schenectady, New York.

When choosing legal representation, some of the discriminating elements are:

- Reputation
- Experience in the type of litigation pertinent to the business represented
- Referrals by colleagues
- Depth of staff
- Qualifications and experience of the attorney assigned to the business
- Communication procedures: frequency and form (written and/or oral)
- Parameters for settlement
- Participation of the defense firm in the risk-management program

Program Administration

Very often, a broker or consultant should be employed to help supervise and oversee the entire administration of the program. Any brokering commissions should be negotiated to eliminate double charges from the transaction. Double charges are commission and administrative fees. A consultant should be used in such situations to completely eliminate any feelings of conflict on the part of the client. This is not to say conflict exists with a broker; however, an arm's-length agreement will help to eliminate concerns.

 ## IDENTIFYING THE NEED FOR INSURANCE

In order to assess the need for insurance versus self-insurance (deductibles, etc.), management must identify how much risk is desirable or appropriate. This process involves a frank assessment by management.

Risk/Reward Scenarios

Using a risk/reward index is one example of a quantitative assessment model useful for comparison of various plans. Simply stated, it is an analysis of out-of-pocket losses expected against the reward anticipated. If the fraction created by this analysis exceeds 1, the risk exceeds the reward expectations. Management then has a simple index system to compare different risk scenarios.

Obviously, this is a simple model. It is not intended to be a panacea but rather a beginning method for analysis of insurance versus no insurance decisions. Also, the calculation of both elements included in this index may involve the use of very sophisticated statistical techniques, which are far beyond the purpose of this chapter. An example of the risk/reward index may be helpful.

Situation: A firm is considering changing its deductible for collision losses. The firm has ten vehicles with a current deductible for each vehicle of $250 per occurrence. How can the risk/reward index be utilized to determine the best alternative? (Note: The numbers in this analysis are illustrative only.)

1. *Decision:* Will increasing the deductible on the fleet be cost effective?
2. *Statement of facts:* Ten vehicles with collision deductibles of $250 per occurrence. Average annual collision loss equals 1.5 collisions/year. Annual premium savings per unit per year:

$$
\begin{aligned}
\$500 \text{ deductible} &= \$100 \text{ per vehicle} \\
\$1,000 \text{ deductible} &= \$140 \text{ per vehicle} \\
\$2,500 \text{ deductible} &= \$150 \text{ per vehicle}
\end{aligned}
$$

3. *Risk Calculation:*

$$\text{Risk} = 1.5 \text{ collisions/year}$$

Formula: New deductible – Old deductible × 1.5 = Losses per year

Risk Values after Formula:

$$
\begin{aligned}
\$500 \text{ deductible} &= 1,(\$500 - \$250) \times 1.5 &= \$1,375 \\
\$1,000 \text{ deductible} &= (\$1,000 - \$250) \times 1.5 &= \$1,125 \\
\$2,500 \text{ deductible} &= (\$2,500 - \$250) \times 1.5 &= \$3,375
\end{aligned}
$$

4. *Reward Calculations:* See Item 2.

   Please note: These calculations are *additional* savings over the existing $250 deductibles.

$$
\begin{aligned}
\$500 \text{ deductible} &= \$100/\text{vehicle} \times 10 = \$1,000 \\
\$1,000 \text{ deductible} &= \$140/\text{vehicle} \times 10 = \$1,400 \\
\$2,500 \text{ deductible} &= \$150/\text{vehicle} \times 10 = \$1,500
\end{aligned}
$$

5. *Risk/Reward Indices:*

$$
\begin{aligned}
\$500 \text{ deductible} &= 1.\$375/1,000 = .375 \\
\$1,000 \text{ deductible} &= \$1,125/1,400 = .804 \\
\$2,500 \text{ deductible} &= \$3,375/1,500 = 2.250
\end{aligned}
$$

The lowest index (0.375) represents the largest gain for the least risk. Depending on management's risk philosophy, the $500 deductible option would offer the best choice for the firm. Many managers will choose higher risk/reward choices. Why? There are as many answers as there are different attitudes.

Qualitative Evaluations

Management philosophies toward risk will play a very large role in any decision process. Some firms are more risk *adverse* than others and would choose a different deductible in the previous example. Also, if lowest net premium cost is important, then the $250 deductible option is most attractive to management. Even though the additional deductible expense must be paid at the time of loss, risk takers may be more comfortable paying the lowest premium now and taking their chances on no losses occurring, less severe losses occurring, or not repairing the damages if the vehicles' operation are only cosmetic. Obviously, there is no single correct answer for everyone.

If management considers *all* elements of long-term cost, the best alternative will involve direct attention to "pre-event" loss-control programs involving prevention, elimination, and reduction techniques as well as "postevent" controls, such as these:

▪ Superior loss adjusting
▪ Claims handling
▪ Medical/occupational rehabilitation
▪ Subrogation
▪ Claims review
▪ Communication techniques

The cost of losses themselves tends to represent only a fraction of the total cost due to unallocated expenses not generally recognized, such as:

▪ Production downtime
▪ Additional expense incurred to correct the situation

- Management and supervisory time to solve problems created by losses
- Loss of customer base through delays and nondelivery of merchandise or services
- Additional resources and time needed to settle losses
- Pain and suffering caused to all involved parties

Earnings Diminution Analysis

Another method of insurance versus noninsurance selection by management is the impact on earnings due to losses. Earning diminution is a very accurate yardstick to judge the risk philosophy of management. Putting a quantitative value on forgone earnings due to property and liability losses will quickly focus attention to the real costs of losses and risk treatment plans.

By using risk/reward scenarios, qualitative evaluations, and earnings diminution analysis, a manager can most readily assess the true cost of losses and insurance and how management sees risk. The preceding suggestions are only a few of the techniques used by management and others in the budget process to identify real cost and select the alternatives most appropriate for the firm.

Once identified, how does a manager select the amount, types, and most efficient insurance products to maximize the firm's objectives?

KEY INSURANCE COVERAGES

It may be helpful to briefly review the primary insurance coverages purchased by most firms. This analysis is not designed to be a complete review of all coverages available or risks to be treated, just a primary discussion of key coverages.

Property Coverages

All organizations own assets and therefore must protect them from physical loss or damage. In addition, most firms have mortgages or lienholders with financial interest in the preservation of these assets. These debt interests may force the organization to purchase insurance to protect their interest as well as the interest of the business firm.

The most important evaluation when purchasing property coverage is *value*. What is the value of the property? There are many value structures, each serving a different financial need. Some of these value structures include:

- Replacement or reproduction cost
- Actual cash value
- Book value
- Tax value
- Debt value
- Functional value/production value/earning value
- Real estate/market value
- Appraised value

Although this discussion may appear confusing, its aim is to help the purchaser or budgeter be aware of these variables and to ask the proper questions to identify which value system will apply at the time of loss. Choosing an inappropriate value system and protecting the incorrect value may render a completely inappropriate settlement and cause financial harm to the firm.

The next most important element in property insurance is the insuring agreements. What perils (causes of loss) is this property protected against? Most commonly, property is protected by two general coverage principals: named perils coverage or open perils coverage.

Specifically, named perils protect the property from only those perils named specifically and *not* excluded. Stated simply, special perils protection defines the actual coverage by the policy exclusions (perils not covered). This means everything is covered except that which is excluded. One needs only to be aware of this situation to properly prepare for the purchase of property insurance.

Generally, open perils coverage is preferred because there are more advantages in a broad policy statement with only the exclusions to manage. Perils such as earthquakes, flood, and property usually in transit are always exceptions and should be treated separately. If one analyzes the exclusions and the property *not* covered, a better picture will be available to the budgeter.

The use of deductibles is probably the largest cost element besides value. Property premiums are determined by many variables, but deductibles make up one of the larger variables. A good manager should investigate deductibles as a means to maximize premiums as well as a proactive management tool for a successful risk or insurance program.

Business interruption is one of the most misunderstood coverages and causes a significant amount of litigation between insureds and insurance companies. Basically, when an asset is destroyed, a resulting loss of revenue may occur. Most business assets are production assets, which add to the firm's revenues; without them, revenues are reduced. As budgeters and managers, analysis of the impact to revenues is extremely important. Business interruption is the property insurance used to cover these losses. The coverage is really analyzed as a "time" function as well as a lost revenue value issue. It is also generally defined by the cost elements in gross revenues regarding continuation or elimination after the loss. It is extremely urgent that a budgeter get assistance in the purchase of this coverage, as it is widely misunderstood but vital to the firm's financial health. Understanding this coverage is extremely important.

Several terms and conditions are generally encountered in the purchase of property coverages: blanket coverage, coinsurance, and agreed amount clauses. All three forms of property coverages help the insured and weaken the defenses of an insurance carrier. Property insurance is first-party coverage (the insured gets payment) and not usually considered adversarial. There are some defenses built into property coverage to assist the insurer maintain a proper premium base from which to pay losses. The most common idea is coinsurance. Simply stated, an insured may be penalized if he or she does not purchase enough coverages when losses are partial. This method puts "value" issues clearly at the door of the insured. To obviate the negative value issues at the time of the loss, insurance carriers commonly allow for exceptions if asked. The use of blanket coverage and agreed-amount clauses are methods that help eliminate value problems at the time of loss. Without enormous detail, a buyer should be aware of these techniques and request their use when buying property coverage.

Larger insureds can utilize other techniques to maximize the purchase of property insurance. Ideas such as dispersion analysis as evidenced by loss-limitation proposals, location or aggregate deductibles, and property retros are techniques available should a firm qualify. Generally, however, property insurance is not a very good candidate for self-insurance treatment, as losses are *not* readily predictable and tend to be too volatile by outcome and size to be insured. A good broker, carrier, or consultant is a must to maximize options.

Casualty Coverages

Casualty coverages are identified by payments being made on behalf of the insured to a third party. The coverages are termed *liability* protection and typically include general liability, product liability, employee benefits liability, auto liability, fiduciary liability, umbrella liability, and workers' compensation. This coverage protects the firm from claims made against it by third parties alleging damages to themselves or their property. This coverage also includes defense of the firm and payment of any judgment up to the limits of liability purchased.

Purchasing the property liability limits is extremely important to any firm. Receiving a judgment in excess of policy limits could easily bankrupt a firm. The purchase of adequate limits has been the subject of a great deal of debate and has evolved into many theories proclaiming the correct answer. A wise buyer will seek assistance from many counselors in this area. The correct answer is the one most suitable to the firm from an expense, security, and risk-attitude perspective.

A buyer should be aware of the variables in the policies confronting them. Most insurance language has been standardized through the Insurance Services Office (ISO). ISO is an organization supported by the insurance companies that conducts policy research for rate and form standardization for its member companies. The purpose for its formation was basically economic in nature. There are many thousands of insurance carriers that cannot afford to conduct individual statistical gatherings for rate-making or policy wording and testing. Very often, the companies did not have the resources or personnel needed for these functions. Therefore, member companies pool resources in ISO to perform these functions.

It is important that policies be reviewed. It is reasonably certain that ISO forms are acceptable, as the wording is standard. Like most insurance policies, the coverages are granted and defined by the exclusions. It is vital that all exclusions be checked and any uncertainty be addressed in writing by the broker, consultant, or insurer. There are several liability forms, which are not standardized.

Fiduciary and employee benefits liability are examples of two such nonstandard forms. Also, workers' compensation is not necessarily an adversarial coverage such as liability. Workers' compensation is heavily controlled by state regulatory authorities. Since the coverage is statutory in nature, both coverages and rates are heavily controlled. Workers' compensation is basically no-fault protection for the employee and his or her family. The coverage provides for on-the-job medical protection as well as reimbursement for lost-time wages due to employment injuries. Coverage disputes are usually settled by a nonlitigious review board, thereby eliminating the right for an employee to sue his employer. Several states currently have an adversarial system, but the majority do not. It is wise to seek competent advice for the firm's situation.

Recently, the insurance market pricing was extremely competitive and did offer the best bargaining power for the firm. It is usually beneficial to shop for all insurance coverages, but the firm's casualty coverage may be the most important. A large firm has a good opportunity for self-insurance options due to the nature of casualty losses. Generally, losses are numerous and are small in severity. However, the exceptional single large loss costing millions of dollars has received much attention. These losses are not the norm. In hard markets, loyalty plays a larger part between insurers and insureds. Multiple yearly quoting often creates a feeling of abuse by underwriters. They may be unwilling to offer terms and conditions to an account seen year after year with no positive outcome. It is wise to plan a complete strategy for optimal use of market resources.

Casualty premiums are usually a function of limits purchased, actual exposure and operations, type of coverage, and geographic area of operations. Specific cost drivers are discussed separately later in this chapter. Casualty coverages tend to cost more in direct relation to the size of the firm. Casualty coverages are also good candidates for deductibles or self-insured retentions as a tool for modified self-insurance options. Also, premium payments may be made on an interval basis without interest charges.

Crime Coverage

The entire issue of crime protection is often overlooked by many insurance purchasers but can be an area of severe losses. Identification of the types of crimes that may affect the firm's net worth are generally divided into employer and third-party crimes. The insurance industry distinguishes crimes further by the type of property taken (i.e., cash versus inventory). Another breakdown is usually where the crime occurs as well as the circumstances (i.e., robbery of money on or off premises versus burglary of merchandise or money on premises only). Each scenario is different and requires specific insurance treatment. Seeking expert counsel is a must in this area.

The largest premium variables are limits purchased, protection, and area of the firm's operation. Managing these variables can be a real challenge. It is also imperative to understand the definitions and exclusions of crime policies, as each is very specifically defined. Some of the largest losses have been linked to crime perils, and protection against these occurrences is a must.

Directors and Officers Liability

Directors and officers liability (D&O) coverage pays damages to third-part claimants against "wrongful acts" by the directors and officers. This coverage indemnifies the corporation and its directors and officers against such suits. The "wrongful acts," which is defined very broadly implies a violation of a duty causing damages. Acts of the board that cause physical injuries to persons or damage to property are covered by the general liability policy of the firm, not the D&O policy. There are many other damages that may be caused by director's decisions; some are covered, many are not:

- Discrimination
- Loss of pension or profit-sharing profits under Employee Retirement Insurance Security Act (ERISA) statutes
- A decision causing the firm to lose earnings or value
- A decision violating human rights
- Use of corporate resources for the personal gain of a director(s)
- A myriad of other breaches of the duties of loyalty, reasonable care, and obedience

As always, competent advice is needed to secure the proper coverage for the firm. D&O liability is a particular specialty and requires special understanding and research on behalf of the buyer or advisor.

There are many variables in the purchase of D&O coverage, including nonstandardized policy forms, deductibles per director as well as per occurrence, percentage deductibles per director, corporate reimbursement deductibles, coordination with corporate bylaws, specific exclusions, different policy definitions of "wrongful acts," and other acts or decisions of a board or individual officer. These variables and others will have a different impact on both premium and coverage availability in the event of a D&O lawsuit.

In addition, special care is needed, as a mistake will affect the most influential persons in the organization who are usually the most powerful. Many careers can be altered forever by a mistake in a firm's D&O coverage. A more detailed analysis of this volatile coverage is beyond the purpose of this analysis but is highly recommended for anyone responsible for purchasing D&O protection.

After this brief discussion of some appropriate coverages, it may be opportune to determine how to purchase insurance, how premiums are determined and carriers rated, how to use the risk-management process, and what this means to the budget function.

Fiduciary/Pension Trust Liability

In addition to D&O needs, diligent attention to two more areas producing substantial litigation activity is necessary. These areas are fiduciary/pension trust liability and employment practices liability. Fiduciary liability has been created by ERISA statutes for employee benefit plans. Employment practices have been created by collective litigation from injured victims.

Fiduciary liability creates responsibility for anyone managing or investing funds for any employee benefit plan. What constitutes an employee benefit plan? Generally, it is any program established or maintained by an employer or employee/organization for the purpose of providing benefits to employees or beneficiaries are usually considered employee benefit plans. Examples include pension, profit sharing, health, 401(k)/403(b), sick pay, vacation pay, or severance pay plans.

One can become a fiduciary in several ways; you, or your position, may be identified as the fiduciary. You, or your position, may manage plan assets or may have discretionary responsibility for plan administration.

What are the responsibilities of a fiduciary? A fiduciary must:

- Conduct all activities for the sole benefit of plan participants.
- Exercise the care and diligence of a prudent person familiar with the administration of similar plans.
- Be sure plan investments are diversified to minimize large losses to plan participants.
- Act in a manner consistent with the legal documents of the plan, or if these documents are confusing, in compliance with the ERISA statutes.

Although these requirements may appear confusing and conflicting, their enforcement is sure and reinforced by the courts in most jurisdictions. Fiduciary/pension trust liability insurance is an inexpensive solution to this morass. The coverage is readily available and moderately priced. Budgeting this coverage into a firm's risk treatment plan may save the career of an uninformed CFO or comptroller. A fiduciary can be individually named in a suit even if he or she has delegated fiduciary duties to a third party, insurance carrier, or bank.

Employment Practices Liability

Another liability created by recent litigation is employment practices liability (EPL). Many societal factors have contributed to these challenges, such as corporate downsizing, discrimination challenges, wrongful termination challenges, sexual harassment, invasion of privacy, defamation, emotional distress, and mental anguish.

The alleged victims are demanding damages from employed individuals, directors and officers, and the corporate entity itself. Some courts have allowed punitive damages in addition to compensatory and special damages. Any person or organization is vulnerable to attack.

Once again, EPL coverage is readily available. The coverage forms are not standard and have been evolving for several years. Deductibles, retentions, claims made forms, and policy warrants are the current arenas for this protection. A wise buyer will require the insurance representative to make a thorough market survey and coverage review or comparison for management's consideration.

Very often, EPL can be added to a firm's D&O policy for a nominal charge. When this is done, the D&O aggregate limit is generally shared, which may prove unacceptable to management. The purchase of additional limits may be a solution. A budgeter should consult with the risk management representative for a complete evaluation of needs and costs.

IDENTIFYING YOUR OWN RISKS

From a planning standpoint, every risk that goes unidentified has the potential to cause an unexpected loss and reduce earnings without ever being treated. An unplanned loss can ruin a successful budget and reduce the collective efforts of the entire firm.

The past indicates the future. Past experiences are an excellent place to begin test assumptions about loss patterns. This is an appropriate technique for casualty losses but not generally acceptable for losses from property perils, such as fire, earthquakes, windstorms, and flood. The reasons for this range from the highly fortuitous nature of property perils to the catastrophic nature of floods and earthquakes. The more unpredictable the loss, the more difficult to predict the likely outcomes. "So," one says, "what aspects can a buyer control and how does one choose the proper limits, perils, and prices?" The next brief discussion assists with the proper thought process.

Property is divided into two distinct categories: (1) real property and (2) personal property. The term "real property" usually applies to buildings and other property permanently attached to the building or pertaining to the service of same. One should check property coverage for an exact definition. The term "personal property" usually applies to all other property owned that is not real property. Often, property coverage is written on a replacement cost basis for real property but an actual cash value basis on personal property representing a depreciated value may be substantially lower.

Real-property values are usually determined from a replacement or functional replacement value. This should not be compared with book value, assessed value, going-concern value, or any other value system in vogue. The safest method of determining property values is by purchasing an appraisal from a reputable insurance appraisal firm. Many good firms can determine replacement cost, actual cash value, and functional replacement cost and defend their findings to an insurer, public adjuster, or court. Brokers sometimes provide this service but usually disclaim the values as they are not generally licensed appraisers.

Should buyers wish to appraise their own property, some appraisal firms sell guides to assist amateurs. Depending on budget constraints, this may offer the only alternative to choosing proper values. Contents values, however, are a bit trickier.

There are too many variables in choosing values for business and personal property to be considered in this presentation; however, a brief analysis is possible. Replacement cost is the cost for like, kind, and quality of the property to be replaced. A buyer should begin with an inventory of all physical assets and update this inventory as property is added and deleted. Usually a firm does not keep a running inventory of personal property and can only estimate personal values from the balance sheet. Unfortunately, the balance-sheet values may be extremely inaccurate, as the original cost may be a far cry from current replacement cost. In addition, physical assets are depreciated, which may further exacerbate the problem. Once again, a professional appraisal is available as a tool to assist the budgeter.

Estimating the cost of raw materials, goods in process, and finished goods inventories are a bit easier as the balance sheet and generally accepted accounting principles rules help to keep inventory values at a consistent value basis. Often the accounting procedures for inventory including the tax ramifications are at odds with each other regarding insurance values. Using a last-in, first-out or first-in, first-out system may alter values considerably during high inflationary periods. The selling price of finished goods may also be insured. This covers the gross margin as well as the actual cost of the product. It is important for a budgeter to know which value system is best for the firm and to then make an educated decision. Since the premium is a direct function of values insured, higher limits means more expense. An alternative to selling price coverage may be accomplished with proper business-interruption protection. A brief discussion is presented next.

Business interruption protection is designed to protect the firm from loss of certain revenues resulting from a property loss to a firm's production facilities. There are many different business interruption forms, and an analysis of their specific terms and conditions is beyond the purpose of this chapter. A budgeter would serve the firm well by assuring a complete understanding of business interruption coverage and limits.

Business interruption forms define gross earnings as "the reduction in gross earnings less non-continuing expenses." In other words, this statement translates to continuing expenses and gross profit lost for the time it takes to restore the operations to capacity. Business interruption is then a function of two variables: production value and the time for restoration. Any analysis of proper limits must involve a complete study of these two variables as well as the exact policy terms and conditions.

Another coverage that may be appropriate for the firm is extra expense coverage. *Extra expenses* are costs necessary to allow a firm to continue operations after a property loss to production facilities. An example might be helpful: A service organization suffers a huge flood, which shuts down its office building for 13 days. Management sets up facilities for customer service in another location. Extra expense would provide funds for the extra cost of telephone, movers, advertising to notify clients, and overtime wages needed to set up the temporary facilities as long as the loss was caused by an insured peril. In this specific case, the firm needed extra expense coverage for flood perils.

Choosing the proper limits for both business interruption and extra expense is aided by the use of worksheets designed to assist the firm in calculating its exposure. A budgeter should consult the firm's broker or carrier for advice and details. There are also other factors to consider when analyzing business interruption exposures, such as insured perils, manufacturing processes, contingent business interruption, disaster planning, alternative locations, construction economy, cost of capital, sales cycles, and modern building codes, which all have an effect on a budgeter's buying decisions. The last area of value assessment for property coverages is the area of irreplaceable or very old equipment. Often production equipment outlasts its book value. Also, the industry does not change substantially to warrant reinvestment: The old equipment still produces efficiently. If there is no active used-equipment market and/or the technology is very specialized, how does one restore or replace the damaged equipment?

Management must plan for the replacement and ascertain specific appraised values on this type of equipment. Machinery appraisers, like jewelry appraisers, are skilled in the valuation of such equipment. Value may still not solve the dilemma of availability. Perhaps this equipment must be operated in a secure environment to be certain it cannot be lost in a catastrophe. Clearly, risk management or loss prevention techniques may be more valuable than insuring to the proper value. Possibly the only answer is to upgrade equipment when a loss occurs. With this scenario, the budgeter may find a severe shortfall between the appraised value and the replacement cost for modern equipment. If this could be the case, it is wise to know before the loss occurs. Having to replace equipment before its time can ruin a firm's capital budget and may severely impair its revenue stream. Such scenarios can easily cost a budgeter's job in the process.

HOW TO BUDGET FOR CASUALTY PREMIUMS

Choosing the best casualty program is a subject of a great deal of analysis and controversy. The proper limits, perils, exclusions, conditions, and rating program requires a discussion far in excess of space available herein. As a buyer, professional help is a must to evaluate all the variables. As a budgeter, casualty coverages are variable expenses, and understanding the premium cost drivers is a must for the budgeting process.

Basically, premiums for workers' compensation and general liability coverages vary directly with payroll and sales. It is important for a budgeter to know the rates applicable per unit of variation (payroll/sales) to project ultimate premiums. The estimated annual premium is exactly that, an estimate. At the beginning of the policy period, estimates for payrolls and sales are used to calculate the policy premium. At the end of the policy period, an audit is conducted and the premium is recomputed based on the actual exposures. Obviously, this can cause great fluctuations in the premium charged and wonderful surprises for the uninformed. Often this audit feature can be used as a capital source when the firm is growing.

Specifically, the firm can understate expected sales and payroll to minimize the estimated premiums and use the *saved* premium to help fund the firm's growth. The bill for this growth must be paid later and could cause great distress for the firm's future earnings and tax implications. This method of funds management has been used effectively by many firms but lasts only as long as the insurance carrier remains unaware (usually one year). This method also has limitations in the areas of cost allocation and financial management and is not recommended as a substitute for good capital management.

Another feature of casualty variables is the audit limitations in both payroll and sales. In other words, not all sales and payroll data are counted. Often there are limits on maximum payroll chargeable per person and certain payroll classes are completely eliminated, such as drivers, driver's helpers, executive officers, clerical workers, and draftsmen. These features are prevalent in general liability, and some are applicable to workers' compensation. A wise budgeter must know how casualty program coverages are priced and the rating rules applicable.

As the firm grows, very often casualty premiums are driven by losses and in programs generally termed "loss sensitive." The plans are largely variations on retro plans, where losses and administrative charges are separated and the loss element drives the ultimate premium costs. These type of plans are most prevalent in workers' compensation coverages but may be combined with liability and automobile coverages for larger firms. Generally these plans maximize administrative costs, cash flow, benefits, and loss-control features, such as elimination and reduction techniques.

From the position of budgeting, the ultimate net costs of these programs are not determined until each loss is ultimately settled. It may take five to eight years before the ultimate costs are absolutely determined.

Obviously, this is an extreme impediment to accurate budgeting. Attention to proper loss reserving will help estimate ultimate costs and relate them to the proper revenue periods. The reserve, when calculated by a credible and recognized expert, may be used as an identified cost element in the current revenue period. For complete analysis, the firm should consult proper accounting and tax expertise.

The remainder of the property and casualty insurance products purchased by the firm are flat-charge premiums with no variation except for the amount purchased, perils, and actual exposure to loss. It should be noted that most insurers will apportion the annual premium into installments if requested. Usually these installments are available for no interest charge or a small administrative service charge. If the carrier refuses to provide installments, the premium may be financed by finance companies at competitive interest rates. In addition, this financing does not impair the firm's credit as the debt is entirely secured by the equity in the policy represented in the unearned premium. As such, the finance agreements are not entered as current liabilities. One should consult proper accounting advice for a complete explanation of this feature. The foregoing discussion has been attempted as a how-to purchase analysis of property and casualty coverages. It is only an outline and requires further study before competent budgeting decisions can be made for each firm. No such treatise would be complete without a discussion of the carriers or insurance companies, as discussed next.

Property and casualty carriers continue to be regulated on a state level through a federal exemption granted under the McCarren Ferguson Act. This federal document continues to grant state authority for regulation of carriers, rates, forms, and the proper conduct of this business. The reasons for this federal exemption are many, and this act is under constant attack for repeal. To date, state jurisdiction remains.

Having 50 separate regulatory bodies may cause some confusion and create some gaps in the administration of this industry due to unequal tax bases, talent availability, and legislative prioritization. All regulation attempts to balance the issues of insurer solvency and unfairly discriminatory rates. If the rates are too high, the carriers may be solvent but the taxpayer is gouged. If the rates are too low, the taxpayer has an immediate benefit in lower premiums but a long-term problem is insurer solvency. Since carriers are regulated by the states, solvency is also state regulated. In order to help a buyer understand the solvency issue, a brief discussion of the types of insurers may be helpful. An insurance company may operate in a state under many legal definitions, including admitted, licensed, nonadmitted, alien, and foreign. The most common types are admitted and nonadmitted insurers. Both are licensed by the state to conduct business, but their status and legal definitions are different.

Admitted Carrier

Admitted carrier is the most desirable status from a consumer standpoint for these reasons:

- There is a larger policyholder surplus requirement making it more secure to pay losses.
- An insolvency of an admitted carrier gives a policyholder access to state insolvency funds to pay losses incurred.
- The state regulatory body spends more time analyzing the financial health of an admitted carrier. This provides an early-warning mechanism for policyholders to enable them to choose another company.

Nonadmitted Carrier

A nonadmitted carrier may be a very secure company but chooses to operate on this legal basis for many reasons. Generally, policyholders of nonadmitted insurers do *not* have the protection of state insolvency funds to help secure their policies. Also, a nonadmitted carrier may have substantially less policyholder surplus required to operate and transact business. The carrier may choose to operate on this basis to avoid regulation for forms and rates. Therefore, a buyer must be more aware of the terms and conditions of policies when dealing with a nonadmitted carrier.

Very often, a buyer must also pay a user fee, known as a surplus lines tax, to use a nonadmitted carrier, which thereby raises the price of the coverage. Why, then, would a buyer use a surplus lines carrier? The primary reasons are:

- Unique coverage needs not readily available in the traditional market, such as errors and omissions, hazardous liability protection (blasting, scaffolding, etc.), or high-limit situations, such as reinsurance or excess umbrella capacity limits over $50 million
- More competitive terms for both form and rate
- Unique needs, such as financial guarantee coverages or substandard risks (vacant buildings or high-crime-area property)

It is always wise for buyers to consider *all* alternatives as long as they have identified the risks inherent in each alternative. In order to rate insurance carriers, buyers may gain access to some available resources, including:

- A. M. Best's rating guides
- Moody's insurance rating guides
- The insurance department in the appropriate state
- A broker or consultant
- Other policyholder in the same carrier

Frequently, large brokers maintain security committees that analyze insurance companies and report to their branch offices. This is clearly a feature that is highly desirable and valuable to the policyholder. Many buyers choose their broker on such capabilities and expertise, not merely on premium cost. A wise buyer analyzes *value*, not only price. In addition, the broker maintaining such a function may create an additional obligation to a client and increase additional benefit to help further secure the contrast.

There really is no absolute guarantee to a policyholder that benefits will be payable at the time of a loss. Features such as those mentioned in this chapter help increase the policyholder's chances of a positive financial outcome but surely they are not a guarantee. Insurance carriers are businesses, and their rates are a function of competition, economies, management, and regulation. A wise buyer tries to manage these variables using the tools of proper information, professional representation, and careful monitoring of the insurer's economic health.

SUMMARY

The purpose of this chapter is to assist persons responsible for the risk-management function in a firm and to apply it to the budgeting process. Only through the understanding of the choices, process, and variables in the purchase of property and casualty coverages can a manager truly help his or her firm. The risks are great and the stakes are high for imprudent or improper decisions.

The most important and overriding element to proper budgeting is the gathering of credible information from professional sources. In property and casualty coverages, the team is usually composed of legal, accounting, and professional insurance advice from an agent, broker, or consultant. Understanding the meaning of some of the coverages is always helpful. Understanding the premium variables, deductible applicability, the hidden cost of losses, and asset valuation is a must for any budgeter. Without this understanding, there are too many variables and too much fluctuation in costs.

The chapter discussed some of these variables:

- The risk-management process
- Available insurance mechanisms
- Role of insurance/risk consultants
- Role of brokers/agents
- Other TPA and service providers
- One quantitative model: risk/reward index
- Identification of risk/values
- Property and casualty coverages
- Managing insurance insolvencies

If this analysis is to be successful, it must be used. Although property and casualty is usually a small expense item as a percentage of gross sales, the impact to asset preservation and conservation as well as maintaining revenues is extremely critical. If a firm's resources of production are destroyed, the firm's ability to generate revenues may also be hampered. Depending on the severity of this destruction, the firm may perish or at least be weakened.

Risk and budgeting managers must avoid this outcome or be a possible party to the detriment of the firm's solvency.

PART FOUR

Budgeting Applications

CHAPTER TWENTY-NINE

Budgeting: Key to Corporate Performance Management

Michael Coveney
Comshare, Incorporated

FUTURE OF BUDGETING

It will come as no surprise to learn that budgeting is one of the most detested management processes. Senior executives view budgeting as an expensive waste of resources for which they receive little return. Budget holders see it as irrelevant to their real work. Because most budgets seem to be out of date within the first few months of operation, there is a great deal of concern that the whole process just is not worth the time, effort, or cost.

For many, budgeting today is mainly an annual ritual in which senior management and budget holders play a game. The game rewards those who exceed set targets, a goal that in itself becomes an incentive to set low targets instead of high—or maybe even realistic—targets. As a result, budget holders pad the budget as much as possible in anticipation of receiving the inevitable top-down budget from senior management; by padding the budget, budget holders ensure they will have enough slack in which to operate. It is a game where, in the long run, everyone loses. Organizational focus is concentrated on who plays the game better rather than on how the organization can beat the competition.

Another problem with the budgeting ritual is that it tends to take place just once a year. This means that the organization is trying to predict events that are up to 16 months away. In today's fast-paced economic environment that sees markets changing on a quarterly basis and product life cycles that are measured in months, an annual budget process makes no sense at all.

Some organizations have tried to get rid of the budgeting process altogether. Doing so, however, is not a realistic proposition; budgeting is the key process through which management can change and direct organizational behavior.

If budgeting is to survive, it has to make sense and it has to add value to the organization. Consequently, it is not good enough just to make the process more efficient. After all, what is the value of shortening the budgeting cycle by one month if the resulting budget is still irrelevant after only a few months? The focus of any revised budgeting process has to be on helping the organization compete more effectively in the marketplace. Budgeting is long overdue for a major overhaul.

ADDING VALUE TO THE ORGANIZATION

To be effective, organizations must develop and implement strategic plans aimed at beating the competition. While many organizations formalize this process, their ability to actually implement their strategic plans is in doubt.

In 2001, more than 250 U.S. organizations—with a combined asset value exceeding $255 billion—failed. At the time this is being written, companies are on track to match that figure in 2002. More than 25 percent of the top 100 U.S. companies that survived in 2001 lost at least 66 percent of their market capitalization.[1] Certainly this level of performance was not planned. Assuming that their strategic plans were good plans, why did those organizations fail to implement them? Perhaps more important, why didn't they manage to change those plans when they saw that they were not going to succeed? What is it about the strategic planning process and its execution that fails?

These are crucial questions that need to be answered. In a survey by Ernst & Young, investors were asked what nonfinancial factors they looked for in a company. The top answer was not the quality of their strategy. It was the ability of management to implement their strategy (see Exhibit 29.1).[2] Without the capability to achieve objectives, executives and managers become mere bystanders in an organization where performance—or nonperformance—"just happens."

If the implementation of strategy is so vital, then the systems that support the process must be equally important. This view is supported by a study of 113 companies located in the United States, Europe, and Asia, half of which had $5 billion or more in annual revenue. The study revealed that companies with a formal strategic performance measurement system performed better in the stock market than did their peers.[3]

Consider the value of combining processes with a supporting system that enables an organization to beat analysts' expectations by a penny a share, that enables strategy to be implemented quickly and successfully, or that warns the organization when current or future performance is unlikely to meet strategic goals. This type of value is the goal of corporate performance management (CPM).

---

[1] Ram Charan and Jerry Useem, "Why Companies Fail," *Fortune,* May 27, 2002.

[2] Ernst & Young, *Measures that Matter*™ (2000), p. 12.

[3] Dr. Stephen Gates, "Aligning Strategic Performance Measures and Results," The Conference Board, delivered to Balanced Scorecard Interest Group, Washington, D.C., November 14, 2001, p. 10.

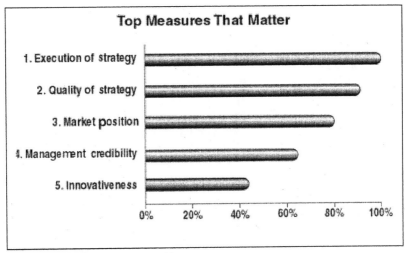

Top Measures That Matter

1. Execution of strategy
2. Quality of strategy
3. Market position
4. Management credibility
5. Innovativeness

0%   20%   40%   60%   80%   100%

Source: Ernst & Young, Measures that Matter™

EXHIBIT 29.1   Investors Value Corporations that Execute Strategies

CORPORATE PERFORMANCE MANAGEMENT

CPM is the term coined by Gartner, the Stamford, Connecticut-based research and advisory firm, which defines it as "an umbrella term that describes the methodologies, metrics, processes and systems used to monitor and manage the business performance of an enterprise."[4] In this context, methodologies include management techniques such as balanced scorecard, economic value added, and activity-based management. Metrics are the specific measures used within those methodologies. Processes are the procedures that an organization follows to implement and monitor corporate performance, while systems are the technology solutions that combine all of the above into a single, enterprise-wide management system focused on the successful implementation and execution of strategy.

In the past, organizations have used a mixture of discrete systems from multiple vendors, employing a variety of methodologies and metrics to measure and manage corporate performance. However, this approach has resulted in fragmented silos of data that are difficult to integrate, that cannot be effectively deployed across the enterprise, and that have little or no focus on strategy. Similarly, organizations that have tried to use their enterprise resource planning (ERP) systems to deliver CPM all have been disappointed. According to Gartner, two reasons for this disappointment include the complexity of those systems and the closed architectures that make it difficult to integrate non-ERP data.[5]

What makes CPM systems different is that they leverage technology and best business practices to answer the key questions around the formulation and implementation

---

[4] Lee Geishecker and Nigel Rayner, *Corporate Performance Management: BI Collides with ERP*, Research Note SPA-14-9282, Gartner, Inc., December 17, 2001, p. 1.

[5] Ibid., p. 3.

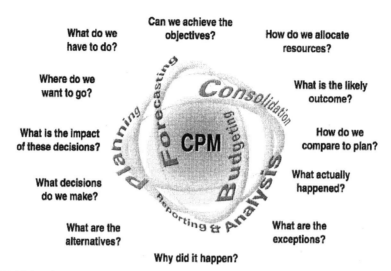

EXHIBIT 29.2 CPM Systems Help Answer Questions Used to Formulate Strategy

Source: Comshare, Incorporated.

of strategy. This is a closed-loop process that starts with understanding where the organization is today, where it wants to go to, what targets should be set, and how resources should be allocated to achieve those targets (see Exhibit 29.2). Once plans have been set, CPM systems then monitor the performance of those plans, highlight exceptions, and provide insight as to why exceptions have occurred. CPM systems support the evaluation of alternatives from which decisions can be made regarding organizational direction.

In summary, CPM systems:

- Integrate planning, budgeting, forecasting, consolidation, reporting, and analysis processes.
- Support methodologies for linking strategy to the allocation of resources (financial and nonfinancial) in support of strategies that can be transformed into action.
- Help executives communicate and drive strategy down throughout the enterprise in a way that enables people to act and make decisions that support strategic goals.
- Help members of the organization focus on key issues and critical data rather than on all the data and events that are possible.
- Deliver the right information to the right people at the right time and in the right context.

DEVELOPING A BUDGET PROCESS FOCUSED ON IMPLEMENTATION OF STRATEGY

The formulation of strategy should be the driving force in designing a CPM solution. The budget process determines how—and how well—the strategies are implemented. Therefore, the budgeting model—that is, the accounts and structures used to enter and monitor a budget—must be designed around strategies and the associated tactical plans. In addition, users must be able to see how the strategies specifically affect them and how their decisions and actions impact the strategies. This strategic focus when creating budgets and reporting actual results is a departure from traditional budgeting and reporting processes that tend to focus on cost centers and charts of accounts.

The design of a CPM system is a big topic and cannot be covered in detail in this chapter. However, the next five steps describe ways in which the budgeting process can be adapted to support CPM.[6]

Step 1: Define Measures Necessary to Implement Strategy

The first step in designing the CPM budget data model is to review the strategic and tactical plans. In this context, tactical plans are the specific action steps that map out how each strategy will be implemented to achieve strategic goals.

As an example, a manufacturer of consumer electronics may have a strategy to improve sales productivity. The goal is to achieve revenue of $250,000 per salesperson. To achieve this goal, operational management has identified the two tactics: to grow the cellular product line by 25 percent and to keep cost of sales to 15 percent of total revenues.

For each tactic and associated goal, these points need to be determined:

- The base measures and their associated business dimensions (i.e., year, region, product, etc.), which are required to plan and measure the associated goals.
- The assumptions being made about the economic and competitive climate that could impact goal achievement. In some industries, this external information can be purchased. Otherwise, some form of research will be required. If it cannot be purchased or researched, consider this saying: If you can't measure it, don't plan for it.
- Key performance indicators (KPIs). KPIs are the critical measures that tell an organization whether a tactic is working. In addition, leading indicators should be employed to warn the organization if a goal is likely to be missed.
- The person(s) responsible for achieving the goal. If no one is responsible, there is nothing to manage.

In Exhibit 29.3, a form has been used to document answers to these questions relative to the example just described.

With this information, the organization can determine how it will plan and track each initiative (see Exhibit 29.4). The KPIs used to monitor the success of each tactic will come from this list. In this example, the KPIs will be revenue, product growth, cost as a percentage of revenue, number of sales representatives, and product volume as a percentage of production. This process needs to be repeated for each strategy, tactic, and goal.

---

[6] For a more in-depth study, refer to Michael Coveney, Dennis Ganster, Brian Hartlen, and Dave King, *The Strategy Gap: Leveraging Technology to Execute Winning Strategies* (Hoboken, NJ: John Wiley & Sons, 2003).

EXHIBIT 29.3 Defining Measures for Strategy Implementation

Strategy: Improve Sales Productivity				
Tactics and Goal(s)	**Budget Center**	**Measures**	**Other Related Business Dimensions**	**Frequency of Measurements**
Achieve sales of $250,000 per sales rep	Sales	Sales revenue	By person	Monthly
Grow cellular product line by 25% over last year		Volume	By product	
Keep sales costs within 15% of total revenues		Cost of goods		
		Salaries		
		Commission		
		Other sales expense		

External Business Assumptions to Be Monitored
Average sales per head of peer organizations
Cellular market share

Internal Threats	**Leading Indicators to Monitor**
Not enough sales reps	Number of sales reps and their level of experience
Production cannot meet demand	
	Cellular product line production levels

Level of Detail to Support Monitoring	**Level of Detail to Support Forecasting**
Revenue and volume by product, customer and sales rep	Volume by product
	Revenue by sales rep

Source: Comshare, Incorporated.

EXHIBIT 29.4 Determine KPIs for Each Strategy, Tactic, and Goal

Planning and Tracking by Initiative	
Base measures and dimensions	Revenue to be monitored by person
	Volume by product
	COGs, salaries, and commissions by department
External assumptions to be tracked	Average sales per head in competitor organizations
	Market share for cellular phones
Leading indicators to be used as alerts	Number of sales representatives and their level of experience (experienced people tend to sell more)
Responsibility	Divisional sales managers

Source: Comshare, Incorporated.

Step 2: Define Additional Measures for Reporting

Once the measures have been determined for strategies, tactics, and goals, the next step is to identify additional measures—by the appropriate business dimensions—that will be required to generate management and financial reports. This will allow the budgeting model to report not only the progress of strategic implementation but also the impact on financial results.

Step 3: Group Measures into Related Schedules

Schedules are simply groupings of accounts that share the same set of business dimensions. Once created, these schedules are presented to budget holders for entering and monitoring their budgets. It is important to ensure that strategic initiatives can be planned and tracked individually. Some measures will appear in multiple schedules and need to be linked so the total value of the measure is held only once in the system.

Step 4: Identify Model Structures

The previous steps have concentrated on determining the accounts to be budgeted. In this step, the various business dimensions, associated members, and structures need to be determined. Some dimensions, such as the organizational structure, may also have multiple versions, such as geographic, responsibility, and alternative structures. Therefore, it is necessary to use a multidimensional system to implement a CPM solution.

Step 5: Define How Strategy Will Be Presented to Users

CPM systems are essentially a portal or gateway through which users plan and monitor performance. These systems are web based. That is, a web browser—such as Microsoft Internet Explorer—is the main mechanism through which users access the system, although options for spreadsheet and PDA device access also may be offered.

Through this portal or gateway, users should be able to access details of organizational strategy and see how they impact that strategy. Information can include a situation analysis, assumptions about the economic environment, and how major competitors are faring. Exhibits 29.5 and 29.6 provide an example of a portal that allows users to see strategies, tactics, and how each department contributes to goals. When the user selects the relevant icon (Exhibit 29.5), the target set by senior management and the progress to date toward that target appear (Exhibit 29.6). The user also sees who is responsible for the target and how often performance will be measured.

When entering budgeting data, users should be shown the expected targets but should also be allowed to comment on their ability to meet those targets. In the next example (Exhibit 29.7), having entered the budget for each tactic, the user is presented with a summary of each tactic and is shown a variance to the targets set by senior management. In addition, text comments were added when the budget was submitted and reviewed, improving enterprise-wide understanding of the numbers that support strategic initiatives.

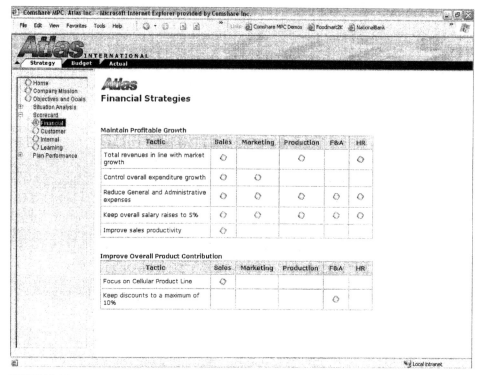

EXHIBIT 29.5 A CPM Portal Allows System Users to View Organizational Strategies, Tactics, and Goals

Source: Comshare, Incorporated.

By adhering to the preceding five guidelines for budgeting, management can easily ask and answer these questions when reviewing the budget:

- Which tactics do we want to fund?
- Which tactics cannot be implemented within the set limits?
- What do budget holders have to say about those tactics?
- If we need to reduce costs, which tactics do we eliminate and how will this impact strategy?

Similarly, once the budget has been approved, the success of each tactic can be monitored. Variances lead to discussions about which tactics are working, which tactics need revision, and what other actions could be taken to improve performance. In all cases, the focus is on implementing strategy.

ROLE OF TECHNOLOGY

CPM systems do far more than simply collect and report numbers. They exist to support users as they perform the various processes necessary to implementing and monitoring

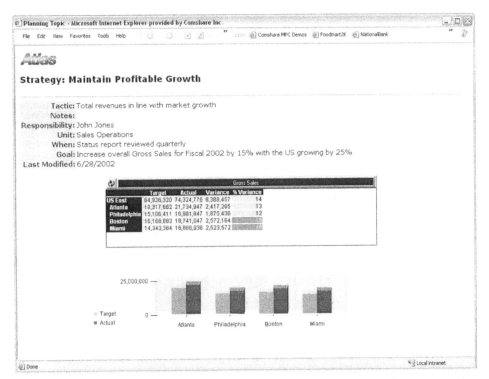

EXHIBIT 29.6   CPM System Users Monitor Their Performance against Strategic Tactics and Goals

Source: Comshare, Incorporated.

strategy. In looking at CPM early adopters, Gartner concludes that "the success of their solutions depended on the capabilities of the vendor chosen for their BI applications."[7] Evaluating a CPM solution is far too big a topic for a single chapter. However, nine characteristics that CPM systems display are described here.

1. *Integrated.* CPM systems encompass planning, budgeting, forecasting, financial consolidation, reporting, and analysis, and treat them as a single, continuous process. They support senior management in the evaluation, selection, and communication of strategic initiatives. CPM systems help budget holders assign money, people, and assets to the chosen initiatives to achieve corporate strategic goals. They embody predictive forecasting techniques that can analyze trends and use the resulting information to predict future performance. For actual reporting, CPM systems highlight those initiatives that are working and those that need attention. Finally, they allow end users to create their own reports, investigate the causes of exceptions, and assess the impact of proposed changes. They do this all within a single application that is maintained centrally, which

---

[7] Nigel Rayner, *Corporate Performance Management Benefits Early Adopters,* Research Note COM-15-9802, Gartner, Inc., May 3, 2002, p. 3.

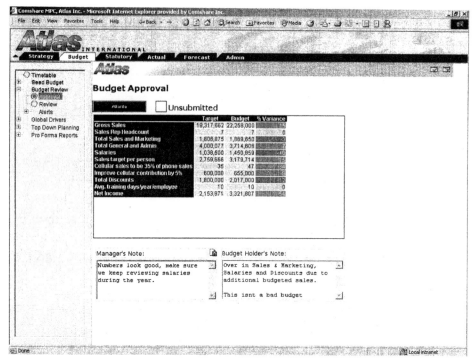

EXHIBIT 29.7   Color-Coded Variance Reports and Text Notes Enhance Communication throughout the Budgeting Process

Source: Comshare, Incorporated.

holds common definitions on calculations and stores a single version of the truth.

2. *Enterprise-wide.* CPM systems are extensible across the enterprise and provide an infrastructure for collaborative processes to take place around the globe. CPM systems are web based, making it possible for users to work from anywhere at any time. Users are not tied to a specific machine or location.

3. *Focus on exceptions.* CPM applications accommodate the reporting and analysis of both financial and nonfinancial data, because the success of strategic initiatives is not always measured in monetary units. They focus users' attention on the unanticipated by highlighting and proactively alerting them to exceptions, eliminating the need for users to search through stacks of reports. If an exception is found, CPM systems allow users to drill down into the detail so they can see what is really happening.

4. *Automate data processing.* CPM systems automate the calculation of ratios, currency conversions, allocations, minority interests, intercompany eliminations, consolidation of results, and more. They can do this on a real-time basis or automatically at set times.

5. *Filter and format data.* CPM systems summarize large volumes of data and present it in a format that is easily understood for the purpose. Examples include the creation

of financial documents, such as the income statement, balance sheet, and cash flow statements, as well as supporting analyses in both tabular and graphical formats.

6. *Provide end users with access to information.* The Web has transformed the way in which business professionals obtain information. It allows organizations to access information in disparate systems, at different locations, and in different formats anytime, anywhere. CPM systems exploit the Web and provide secure user access to any relevant information such as timetables, assumptions, comments, reports, analyses, actual results, and forecasted results.

7. *Support collaboration.* CPM systems are designed with collaboration in mind. They support existing collaboration facilities such as e-mail, instant messaging, bulletin boards, and comments. This support means that, for the first time, users can collaborate with colleagues no matter where they are or what time it is.

8. *Provide insight.* One of the main purposes of a report is to reveal something that was previously unknown or unexpected. If that information is presented as a page of numbers, however, it can be difficult to spot trends and exceptions. CPM systems provide strong analytical capabilities such as trend analysis, sorting, charting, and exception reporting to transform data into insight.

9. *Automate monitoring of vital signs.* Reports have a number of limitations. For example, they are static and accurate only at the exact time they are produced. They also tend to consist of summarizations that mask problems lurking in the detail. CPM systems, in contrast, are "live," searching the details on a continuous basis. They can proactively warn users when exceptions occur or are predicted to occur, thereby highlighting issues that would be hidden in a "normal" report.

By combining these nine characteristics, CPM systems provide end users with instruction and knowledge on how to perform their roles in implementing strategy. However, although CPM systems may improve efficiency, they cannot ensure effectiveness by themselves. They are only as good as the methodology, metrics, and processes they support. Often organizations believe they will solve their planning, budgeting, reporting, or analysis problems by implementing a new system. But if budgeting or another process is broken, a new system will not fix it. The result will still be a broken process, only now it will be supported by a high-tech system.

 ## OVERCOMING ORGANIZATIONAL RESISTANCE

Because CPM systems impact all areas of the business, their implementation will likely incur resistance from within the organization. This resistance needs to be dealt with; it will not dissipate on its own. Resistance can come from all levels of the organization, but it is particularly serious when it comes from senior managers and others who can affect the success of the CPM initiative. The organization can do several things to minimize the occurrence and effects of this resistance.

1. *Secure senior management sponsorship for the project.* From the outset, the CPM project must be seen as having senior management sponsorship and full endorsement.

Members of the project team must have—and be seen to have—the delegated authority of the senior management team, and must, where necessary, have access to any person or necessary resource within the organization.

2. *The team must communicate objectives and benefits.* The project must be publicized among those who will be impacted. This communication should consist of clear, concise, forward-looking documents that outline the short- and long-term objectives and that outline the business benefits that will be gained from the solution. Other methods of communication could include presentations by the chief executive or other senior managers, videos, e-mail, newsletters, and more. Whatever method or combination of methods is used, the communications must emphasize that the solution is strategic in nature and is an essential system that will help individuals meet organizational objectives.

3. *Bring known issues—and detractors—into the open.* When the proposed solution has influential skeptics and detractors, bring the skeptics together with key supporters so that the issues can be properly discussed in the open. This meeting should have an agreed-on agenda that outlines the issues in advance. Comments and action points raised in the meeting should be documented and followed up. Recognize that often detractors can be transformed into supporters by involving them in defining requirements to solve business issues. Ensuring that the system does something for them specifically in a first release, when possible, can help emphasize the benefits of the CPM initiative.

4. *Never make it personal.* Although detractors may have a personal agenda, comments and actions should not be targeted at them personally. Instead, the business benefits of the CPM initiative should be reemphasized. Also emphasize the likely results of not doing anything at all.

5. *Build a sense of ownership.* The purpose of a CPM system is to make the organization more competitive and enable individuals to play a part in that success. Progress toward those goals needs to be communicated on a regular basis so that everyone knows this is not just a passing fad. Eliciting feedback from the different user communities can help generate this sense of ownership.

PLANNING AND CONTROLLING IMPLEMENTATION OF A NEW SYSTEM

Successful implementations are planned—they do not just happen. Implementations are a partnership between all the parties involved, including the software supplier, the information technology (IT) department, the finance department, and the project team that is involved in developing a solution. Each party has various skills to bring: The software vendor supplies software, training, and technical advice; finance and other system users supply requirements; and IT provides the hardware/software infrastructure on which the solution will run.

Implementation methodologies are an agreed-on way of working together that will deliver the solution on time and within budget. Methodologies break down the scope of an implementation into definable phases, each having a deliverable. Exhibit 29.8 shows the typical steps involved in implementing a CPM project. While this chapter does not

EXHIBIT 29.8 Typical Implementation Steps

Step	Deliverable
Project scope: Defines the problems being experienced and the scope of a new system	*Project scope document*
Application specification: Defines in detail exactly how the system will be put together, including how data will be gathered, processed, and reported back to users, and how the system will look and feel	*Detailed specification*
Technical design: Defines how the system will be implemented in harmony with the organization's current IT infrastructure	*Technical design document*
Development: Builds the system using the software package and writes any additional code that may be required	*Draft solution*
Acceptance testing: Tests the system thoroughly according to a predetermined plan to check that it performs as specified	*Signed acceptance test plan*
System rollout: Moves developed system into the production environment for access by users; includes end user training, setting up a help desk, defining support procedures, and loading historic data so that the system is ready for live use	*End-user/administrator documentation Training materials*
Live use: System is used "live" for the first time	
Postrollout review: Surveys users to ensure the system meets the defined need	*Project signoff document*

Source: Comshare, Incorporated.

provide all the details of planning and controlling an implementation, the next key points are offered as a partial guideline to successful project implementation.

Set Expectations

The first key point is to make sure that everyone impacted by the system knows why the system is being developed, what business problem(s) it will solve, what functionality is going to be delivered, and when it is going to be delivered. Too often users are disappointed with a new system because it does not do what they think it should do. To help avert this potential issue, it is useful to create a CPM "road map" that details how the organization is going to move from its current processes and systems to one based on planning and monitoring strategic performance. This road map should ensure that any pain points (the things that make it most difficult for employees, managers, and executives to do their jobs efficiently and effectively) being experienced in the planning, budgeting, and reporting processes are addressed first, but that the design takes into account what is to be achieved in the long term.

The CPM road map, along with the rationale for the priorities that have been established, should be shared with and explained to the organization. Do not oversell the system, but do make clear the business benefits that will be achieved with the new solution.

Establish Accurate Specifications

Many projects fail because there is not a well-communicated and understood set of requirements at the start of the implementation. An inaccurate specification typically manifests itself during the project as a constant debate over what the project is intended to deliver. At the end of the project, the result of an inaccurate specification is a system that is unlikely to solve the original problem, will cause other issues to arise, will be considered a failure, and will need to be reimplemented at additional cost.

For a CPM application, the specification stage may take longer than any other stage. Although modern-day software solutions can be implemented in a fraction of the time of older systems, the time needed to specify requirements has not been reduced. Assuming that the project scope has been accurately defined, five items need to be specified in detail:

1. *The CPM data model.* Clarify what information is to be held within the model and the associated business rules. The model is specified in terms of data stores, business dimensions, organizational structures, currencies, measures, and any calculated variables such as ratios and allocations.
2. *User workflow.* Determine how users will interact with the system. The user workflow describes how users will be led through the affected processes and the information they will need to complete a task.
3. *Reports and analyses.* Describe in detail the reports, analyses, and alerts that the new system will generate.
4. *Data load formats.* Identify the different data sources and how they are to be integrated into the CPM data model.
5. *Security.* Specify which users get access to the defined processes and data.

Select Suitable Software

When compiling a list of potential vendors, use all the resources available today. These can include Internet searches, webcasts, electronic newsletters, magazines, hardcopy newsletters, direct mail, and more. Pay particular attention to third-party analysts (e.g., Gartner, IDC, META Group, and others) as a means of identifying the proven performers.

Once an organization has chosen its candidates and is ready to begin reviewing vendor proposals, several issues need to be considered. First, the organization should be wary of any vendor that is ready to demonstrate a product without first investigating and understanding the organization's unique business challenges. If the vendor has not taken time to understand the enterprise's current and future needs, how can the vendor be confident that its system will meet the organization's requirements?

Next, when the vendor demonstrates its solution, the CPM selection team should not be a passive audience. Change some numbers "live" and see what happens. Ask the vendor how its own company uses the solution in-house. Salespeople are very good at presenting a standard demonstration in which everything runs according to a predetermined script. Their responses when they have to deviate from the script may give you a more realistic idea of how the solution functions in practice, not just in theory.

Solicit input from everyone who will be affected by the new performance management system (managers, budget holders, other business users, system administrators, IT staff). In addition to the insights gathered from these individuals' specialized knowledge in evaluating the solution, this involvement will benefit the project by creating a sense of teamwork and buy-in around the project.

During the demonstration, make sure the vendor demonstrates how the solution is specifically addressing each of the problems the organization identified during its business review process. In addition, be open to alternative solutions the vendor suggests. After all, the vendor may have insight into current best practices based on real-world experiences with other companies.

Finally, investigate the vendor's implementation methodology, not just the software. This is an essential step, often overlooked, which can result in an implemented solution that is quite different from what the company thought it was buying. Verify that the vendor has a systematic, documented implementation methodology. Understand how—or whether—the vendor guarantees the success of a solution as defined by the organization's needs.

Plan for IT Involvement

Most packaged financial applications, including CPM systems, are designed to be set up and maintained by the finance department. Typically, system administrators are given easy-to-use facilities for maintaining the data model, business rules, data-entry screens, reports, and analyses. In essence, everything they need to accommodate changing business requirements is provided.

However, CPM systems involve many people and cut across departmental boundaries. As a result, they rely heavily on the supporting IT infrastructure. For this reason, IT must be involved in the CPM project. Their active involvement is required to:

- Provide the appropriate hardware/software environment for development and production use.
- Load and maintain access to the application software, data model, and associated user interfaces.
- Perform the initial setup of the database workspace.
- Provide user-access security over and above that delivered by the application. This is usually directly related to the technology being used and typically involves database and web-access security.
- Ensure users have the appropriate communication links to the application.
- Extract data from any transactional systems in accordance with the agreed-on formats for loading it into the application.
- Tune the database and network for performance once the application has been created.
- Provide application and database backup.
- Provide end user technical assistance.

Control the Project

Development team members must meet regularly to monitor progress of the CPM implementation. They should ensure that the solution being developed continues to meet the business case for the implementation and the needs of users and that it fits within the organization's IT infrastructure. The discussions, actions, and conclusions of these meetings should be recorded and distributed as appropriate.

During CPM implementations, project specifications and deliverables do change. There is no point in delivering a solution that does not meet real requirements. All potential changes should be reviewed using an agreed-on change control procedure that includes documenting the change and circulating it to each member of the CPM direction team. Team members should then assess the impact on their area of responsibility.

To help stay on schedule and within budget, any proposed changes should be saved for a future phase of the implementation, where possible. When changes are to be included in the current phase, however, revised specifications and project plans will need to be generated and circulated to all members of the development team. Should a change cause the project to go outside the terms of the original business case and project scope, the project should be suspended until those terms can be adjusted and the project planned again.

Provide Ongoing Training and Support

Training for administrators, budget holders, managers, and support staff must take place before the solution goes live. Training should include instruction regarding:

- Goals of the new system and how it will aid competitiveness
- Changes to the organization's business processes and any related terminology
- How users will benefit from the new system
- How to use the system
- How to obtain help and support

Whatever form training takes, materials should be prepared knowing that most users are not accountants. Any terminology should be easy to understand for all users. The training should be relevant and to the point. By educating users and informing users of the business benefits, the organization is more likely to achieve user acceptance of the system and the associated processes.

Two types of support will be needed. The first type relates to processes. The support staff must know about the organizational processes as well as how the system carries these out. The second type of support relates to the technology, including machines and accessibility issues.

The support team must be prepared, educated, and available. If they are not, users who encounter problems—even those of their own making—will soon become frustrated and disillusioned with the process and the system. Bad experiences can soon overshadow the benefits that were expected of the new system. To train their employees and reduce the potential for bad experiences, one organization, for example, set up a special room in which system users worked during the first few weeks after the system went live. In this room, they could access the system and complete their tasks but also had immediate access to the development staff who helped system users immediately work through any issues that arose.

Never assume that everyone knows what is going on or knows how to use the CPM system. People leave organizations and new, untrained people take their places. Therefore, a continuous education program should be established. One way to accomplish this is through scheduled formal training sessions. Another way is through informal methods such as newsletters and web-based training solutions.

Organizations often find they want to train additional people as new phases of the implementation are completed and new functionality is delivered. A California-based software firm, for example, initially trained 150 people when its CPM system went live. When the second phase was implemented, it trained 250 more people. Today, more than 700 people have access to the system. The organization's finance director says the company wanted everyone to be aware of the information and to be able to manage it.

Deliver Often

Phases of successful CPM solution implementations are delivered on an incremental basis, such as every six weeks. Typically, some basic processes that address major pain points or solve nagging problems are implemented first. Delivering new functionality and the associated business benefits incrementally reinforces that continuous progress is being made, keeps people interested in and supportive of the project, and allows users to become familiar with the system and build their skills gradually.

This phased approach to implementation also greatly reduces the initial support requirements because only a few functions need to be supported at a time. As users build up their experience and confidence, support requirements for those features will be reduced, allowing newer features to be introduced with the same level of support.

 CONCLUSION

Early adopters of CPM are visionaries. They have turned against conventional approaches to planning, budgeting, and reporting in the belief that there is a better way to manage the implementation and execution of strategy.

Development of the early CPM solutions always started with a pressing problem that needed to be solved. For most early adopters, the most pressing problem was that their budgetary planning and reporting systems did not meet their needs. The systems were fragmented, disconnected from strategy, and expensive to maintain in terms of both cost and effort. In fact, Gartner notes that one of the common themes among CPM solution implementations has been the integration of disparate applications and processes such as budgeting, forecasting, consolidation, and financial reporting.[8]

Early-adopter system designs and implementations typically were led by chief financial officers. The CPM systems are used by senior executives and operational managers to run their companies. These systems are seen as strategic to the organization's ability to manage corporate performance; they are not seen as just another software package for budgeting. While some of these systems are not yet fully operational CPM solutions

---

[8] Ibid., p. 1.

covering all aspects of performance management, they have all been designed to deliver broad and expanding CPM capabilities over time.

Today's CPM early adopters report a number of benefits, including more realistic budgets. Many remark on dramatically reduced cycle times, allowing them to complete tasks they never would have attempted with their old systems. Others comment on how they are better able to use their time. Rather than spending it collecting data, looking for errors, and replicating information, they report using their time to analyze results and test scenarios. They appreciate the improved quality of their data, which in turn inspires confidence among managers about the decisions they make. Early adopters believe that they are now better able to respond to changing business and customer needs, which leads to competitive advantage and increased shareholder value.

Gartner has predicted that organizations that effectively deploy CPM solutions will outperform their industry peers and that all enterprises should understand the implications of CPM and immediately start building their strategy.[9] For most organizations, that strategy will include updating processes and technology to transform budgeting from a low-value, time-consuming activity into one that drives organizations in their chosen strategic direction.

---

[9]   Lee Geishecker and Nigel Rayner, *Corporate Performance Management: BI Collides with ERP*, Research Note SPA-14-9282, Gartner, Inc., December 17, 2001, pp. 1, 6.

CHAPTER THIRTY

Zero-Based Budgeting

Peter A. Pyhrr
Magnetic Ticket & Label Corp.

INTRODUCTION

Zero-based budgeting (ZBB) is nothing conceptually new, is not a budgeting process, and is not "reinventing the wheel." It is, however, a management approach, and it can be a key decision-making tool for the chief executive officer (CEO).

The term "zero-based budgeting" was launched into vogue by former President Jimmy Carter, who installed the process while governor of Georgia and who attempted to install it throughout the federal government. However, the process was developed in industry, at Texas Instruments, and is currently being used by industrial companies. There are several key characteristics about the process in its application to date:

- The decision to implement ZBB is usually made by the CEO or other key operating managers, not by the vice president of finance or the controller.
- It is being used by companies noted for their good management. ("Good management is always looking for better decision-making tools.")
- The process is difficult, requires a great deal of effort to implement effectively, and may be perceived as a threat by many managers. It has failed in a few organizations and is no panacea, yet most companies have found that the benefits far outweigh the costs of implementation.

Those organizations that have had the most success with ZBB have learned that it is not a budgeting process but a management approach.

The chief beneficiaries of the zero-based management approach are the CEO and top-level managers with profit and loss responsibilities. The purposes of this chapter are to focus on the problems of top management with the traditional management,

677

planning, and budgeting systems; to explain the zero-based approach; and to identify the potential benefits (and problems) that the approach might offer.

 PROBLEMS WITH TRADITIONAL TECHNIQUES

Top-level executives are faced with the difficult tasks of management and decision making in a complex and dynamic environment. Managers often must face conflicting demands, typified by the demand for growth that many times requires a significant allocation of today's funds for tomorrow's new product or market versus the requirement to produce this year's profit. Managers are continuously besieged for funds for diverse activities such as research, marketing, maintenance, and data processing, for which they must play Solomon in determining how the baby will be divided. The individual executive is not an expert in each of the specialties competing for funds, yet he or she must make the ultimate funding allocation decisions. The environment is becoming more complex, with increased government regulation, increasing worldwide competition, rapidly changing technology, and increasing difficulty in raising prices. The only constant seems to be the continual rise in costs.

Although the business climate is continually evolving, the management tools available to top management have remained basically static. The traditional tools, especially planning and budgeting, have not evolved at the same pace in order to provide top managers with an effective tool for managing their business.

Under the traditional planning and budgeting procedures, management's attention is focused primarily on planned changes from the previous year's expenditure level. This is usually referred to as *incremental budgeting*. Although considerable thought goes into the development of these plans, it is primarily the year-over-year increment that receives the most critical and analytical attention by senior management. Thus, in many cases, the "base" to which the increment is added is treated as if it were already authorized and required little additional review or evaluation.

This traditional incremental approach often creates several typical problems for top management:

1. *Budgeting requests exceed funding availability, often forcing management to recycle the process.* The incremental approach usually aggravates this problem. Because managers know their initial budget requests will be slashed, they usually inflate these requests. (Managers who turn in low requests on the initial budget submission quickly learn that they will often receive a cut—often in similar proportion to managers who inflate their initial budget requests.)
2. *Difficulty in translating long-term objectives into action plans (and budgets).* Long-term projections are often wish lists and economic forecasts, although specific projects must be funded to achieve growth. New projects, however, are often the first items cut from the budget request when funding requests exceed funding availability.
3. *Key problems and decision areas are not highlighted.*
4. *Alternatives are not identified.* One set of numbers is submitted without an identification of alternative means of performing the function or alternative funding levels (especially lower levels).

5. *Difficulty in adjusting budgets and operations readily to changing situations*, because work-loads are not clearly identified (except direct manufacturing costs that are controlled by standard costing systems) and priorities are not established throughout the organization.
6. *Trade-offs among long-term goals and programs, operating needs, and profits are not clearly identified.* Projects and priorities are not clearly identified, and new development funds are often the first to be cut when the "cut 10 percent" dictate is given.

Top managers will readily nod in agreement to these problems, but then ask what alternatives they have. The zero-based management approach is a major alternative and can be a significant tool enabling top management to focus on key problems, alternatives, and priorities throughout the organization.

ZERO-BASED APPROACH

ZBB is nothing conceptually new. It is a logical process, combining many elements of good management. The five key elements of ZBB include:

1. Identification of objectives
2. Evaluation of alternative means of accomplishing each activity
3. Evaluation of alternative funding levels (elimination, lower levels, current level, and increased levels)
4. Evaluation of workload and performance measures
5. Establishment of priorities

However, the key word in the statement that ZBB is nothing conceptually new is *conceptually.*

Although the process is nothing conceptually new, it is radically different from the traditional planning and budgeting process generally practiced today. What ZBB does that is different is to recognize that the budgeting process is, in fact, a management process. It also recognizes budgeting as a key decision-making process and a driving force. (Managers must perform the ZBB analysis in order to get any budget at all.)

Thus, ZBB is not a budgeting process in the traditional sense of the word—it is first a management process, second a planning process, and only third a budgeting process. The term "zero-based" does not mean that everybody's position is automatically "zeroed" or that we must reinvent the wheel, which would be entirely unrealistic in a pragmatic world. What it does mean is that we must reevaluate all activities to see if they should be eliminated, funded at a reduced level, funded at a similar level, or increased. Which of these funding levels—from zero to a significant increase—is appropriate will be determined by the priorities established by top management and by the availability of total funding.

ZBB applies to all actionable or discretionary activities, programs, and costs for which we can identify some cost–benefit relationship—even if this relationship is highly subjective. In government, ZBB can be applied to all operations. In industry, it can be applied to all costs except direct labor, material, and fixed overhead, since these costs are normally handled by a standard costing system. ZBB can therefore be applied to all administrative and staff functions (data processing, financial, supervision, legal), technical and manufacturing indirect costs (research and development [R&D], laboratory, engineering, maintenance, quality control, production planning), and commercial functions (sales, marketing, purchasing, traffic).

These manufacturing indirect and overhead costs to which ZBB directly applies may make up only a fraction of the total budget of a heavy manufacturing operation, but they represent activities that are usually the most difficult to plan and control, and they offer management the greatest lever to use in affecting profits. Consider these three areas of activity that are subject to ZBB analysis and how resource allocation could affect them as well as the entire organization:

1. Marketing and R&D programs determine the future course of an organization. If development funds are not adequate, or if marketing support is not sufficient to handle expected sales volume, long-term plans for growth may not be achieved.
2. Funding for R&D, capital, industrial engineering, production planning, and so forth can directly affect manufacturing technology and heavily influence direct manufacturing costs.
3. Arbitrary cost reductions in the service and support functions without a full understanding of the consequences can create severe problems, with the cost savings proving minor compared to the resulting production problems and increased direct manufacturing costs.

ZBB addresses those areas where management has a difficult time evaluating efficiency and effectiveness, because budget variances are not necessarily good indicators of performance. In a pure manufacturing environment, it makes sense to evaluate a manager on the basis of actual versus budgeted costs. If the budget for production of a million widgets is $3 million, and if a manager has produced a million widgets for $2.8 million, he or she is usually credited with having done a good job if the widgets are up to specification. But if a manager were told to spend $3 million on R&D and came back a year later having spent only $2.8 million, one would be hard put to say whether the manager had done a good job or not. The distinction is that the first manager produced something tangible; there should be no question as to whether or not a million acceptable widgets were actually produced. However, given the very tenuous connection between dollars going into the R&D pipeline and the value coming out, it is impossible to say whether the second manager "produced" the right amount of R&D. Obviously, if one does not know how costs affect output, it is not possible to measure outputs by measuring costs. This problem is compounded for the CEO who has this problem with R&D, advertising, data processing, maintenance, and numerous other specialties for which he or she is not an expert.

ZERO-BASED BUDGETING PROCEDURES

The zero-based approach requires each organization to evaluate and review all programs and activities (current as well as new) systematically, to review activities on a basis of output or performance as well as cost, to emphasize manager decision making first, number-oriented budgets second, and to increase analysis. However, it should be stressed that ZBB is an approach, not a fixed procedure or set of forms to be applied uniformly from one organization to the next. The mechanics and management approach differed significantly among the organizations that have adopted ZBB, and the process must be adapted to fit the specific needs of each user.

Although the specifics differ among organizations, there are four basic steps to the zero-based approach that must be addressed by each organization:

1. Identify decision units.
2. Analyze each decision unit in a decision package.
3. Evaluate and rank all decision packages to develop the budget request and profit and loss statement.
4. Prepare the detailed operating budgets reflecting those decision packages approved in the budget.

Defining Decision Units

ZBB attempts to focus management's attention on evaluating activities and making decisions. The meaningful elements of each organization must be defined so that they can be isolated for analysis and decision making. For the sake of terminology, these meaningful elements have been called decision units.

For those organizations with a detailed cost center structure, the decision unit may correspond to the cost center. In some cases the cost center manager may wish to identify separately different functions or operations within the cost center if they are significant in size and require separate analysis. For example, a single cost center for the controller's office might be divided into general accounting, financial analysis, cost accounting, and credit and collection. Decision units might also be projects (R&D, management information systems, engineering), services provided or received (data processing charged to each major user), objects of expense (advertising by product and market, legal or consulting fees), or capital projects.

DECISION PACKAGE

The decision package is the building block of the ZBB process. It provides a description and evaluation of each decision unit for management review and decision making. The decision package form is designed to produce an evaluation of each decision unit that will describe the:

- Purpose or objective
- Description of actions (what are we going to do, and how are we going to do it?)
- Costs and benefits
- Workload and performance measures
- Alternative means of accomplishing objectives
- Various levels of effort (what benefits do we get for various levels of funding?)

The key to developing decision packages is the formulation of meaningful alternatives. Types of alternatives that should be considered in developing decision packages include:

▪ *Alternative methods of accomplishing the objective or performing the operation.* Managers should identify and evaluate all meaningful alternatives and choose the one they consider best. If an alternative to the current method of doing business is chosen, the recommended way should be shown in the decision package, with the current way shown as the alternative not recommended.
▪ *Different levels of effort of performing the operation.* Once the best method of accomplishing the operation has been chosen from among the various alternative methods evaluated, a manager must identify alternative levels of effort and funding to perform that operation. Managers must establish a minimum level of effort, which must be below the current level of operation, and then identify additional levels or increments of separate decision packages. These incremental levels above the minimum might bring the operation up to its current level and to several multiples of the current level of effort.

A decision package is defined as one incremental level in a decision unit. Thus, there may be several decision packages for each decision unit, as shown in Exhibit 30.1. In evaluating each level, managers are evaluating the incremental benefit they get for incremental expenditures. For example, looking at level 2 in Exhibit 30.1, managers will be evaluating the additional benefit they get from spending an additional 20 percent, or $20,000 (not the 100 percent total). It is these incremental levels that get ranked. By identifying a minimum level of effort, plus additional increments as separate decision packages, each manager thus presents several alternatives for top management decision making:

▪ *Elimination.* Eliminate the operation if no decision packages are approved.
▪ *Reduced level.* Reduce the level of funding if only the minimum-level decision package is approved.
▪ *Current level.* Maintain the same level of effort if the minimum level and the one or two incremental levels (bringing the operation from the minimum level to the current level of effort) are approved. (Note: The current level of effort refers only to the level of output or performance, sometimes called *maintenance level.* However, even at the current level of effort, managers may have changed their method of operation and made operating improvements, so that the current level of effort may be accomplished at a reduced cost.)
▪ *Increased levels.* Increase the levels of funding and performance if one or more increments above the current level are approved.

Identifying and evaluating the minimum level of effort is the most difficult element in the zero-based approach—especially identifying a minimum level that is usually 70 to 80 percent of current and may be much less for some discretionary activities, such as advertising. Maintenance is not worried about being eliminated, but the maintenance manager will be extremely concerned about identifying a lower level of effort. If the requirement for a minimum level is so difficult, why does ZBB emphasize this requirement?

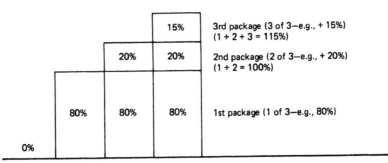

EXHIBIT 30.1 Graphic Representation of Levels of Effort (Decision Packages) for Each Decision Unit

There are two fundamental reasons for defining a minimum level.

1. The minimum level forces managers to make an in-depth evaluation of their operations. This requirement of identifying a minimum below the current level of effort forces managers to consider alternatives, identify what is most important (all things are not equal), and quantify workload and performance measures to justify their conclusions. If only one level was required, reflecting the total funding desired, managers in mandatory functions such as maintenance could avoid an in-depth analysis and would normally recommend continuing past practices.
2. Top management needs the option of elimination and reduction if funds are to be reallocated, and elimination is viable only in a limited number of programs. If only one level of effort was analyzed (probably reflecting the funding level desired by each manager), top management would be forced to make a yes-or-no decision on the funding request, thus funding at the requested level, eliminating the program, making arbitrary reductions, or recycling the budget process if requests exceeded funding availability.

The minimum level of effort is the most difficult level to identify, since there is no magic number (i.e., 75 percent of the current level) that would be meaningful to all operations. The minimum level must be identified by each manager for his or her operations. The minimum level must be below the current level of effort and should attempt to identify that critical level of effort below which the operation would be discontinued because it loses its viability of effectiveness. Five considerations can aid managers in defining the minimum level of effort:

1. The minimum level may not completely achieve the total objective of the operation. (Even the additional levels of effort recommended may not completely achieve the objective because of realistic budget and/or achievement levels.)
2. The minimum level should address itself to the most critical population being served or should attack the most serious problem areas.
3. The minimum level may merely reduce the amount of service (or number of services) provided.

4. The minimum level may reflect operating improvements, organizational changes, or improvements in efficiency that result in cost reductions.
5. Combinations of considerations 1 through 4.

By identifying the minimum level, each manager is not necessarily recommending that his or her operation be funded at the minimum level but is merely identifying that alternative to top management. If a manager identifies several levels of effort, he or she is recommending that all levels be funded.

The operating manager responsible for the decision unit normally does the analysis of the unit, since he or she is the most knowledgeable about its operation and will be responsible for carrying it out. However, this analysis will be reviewed by higher management levels and the financial staff. Thus, we can get the analysis workload spread among many managers, yet we have the review and ranking process that will allow top managers to play their normal devil's advocate role and require decision package revisions where appropriate.

Example Decision Package Analysis and Forms

This example of materials handling (which is the decision unit) is an actual decision package analysis taken from a specialty steel mill. The description provides the highlights of the analysis, which is translated into the completed decision package forms shown in Exhibit 30.2 (levels 1 and 2 are shown, with each level described on a two-page form).

DECISION PACKAGE				Page 1 of ____	
(1) PACKAGE NAME	**(2) DEPARTMENT**		**(3) PREPARED BY**	**(4) DATE**	**(5) RANK**
MATERIALS HANDLING – (1 of 4)	409	Materials Handling	J. JONES	7/28/78	

(6) PURPOSE/OBJECTIVE

Provide materials handling from raw materials stores thru all production departments to finished goods inventory.

(7) DESCRIPTION OF ACTIONS (OPERATIONS) FOR THIS LEVEL

Twenty vehicle operators using forklifts; two dispatchers and two head men to provide minimal service to move output from three shifts by reducing frequency of service and elimination of some shift coverage. This level would increase average WIP inventory 12% due to some additional queuing on first and second shifts, and by eliminating the third shift in the Cold Mill by queuing all materials for the third shift by the end of the second shift. This will require some limited movement of material by production personnel on third shift. Handling for maintenance and reclamation would be reduced from scheduled to an on call basis, which would require an additional queuing of material and some additional work space or palletizing for the additional storage required. Shop mule service reduced from 4 to 2 routes per day.

Staffing: 21 vehicle operators, 2 dispatchers, 2 head men

(8) CHANGES/IMPROVEMENTS FROM CURRENT OPERATIONS (CAPITAL EQUIPMENT)

 – Cold Mill – elimination of third shift
 – Hot Mill – reduced frequency but maintaining 3 shift coverage
 – Roll & Grind – reduced frequency of service
 – Maintenance and Reclamation – reduced from scheduled to on-call basis
 – Shop mule service reduced from 4 to 2 routes per day

(9) WORKLOAD/PERFORMANCE MEASURES	1977	1978	1979	(10) RESOURCES REQUIRED	1977 Actual	1978 Budget	1978 Revised	1979 Proposed
Production pounds/year (mil.)	9.8	10.1	12.6	Positions – this level	////	////	////	25
Average daily work-in-process (lbs.)	8,580	8,700	9,700	– cumulative	27	29	29	25
Metered fork lift hours per vehicle	1038	1045	1185	Expense – this level	////	////	////	590.0
Number of fork lift trucks	11	11	9	– cumulative	621	671	671	590.0
				% of Prior Year	////	108	100	88
				Capital	////	////	////	0

EXHIBIT 30.2   *(Continued)*

DECISION PACKAGE Page 2 of ____

(1) PACKAGE NAME	(2) DEPARTMENT		(3) PREPARED BY	(4) DATE	(5) RANK
MATERIALS HANDLING – BASE LEVEL (1 of 4)	409	Materials Handling	J. JONES	7/28/78	

(11) CONSEQUENCES OF ELIMINATING THIS PACKAGE

Disapproval of this package will require this function to be de-centralized and absorbed into individual production departments and will be done at a 15–20% increased cost to the Division.

(12) OTHER LEVELS OF EFFORT IDENTIFIED	func. #	exp. #	(14) DETAIL EXPENDITURES	1977 Revised	1978 Proposed
2 of 4 $81.0K Add 4 Veh. Operators to support Hot Mills and restore third shift coverage to Cold Strip Mill			Salaries (Hourly)		342.8
			Wage Premium		17.7
3 of 4 $56.1K Add 1 Veh. Operator & 1 headman to provide support for Hot Mill and Maintenance dispatching			Total Labor		360.5
			Fringes		180.9
			Propane Fuel		28.6
4 of 4 $106.2 Add 2 Veh. Operators to increase frequency of service to Roll Grind and shipping departments			Maintenance		20.0
(13) ALTERNATIVE MEANS OF ACCOMPLISHING THIS PACKAGE					
1. Return the Material Handling function to the individual production departments. This was rejected due to productivity declines, loss of flexibility within the division, and higher costs. The material handling was decentralized until 1975, with the current structure producing a 15% savings when this function was centralized.			Total		590.0
2. Combine this function with Work Stores. This alternative was rejected due to potential bargaining unit problems and decreases in flexibility because of contract negotiated work rules in the stores area.					

DECISION PACKAGE Page 1 of ____

(1) PACKAGE NAME	(2) DEPARTMENT		(3) PREPARED BY	(4) DATE	(5) RANK
MATERIALS HANDLING – (2 of 4)	409	Materials Handling	J. JONES	7/28/78	

(6) PURPOSE/OBJECTIVE

Provide materials handling from raw materials stores thru all production departments to finished goods inventory.

(7) DESCRIPTION OF ACTIONS (OPERATIONS) FOR THIS LEVEL

Add four Vehicle Operators to provide additional second shift material handling service for the Bar Mills, Annealing and Pickling Department in the Hot Mill building. This will free the dispatch truck to move released material from Hot Mill Hold area and speed production flow. Provide added frequency of shop mule service from 2 to 4 routes per day, and improve service to the Hot Mill on first shift. Add third shift coverage to the Cold Strip Mill.

Staff: Add 4 Veh. Operators

(8) CHANGES/IMPROVEMENTS FROM CURRENT OPERATIONS (CAPITAL EQUIPMENT)

Hot Mills – Reduced frequency and some additional WIP (5%).
Maintenance & Reclamation provided on on-call basis only.

(9) WORKLOAD/PERFORMANCE MEASURES	1976	1977	1978	(10) RESOURCE REQUIRED	1976 Actual	1977 Revised	1977 Revised	1978 Proposed
Production pounds/year (mil.)	9.8	10.1	12.6	Positions – this level	/////	/////	/////	4
Average daily work-in-process (lbs.)	8,580	8,700	9,300	– cumulative	27	29	29	29
Metered fork lift hours per vehicle	1038	1045	1150	Expense – this level	/////	/////	/////	81.0
Number of fork lift trucks	11	11	11	– cumulative	621	671	671	671.0
				% of Prior Year	/////	108	100	100.0
				Capital	/////	/////	/////	5

EXHIBIT 30.2 *(Continued)*

DECISION PACKAGE			Page 2 of ____	

(1) PACKAGE NAME	(2) DEPARTMENT		(3) PREPARED BY	(4) DATE	(5) RANK
MATERIALS HANDLING – (2 of 4)	409	Materials Handling	J. JONES	7/28/78	

(11) CONSEQUENCES OF ELIMINATING THIS PACKAGE

Will result in some production departments providing their own materials handling (Zero-incremental cost); but excess WIP inventories and less efficient production activity could result. Delayed shipments could cause a shift delay in movement in Hot Mill.

(12) OTHER LEVELS OF EFFORT IDENTIFIED	func. #	exp. #	(14) DETAIL EXPENDITURES	1977 Revised	1978 Proposed
(1 of 4) $590.0 Minimum materials handling coverage for the Mill reducing frequency and shift coverage; 25 people			Salaries (Hourly)		38.1
			Wage Premium		12.2
(3 of 4) $56.1K Add 1 Veh. Operator & 1 headman to provide support for Hot Mill and Maintenance dispatching			Total Labor		50.3
			Fringes		20.4
			Propane Fuel		2.3
(4 of 4) $106.2 Add 2 Veh. Operators to increase frequency of service to Roll Grind and shipping departments			Maintenance		8.0
(13) ALTERNATIVE MEANS OF ACCOMPLISHING THIS PACKAGE					
1. Return the Material Handling function to the individual production departments. This was rejected due to productivity declines, loss of flexibility within the division, and higher costs. The material handling was decentralized until 1975, with the current structure producing a 15% savings when this function was centralized.			Total		81.0
2. Combine this function with Work Stores. This alternative was rejected due to potential bargaining unit problems and decreases in flexibility because of contract negotiated work rules in the stores area.					

EXHIBIT 30.2 Decision Package Analysis Forms

Situation: Centralized materials-handling department, handling from raw material stores through all production phases to finished goods inventory.

Different Ways of Performing the Same Function: Recommended alternative is to maintain current organization with multiple shift coverage using forklift trucks and palletized production loads. Alternatives not recommended are (1) returning materials-handling function to individual production departments and (2) combining function with work-stores department (which has a separate materials-handling function).

Different Levels of Effort for Performing This Function:

1. Materials handling (1 of 4): cost $590,000; 25 people. Twenty vehicle operators using forklifts; two dispatchers and two head persons to provide minimal service in moving output from three shifts by reducing frequency of service and elimination of some shift coverage. This level would increase average work-in-process inventory 12 percent because of some additional queuing on first and second shifts and by eliminating the third shift in the cold mill by queuing all materials for the third shift by the end of the second shift. This will require some limited movement of material by production personnel on third shift.

2. Materials handling (2 of 4): cost $81,000; 4 people (levels 1 + 2 = $671,000). Add four vehicle operators to provide additional second-shift materials-handling service for the bar mills, annealing, and pickling department in the hot mill building. Provide added frequency of shop mule service from two to four routes per day, and

improve service to the hot mill on the first shift. Add third-shift coverage to the cold strip mill.

3. Materials handling (3 of 4): cost $56,100; 2 people (levels 1 + 2 + 3 = $727,100). Add one vehicle operator and one head person to provide full service in the hot mill and hot mill service areas on the first shift. Provide full service to all departments on the first-shift basis. Provide work direction for materials-handling functions on the third shift.

4. Materials handling (4 of 4): cost $106,200; 2 people (levels 1 + 2 + 3 + 4 = $833,300). Add two vehicle operators to increase frequency of service to the roll grind and shipping departments, plus purchase $60,000 of skids and hoppers.

In reviewing this example, you should note several factors:

▪ Only one alternative was proposed, with the other alternatives listed with the reason for rejection. Top management might challenge the reasoning or ask why other alternatives that might be identified were not considered.

▪ The minimum level is 88 percent of the 1978 revised estimate of current year's costs—yet in previous sections minimum levels of 70 to 80 percent of current were discussed. However, if you look at the workload measures, you will see that production pounds per year (in millions) has increased from 10.1 to 12.6 (a 25 percent increase); normal inflation might have accounted for an additional 6 to 8 percent increase in costs. The production workload was a planning assumption used by all departments, and it is not meaningful in this example to cut to 88 percent as a minimum by reducing the amount of materials handled. There may be some examples where there might be a reasonable alternative not to handle all material or provide all the prior services.

▪ The narrative and data sections combine to give a complete picture of the operation. Even traditional reviews to evaluate items of expense are augmented by narrative sections and the workload and performance measures, which can raise many red flags for the expense analysis.

Top management might be very pleased to reduce these materials-handling costs to a minimum, but the decision package also describes the negative consequences of such actions. The final determination as to the number of decision packages that will be funded will be determined in the ranking process.

RANKING PROCESS

The ranking process attempts to provide management with a technique for allocating its limited resources by answering two questions: (1) What objectives should we attempt to achieve? and (2) How much should we spend in this attempt?

Management can attempt to answer these questions by taking the decision packages identified and listing (ranking) them in order of decreasing benefit to the organization, as shown in Exhibit 30.3. Management could then identify the benefits to be gained

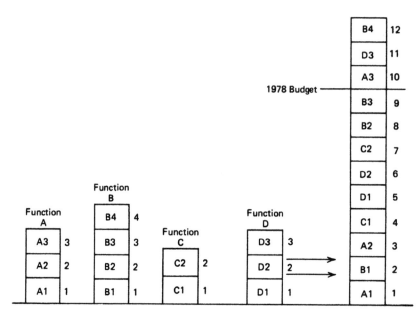

EXHIBIT 30.3 Ranking Process

at each expenditure level and the consequences of not approving additional packages ranked below the expenditure level. The total request, or traditional budget, would be the sum of all decision packages proposed. However, management would have the option of funding all packages, no packages, or any number of packages. Regardless of the number of packages funded, top managers can assure themselves that they are funding the most important packages—current or new.

The ranking process establishes priorities among the functions as described in the decision packages. If a company wanted to severely limit its ranking, it could have only those managers preparing packages rank their own packages. However, this approach is obviously unsatisfactory, since it does not offer top management and the CEO any opportunity to trade off expenditures among cost centers or other, larger divisions of the company. The burden would be on division managers to establish trade-offs among industrial engineering, production planning, and maintenance as well as sales and administrative functions.

At the other extreme, a single ranking of decision packages could be required for an entire company. This ranking would be made by top management. Although this single ranking would identify the best allocation of resources, ranking and judging the high volume of packages created by describing all the discrete activities of a large company would impose a ponderous—if not impossible—burden on top management. One realistic compromise (depending primarily on organizational size) might be to stop the formal ranking process at some intermediate organizational level—for example, at the level of the plant manager or profit center. Many companies solve the dilemma by grouping cost centers or profit and loss units together naturally, according to kinds of activity, and producing consolidated rankings for each grouping. Top management will use these rankings to analyze the trade-offs among profit centers and specifically to compare the marginal benefits of funding additional decision packages against the organization's profit needs.

Continuing with the steel mill example in which materials handling is only one out of 16 decision units, the mill manager had to make a single ranking of 52 decision packages encompassing all 16 decision units within the mill. Exhibit 30.4 shows the matrix of all 16 decision units within the mill, which have from two to four levels of effort for each decision unit. The resulting ranking is shown in Exhibit 30.5.

EXHIBIT 30.4 Decision Unit Summary for Steel Mill Operations

Decision Unit	FY'XX Estimate	Base Pkg.	Pkg. 2	Pkg. 3	Pkg. 4	Pkg. 5	Total Request
145A Supervise air melt	$277	$234	$56	$39	$36	$	$365
146A Supervise vac melt	281	260	39	35	—		334
147A Supervise hot mills	567	565	36	78	—		679
168A Supervise manufacturing service area	203	178	36	36	17		267
190A Supervise cold strip mill	289	308	39	15	—		362
409A Material handling	686	590	81	56	105		832
409B Vehicle operators	106	63	50	27	27		167
409C Grounds maintenance	207	187	42	25	27		281
409D Garage vehicle repair	330	377	56	35	36		504
409E Utility labor pool	15	7	7	—	—		14
409F Department supervision	104	92	34	31	—		157
446A Shop floor control	284	203	92	21	—		316
446B Work stores	293	255	63	70	—		388
454A Mill process engineering	641	517	172	78	66		833
454B Mill process engineering—other	43	46	83	—	—		129
461A Mill management	199	130	46	—	—		176
Total	$4,525	$4,012	$932	$546	$314		$5,804
Cumulative		4,012	4,944	5,490	5,804		
Cumulative %		88.7%	109.3%	$121.3%	$128.3%		

COMPLETING THE PROFIT AND LOSS

With the decision packages ranked in order of priority, management can continually revise budgets by revising the cutoff level on any or all rankings—that is, it can fund package numbers 1 through 41 but not package numbers 42 through 52. Doing this

DECISION PACKAGE RANKING

(1) RANK	(2) PACKAGE NAME	(3) 1978 PROPOSED		(4) 1979 CUMULATIVE		
		Positions	Expense (excl. cap.)	Positions	Expense (excl. cap.)	% of 1978 Revised
1	Supervise Air Melt Shop, Material Reclaim & Weighroom (1 of 4)	7	235	7	235	5
2	Supervise ESR, Vac Arc Remelting, VIM & EB Melt (1 of 3)	8	260	15	495	11
3	Supervise & Operate Hot Mills and Forging (1 of 3)	18	566	33	1061	23
4	Supervise & Operate Cold Strip Mill (1 of 3)	10	309	43	1370	30
5	Supervise & Operate Manufacturing Service (1 of 4)	6	179	49	1549	34
6	M. P. E. Std. Practice Control & Trouble Shooting (1 of 1)	17	518	66	2067	45
7	Mill Management (1 of 2)	3	130	69	2197	48
8	Material Handling (1 of 4)	25	591	94	2788	61
9	Garage Vehicle Repair (1 of 4)	8	378	102	3166	69
10	Yard Departmental Supervision (1 of 3)	3	92	105	3258	71
11	Supervise Air Melt, Material Reclaim & Weighroom (2 of 4)	3	56	108	3314	73
12	Supervise ESR, Vac Arc Remelting, VIM & EB Melt (2 of 3)	2	39	110	3353	73
13	Supervise & Operate Hot Mills & Forging (2 of 3)	2	36	112	3389	74
14	Supervise & Operate Cold Strip Mill (2 of 3)	2	39	114	3428	75
15	Supervise & Operate Manufacturing Area (2 of 4)	2	36	116	3464	76
16	Shop Floor Control (1 of 3)	7	204	123	3668	80
17	M. P. E. Statistical Process Control & Process Optimization (2 of 1)	6	172	129	3840	84
18	Shop Floor Control (2 of 3)	4	92	133	3932	86
19	Grounds Maintenance (1 of 4)	7	178	140	4110	90

ORGANIZATION BEING RANKED	PREPARED BY	DATE	Page 1 of 3
MILL PRODUCTS	MILL MANAGER	7/29/78	

(1) RANK	(2) PACKAGE NAME	(3) 1978 PROPOSED		(4) 1979 CUMULATIVE		
		Positions	Expense (excl. cap.)	Positions	Expense (excl. cap.)	% of 1978 Revised
20	Work Stores (1 of 3)	10	255	150	4365	96
21	Vehicle Operator (1 of 4)	3	63	153	4428	97
22	Material Handling (2 of 4)	4	81	157	4509	99
23	Garage Vehicle Repair (2 of 4)	2	56	159	4565	100
24	Division Utility Labor Pool (1 of 2)	8	7	167	4572	100
25	Yard Departmental Supervision (2 of 3)	2	34	169	4606	101
26	Material Handling (3 of 4)	3	56	172	4662	103
27	Grounds Maintenance (2 of 4)	2	42	174	4704	103
28	Grounds Maintenance (3 of 4)	2	25	176	4729	104
29	Work Stores (2 of 3)	4	63	180	4792	105
30	Supervise ESR, Vac Arc Remelting, VIM & EB Melting (3 of 3)	2	35	182	4827	106
31	Supervise & Operate Manufacturing Service Area (3 of 4)	2	36	184	4863	107
32	Vehicle Operator (2 of 4)	2	50	186	4913	108
33	Garage Vehicle Repair (3 of 4)	2	35	188	4948	108
34	Vehicle Operator (3 of 4)	2	27	190	4975	109
35	Supervise & Operate Hot Mills & Forging (3 of 3)	3	78	193	5053	111
36	Supervise & Operate Cold Strip Mill (3 of 3)	2	15	195	5068	111
37	M.P.E. (other than Mill Service) (1 of 1)	2	46	197	5114	112
38	Division Utility Labor Pool (2 of 2)	8	7	205	5121	112

ORGANIZATION BEING RANKED	PREPARED BY	DATE	Page 2 of 3
MILL PRODUCTS	MILL MANAGER	7/29/78	

EXHIBIT 30.5 *(Continued)*

DECISION PACKAGE RANKING

(1) RANK	(2) PACKAGE NAME	(3) 1978 PROPOSED		(4) 1979 CUMULATIVE		
		Positions	Expense (excl. cap.)	Positions	Expense (excl. cap.)	% of 1978 Revised
39	Supervise Air Melt, Reclaim & Weighroom (3 of 4)	2	39	207	5160	113
40	Mill Management (2 of 2)	2	46	209	5206	114
41	M.P.E. – Eng. Relief on Conversion Coverage (3 of 1)	3	78	212	5284	116
42	Supervise & Operate Mfgr. Services Area (4 of 4)	2	17	214	5301	116
43	Grounds Maintenance (4 of 4)	2	27	216	5328	117
44	Material Handling (4 of 4)	3	106	219	5434	119
45	Yard Departmental Supervision (3 of 3)	2	31	221	5465	120
46	Supervise Air Melt, Reclaim & Weighroom (4 of 4)	2	36	223	5501	121
47	M.P.E. (2 of 1)	2	83	226	5584	122
48	Vehicle Operators (4 of 4)	2	27	228	5611	123
49	Garage Vehicle Repair (4 of 4)	2	36	230	5647	124
50	M.P.E. (Off-shift Coverage) (4 of 1)	3	66	233	5713	125
51	Shop Floor Control (3 of 3)	2	21	235	5734	126
52	Work Stores (3 of 3)	3	70	238	5804	127

ORGANIZATION BEING RANKED	PREPARED BY	DATE	Page _3_ of _3_
MILL PRODUCTS	MILL MANAGER	7/29/78	

EXHIBIT 30.5   Decision Package Ranking

ensures that the highest-priority decision packages have been funded. It means that some of the new high-priority programs have been funded by eliminating or reducing lower-priority, ongoing programs rather than by reducing profits.

Top management and the CEO complete the profit and loss by taking sales and other income; less direct labor, material, and fixed overhead; less some number of decision packages. This is graphically shown in Exhibit 30.6. Top management can make

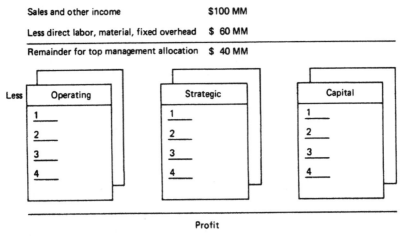

EXHIBIT 30.6   Top-Management Decision Making

a direct trade of decision packages in various rankings versus profit. To aid top management focus, decision packages and rankings may be segregated to show operating activities, strategic and long-range development programs, and capital (showing cash and depreciation expense). Top management must now make the very difficult decisions on funding allocations. The zero-based approach has systematically laid out the alternatives and priorities, not to make the decision process easier but to make it better.

PREPARING DETAILED BUDGETS

After the CEO has made the final funding decisions and established the division and corporate profit and loss, the approved decision packages are handed back to each manager for preparation of the detailed budget. The approved decision packages identified not only approved budget and manpower levels but also the accomplishments that were expected from each manager. Each manager then prepared his or her detail budgets, showing detailed expense accounts by month, which may be fed into the computer for monthly reporting purposes.

Traditional versus Zero-Based Budgeting

Exhibit 30.7 depicts traditional and ZBB as they flow through each of these stages. To simplify the comparison, let us assume that each process is preceded by a long-term plan. During the initial stages of the operating plan and budget, both processes develop sales forecasts from which the costs of direct labor, material, and overhead are calculated using standard costing procedures.

Until this stage, both standard and zero-based procedures are similar; however, at this point, they part company. Under the traditional method, each operating manager's (or financial staff's) next step is normally to estimate the cost of continuing current activities. This cost is usually not challenged in depth and is considered as a fixed base for the following year's operating plan. Managers then focus their time on developing costs for new activities proposed for the upcoming year. (This procedure is sometimes reversed if an entire organization must reduce its budget, with managers asked what they must do to cut X percent of their budget. However, the same basic problems still apply, except that the increment focused on is down instead of up.) In many organizations, each manager's request for new costs is often combined with a cost estimate for continuing current operations. The manager then provides to higher levels of management a detailed budget combining all proposed costs, which is usually accompanied by a narrative highlighting the new programs as well as next year's anticipated operations. These detailed budgets are then presented to top management.

Top management is now in the unhappy position of attempting to evaluate the detailed budgets and to reconcile them against the organization's goals and objectives. As all-too-frequently happens, budget requests exceed funding availability. When a budget is rejected, it is normally returned to the budget unit, where the budget development process is repeated and a revised detailed budget is prepared. Evaluation is not an easy task. Managers often are unable to determine whether appropriate actions have been planned or budgeted to achieve established goals. They must test the detailed budgets

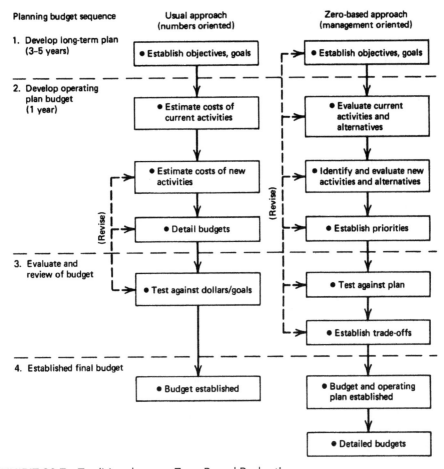

Planning budget sequence	Usual approach (numbers oriented)	Zero-based approach (management oriented)
1. Develop long-term plan (3–5 years)	• Establish objectives, goals	• Establish objectives, goals
2. Develop operating plan budget (1 year)	• Estimate costs of current activities	• Evaluate current activities and alternatives
	• Estimate costs of new activities	• Identify and evaluate new activities and alternatives
	• Detail budgets	• Establish priorities
3. Evaluate and review of budget	• Test against dollars/goals	• Test against plan
		• Establish trade-offs
4. Established final budget	• Budget established	• Budget and operating plan established
		• Detailed budgets

EXHIBIT 30.7   Traditional versus Zero-Based Budgeting

against dollar goals; typically they find that alternatives and lower levels of expense, and their consequences, are not identified.

Under ZBB, current activities and alternatives are evaluated at the same time as new programs are identified and considered. Operating managers establish their priorities and thereby identify the trade-offs between expenditure levels and operating needs. New activities can be ranked higher than current ones, and thus new programs can be funded within existing funding levels. Top management makes the final evaluation and funding decisions on the basis of the decision package and the ranking analysis.

Using ZBB, top management can readily test the budget against the operating plan, since it is looking at an evaluation in terms of priorities rather than in terms of numbers. It can identify trade-offs, determine the consequences of alternative expenditure levels, and, based on its evaluation, come up with a new and better set of allocations for the upcoming budget year. From its analysis of decision packages, management gets not only a budget but an operating plan, and the budget is a product of operating decisions.

(All too often, companies make budget decisions first, and these decisions become a rigid framework within which line managers must make their operating plans.)

Additional Applications

Top managers have two additional key benefits that they can derive from the zero-based approach: (1) ability to react effectively to changing situations and (2) ability to focus on strategic development efforts in a program matrix.

Changing Situations

The environment seems to be getting more and more unpredictable, and the sales and other projections made by management at the beginning of the planning and budgeting cycle versus the actual situation are sometimes very different by the time the budget cycle is complete—and even more at variance during the operating year. Some companies try to counteract this problem by building contingency plans.

The zero-based approach, however, is a built-in contingency plan, based on the decision packages and priorities. If sales or other assumptions change or if actuals differ from budget, one can quickly take four steps:

1. Adjust direct labor, material, and fixed overhead budgets based on the standard costing system.
2. Identify on an exception basis those decision packages directly affected by the change—usually a small percentage of the packages (e.g., if sales change, maintenance and quality control packages will be modified, but accounting and research will not be affected).
3. Modify rankings, if required, for changes in priorities or ranking of new or expanded programs.
4. Add or delete decision packages in priority order.

This process can be done rapidly even in large organizations because decision packages and rankings can be modified on an exception basis—the entire process does not have to be recycled. These revisions can be made during the planning and budgeting process as planning assumptions change or during the operating year as actuals differ from plan (reflecting, of course, that once midway through the year, the decision package costs that can be affected will be reduced accordingly).

Strategic Development

Strategic planning is one of the most difficult tasks facing top management. It deals with futures and many uncertainties and cuts across organizational lines; these programs are often among the first to be cut, because they are new and are easier to cut than operations such as maintenance. Many organizations have three- to five-year projections showing sales and profit growth, yet their five-year plan becomes a six-year plan when the final "cut 5 percent" eliminates or severely reduces many of those development programs required to achieve growth. The responsibility for strategic development rests heavily with top management and should be a major focus during the planning and budgeting review.

The zero-based approach offers top management a vehicle to use in translating long-term plans into action plans and budgets by way of the decision package and ranking. Decision packages may be prepared for the research, marketing, engineering, manufacturing, and capital requirements of each strategic plan. These decision packages can then be ranked by major program or objective (rather than by organization). Top management can then focus on these strategic development plans, ensure a coordinated approach (e.g., the research department's setting a high priority on the program while marketing eliminates its efforts), and determine the funding trade-offs among elements of the strategic program, among strategic programs, and among strategic/operating/profit needs (as shown in Exhibit 30.6).

SUMMARY

The zero-based approach is not a panacea and is not without its problems. The major problem is that many managers feel threatened by a process that evaluates the effectiveness of their programs. The zero-based process also requires a great deal of effective administration, communication, and training of managers who will be involved in the analysis. Managers may also have problems in identifying appropriate decision units, developing adequate data to produce an effective analysis, determining the minimum level of effort, ranking dissimilar programs, and handling large volumes of packages. For many programs, work-load and performance measures may be lacking or the program's impact may not be well defined so that the analysis will be less than perfect. Therefore, ZBB should be looked upon as a longer-term management development process rather than a one-year cure-all.

If done properly, the zero-based approach is not subject to the gamesmanship one might anticipate. The traditional budget approach offers maximum opportunity for gamesmanship because current operations are seldom evaluated, and many discrete decisions are never explicitly identified and get buried in the numbers. However, the zero-based approach removes the umbrella covering current operations and requires managers to identify operating decisions clearly. In ZBB, the most obvious forms of gamesmanship would be to avoid identifying reasonable alternatives, to include the pet projects within the minimum-level package, and to rank high-priority programs low in order to obtain additional funding. If the decision packages are formatted to display the alternatives considered, the workload and performance data, the descriptions of actions, and enough cost data so that discretionary items cannot be built into the cost estimate, it becomes very obvious when such gamesmanship is attempted. Also, because the entire ranking of decision packages must be displayed, it is very easy to challenge a high-priority item that received a low ranking or a low-priority item that received a high ranking.

The problems in implementing ZBB are not to be minimized. The specific needs, problems, and capabilities of each organization must be considered in adapting the approach. Although most of the basic concepts of the approach have been maintained, the specifics of administration, formats, and procedures have been different for each organization that has adopted the approach. ZBB can be applied on an intensive basis throughout all levels of an organization, only to selected programs, or only at major program levels rather than involving all operating managers. The strategy of implementing the zero-based approach must be developed for each organization, depending on its specific needs and capabilities.

Top management must play a major role in implementation. Because the process is difficult, managers must stand behind it, understand it, and use it. Finally, managers must be willing to make the tough decisions and trade-offs that the process requires.

CHAPTER THIRTY-ONE

Bracket Budgeting

Michael W. Curran
Decision Sciences Corporation

INTRODUCTION

Annual budgeting is a way of life in most organization. Planning and control, the two phases of operational budgeting, receive considerable attention at all levels of management. All too often, however, the actual profit differs significantly from the target. This difference is generally attributed to the vagaries of modern business, and rightly so. But this is simply an admission that conventional budgeting is often incapable of coping with business realities.

The reason for this deficiency is fundamental. With conventional budgeting, the forecast of each element in the budget must ultimately be represented as a single number, even though management may know beforehand that thousands of other values are possible. If there are more than a few such elements, the number of possible ways in which they can combine and their effects cascade to the bottom line defies analysis. Bracket budgeting, an analytical procedure that complements conventional budgeting techniques, overcomes this serious inadequacy. This relatively new methodology is a synergistic combination of basic concepts in modeling, simulation, and heuristics that gives management an unequaled understanding of the future.

It must be emphasized that the personal computer plays an integral and indispensable role in bracket budgeting. This means, of course, that it must be programmed to perform the myriad calculations required. Although bracket budgeting can be successfully employed by any manager, development of the necessary computer programs requires substantial technical expertise. The purpose here is to explain the general theory of bracket budgeting and how it is applied by management. Technical issues underlying the theory are discussed only in terms of their practical interpretation and application. No attempt is made to adequately cover this complex subject.

APPLICATION OF BRACKET BUDGETING

The profit or cost center is the basic level of application of bracket budgeting. (Hereafter, profit and cost centers will be referred to as budget centers, with the bottom line of the cost center considered as negative profit.) The scope of the budget center depends on such factors as the size of the company, its organizational characteristics, and the manner in which budgetary responsibilities are defined. A small firm may consist of a single budget center. In larger organizations, each division may be composed of numerous budget centers such as production departments, sales branches, or product lines. Since bracket budgeting is merely an adjunct of conventional budgeting, its wholesale application throughout an entire company or division is not required; only those budget centers that can benefit from the technique should employ it. The determining factors are uncertainty, complexity, controllability, and commitment. Each of these must be in evidence to a significant degree for a budget center to implement and utilize bracket budgeting successfully.

A budget center is a candidate for bracket budgeting if any possible variance from its targeted bottom line would, in management's eyes, constitute a significant change in the bottom line of the operational unit of which it is a part. In other words, the degree of uncertainty about its bottom-line performance must be substantial enough to cause concern at higher levels of management. In companies organized by divisions, this criterion tends to eliminate from consideration a number of budget centers in each division and, in some cases, entire divisions.

Assuming that the budget center demonstrates the requisite degree of uncertainty, it must then be shown to possess significant complexity. In this sense, "complexity" means that there is a significant number of elements in the budget and that the ways in which they interact to produce changes in the bottom line are not patently obvious. Complexity should not be confused with size. Many budget centers that are large insofar as their bottom lines are concerned are rather simple in operation. Yet many small budget centers are quite complex.

Next, there is the matter of controllability. If the nature of the budget center is such that management has a very limited range of decision options with which to influence bottom-line results, there is little point in applying bracket budgeting. The principal benefit of the technique lies in its ability to identify potential problems and opportunities related to future bottom-line performance. If management cannot then change the probable course of events by exercising its influence over those critical elements of the business that account for these potentialities, the major benefit of bracket budgeting is obviated.

Finally, and perhaps most important, there must be a genuine commitment by the budget center's management to apply and aggressively exploit the capabilities afforded by bracket budgeting. More than lip service is needed. Management must attach the utmost importance to the planning process and recognize that its benefits result from diligence, not default.

PREMISES TO PROFITS?

"Profit planning and budgetary control," a phrase in common use, implicitly differentiates between the terms "profit plan" and "budget." The profit plan, an antecedent of the budget, is management's assessment of the coming fiscal year, along with a planned course of action to attain acceptable financial performance for that period. The degree of formalization of the profit plan varies according to the needs and attitudes of management. Generally, the larger and more complex the business, the more formal the profit plan. In some cases, it may simply be a verbal consensus on the most critical components; in other cases, it may receive much attention in all stages of its development. Elaborate details may be injected regarding industry and market share trends, advertising, key accounts, production, distribution, and so forth. Page after page of supporting narrative may be included to explain the overall thrust of the plan and its various intricacies.

In simplest terms, however, the profit plan is a set of premises upon which management charts a course of action for the coming fiscal year. The budget is the quantification of the profit plan into accounting formats. Of principal concern here is the pro forma income statement and its supporting detail. In essence then, the budgeted bottom line on the income statement is a fairly accurate estimate of the actual bottom line—*if* the set of premises (the profit plan) is essentially valid *or if* "compensating factors" occur. Herein lies the problem.

A firm's track record with budgeting usually reflects the complexity of its business and the uncertainty conditions under which it must operate. An organization with few products or services operating in a relatively stable environment tends to have little difficulty in forecasting profit within an acceptable margin of error. A firm offering a multitude of products or services under volatile conditions, however, is more apt to experience a large variance from forecast. This is particularly true of individual budget centers within such an organization. In a budget center where a significant profit variance is possible, the value of budgeting is called into question. What can management hope to accomplish? This question is appropriate to both the planning and control phases of operational budgeting.

With regard to budgetary control, consider the case of a budget center experiencing a substantially unfavorable year-to-date profit variance. Management carefully reviews the operation and, as a result, decides to do something differently. In other words, it changes tactics. What, exactly, is its reason for doing this? One is tempted to say that the purpose is to achieve the annual profit target. In fact, however, this is not the basic objective. Consciously or otherwise, management is attempting to improve its chances, or probability, that actual profit will be at least as much as the target. As it turns out of course, increasing this probability increases profit—even if the target is not reached. Recognition of this subtle but important difference leads to the conclusion that conventional budgeting falls far short of management's objective. There is no mechanism to measure, monitor, and manage this probability throughout the budgeting period. More important, potential profit problems and opportunities that influence this probability cannot be identified and ranked in order of decision priority so that management can take early and appropriate action to improve the odds for success.

Similar shortcomings are apparent in the annual planning phase. What chance is there of attaining next year's profit target? Is it close to 75 percent or nearer to 10 percent? (Managers are often shocked to learn it is inordinately low or high.) What factors, ranked in order of importance, account for this low or high probability? Which of these factors can something be done about now to improve the chance of success? Practically speaking, what is the lowest potential profit next year? The highest? Will this proposed marketing plan increase the probability of reaching the annual profit target? By how much? With bracket budgeting, critical questions such as these can be adequately answered to avoid surprises later.

DEVELOPING A TACTICAL BUDGETING MODEL

Once it is determined that bracket budgeting should be implemented in a budget center, a tactical budgeting model must be developed. Prior to actually developing the model, a careful examination is made of the budget and its supporting detail. Wherever possible, significant line items in the budget are analyzed in terms of their basic elements. Thus, sales may be stated by product and, if appropriate, each product considered in terms of unit demand and selling price per unit. In some cases this may be further refined to major customers or some other subcategory. Once these basic elements are identified, they are used to develop a tactical budgeting model, which is generally a series of simple equations showing how the elements combine to produce the bottom line.

Effective use of bracket budgeting largely depends on the complexity of the tactical budgeting model. Strange as it may seem, the more time devoted to developing this model, the less useful it probably will be. The reason is quite simple. Spending a considerable amount of time attempting to make the model as realistic as possible inevitably leads to a level of complexity that the budget center manager will find neither necessary nor understandable. The objective here is not to make mathematicians out of managers but to provide them with a fairly simple and highly useful model.

It must be remembered that this model will be used in tactical budgeting, an area of application where the period being forecasted does not extend years into the future as it does in strategic budgeting problems. This permits the inclusion of many simplifying assumptions, assumptions that would not hold water if the model were to be used in a capital investment analysis, for example. Unlimited production capacity and products having no market elasticity are good examples of simplifying assumptions that can very often be made in developing a tactical budgeting model. In those few cases in which such an assumption would be inappropriate for whatever reason, the model can be expanded to describe the situation adequately. Again, however, these exceptions should be treated as simply as possible. If developing a tactical budgeting model requires more than a few hours or days, there is every likelihood that it will be more complex than is necessary or desirable. And that would be a serious error indeed.

One technique often used to simplify development of a tactical budgeting model deserves special mention. It is particularly helpful in developing a model of a budget center having a substantial number of products: from a hundred up into the thousands. Almost a century ago, Vilfredo Pareto observed that a small number of people accounted for a large portion of total wealth. This phenomenon of a relatively small percentage of a population accounting for a very large portion of a characteristic of the population can be found in innumerable situations and is referred to as Pareto's law or the 80/20 rule. Pareto's law is well known to most managers but exploited by few. It frequently manifests itself in a budget center having a very large number of products: A relatively small number of them will account for a very large portion of the bottom line. The best measure of a product's contribution to the bottom line is its gross profit, in dollars. Those relatively few products that are important can be readily identified by a stratified-cumulative gross profit analysis, as is later demonstrated. The number of elements in the tactical budgeting model can therefore be drastically reduced by enumerating only the important products and accounting for the remainder in just two elements: sales of all other products" and "cost of goods sold of all other products," for example.

Identifying the Critical Elements

A principal feature of conventional budgeting is its ability to analyze past performance—last month or year-to-date, for example. Bracket budgeting also tracks actual performance, albeit in a much different way. However, bracket budgeting's primary focus is on the future—next year during annual profit planning and next month or next quarter in the budgetary control phase.

In the budgetary control application, bracket budgeting enables management to challenge tactics in order to determine whether there is a high probability they will lead to the desired result—achieving targeted profit for the next quarter, for example. If current tactics are demonstrated to be unequal to the task, bracket budgeting highlights those areas that deserve attention. With these hot spots identified and ranked, management then concentrates its effort where it is needed most—in developing one or more alternate methods of achieving the goal. Bracket budgeting is reemployed to test these alternatives and management then implements that alternative which maximizes the chance for success. In many organizations, applying this concept on a monthly rather than a quarterly basis would be ineffective; an appreciable part of the month will have gone by before any benefits would be realized from a change in tactics.

Once the budget center's basic elements are identified and a tactical budgeting model is developed, the next quarter's budget is analyzed to determine each element's impact and critical variance. Each element, in turn, is set at a value that is 1 percent more favorable than its target (while all other elements are held at their respective targets), and the resultant change in the budget center's bottom line is determined. This change is called that element's 1 percent impact. Since all elements are varied each in turn by this same percentage, their impacts can be compared. Management then specifies the maximum percentage change from the profit target that it is willing to accept as attributable to any one element. In most budget centers, 2 percent works quite nicely. This cutoff value, along with the impact, is then used to determine the critical variance of each element.

For example, if the profit target is $100,000 and the 2% figure is used, then the cutoff value at the bottom line is $2,000. If a given element's 1 percent impact is $250, the critical variance for that element is 8 percent, as is found by dividing 2,000 by 250. Looking at it another way, for every 1 percent variance from target on this element, the bottom line is changed by $250. Thus, an 8 percent variance would change the bottom line by $2,000. However, that is the cutoff value stipulated by management; therefore, the critical variance for the element must be 8 percent. Management generally finds it more helpful if critical variances are expressed in units rather than percentages. For example, if a sales element has a target of 3,000 gallons and a critical variance of 3 percent, the critical variance would be expressed as 90 gallons.

If, for the next quarter, it is conceivable that the variance of any given element can exceed its critical variance either favorably or unfavorably, then that element is classified as a critical element. Pareto's law predicts there will be relatively few. In actual practice, a budget center typically has between 10 and 20 critical elements—regardless of the budget center's size or complexity. Thus, management's attention can be sharply focused on those relatively few elements of the business that play such vital roles in its bottom-line performance.

Fishing Supplies Company

Fishing Supplies Company, a hypothetical budget center, may be thought of as a small firm or as a profit center in a larger corporation. The management team consists of a general manager (Gene), a marketing manager (Mary), a production manager (Paul), and a controller (Carl). Fishing Supplies is just about to complete the fifth month of its current fiscal year. The budget for its upcoming third quarter is shown in Exhibit 31.1.

EXHIBIT 31.1   Fishing Supplies Company's Third-Quarter Budget

Sales		$500,000
Cost of goods sold		360,000
Gross profit		$140,000
Operating expenses		
Commissions	$45,000	
Advertising	9,000	
Other selling expenses	6,000	
Administrative expenses	32,000	
Total operating expenses		92,000
Net operating income		$48,000
Other income	$3,000	
Other expense	1,000	2,000
Net income before taxes		$ 50,000

EXHIBIT 31.2   Fishing Supplies Company's Third-Quarter Budget—Gross Profit Before and After Fixed Costs

Sales	$500,000
Cost of goods sold (variable costs only)	270,000
Gross profit (before fixed costs)	$230,000
Cost of goods sold (fixed factory overhead)	90,000
Gross profit (after fixed costs)	$140,000

(Since any example must necessarily be brief, much fault can be found with this one. Undoubtedly, the real world is not as simple as suggested here, but this lack of reality in no way impairs a serious treatment of the bracket budgeting methodology.)

Carl took the first step in developing the tactical budgeting model by preparing an analysis of the third-quarter budget in terms of gross profit, both before and after fixed costs. The results are depicted in Exhibit 31.2. The management team feels that exclusion of the fixed portion of cost of goods sold from gross profit more faithfully represents the bottom-line contributions of the products. (Gross profit before fixed costs will hereafter be referred to simply as gross profit.) In effect, Carl treated these data as if Fishing Supplies were operating under a direct costing system. It needs to be pointed out, however, that bracket budgeting requires no specific method of costing; it operates equally well with standard, direct, activity based, and other types of accounting systems.

Next, Carl prepared Exhibit 31.3 showing the sales, variable cost, and gross profit for each of the six product lines. He identified the importance of each product line by indicating its rank according to the magnitude of its budgeted gross profit in the third quarter. Carl was not surprised to see that lures are the largest contributor to Fishing Supplies' bottom line and bait buckets the smallest. After reviewing this information, he was able to quickly prepare the stratified-cumulative gross profit analysis shown in Exhibit 31.4. Carl simply listed the product lines in descending order of gross profit, indicating the percentage each accounts for of the total gross profit and, in the last column, the cumulative percentage. The Pareto effect is quite

EXHIBIT 31.3   Fishing Supplies Company's Third-Quarter Budget—Gross Profit (Before Fixed Costs) by Product Line

Product Line	Sales	Variable Cost	Gross Profit[a]	Rank
Rods	$26,404	$14,028	$12,376	4
Reels	135,999	95,046	40,953	3
Lures	190,402	97,691	92,711	1
Bait buckets	12,012	6,258	5,754	6
Minnow traps	19,596	13,156	6,440	5
Tackle boxes	115,587	43,821	71,766	2
Total	$500,000	$270,000	$230,000	

[a] Before fixed costs.

EXHIBIT 31.4 Fishing Supplies Company's Third-Quarter Budget—Gross Profit (Before Fixed Costs) by Product Line, Using Stratified–Cumulative Analysis

Product Line	Rank	Gross Profit[a]	Percentage of Total	Cumulative Percentage
Lures	1	$92,711	40.3	40.3
Tackle boxes	2	71,766	31.2	71.5
Reels	3	40,953	17.8	89.3
Rods	4	12,376	5.4	94.7
Minnow traps	5	6,440	2.8	97.5
Bait buckets	6	5,754	2.5	100.0
Total		$230,000	100.0	

[a] Before fixed costs.

obvious here; half of the products account for 89.3 percent of total gross profit. Since Fishing Supplies does not have that many products to start with, the management team decided to include all of them as individual elements in the tactical budgeting model.

After Gene, Mary, and Paul reviewed all this information, Carl prepared Exhibit 31.5 showing the third-quarter budgeted unit sales, unit selling prices, and unit variable costs for all six product lines. Upon meeting and discussing all of these analyses, the management team developed a simple tactical budgeting model. Its elements are described in Exhibit 31.6, and their logical relationships to the bottom line are given in Exhibit 31.7. The model consists of 25 elements, 19 of which pertain to sales and cost of goods sold. Because commissions are a variable expense, they are stated as a percentage of sales, the element on which they depend.

The model was then used to analyze the third-quarter budget and to calculate the impact and critical variance of each element. The results are given in Exhibit 31.8. Reviewing the data for just one of the elements will clarify the very important concepts of impact and critical variance. The unit sales of reels was favorably varied by 1 percent from its target of 7,300 units, in effect making it 7,373 units, while all

EXHIBIT 31.5 Fishing Supplies Company's Third-Quarter Budget—Unit Sales With Unit Selling Prices and Unit Variable Costs

Product Line	Sales	Variable Cost	Unit Sales	Selling Price per Unit	Variable Cost per Unit
Rods	$26,404	$14,028	2,800 ea.	$9.43	$5.01
Reels	135,999	95,046	7,300 ea.	18.63	13.02
Lures	190,402	97,691	8,300 doz.	22.94	11.77
Bait buckets	12,012	6,258	2,100 ea.	5.72	2.98
Minnow traps	19,596	13,156	4,600 ea.	4.26	2.86
Tackle boxes	115,587	43,821	8,100 ea.	14.27	5.41
Total	$500,000	$270,000			

EXHIBIT 31.6 Fishing Supplies Company—Elements of Tactical Budgeting Model

Element	Description of Element	Unit
E1	Rods—unit sales	ea.
E2	Rods—selling price	$/ea.
E3	Rods—variable cost	$/ea.
E4	Reels—unit sales	ea.
E5	Reels—selling price	$/ea.
E6	Reels—variable cost	$/ea.
E7	Lures—unit sales	doz.
E8	Lures—selling price	$/doz.
E9	Lures—variable cost	$/doz.
E10	Bait buckets—unit sales	ea.
E11	Bait buckets—selling price	$/ea.
E12	Bait buckets—variable cost	$/ea.
E13	Minnow traps—unit sales	ea.
E14	Minnow traps—selling price	$/ea.
E15	Minnow traps—variable cost	$/ea.
E16	Tackle boxes—unit sales	ea.
E17	Tackle boxes—selling price	$/ea.
E18	Tackle boxes—variable cost	$/ea.
E19	Fixed factory overhead	$
E20	Commissions (% of sales)	%
E21	Advertising	$
E22	Other selling expenses	$
E23	Administrative expenses	$
E24	Other income	$
E25	Other expense	$

EXHIBIT 31.7 Fishing Supplies Company—Tactical Budgeting Model

Sales = (E1 × E2) + (E4 × E5) + (E7 × E8) + (E10 × E11) + (E13 × E14) + (E16 × E17)

Variable costs = (E1 × E3) + (E4 × E6) + (E7 × E9) + (E10 × E12) + (E13 × E15) + (E16 × E18)

Total cost of goods sold = Variable costs + E19

Gross profit = Sales − Total cost of goods sold

Commissions = 0.01 × E20 × Sales

Total operating expenses = Commissions + E21 + E22 + E23

Net operating income = Gross profit − Total operating expenses

Net income before taxes = Net operating income + E24 − E25

EXHIBIT 31.8   Fishing Supplies Company's Third-Quarter Budget—Impact and Critical Variance Analysis

Description of Element	Unit	Target	1% Impact ($)	Critical Variance
Rods—unit sales	ea.	2,800	100	280
Rods—selling price	$/ea.	9.43	240	0.39
Rods—variable cost	$/ea.	5.01	140	0.36
Reels—unit sales[a]	ea.	7,300	287	254
Reels—selling price[a]	$/ea.	18.63	1,238	0.15
Reels—variable cost[a]	$/ea.	13.02	950	0.14
Lures—unit sales[a]	doz.	8,300	756	110
Lures—selling price[a]	$/doz.	22.94	1,733	0.13
Lures—variable cost	$/doz.	11.77	977	0.12
Bait buckets—unit sales	ea.	2,100	47	449
Bait buckets—selling price	$/ea.	5.72	109	0.52
Bait buckets—variable cost	$/ea.	2.98	63	0.48
Minnow traps—unit sales	ea.	4,600	47	984
Minnow traps—selling price	$/ea.	4.26	178	0.24
Minnow traps—variable cost	$/ea.	2.86	132	0.22
Tackle boxes—unit sales[a]	ea.	8,100	614	132
Tackle boxes—selling price[a]	$/ea.	14.27	1,052	0.14
Tackle boxes—variable cost[a]	$/ea.	5.41	438	0.12
Fixed factory overhead[a]	$	90,000	900	1,000
Commissions (% of sales)	%	9.0	450	0.2
Advertising	$	9,000	90	1,000
Other selling expenses	$	6,000	60	1,000
Administrative expenses[a]	$	32,000	320	1,000
Other income	$	3,000	30	1,000
Other expense	$	1,000	10	1,000

[a] Critical element.

other elements were held at their respective targets. The model then calculated the bottom line and found it to be $50,287 rather than the $50,000 target. Thus, selling 73 additional reels would increase the bottom line by $287, the element's 1 percent impact as shown in Exhibit 31.8. This is verified rather easily by noting that the element's unit selling price of $18.63 yields an additional $1,359.99 in sales when multiplied by the 73 additional units, and its unit variable cost of $13.02 results in an additional $950.46 in cost of goods sold when multiplied by the same 73 units. Thus, the difference between the $1,359.99 additional sales and the $950.46 additional cost is $409.53 additional gross profit.

Commissions would have to be paid on these additional sales, a fact considered by the model. (Like all the other elements, commissions were held at a target value, but that value is a rate, not dollars. Thus, the model will reduce any additional sales by the appropriate amount of commissions to reflect the correct net effect at the bottom line.) At the rate of 9 percent, there would be an additional commission cost of $122.40 on the additional $1,359.99 of sales. Subtracting this $122.40 from the $409.53 additional gross profit previously calculated leaves $287.13, which, to the nearest dollar, is the 1 percent impact for the unit sales of reels shown in Exhibit 31.8.

Now, since a 1 percent change in the unit sales of reels would result in a $287 change in the bottom line, for the bottom line to swing by as much as the cutoff value of 2 percent (which is $1,000), the unit sales of reels would have to vary by 3.48 percent, as is found by dividing $1,000 by the $287.13 impact figure. Therefore, the critical variance is 3.48 percent or, as is found by multiplying 7,300 by 3.48 percent, 254 units. This is the critical variance for the unit sales of reels as shown in the exhibit.

Upon reviewing the information in Exhibit 31.8, Fishing Supplies' management identified ten critical elements. Each of these is noted in the exhibit. As an example, the unit sales of reels was deemed critical since, according to Mary, its third-quarter performance could easily vary from target by more than 254 units, its critical variance. Conversely, Paul stated that the maximum potential fluctuation in the variable cost of rods is less than its critical variance of $0.36 per unit. That explains why this particular element is not critical. Commissions is not a critical element since management rightfully expects its actual value to be identical to its target, which is expressed as a rate rather than as dollars.

Scientific Guessing

If uncertainty is to be dealt with effectively, it must be measured. The bottom-line target reposes in a two-dimensional world: dollars and the chance of achieving those dollars. (In this sense, "achieving" means an actual value at least as favorable as the target.) Managers are aware of this second dimension, but, lacking a yardstick to measure it, they are forced to deal with it in a qualitative, often disastrous, fashion. The uncertainty associated with the bottom-line target results from the uncertainties of the critical elements above it on the budgeted income statement. If the number of such elements is more than a few, as is usually the case, the human mind finds itself incapable of adequately evaluating their concurrent potential effects on the bottom line.

However, this is exactly what conventional budgeting asks management to do. Bracket budgeting, however, breaks the problem down into its component parts. Management is asked to assess the uncertainty of each critical element. Then, with the use of the tactical budgeting model and a personal computer, bracket budgeting puts all of these individual uncertainties together in such a way that the uncertainty related to the bottom line can be determined and presented to management for decision-making purposes.

A critical element's uncertainty may be assessed in a number of ways. Most of these, however, require a basic understanding of probability theory and statistics, technical knowledge that all managers cannot be presumed to have. There is one simple but effective measure: the range. The manager determines the range by specifying the highest value that the element's actual can assume, the lowest value that the element's actual can assume, and the probability that the element's actual value will be at least as favorable as its target. By measuring uncertainty with the range, the manager "brackets" the element's ultimate true value, a process analogous to skeet shooting: High scores are achieved with a shotgun, not a rifle.

The lowest and highest estimates in the range have no importance per se; they merely serve as boundaries. The greater the uncertainty, of course, the farther apart these boundaries and the broader the range. The element's target is also a boundary in that it divides the range into two parts, favorable and unfavorable. (If the target is infeasible, then the entire range is either favorable or unfavorable.) The probability factor is simply management's confidence that the element's actual value will materialize anywhere in the favorable part of the range. For that reason, this probability is often called the *confidence factor.* The confidence factor's complement is the risk. For example, if a confidence factor of 75 percent is specified for a given element, then the chance of unfavorable performance (i.e., risk) is 25 percent.

By assessing each critical element in this manner, management can better articulate its perception of the future—certainly much better than by mentally wrestling with all the elements simultaneously. This approach also has the advantage of putting the target into perspective. Assuming it is attainable, the target is but one point in a spectrum of feasible points. Unfortunately, the target is often referred to as the "best estimate." This implies that there is at least a 50 percent chance that the actual will be at least as favorable as the target. Although this may indeed be true, it can be misleading in that it says nothing about how far the actual might be from that target, in either direction. A range is much more practical than a target or average figure—imagine a person who cannot swim, about to wade across a river, being told the average depth is three feet. Also, ranging tends to minimize the differences between bullish and bearish managers; the capability of looking at an element in terms of its potential extremes begs for a realistic assessment of its uncertainty.

When specifying a critical element's range, management takes into account all foreseeable circumstances. Ideally, the lowest estimate should be determined in such a manner that there is slightly less than a 1 percent chance of the actual going beyond that boundary of the range. The highest estimate should be determined in similar fashion. In essence, then, the chance that the actual will fall within the range is better than 98 percent or, for all practical purposes, 100 percent.

In qualitative terms, the lowest and highest estimates should each be far enough out to capture the extremely improbable, but not the slightly absurd. When first faced with making a judgment of this type, some managers are uneasy about the procedure since it involves "a lot" of guesswork. But that is precisely why conventional budgeting comes up short in many cases; working solely with targets involves only a little guesswork. So little, in fact, that the potential variability of the bottom line cannot be adequately ascertained. There is nothing wrong with guessing, as long as proper recognition is given to inherent error. After all, Nobel Prizes have resulted from shrewd scientific guessing. A ranging error in bracket budgeting has far less import than a comparable percentage error in the target if the target is the only measure of future performance. In terms of informational enrichment, the target often suffers in abject poverty. The range, no matter how subjective it is, has much more informational reliability than any single point from within it, including the target.

Fishing Supplies Company

One month from now, Fishing Supplies' third quarter will begin. Four months from now, no one will be able to do anything about it. Potential problems must be uncovered now before they become realities later. Management cannot afford to wait until the middle of the quarter for a report showing the actuals for the first month of that quarter. (That is like steering a car along an interstate highway by watching nothing other than the white line in the rearview mirror.)

Yesterday morning the management team reviewed the third-quarter budget, considering all currently available information and under the assumption that business will be conducted according to the tactics originally outlined in the profit plan. The greatest portion of this meeting was devoted to establishing ranges for the critical elements. Two targets were found to be infeasible since they fell outside of their respective ranges. However, the managers did not establish new targets for these elements. Instead of rebudgeting, they merely reassessed the reasonableness of the original targets by stating ranges. No time was spent ranging the noncritical elements. The forecast of each of these was "frozen" at its target, unless management believed another value was a better estimate; then the element was frozen at that value instead of its target.

The data developed during yesterday morning's meeting are given in Exhibit 31.9. By having this opportunity to tell it like it is, Fishing Supplies' managers have come to grips head on with the problem of uncertainty. It is evident that they know much more about the current status of each critical element than they could possibly convey in any single-value forecast. This informational reservoir has previously gone untapped at Fishing Supplies—untapped, at least, by any reliable method.

Mary stated that, under the poorest conditions she could imagine, sales of reels would not fall below 6,500 units. Nor she could not envision demand rising above 8,000 units. (This assessment spans 1,501 possibilities, one of which is the target of 7,300 units.) Furthermore, she was rather confident that the actual value would be at least as favorable as the target, believing that there were three out of four chances this would occur. She therefore specified a confidence factor of 75 percent. The target for the selling price of reels was deemed infeasible, in an unfavorable way. Conversely, the target for administrative expenses was judged infeasible, in a favorable way.

Last week, Mary met with one of Fishing Supplies' major customers. During the course of conversation, she learned that the customer was experiencing considerable shifts in sales activity, including a dramatic reduction in the demand for tackle boxes. In fact, at the current rate of sales, the customer had enough in inventory for the next five months. Unfortunately, Mary had no way of predicting this when she prepared the annual profit plan; the third-quarter budget assumed continued high demand for tackle boxes from this major customer. (One of those premises just turned sour!) This is the primary reason why Mary's range for the unit sales of tackle boxes was so unfavorable compared to its target.

EXHIBIT 31.9   Fishing Supplies Company—Management's Assessment of Third Quarter, Based on Original Plan

Description of Element	Original Target	Confidence Factor	Lowest Estimate	Highest Estimate	Frozen Value
Rods—unit sales	2,800				2,600
Rods—selling price	9.43				9.58
Rods—variable cost	5.01				5.05
Reels—unit sales	7,300	75%	6,500	8,000	
Reels—selling price	18.63	0%	18.05	18.55	
Reels—variable cost	13.02	80%	12.75	13.10	
Lures—unit sales	8,300	40%	7,500	8,700	
Lures—selling price	22.94	75%	22.65	23.25	
Lures—variable cost	11.77				11.75
Bait buckets—unit sales	2,100				2,100
Bait buckets—selling price	5.72				5.72
Bait buckets—variable cost	2.98				2.98
Minnow traps—unit sales	4,600				3,900
Minnow traps—selling price	4.26				4.35
Minnow traps—variable cost	2.86				2.90
Tackle boxes—unit sales	8,100	20%	4,700	8,600	
Tackle boxes—selling price	14.27	50%	13.70	14.70	
Tackle boxes—variable cost	5.41	60%	5.30	5.55	
Fixed factory overhead	90,000	60%	87,000	93,000	
Commissions (% of sales)	9.0				9.0
Advertising	9,000				8,200
Other selling expenses	6,000				5,400
Administrative expenses	32,000	100%	30,000	31,500	
Other income	3,000				3,400
Other expense	1,000				1,000
Net income before taxes	50,000	?	?	?	

Although some of these ranges are rather broad, compared to many budget centers in the real world, Fishing Supplies' uncertainties are mild indeed. For that reason, and primarily because of the simplistic nature of this example, it is not difficult to see that Fishing Supplies' third-quarter pretax income target is in jeopardy. But what is the most urgent problem and how important is it? Even in this simple example, that question is not so easily answered. Considering only the unfavorable end points of the ranges, the lowest possible third-quarter pretax income is $3,224. Similarly, considering only the favorable end points, the highest pretax income is $74,489. However, the chance of the future unfolding close to either of these extremes is ridiculously small; these theoretical income limits are thus useless for all practical purposes.

Tapping the Power of the Personal Computer

Even with the few ranges in Fishing Supplies' case, there is an astronomical number of ways for the elements to combine to produce third-quarter pretax income. Not one of these combinations is important since the chance of it actually occurring is extremely small. What is important is the manner in which they compare with one another in what is known as the *income profile*. There is no need to consider each and every combination to determine the income profile, any more than it is necessary for a pharmaceutical company to inspect millions of tablets to reliably determine the quality of a given production run. Indeed, the quality can be determined by scientifically sampling a very small number of tablets.

In Fishing Supplies' case, a personal computer scientifically sampled relatively few combinations to develop a highly reliable income profile. In each sample, the computer selected a value from within the range of each of the 10 critical elements. (Any value contained in a range was available for selection, although all values did not have the same chance of being selected.) The computer then used these 10 values, along with the 15 frozen values of the noncritical elements, to compute the pretax income for that particular sample. This procedure was repeated many times over to develop the income profile. In any one of these samples, the value selected from within one range was in no way related to the value selected from within any other range, any more than in the "real world" the unit sales of reels is related to the variable cost of bait buckets. Thus, one sample might have reflected a high demand for reels and a low variable cost for bait buckets, whereas the next sample might have been the reverse of this, or any other possible combination of these two elements. In any case, the computer did nothing more than what management said was feasible. For example, considering unit sales of reels in any one sample, the computer selected one of the 1,501 possibilities that lie within its range. Furthermore, for each sample, there was a 25 percent chance of the computer's selecting a value less than the 7,300 target.

The computer sampled a total of 1,000 possibilities. In effect, it prepared 1,000 income statements of the third quarter, remembering the pretax income in each case. This number of samples is in excess of the reliability called for in this problem, but the computer required just a few seconds to complete the task. After completing the sampling process, the computer sorted the pretax income figures into an array of descending values. As a result, the topmost value was $63,128 and the bottommost $18,863. In other words, in the 1,000 samples, the computer did not find a value either less than $18,863 or greater than $63,128. Thus, for all practical purposes, the odds are greater than 1,000 to 1 against the actual third-quarter pretax income falling outside of these two values. For this reason, these values are referred to as the *practical income limits*.

Having been told that the target is $50,000 pretax income, the computer then searched the ranked array, starting at the topmost (largest) value. It continued searching down the array until it found the first value that was less than the $50,000 target. This occurred at the 278th position from the top. The value located there was just a few dollars less than the target. This means that 277 (or 27.7 percent) of the 1,000 values were at least as large as the target. Therefore, the computer reported that Fishing Supplies has a 28 percent chance of achieving its third-quarter pretax income goal. Conversely, since 723 of the 1,000 values were less than the target, the chance of an unfavorable result (i.e., the risk) is 72 percent.

The chance that actual pretax income will be at least as much as any given figure in the ranked array can be similarly determined. For example, the 900th value from the top was $30,362 pretax. Thus, there is a 90 percent chance that the actual will be at least $30,362. Printing all of these 1,000 pretax income figures on a report is unnecessary. The computer merely selects representative values and displays them in tabular or graphical form.

Finally, the computer examined all of the critical elements in Fishing Supplies' budget to determine the relative proportion that each accounts for of all potential income problems and opportunities. (This can be accomplished with a heuristic which jointly considers the element's importance to the bottom line, the magnitudes of its potential favorable and unfavorable variances as specified by its range, and management's confidence that the element's actual value will be at least as favorable as its target.) The noncritical elements were evaluated as a group in a different, but comparable, fashion. The results of these analyses are given in Exhibit 31.10.

As could have been expected from Pareto's law, a relatively small number of elements accounts for the greatest portion of Fishing Supplies' potential income problems. Unit sales of tackle boxes accounts for 56 percent, the selling price of reels 17 percent, and unit sales of lures 12 percent. Thus, 85 percent of all potential income problems in the third quarter can be attributed to these three elements alone. None of the three contributes any significant potential income opportunity since, as can be noted from their ranges, little or no favorable variances from their targets are possible. Administrative expenses present no potential income problems since, according to their range, no unfavorable variance is foreseen. All things considered, Fishing Supplies is heading into a troublesome third quarter. There is only one way to improve the prognosis: Change tactics. Having recognized this after reviewing these results late yesterday morning, the managers decided to continue their meeting into the afternoon.

A Plan Is Nothing—Planning Is Everything

Right now, the management team at Fishing Supplies has a better chance of winning a coin toss than of meeting its third-quarter pretax income goal. Some tactical replanning is clearly in order. The purpose of yesterday afternoon's meeting was to develop an alternative plan to improve the odds for success. Naturally, attention was immediately trained on the most important potential income problem: unit sales of tackle boxes. After the four managers explored several options that proved unpromising, Mary hit on an idea. For some time, Fishing Supplies recognized a need to introduce tackle boxes into the Dallas market. This was carefully reviewed when this year's profit plan was developed. As a result, the introduction of tackle boxes into the Dallas market was

NET INCOME BEFORE TAXES			PROBABILITY OF ACHIEVING TARGET
LOWEST $18,863	TARGET $50,000	HIGHEST $63,128	28%

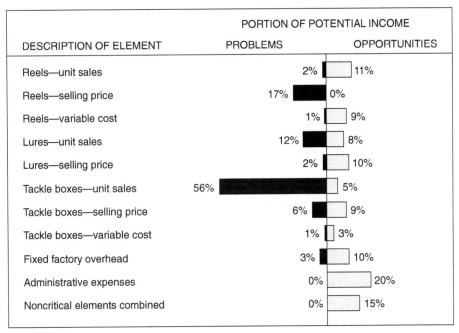

	PORTION OF POTENTIAL INCOME	
DESCRIPTION OF ELEMENT	PROBLEMS	OPPORTUNITIES
Reels—unit sales	2%	11%
Reels—selling price	17%	0%
Reels—variable cost	1%	9%
Lures—unit sales	12%	8%
Lures—selling price	2%	10%
Tackle boxes—unit sales	56%	5%
Tackle boxes—selling price	6%	9%
Tackle boxes—variable cost	1%	3%
Fixed factory overhead	3%	10%
Administrative expenses	0%	20%
Noncritical elements combined	0%	15%

EXHIBIT 31.10   Fishing Supplies Company—Results of Computer Simulation of Third Quarter, Based on Original Plan

scheduled for the fourth quarter this year. That would give the production department an opportunity to build the necessary increase in inventory during the slack season, the third quarter.

Mary's proposal is to move the target date ahead three months and to open up this new market in the third quarter rather than the fourth. This action would not simply displace sales from one quarter to another since strong demand for the product can reasonably be expected to continue throughout the remainder of the year. Assuming this alternative is implemented, Mary stated that third-quarter sales of tackle boxes will be between 7,200 and 11,600 units. Whereas she previously had said there was only a 20 percent chance of achieving the target of 8,100 units, she now believes there are about eight chances out of ten that a favorable sales variance will occur on this product. However, third-quarter advertising expenses are expected to be $1,600 higher and other selling expenses $500 higher than their frozen values in Exhibit 31.9.

Paul voiced concern as soon as he heard that sales could increase by as much as 3,000 units over the original range, stating that production did not have enough inventory to meet this much demand and that customer service would deteriorate as a result. Everyone agreed this could not be tolerated, especially when opening up a new market. At that point Carl suggested building inventory during the first several weeks of the quarter by manufacturing the product on an overtime basis. This seemed feasible, so Paul reassessed the variable cost of tackle boxes to reflect this additional labor. He concluded that, spread over all units of the product, the variable cost in the third quarter would be somewhere between $5.50 and $5.80 per unit. This would make his $5.41 target unfavorably infeasible, but this alternative plan must be judged on the basis of what is best for the entire budget center: Will it improve the odds of reaching the bottom-line goal?

The revised values of the four elements affected by this proposed change in tactics are shown in Exhibit 31.11. The assessments of all other elements remain unchanged. Using these new data, the computer again simulated the third quarter, but on the assumption that management would implement this alternative plan. One thousand samples were again taken. The results are given in Exhibit 31.12.

The chance of achieving the third-quarter pretax income goal is now 56 percent, and, as is evident from the increases in the lowest and highest pretax figures, the entire income profile has shifted upward. The potential income problem associated with unit sales of tackle boxes is significantly less than it was before. In fact, this element now represents the largest potential income opportunity. As had been expected, the variable cost of tackle boxes rose on the problem list; of all remaining potential income problems, 22 percent can be attributed to this element alone. The unfavorable reassessments of advertising and other sales expenses are also apparent in the shifting of the noncritical elements into the problem column. Obviously, however, all of these unfavorable changes are more than offset by the improvement in unit sales of tackle boxes.

Upon studying the results shown in Exhibit 31.12, the management team decided to investigate the advisability of increasing the selling price of reels, the top remaining potential problem. Gene noted from Exhibit 31.8 that the 1 percent impact for the selling price of reels is $1,238 whereas the 1 percent impact for their unit sales is $287. Since the ratio of these two impacts is about 4.3 to 1, this means that the bottom-line churn from a 1 percent increase in the product's selling price is 4.3 times greater than that due to a 1 percent increase (or decrease) in its unit sales. Roughly speaking, this means that management can increase selling price by 1 percent, lose as much as 4.3 percent in unit sales, and still stay even at the bottom line.

EXHIBIT 31.11　Fishing Supplies Company—Management's Assessment of Third Quarter, Based on Introducing Tackle Boxes Into Dallas Market

Description of Element	Original Target	Confidence Factor	Lowest Estimate	Highest Estimate	Frozen Value
Tackle boxes—unit sales	8,100	80%	7,200	11,600	
Tackle boxes—variable cost	5.41	0%	5.50	5.80	
Advertising	9,000				9,800
Other selling expenses	6,000				5,900
Net income before taxes	50,000	?	?	?	

NET INCOME BEFORE TAXES			PROBABILITY OF ACHIEVING TARGET
LOWEST $32,930	TARGET $50,000	HIGHEST $81,530	56%

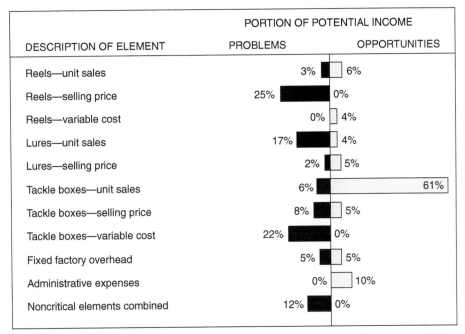

EXHIBIT 31.12 Fishing Supplies Company—Results of Computer Simulation of Third Quarter, Based on Introducing Tackle Boxes into Dallas Market

Carl reminded everyone that such a conclusion is correct only if the relatively small effect of the joint change in both price and demand is ignored. (The bottom-line effect of this joint change becomes significant for larger changes in price. For example, it would be incorrect to use the ratio of 4.3 to 1 to conclude that management can increase the selling price by 10 percent, lose as much as 43 percent in unit sales, and still stay even at the bottom line.) Since Gene and Mary were contemplating a price increase of 10 percent, Carl used a joint effects formula to quickly determine that 30.1 percent is the maximum decrease in demand that could be tolerated without eroding the bottom line.

Mary was delighted to learn this because she had already estimated that a 10 percent price increase on reels would result in a maximum decrease of 12 percent in unit sales. In fact, she felt that the decrease could be as low as 4 percent.

The management team therefore decided to evaluate this alternative. The previous range for the selling price of reels was revised to show a 10 percent price increase of $1.86 per reel; thus, the previous lowest and highest estimates were each increased

EXHIBIT 31.13 Fishing Supplies Company—Management's Assessment of Third Quarter, Based on Introducing Tackle Boxes Into Dallas Market and Increasing the Selling Price of Reels

Description of Element	Original Target	Confidence Factor	Lowest Estimate	Highest Estimate	Frozen Value
Reels—unit sales	7,300	10%	5,720	7,680	
Reels—selling price	18.63	100%	19.91	20.41	
Net income before taxes	50,000	?	?	?	

by this amount. This resulted in a lowest estimate that was greater than the target, thus making the confidence factor 100 percent on the selling price of reels. To reduce the previous range for unit sales of reels, Mary reduced the previous lowest estimate by 12 percent, making it 5,720 units; similarly, she reduced the previous highest estimate

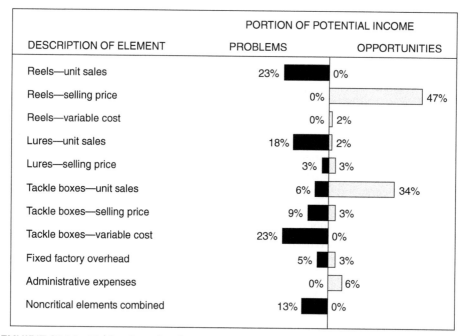

NET INCOME BEFORE TAXES			PROBABILITY OF ACHIEVING TARGET
LOWEST $39,615	TARGET $50,000	HIGHEST $92,364	93%

DESCRIPTION OF ELEMENT	PROBLEMS	OPPORTUNITIES
Reels—unit sales	23%	0%
Reels—selling price	0%	47%
Reels—variable cost	0%	2%
Lures—unit sales	18%	2%
Lures—selling price	3%	3%
Tackle boxes—unit sales	6%	34%
Tackle boxes—selling price	9%	3%
Tackle boxes—variable cost	23%	0%
Fixed factory overhead	5%	3%
Administrative expenses	0%	6%
Noncritical elements combined	13%	0%

PORTION OF POTENTIAL INCOME

EXHIBIT 31.14 Fishing Supplies Company—Results of Computer Simulation of Third Quarter, Based on Introducing Tackle Boxes into Dallas Market and Increasing the Selling Price of Reels

by 4 percent, making it 7,680 units. She then felt there would only be one chance in ten of having a favorable variance in unit sales on this product.

These two new ranges pertaining to the alternative of increasing the selling price of reels are given in Exhibit 31.13. One thousand samples were taken based on the second alternative plan—introduce tackle boxes into Dallas *and* raise the selling price of reels. The results of the computer simulation are shown in Exhibit 31.14.

Obviously, these results indicate that a 10 percent increase in the selling price of reels should be implemented as soon as possible since, all things considered, the probability of Fishing Supplies achieving its targeted bottom line is increased to an enviable 93 percent. The income profiles of the original and two alternative plans are graphically compared in Exhibit 31.15. After the management team reviewed these results early this morning,

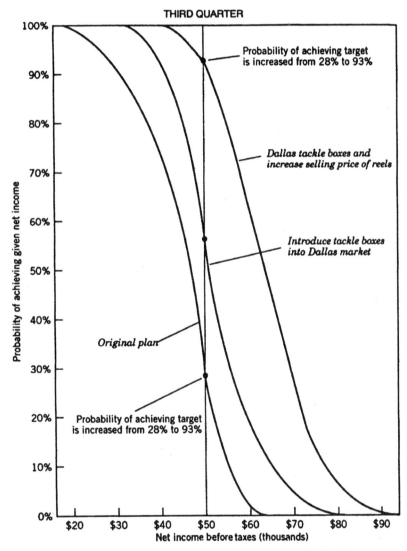

EXHIBIT 31.15 Fishing Supplies Company—Income Profiles of Third Quarter

all agreed that the alternative plan must be adopted. Mary prepared a formal announcement of the impending changes for the field sales force and then everyone moved into high gear for introducing tackle boxes into the Dallas market and increasing the selling price of reels. By concentrating on the residual problems indicated in Exhibit 31.14, they might well have been able to develop another alternative to further improve the odds for success. For brevity's sake, however, it is assumed that no other options were available.

Tracking and Feedback Mechanism

Fishing Supplies' third quarter came to an end about ten days ago. Today the management team is reviewing the results summarized in Exhibit 31.16. The actual pretax

EXHIBIT 31.16   Fishing Supplies Company—Tracking Data on Third Quarter

Description of Element	Unit	Original Target	Forecast	Actual	Error at Bottom Line
Rods—unit sales	ea.	2,800	2,600	2,561	$ 143+
Rods—selling price	$/ea.	9.43	9.58	9.47	260+
Rods—variable cost	$/ea.	5.01	5.05	5.02	78–
Reels—unit sales	ea.	7,300	6,829	6,574	1,376+
Reels—selling price	$/ea.	18.63	20.16	20.33	1,056–
Reels—variable cost	$/ea.	13.02	12.95	12.86	615–
Lures—unit sales	doz.	8,300	8,190	8,024	1,522+
Lures—selling price	$/doz.	22.94	22.99	22.95	298+
Lures—variable cost	$/doz.	11.77	11.75	11.79	328+
Bait buckets—unit sales	ea.	2,100	2,100	1,935	367+
Bait buckets—selling price	$/ea.	5.72	5.72	5.67	96+
Bait buckets—variable cost	$/ea.	2.98	2.98	3.04	126+
Minnow traps—unit sales	ea.	4,600	3,900	3,764	144+
Minnow traps—selling price	$/ea.	4.26	4.35	4.31	142+
Minnow traps—variable cost	$/ea.	2.86	2.90	2.89	39–
Tackle boxes—unit sales	ea.	8,100	8,995	8,879	849+
Tackle boxes—selling price	$/ea.	14.27	14.25	14.03	1,801+
Tackle boxes—variable cost	$/ea.	5.41	5.65	5.78	1,169+
Fixed factory overhead	$	90,000	89,800	89,603	197–
Commissions (% of sales)	%	9.0	9.0	9.0	0–
Advertising	$	9,000	9,800	9,855	55+
Other selling expenses	$	6,000	5,900	6,294	394+
Administrative expenses	$	32,000	30,750	30,778	28+
Other income	$	3,000	3,400	3,512	112–
Other expense	$	1,000	1,000	1,473	473+
Error due to joint effects					13+
Net income before taxes	$	50,000	62,264	54,803	$7,461+

income of $54,803 exceeded the target by nearly 10 percent. The income forecast of $62,264 was determined by the tactical budgeting model using the data shown in the forecast column of the exhibit. (The forecast column reflects introducing tackle boxes into the Dallas market and increasing the selling price of reels.) The difference between the forecast and actual pretax income is shown in the last column as $7,461+, signifying that the forecasted income overestimated the actual bottom line by $7,461. In turn, this $7,461 overestimate is traced back to individual elements. (All figures shown in the "Error at Bottom Line" column are pretax income dollars. Plus signs denote overestimates and minus signs underestimates.)

The forecast figure given for each noncritical element is simply the value at which management froze that element for the simulation. In the case of a critical element, the forecast value shown is the weighted average of the element's range. In other words, if an infinite number of values were scientifically sampled from within the range, the average of those values would be identical to what is labeled as the element's forecast value in Exhibit 31.16. This figure may also be thought of as the range's center of gravity. By comparing it to the element's actual value, it can be quickly determined whether the manager who prepared the range was optimistic or pessimistic about the element's performance.

For example, the forecast for sales of tackle boxes was 8,995 units. This is 116 units greater than the actual of 8,879. Thus, Mary was somewhat optimistic about third-quarter unit sales of the product. (Perhaps the Dallas market was not quite as large as anticipated.) This overestimate of 116 units of tackle boxes was traced all the way to the bottom line and, in effect, was found to have overestimated pretax income by the $849 figure shown. Conversely, the selling price of reels was underestimated, which in turn underestimated pretax income by $1,056.

By monitoring this tracking information quarter by quarter, managers can identify any bias that might be consistently present in the range estimates of any critical element. Such undue optimism or pessimism may then be tempered by adjustments in the future ranges for that element. By identifying those elements that contributed large errors in the forecast of the bottom line, management can give them the additional attention they deserve when they are ranged in future quarters. This is particularly helpful to new managers who are trying to get a better grip on their operations.

BRACKET BUDGETING IN ANNUAL PLANNING

The traditional approach to annual profit planning generally involves preparation of a "realistic" budget. But what is realistic? In the marketing function, it may mean a pretax goal that management is 50 percent confident of achieving. In the financial area, it may mean a target that has a 75 percent chance of attainment. If "realistic" means a 50 percent confidence factor, then it would seem that all elements in the budget should be targeted at the 50 percent confidence level. However, this rarely results in what is expected; the probability of meeting the targeted bottom line may be substantially lower or higher than 50 percent. If all elements are targeted at the 75 percent confidence level, the resultant pretax target would have nearly a 100 percent chance of attainability and correspondingly would probably not represent an acceptable level of performance. Thus, management must grapple with the problem of balancing the planned profit with the chance of attaining that profit. If the latter is not measured in critical budget centers, top management is flying blind. Measuring this uncertainty not only results in a clearer and more realistic portrayal of the coming fiscal year, it also provides for more effective communication among the members of the management team.

The application of bracket budgeting in annual planning is similar to its use in budgetary control. The primary purposes are to maximize the odds of achieving an acceptable profit and to identify potential profit problems and opportunities. Instead of dealing with quarterly figures, however, the elements' proposed annual targets are evaluated. By addressing the annual planning problem in this manner, management can easily test many different alternatives, thus eliminating the need to prepare two or more budgets before the final version is approved. This tends to streamline the planning process and reduce managerial frustration.

CONSOLIDATING INCOME STATEMENTS

Although its application is selective at the budget center level, bracket budgeting can be used to present a unified picture of an entire division by linking together its budget centers, including those operating with conventional budgeting only. Likewise, a composite of the entire company may be obtained by chaining together all of its divisions and corporate overhead departments, even though some of those units may not be using bracket budgeting.

Exhibit 31.17 demonstrates the manner in which such a consolidation is made. In this example, the Fun Time Company, a hypothetical corporation, consists of 11 critical budget centers. Next year's income profile of each was used as input for a computer simulation of corporate earnings per share. As a result, it was determined that there is a 72 percent chance that next year's earnings per share will be at least as much as the $1.27 target. As is also noted, three profit centers collectively account for 68 percent of all potential corporate earnings problems next fiscal year. If management wishes to be more confident with its forecast, the appropriate figure can readily be found in the earnings per share profile (not shown). For example, management can be 90 percent confident that next year's earnings will be at least $1.22 per share.

SUMMARY OF BENEFITS

When it is properly implemented and applied, bracket budgeting:

- Recognizes the unique nature of any given business. The tactical budgeting model is tailored to the specific needs of management.
- Is an early warning system. Potential earnings problems and opportunities are identified well in advance. In other words, management can act rather than react.

ANNUAL EARNINGS PER SHARE			PROBABILITY OF ACHIEVING TARGET
LOWEST $1.10	TARGET $1.27	HIGHEST $1.45	72%

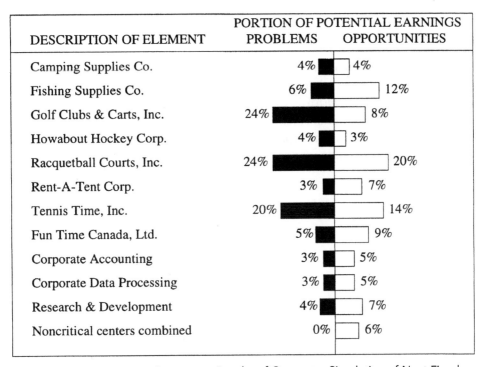

DESCRIPTION OF ELEMENT	PORTION OF POTENTIAL EARNINGS	
	PROBLEMS	OPPORTUNITIES
Camping Supplies Co.	4%	4%
Fishing Supplies Co.	6%	12%
Golf Clubs & Carts, Inc.	24%	8%
Howabout Hockey Corp.	4%	3%
Racquetball Courts, Inc.	24%	20%
Rent-A-Tent Corp.	3%	7%
Tennis Time, Inc.	20%	14%
Fun Time Canada, Ltd.	5%	9%
Corporate Accounting	3%	5%
Corporate Data Processing	3%	5%
Research & Development	4%	7%
Noncritical centers combined	0%	6%

EXHIBIT 31.17   Fun Time Company—Results of Computer Simulation of Next Fiscal Year

- Enables management to establish a list of decision priorities to influence future earnings performance.
- Minimizes the amount of information presented to management for decision making. The more complex the business (e.g., many products, varying gross profit percentages), the more beneficial it is.
- Complements, not replaces or alters, conventional methods of budgeting.
- Integrates easily with all costing methods—standard, direct, activity based, and so forth.
- Capitalizes not only on what management knows about the future but also on what management knows it does not know.
- Has tutorial feedback mechanisms to assist managers in refining their future inputs. This is particularly helpful to newly appointed managers who have significant bottom line responsibilities.

- Allows tactical budgeting models to be developed very rapidly, many times within a matter of hours. Consequently, for the few times that they require changes, models can be revised in minimal time.
- Requires no understanding of higher mathematics or computer programming to be used effectively.

SUMMARY

In some firms, the application of bracket budgeting would be equivalent to killing a fly with an elephant gun. In others, the sole use of conventional budgeting is not unlike trying to kill an elephant with a fly swatter. For businesses in which major uncertainties can play havoc with the bottom line, bracket budgeting provides management with the means to cope effectively with the problems that such uncertainties pose and with little more effort than is currently exerted.

CHAPTER THIRTY-TWO

Program Budgeting: Planning, Programming, Budgeting

William B. Iwaskow, MBA, JD

INTRODUCTION

As noted in the previous chapters, budgeting has evolved into a major integrating tool for planning and control. It can bridge the gap between strategic planning, long- and medium-range planning, and current actions. Without an adequate union, planning can be out of touch with the constraints of scarce resources, and budgeting can be divorced from the direction of plans and programs.

This chapter provides a broad, comprehensive approach to integrating planning and budgeting, called *program budgeting* (PB), which is another designation for planning, programming, and budgeting. This approach represents a significant stage in the continuing evolution of planning and budgetary techniques and the general technology of management decision making.

The PB integration is basically accomplished by the use of strategic output-oriented programs that are based on goals, purposes, and objectives. Providing output-oriented budget information with a long-range perspective to allocate resources more effectively in PB's basic objective. The output-oriented program expenditures are later translated into traditional line-item appropriation budget requests. A budget based on PB concepts is a statement of policy for a planning period and a means for implementing it. Because of the output orientation of PB, designating it as "output budgeting," the term used in the United Kingdom, might be more descriptive.

PB was introduced into the U.S. Department of Defense (DOD) in 1961 with considerable publicity because of its revolutionary approach to government planning and budgeting techniques. By 1968, its utilization became epidemic in the federal government as well as in various state and local governments. Both public and private sectors have since utilized the concepts and lessons of PB, sometimes under different labels and forms.

PB applies not only to government but also to industry and nonprofit organizations. The concepts of PB have origins in both the private and public sectors. This chapter address the concepts, background, requirements, and lessons of PB.

DESCRIPTION OF PROGRAM BUDGETING

PB does not have a standardized definition because of its encompassing nature. Its many aspects include concepts; a system and process; a technique and format; and, in some cases, almost a management philosophy. Essentially, it is a management decision-making system that ties together strategic and long-range planning with conventional budgeting and supporting analysis so that an organization can most effectively assign resources to achieve both its short- and long-range objectives. It utilizes a planning and budgeting process in an output-oriented program format, which is oriented to its objectives to facilitate developing and evaluating alternatives and making decisions. This process ultimately leads to an allocation of resources over a planning period. This is then a basis for constructing a budget, which supports the goals, strategies, and decisions.

Under PB, a program contains a specified combination of resources or manpower, materials, facilities (including equipment), and capital, which operate together to achieve a set of common objectives within a planning period. A program resource matrix extended over time in a program hierarchy is shown in Exhibit 32.1. The matrix shows an allocation of resources to various programs over time. The development, structuring, and hierarchy of programs are explained in a subsequent section.

Concepts

The functions of management can be summarized as planning, implementation, and control. PB is one of the most comprehensive decision-making systems designed to accommodate and integrate these multiple management functions. It integrates all of the organization's planning activities (from conceptual to partially implemented stages) and budgeting into a total system. It relates and integrates into one conceptual framework all plans (strategic, long-range, medium-range projects, etc.) and budgets, objectives and costs, key activities and operations, organizational units, resource allocations, analysis and measurements, including reengineering studies, controls, and results. Great emphasis is continually placed on the analysis of alternatives (including the effectiveness of existing programs) and on estimating the cost of accomplishing objectives and fulfilling purposes and needs.

A schema of a PB process cycle is shown in Exhibit 32.2 in the process context of management requirements and decision making.

The schema shows an organization's policies, missions, and objectives serving as the basis for the cycle, with various key decision-making and analysis checkpoint intervals operating within the existing information systems. The planning–programming–

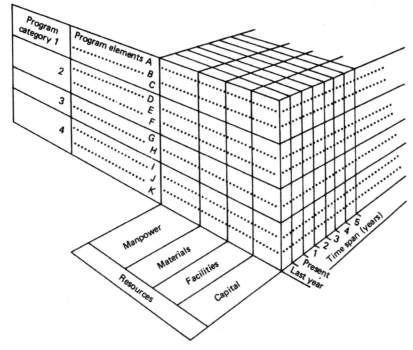

EXHIBIT 32.1   Program, Resources, and Time Matrix

budgeting steps have separate interlocking and interactive time intervals, with different requirements in increasing detail.

From the standpoint that budgeting has already evolved to a significant extent as a major integrating tool for planning and control, there is a bit of PB in every budget system. Traditionally, however, most budget systems have been primarily structured for the implementation of ongoing activities and the attendant spending control. There are many differences between traditional budgeting and PB.

To begin with, the flow of decisions is generally different in a PB system than in one utilizing traditional line budgeting. In the latter, especially when outside a planning context, the flow of budgetary decisions is primarily upward, with an aggregative information flow. In PB, however, the budget is a means of implementing the long-range plans, and the decision making is primarily downward and disaggregative to the information database.

Traditional budgeting has also generally emphasized the current means or objects of work achievement and the attendant efficiency with appropriate controls whereas PB is also concerned with the purpose of the work. PB requires that budgetary decisions be made by emphasizing output categories, such as goals, objectives, purposes, and products or services, instead of inputs, such as salaries, materials, and facilities.

Traditional budgetary approaches have also generally taken a retrospective focus in measuring what was done with current means in estimating the next budget year. In contrast, PB is more prospective, with its focus on the future impacts of current major decisions or choices. *The PB focus rests on the premise that more resources are wasted in*

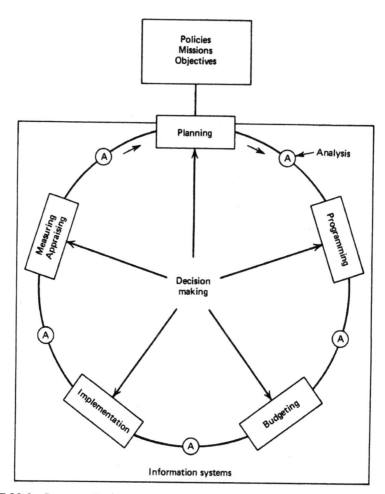

EXHIBIT 32.2 Program Budgeting Process Cycle

implementing wrong decisions efficiently than in implementing right decisions inefficiently.
The system aims at the major issues facing an organization and incorporates policy,
goals, objectives, and strategy directly into the budget process.

A budget in a PB system is initially decided in a planning framework, with the
expenditures expressed in an output-oriented program structure. It is then translated
into a traditional line-item appropriation form by means of a "crosswalk," as shown in
the schema in Exhibit 32.3. The schema shows the basic and smallest program entities,
or *program elements*, extended over a planning period and aggregated into the more
encompassing program categories. It also shows their respective connections to a traditional line budget for year 1. (The different types of program groupings are discussed
in the section later in this chapter titled "Program Hierarchy.")

This crosswalk reconciliation, or cross-classification, allows data to be converted
from a PB planning framework in year 1 (by moving to the left) into a traditional line
budget, which generally represents a management and control framework. It also allows

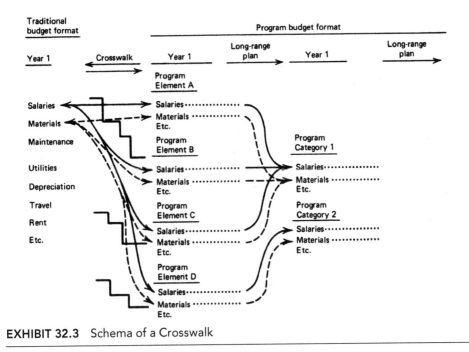

EXHIBIT 32.3 Schema of a Crosswalk

data to move in both directions and is constructed only for the budget year. Although PB gives a major role to planning in the construction of a budget, it also embraces the control functions of budgeting with provisions like the crosswalk. This is elaborated on further under the section later in this chapter titled "Crosswalk."

The novelty of PB is not with the various ingredients just indicated. Each of them is familiar, reflecting past and current practices to some degree. What is novel is the combination of a number of these ingredients into a comprehensive package and system with an output focus. PB gives a coherence to the various ingredients that were not consciously or sufficiently related previously.

The PB approach is a significant shift from traditional budgeting, especially in government. Industry's "profit center" approach of relating product or service line revenues to costs has many similarities to PB, but the comprehensiveness and completeness is often limited in the budgeting, planning, or analysis phases.

Managerial Needs

PB came into being for some of the same reasons that other management techniques, such as management by objectives; strategic planning, zero-based, flexible, and bracket budgeting; and cost accounting developed. Managerial tools need to be updated and new ones developed. Solutions must be found for problems arising from technology, diversification, growth, size, government regulations, economic conditions, international interplay, general complexity, or new needs.

Many executives are swamped with studies, information, and rapidly changing events. They are inclined to believe, however, that a relatively small number of their decisions dealing with strategies and policy ultimately determines 80 to 90 percent of their success or failure, in the context of Pareto's law, or the 80/20 rule. Strategic planning allows the isolation of a small number of decision areas that can have a big impact. PB is of particular interest as a management decision-making tool since it links the broad strategic planning process to the detail-oriented budget process, which at least provides a semblance of rational direction and control in organizations of overwhelming size or complexity. A PB system is one of the few strategic management tools that can help manage large, diverse organizations and bring top management and policy makers into the total decision-making process, from planning to the primary budgetary areas, in a comprehensive and disciplined fashion.

Unfortunately, new management approaches are sometimes taken literally in a cookbook fashion and are regarded as panaceas rather than as guiding concepts. In any case, they will continue to be sought after as a means of overcoming many of the perennial shortcomings of budget and planning systems, which include:

- A generally dim focus of budgets on strategic or key decision areas
- Gaps between planning and financial management
- Lack of comprehensive, integrated, multipurpose data systems
- Piecemeal departmental plans and budgets lacking comprehensive, organization-wide perspective and linkage
- Limited coping with uncertainty and changes in the world, including global interplay
- Limited time horizon and perspective of budgets to provide the full cost implications of current decisions
- Limited examination of alternatives and lack of sufficient relationship of benefits to costs or effectiveness
- Arbitrary budget allocations (or cuts) resulting from an inability to judge the relative worth of a multitude of budget requests

What Program Budgeting Is Not

PB does not reduce decision making to a formula that eliminates the need for judgment and intuition. Its function is to provide a comprehensive framework and system within which effective decisions can be made.

PB is not a new accounting system, and it does not necessarily require changes in an existing accounting system to accommodate its output program classifications. It is not a management information system, although the availability of one in good form is beneficial.

PB is not a plan for reorganization to fit its output program structure. However, an organization structured to its purposes and goals would be considered ideal.

PB is not a mathematical model or a computerized form of management. It does not depend on the use of computers or complicated mathematics.

HISTORY

PB has origins in both U.S. industry and the federal government. Its approaches were initially utilized by industry in the 1920s, with analyses utilized by Bell Laboratories and a system introduced by the DuPont Company into General Motors. In the early

1940s, the federal government started a wartime materials-control system that utilized many of the principles of PB in its concept. Although the term "program" occasionally appeared in some government documents prior to the 1940s, it had no connection with the concepts described here.

There also are a number of other antecedent paths from both the private and the public sectors that converged in the 1950s to develop PB. They include:

- Growing sophistication of macroeconomic analyses and modeling
- Use of microeconomics for appraising public projects
- Increased use of government economic analyses for formulating fiscal policy
- Refinements in scientific management and decision-making techniques
- Improved information-handling technologies and computers
- Increased use of analytic tools, such as systems analysis and operations research, especially in the DOD
- Continuing improvement of planning and budgeting techniques

The most extensive use of PB ever embarked upon was by the U.S. federal government. The scope and scale of its application has never been matched by any other budgetary technique for a single organizational entity (other than the traditional line-item approach). PB became an official budget approach utilized throughout the federal government by the mid-1960s, which was well documented]. It is presented here in considerable detail, therefore, and in much of its original nomenclature.

Industry

Bell Laboratories employed a systems analysis in the 1920s that included some economic, political, and social considerations, but it was primarily hardware oriented.

DuPont used a form of PB around 1915 and introduced a similar concept to General Motors in the early 1920s, when the company made a major investment in GM. Since then, the automobile industry has utilized many PB concepts through its longtime concern with:

- Planning models into the future
- Identifying clear objectives (models and price classes)
- Establishing programs to achieve objectives
- Allocating resources to program potentials
- Utilizing forecasts, studies, and analyses

Over the years, many private and public organizations have been using various concepts of PB, under categories such as strategic planning and project management. However, most companies treat their management systems as proprietary matters and do not allow general publication. A few companies, such as General Electric (in the research and development [R&D] area) and John Hancock Insurance, have published their experience with PB approaches. The strategic planning at GE, which was developed in concert with the McKinsey management consulting organization, utilized strategic business units (SBUs). These SBUs had many similarities to the strategic program groupings of PB.

Federal Government

Over the past 70 years, the federal government has made three basic alterations to its budgeting approaches.

Between 1921 and 1949, emphasis was on the expenditure control of cost inputs such as salaries, rent, materials, and so forth, which is generally characterized as a line-item type of budgeting. The connections of these items to goals, objectives, or results were very limited; the primary focus was on accountability.

Between 1949 and the early 1960s, "performance-type" budgeting, emphasizing efficiency, was implemented. In 1949, the Hoover Commission recommended that the entire budgetary concept be refashioned into a budget based on functions, activities, and projects. Its focus was work–cost measurement and managerial efficiency. That is, cost and production goals were established and then compared to actual performance. Limited attention was paid to whether the chosen goals addressed public needs or whether they were effective.

Between 1965 and the present, additional attention has been paid to strategic and long-range planning and the effective allocation of limited resources among varying public needs, along with efficiency. An across-the-board application of PB in the federal government started in 1965, after a news conference held by President Johnson formally launched it. At that news conference on August 25, 1965, President Johnson announced "a very new and very revolutionary system of planning and programming and budgeting throughout the vast government—so that through the tools of modern management the full promise of a finer life can be brought to every American at the lowest possible cost."[1]

The federal government PB antecedents, however, go back to World War II in the controlling of critical materials and to DOD analyses in the mid-1950s.

World War II

During World War II, a shortage of critical materials necessitated a wartime materials control system. It was essentially the first type of program budget utilized in the government. It translated major U.S. goals (combat and civilian) into specific programs for allocating materials, crossed organizational lines (land, sea, air), extended the budget time frames a number of years out, and examined alternatives through systematic analyses. This approach fell into disuse after the war.

Rand Corporation

In 1953, the Rand Corporation, a not-for-profit think tank specializing in military-type planning and research, proposed a program budget format to the air force for weapon systems. Rand had already been performing systems analyses for weapons, taking into account such nontraditional considerations as social, political, and economic factors. The proposal was never acted on until Rand published some studies on the subject that came to the attention of the Kennedy administration.

---

[1] "Transcript of the President's News Conference on Foreign & Domestic Affairs," *New York Times*, August 26, 1965.

Kennedy Administration

In 1961, under the direction of DOD Secretary Robert McNamara, PB was introduced into the DOD. Before that time, there was almost a complete separation between military planning and budgeting in DOD, resulting in unbalanced forces not readily deployable for combat duties. Moreover, the branches of the armed services (army, navy, air force) were each vying for control over different weapons systems without an overall coordinated defense policy. Although each had been conducting long-range planning and using systems analysis and operations research in allocating funds, these studies were essentially conducted independently by each service branch. In fact, they were not always concerned with the same war possibilities.

Johnson Administration

PB worked so well for the DOD that it was officially established throughout the federal government in 1965 by Lyndon B. Johnson in response to the growing complexity of budget requests and to the need to better allocate resources across the spectrum of the nation's needs. By 1967, the Bureau of the Budget, which administered PB, had implemented it in 21 federal agencies. It was found to be particularly helpful in foreign aid planning and in defining the Peace Corps missions. It was beginning to be recognized as the greatest advance in the art of government since the introduction of a competency basis into the Civil Service 100 years before. Bureaucracies generally perform poorly in innovating or generating effective forward motion; their best performance is limited to routine tasks. PB had the potential to correct this old defect.

In 1968, the federal government also financed the introduction of PB (for a year) in five states, five cities, and five counties under a 5-5-5 Program.

Nixon Administration

In 1970, under President Nixon, the Bureau of the Budget was renamed the Office of Management and Budget (OMB), emphasizing efficiency, effectiveness, and realism in response to the fiscal pressures brought on by the Vietnam War.

In 1971, the OMB indicated that it was no longer necessary to submit a budget under the rigid PB format. Efficiency, again, became the primary concern. The OMB's instructions did not eliminate the utilization of the PB concepts but only the rigid format that had evolved. It was sometimes characterized as a management by objective approach or an attenuated PB. Some of the PB-type requirements were maintained for special situations. That is, multiyear costing beyond the budget year was required for special OMB requests or whenever legislation was needed for resource authorization; cost–benefit analysis was necessary whenever something different or novel was advanced into the budget. Another favorable sign was the retention of the PB units in the various federal agencies for continuing analysis and strategy development. Moreover, President Nixon's message on the fiscal 1972 budget stressed the need to emphasize outputs, long-range planning, and the allocation of resources instead of a view limited to cost activities.

PB led many federal agencies to reappraise their missions and functions. In addition, an increased use of cost–benefit and cost-effectiveness analysis, and a greater concern and involvement with goals and objectives, generally remained. Thus, many of the aspects of PB continued, as well as its spirit, although the concepts were presented differently.

Carter Administration

President Carter introduced zero-based budgeting (ZBB) to the federal government in the mid-1970s, following his experience with it as the governor of Georgia. ZBB was, among other things, an organizational departure from PB in that it developed budgets from the bottom up rather than PB's top-down approach. This hierarchical direction distinction is fading in budgeting and planning systems with the growing horizontal, global type of organizations in the twenty-first century era of global capitalism.

In a short time, ZBB became unwieldly and was disbanded due to its burdensome requirement as essentially a 100 percent annual review system and its inability to easily integrate into long-range planning.

Federal Phase-Out

Some of the reasons that the official PB format was phased out of the federal government include:

- The availability of funds became tight with the Vietnam conflict, and the emphasis reversed to the old standbys of budgeting: control and accountability.
- President Nixon's management style emphasized shorter-range performance by the agencies in meeting agreed-to objectives. This course was supported under the constrained resources situation and by the fact that many of the public welfare programs of the Johnson administration were expensive and not meeting expectations.
- Policy development was being concentrated within President Nixon's office through the Domestic and National Security Councils. In effect, increased layers of authority were placed between the budgeters and the top policy makers. The PB system that had been developed was geared to develop a great deal of policy at the agency level.
- President Nixon was trying to reorganize many of the agencies into decision-making entities along many of the developing PB program lines, which to a degree subordinated the need for a PB structure.
- The special PB plans and analyses were essentially designed for and used by the executive branch and were not appropriately incorporated into the operational flow of data to Congress, with its various committee requirements and politics.
- The routines became burdensome, with too much paperwork and time consumption.
- Linking the PB analytical process, particularly the policy analysis, to the budget process was difficult and generally was resisted. Also, too many issues were raised in regard to the scarce analytical capabilities, and many times they were not relevant.
- Gaps in coordination and compatibility between the special PB and regular budget staffs caused problems.

- The PB format was basically the one developed by the DOD, with insufficient consideration given to the individual needs of civilian agencies or to the status of their existing information systems. More tailoring was necessary with a much lesser emphasis on format and procedures.
- President Carter's introduction of ZBB and its lack of success gave further impetus to the bureaucratic and legislative entities to ease back to the old, comfortable, politically more manipulative standby: line-item budgeting.

Some caution is offered regarding a possible negative evaluation of PB's basic merits based solely on its experience in the federal government. It is important to make the evaluation with the perspective that the federal government is very complex and one of the largest fiscal units in the world, with its spending having a value of more than 20 percent of the country's gross national product. In the years PB was formally utilized, the annual federal spending was $300 billion. In addition, the entire decision-making process operated within a highly complex governmental apparatus containing several conflicting layers of decision makers within a traditional, fragmented, and intensely political legislative environment.

In short, the federal phase-out was attributable to many factors that do not negate PB's basic concepts, validity, or contributions. PB never truly became a tool for both the executive and the legislative branches. It is only when people use a management system that it can have vitality. Also, to have expected PB to perform miracles was unrealistic. There is no magic in PB, as there is none in any management system or technique. Even under the most favorable of circumstances, PB can only organize and improve the data for decision making and management. It does not make decisions. It only provides a long-range perspective regarding the consequences of budgetary decisions.

Utilization Overview

PB has been tried in whole and in piecemeal and has been modified and incorporated into the decision-making processes of many areas outside the federal government. It has taken many different forms, different emphases, and even different names over the years. Many school districts in the United States have termed their version of PB *educational resources management system;* in the United Kingdom, it is sometimes referred to as *output budgeting.* The different names and modifications, in fact, present difficulties in tracking and evaluating PB. Perhaps some of the changes in designation reflect a disassociation with the federal government approach or an increasing management sophistication in not adopting novel techniques literally.

The system has also been introduced in industry and in various states, counties, cities, school districts, universities, libraries, and not-for-profit institutions in the United States as well as in several foreign countries. California, in particular, has had numerous successes. The results appear to be mixed, however, and the system seems least successful where PB's application was rigid and not tailored to individual needs or insufficiently integrated into political environments.

Cynical economists and budgetary analysts have felt that for the public and government sectors, in particular, with their inherent significant political dynamics, only the line-item type of budgeting is feasible. They feel the bureaucrats and politicians do not want to relinquish their easier control of allocating resources via the line-item approach or discipline themselves in reviewing the consequences of their budgetary decisions.

Some of the disappointments reflect unusually high initial expectations or an over-selling of the management tool in relation to the human and institutional realities and the multiple demands of a budgetary process. Budgeting, for example, with its control orientation, is geared to demanding routines and deadlines, which can clash with the varied PB analysis and timing requirements. Many organizations also have encountered difficulties in trying to identify their objectives and in relating activities to them in program terms. Many assumed that programs would define themselves through some black-box magic formula of strict rote technique. There generally appears to have been an excessive preoccupation with technique and format rather than the development of disciplined thinking about what an organization is and what it should be producing with its budget allocations, the basic concept of PB. More than 1,000 years ago, Chinese philosopher Lao-tse advised: "Govern a great nation as you would cook a small fish. Do not overdo it."

It is interesting to note, however, that the beginnings of PB in Europe appear to have been somewhat smoother than in the United States. Although there have also been difficulties, generally the approach has been slower and more cautious. More attention has been paid to understanding the concept and to preparing for potential difficulties.

Although the utilization of PB has taken many forms and its efficacy varies, interest continues as organizations grow in size, scope, and complexity and find themselves with management tools inadequate for coping with change and the allocation of limited resources.

FRAMEWORK OF PROGRAM BUDGETING

A major aim of PB is to convert the annual routine of preparing a budget into a conscious appraisal and formulation of an organization's goals by providing a long-range perspective. A PB framework requires the fusion of strategic and long-range planning with budgeting processes through the use of various structural, analytical, and informational elements.

A generalized PB system does not exist. In applying PB to an organization, managers must tailor it to the organization's particular context and needs. There are several key processes and elements, however, that are common to most PB systems.

Process Phases

PB operates within three basic interlocking and interactive process phases in its annual cycle: *planning, programming,* and *budgeting.* They have separate time allotments, with reviews and key decision checkpoints at each juncture, providing progressively more detailed views. A schema of a PB process cycle was shown in Exhibit 32.2 in the context of management requirements and decision making.

The planning phase should provide ample time for identifying and studying challenges, objectives, and alternatives and for resolving the basic strategy and program structure. The programming phase should provide time for the assembly and review of detailed planning forecasts (inputs and related outputs in a program structure). The budgeting phase should provide sufficient time to translate the previous efforts into a traditional line-item budget.

The progressively more detailed views are likely to involve different kinds and magnitudes of change or direction. The planning phase may trigger significant changes, and the programming phase generally results in some adjustments of the plans. Although the budgeting phase may still bring more significant light to bear, it generally only modifies earlier decisions. All of the phases, however, are expected by design to trigger major changes if required by further information or analysis.

Planning Phase

The planning phase deals with the development of missions, goals, objectives, and alternatives and with the strategies and general resource allocations for achieving them over a long-range time frame expressed in a basic program structure. A basic program structure classification should be developed or updated in this phase.

The planning phase can be viewed and conducted sequentially. Strategic planning is the first consideration. This means planning for an entity as a whole, not merely adding up the separate plans of the respective parts without a common and guiding thread. When dealing with a company as a whole in industry, this strategic planning is sometimes referred to as *corporate planning*.

Strategic planning is basically concerned with the long-term destiny of an organization. It is the guiding light. Whatever the organization's size, its destiny will generally depend on two, three, or four key decisions. If they are right, the organization will be well positioned to take advantage of most opportunities or to solve most problems that come along. If they are wrong, it may not just mean having the wrong foot on the playing field but playing the wrong sport in the wrong stadium. The result can be a serious deterioration in, or the demise of, an organization.

Strategic planning consists of identifying what those few decisions are and getting them right. Although strategic planning is deceptively simple, this does not mean that it is easy. Difficulties arise because the decisions are pivotal, with big impacts, and they depend largely on judgment and intuition in an uncertain future. A strategic plan should summarize in very broad terms and quantification what the key decision makers believe the organization should look like in the next five to ten years, together with a realistic statement as to how it will be done. Apart from the instrinsic value of the strategic plan, a sense of consensus and cohesion in an organization generally follows its development, with more members pulling in the same direction and at the same speed. This is especially so if the planning process was interactive up and down the line. If an organization is big and diverse, the major component entities should also develop supporting strategic plans, which, of course, must ultimately be governed by the organization's overall requirements and program structure.

In all cases, the initial broad focus of strategic planning generates the major options and aids in decisions on the missions, objectives, policies, and major PB program groupings and on the general acquisition, use, and disposition of resources necessary to attain the objectives. This must be done in the realistic context of an organization's status quo and critical issues. This then serves as a basis for the more detailed planning and quantification of the planning phase, which is sometimes referred to as *long-range planning*. It generally represents further translation toward implementation and is sometimes not much more than additional long-range details of the chosen options.

The long-range planning, then, as distinguished from strategic planning, moves closer to the planning of current operations and of all the units of an organization. This further planning could include completing the PB program structure hierarchy, additional analysis of alternatives, data development, inclusion of more organizational units, further operational and functional area considerations, reengineering studies, and generally more details. In industry, it might also include product and market planning, finance and manpower planning, and R&D and manufacturing planning; these would be expressed within the chosen program structure, with their respective resource allocations.

The major considerations for the various kinds of planning can begin with the taking of a situational inventory. This is done by identifying and studying the critical issues or challenges facing an organization or planning unit that revolve around its competition, major problems, needs, threats, opportunities, strengths, and weaknesses. Various alternatives and strategies are then generated in response to the issues. This process also serves as a creative stimulus by exposing the decision makers to situations demanding solutions. The evaluations and directions that result are measured against the existing goals and objectives in order to confirm, change, or update them as well as the strategic responses. The strategic responses are then expressed in output-oriented programs, with estimates and data that are not detailed. Again, strategic planning would have the most general data, whereas long-range planning would start to provide more details and forecasts to fit into current operations.

The next significant level of detail would be accomplished in the next phase: programming. In some planning systems, this activity could still be regarded as being in the planning phase, as part of the long-range planning mentioned previously, and would involve the assembly and review of long-range plans in further forecast detail. This distinction is not critical, as long as a planning system's process and data provide a comprehensive decision-making base in increasing detail and in a program structure for building a connected, supportive, and consistent budget. In many cases, however, the details of the long-range plans are too limited or disconnected for easy conversion to a budget. The programming phase, in particular, addresses such deficiencies.

The planning and programming phases as described here, therefore, are essentially parts of the same activity, differing primarily in planning detail. The major strategic considerations, however, should be resolved in the planning phase. The key decision makers should be integrally involved in both phases and should review the results before moving to the budgeting phase.

Programming Phase

The term "programming" can be a bit confusing in PB jargon and should be differentiated from the term "program." The creation of the major PB program groupings is generally handled in the planning phase, with the term "program" indicating an output-oriented strategic classification. Probably the programming phase could have more appropriately been designed as "multiyear forecasting."

Programming primarily deals with the more detailed application of resources (manpower, materials, facilities, and equipment) and schedules to the plans and programs. That is, it is the programming of resource expenditures (capital planning) for the programs in significant detail for incorporation into a budget. It is the level of detail after planning that bridges the gap to budgeting and reflects all of the strategic decisions and projected expenditures in a program format for a planning period. In a sense, it represents a multiyear budget in a program format.

Objectives should be well defined by the programming phase, but they should still be challenged. The attention should now be focused on translating the preferred alternatives for implementation and the deployment of resources. Quantification data in considerable detail are necessary at this stage because the budgeting consequences of the approved programs should be anticipated. Assembly of the various multiyear financial forecasts of the planning period is completed in this phase according to all the program groupings, with the resources allocated within financial capabilities. The crosswalks are also completed in this phase. The multiyear forecasts need only be in a program structure format. It is not necessary that they also be in a regular line-item format. Only the budget year is translated into a line-item format, as is discussed later.

After the programming phase is completed and approved, preparation commences on the budget or the annual profit plan, as it is often called in industry. The first year of the multiyear forecasts in the PB format is now fully translated into a regular line-item budget format through the crosswalks (described later). Such details significantly facilitate the preparation of the budget with a soundly conceived foundation regarding the likely future requirements. It is expected that much of the annual budget debate can take place in the programming phase and can result in the basic budget assumptions, guidelines, and decisions.

Budgeting Phase

In the budgeting phase, final allocations of resources and more detailed reviews are made in a traditional line-item format to accomplish and control the approved programs for the first year of the plan. They are based on the latest information, the crosswalk translations, and the basic budget decisions made in the programming phase. Here, again, there should still be an allowance for decisions that may be necessary to modify program choices, but, obviously, at this late stage, changes must be applied judiciously. If the budget changes are significant, the multiyear forecasts of the programming phase should be recast promptly in order to balance inputs and outputs and to view the ramifications to allow for possible strategic adjustments.

Key Elements

There are commonalities in all PB systems. They include various key *structural, analytical*, and *informational elements* in the process leading to a budget. Although there is some overlap among them, and although they are balanced differently in some PB systems, they are presented here as separate entities for clarity and emphasis. They include various key activities and components that should take a written form for proper communication and reference.

Throughout this chapter, considerable reference is made to the federal PB terminology because of its vast influence on all systems. A separate section titled "Federal Program Budgeting Format" is provided later, more fully describing the components.

Program Structure

A program structure is the basic framework of PB. An output-oriented program structure should be established in the planning phase and should be based on a translation of an organization's fundamental missions, goals, objectives, or purposes. The translation establishes the strategic program classifications in a program hierarchy. The hierarchy ranges from the largest program category classification to the basic and smallest constituents, termed *program elements*. Each program should represent activities and resources with a common purpose that will produce the same outputs.

The program groupings, however, will not likely conform to an existing organizational structure, and they need not be so constructed. In the early evaluation stages, the programs can overlap the existing organizational structure in the deployment of resources. The program structure should provide insights into an organization's objectives as well as its priorities, according to the allocations made with the programs. The possible overlaps can be resolved in the later stages of the planning phase or in the programming phase.

The basic considerations in developing a PB program structure are provided later in the section on program structuring because of the special significance of this aspect.

A program structure analysis should contain the program choices made, the alternatives considered, and the rationale and broad strategies on which the programs are built, including the attendant long-range goals and anticipated program accomplishments. The calculations supporting the chosen program groupings should also be included, with as much history along the basic program structure lines as is feasible. This analysis can be part of the strategic and long-range plans and can represent a part of their basis. In the federal PB terminology, this type of analysis would be a basis for a program memorandum (PM). It could also be characterized as a kind of strategic position paper.

Issues Analysis

A continual conducting of key studies is necessary to provide an analytic foundation for decisions made in a PB system. These studies include the identification and review of critical issues and challenges facing an organization that must be made periodically and injected into a PB cycle for strategic consideration, addition, confirmation, or rejection. This can be part of the strategic planning and its periodic updating. This activity has been referred to as an *issues analysis*. In the federal PB format, it was called *special studies*, which are basically of two kinds. Some were carried out for the purpose of resolving issues in the budget year, whereas others had time frames that extended beyond the budget year in order to serve the development of future recommendations and actions.

Without these analytical inputs, the process of planning, programming, and budgeting can become overly procedural, with limited vitality and substance. They can deteriorate into an exercise in numerology without interactive analytic inputs on the key issues. In the context of more current management lexicon, some of these studies could include or be part of *reengineering-type audits/studies*.

Strategic and Long-Range Plans

The strategic and long-range plans may be completed and considered as one unit or be separate, but connected, entities. As indicated earlier, this distinction is not critical. It depends a great deal on the characteristics of an organization and its current planning system and needs. It is certainly critical, however, that a strategic plan be developed for the basic organizational direction and program structure.

A *strategic plan* should deploy the major resources of an organization. It summarizes an organization's future direction, objectives, and rationale for the chosen program groupings, with their broadly estimated resources, costs, and returns. A strategic plan can be largely qualitative and should serve as a good basis for developing more planning details. It should not require extensive revision every year and should consist of only a few pages as the foundation of the various plans. Separate subordinate strategic plans may also be necessary for the major entities of large or diverse organizations. The federal government PB PMs had many similarities to strategic plans.

Related *long-range plans*, which support the strategic plan and provide additional definition of current operations, program groupings, organizational units, functional areas, objectives, strategy, and financial details, should be developed and updated each year. They serve as a basis for more detailed multiyear comprehensive forecasts in a program format for ultimate conversion to a budget. In PB, these details are represented in multiyear program forecasts.

Multiyear Program Forecasts

Detailed long-range forecasts of inputs and outputs resulting from the strategic and long-range planning that includes the budget year should be developed in a program for-mat along with as much history as is feasible. In the federal PB terminology, this forecast had also been called a multiyear *program and financial plan* (PFP). These forecasts show the probable impact of current decisions on future revenues and expenditures for all the programs from the broad program category level to the narrower program element level. Although these forecasts were in considerable detail, they were less detailed than a budget and were the result of completing the programming phase. They provided all the pertinent data related to the outputs, costs, capital, and financing of the programs in sufficient enough detail for the traditional budget preparations.

In short, these multiyear forecasts were the basic quantitative and comprehensive statistical planning documentation of PB. It relates the quantitative measures of the program outputs to the respective operating and capital expenditures. It is generally a statistical tabulation, covering a planning period, as outlined in Exhibit 32.4 at a pro-gram category level. Expenditures are indicated only for the budget year for purposes of simplicity.

EXHIBIT 32.4   Outline of a Multiyear Program and Financial Plan ($ Thousands)

| | | Program Category I | | | | | | |
	History	Budget Year 1	Year 2	Year 3	Year 4	Year 5	Total Costs
Expense Outlay							
Salaries		$15,000					
Materials		10,000					
Maintenance		3,000					
Utilities		2,000					
Depreciation		2,000					
Travel		5,000					
Rent		7,000					
Total expense		$44,000					
Capital Outlay							
Buildings		$3,000					
Property		1,000					
Equipment		5,000					
Fixed capital		9,000					
Working capital		4,000					
Total capital		$13,000					
Select output							
Indicators and benefits							

In industry, these forecasts could include profit and loss, cash flow, and capital expenditure statements or tabulations. The outputs would include the sales of key related product or service areas, with their respective profits and returns.

In nonindustry organizations where the outputs cannot be measured in monetary terms, it is also necessary to conceive of output indicators in addition to a program structure. This is necessary in order to measure in physical terms the outputs of the various programs. The output measure chosen should be the most important quantitative performance indicator of a program. For example, for an on-the-job training program, it could be the number of workers trained; for a health program, it could be lowered disease incidence; for highway construction, it could be the number of lane miles built or reduced traffic accidents per mile.

New circumstances or thinking may dictate significant changes in the budgeting, and these changes, in turn, may require a timely rebalancing of the multiyear forecasts to evaluate the impacts on the basic thrust of the plans.

A multiyear forecast will also generally have an accompanying crosswalk (or reconciliation tabulation), cross-referencing a PB program format to the existing appropriation and fund accounts for the first year of the planning period. The purpose of the reconciliation is to ensure that the budget submissions are consistent with the intent of the program decisions and that they can be implemented through the existing budget structure.

Crosswalk

If a program structure differs from an existing budget structure, as is very likely, then a crosswalk reconciliation, or cross-classification, must be established to connect them and to transform the first year of a PB format into a line-item budget. By the use of a crosswalk, the information from the existing database can first be allocated and programmed into the strategic program groupings more appropriate to policy making and later regrouped for implementation and control.

The crosswalk allows the movement of data between planning and budgeting. The approach can be an elaborate one, utilizing an extensive reconciliation between a PB budget coding and a regular budget appropriations coding and the use of a computer. It also can be a simple tabular and manual cross-classification in a two-dimensional array with a less elaborate reconciliation, especially used for initial purposes as shown in Exhibit 32.5. It need only be constructed for the budget year.

Exhibit 32.5 shows an expenditure crosswalk tabulation for year 1, or the budget year, for three program categories. A reconciliation could even be carried down to a program element level. (Distinctions among the levels in a program hierarchy are discussed later.) However, this is very much a circumstantial decision in which judgment must be applied for particular needs and merits. Certainly, some kind of cross-reference must be maintained to construct and explain, if necessary, the building of the larger

EXHIBIT 32.5 Sample Expenditure Crosswalk: Year 1

Traditional Cost Categories			PB Format		
		Crosswalk ← →	Program Category	Program Category	Program Category
Account No.	Account	Totals	1	2	3
100	Salaries	$25,000	$15,000	$5,000	$5,000
200	Materials	50,000	10,000	35,000	5,000
300	Maintenance	5,000	3,000	1,000	1,000
400	Utilities	5,000	2,000	2,000	1,000
500	Depreciation	10,000	2,000	7,000	1,000
600	Travel	15,000	5,000	5,000	5,000
700	Rent	60,000	7,000	50,000	3,000
Etc.	Etc.	—	—	—	—
	Operating expense outlay	$170,000	$44,000	$105,000	$21,000
1100	Buildings	20,000	3,000	12,000	5,000
1200	Property	10,000	1,000	7,000	2,000
1300	Equipment	15,000	5,000	9,000	1,000
1400	Fixed capital outlay	$45,000	$9,000	$28,000	$8,000
1500	Working capital outlay	15,000	4,000	8,000	3,000
	Total capital	$60,000	$13,000	$36,000	$11,000

program categories from their basic program elements and resource allocations. Most budget submissions would not likely include crosswalks at a detail level below that of a program category, the largest program grouping used.

The crosswalk tabulation indicates how each traditional line item and its account numbers (shown in rows) are allocated and cross-classified to the various program categories (columns) for the budget year through the same crosswalk totals. Also note that program category 1 ties back to the multiyear program forecast tabulation shown in Exhibit 32.4.

The PB format does not eliminate the need for the more traditional formats dealing with administrative, operational, organizational, and performance requirements. The system is not intended or designed to increase the efficiency in the performance of daily operations or to improve the administrative control of the expenditure funds. It primarily ties planning, analysis, and budgeting together. It is necessary, however, that the various budgetary formats used be connected to a PB format by a crosswalk.

Change Analysis

Change may be characterized as the lifeblood of PB. The handling of change keeps a PB system alive and lively. It is especially necessary to determine periodically the need for strategic redirections. Provisions should be established in the annual planning and budgeting processes for necessary revisions. This should include at least a definite review period in the planning phase and flexible procedures and time allowances through the budgeting phase for ad hoc situations. It is difficult to schedule exact times throughout the year because of the ever-present uncertainties and the interlocking and interacting nature of the PB phases that provoke change. For certain, the major issues should always be resolved before considering the dependent ones, and flexibility must be available. In PB terminology, these revisions, particularly major ones, have sometimes been referred to as *change proposals*.

The changes may be the result of shifts in significant external and internal factors or assumptions. In industry, for example, significant changes could come from new information dealing with technology, competition, customers, or pricing; from shifts in the general economy or political or social climate; from more detailed analyses of resource requirements or outcomes; and so forth. A proposal for change, therefore, might cover a new product, service, or approach; a revision of an existing program or its cancellation; and so on. It would include the quantitative ramifications, the rationale, and all the relevant information. This could serve as a basis for redoing the multiyear program forecasts or could stand alone as an interim revision for further reflection and later incorporation. Such considerations, as well as a format, depend on the particular circumstances of an organization.

A change analysis should contain at least an outline of the major considerations and information, including summary quantification impacts.

Annual Calendar

An annual PB cycle must be established, with regular intervals for the planning, programming, and budgeting phases. This is to allow sufficient time for analysis and decision making at all levels of management.

An annual PB cycle should provide a year-round process of addressing program objectives, performance, and costs with a disciplined approach to change. It should also allow sufficient time for the program-oriented data to be translated into the budgeting phase with the required control details. Appropriate checkpoints should be included in order to ensure that all the essential steps are taken and that current reviews, revisions, and recommendations are given consideration at appropriate times in the cycle. A typical federal annual PB cycle is shown in Exhibit 32.6.

Systematic Analysis

An outstanding feature of PB is the emphasis on analysis throughout all its phases. Systematic analyses must be performed to clarify the conceptual framework in which decisions are made, to define possible alternative objectives, and to explore the cost and effectiveness of alternative courses of action. The system itself is an analytical tool. Because of the importance of analysis to PB, this topic is covered in greater depth in the section later in this chapter called "Types of Analysis."

Information Systems

PB should derive its information primarily from existing management records and practices. The existing database and accounting systems should provide information (or be adapted) to the planning, programming, and budgeting phases in a program structure

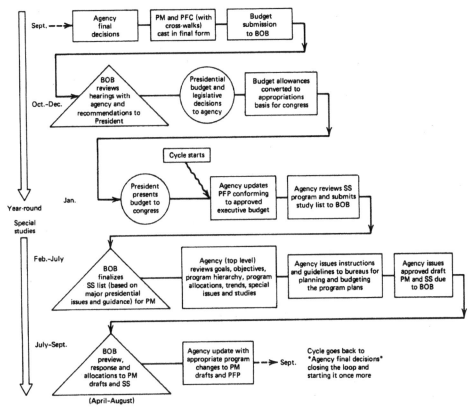

EXHIBIT 32.6 Typical Annual PB Cycle for a Federal Government Agency

hierarchy. It should allow the basic forecasting, implementation, and analysis, as well as the progress reporting and control with updating procedures. The basic requirements need not be difficult to set up. Various considerations for setting up a PB system are provided in the section on installation considerations.

Federal Program Budgeting Format

Combinations of the various PB elements can, of course, take many forms. More specifically, the format that was developed in the federal government is of greatest interest because of its wide use, publicity, and extensive scope.

Documents

Three kinds of federal PB documents were generated annually along with the traditional budget addressing various qualitative and quantitative considerations.

PMs were provided by each federal agency, containing its program structure recommendations to fit its objectives for the forthcoming period. These objectives were required to be defined in quantifiable and measurable terms, to allow for meaningful program analysis and implementation. PMs were basically strategic decision documents. They essentially are strategic plans that include a program structure analysis.

PMs were expected to be brief written documents explaining the program issues, the rationale of alternative program groupings recommended or rejected, and their costs and effectiveness. They also were to include the results of special studies, which are described subsequently. PMs encouraged policy debate among decision makers in the executive branch and communicated the final policy.

Aspects of ZBB are also in PMs because they include a defense and review of total expenditures proposed for a program rather than just indicating the changes from previous appropriations. The government instructions pointed out that as much attention should be paid to reducing and modifying obsolete and low-priority programs as to expanding others and introducing new ones. However, the government ultimately retreated from a full embracing of ZBB. It gravitated somewhere between incremental budgeting and a zero-based review of all programs.

The multiyear PFP summarized in tabular form the data from each agency that were pertinent to its program outputs, costs, and financing for the past two years, the budget year, and four additional years. The time span could be longer for special situations, such as for timber production or water resource projects.

The PFP was the result of the programming phase and was meant to be a record of the consequences of the current year's decisions. The data of PMs, however, did not have to be so confined and could reflect on consequences outside the budget-year decisions.

The outputs enumerated in the PFP were the measurable end products or services that were produced by the individual program elements. For example, a health program might use mortality data; an on-the-job training program could cite the increase in the income of the workers trained.

The PFP also included tables on the financial requirements for all the major program groupings, down to the smallest program element. The financial data included total program costs, which encompassed program-oriented R&D and all related operating costs and capital investments. Each program element was assigned a program budget code based on the regular appropriation code in order to provide a crosswalk reconciliation. This crosswalk was a tabulation in the PFP and made it possible to translate the program costs back into conventional budget requests through the existing organizational structure. This was necessary since the president was required to recommend his budget to the Congress in an established appropriations structure and also to monitor the consistency of the budget submission with the program decisions. The crosswalk did not have to show a reconciliation down to a program element level but only to the major program groupings, the program categories.

Special studies (SS) provided the basic data and analytical foundation for the program decisions of the PMs regarding the program choices and rejection of alternatives. They usually covered specific aspects of programs. They showed the costs and benefits of prior programs and compared alternative program mixes.

These analyses were for decision-making purposes and considered economic opportunity and marginal costs in addition to regular budget-type costs. The costs in the PFP, however, were more limited and in a regular budgetary mode. The PFP constituted a link between the mixed bag of analytical costs covered in both the SS and the PMs to the regular budget financing needed to implement the programs.

In addition, the SS served as a vehicle for general policy issue analyses in which the major issues were identified, analyzed, and then incorporated into the budget. There was no fixed length or format for SS. It was performed and issued year round to support an agency's strategic directions or on request from the BOB. It was not part of the final submitted budget package. Yearly, the BOB and the agencies jointly agreed to a list of program issues requiring detailed analysis. Some of them were for resolving issues in the budget and others were for future actions.

The basic quality of the various PB documents was judged on some of these criteria: For the PM, it was the concentration of major policy decisions and the identification of major alternatives; for the PFP, it was the accuracy of cost and output estimates; and for the SS, it was the usefulness of the information and the identified alternatives for achieving the program objectives.

Final Federal Submission

PB became the third way in which each federal agency was required to display its annual budget. Each agency was required to identify the major objectives it was pursuing and to display its budgetary data in these terms:

- Appropriations for control of expenditures (line-item traditional cost format)
- Activity for management efficiency ("performance" format)
- PB format, which included the PM and PFP as integral parts of the traditional budget submissions and reviews

Annual Federal Cycle

The federal PB cycle was an annual comprehensive process of addressing program objectives, performance, and costs by systematically bringing planning, analysis, and budgeting together. It provided checkpoints to ensure that essential steps were taken and that current reviews, revisions, and recommendations were given consideration at appropriate times in the budget process. Throughout the process it utilized the basic PB documents: the PM, PFP, and SS.

Each federal agency had latitude for tailored modifications in the cycle as long as it met the BOB's basic legal and legislative schedule requirements. Each agency head was expected to receive recommendations from his or her principal managers on all the major program issues. It was the responsibility of each agency head to ensure that line managers at appropriate levels participated in the cycle.

An outline of a typical annual PB cycle utilizing the various PB process steps for the federal agencies is shown in Exhibit 32.6 within a year around special studies activities. The cycle shown is basically for an established PB system. It breaks into the cycle in the September activities to highlight the beginning context of the cycle that starts in January. The cycle begins in January with an updated multiyear program and financial plan conforming to the approved executive budget soon after the president's submission of the administration's budget to the Congress the same month. This is the basis for the various planning activities that proceed through August. Also in August are the programming activities that are reflected in the updating and program changes of the PFP before the start of the September budgeting activities. The budgeting activities of the cycle go from September through January and end with the president's budget presentation for the next fiscal year. There is some overlap or combination of PB process activities in some of the checkpoint intervals. This is to be expected, with the interlocking and interactive nature of the PB to provide the most timely and comprehensive decision-oriented data.

PROGRAM STRUCTURING

Program structuring is a vital ingredient of PB that transforms an organization's existing cost structure into strategic output-oriented information. It arranges an organization's activities into a hierarchy of strategic program groupings with common outputs and objectives. It is a way of organizing information to show how much is spent or should be spent for an organization's various purposes, irrespective of its existing organizational structure. As indicated previously, the SBUs employed in the GE/McKinsey strategic planning technique have many similarities to the strategic program groupings of PB. The term "profit center," utilized in industry, also has many similarities.

A number of key considerations to be aware of in developing and structuring PB programs for both private and public-sector organizations are discussed next.

No Set Formula

There is no set formula for creating programs or a program structure. There are as many ways of conceiving programs as there are of organizing activities.

The possibilities for regrouping activities are almost endless, and different program grouping schemes may be necessary for different organizational needs and circumstances. Rigidity and inflexibility should be avoided. A test of satisfactory program structure is its utility in facilitating and clarifying an organization's current decision-making processes for strategically allocating resources.

Programs in a planning development stage need not be mutually exclusive because an organization's objectives may require some overlapping structures between business, geographic, and functional areas. This can help in evaluating programs, in making trade-offs, and ultimately in choosing a final program and in resolving the budget.

Traditional versus Program Budgeting Format

Examples that vividly differentiate a PB program structure from one of traditional budgeting with a more limited output orientation are shown next.

Possible Program Structures	
Traditional Structure	**PB Structure**
Coast Guard	Coast Guard
Vessel operations	Search and rescue
Aviation operations	Aids to navigation
Repair and supply facilities	Law enforcement
Export Service	Forest Service
Forest protection	Timber production
Range improvements	Outdoor recreation
Land acquisition	Natural beauty
Access roads	Wildlife

The PB program structure clearly emphasizes the purposes and objectives of the Coast Guard and Forest Service, whereas the traditional structure emphasizes the methods or means used.

A PB program structure can provide a better framework for strategic decision making and resource allocations between the various activities. This factor does not negate the need for other kinds of budgeting structures that can be more helpful in dealing with operations, performance, and efficiency. Different views can provide an additional basis for sound decision making and controls.

Program Hierarchy

Program structuring involves defining a hierarchy of programs. The concept of a program hierarchy presents the logic of moving from defined objectives into programs and operating activities in meaningful implementation terms. In PB terminology, they can range from the largest aggregation of activities, *program categories* (which address the broad objectives or missions); to intermediate categories, *program subcategories* or *program packages*; to the smallest program units, *program elements*. The designation distinctions among these category levels are not important. It is important to have meaningful hierarchical program groupings to assist in choosing among program alternatives and for making fund allocations across the program spectrum of an organization.

Probably the missions of an organization, particularly the market missions in industry that assume a "purposes" tone and that relate to encompassing (or the highest) levels of an organization's activities, can best help define the broad program categories.

A program element is the smallest program unit that is self-contained. In the industry sense, it might be called a *profit center* or *key product area*. It is a complete, identifiable, self-contained activity or decision unit, such as a system, a product, or a service, that contributes to an organization's purpose and objectives. It serves as a building block of a program structure.

All major costs, facilities, major equipment, manpower, and other resources directly related to the programs must be identified (see Exhibit 32.1 for a matrix view).

Program Development

Programs can be generated by focusing on broad objectives related to purposes, by separating costs into generic activities, by separating means from ends, by considering current strategic requirements, by breaking a major area into its primary components, and so forth. A creative approach could utilize many of these approaches concurrently, with a choice ultimately being made according to an organization's particular circumstances and needs.

A hierarchy of programs can be constructed from two directions, that is, from smaller units into larger ones or from purposeful generic umbrellas broken down into smaller units. The main approach is the latter. The upper levels of major programs should focus primarily on outputs whereas the lower levels can focus more on means to achieving objectives. The development process is iterative and very subjective to an organization and circumstances.

Classification Schemes

A variety of classification schemes can be utilized for creating program categories. The groupings should all focus on objectives and purposes and can cover a wide range, such as customers, markets, age–sex–type groups, geography, primary function, product, or service lines.

Industry

A hypothetical conglomerate industrial organization could include plant and toiletry products with this possible program hierarchy:

Industry Program Hierarchy	
Plant Products	**Toiletry Products**
1. Fertilizer	1. Hair care
a. Industrial	a. Cleansing
b. Home and garden	b. Coloring

or	or	or
Chemical types	Shampoo	Consumer
	Dyes, tints	Institutional

2. Pesticides
    a. Industrial
    b. Home and garden

or		
Destruction		
means:		
Mechanical		
Chemical		
Biological		

2. Mouth care
    a. Cleaning
    b. Deodorizing

or	or
Toothpaste	Consumer
Mouthwash	Institutional

3. Skin care

Federal Government

A segment of program hierarchies from two federal agencies are:

Federal Program Hierarchy	
Department of Health, Education & Welfare (February 1968)	**Department of Labor (May 1968)**
Education	*Manpower Development Assistance*
1. Basic skills department	1. Training
a. General population	a. On-the-job
b. Economically disadvantaged	b. Institutional (classroom)
c. Handicapped	2. Special manpower program
Health	a. Experimental projects
1. Development of health resources	3. Work programs
a. Increasing knowledge	a. Neighborhood youth corps
Heart disease	b. Community employment
Cancer	c. Work incentive program
b. Providing facilities/equipment	*Employment Assistance*
2. Prevention/control health problems	1. Employment market information
a. Disease control	2. Job development/placement
3. Health services provision	a. Assistance
a. Aged	b. Agricultural
b. Poor	c. Veterans
c. Indians	3. Employability assistance
d. Children and mothers	4. Civil rights compliance

It can be seen that a variety of program classifications can be established for the programs described here, and they could all be valid in accommodating various organizational needs. It is interesting to note the scope that PB took in the DOD with about 10 program categories and more than 800 program elements.

Problems

Several problems in establishing a PB program structure should be taken into consideration. These include:

- *Increased paperwork and manpower time, and possible increased costs to do the work.* For example, superimposing a program structure onto a conventional accounting system will require a reconciliation through a crosswalk.
- *Power struggles with program delineation.* Since program delineations may be arbitrary and may not respect organizational lines, struggles to retain budgetary control may ensue.
- *Confusion with cost allocations.* Differences are bound to occur regarding the apportionment of costs that cut across jurisdictional lines.

Although there are formidable problems to consider in structuring programs, they can be managed if one anticipates them. The payoff can be improved results and viability.

TYPES OF ANALYSIS

The cornerstone of PB is the systematic identification and analysis of alternatives, which are examined in relation to benefits and costs. As mentioned, some of the current management jargon in this genre would include reengineering audits/studies. Buzzwords such as *cost–benefit,* however, became strongly identified with PB in its heyday at the Pentagon and are still very much a part of the lexicon. The distinctions among the various types of applicable analyses, however, are not always clear.

Three basic types of analysis have been associated with PB: (1) *systems analysis;* (2) *cost–benefit* and *cost-effectiveness* analysis, which are similar terms and are sometimes used synonymously; and (3) *operations research.* These types are sometimes used interchangeably because of the overlap among them. In a sense, they represent an analytical hierarchy, with the differentiating factors being the degree of problem scope, complexity, and uncertainty. Reviewing the similarities and differences between these analyses should shed some light on their key elements and applications.

The approach of all of these analyses to solving problems is the scientific method: analysis, synthesis, and verification. All of them are a form of systems analysis in that they all relate to inputs and outputs within defined boundaries. They all break a given area or system into its component inputs and outputs, which collectively serve as a model.

Systems Analysis

A systems analysis has the broadest orientation and is generally concerned with broad or ill-structured problems (bordering on policy, goals, and strategy) having choices that cannot be reduced solely to an economic basis.

Systems analysis has been characterized as a way to a solution, or as quantitative common sense. This means, of course, that for very complex problems dealing with the future, particularly those dealing with strategy or significant political, social, or public factors, a solution is generally not obvious in a quantitative sense. In such cases, a systems analysis aids a decision maker in creating alternatives and in selecting one. It provides a comprehensive summary of all the relevant information. It is more concerned with widening the range of alternatives or creating sensible objectives rather than with selecting the best one from a limited given range. It attempts to ensure the achievement of a larger objective more effectively rather than solely focusing on optimizing a few component parts. Its premise is that it is better to be roughly right rather than exactly wrong. It seeks to avoid gross error. In this sense, it is a rough kind of grand optimum for a broad set of circumstances.

Limited Mathematics

Systems analysis involves applying broad concepts to situations having a significant number of uncontrolled and unpredictable factors. The extensive use of mathematical statistical techniques in such cases is limited. One can deal with uncertainty through the use of scenario alternatives, sensitivity tests, and quantitative ranges. The calculations generally utilized are relatively uncomplicated in the context of the broad basic concepts of macroeconomics, where informed judgment still plays the bigger role. Although systems analysis uses calculations, it puts less emphasis on them relative to the other types of analysis.

Breaking up a complex management system into a conceptually oriented framework of smaller component systems or subsystems, such as in PB, with various inputs and outputs, is a form of systems analysis. Systems analysis is not some arcane, heavily computerized or mathematically oriented form of analysis. Strategic and long-range planning in industry are forms of systems analysis, as is an analysis of strategic weapons systems in the military.

Iterative Process

As with strategic or long-range planning, the analytic process is highly iterative in the mold of the scientific method and in trial and error. A sequence of the process could be defining the problem (or opportunity), selecting objectives, designing alternatives, collecting data, building models, evaluating costs attendant to benefits, testing for sensitivity, reviewing original premises against the forecast results, reexamining the objectives, designing new alternatives, reformulating the problem, determining new or modified objectives, and so on to a solution (or strategy).

Cost–Benefit and Cost-Effectiveness Analysis

Every systems analysis must reach the point, after getting past the grand objectives and strategies, of evaluating the costs, benefits, or effectiveness of specific alternatives or subsystems for achieving specified objectives. At this juncture, the broad qualitative policy issues are either minimized or well defined. The analyses of such alternatives has generally been termed cost–benefit or cost-effectiveness analysis. Because these analyses often receive the most attention, the entire analysis, including the systems analysis portion, often is called cost–benefit or cost-effectiveness analysis.

Both types of analysis require the measurement of inputs and outputs for a given alternative and measure costs in monetary terms. Their distinction lies basically on the output side. In cost–benefit analysis, the outputs can be computed in monetary terms, whereas in cost-effectiveness analysis, the outputs can be quantified only in physical units. Some problems may have combinations of both kinds of analysis.

Different Evaluation Values

A cost–benefit analysis is quite common in industry where, for example, major new capital projects require extensive cost–benefit calculations, including profit and loss, break even, cash flow, payouts, return on investment, discounted rates of return (internal rate of return, net present value), and cost–benefit ratio analyses. However, this technique has evolved to the point where it is capable of handling broader problems than those traditionally found in business. In situations where monetary values are only a part of the total value, or where important quantitative value factors cannot be expressed in monetary terms, a combination cost–benefit and cost-effectiveness analysis is helpful.

In government, educational, and various nonprofit institutions, many of the major decisions reflect social benefits and costs and political considerations. The cost-effectiveness approach is used primarily in such cases, with the outputs measured in physical outputs. The benefits may include workers trained, disease reduced, fatalities prevented, junk yards beautified, billboards removed, or youth trained.

When the costs or benefits cannot be well quantified, one has to fall back on a systems-analysis mode. When costs can be quantified but benefits or effectiveness cannot be, one is faced with a hybrid structure. The approach to utility theory used in Bayesian decision theory, statistics, and economics can be helpful in such cases. The utility (satisfaction, value, worth) preferences of people can be represented in numerically useful ways, with probability distributions or degrees of "yes" or "no" for policy decisions. Such approaches have significant implications for welfare and ethics economics.

The cost–benefit and cost-effectiveness types of analysis provide a method by which many of the major relationships in a problem capable of being reduced to a quantitative basis are so translated, thereby leaving the decision maker with a better basis for applying judgment and intuition to the remainder.

In its collective utilization, PB, including that of the federal government, has probably put more people to work trying to learn how to do analyses of social systems than any other management effort in history.

Basic Approaches

A cost–benefit and cost-effectiveness analysis can be approached from a few basic points of view: The cost is constrained or fixed, and the solution is the maximum benefit or effectiveness; the level of benefit or effectiveness is fixed, and the solution is the option with the lowest cost. Also, in the case of cost–benefit analysis, and dealing strictly in monetary terms, a solution may be to maximize net benefits (benefits minus costs). Generally, however, all of these analyses are constrained by the limited resources of a budget.

In reaching a decision, the risk and returns should be evaluated on both a quantity and a ratio basis. The various measurements may include cost–benefit or cost-effectiveness ratios, net present values, internal rates of return, and the like. Of course, intuition and judgment are also important in considering the relevance of the qualitative factors and sometimes the primary basis after the number crunching.

Cost–Benefit Example

A cost–benefit analysis may mix quantitative and nonmonetary-oriented data in order to enable choosing among alternatives. Consider this example: An industrial corporation has decided to put up a new combination headquarters/research building next to its primary manufacturing facilities. The facilities for research and administration had previously been rented. A simplified cost–benefit structure is shown in the next table, which highlights the various cost and benefit considerations for five alternatives:

	Owned Facility	Rented Facility
	Alternatives	
	1 2 3	4 5
Benefits		
New product sales		
Improved existing product sales		
Enhanced company image		
Improved morale and productivity		
Savings (rental removal)		
Tax benefits		
Better communications, cross-fertilization		
Reduced turnover		
Reduced staff travel time		
Increased new products introductions		
Percentage increase in manufacturing efficiency		
Higher-caliber technical staff attraction		
Increased customer service and contact		
Government contract enhancement		
Increased patent production		

(Continued)

	Alternatives	
	1 2 3	4 5
Improved university relationships		
Improved team spirit		
Cost		
Capital investment		
Operating cost		
Depreciation		
Salaries		
Maintenance		
Rental		
Equipment		
Other		

A complete cost–benefit analysis could also take into account appropriate time spans and additional financial considerations, including cost–benefit ratios, cash flow, internal rates of return or net present values, payouts, returns on investment, and so on.

Industry Applications

The cost–benefit and cost-effectiveness approach has largely been utilized by government and not-for-profit institutions (e.g., educational institutions, libraries) to deal with social and political factors; the complete approach has been little used by profit-making organizations. As nonmonetary factors become more important to industry decision making, undoubtedly the broader aspects of these analyses will be increasingly utilized. Such analyses already have many existing useful applications for preparing budgets in nonrevenue departments, such as personnel, finance, and public relations. Generally, those budgets are approached on a limited incremental basis from year to year or requirements are injected into the department. In both approaches, the potential results are not adequately measured against costs.

The emphasis in preparing budgets for nonrevenue departments should be on identifying and, if possible, measuring the derived benefits or effectiveness against the costs and on determining whether greater advantage might not be obtained by shifting the directions (or even aborting some) in which the available funds are spent. Obviously, there are aspects of ZBB to this approach. All of this encourages economics in the large sense rather than in the small, as with incremental budgeting. In addition, these types of analysis provide a mechanism for establishing a comprehensive dialogue between the involved parties to discuss policy issues of a department in the concrete terms of constructing a budget.

Operations Research

Operations research involves the application of sophisticated applied mathematics and scientific methods to problems in order to provide optimum solutions. The term was coined during World War II. The beginnings of systems analysis appear to be the successful operations research that was employed during World War II to handle military problems of defense and logistics. It initially dealt with military operations, such as preferred bomb mixes for different bombing missions, and gravitated into the broader considerations of strategic weapons systems. The label that is generally preferred for the broader type of problems, though, is systems analysis.

Operations research is concerned primarily with efficiency and far less with the construction of choices, as contrasted with systems analysis. It tries to select an optimum solution from a predetermined set of alternatives and in a sense is a form of cost–benefit or cost-effectiveness analysis in which the numerical results have a high reliability in decision making. It generally deals with the optimization of smaller subsystems in which the data are assumed to be sufficiently accurate to allow sophisticated and detailed calculations within a range of statistical validity.

Operations research emphasizes applied mathematical techniques for discrete problems or for those that are better defined, narrower, or subject to constraints. Such problems are sufficiently defined so that they can be adequately described by a mathematical model in which the element of calculation is dominant; therefore, in a sense, the mathematics substitutes for the need for judgment. The mathematics includes linear and dynamic programming, queueing theory, decision theory, Monte Carlo techniques, search theory, inventory theory, control theory, and the like. The assumption is, again, that the empirical data are sufficiently accurate for the sophisticated calculations. In such cases, of course, computers can be extremely helpful and fast.

Good examples of operations research-oriented analyses deal with materials and inventory management in industry or the military and with the routing and scheduling of transportation-related activities (trucking, airlines, rail, etc.).

Comparison of the Analyses

There are similarities among systems analysis, operations research, and cost–benefit and cost-effectiveness analysis, because they all employ the scientific method to problem solving and because there is some overlap. At the extremes, however, systems analysis is more complex and less neat and quantitative. Although they are all quantitatively oriented, systems analysis tends to include a much large proportion of nonquantitative elements influencing the outcomes. In the cases of developing a new consumer or industrial product, designing a new weapons system, or developing an urban renewal plan, a systems analysis could be employed, and although operations research or a cost–benefit or cost-effectiveness analysis could be a part, they would likely have a more limited role. Again, a systems analysis is more concerned with avoiding strategic gross error and focuses on providing a wider range of choices or on designing a new solution. If there is an optimum with a systems analysis, it is with the large scope (in the grand sense) rather than with the small.

Although the differences among systems analysis, cost–benefit and cost-effectiveness analysis, and operations research are not absolutely clear, an analogy that has been used points to the differences that exist between strategy and tactics.

Modeling

All of the analyses that have been described utilize models as a simplifying mechanism to simulate the behavior of the real world. A *model* is essentially a simplified representation of an operation that contains only those aspects of primary importance to the problem under study. Although models generally take the form of a set of equations, they can be cast in several different quantitative and qualitative forms. They may vary from objects to verbal pictures to precise mathematical formulas.

Pro forma balance sheets, profit and loss statements, and break-even charts are good examples of quantitative models simulating the financial processes of an organization. An accounting system is also a model; it is a simplified representation on paper, in the form of accounts and ledgers, of the flow of goods and services through a business enterprise.

There are also many nonquantitative types of models that must be employed, because not all situations can be easily or fully translated into a neat quantitative framework or equation. These models are frequently utilized in strategic planning, systems analysis, or policy development, and they mostly rely on the informed judgment of experts on the issues. They include:

- *Scenarios.* A future is described under a possible chain of events in order to discuss policy options.
- *Delphi technique.* Experts forecast and interact indirectly on the future through a questionnaire. This is particularly useful in single-discipline situations.
- *Gaming.* A role-playing approach for simulating the interactions of people in the real world. This is particularly useful in situations requiring multidisciplines.

Two Types

Models may be characterized as one of two general types: deterministic or probabilistic. The distinction is not so important in actually constructing a model as it is in utilizing the appropriate mathematics for a set of circumstances.

A deterministic model is used to represent operations or processes in which the degree of predictability is very high and the circumstances can be significantly controlled. Many operations research models fall into this category with the mathematics largely dictating the decision.

A probabilistic model is used to represent situations that have many uncertainties, the interactions of which are difficult to relate and control, with the ultimate consequences thus being extremely difficult to predict. Systems analysis and planning models generally fall into this category, as does PB as a model. Most of the submodels of PB tend to be probabilistic.

New Emphasis

There is very little that is new about modeling techniques, as they date back to ancient times. What is new is the emphasis in all kinds of organizations, government through industry, on developing larger comprehensive conceptual frameworks, as in PB, that will:

- Better elucidate the various relationships
- Better cope with the greater recognition of the existing uncertainties
- Better quantify outcomes
- More clearly demonstrate the consequences of various decisions

Handling Uncertainty

Through the manipulation of a model, one can demonstrate the influences of various kinds of uncertainty. For example, in the government, uncertainty can range from unpredictable congressional or citizenry attitudes to ally or enemy reactions. In business, uncertainty may result from new technology, energy crises, competitive reactions to pricing, product shifts in customer or consumer attitudes and demand, changes in interest rates, or the availability of capital, inflation, recession, and so on.

In such cases, a sensitivity analysis can be performed, using a model to determine the relative sensitivity of the significant variable factors to the outcomes. *Sensitivity analysis* is nothing more than a measuring of the degree to which costs or benefits may change with varying assumptions. Such an analysis in industry could include changes in profitability under varying levels of pricing, product mix, sales volume, cost, and capital. The model facilitates this kind of analysis, uncovering the important relationships so that appropriate actions may be taken.

Acid Test

The acid test for determining the value of a model does not rest with the model's complexity or mathematical elegance but with its ability to provide insights into the problems raised and the solutions required and to predict the likely outcomes with sufficient accuracy—and, of course, in the end to facilitate sound decision making.

Overview of Analyses

PB is concerned primarily with the methodology of systems analysis and cost–benefit and cost-effectiveness analysis rather than with that of operations research because many of the significant factors elude sophisticated quantification. However, the benefits of operations research can be substantial when the quantitative approach is appropriately utilized in total or in part. Operations research correctly applied can provide firm and reliable answers rather than just uncovering additional remedies of unknown or unverifiable success potential.

Systems analysis utilizes the scientific method, but it is more an art than a science. It generally is an approach to complex problems of choice under conditions of significant uncertainty, and its focus is with uncovering remedies. No single methodology can be employed. Performing a systems analysis helps decision makers recognize that they are managing a total and complex system with many relationships that cannot be managed by brushfire fighting or a mathematical formula. It helps focus on the importance of a central role and direction in managerial decision making, particularly in the strategic considerations.

Analysis is an aid, but not a replacement, for the decision maker. It sharpens intuition and judgment, stimulating the right questions and putting them in a logical array of priorities. How much of a budget should be allocated among competing programs in an organization is a decision problem that must finally depend on judgment, intuition, and faith in large part alongside the numbers and forecasts.

PB can be viewed as a model of an organization's overall input–output process. It, therefore, is itself an analytical tool, because it generates objectives and alternatives, summarizes the costs and benefits, draws out the criteria, and provides a decision-oriented array in a distilled form.

INSTALLATION CONSIDERATIONS

The framework, program structuring, and analytical aspects of PB have been covered in previous sections. There are additional aspects to be taken into account when installing a complete, modified, or partial utilization of PB in an organization. They involve information and accounting systems, assessing and organizing, and tailoring and staffing. In many organizations, a PB installation will be more a process of consolidating and systematizing the ingredients already in place.

Information System

A critical ingredient of PB is data. An inadequate information system can be a major constraint to PB's operating effectively. A PB system may require restructuring data from existing systems, modifying some of the existing systems, or developing new supporting systems.

Many of the required information sources, reporting subsystems, and processing capabilities already exist in most large or up-to-date organizations. One may employ expedient stopgap approaches to get a PB system started, but, in all cases, the primary effort is with strategic and long-range planning rather than with the mechanical manipulation of data.

Role in Program Budgeting

PB is not a management information system. In some instances management information systems were undertaken as a substitute for major PB features. However, PB is not synonymous with the installation of a new computer system or related techniques for making management data more readily available. It is not the sole, or even the prime, reason for an organization to undertake company-wide information systems improvement programs. Even though a good management information system is very useful to PB operations, alone it lacks the planning emphasis, program structuring, and alternative analysis that are so vital to PB. Increasing the amount of hardware, firepower, and automatic processing does not provide these key PB elements. If an organization has the sophistication to consider a better link between its planning and budgeting systems, it very likely has the existing data systems adequately set up to utilize or readily adapt to PB techniques.

Program Budgeting Matrix

The existing information system should allow the construction of a resources and cost matrix in a program format. It should allow displays and summaries by program, cost, organizational unit, function, or resource category in sufficient detail and validity to make decisions. Of course, if any of the existing systems are inadequate, they should be improved or eliminated, irrespective of installing a PB system.

Management's Needs

Most management information system accomplishments have been in the areas of mechanization or computerization of record keeping and other routine operational activities and with middle management–type problems. They have been structured primarily for control and do not sufficiently serve the multiple needs of all levels of management, particularly in the areas of information and analytical support for the planning and policy decision making of the PB type. With the widespread availability of minicomputers and microcomputers and sophisticated software programs, there is increasing potential for building dynamic, multifactor models for analysis and resource allocation.

Accounting System

It is unnecessary to change an existing accounting or reporting system to conform to a program structure; in fact, it may be undesirable. A PB program structure is not a static framework to be maintained despite significant external and internal changes or new strategic insights. The basis of PB is a periodic reexamination of program results in order to evaluate and restructure programs and objectives. A PB system and structure, like all planning systems, must be dynamically oriented to be valuable. Since programs and objectives are subject to change, it would be very disruptive to parallel changes each time with the accounting and reporting systems. Moreover, it would be equally chaotic to make organizational changes based solely on a program structure. If an organization is comfortable and knowledgeable with its existing accounting system, and the system can be used, PB can be introduced more smoothly.

The existing accounting system must allow data to be consolidated into the large aggregative program categories from a program element level. Both direct and indirect costs must be in proper form and appropriately coded. The adjustment of the data should be kept to a minimum when accumulated into the larger categories. In the beginning, methods should be developed to eliminate arbitrary allocations of indirect costs. Moreover, the system should permit a summation of detailed cost elements from all cost elements to responsible organizational units (indicating the magnitude of the work load and resources each program requires). Also, appropriate coding or initial tracking for a crosswalk should be developed for transforming a PB format into an existing budget format.

Assessment and Organization

Before organizing a PB system, it is helpful to take an inventory of the existing decision-making processes, including an assessment of the analytical capabilities and data system operations and support. This sampling of questions could be included:

- What are the objectives and key issues of the organization? Strengths and weaknesses? Threats? Opportunities?
- Who makes the strategic decisions? The chief executive officer? The board of directors? Individuals? A committee? At what level?
- Who brings the strategic issues to the decision makers, and how? What is the size and experience of the analytical staff?
- What are the external influences and constraints in the general managerial processes, and how are they handled?
- What special studies, policy issues, analyses, and data are considered? Who prepares and analyzes them? How far into the future are these studies and forecasts generally made? How are benefits measured? Are the current data valid and up to date? Can history be reconstructed? What kinds of forecasts or projections are generally made from the database? Where and how are data collected, processed, and displayed?
- What controls, measurements, and appraisals exist to indicate actual costs, benefits, and accountability?
- What kind of planning exists? How is it coordinated for different programs and resources?
- How is the budget prepared? On what basis? What are the accounting systems utilized?
- What is the timetable for the key decision making in the organization? Is there a regular schedule or cycle for planning and budgeting? For capital requests? For new ventures?

Alternatives

Some of the alternatives to be considered in applying PB in an organization are listed next.

- Integrate it into the existing managerial and financial systems.
- Superimpose it over the existing systems.
- Implement it company-wide.
- Implement it on a select organizational basis.
- Do it piecemeal; for example, do program structuring without extensive analysis.

Tailoring

All questions and alternatives, such as those listed, should be addressed in order to tailor a PB approach to an organization. The installation can be a crash effort, a methodical piecemeal approach, or something in between. The success of a chosen approach depends on a realistic evaluation of the various considerations and on the leadership and active participation of top management, not just on their approval. The key decision makers should fully understand the need for a PB-type system and that, although it facilitates strategic decision making, it does not make decisions. They must also encourage the use of analysis. Good judgment is improved only when operating on the basis of good data and analysis. The final decisions still must finally reflect the judgment and intuition of the decision makers in determining the important goals and objectives to pursue.

The existing systems should be utilized as much as possible initially. Practicality and flexibility should be employed in introducing a PB system. Choices are available between across-the-board and step-by-step approaches regarding the parts of the organization covered and the parts or scope of the methodology applied.

Some clashes can be anticipated between organizational jurisdictions with possible overlapping PB program structures in the unresolved planning stages as well as with the time-consuming analysis requirements conflicting with demanding budget schedules. These possible problems can be minimized with preplanning, timely communication, and flexible approaches.

One premise is certain: The pace of PB implementation should match the capacity of the organization and its parts to absorb it. If the organization is large, parts of it may adjust to PB at different rates and levels of sophistication. If the approach is not tailored, the utilization of PB can be jettisoned before it really starts, possibly for the wrong reasons.

Staffing

Most major private and public-sector organizations already have the staff expertise and capability to consider and implement a PB approach without personnel additions. In many instances there are special groups to perform capital projects analysis, venture analyses, acquisitions, make-or-buy analyses, and so on. The central PB coordination in a large organization can be managed by a corporate long-range planning group or a corporate financial group. If the organization is large enough to have divisions, a PB planning coordinator should probably be designated in each division to facilitate the process and gain the necessary commitment. Reporting to a division head is preferable. In addition, the active support and involvement of the head of the organization is essential. To be effective, PB requires strong leadership and interest at the top, especially for the extensive analysis of alternatives. The strategic decision making that PB involves, however, should not be delegated to analysts. Analysts should primarily facilitate the process and fully analyze the ramifications of the chosen options and decisions.

There are three ways in which a PB staff can be acquired:

1. It can be recruited from the outside.
2. The existing staff can be oriented and trained for the new approaches.
3. A combination of items 1 and 2 can be used.

Because of PB's emphasis on analysis, it requires individuals who have had significant experience with analytical approaches or some related training or education. Planning and financial analysis experience provides a good foundation.

These requirements are not necessarily met by new elaborate personnel recruiting, education, or training efforts. Generally, what is needed is some orientation and redirection of existing personnel. However, organizations should also consider the prospects of some staff additions and the costs and time associated with installing a PB approach.

A PB system is interdisciplinary in nature and therefore must draw on many types of specialists or properly experienced generalists. No single academic discipline is de rigueur, although it is very helpful for one to have studied a quantitatively oriented subject.

The ideal staff member would have a good knowledge of macroeconomics, microeconomics, mathematics, statistics, engineering, computers, or finance. Experience in budgeting, planning, financial analysis, project management, marketing, or management processes in general is also very helpful. Some line experience, moreover, can be helpful in taking practical approaches. The person should be creative, curious, flexible, courageous, communicative, and results-oriented and should have integrity. Obviously, the ideal individual would have the potential to become an executive within the organization. In addition, it is preferable that the individual have a practical working knowledge of the areas in which the work will be involved. This should be gained within a short time, if the individual does not start with such knowledge. Usually analysis cannot be applied in some sort of pure fashion with significant effectiveness without some working insight or experience.

The entire staff, however, need not have all the ideal characteristics mentioned. A group can be built around one or two solid staff specialists. The others can be trained through the involved cross-disciplinary processes of PB. An interesting statistic is that the federal government built up a cadre of about 1,200 individuals who were essentially dedicated full time to PB activities.

Realistically, the expectation of instant results should be viewed with suspicion. The development of analytical skills for PB, which essentially entails a wide and complex form of analysis, must have a gestation period. The entire organization and the information system are similarly involved with a complex learning process that requires time. An overzealous effort can be counterproductive.

SUMMARY

It is through budgetary decisions that an organization's policy is put into effect. Budgeting is increasingly being regarded as the cutting edge of planning and policy development. Strategic and long-range plans that disregard the realities of budgetary needs and resource constraints become exercises of limited value. Budgeting has traditionally been primarily associated with financial data rather than with the policy making and planning that lie behind the numbers.

Historically, budgetary data were presented in terms of administrative units, cost object classes, or line-item details. Budget determinations were generally restricted to how things should be done or the means used, with very limited consideration given to whether they should be undertaken at all. How effective the existing organizational goals and activities or programs are in satisfying fundamental purposes and needs is at the heart of program budgeting.

Also, the future costs of decisions in the budget process are frequently ignored or not well considered, and the search for more effective ways of achieving goals through the expenditures is limited. Formal planning and the analysis of alternatives in many instances have a limited effect on budget decisions, particularly the ones in government. PB was designed to overcome many of these shortcomings.

Whether a budget system is of the PB type or not, it should be made a part of a comprehensive planning program. In a sense, budgeting disciplines the entire planning process. It is a major operational fault not to tie a planning system and budgeting process together. An integration link ensures a satisfactory degree of coordination among the various operating areas of an organization. The integration relationships can range from loose to tight, and PB has much to offer in any case. The right formula should be tailored to fit a particular organization and should be one that encourages creativity and develops strategic thinking and interactions along with the necessary controls. In striking a proper balance, one should consider an organization's size, stability, structure, scope, resources, management style, function, business, and needs.

PB is not only a linking system for planning and budgeting but also a strategic decision-making system for allocating resources. The PB system provides the key decision makers with the relevant data, both past and future, appropriately structured into a goal-, purpose-, and objective-oriented format and analyzed into a decision-making mode. Decision makers then use intuition and judgment to act on these data. These elements, in concert, allow management to make better decisions regarding the strategic allocation of resources.

PB has three distinct process phases, which interlock, interact, and are progressively more detailed: *planning, programming,* and *budgeting.* Programming is the intermediate connecting phase for making comprehensive and detailed resource and cost allocations in a program format for translating strategic and long-range planning into a proper form to serve budget preparations. The assembly of detailed input–output forecasts for the planning period is completed in the programming phase, ending in a tabular fashion similar to a multiyear budget in a program format. A crosswalk reconciliation connects the first year of the plan in the program format to an existing budget format for translation into a traditional line budget for control and implementation.

A PB system embraces three basic kinds of elements in its framework: *structural, analytical,* and *informational.* The structural program framework is used to process and classify data for ultimately making strategic budgetary decisions. It emphasizes the long-range perspective in an output-oriented program format. The structural hierarchy of programs makes a logical progression in meaningful terms from stated objectives to operating activities. The analytical processes, primarily system analysis and cost–benefit and cost-effectiveness analysis, emphasize a systematic examination of alternative courses of action and their implications, resulting in sharpened intuition and judgment. The informational portion provides the data from which objectives can be specified, analyses made, and progress reported and controlled. In order to keep a PB system alive and lively, it must also provide for disciplined change and analyses of key issues. Periodic updating is also one of the important PB keys.

The PB system has probably put more people to work trying to learn how to do analysis of social systems than any other management effort in history. In its early utilization it took on an aura of magic with the cost–benefit analysis mystique, but it relies heavily on intuition and judgment along with a great deal of hard work and simple arithmetic.

Like many new managerial techniques, PB was initiated with a great deal of publicity, exaggerated expectations, and much overselling. Many organizations wanted to install a functioning PB system instantly. It was often assumed that devising such a format was the only or the primary task and that its accomplishment had some automatic qualities for developing strategic programs. New management information systems, accounting systems, organization charts, or the frequent use of the term "program" in traditional budget systems are not in themselves PB. They cannot provide the vital analytical program structuring or future perspective improvements for decision making.

The costs, time, paperwork, staffing, and organizational impact of installing PB can be significant for some organizations. Most, particularly those that are up to date or large, should not have any special problems if they tailor their approach.

Originally, it was thought that a complete PB system must be installed at the outset. However, it appears that a piecemeal approach is feasible; that is, partial applications of either organizational units or PB methodology are possible. Whichever approach is chosen, an essential ingredient to effectiveness is strong leadership at the top, especially for the required analysis of alternatives at key stages in its cycle.

The pace and the efficacy of adopting PB have varied, but interest in it and its concepts continues as organizations grow in size, scope, and complexity, with the need to better allocate resources. Because of the many changes in the PB designation, there is difficulty in tracking its utilization and efficacy. It is likely that the changes reflect a disassociation with the mixed federal government experience or increased management sophistication in not taking new techniques literally.

Even in the federal government, however, it is generally acknowledged that PB was a significant step forward in its budgetary, planning, and decision-making practices. The bureaucracy was challenged, and on a continuing basis there is a greater consciousness about balancing problems, objectives, programs and alternatives, and benefits and costs. Moreover, there generally is a greater emphasis on the long-range considerations of decisions. Many budget areas are now forecast beyond one year.

The concepts, approaches, and spirit of PB endure, therefore, albeit under other labels and forms. No other budgetary approach has provided the futurity and comprehensiveness for resource allocations, especially for public-sector organizations.

It generally appears that, even in those cases where the complete application of PB has been less than successful, there are residual benefits, such as these.

▪ It helps strategic and long-range planning find an expression in the budget process.
▪ The use of cost–benefit analysis (including reengineering audits/studies) generally increases the analytic proficiency and the employment of analysis for alternatives. That is, analysis is better perceived and utilized as an integral part of decision making.
▪ The PB process helps to better define an organization's missions, goals, objectives, and strategies. It facilitates the rethinking of roles for an organization and its personnel.

While PB history is a great teacher, many are destined to repeat the lessons. It is clear that we need to think of budgets longer than one year and the consequences, especially as we enter the twenty-first century. Information, ideas, technology, and money flow easily and quickly across borders, and businesses and jobs go where they can best be performed. Global economic forces are making cataclysmic, fast-paced changes. A variety of threats, instabilities, and opportunities must be addressed in shorter time frames with ever-greater consequences. This demands more from public and private organizations as they redefine their goals and roles and allocate their resources. Futurity and its importance in budgets and current decision making grows. PB is a strategic tool that can provide guidance through these uncharted and opportunistic seas. The traditional line-item budget cannot serve all of these critical needs.

Even if an organization has initially focused only on the important PB element of defining goals and objectives for program structuring, this would be a major management activity by itself. Defining goals, as Peter Drucker has urged, is a vital initial management activity in shaping the strategic direction of an organization:

> It is not possible to be effective unless one first decides what one wants to accomplish. It is not possible to manage, in other words, unless one first has a goal. It is not even possible to design the structure of an organization unless one knows what it is supposed to be doing and how to measure whether it is doing it. In fact, it is never possible to give a final answer to the question, "What is our business?" Any answer becomes obsolete within a short period. The question has to be thought through again and again.
>
> But if no answer at all is forthcoming, if objectives are not clearly set, resources will be splintered and wasted. There will be no way to measure the results. If the organization has not determined what its objectives are, it cannot determine what effectiveness it has and whether it is obtaining results or not.[2]

PB addresses the challenges of goal setting and change and matches them to an organization's resources and capabilities for effectiveness through an integrated planning and budgeting process in a program format. Its concepts have many applications for planning and budgeting systems. Management must continually explore advances in decision-making technology, such as PB, for potential use. A greater measure of success is likely for those who explore, plan, and manage change.

---

[2] Peter F. Drucker, *The Age of Discontinuity: Guidelines to Our Changing Society* (New York: Harper & Row, 1968), pp. 190–191.

CHAPTER THIRTY-THREE

Activity-Based Budgeting

James A. Brimson, MBA
IPM, Inc.

John J. Antos, MBA
Value Creation Group, Inc.

Edward Mendlowitz, CPA
WithumSmith+Brown

INTRODUCTION

The purposes of this chapter are to discuss problems with traditional budgeting, define activity-based budgeting (ABB), and discuss the ABB process.

A budget is a financial expression of a plan. Traditional budgeting focuses on planning resources for an organizational unit. Each year managers look at history and any significant changes and create an annual budget. The budgeting process starts with the senior executive's announcing budget goals. These may consist of revenue and profit goals as well as goals for new services.

Many managers respond by looking at last year's numbers and increasing their budget for the year based on inflation and/or the amount of the increase in revenues (see Exhibit 33.1). For example, if revenues increase 10 percent, then the

This material has been adapted from James A. Brimson and John J. Antos, *Activity-Based Management for Service Industries, Government Entities, and Not-for-Profit Organizations* (New York: John Wiley & Sons, 1994).

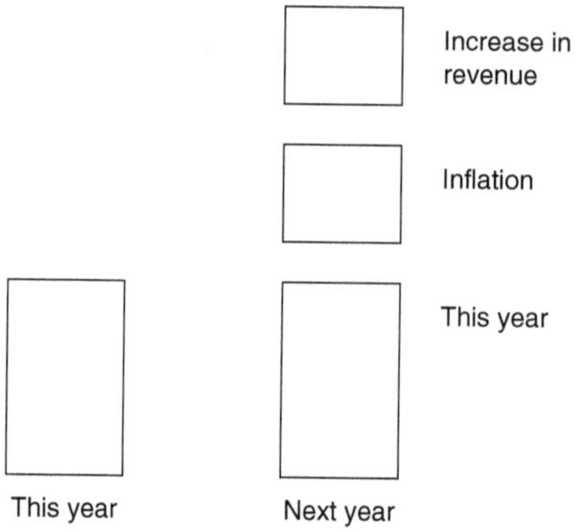

EXHIBIT 33.1　Manager's Response to Next Year's Forecast

various department managers might increase the budgets for their departments by 10 percent.

The problem with this approach is that last year's inefficiencies are incorporated into this year's budget. Often little attention is paid to improvements in each department. Finally, little incentive is incorporated into the budgeting process for continuous improvement. Changing workload for each department often is not considered.

Senior managers, during budgeting, often make arbitrary cuts across the board. A potentially negative consequence is that the better-managed departments may have already cut the majority of waste and now may have to cut into necessary resources. Instead, other, less efficient departments should make more radical reductions to bring them to the same level of efficiency as the better-managed departments.

Budgets in this environment often become wrestling matches in which those who are the best presenters are given larger budgets. The theory goes that the best at presenting the reasons for the larger budget deserves the larger budget.

Once the budget is agreed on, it is often cast in concrete for the year.

TRADITIONAL BUDGETING DOES NOT SUPPORT EXCELLENCE

Budgeting is a generic term for what many managers assume is a perfunctory exercise and they do not apply the seriousness to it that is truly needed.

First, the budgeting process should highlight cost reduction and the elimination of wasteful activities and tasks. Traditional budgeting does not make visible what the organization does. Instead, managers look at their history of spending and simply increase last year's budget and/or actuals based on inflation and/or increases in revenue.

Second, budgeting should be a formal mechanism for reducing workload to the minimal level to support enterprise objectives. Excess workload due to poor structuring of activities and business process drives up cost and does not improve customer satisfaction. The budgeting process itself should give insight into how to reduce workload and how to set workload reduction goals.

Third, budgeting should consider all costs as variable; yet budgeting often formalizes the laissez-faire attitude toward occupancy and equipment costs. Most are familiar with the concept of fixed and variable costs. The problem with this classification is a psychological one. The term "fixed costs" seems to imply that these costs cannot be eliminated because they are fixed. Yet we all know that buildings and equipment can be put to alternative use, sold, demolished, or leased. Often many assets are dedicated to specific activities. By making these assets more flexible, the total capital base of an enterprise can be lowered. Even property taxes and property insurance can be reduced. A budget based on variable and fixed costs often focuses attention on the variable costs and implies that the fixed costs are not controllable.

A better classification would be utilized and unutilized capacity. This classification simply shows that some assets are being used and some are not. It does not present the psychological barrier to change that the term "fixed costs" does. Unutilized capacity can be saved for future growth, eliminated, used for other purposes, or consolidated with another division.

An important goal of budgeting should be to improve each process on a continuous basis. Traditional budgeting, as it is commonly practiced, seems to focus on simply repeating history. Activity budgeting sets improvement targets by activity/business process. Thus, this approach is something everyone can understand and use to work toward improvement. However, traditional budgeting sets goals like "reduce costs" by a specific percentage, without giving employees insights on how to achieve those targets.

Activity budgeting works to synchronize activities and thus improve business processes. Traditional budgeting may take the approach of "every department for itself." Managers pay lip service to coordinating between departments; however, managers will almost certainly respond in a way that will maximize their own department's performance. The inevitable consequence is to lower the performance of the organization as a whole.

Activity budgeting sets business process improvement goals, which requires the joint efforts of employees from a variety of departments. Because the goal is to improve the business process, old barriers between departments begin to crumble.

Traditional budgeting does not formally consider external and internal suppliers and customers. However, activity budgeting requires asking the internal and external suppliers and customers to describe their needs and their respective workload requirements.

Too often, the focus in traditional budgeting is to control the result. For example, consider the organization that closes its financial books in 4 to 15 days. Each month managers focus on information that is 34 to 45 days old. It makes more sense to control the *process* rather than to try to control the *result* through financial statements. Activity budgeting and activity management focus on controlling the process. Only by controlling the process can results improve.

In a similar vein, traditional budgeting tends to focus on the effects rather than the causes. For example, hiring new employees or introducing a new service often requires a long time. In reality, organizations should focus on the causes of these long lead times.

A culture needs to be developed where managers come to meetings asking their peers for suggestions to solve their problems rather than managers thinking that a request for help as a sign of weakness. Managers therefore make up excuses to explain the reasons they were over budget rather than concentrating their efforts on how to improve operations.

Because activity budgeting focuses on the root cause of problems, everyone can work to identify how to reduce or eliminate them. Only by eliminating the root cause of the problem can the cost be permanently eliminated.

Activity budgeting requires that customers be asked for their requirements. Only by asking the customer can an organization understand whether it has properly applied resources to meet the customer's needs (e.g., do the patrons of the U.S. Postal Service want two- to three-day delivery, or do they want consistent delivery within some stated time period?). By asking the customer, the workload connected with the activities necessary to please the customer can better be determined.

Activity budgeting focuses on output, not on input. It focuses on what work is done, how the work is performed, and how much work is done. The required resources are only a consequence of the activities. The problem with traditional budgeting is that it lacks ownership. Even if the department manager "owns" the budget, seldom do the individual employees in that department own the budget. Activity budgeting asks each person to look at the activities he or she performs and set performance targets for those activities in the context of customer requirements and organizational objectives.

Activity budgeting allows people to be empowered to manage their activities properly. If something is wrong, if there is a better way to perform the activity or business process, or if a quality issue arises, the employee(s) who performs the activity or business process should make the necessary improvements or corrections without requiring management approval. (This assumes that the employee is not changing the service or the quality provided to the customer, and is improving the service or business process at a lower cost.)

Senior management needs to remember that people will not work themselves out of a job. People will contribute ideas to improve operations only if they understand that improvement in value-added activities allows the transfer of resources to growth-enabling activities.

Under activity budgeting, mistakes are acceptable, but repetition of mistakes is unacceptable. An executive told Sam Walton of a $10 million mistake and submitted his resignation. Walton told the executive he could not resign because the company had just spent $10 million training him. People need to know they can make mistakes, but they must learn from those mistakes and not repeat them.

Activity budgeting uses a common language—the language of the activities or business processes that everyone is performing. Traditional budgeting uses terms that only the accountants are familiar with. This Tower of Babel makes communication more difficult and encourages specialization at the expense of cooperation.

Activity budgeting looks for consistency of the output. This means that the activity should be performed in a consistent way over time. Continuous improvement must be encouraged, but the activity should be performed only in accordance with current best practice. Success depends on finding the best possible way to perform an activity or business process and consistently looking for ways to improve it while performing the activity/business process in a consistent manner.

Activity budgeting requires setting activity or business process targets as the minimum level of performance rather than the absolute level. These activity or business process targets should identify the minimum level of performance necessary to support organizational objectives. Managers should not try to exceed these minimum levels. Instead, they should look at ways to reduce waste and non–value-added portions of various activities.

ACTIVITY-BASED BUDGETING DEFINITIONS

Activity-based budgeting is the process of planning and controlling the expected activities of the organization to derive a cost-effective budget that meets forecast workload and agreed strategic goals.

ABB is a quantitative expression of the expected activities of the organization, reflecting management forecast of workload and financial and nonfinancial requirements to meet agreed strategic goals and planned changes to improve performance.

The three key elements of ABB include:

1. Type of work to be done
2. Quantity of work to be done
3. Cost of work to be done

Principles of Activity-Based Budgeting

ABB must reflect what is done (i.e.,, the activities or business processes), not cost elements. Resources required (cost elements) must be derived from the expected activities or business processes and workload. *Workload* is simply the number of units of an activity that are required. For example, in the human resource department, the workload for the activity "hire employees" might be to hire 25 employees. The cost elements to perform that activity might be the wages and benefits of the recruiter, travel, advertising, testing, supplies, and occupancy costs for the space occupied by the recruiter and for interviewing. If a hiring freeze occurs, then the workload for this activity would be zero.

Budgets must be based on the future workload in order to meet:

▪ Customer requirements
▪ Organizational/departmental goals and strategies
▪ New/changed services and service mix
▪ Changes in business processes
▪ Improvements in efficiency and effectiveness
▪ Quality, flexibility, and cycle-time goals
▪ Changes in service levels

The final budget must reflect the changes in resource cost levels and foreign exchange fluctuations. However, it is better to initially budget using constant cost and foreign exchange rates to facilitate comparisons and then to add inflation and foreign exchange adjustments at the conclusion of the budgeting process.

As part of the activity budgeting process, it is important to highlight continuous improvement. Each department should identify the activities or business processes to be improved, the amount of improvement, and how it plans to achieve its improvement targets.

Requirements for Successful Activity-Based Budgeting

The organization must be committed to excellence. If the organization does not have this commitment, then resources will be wasted on data-analysis activities that will never be implemented. Changing is not easy. It is easier to study the problem than to make the difficult decisions required to improve.

Process Management Approach

The organization must use a process management approach to improvement. Doing this requires defining each activity as part of a repeatable, robust business process that can be continuously improved and the variability removed. Activities defined this way can use various techniques to decrease time, improve quality, and reduce the cost of those activities.

Process management is crucial to excellence, because high levels of performance are possible only when activities are done to best practices, the unused capacity is minimal, the best practices are continually made better, and the activities are executed perfectly. Activity definitions must support process management. Activities must be in the form of verb plus a noun. There must be a physical output. Two-stage definitions of drivers are usually not adequate. For example, the activity "pay employee" is compatible with process management. To define an activity as "supplies handling" and the output measure as the "number of service production runs" would not be compatible activity definitions. Two-stage activity definitions might be used in assigning costs to a service, but it does not help in improving operations. A better way to define this sample activity would be "move supplies," with the output measure defined as the "number of moves."

One of the first steps that an activity manager may have to take is to review activity definitions to make sure that they are compatible with a process approach.

Culture Encourages Sustaining Benefits

The organization culture should encourage sustaining benefits. These benefits should not be something that lasts for only a short while, after which everyone goes back to the old way. These benefits should change the way the people in the organization think and act. Often this means changing the way the employees are compensated, so that they share in the productivity improvement.

Organizations must overcome the cultural barriers shown in Exhibit 33.2. Next to these barriers are actions the organization must take in order to overcome these cultural barriers.

EXHIBIT 33.2   Cultural Barriers

Cultural Barriers	Actions
Departmental structure often interferes with departments interacting, in order to minimize total enterprise cost.	Change information systems so the organization can see total cost of business processes rather than just the costs in a specific department.
Policies and procedures provide guidelines for employee behavior. These were often set up to ensure consistency and to make it easy for employees to handle specific situations.	Empower employees to handle various situations to ensure customer satisfaction. Use policies to set general guidelines and train, support, and empower employees to satisfy the customer.
Suggestion programs are only for changes to the service or for capital requests. Changes to efficiency should be made by employees without management approval.	Suggestion programs usually require the approval of management to implement change. This slows the change process.
Measurement systems tend to focus on the department level.	Abolish micromanagement. Give managers/ employees the tools, authority, and responsibility to do their jobs. Make them responsible for outputs and a budget level of resources to do their work.
Specialization assumes that lowest cost is achievable through economies of scale.	Today flexibility is critical. People must be cross-trained for a variety of tasks because: (1) as slack or heavy periods occur, employees can help out in other departments and (2) they need to understand how what they do affects other departments and how what other departments do affects them.

Activity-Based Costing Compared to Generally Accepted Accounting Principles

Activity-based costing (ABC) requires new thinking and is contrary to generally accepted accounting principles. In general, companies working with traditional costing systems find implementation of an ABC system much easier. Following is a brief comparison of some of the differences.

	GAAP	ABC
Expenses	Booked when incurred	Booked when put into product; the cost is more properly matched with cash flow it generates
Indirect expenses and costs	Deducted when incurred	Deducted when product they relate to is shipped
Costs	Except for inventoryable items, all costs are deducted when incurred	Deducted on a true economic consumption measure
Salaried personnel	Deducted when period is charged for salary	Deducted when applied to end product when it is shipped

(Continued)

	GAAP	ABC
Purchasing personnel payroll	Deducted when period is charged for salary	Deducted when raw materials that they ordered are converted into finished product and that product is shipped
Shipping personnel payroll	Deducted when period is charged for salary	Deducted when products they worked on are shipped to customer
Depreciation	Deducted in accordance with fixed measures—usually time based	Deducted over some economic measure as equipment is utilized in end product; needs a true economic consumption life cycle costing
Sales commissions	Deductible when "earned"	Charged to product when it is shipped to customer
Postage	Booked when spent	Booked when function or activity is made part of end product
Preproduction design, development, and planning and/or postproduction customer support	Deducted when incurred	Deducted when finished products they relate to are shipped
Training, marketing, and other expenses	When committed	When related cash flow actually occurs
Cost of generating an invoice, maintaining customer files, keeping track of sales commissions, getting payment, and time cost of money	When incurred	When product is shipped
Overhead	Allocated based on a large variable expense, such as labor	Each item broken down into components and allocated as it results in a completed sales activity

Commitment to Excellence

Many organizations take a short-term approach to improving operations. Costs are easy to control: Simply stop spending money. This approach is similar to a crash diet. The problem with crash diets is that the dieter usually regains what he or she lost and often gains even more weight. If an organization is committed to excellence, then its goal is to change the way it does business. This is similar to changing eating habits. For example, organizations must start compensating people based on business-process performance rather than the traditional actual versus budget of cost elements that most organizations historically have used.

ACTIVITY-BASED BUDGETING PROCESS

The ABB process begins with the customer. The organization must determine who the customer is and what the customer wants. It must look to its competitors. Competition consists of both direct competitors and alternate services that might compete with the organization's services.

Then the organization must develop a strategy to meet customer needs. A restaurant must decide whether to be a five-star restaurant, with crystal and linen tablecloths, or to provide good food in a clean environment with less sophisticated decor but with good value to the customer.

Next, the organization should forecast workload. Management and sales determine what sales levels will be, and managers need to estimate their workloads as a result of these sales levels. Often, the sales forecast includes new services and new markets, as well as any changes in strategy.

Planning guidelines must be articulated to each manager to establish the specific activity-level targets within a business process context. Eventually, every activity manager should have targets for improving his or her respective value-added activities and eliminating non–value-added activities.

Next, interdepartmental projects should be identified. Because these projects will affect the workload as well as the activities in several departments, they must be coordinated and done prior to each manager improving his or her own activities.

At this point in the budgeting process, specific activity-level projects can be identified. These are projects to improve operations at the individual activity level. However, improvement should always be within organizational objectives, a business-process context, and a customer satisfaction context.

Activity-based investment analysis consists of defining improvement projects, evaluating those projects, and then using committees to select projects that will meet the organization's goals and meet customers' needs.

The final step is to determine the activities and workload for the coming year.

LINKING STRATEGY AND BUDGETING

One of the problems with traditional budgeting is that a clear link between the enterprise's strategy and budgeting often does not exist. Therefore, operating managers do not know how to incorporate strategy into their budgets.

Principles of Strategic Management

There are various seminars and books available on the subject of strategic management. This chapter does not discuss those techniques but simply assumes that a strategic plan exists. The role of senior management is to set performance targets based on the strategic plans. The performance targets might be for sales, number of new services and/or markets, cycle time, cost, quality, or customer service levels. The role of the activity manager is to achieve or exceed those targets.

Strategic objectives and performance targets must be translated into activity-level targets. Activity managers must ensure that service requirements are a direct derivative of customer needs.

The translation process starts with customer requirements and an analysis of competitive strategies. Then strategic objectives are set. The price for services allowable by the market are determined, as are time, quality, and cost targets. Then these targets are translated into activity-level targets.

There are several important strategic management tools to assist with this process. The key ones include:

- Customer surveys
- Core competency analysis
- Benchmarking
- Activity Function Deployment
- Reverse engineering

Customer Surveys

One of the first steps in the strategic management process is to perform a customer survey. The customer survey can be done in person, by telephone, by e-mail or postal mail. The survey asks a variety of questions, but the focus is on the factors that are important to the customer, a ranking of those factors by the customer, and, finally, the customer's perception of the organization's performance regarding those factors.

Based on this survey, the organization needs to start with the factors most important to the customer and determine whether it is satisfying the customer on those factors of performance. Activity or business process and investment preference must be given to those activities or business processes that the customer feels are most important. Especially in the case where satisfaction levels are not satisfactory to the customer, the organization needs to change, improve, or increase resources and effectiveness of those activities or business processes.

For example, if an organization determines that it needs to allow nurses to spend more time with patients and less time doing paperwork, then it could create an activity budget in this way:

For the activity "complete medical charts":

Total Cost	Salaries	Depreciation	Supplies	Phone	Occupancy
$24,410	22,000	400	900	150	960

The assumptions are that a person would be hired to "complete medical charts." The employee's salary and benefits would be $22,000 per year. Depreciation on his or her desk and computer would be $400. Supplies connected with filling out the charts are estimated to be $900. Because this person would be communicating with other departments, a phone would be necessary for interhospital calls. The fully loaded cost of hospital space (including depreciation, heat, electricity, building maintenance, and janitorial cost based on the number of square feet occupied) equals $960.

Hiring this person will enable ten nurses to spend 10 percent of their time comforting, informing, and answering questions for patients. A nurse earns $36,000 annually, including benefits.

For the activity "communicate with patients":

Total Cost	Salaries	Depreciation	Supplies	Phone	Occupancy
$46,320	36,000	1,000	2,000	320	7,000

These assumptions were made. Annual salaries and benefits for ten nurses at $36,000 per nurse equals $360,000. Because they will spend 10 percent of their time on this activity, the salary portion of this activity cost equals $36,000. There would be some depreciation on the desk for the portion of time performing this activity. Some educational literature would be given to the patients, which would total approximately $2,000. Nurses would need a phone line for tracking down answers to patient questions, and a reasonable percentage of the total phone cost was estimated at $320. Because the nurses spent some time sitting at a desk for this activity, 10 percent of their total occupancy costs was apportioned, which amounted to $7,000.

Now senior management can look at the customer survey and performance as it relates to nurses communicating and comforting patients—a high-priority item in the eyes of the customer. Then they can determine if it is worth spending a total of $70,730 ($24,410 plus $46,320) to improve customer satisfaction in this area.

Core Competency Analysis

An organization starts by asking what activities or business processes are critical to its industry. These activities or business processes become the *core competencies* of that industry. Then the organizations can ask themselves which activities or business processes they perform well. They need to compare themselves with external benchmarks and determine where there is a core competency gap. Then the organizations can set budget targets in terms of cost, quality, and time.

Industry	Core Competency
Banking	Accuracy, fast turnaround, full service
Insurance	Low rates, knowledgeable representatives, fast claims handling
Hospitals	Friendly nurses, full service, high success rate
Airlines	On-time, convenient departures, reasonable fares
Fast food	Quality, service, cleanliness
Internal Revenue	Rules that are easy to comply with, fairness, easy access
Fundraisers	Good cause, large percentage of funds directly to cause

An auto dealer decided that a core competency of the repair shop was to provide quality repairs the first time. A further analysis revealed an opportunity to improve performance by conducting auto repair training seminars for the mechanics. Four seminars for 20 mechanics who earn $14 per hour were planned. Each seminar was to be five hours long with $500 in training supplies. A consultant will charge $3,000 per training session.

For the activity "train mechanics":

Total Cost	Salaries	Supplies	Phone	Consultant
$18,100	5,600	500	0	12,000

Benchmarking

The benchmarking process compares performance to other organizations, either internally or externally. Benchmarks may measure:

- Activities
- Business processes
- Time
- New service introduction
- Customer service
- Quality
- Cost

Comparisons should be made, where possible, across divisions, with competitors, and with the best organizations in the world. For example, one telephone company can process a request for new phone service within 43 seconds. This is a speed few other organizations can duplicate and would serve as a great benchmark for the activity "process new customers' credit requests."

One association felt it was important to answer the phone after only two rings. This would be a high-quality service to the members and would avoid lost sales of books and seminars because people tired of waiting for someone to answer the phone. The association's operators were currently answering the phone on the third or fourth ring. The association decided to increase the number of telephone operators by three. Telephone operators could be hired for $18,000 per year. They would need a desk, a computer, a phone, and supplies for order taking. Fully loaded occupancy costs were running $10 per square foot. Each operator would need 64 square feet of space.

For the activity "answer phones":

Total cost	Salaries	Depreciation	Supplies	Phone	Occupancy
$60,120	54,000	2,000	1,200	1,000	1,920

Activity Function Deployment

Activity function deployment (AFD) is a concept similar to quality function development, which originated in the quality field, and is applicable to activity budgeting. In

AFD, the organization compares the customers' requirements with the activities or business processes necessary to meet those requirements. For each activity or business process, a comparison is also made with the competition to determine how the organization is doing against the competition. Also, a correlation is made between activities to show which activities have a strong positive or strong negative correlation with meeting customer requirements. Some activities will have no correlation with each other. Finally, a correlation is made between various activities and customer requirements. Thus, the organization can determine which activities are critical to greatest customer satisfaction. Customer requirements are ranked as part of this analysis.

Although a complete explanation of this technique can be found in a number of quality books and seminars, a simple example is discussed here. An airline is looking to increase market share by better satisfying its customers. Using AFD, the airline determines that quick turnaround time is important in order to have on-time departures. One way to improve in this area is to have two jetbridges to load passengers instead of only one. There are two activities—"move jetbridge" and "maintain jetbridge"—connected with this second jetbridge.

The airline determines that 10 percent of a ticketing agent's time is needed to handle this second jetbridge. A ticketing agent earns $32,000 per year. Two hundred ticketing agents will be affected. This means that salaries with benefits dedicated to the activity "move jetbridge" would be $640,000 (200 × 10% × $32,000). An additional 100 jetbridges would have to be purchased, at the rate of $10,000 per jetbridge. Therefore, the depreciation on $1,000,000 (100 × $10,000) using a five-year life would be $200,000 per year. The annual cost of maintenance labor is $100,000 on these jetbridges and is $50,000 on maintenance parts. Occupancy costs are $20,000 for the maintenance space needed for these jetbridges.

For the activities "move jetbridge" and "maintain jetbridge":

Activity	Activity Cost	Salaries	Depreciation	Parts	Occupancy
Move jetbridge	640,000	640,000			
Maintain jetbridge	370,000	100,000	200,000	50,000	20,000
Total cost	1,010,000	740,000	200,000	50,000	20,000

Reverse Engineering

Reverse engineering involves studying a competitor's services. At first glance, one would think that reverse engineering is a concept that applies only to products. However, applying reverse engineering to a service and seeing how competitors perform the service is a very useful tool.

For example, consider a company that has a regulatory affairs department that must file with the Food and Drug Administration (FDA) to get regulatory approval. The company's managers studied the competitor's process of filing for regulatory approval. The objective was to determine how to perform the process more effectively.

Using reverse engineering principles, they started by asking the customer, in this case the FDA, the testing requirements in order to get this new product approved. Then, based on the FDA comments, they improved how they designed their products and their testing procedures in order to get approval more quickly.

For the activity "improve the FDA approval process," these activity costs are determined: Regulatory personnel with salaries of $50,000 will spend 10 percent of their time on this project. They will have travel costs amounting to $3,000. Supplies are expected to run $600. A seminar on this topic will cost $1,700. A 10 percent share of their office occupancy cost is running $2,000 per year.

For the activity "improve FDA approval process":

Total Cost	Salaries	Travel	Supplies	Seminar	Occupancy
$12,300	5,000	3,000	600	1,700	2,000

TRANSLATE STRATEGY TO ACTIVITIES

Strategy must be translated to an activity level to identify necessary changes. An example of a translating procedure is shown next.

Steps	Example
Define mission statement with enterprise goals	Dominate the market and diversify where advantage can be applied
Establish critical success factors	Grow market share; increase new service sales as percent of total sales
Establish service targets	Increase market share: Service 1 by 7%; Service 2 by 8%; discontinue Service 3
Establish service-level targets	Service 1: increase sales 5%; decrease cost 8%; deliver in 2 hours

Identify Activity Targets by Bill of Activities

The next step is to identify activity targets for each service.

For example: The mission might be to dominate the consumer loan business in Dallas; the critical success factor might be to grow market share; the service target might be to grow auto loan revenue by 7 percent; and the service-level targets might be to increase auto loan sales by 5 percent and decrease cost by 8 percent.

Bill of Activities

Activity Description	Cost/ Output $	Units of Output	Cost of Service $	Target Activity Reduction (%)	Target Activity Reduction ($)	Target Cost of Service ($)
Take application	100	1	100	(5)	(5)	95
Order reports	50	3	150	(10)	(15)	135
Review loans	200	1	200	(7)	(14)	186

Activity Description	Cost/ Output $	Units of Output	Cost of Service $	Target Activity Reduction		Target Cost of Service ($)
				(%)	($)	
Complete paperwork	25	4	100	(30)	(30)	70
Disburse funds	250	1	250			250
Totals			800	(8)	(64)	736

This table shows that the employees have established cost reduction targets for four of the five activities. The total reduction of $64 is an 8 percent reduction from last year's bill of activity cost.

Once these strategic management tools are employed, then cost, time, and quality targets can be set by the employees for each activity. An example of cost, time, and quality targets is presented next.Strategic Management Tools and Target

Strategic Management Tools and Targets

Tool	Activity	Cost	Time	Quality
Customer survey	Communicate with patients	C: 46,320 T: 40,000	C: 10 minutes T: 30 minutes	C: 80% satisfaction T: 90%
Core competency	Train mechanics	C: 18,100 T: 22,000	C: 20 hours T: 24 hours	C: 9% redos T: 5% redos
Benchmarking	Answer phone	C: 60,120 T:	C: 4 rings T: 2 rings	C: T:
QFD	Move and maintain jetbridge	C: 1,010,000 T: 900,000	C: 45 minutes T: 30 minutes	C: 85% T: 90% on time
Reverse engineering	Obtain FDA approval	C: 12,300 T: 10,000	C: 5 years T: 2 years	C: 75% T: 80% approval

C = current; T = target.

Match Resource to Goals

Next, match resources to goals. Goals should be set to be achievable. Resources should be oriented toward goals. Identify improvements to business processes as well as activities.

 DETERMINE WORKLOAD

There are three major steps in determining activity or business process workload. These include:

1. Forecast service-determined activities or business processes.
2. Forecast non–service-related activities or business processes.
3. Forecast special projects.

Workload of Service-Determined Activities or Business Processes

The first step in forecasting total organization workload is to forecast workload for service-determined activities:

- Identify activities for new services.
- Identify planned changes to services.
- Create/update a bill of activities for each service line.
- Forecast services by service lines rather than individual services, in most cases.
- Explode bill of activities to determine activity quantity for each service line.

Service	Units of Service	Bill of Activity Units required for Each Service	Activity Quantities
Mortgages	5,000	Order report 3	15,000
Auto loans	1,800	Order report 1	1,800
Personal loans	1,000	Order report 1	1,000
		Total reports	17,800

Workload for Non–Service-Related Activities

The second step is to forecast workload of non–service-related activities. Non–service-related activities are those performed by support departments such as management information systems, human resources, security, and accounting.

Activity Class	Activity Measures
General management	Number of employees
Financial reporting	Number of financial reports
Corporate advertising	Number of TV advertisements
	Number of promotions
Marketing	Number of trade shows
	Number of market surveys
Research	Number of new services
Facilities	Number of square feet

Workload for Special Projects

The third step is to forecast workload for special projects. Examples of special projects include:

- Install activity-based management.
- Install ABB.
- Install new computer system.
- Expand office.

Then the organization needs to set up a calendar for each special project, with the activities and tasks listed by time period.

Activity-Based Budgeting Calendar

Brief senior management	*
Select team	**
Select departments/services	**
Review activity definitions	****
Review strategic plan	****
Explode bill of activities	****
Start improvement projects	***

Each * equals one week.

CREATE PLANNING GUIDELINES

An organization should identify activity or business process–level projects with the goal of continuous improvement. Look at the budgeted workload and divide it into mandatory, discretionary, and optional units for each activity or business process. Doing this split helps to decide what portion of value-added activities to eliminate. For example, an organization might determine that it needs only one quote to purchase supplies. The workload to obtain quotes is the minimum mandatory work. Discretionary work occurs when the purchasing agent believes a lower price is obtainable through two quotes. For optional work, the agent feels better by getting three or four quotes, some of which are from noncertified vendors.

IDENTIFY INTERDEPARTMENTAL PROJECTS

The organization should look at its business processes to eliminate duplicate activities and synchronize the remaining ones. Consider this business process to "procure supplies."

Activity-Based Budget for Procuring Supplies

Activity	Labor	Technology	Facility	Utilities	Supplies	Travel	Other	Total
LYPQ TY	89088		7827	1293	1075	4000	162	103445
LYIP TY	101479		8915	1472	1225	4000	175	117266
LYAP TY	108404	190299	9524	1573	1308	4000	187	315295
LYSS TY	29211		2568	424	353	5562	50	38168
LYMA TY	65545		5871	938	578	200	111	73243

LY = last year; PQ = prepare quotes; TY = this year; IP = issue purchase order; AP = administer purchase order; SS = source supplies; MA = manage area.

After reviewing last year's total costs for each activity, the next step is to calculate last year's unit cost for each activity. For example, the activity "prepare quotes" cost $103,445. Last year, 2,000 quotes were prepared. By dividing annual quotes into total cost, the unit cost for this activity is $51.72 per quote.

Activities	Workload Measures	Volume	Total Cost $	Unit Cost $	Target Cost $
Prepare quotes	Quotes	2,000	103,445	51.72	50.00
Issue purchase order (PO)	PO	5,679	117,265	20.65	19.65
Administer PO	PO	5,679	315,295	55.52	53.00
Source supplies	New suppliers	100	38,167	381.68	375.00
Manage area	Staff	28	72,243	2,580	2,200

Activity-Based Budgeting Example of Target Cost

The organization has set a target of $50 per quote. This is a reduction of $1.72 from last year's cost of $51.72 per quote. The improvement process for 2,000 quotes at $1.72 per quote results in a savings of $3,440. Managers feel that they can reduce supplies by $440 by keeping more information on the computer and less on paper. Travel could be reduced $1,000 by having more vendors come to the organization's offices. Because quotes will be kept on the computer, there will be a reduction in the filing activity, saving $2,000 for part-time employee wages and benefits.

Creative Thinking Approaches

Continuous improvement requires innovative approaches to streamlining the way an activity is done. Although creativity is a very personal trait, studies have shown that certain environments and methods are better suited to drawing out creative ideas. Some of the more effective methods are:

1. Challenging assumptions about:
   - People
   - Supplies
   - Business processes
   - Location
   - Capital
   - Automation
   - Activities
2. Viewing activities or business processes based on new assumptions
3. Perceiving patterns from other:
   - Divisions
   - Offices

- Services
- Departments

4. Making connections with other organizations
5. Establishing networks among suppliers, suppliers' suppliers, you, customers, and end users
6. Exploiting failures (e.g., the glue for Post-it notes was too weak)
7. Performing activity or business process backward and from the middle
8. Using idea triggers (e.g., a new idea for each of Baskin & Robbins' 31 flavors)
9. Creating superheroes
10. Imagining you are the service, activity, or business process

Brainstorming

Brainstorming techniques are fairly common today. They consist of:

- Suspending judgment until all ideas are on the table
- Emphasizing quantity of ideas without worrying about quality
- Stimulating a freewheeling session, with wild ideas encouraged
- Involving people from throughout the organization
- Reminding people that wild ideas often will fertilize the thinking process

Storyboarding

Storyboarding is a creativity tool that consists of using colored index cards to show business processes, activities, and tasks. The first step is to define the department mission statement. For a hotel, the department mission for the maids might be "to keep rooms clean in order to delight customers at a minimum cost."

	Activities		
	Stock Cart	**Clean Rooms**	**Empty Carts**
T	Stack towels	Empty trash	Dispose garbage
A	Stack linens	Change bedsheets	Separate linens/towels
S	Stack toiletries	Clean bathroom	Store cart/vacuum
K	Stack stationery	Restock toiletries	
S	Stack cleaning supplies	Replace towels	
		Dust room	
		Vacuum room	
		Refill stationery	

Value Management

Value management is an organized way of thinking. It is an objective appraisal of functions performed by services and procedures. The focus is on necessary functions for the lowest cost. It increases reliability and productivity. Costs are decreased. Value management challenges everything an organization does.

It starts by gathering information such as:

- The purpose and use of each service
- The operating and performance issues
- The physical and environmental requirements

For example, fresh fish must be kept cold. Jewelry must be kept in a secure environment. What types of support requirements are there? What problems exist? Which and how many liaison personnel are required? What are the economic issues?

These requirements are translated into required functionality of the service. Begin by determining the worth of each portion of the service. Then calculate the value improvement potential. What part of the service does the customer want? Which parts add cost? Which part is the customer willing to pay for?

Begin by being creative. Ask the customers to value different features. Ask suppliers for ideas. Use cross-functional teams and brainstorming. Use reverse engineering techniques and look at the competitor's services. Benchmark in other industries. Find the best customer service, warehousing, and order fulfillment organization. Eliminate part of the service. How can the organization create more commonality of services and support services as well as common reports and forms?

Evaluate whether it would be better to buy a portion of the service from outside (e.g., catering/training/maintenance for airlines; check processing and management information systems for banks; bodywork for car dealers; janitorial, engineering, waste collection for cities) or to perform those services and support services in-house. Analyze customer trade-off of cost and features. Calculate value versus cost to produce various portions of the service. Eliminate functions, procedures, and reports. Simplify procedures, business processes, and functions. Use alternate supplies, specifications, and methods. Shorten the service operation cycle with cross-training of departments.

Task-Level Analysis

Sometimes it is useful to analyze the tasks of an activity in order to determine the improvement potential. For example, the activity "pay vendor invoice" has these tasks:

Task	Total	Non–Value-Added	Value-Added	Best Practice
Receive purchase order (PO)	.50	.50		
Locate receiver (R)	.50	.50		
Get vendor invoice (I)	.50	.50		
Match PO, R, I	2.00	2.00		
Enter data	4.50		4.50	2.00
Determine errors	2.50	2.50		
Expedite payment	1.25	1.25		
Make payment: computer	3.00		3.00	2.75

Task	Total	Non–Value-Added	Value-Added	Best Practice
Make payment: manual	1.00	1.00		
Document file	3.00	1.50	1.50	1.25
	18.75	9.75	9.00	6.00

IMPROVEMENT PROCESS

The improvement process starts with creative thinking to determine solutions. Then an investment proposal is prepared. Management selects the projects that have the highest priority in meeting customer needs. The solution is implemented and incorporated into the activity budget.

Ranking Budget Requests

After all the budget requests have been made, they are ranked. One convenient way to rank them is through a rating system in which management looks at the budget requests in comparison with the customer needs. Another useful tool is to classify them according to whether they support the current level of service or whether they are at the minimum or intermediate. "Current" implies that this is the cost of activities as they are presently performed. "Minimum" implies that this is the minimum level of service for an activity. "Intermediate" implies that this is not a final solution.

Impact of Projects

Then the organization should look at the impact of these projects in terms of the change in workload but also in terms of the changes in activity or business process cost.

FINALIZING THE BUDGET

Budget proposals are created for the most promising projects. They should be reviewed, and the highest-priority projects should be selected. An implementation plan should be conceived. An activity impact report should be generated to include its cost impact, assuming no inflation or foreign currency issues. This allows for comparisons with previous activity or business-process performance. Finally, inflation and foreign currency should be incorporated into the budget.

Budget Review Panels

Budget review panels should consist of cross-functional teams whose purpose is to question and review the budget. A review panel might consist of the directors, support departments such as human resources, administration, quality, finance, and operations.

Budgeting Options

An organization has two options for activity budgeting: (1) budget and report by activities; and (2) budget by activities and convert the activity budget into a traditional cost element budget. In the second approach, the organization plans on an activity or business process basis. Managers would use activity costs per unit to determine cost elements. Then they would summarize by cost elements. This second approach is only temporary until the organization better understands how to manage by activities, and usually lasts for only a year.

Steps in Implementing Budget

Activities/Tasks	Months			
	1	2	3	4
Train and educate	**			
Perform strategic analysis	****			
Foreast work load	******			
Establish planning guidelines	****			
Propose interdepartmental improvement	****			
Propose activity improvement	********			
Select improvement options	*******			
Finalize budget	***			

Each * equals one week.

Initial Project

A steering group of three to five members should be created. A series of panels with five to six members from different departments should be created to discuss cross-departmental issues. Each budgeting unit should have a budgeting manager, which could be someone other than the department manager. There would be 10 to 20 budgeting units per in-house coordinator or per consultant.

PERFORMANCE REPORTING

Remember that the most effective reports are those that do not have to be made. Therefore, introduce proactive control rather than reactive cost monitoring wherever possible. ABB encourages this approach.

Aim to control the process so that output is managed with quick reallocations of resources or production possible. Also, make sure resources can be shifted when workload varies—workload seldom stays the same throughout the year. Plan and budget for using those slack times to improve the organization.

Data Capture

There are three methods for data capture within an ongoing system.

1. There are *dedicated resources.* Set up cost centers and define workload measures at the activity or business process level.
2. There are *shared resources,* in which an organization does time reporting by activity.
3. Use a *surrogate* in which actual outputs are used at a standard activity cost. Actual costs would be compared to total department earned cost in this approach. Total actual cost could also be compared to best-practices earned value.

Activity-Based Budget Reconciliation

Department Total			Activity Analysis			
Expense	Budget $	Actual $	Issue Purchase Order	Certify Vendor	Expedite Order	Other
Wages	180,000	180,000				
Supplies	40,000	38,000				
Space	30,000	30,000				
Equipment	18,000	18,000				
Travel	22,000	20,000				
Other	10,000					
		8,000				
Total	200,000	194,000				

In this example, the organization budgeted the activity "issue purchase orders" at $50 per purchase order. It budgeted 3,000 purchase orders. This yielded a budgeted value for the "issue purchase order" activity of $150,000. The same activity budgeting process was followed for the remaining activities, including an "other" or miscellaneous category of activities. This yielded a total activity budget for this department of $200,000, which was backflushed into expense categories.

The actual expenses for the period were $194,000. Compared to the original budget of $200,000, this looks very good. However, when the earned value is calculated, the department is shown to have an earned value variance of $13,000. Earned value is calculated for each activity by multiplying the actual volume for each activity by that activity's charge rate. For the "issue purchase order" activity, the actual volume of 2,700 purchase orders when multiplied by the charge rate of $50 yields $135,000. The same calculation is made for all activities and the answers added for each department. This earned value total of $181,000 is compared to actual expenses of $194,000 to yield an earned value variance of a negative $13,000. This is a different picture than simply comparing actual ($194,000) with budget ($200,000), which yielded a favorable variance of $6,000. Managers can now use this as a planning tool as well as a means to operate the organization more efficiently.

Business-Process Reporting

In business-process reporting, activity cost could be shown for each department as well as for each business process that delivers a service. This is an exercise for organizations that are more advanced in ABB techniques.

SUMMARY

ABB gives managers the tools they need to make better decisions about running their organization. This budgeting technique spends most of the time on improvement rather than filling out forms, which is often the case with traditional budgeting. This technique gives managers a method to improve activities as well as business processes.

PART FIVE

V

Industry Budgets

CHAPTER THIRTY-FOUR

Budgeting for Corporate Taxes

Scott M. Cheslowitz
Stewart Berger

INTRODUCTION

When budgeting for corporate taxes, should it be done annually, semiannually, monthly, or on a transaction by transaction basis? Like any transaction, you should know what your costs are, in order to determine if the transaction makes financial sense. Budgeting for corporate taxes can be quite complicated and quite demanding. The materiality of a transaction or a group of transactions generally plays a role in what transactions get the attention of the tax department. Today Financial Accounting Standards Board (FASB) Interpretation No. 48 (FIN 48) for financial accounting purposes and Schedule UTP for corporate income tax purposes may need to be considered when determining if you have an uncertain tax position (UTP). FIN 48 considers all jurisdictions, from the federal right down to state and local taxes. Schedule UTP, however, seeks disclosure relative to federal UTPs. An accountant must consider the standard of more likely than not in determining a UTP or risk potential preparer penalties in the process, which is a form of self-monitoring. These UTPs may arise at the state level, where nexus is involved, or at the federal level, where transfer pricing issues are involved, to give just a few examples. Again, the Internal Revenue Service (IRS) Schedule UTP only involves federal level uncertain tax positions. Not only do the readers of financial statements want to know, or even the government wants to know, but the inside financial people would want to know what their additional corporate tax exposure may be regarding transactions that their entities are considering. The purpose of this chapter is not to focus too much on any one area of taxation but to touch on a few areas that may need to be considered when budgeting for corporate income taxes. Again, we touch on a few areas here, with examples ranging from the start of a corporation to the conclusion of one, and a few types of transactions in between.

Taxes are something that have to be considered every step of the way. Forming an entity may bring about unexpected tax consequences. If, for example, a company is formed and funded with property in exchange for stock in the corporation, should the shareholders as a group not be considered to be in "control," then the 80 percent test would give rise to a taxable event. Also, if property is transferred in exchange for stock of the corporation but the property is subject to liabilities, then the assumption of that liability by the corporation would give rise to a taxable event to the shareholder if the liability exceeds the cost of the asset. In both cases you failed what would have ordinarily been a tax-free event under Internal Revenue Code Section (IRC) 351.

TAXATION OF C CORPORATIONS

C corporations typically calculate taxes on the net of gross income minus deductions from gross income and then minus special deductions, which equal taxable income. Gross income consists of sales, receipts from services, interest and dividends, net gain on sale, and exchange of assets, to name a few examples. Deductions from gross income include categories such as cost of sales, officers compensation, rent expense, taxes, and depreciation. Special deductions typically are net operating losses and the dividends-received deduction. Taxable income is then calculated based on the rates in effect and further reduced by items such as the foreign tax credit and combined business tax credits while potentially increased by category items such as alternative minimum taxes.

You might say that some of the easier planning for corporate income taxes may occur when a corporation is a subchapter S corporation. A subchapter S corporation is an entity that by unanimous consent of its shareholders elects to have its income and deductions taxed on the individual shareholders' personal returns. In order to be treated as an S corporation, an entity must satisfy certain criteria, including a shareholder limit. Under current law, the shareholder limit is up to 100 shareholders.

You may wonder why you are budgeting for taxes for the S corporation level when all of the income and deductions flow through to the shareholders? The answer is that if in fact the entity was engaged in a trade or business as a C corporation prior to becoming an S corporation, there potentially could be a tax at the corporate level. Any further discussions about the taxation of an S corporation for federal tax purposes assume that the entity was a prior C corporation.

The S corporation may have been engaged in a trade or business as a C corporation prior to electing to become an S corporation; therefore, potentially there could be a tax at the corporate level. Any further discussions about the taxation of an S corporation for federal tax purposes assume that the entity was a prior C corporation. An S corporation may also incur a corporate-level tax when it acquires assets with a built-in gain from a C corporation in a tax-free acquisition and sells those assets within a ten-year period, which begins on the date of asset acquisition. An S corporation may also be subject to a corporate level tax if more than 25 percent of its gross receipts constitute passive investment income. Certain types of passive investment income are rents, royalties, dividends, interest, and sales of stock, just to name a few. Two other scenarios in which an S corporation can be subject to a federal corporate-level tax is when there is a last-in, first-out (LIFO) recapture tax or a tax on the prior year's investment credit.

The tax on built-in gains is based on assets disposed of by an S corporation that were either acquired from or appreciated in a C corporation (acquired in a tax-free exchange) and sold during that ten-year window discussed earlier. During recent legislation, the ten-year window has changed but provides only temporary relief.

The built-in gains tax is applicable only to S elections after 1986, and the entity recognizes a gain from its calculated net unrealized built-in gain. The net unrealized built-in gain was calculated on conversion to an S corporation or from the acquisition of assets from a C corporation in a tax-free exchange. The net recognized built-in gain is the lesser of the recognized built-in gains and losses taken into account compared to the corporate taxable income. If the entity has a tax loss, then the recognized built-in gain gets carried forward.

In calculating the tax we use the highest rate today of 35 percent. However, the government, in a way to reduce the effect of a double taxation, allows S corporations to reduce the recognized built-in gain passed through to the shareholder by the federal corporate tax imposed. For example, if the S corporation has a $1 million recognized built-in gain and pays $350,000 in taxes at the federal level, it will pass through a $650,000 gain to its shareholders.

These are just some of the basics involved with the built-in gains. It should be noted that certain credits and credit carryforwards would be allowed against the tax under IRC Section 1374 to help mitigate the tax bite.

Other areas that can create a corporate-level tax for an S corporation are excessive net passive income and the LIFO recapture. We described some examples earlier of what makes up net passive income. If an S corporation derives this type of income in its ordinary course of its trade or business, the income will not be considered passive investment income. Now net passive income is reduced by any allowable deduction directly connected with the production of that income. If the corporation has a tax loss in a year that also has excess net passive income, a tax is not due, and unlike the built-in gains tax, there are no carryforwards. The LIFO recapture is where a C corporation maintains its inventory using the LIFO method in its last year before electing S corporation status, or in a tax-free exchange. The basic recapture amount is determined by measuring how much the first-in, first-out (FIFO)method exceeds the inventory amount over the LIFO method. Taxes for LIFO recapture are due annually in four equal installments.

These are just some exposures to corporate income taxes potentially suffered by an S corporation. For example, what if a C corporation owned an interest in a partnership that was using the LIFO inventory method and the C corporation became an electing S corporation? Now proposed regulations would have you look to the amount of income that would be allocated to the corporation as if the partnership had sold its LIFO inventory for FIFO inventory by taking into account IRC Section 704(c) and Regulation 1.704-3; however, the results in the *Coggin Automotive Corp.* case point to certain facts whereby the electing S corporation would not be always subject to taxation. The underlying point is that circumstances need to be investigated and transactions need to be scrutinized in order to properly budget for taxes. It should also be noted that there are state-level taxes, city taxes, fees, and so on. One very important factor in budgeting for taxes is that shareholders who owe taxes based on the flow-through income need to get their money from somewhere to pay those taxes. A good budget may also factor in what needs to be distributed to the corporation's shareholders in order for them to pay the taxes on the income that has been distributed. Currently the highest federal rate that an individual may pay is 35 percent. After factoring in state and local rates, depending on where the shareholder resides, and you may end up above 47 percent. If an S corporation generates ordinary income of $2 million, with rounding, it would need to budget around $1 million for distributions just to cover shareholders' tax burden.

Before we go any further, let us compare a subchapter S corporation to a C corporation. Subchapter S corporations are a standard corporation that has elected a special tax status with the IRS. S corporations carry the same benefits as C corporations, generally protecting the shareholders' personal assets from the debts and liabilities of the business, unlimited life and tax deductibility of certain business expenses. The primary differences between S corporations and C corporations are the way they are taxed and the ownership restrictions imposed on S corporations.

When deciding which entity structure is most appropriate for their business, small business owners often view the potential double taxation of profits associated with C corporations as the primary disadvantage to forming a standard corporation. With C corporations, the profits are taxed first at the corporate level and then again at the individual level if they are distributed to shareholders in the form of dividends. Shareholders must report dividends as personal income and pay taxes on that income.

Double taxation can be eliminated by completing the S corporation election with the IRS. S corporations are taxed as pass-through entities, similar to partnerships. While the profits of an S corporation are reported at the corporate level, taxes are not paid at the corporate level. Instead, the profits or losses are passed through to the individual tax returns of the shareholders and are taxed at the individual rate.

Note that not all C corporations can make the S corporation election. Shareholders must number fewer than 100, and all shareholders must consent in writing to the S corporation election. S shareholders must be individuals, estates, or certain qualified trusts. They cannot be nonresident aliens, and S corporations can have only one class of stock.

Readers should seriously consider whether the S corporation structure is best for their particular business or for the future plans of the entity.

The standard corporation, also called a C corporation, is a very common business structure. Corporations are separate legal entities that are owned by shareholders. The primary advantage of incorporating a business is the limited liability of the corporate entity. Typically, shareholders are not personally liable for the debts and obligations of the corporation (although there may be some exceptions, such as fraud or trust fund liability).

We will not go through the pros and cons of being a corporation as that is not the focus of this chapter. However, one main disadvantage to forming a C corporation is often considered to be the potential for double taxation. C corporations are considered separately taxable entities by the IRS and taxes must be paid on the profits of the corporation. If a corporation then distributes its profits to shareholders in the form of dividends, the dividend income is also taxed at the shareholder level. With that you can see the double tax.

In order to eliminate the possibility of double taxation, a C corporation can pay a reasonable salary to its shareholder-employees for services that they have provided in order to reduce the income subject to tax at the corporate level. Another possibility is for a C corporation to elect to be taxed as an S corporation with the IRS. S corporations profits and losses are reported on the individual tax returns of the shareholders, and any necessary tax is paid at the individual level. Categories are broken down on Schedule K-1 of the return to reflect what is known as separately stated items to the shareholders of the S corporation. Some categories include, but are not limited to, ordinary income, dividends, interest, and capital gains, both long and short term.

Now that we have made a distinction for tax purposes between C corporations and S corporations, let us take a look at certain tax consequences of C corporations.

Let us start with the personal service corporation. For a corporation to be a personal service corporation, it must meet all of these requirements:

- Its principal activity during a "testing period" is performing personal services, and its employee-owners substantially perform the services. This requirement is met if more than 20 percent of the corporation's compensation cost for its activities of performing personal services during the testing period is for personal services performed by employee-owners.
- Its employee-owners own more than 10 percent of the fair market value of the outstanding stock on the last day of the testing period.

Personal services include any activity performed in the fields of accounting, actuarial science, architecture, consulting, engineering, health, law, and the performing arts. A person is an employee-owner of a personal service corporation if *both* of these points apply:

- The person is an employee of the corporation or perform personal services for, or on behalf of, the corporation on any day of the testing period.
- The person owns any stock in the corporation at any time during the testing period.

Note that a personal service corporation does not enjoy the benefits of a graduated rate system; however, it pays taxes at the highest corporate rate from the first dollar of income. Again, reasonable compensation can mitigate the effect both from a corporate tax standpoint and from a double tax standpoint.

The financial people of a C corporation do need to understand the tax consequences of the corporation's every move; they also need to understand the tax consequences of its nondecisions. Let us now focus on a few of a C corporation's pocketbook taxes. These taxes are assessed in addition to the regular corporate level tax.

A corporation is allowed to accumulate its earnings for bona fide business reasons; however, if a corporation allows earnings to accumulate beyond the reasonable needs of the business, it may be subject to a 15 percent tax on its accumulated earnings.

The measurement to determine if the corporation is subject to the accumulated earnings tax is an accumulation of up to $250,000 within the reasonable needs of most businesses and up to an accumulation of $150,000 for a personal service corporation.

"Reasonable needs" of a corporation include expansion of a business or a possible redemption of corporate shares from its shareholders.

The fact that a corporation has an unreasonable accumulation of earnings is sufficient to establish liability for the accumulated earnings tax unless the corporation can show that the earnings were not accumulated to allow its individual shareholders to avoid income tax. This tax under IRC Section 531 applies to any domestic or foreign corporation whose intent is to avoid or prevent the imposition of the individual income tax on its shareholders, by permitting earnings and profits to accumulate instead of distributing them. Certain exceptions do apply in the case of personal holding companies, foreign personal holding companies, and certain exempt corporations under Subchapter F of the code.

Section 531 applies to any foreign corporation, with respect to any income derived from sources within the United States, if any of its shareholders are subject to income tax on the distributions. For a group filing a consolidated return, the accumulated earnings tax under Section 531 is imposed on consolidated accumulated taxable income. The tax applies to any group that attempts to avoid the imposition of the individual income tax on the shareholders of any of its owners by not distributing earnings and profits to its shareholders. Section 531 does not apply to a group that is treated as a personal holding company. Special rules apply for other groups, including one or more personal holding companies.

Under Section 533(a), if the group's earnings and profits are permitted to accumulate beyond the reasonable needs of its business is reflective for the purpose to avoid the income tax at the shareholder level, the group must be ready to provide evidence to the contrary or be in danger of the accumulated earnings tax. It may be concluded that a group is a mere holding or investment group as evidence that the group's purpose is to avoid the income tax at the shareholder level. Noteworthy is where a member, such as a personal holding company, is not taken into account in determining if the group is a mere holding or investment group. With respect to earnings and profits, if no member of the group is a personal holding company, the group's earnings and profits are the aggregate of the earnings and profits of each corporation that is a member at the close of the taxable year.

The reasonable needs of the group's business include the reasonable needs of the business of any corporation (other than a personal holding company) that is a member at the close of the taxable year. Thus, the earnings and profits of one member may be accumulated with respect to the reasonable business needs of another member.

If a member is a personal holding company for the taxable year, the consolidated liability for tax is reduced by the portion thereof allocable to that member. For purposes of this section, the consolidated dividends paid deduction is the aggregate of the members' deductions under Section 561(a) (1) and (2). This deduction is determined by excluding deductions for dividends paid to other members. Dividends paid are amounts treated as dividends paid during the taxable year under Sections 562(b) (1), 563, and 565.

PERSONAL HOLDING COMPANY TAX

The term "personal holding company income" refers to the portion of the gross income that generally consists of dividends, interest, rents, royalties, annuities, personal service contracts and capital gains.

Personal holding company income also includes amounts from the sale or other disposition of any interest in an estate or trust. Potential compensation for the use of property may fall under the definition of personal holding income in certain cases when certain criteria are met. There are planning techniques to avoid the personal holding company tax; consent dividends is one example. However, should a corporation be subject to a personal holding company tax, the current tax rate would be 15 percent. The consent dividend is where the shareholders increase the capital structure of the company as paid-in capital and decrease retained earnings by the same amount for the deemed dividends. The shareholders are taxed on these dividends at the 15 percent rate without the benefit of having received the dividends paid to them in cash. We mentioned the benefits of a net operating deduction as a special deduction. Corporations that are eligible for the deduction get to reduce their taxable income by the net operating loss (NOL) deduction. Most C corporations are eligible to take the NOL deduction, but careful consideration needs to be taken when calculating your tax. A personal holding company, for example, can apply the NOL from only the preceding tax year as opposed to the standard NOL carryforward available when calculating the regular corporate tax. A C corporation that is subject to the accumulated earnings tax, however, does not get to utilize an NOL when calculating the tax, so the NOL is not applicable to it. Applicability needs to be understood when calculating a C corporation–level tax on a subchapter S corporations or between a corporation and its successor.

NET OPERATING LOSS UTILIZATION

In general, C corporations that are ordinary taxable business corporations are fully eligible to take NOL deductions. One important note is that a C corporation and its shareholders are distinct from one another and losses of one cannot offset gain from another. One exception is the ability of an affiliated group of corporations to file a consolidated return and take advantage of the subsidiary's loss for the year, thus reducing the taxable income of the group.

Because each corporation is a separate taxpayer, the NOLs of one corporation do not carry over or carry back between one corporation and its successor corporation. An important exception exists in the context of subsidiary liquidations and reorganizations.

A corporation in the process of liquidating may carry back the NOLs generated during the liquidation process. Once a corporation has completed its liquidation, the ability to carry back NOLs ends.

Corporations controlled by five or fewer individuals are subject to these sets of rules. Limitations on the ability to deduct losses are the at-risk rules and the passive activity loss rules. The at-risk rules limit the ability to deduct losses arising when the investing corporation bears no economic risk of loss. The passive activity loss rules restrict the deductibility of losses from a passive business whereby the corporation does not materially participate. Only limited classes of corporations are subject to these rules. The only other corporate entity affected is personal service corporations, which are subject to the passive activity loss rules.

Corporations that invest through disregarded entities consolidate their own operations with those of the disregarded entities for purposes. The disregarded entity could be a single-member limited liability company. At-risk rules and passive activity loss rules may apply to a limited class of corporations that invest through disregarded entities.

No items carry back or carry over at the corporate level from S corporation years. If a C corporation becomes an S corporation, NOLs from C corporation years cannot carry over to S corporation years.

A few more examples are where cooperative organizations are permitted to take NOL deductions for purposes of determining their corporate income tax liability. Tax-exempt organizations that are subject to corporate tax on their unrelated business taxable income can also deduct NOLs for purposes of applying the unrelated business income tax. The determination of NOLs is adjusted to ensure that NOLs are not affected by, and do not affect, the organization beyond those transactions that generate the unrelated business income.

Tax attributes belong to the corporation that created them. However, in certain asset acquisition transactions, another corporation may acquire a target corporation's tax attributes. Code Section 381 provides rules for the transfer of corporate tax attributes. Net operating losses are corporate tax attributes. If the acquiring corporation receives assets in an A, C, D, or F reorganization, the acquiring corporation succeeds to all of the NOLs of the target corporation. This is also true if a corporation receives assets in a subsidiary liquidation. No acquiring corporation NOLs may be carried back to any target corporation tax year. However, they may be carried back to a preacquisition tax year. The target corporation's NOLs may not be carried back to the acquiring corporation's preacquisition years.

CHARITABLE CONTRIBUTIONS

The IRC prohibits a double deduction for charitable contributions through an interrelationship with net operating losses.

When a corporation donates ordinary income property, the deduction is generally limited to its basis in that property. In most instances, the amount of the corporation's deduction for a contribution of property is reduced by the amount of the gain that would have been ordinary income or short-term capital gain if the contributed property had been sold by the taxpayer at its fair market value. An exception applies to certain corporate contributions of inventory that is donated to a qualified public charity. When all applicable requirements are met, typically the corporation may deduct its basis in the contributed property plus one-half of the property's appreciation in value. Thus, taxes are a consideration when giving to charity.

Taxes are also a consideration when determining whether to have a retirement plan and of what type. There exist, for example, defined benefit plans, defined contribution plans, employee stock ownership plans, and nonqualified deferred compensation plans.

Important note deductions for contributions to a qualified plan are generally deductible in the year in which the contribution or compensation is paid. A contribution is deemed to have been made on the last day of the preceding tax year if it is made on account of that tax year and is made no later than the time for filing the return for that tax year, including extensions. For example, if a calendar-year employer makes a contribution to the company retirement plan by March 15, the contribution may be deducted from its taxes for the previous year.

Another area where taxes need to be considered is when a corporation sells its business by selling its assets. Here are some basics generally gain or loss recognition takes place when selling assets. Corporations recognize gain but not loss when distributing assets not in liquidation. Parent and subsidiary corporations recognize no gain or loss on liquidation of subsidiary. Shareholders generally recognize gain or loss on liquidation of stock. Shareholders of the corporation must weigh the overall advantages and disadvantages of the deal when deciding to sell either the assets of the entity or stock in it.

An asset sale by a C corporation generally results in an unfavorable tax result for the selling shareholders. Double taxation occurs when the asset sale is taxed both at the corporate level and then the proceeds distributed out to the shareholder for the purposes of redeeming the shares are taxed at the individual shareholder level.

An asset sale is usually the favored structure for buyers because it allows them to take a stepped-up basis in all of the purchased assets. Of course, a stepped-up basis allows buyers to obtain larger depreciation and amortization deductions.

An asset sale of a corporation can either be a direct sale or a forward merger, whereby the corporation is merged into the buyer or its subsidiary and the shareholders of the seller receive cash.

The character of the gain or loss is determined by the category of the underlying asset in an asset sale; in a stock sale, capital gain or loss is generally recognized unless there is a tax-free exchange.

In an attempt to have every corporation pay its fair share of taxes, the tax law imposes an alternative minimum tax (AMT). For the purposes of this chapter, we briefly discuss the corporate AMT. Corporations utilize the laws in effect to reduce their regular taxes. The corporate AMT ensures that corporations pay at least a minimum amount of tax on their economic income. A corporation that is not a small corporation exempt from the AMT owes AMT if its tentative minimum tax is more than its regular tax.

A corporation is treated as a small corporation exempt from the AMT for its current tax year if that year is the corporation's first tax year in existence or it was treated as a small corporation exempt from the AMT for all prior tax years and its average annual gross receipts for the three-tax-year period did not exceed $7.5 million (or $5 million if the corporation had only one prior tax year).

Last, but not least, budgeting for taxes ultimately has a day of reckoning. Certain transactions involving cash outlays that we have touched on, such as charitable contributions and retirement plan contributions, will yield certain tax benefits. A corporation that owes taxes needs to know its tax burden on a quarterly basis or risk being subject to an underpayment penalty. An underpayment penalty is really interest for the use of money, again measured on a quarterly basis. Estimated taxes are paid in four installments. They generally must equal 100 percent of tax shown on current year's return or 100 percent of tax shown on previous year's return. Large corporations can base only the first installment payment on the prior year's tax. Payments may also be based on annualized income whereby income is broken down into the quarter's earnings so the estimates due would be more in line with that quarter's income. State requirements for estimated tax payments differ greatly, based on different thresholds, a fact that tax people must be aware of.

Last, and sadly, C corporations need to consider in which states or countries they want to do business, buy their supplies, or achieve their goals for the lowest cost in order to save on taxes. The international taxation arena, like many other areas of domestic taxation, cannot be overlooked when budgeting for corporate income taxes.

TAXATION BUDGET

Every company that is in business to make a profit must file and pay taxes. The taxes that are paid can take the form of payroll taxes, property taxes, sales taxes, and income taxes.

The definition of a budget on taxation is a systematic plan or forecast of future tax liability. The need for such a plan arises because of the timing differences between business income and taxable income.

Payroll Taxes

Payroll taxes expense and liability is based on salaries estimated to be paid as budgeted in the income and expense budget. The tax expense includes employers' estimated amounts to be paid to employees for Social Security tax, Medicare tax, and state unemployment insurance as well as related fringe benefits. Fringe benefits should take into consideration workers' compensation rates for different classifications of workers and employers' portion of health and pension costs. Analysis of estimated commissions paid to salespeople is made to determine whether these costs should be considered as labor costs and therefore included in budgeted payroll costs or whether they meet the requirements of independent contractorsand therefore not considered as labor costs.

Property Taxes

Real estate taxes are based on estimated values of real property owned and tax rates in effect. The budget for real estate taxes is based on past history and/or correspondence with local assessor's office of the municipality and the determination of the rates.

Intangible Taxes

Intangible taxes are based on the cost basis and/or book value of the fixed asset after depreciation based on tax rates established by the local municipality.

Sales Tax

The tax budget for sales tax is based on the taxability of retail sales as determined by the budget for retail sales as well as a reasonable estimate for sales and use tax for purchases of equipment and expenses for own use where no sales tax is charged by vendor.

Corporate Taxes

The management of corporate taxes increases in importance and complexity each year due to changes in federal, state, and local tax law changes. Rates in existence should be determined, and the income should be budgeted based on estimated income after expenses.

FEDERAL CORPORATE TAX

The corporate taxable income may be different for income tax reporting from that for financial reporting because of permanent and temporary timing differences. The differences can be attributable to, but are not limited to, these points:

Inventory

- Switch from FIFO to a LIFO valuation of inventory.
- *Unicap capitalization rules.* Uniform capitalization rules are a tax concept, not an accounting concept. The rules are a method of valuing inventory for tax purposes that requires capitalization of direct costs (such as material and labor costs) and an allocable portion of indirect costs that benefit or are incurred because of production or resale activities. Certain expenses must be included in the basis of property produced or in inventory cost rather than currently deducted.

Depreciation

- For financial reporting purposes, the company may depreciate or amortize its fixed assets using the straight-line method of depreciation while for income tax reporting, it uses an accelerated method of depreciation to reduce its taxable income, thus reducing its income tax liability and increasing its cash flow. Accelerated methods of depreciation include:

  - *Bonus depreciation.* Under current federal tax law, new personal property assets including leasehold improvements acquired after September 8, 2011, and 2012 can be taken as a deduction for their full cost, thus reducing taxable income.
  - *Cost segregation.* The purchase of real estate property is segregated into its component parts as building, land improvements, and equipment. The company hires a cost segregation expert who issues a report that segregates the purchase price of the real estate into its component parts. The estimated useful lives of the component parts can be as low as 5 years and as high as 39 years.
  - *Declining balance method of depreciation.* The asset is depreciating using either 150 or 200 percent of its estimated life.

▪ *Goodwill.* For financial reporting purposes, goodwill is an expense and reduces corporate income when the asset is impaired. For income tax purposes, goodwill is amortized over a 15-year life.

▪ *Meals and entertainment.* For financial reporting purposes, this category is deductible in full; for income tax reporting, only 50 percent of these expenses are deductible.

▪ *Bad debts.* Reserve for bad debts is deductible in arriving at financial reporting purposes. Bad debts are deducted as incurred for income tax reporting.

▪ *Provision for warranty costs.* Warranty costs are deductible for financial reporting on the reserve method but may be deductible as incurred for income tax purposes.

PURPOSES

Recently the IRS has come out with disclosure of uncertain tax positions. This IRS disclosure is an outgrowth of FIN 48 and must be disclosed in tax reporting. The accounting policies of the company are to be evaluated to determine whether they are in conformity with IRS tax regulations and procedures. If these procedures are not in conformity, disclosure must be made in the tax return and deferred taxes must be recorded for financial reporting.

TAX RETURN

In the current economic situation, states are looking to increase their collection of revenue either by changing tax regulations and law or by nexus. Each state has its own criteria for nexus. Nexus is the means by which states bring corporate operations into the state, thus making the company's operations taxable in that state. Adjustments made to determine state taxable income include, among others:

▪ State income taxes
▪ Municipal bond interest income
▪ Adjustments to federal depreciation due to decoupling

Most states allow companies to allocate their income by apportionment. The apportionment factors are property sales and payroll. Property factors including allocation of inventory, fixed assets and rent multiplied by eight, and real estate owned in and out of the state. Sales and payroll are apportioned by sales and payroll in and out of the state, to total sales and payroll. The apportionment is the total value of items particular to that state to the total everywhere. Recently some states have adopted the single-factor formula by apportionment of sales; other states have adopted the throw-out sales in the computation of the apportionment factor. Under the throw-out sales rule, which has been found to be constitutional, the sales not reported to other states by filing a franchise tax is reduced from total sales for the year thus increasing the sales apportionment factor.

CHAPTER THIRTY-FIVE

Budgeting in the Global Internet Communication Technology Industry

Michael Kraten, PhD, CPA
Providence College

OVERVIEW

The Internet communication technology sector is a natural extension of an industry that has flourished for 160 years. Western Union, for example, traces its roots back to the 1851 birth of its ancestor firm, Ntew York & Mississippi Valley Printing Telegraph Company. Nevertheless, the Internet itself has only existed for a single generation: Google, for instance, was created as recently as 1996 and Facebook in 2004.

This marriage of a relatively ancient industry service with a fledgling electronic delivery platform presents numerous challenges to accountants in the field of budgeting. Although many of the terms and techniques of budget planning in this sector are consistent with those utilized since the 1800s, the characteristics and complications of Internet connectivity have produced a number of unique considerations.

The purpose of this chapter is to extend selected material from the first four parts of this book by elaborating on how the content should be applied to the global Internet communication technology industry. It introduces new concepts that address a number of emerging trends in the accounting profession, involving issues that extend beyond Internet communications, and that are relevant to many different entrepreneurial sectors.

For instance, in the "Essentials from Earlier Chapters" section of this chapter, we revisit the planning cycle as described in Chapter 3, business valuation issues as described in Chapter 7, break-even analysis as described in Chapter 13, budgeting for international operations as described in Chapter 28, and activity-based budgeting as described in Chapter 33. Budget planners in the global Internet communication technology industry are advised how to modify the practices that are described in earlier chapters to address the unique characteristics of their own industry.

Then, in the section titled "Freemium Strategies," we discuss why the freemium service pricing and distribution strategy has become prevalent in the industry. We also address how such services should be managed by budget professionals, considering that freemium services are strategically positioned as "loss leaders" that may significantly impact volume estimates; nevertheless, they usually do not burden firms with significant additional marginal costs.

We then proceed to address volunteer services, focusing in particular on the contributions of nontraditional (and often uncompensated) activities of student programmers, amateur journalists, and aggregators of information from the public domain. Relationships between these stakeholders and Internet technology firms must be negotiated in unusual and innovative ways, impacting the cost structures of these firms and the internal budgets that quantify them.

Finally, in the last section of this chapter, we discuss how the discipline of enterprise risk management (ERM) impacts the development, review, and modification of static budgets. Although risk management is a well-established discipline, the contemporary integrated model of ERM was introduced by the Committee of Sponsoring Organizations of the Treadway Commission (COSO) in 2004, at roughly the time when Facebook and other newly emerging Internet communication technology firms were launched.

Although much of the ERM integrated model has been designed to address general business concerns, its relatively recent genesis has led it to emphasize certain features that are particularly significant for newly emerging industries. Its heavy reliance on measurement indicators, for instance, is particularly meaningful for a service industry in which every "click" (i.e., every minute move) of every consumer can be measured and analyzed for planning purposes.

Furthermore, the ERM model's emphasis on preventive controls is particularly relevant in cloud-based service architectures, where upgrades can be implemented at the host server level and not laboriously rolled out through geographically remote client-service activities.

The global technology industry and other emerging industries of the twentieth and twenty-first centuries have served as the breeding grounds of innovations in budget management, innovations that have later become established tenets throughout the economy. The balanced scorecard methodology described in Chapter 1, for instance, was first pioneered during the twentieth century in the process engineering industry. And the manufacturing cost accounting systems discussed in Chapter 12 first emerged as modernizing nations entered the Industrial Revolution of the 1800s and early 1900s.

Thus, the methodologies that are explored in this chapter are likely to eventually enter the lexicon of all of our established industries, as the global Internet communication technology industry matures into an established pillar of the world's economy. As this occurs over time, these budget techniques will evolve as well, becoming less of a set of specialized industry applications and more of a collection of general budgeting policies and procedures.

ESSENTIALS FROM EARLIER CHAPTERS

Accountants with budget management responsibilities at Internet communication technology firms should adhere to the policies and procedures described throughout the first four parts of this text. All of the guidance described therein is relevant to the fiscal activities of contemporary organizations.

There are, however, five specific topics that demand special consideration from budget professionals in this industry sector. The topics are described next, accompanied by brief explanations of the considerations that will likely result in modified budgeting practices.

Planning Cycle

Chapter 3 of this book describes the planning cycle in terms that apply to most business and governmental organizations. Budgets are typically prepared on an annual basis, although certain firms (such as publicly traded corporations) tend to revise their budgets on a quarterly basis. Furthermore, a few organizations (such as real estate management companies with rental properties) tend to budget revenues, expenses, and cash flows on a monthly basis.

In the Internet communication technology industry, however, budgets are generally prepared for each new upgrade of a product or service, regardless of the timing of the release of the upgrade. This can result in budget planning cycles that fall into irregular time frames; the Apple iPad, for instance, was initially launched on January 27, 2010; its second generation was released 13 months and three days later on March 2, 2011.

Business Valuation Issues

Chapter 7 of this book explains business valuation practices by utilizing common financial accounting terms and concepts. Revenues, net earnings, operating cash flows, and dividends, for instance, are financial performance indicators that are utilized to derive valuation estimates.

Internet communication technology firms, however, are often valued on the basis of market usage statistics that bear little or no relationship to such financial accounting measurements. Facebook, for instance, was assigned a valuation of $50 billion by Goldman Sachs in early 2011 for a variety of reasons, one of which was the investment public's admiration of its success in building a consumer base of over 500 million active users as of July 2010, an increase of 150 million over the 350 million users that it served as of December 2009. This explosive growth served to magnify the public's excitement about the market usage statistic, which in turn impacted Facebook's valuation estimate.

Break-Even Analysis

Chapter 13 of this book describes break-even analysis as the process by which a target level of volume can be estimated as the point where contribution margins (i.e., sales revenues less variable operating costs) equal fixed operating costs. Firms with relatively high levels of fixed operating costs tend to have relatively high target levels of break-even sales volume; conversely, firms with relatively low levels of fixed operating costs tend to achieve break-even results at fairly low levels of volume.

Internet communication technology firms tend to maintain budgets that are relatively low in *both* variable and fixed operating costs; instead, most of their costs of doing business are embedded in their extensive preoperational (or prelaunch) software development activities. As is the case with biopharmaceutical drugs, military hardware, and other industry sectors that feature similarly significant preoperational research and development costs, such Internet firms must place more emphasis on estimations of payback periods (defined as the lengths of time that are required to earn sufficient profits to cumulatively pay back initial required investments) than on break-even points.

International Operations

There are the unique fiscal and managerial budgetary considerations of operating extensive global enterprises. Special consideration must be given to currency translation issues, customs fees, and other concerns that are typically not relevant for purely domestic organizations.

Because Internet communication technology firms are in the business of providing services that can be instantaneously routed through various global destinations and jurisdictions, such organizations can often exploit opportunities to reconfigure the manner in which they serve consumers in order to minimize operating costs and taxation expenditures. Google, for instance, has been known to minimize its taxation levels in the United States by routing certain services through its Irish server farms.[1]

Activity-Based Budgeting

Chapter 33 of this book illustrates how the volume drivers of various operating activities can be quantified and utilized to allocate costs and expenditures across different products and services. The true costs of production and distribution can thus be matched against the revenue produced by the sale of each unit in order to accurately prepare budget estimates of the actual profit or loss derived by the firm.

As noted, however, most of the overall costs that are incurred by Internet communication technology firms are generated during the development stage, not during the sales and operations stages. Thus, although activity-based budgeting can indeed be utilized to quantify the operating profits per unit of service, these profits are not likely to be affected significantly by the operating expenses that are expressed in firm budgets. In other words, the incremental marginal cost of allowing each additional consumer to use an Internet communication service is relatively close to zero, assuming that the technology firm possesses sufficient excess capacity to serve each consumer.

FREEMIUM STRATEGIES

In addition to serving as incubators of software innovation, Internet communication technology firms have served as innovators in pricing and distribution business strategies.

---

[1] See www.guardian.co.uk/business/Ireland-business-blog-with-lisa-ocarroll/2011/mar/24/google-ireland-tax-reasons-bermuda and http://sociable.co/2011/08/10/google-irelands-dublin-staff-put-on-a-performance-for-the-google-street-view-cameras/

For instance, this industry sector has pioneered what is commonly known as the freemium model of service.

Traditionally, industrial-era firms like General Motors built layers of brands, with more spartan products and services bearing lower consumer prices and more luxurious offerings bearing higher prices. Although the relatively spartan items cost less to produce and distribute than the luxury items, the production *cost* differential per unit is usually far smaller than the consumer *price* differential per unit (i.e. the *cost* discount is customarily lower than the *price* discount), thereby leading organizations to budget much lower profit margins per unit for their entry-level brands. This explains why, for instance, subcompact automobile models generally yield lower profit levels per unit than luxury models.

The "Free" in Freemium

The definition of a freemium strategy can be stated in this way: "Simply give a basic (or spartan) level of service away for free." In other words, a management accountant quite literally budgets no consumer revenues at all for a freemium service.

How can an accounting budget ever call for a reasonable level of profit (or even a break-even outcome) when revenues are budgeted to be zero? It obviously can never do so; losses are indeed inevitable whenever a firm adopts a freemium strategy. And as long as marginal costs exceed zero (i.e., as long as there is some measurable additional cost of providing each new free service), the losses must inevitably mount as volume increases.

Nevertheless, as noted previously, Internet communication technology firms tend to maintain very low marginal cost structures and thus tend to only suffer modest losses from the distribution of freemium services. As a result, a basic level of freemium service can often be established as an affordable strategic "loss leader," as long as some measurable benefit can be derived from the practice.

The "Premium" in Freemium

Typically, the benefit that is derived from providing a freemium service is the likelihood that a number of freemium customers will upgrade to a premium level of service, thereby generating profits for the organization. Because the marginal cost of serving each freemium customer is quite low, the percentage of freemium customers who upgrade to the premium level can actually be quite low as well while still appearing to be reasonable in comparison to the modest cost of offering a basic level of service.

For instance, let us assume that the marginal cost of serving each freemium customer is $1 per month. Let us also assume that each premium customer generates $10 per month of profit for an Internet communication technology firm. Under such circumstances, the firm could generate sufficient profits to serve ten freemium customers by simply persuading one of them to upgrade to the premium level, a mere 10 percent conversion rate.

VOLUNTEER SERVICES

In most industries, budget accountants tend to work with revenue and cost items that generate or drain their organizational coffers of cash. Sales transactions bring in revenue and then cash receipts whereas operating activities lead to expenses and then cash disbursements; even noncash journal entries such as depreciation and amortization tend to be based on prior asset purchase transactions that were initially triggered by cash-based transactions of some kind.

Nonprofit organizations, though, have traditionally been required to modify their management accounting budget practices to reflect a different type of transaction, namely, the contributions of volunteers. Such services must also be budgeted, albeit as nonoperating revenues or noncapital contributions because they represent increases in the value of resources received by the organization.

Nevertheless, volunteer services also represent costs to such organizations because of the need to develop and maintain oversight activities and other internal controls related to the activities of volunteers. Furthermore, if the value of volunteer services is recorded as a nonoperating revenue or noncapital contribution item, then it should also be recorded as an accrued noncash expense item. In other words, the management accountant budgets the value of the voluntary work activity as an expense of the entity and budgets the voluntary contribution of time and resources as an increase in the equity value of the firm.

From Nonprofits to Technology Firms

Interestingly, for-profit Internet communication technology firms often have been able to inspire student programmers, amateur journalists, information aggregators, and other volunteers to donate time and resources to improve their products or services, without any expectation of compensation by these contributors. News organizations from CNN to the BBC, for instance, have accepted and posted photographs and videos from amateur reporters around the world. And most productivity application providers maintain online forums and message boards where volunteers help users learn about software features.

Such for-profit organizations must modify their budgets, as nonprofit organizations do, to account for the fiscal impact of these volunteers. The value of their time and contributions, based on the market value of the resources contributed by the volunteers, should be budgeted as revenues or capital contributions. And the replacement cost of their activities, defined as what the firms would need to spend to perform the organizational functions that have been assigned to the volunteers, should be recorded as accrued expenses.

Would these revenues or capital contributions always necessarily balance out these accrued expenses? Not necessarily; variations may exist because of mismatches between resources and activities. A programmer with a PhD in software engineering, for instance, would represent a significant resource and yet an insignificant accrued expense if his or her volunteer time is "wasted" on helping novice users learn how to create user accounts and passwords.

Role of Negotiations

Expectations about the quantity and quality of the services provided by volunteers must be negotiated by the organization; ancillary benefits and other valuable tokens of gratitude must be negotiated as well. Internet communication technology firms may, for instance, agree to terms that permit volunteers free access to premium content or provide them with early access to service upgrades that are not yet available to the general public.

Many fiscal executives with budgetary responsibilities are accustomed to allowing transfer prices and other budgetary variables to be negotiated by divisional managers, but they may not be familiar with the practice of negotiating relationships with volunteers and formalizing their terms within managerial budgets. When Internet communication technology organizations place heavy reliance on the contributions of volunteers, though, such practices are indeed necessary.

ENTERPRISE RISK MANAGEMENT

Chapter 3 addresses contingency planning, a topic that addresses the need to modify budgets on the fly when difficult circumstances require organizations to change their strategic plans. Because Internet communication technology firms typically experience extremely brief and highly volatile planning cycles, such organizations often must place considerable emphasis on this element of the budgeting process.

The discipline of ERM provides the budget accounting professional with valuable tools and techniques for developing such contingency planning activities. The material is summarized in a set of guidelines known as the ERM Integrated Framework; it is available for purchase on the Web sites of the COSO[2] and of the American Institute of Certified Public Accountants (AICPA).[3]

The framework focuses on four core steps that summarize how budget professionals should define organizational priorities, prioritize contingent events and concerns, and identify pragmatic preventive controls and crisis response functions that must be maintained by organizations. Although the framework is a general practitioner model that is not exclusively focused on Internet communication technology firms, its emphases on measurement indicators and preventive controls make it particularly useful for such organizations.

Four Core Steps

The first core step of the COSO model of ERM is called *event identification*, that is, the preparation of a list (or an "inventory") of potentially destabilizing or damaging incidents. The second core step is called *risk assessment*, that is, the prioritization of events on the basis of: (a) their *likelihood* of occurrence and (b) their potential *impacts* of occurrence.

When high-priority events feature *likelihood* estimates that exceed tolerable threshold targets, firms are expected to develop preventive *control activities*, the third core step, that reduce these estimates to acceptable residual levels. Likewise, when high-priority events feature *impact* estimates that exceed such targets, firms are expected to develop *risk response* activities that do so, which is the fourth core step.

---

[2] See http://coso.org/guidance.htm.
[3] See www.cpa2biz.com/AST/Main/CPA2BIZ_Primary/InternalControls/COSO/PRDOVR~PC-990015/PC-990015.jsp.

The direct costs of designing and maintaining these preventive controls and risk (or crisis) response capabilities must be incorporated into management budgets. Internet communication technology firms must rely on relatively unpredictable resources (such as the time contributed by volunteers) to develop and implement systems service upgrades on extremely short-term planning cycles; they must therefore place particular emphasis on such activities.

Applications: Measurements and Controls

COSO's emphasis on measurable threshold targets is especially relevant to Internet communication technology organizations because user behaviors can be tested and measured on an every-click, every-second basis of extreme precision. Google, for instance, has been known to extensively field test new innovations on consumer behaviors before deciding whether to incorporate such new business opportunities into its collection of products and services.

The industry's evolving reliance on cloud-based service architectures, with its emphasis on storing most software programming code on the servers of Internet communication technology firms instead of downloading them onto the mainframes and personal computer hard drives of end users, tends to minimize the likelihood and damage estimates of certain events within ERM analyses. Computer viruses, for instance, can be more easily quarantined, analyzed, and then neutralized when targeted software programs reside on the servers of firm service providers instead of in the hands of hundreds of thousands of geographically dispersed end users.

About the Editor

William Rea Lalli, is certified public accountant in New York and was the founder and chief financial officer of WillCo LLC, a premier provider of continuing professional education in the study of budgeting, planning, forecasting, corporate finance, auditing, accounting, and taxation. After a successful career in public accounting with the world's largest firm and AICPA, Mr. Lalli held progressively more responsible executive positions with the world's largest conference organizers. He has been published many times by the AICPA and is on the board of advisors of the *Journal of Corporate Accounting & Finance.*

About the Contributors

John J. Antos, MBA, is president of Value Creation Group, a management consulting firm specializing in activity-based management, quality costs, acquisitions, planning, and modern cost systems. He consults and lectures around the world to major companies and is a recognized professional in his field. He has been a chief financial officer, director, and controller within industry and has turned around a company on the verge of bankruptcy. He has consulted on such topics as ABM, ABC, ABB, accounting systems, strategic planning, plant expansion studies, acquisitions, and marketing. Mr. Antos has an MBA in accounting and marketing from the University of Chicago and a BS in business administration from the University of Illinois–Urbana. He is also a certified management accountant and a certified financial planner.

Robert Dale Apgood, PhD, MBA, CPA, is a leasing and financial consultant, specializing in international leasing, accounting, and finance. Dr. Apgood has served as chairman of the Accounting Standards Committee for the broadcast industry, as vice president of finance for a broadcasting and telecommunications conglomerate, and as a full professor of accounting. In addition to his consulting practice, he is currently vice president of Canterbury Group, a high-tech bioremediation firm.

Paul Barber is president of PROPHIX Software, based in Mississauga, Ontario. He has over 20 years' experience in the computer software industry and has been involved in the development, application, and implementation of decision support systems, executive information systems, financial reporting systems, OLAP databases, and budgeting software. Mr. Barber has an MA in mathematics from Cambridge University and an MBA from the Ivey Business School of the University of Western Ontario.

Jeffrey L. Bass, MA, MPA, is principal at the firm of Margolin, Winer & Evens, LLP, where he directs and manages the firm's practice in strategic business planning and corporate finance. Mr. Bass is chair of the Long Island Venture Group and the Long Island Forum. He serves as director of the Long Island Community Development Corporation, the Long Island City Business Development Corporation, and Turnaround Management Association (Long Island Chapter). Mr. Bass received his MA. from the City University of New York and his MPA from New York University.

Carl Benner is with the consumer and industrial manufacturing practice at PricewaterhouseCoopers L.L.P.

Stewart Berger, CPA, Tax Principal, has over 30 years of experience providing tax and estate consulting services to closely held companies and high net worth individuals. He is a member of the fiduciary service group of Rosen Seymour Shapss Martin & Company.

Mr. Berger received his B.S. from Brooklyn College. He is a member of the American Institute of Certified Public Accountants and the New York Society of Certified Public Accountants ("NYSSCPA"). He served on the Nominating Committee of the NYSSCPAs and also a member of the Closely Held and S Corporation Committee where he was past chairman of the committee. He is currently serving on the Rapid Response Committee of the Tax Division Oversight Committee of the NYSSCPA. Also, he is currently the co-chair of the Closely Held and Flow Through Entities annual conference and previously served as Chairman of the Evening Technical session of the Closely Held and S Corporation committee for the NYSSCPAs. He has also written several articles for professional publications and has been quoted in various industry trades and regional newspapers.

James A. Brimson, MBA, is president of IPM, Inc., an international confederation of consulting, training, and software companies who specialize in activity-based management. Prior to IPM, Inc., Mr. Brimson served as partner-in-charge of PricewaterhouseCoopers LLP, Deloitte's worldwide activity-based management consulting practice in London, England. He also served as director of CAM-I (an international consortium) with over 13 years of industry experience concentrating in cost management and systems development activities primarily in the manufacturing industry. Mr. Brimson is the author of *Activity Accounting: An Activity-Based Costing Approach*, published by John Wiley & Sons, Inc., and coeditor of *Cost Management for Today's Advanced Manufacturing: The CAM-I Conceptual Design*, published by Harvard Business School Press. He has a BS from Auburn University and an MBA in quantitative science from Arizona State University.

Scott M. Cheslowitz, CPA, a Member/Partner at Rothenberg & Peters, PLLC, has provided business services for many years in the public accounting arena. He has been a general practitioner for almost 25 years, working with closely held entities and high-net-worth individuals. Those services provided include accounting and tax, and business planning for corporations, partnerships, and individuals. He also provides for estate planning and estate tax work, along with estate and fiduciary income tax preparation.

Scott is a member of the AICPA, serves as the current Chair of the NYSSCPA Tax Division Oversight Committee, is a former Chair of the Closely Held and S Corporations Committee, and has served as a Chair for several NYSSCPA tax conferences. He has written tax questions for the AICPA Uniform CPA Exam; has been published several times; has appeared on FOX Business News, Bloomberg Television, and Business-Week TV programs; and also has been quoted in the media. He graduated with a degree in Accounting from Queens College of the City University of New York, where he returned to teach, and is a former Adjunct Professor. He is a CPA licensed in the State of New York.

Gary Cokins, CPIM, is a strategist, Performance Management Solutions, with The SAS Institute, Cary, North Carolina. He was formerly with ABC Technologies (acquired by SAS in 2002). SAS continues to be the leading provider of activity-based information software. Mr. Cokins is an internationally recognized expert, speaker, and author in advanced cost management and performance improvement systems. He began his career as a strategic planner at FMC's Link-Belt Division and then served as financial controller and operations manager. In 1981, he began his management consulting career at Deloitte & Touche and then KPMG Peat Marwick. He was trained on ABC by Harvard Business School professors Robert S. Kaplan and Robin Cooper. More recently, Mr. Cokins headed the National Cost Management Consulting Services for Electronic Data Systems (EDS). He is the author of several books: *An ABC Manager's*; *Activity-Based Cost Management: Making It Work (McGraw-Hill)*; *Activity-Based Cost Management: An Executive's Guide (John Wiley & Sons)*; and *Activity-Based Cost Management in Government (Management Concepts)*. He can be contacted at garyfarms@aol.com.

Michael Coveney, senior director of Strategy Management, spearheads Comshare's successful best practices consultancy, helping enterprises improve the efficiency and effectiveness of their corporate performance management processes. With more than 28 years of experience in the financial analytical software industry, Mr. Coveney has been involved in the design and implementation of performance management systems for many of the world's leading organizations, including BP, Guinness, and British Aerospace. His extensive experience has led him to become a regular speaker and course leader at many international events.

Bryan Crawford is the team lead for budget and finance in the Fish & Wildlife group at the Bonneville Power Administration. Prior to this position, he was the lead of the Capital Investment Review Team. This cross-agency team was charged with developing a revised capital investment review process that incorporates industry best practices and leads to more efficient and effective investment analysis, review, selection, and performance measurement. Mr. Crawford holds a BA and MA in art history and a master's in management from the Atkinson Graduate School of Management at Willamette University. He has 13 years' experience in finance, accounting, and budget development and execution.

Graef S. Crystal has many years of business experience, including vice president and member of the board of directors of Towers Perrin, where he headed the firm's compensation consulting practices. He served as an executive compensation consultant to the senior management and their boards of more than 30 multibillion-dollar companies. He also held management positions at Booz, Allen & Hamilton, Pfizer International, and General Dynamics. He has written several hundred articles on executive compensation topics and is a frequent contributor to major publications. He is currently a columnist for *Pensions & Investments* and the *New York Observer*. He is the author of six books, including *In Search of Excess: The Overcompensation of American Executives (Ecco Press)* and *What Are You Worth? (Whittle Communication)*. In addition, he has contributed chapters to 11 other books.

Michael W. Curran is president and principal consultant of Decision Sciences Corporation, a St. Louis–based consulting and software development firm he formed in 1968. He is the developer of the theories of bracket budgeting and range estimating. He is listed in *Who's Who in Consulting*, *Who's Who in Industry and Finance*, *Who's Who in America*, *Who's Who in the World*, and other biographical references. He has chaired or appeared as a guest speaker at over 200 courses and conducts seminars for top managers in many foreign countries.

William E. Dailey is a Managing Director in KPMG LLP's Risk Advisory Services. He is based in the firm's Boston office, where he serves as the product leader for the Budget and Forecasting service offering. In addition, Mr. Dailey is one of the prime architects of the Quality Close and Manufacturing Cost Accounting services.

Since joining KPMG, LLP in 2000, Mr. Dailey has provided a wide variety of advisory services to clients in commercial, industrial, electronics, high-technology, and financial services markets. Prior to joining KPMG, he spent over 22 years with Digital Equipment/Compaq Computer Corporation (now HP). During his tenure at Digital/Compaq, he held a variety of senior financial management positions, including plant controller, group/divisional controller, manufacturing controller, corporate reporting manager, and global SAP implementation manager for Manufacturing. Mr. Dailey has also held finance and operational positions in retail management and consumer products. He can be reached at wdailey@kpmg.com.

Frank C. Evans, CBA, ASA, CPA/ABV, a certified business appraiser, an accredited senior appraiser in business valuation, and a certified public accountant/accredited in business valuation, is a principal in Smith Evans Strimbu, Valuation Advisory Services. His practice is concentrated in valuation-based strategic planning and transaction advisory services. He works primarily with privately held companies but has worked as a valuation consultant with various public firms, including ExxonMobil, Ford, UPS, Caterpillar, and Accenture. His book, coauthored with David M. Bishop, *Valuation for M&A: Building Value in Private Companies*, is published by John Wiley & Sons and can be ordered at www.wiley.com. He earned a master's in business administration and a BA in economics from the University of Pittsburgh, after which he began his career with what is now Deloitte & Touche, LLP.

Robin Fraser, BSc(Eng), FCMA, FIMC, is one of the founders and a director of the Beyond Budgeting Round Table (BBRT), a research consortium group open to organizations seeking to develop continuous planning and adaptive control processes. Mr. Fraser leads BBRT's advisory services. Formerly a management consulting partner with Coopers & Lybrand (PwC, now IBM), he has 30 years of experience in business planning, performance improvement, and cost reduction and has worked in all sectors. In C&L, he led the development of Priority Base Budgeting, and headed the firm's Activity Based Management practice. He coauthored with Jeremy Hope the book Beyond Budgeting—How Managers Can Break Free from the Annual Performance Trap, published by Harvard Business School Press, 2003, and the HBR article, Who Needs Budgets? He is a regular speaker on "Beyond Budgeting" at conferences, public courses, and in-company workshops. He can be reached at robinfraser@bbrt.org.

Albert A. Fried is an expert in the practical applications of the strategic planning process.

Terrence B. Hobdy, BBA, MBA, president of Management Information Specialists, Inc., has over 14 years' experience assisting domestic and international companies achieve measurable improvements in profitability, productivity, and efficiency through the implementation of processes, organization designs, and enabling technologies. He is an expert in assisting companies implement proven cost-management strategies to accurately measure customer, product, and/or channel profitability. Additionally, Mr. Hobdy has specialized in benchmarking, reengineering financial business processes both transactional and decision support (e.g., budgeting and forecasting) and developing performance measures (e.g., balanced scorecard). Mr. Hobdy has coauthored three books, *Lessons from the Activity-Based Management Battlefield*; *Handbook of Budgeting 2002*; and *Handbook of Budgeting 2003*. He has also contributed to *Business Finance* and *Management Accounting* magazines. His diverse industry experience includes telecommunications, electric utilities, financial services, software, retail, oil and gas, distribution, and manufacturing industries. Mr. Hobdy received a BBA with a concentration in accounting from the University of Houston and an MBA with a concentration in finance from the Pennsylvania State University.

Jeremy Hope has led the Beyond Budgeting Round Table research program since 1998. He is one of the world's foremost thought leaders in the field of performance management and has written dozens of articles and cowritten three books; Transforming the Bottom Line (1995), Competing in the Third Wave (1997), and Beyond Budgeting (2003), all published by the Harvard Business School Press. He has been keynote speaker at many conferences on performance management around the world. He is a Chartered Accountant and after spending eight years with 3i and 10 years in business management, he became a writer and management educator.

William B. Iwaskow, MBA, JD, is a consultant, business executive, and adjunct professor of management. He was formerly an executive vice president at Hoffman-La Roche; a division president and general manager of Allied Chemical; a director of business development and planning for the International Division of American Cyanamid; and a principal at Korn Ferry International. Mr. Iwaskow is currently an adjunct professor of management at William Paterson College; previously, he served in the same capacity at Pace University. In addition, he has conducted many management seminars and developed a variety of multimedia products for several trade associations. He has a broad education with degrees in engineering, business (MBA), and law. He also received President Reagan's citation for "Private Sector Initiatives" at the White House for raising $7 million for New Jersey doctoral engineering scholarships.

Mike Kaufman is president of Management Advisory Group, a New York consulting firm specializing in business planning and profitability improvement. His previous experience includes the New York director of Corporate Finance Associates, a financial consulting consortium; corporate director of operations improvement for Lever Brothers Company, where he was responsible for capital planning and analysis; and the Sperry Corporation, where he held a similar position. Mr. Kaufman teaches corporate finance at the graduate school of Pace University and has authored a book on capital budgeting. He also lectures on financial and general management topics and conducts ongoing research regarding corporate practices in areas of finance, including cost of capital determination and other capital budgeting criteria.

Malcolm M. Knapp, MBA, is president of Malcolm M. Knapp, Inc., a leading consultancy to the foodservice industry. He is an advisor to many CEOs of major companies, frequently addresses trade associations, and is often quoted in the national and trade press. Mr. Knapp received a BA from Columbia University and an MBA from Harvard University's School of Business.

Eugene H. Kramer, CPA, was previously a principal in the firm of E.H. Kramer and Company.

Michael Kraten, PhD, CPA is a member of the Accounting faculty at Providence College in Rhode Island, where he teaches the capstone course in accounting policy. The course curriculum emphasizes case discussions and simulation activities regarding ethics, leadership, global business planning, and enterprise risk management.

Dr. Kraten's research specialty involves the use of communication technologies and social media for business negotiation activities. He is currently conducting outsourcing negotiation simulations with transfer pricing taxation implications for a network of institutions in Africa, Asia, Australia, Europe, and the United States.

Dr. Kraten is a Certified Public Accountant who spent nine years in the auditing, accounting, and consulting divisions of Deloitte & Touche and BDO Seidman, the second and fifth largest public accounting firms in the world, respectively. He resigned from a consulting partnership at BDO in 1995 to become co-founder and President of Enterprise Management Corporation (EMC), a Connecticut based consulting firm with centers of excellence in negotiation, entrepreneurship, and social policy.

Dr. Kraten has earned a PhD in behavioral and managerial accounting from the University of Connecticut. He previously earned an MPPM in public and private management from Yale University, and a BBA in public accounting from Baruch College-The City University of New York.

James E. Kristy is an internationally known lecturer, writer, and consultant specializing in financial management. His background comprises an active career in business and advanced degrees in management. He was a former senior vice president and chief financial officer of a statewide California bank. He has practiced financial management for over 25 years in such diverse settings as the cement, motion picture, computer industries, and commercial banking. He is the creator of the Commercial Credit Matrix, a rating system for measuring a firm's financial strength. His booklet, *Analyzing Financial Statements: Quick and Clean*, describes the system, and there is a software version for personal computers. Other writings include *A Guide to Financial Planning*, *Finance Without Fear*, and a computer tutorial, *Analyzing Financial Statements with Electronic Spreadsheets*. He is listed in *Who's Who in Finance and Industry* and *Who's Who in the World*.

Jay H. Loevy, CPA, CFE, is a retired partner of KPMG Peat Marwick. His present practice includes management consulting, litigation support, and forensic accounting. Mr. Loevy is also chairman of the MCS Technical and Industry Consulting Practices Subcommittee of the AICPA.

Maria Theresa Mateo, MBA, is a managing associate in the Manufacturing Industrial Practice of PricewaterhouseCooper Consulting. Ms. Mateo has over eight years' consulting experience in strategic planning, business reengineering, cost reduction, operations management, supply-chain management, in-controls risk management, and organizational analysis. Prior to consulting, Ms. Mateo capitalized on a fad and established a company to domestically manufacture and distribute novelty boxer shorts. She has a BS degree in biology, an MBA from Columbia Business School, and a psychology and economics degree from the University of Michigan.

Edward Mendlowitz, CPA, ABV, PFS, CFF, is a partner in WithumSmith+Brown and is a member of the AICPA, NYSSCPA and NJSCPA. He is also admitted to practice before the United States Tax Court; testified twice before the House Ways and Means

Committee on tax policy, reform and equity; and has testified as an expert witness in federal and state court regarding business valuation.

Ed has served on committees of the NYSSCPA and NJSCPAs, and was chairman of the committee that planned the NYSSCPA's 100th Anniversary. The author of 18 books, Ed has also written hundreds of articles for business and professional journals and newsletters. He has been a contributing editor to the *Practitioners Publishing Company's 706/709 Deskbook*, various editions of the *Corporate Controller's Manual and the AICPA's Management of an Accounting Practice Handbook*, is on the editorial board of *Bottom Line/ Personal* newsletter, and *Journal of Accountancy's* Member Panel for business valuation and forensic services. He is the recipient of the Lawler Award for the best article published during 2001 in the *Journal of Accountancy*. Ed has also taught for 11 years in the MBA program at Fairleigh Dickinson University, and is the author of continuing education programs and webinars on cost accounting and budgeting. Additional information is available at www.edwardmendlowitz.com and www.withum.com.

C. Eugene Moore is principal of C. Eugene Moore & Associates. For over 25 years, he has been a manufacturing executive with profit and loss responsibility as well as a lecturer and seminar leader. In his executive capacities, he has participated in and directed notable profit improvement and growth processes for E.M.D., Crown Cork and Seal Company, Mack Truck, Crompton and Knowles, Singer, and Littell Machine Company. Mr. Moore has completely planned, contracted, and managed the construction and occupancy of manufacturing plants in the United States, Europe, and South America.

Antosh G. Nirmul has led executive and board-sponsored projects to implement enterprise-wide management improvement and change in multiple industries. Mr. Nirmul currently works with Drs. Robert Kaplan and David Norton, originators of the balanced scorecard, as a manager for the consulting practice of the Balanced Scorecard Collaborative. Mr. Nirmul has led multiple large and small projects to implement the balanced scorecard and strategic management systems for companies in various industries, with a special emphasis in utility and telecommunications companies. He holds a degree in chemical engineering from the University of Michigan.

Thomas F. Norris is a managing associate in the consumer and industrial manufacturing practice of the New York metro consulting office of PricewaterhouseCoopers LLP. Mr. Norris has over 20 years' experience in operations, materials management, accounting, and information technology. His experience also includes both centralized and decentralized management in global environments. He has a BBA from Siena College in Accounting and has both CPIM and CIRM designations from the American Production and Inventory Control Society.

Joseph M. Orlando is the National Partner-In-Charge of KPMG LLP's CFO Advisory Services practice. He oversees a team of professionals who provide business process, program management, and regulatory advisory services for today's finance organizations. He helps champion the role of chief financial officers, controllers, and financial executives with an emphasis on budgeting and forecasting, financial closing/reporting, shared services, and finance transformation.

Some of Mr. Orlando's recent client accomplishments include: transforming the financial close and reporting processes to help clients meet regulatory compliance, enhance processes, and improve resource allocation; developing/advising on the implementation of a balanced scorecard/performance management process; construct-ing/project managing an activity-based costing system; assisting with financial systems guidance; designing finance organization investment plans; and managing an aggres-sive finance transformation initiative. Industries served range from manufacturing, publishing, energy and chemicals, automotive, gaming, aerospace, entertainment and hospitality, and more.

Prior to joining KPMG, Mr. Orlando served for over 12 years in various financial leadership roles while also acquiring treasury, tax, and international experience. Nota-bly, he was vice president of a large manufacturing company and corporate controller for an established network communications company. Today he continues to deliver speeches and facilitate workshops emphasizing the challenges, vision, and leading prac-tices of the finance function. Mr. Orlando can be reached at jorlando@kpmg.com.

Robert E. Paladino, Senior Vice President of Global Performance, reports to the CEO of Crown Castle and is a highly skilled executive with demonstrated results in developing and implementing enterprise-wide and operational strategies for improving the performance of national and international companies impacted by deregulation, convergence, globalization, and competition.

He now plays a critical role in directing Crown Castle's global performance improve-ment programs to drive its Operational Excellence strategy. He draws on proven expe-rience implementing GE and Motorola Six Sigma, balanced scorecard, activity-based management, and process improvement disciplines. Prior to this appointment, he served as Vice President and Global Leader of the Telecommunications and Utility Practice for Robert Kaplan and David Norton's company, The Balanced Scorecard Collaborative, in affiliation with Harvard Business School. Prior to that he was a Principal Consultant with PricewaterhouseCoopers (PwC).

Mr. Paladino has a dual MBA in Finance and Management from the Wharton Graduate School of Business at the University of Pennsylvania. He holds a BA degree in Accounting Cum Laude from the University of Massachusetts. He completed Executive Education at Harvard Business School and Massachusetts Institute of Technology. He is a certified public accountant and is a member of AICPA and MSCPA. He is published in leading journals and is an active speaker at industry and trade events.

Steve Player serves as the North American Program Director for the Beyond Bud-geting Round Table, a research consortium group open to organizations seeking to develop continuous planning and adaptive control processes. BBRT was founded in Europe in 1998 and expanded to North America in 2002.

Mr. Player spent over 20 years with Arthur Andersen, where he was the Managing Partner of Andersen's Advanced Cost Management Team and served as Practice Leader for the National Baan Software Practice. He has co-authored or edited five books on cost and performance management, including Arthur Andersen's Global Lesson in Activity-Based Management and Cornerstones of Decision-Making: Profiles in Enterprise ABM.

Mr. Player founded and runs the Activity-Based Management Advanced Imple-mentation Group, whose members include Bell South and Bell Canada. He served on the board of directors of the Consortium for Advanced Manufacturing—International and provided insight for the AICPA Industry and Management Accounting Executive

Committee. Clients include American Express, Colgate Palmolive, Hewlett-Packard, The Covey Leadership Center, and World Vision

Peter A. Pyhrr is chairman of three specialty printing companies in Dallas, Texas (Hospital Forms & Systems Corporation, Magnetic Ticket & Label Corporation, and Inkless Image Corporation). He was formerly president of his own consulting company and controller of two divisions of Texas Instruments. He is invariably identified as developing the concept of zero-based budgeting. He served as a consultant to then–Georgia governor Jimmy Carter for the first government implementation. He has many years of consulting experience in both industry and government, specializing in long-range planning, operational planning, budgeting, and control. He has lectured and written extensively on the subject of zero-based budgeting.

John N. Trush is with the consumer and industrial manufacturing practice at PricewaterhouseCoopers LLP.

Ronald K. Tucker, BBA, CPCU, ARM, is a vice president with Hagedorn & Company and was previously vice president in the Johnson & Higgins Middle Market Division, where he was responsible for new business sales activities. Mr. Tucker has served in various sales and management roles with another national broker; was responsible for wholesale and retail sales at the Rhulen Organization; has owned his own insurance agency; and has worked for two large insurers, Reliance Insurance Company and American International Group.

Vicki L. Tucker, MS, ARM, is with Good Samaritan Hospital. She has developed risk-management systems within the healthcare industry. Her prior experience includes president, Risk Management & Quality Assurance Consulting Services, Inc.; administrator for Professional Services for the Lake County Health Care Systems, Inc.; and director of Medical Staff Services/Risk Management/Quality Assurance. Ms. Tucker is currently an administrator with the Center for Rehabilitation.

Paul D. Warner, PhD, LLM, CPA, is chairperson and professor of accounting and business law, Frank G. Zarb School of Business, Hofstra University. Dr. Warner was also active in public accounting, holding various positions, the most recent as the National Director of Auditing at BDO Seidman, LLP, and previously was director of management services as well as a tax and an audit partner in other regional and national CPA firms. Dr. Warner is currently a member of the New York Society of Certified Public Accountants' Auditing Standards and Procedures Committee, its General Committee on Higher Education and Entry to the Profession, and the Scope of Practice Task Force. He recently completed a three-year term as a member of the American Institute of Certified Public Accountants' Computer Audit Committee of the Auditing Standards Board. Dr. Warner received his PhD in accounting and computer applications and information systems and an MBA in Accounting from the Graduate School of Business Administration, New York University. He also received JD and LLM (taxation) degrees from the New York University School of Law. He is a CPA, a member of the New York and federal bars, and holds a certificate in data processing.

R. Layne Weggeland was formerly vice president of business operations and planning for UNIX International, Inc. He also served as president of Maple Business Consultants, Inc.; president of Royal Worcester Spode, Inc.; and vice president of finance for Estee Lauder International, Inc. He has served as director of the Internal Audit

Department for Estee Lauder. Mr. Weggeland received his BA from Drew University and attended New York University's Graduate School of Business.

Serge L. Wind, PhD, is special project and analysis director at Lucent Technologies, with responsibility for identifying and targeting financial measures, monitoring the capital and investment program, establishing financial targeting via competitor analogs, generating financial models, overseeing transfer pricing, and performing special analytical studies (including analyzing corporate mergers and acquisitions). Mr. Wind holds PhD and BA degrees in statistics and economics from Columbia University.

Maurice I. Zeldman is president of Emzee Associates of Pittsburgh, Pennsylvania. His technical consulting group works in all of the interface activities associated with product or process development, including research and development, engineering, marketing, production, and transfer of technology. His prior experience includes director of technical development for Rockwell International, where he planned, staffed, and operated a development center that was responsible for developing new products and a new business. He was also responsible for technological planning for 14 industrial divisions. Mr. Zeldman has written several books, is a frequent lecturer, and is a licensed professional engineer in the state of New York.

Index

CPSIA information can be obtained
at www.ICGtesting.com
Printed in the USA
LVHW060138021221
704600LV00031B/117